Third Sex, Third Gender

Third Sex, Third Gender

Beyond Sexual Dimorphism

in Culture and History

Edited by Gilbert Herdt

ZONE BOOKS · NEW YORK

1996

© 1993 Gilbert Herdt

ZONE BOOKS

611 Broadway, Suite 608

New York, NY 10012

Printed in the United States of America.

Distributed by The MIT Press,
Cambridge, Massachusetts, and London, England

Library of Congress Cataloging-in-Publication Data

Third sex, third gender : beyond sexual dimorphism in
culture and history / edited and with an introduction
by Gilbert Herdt.

    p.   cm.

    Includes bibliographical references and index.

    ISBN 0-942299-82-5

    1. Sexual deviation—History. 2. Hermaphroditism—
History. I. Herdt, Gilbert H., 1949– . II. Title:
3rd sex, 3rd gender.

HQ71.T57   1993

305—dc20   93-2276

                                            CIP

Contents

This book is dedicated to

Martin P. Levine

Naar Vriendschap Zulk een Mateloos Verlangen.*

(For friendship, such an endless longing.)

*Cited in Karin Daan, "Het homomonument," in Gert Hekma and D. Kraakman (eds.), *Goed Verkeerd: Een geschiedenis van homoseksuele mannen en lesbische vrowen in Nederland* (Amsterdam: Meulenhoff, 1989), pp. 199–200.

Nature is never constrained to change, and that which
is once formed cannot simply will to reverse itself
wrongly, since desire is not nature. Desire can alter
the character of something already formed, but it
cannot remake its nature. It is true that many birds
change with the seasons, both their colors and their
voices.... But they cannot change a whit of their
actual nature.... Nor can it be believed that the hyena
ever changes its nature or that the same animal has at
the same time both types of genitalia, those of the
male and the female, as some have thought, telling of
marvelous hermaphrodites and creating a whole new
type – a third sex, the androgyne, in between a male
and female. They are certainly wrong not to take into
account how devoted nature is to children, being
the mother and begetter of all things.
                    – Clement of Alexandria (d. ca. 215 A.D.)*

Two sexes are not the necessary, natural consequence of
corporeal difference. Nor, for that matter, is one sex.
                                        – Thomas Laqueur†

Navaho and Pokot take, in their different ways, the view
that intersexuals are a product, if a somewhat unusual product, of the normal course of things – gifted
prodigies, botched pots – where the Americans...
apparently regard femaleness and maleness as exhaust-
ing the natural categories in which persons can
conceivably come: what falls between is a darkness,
an offense against reason.
                                        – Clifford Geertz‡

*"Paedogogus 2.10," trans. John Boswell, in Christianity, Social Tolerance, and
Homosexuality (Chicago: University of Chicago Press, 1980), p. 356.
†Thomas Laqueur, Making Sex: Body and Gender from the Greeks to Freud (Cam-
bridge, MA: Harvard University Press, 1990), p. 243.
‡Clifford Geertz, Local Knowledge (New York: Basic Books, 1984), p. 85.

Preface

For centuries the existence of people who did not fit the sex/gen-
der categories male and female have been known but typically
dismissed from reports of certain non-Western societies, while
in the Western European tradition they have been marginalized,
stigmatized and persecuted. Although much has been written
about gender variations and sexual deviations of late, especially
within the historical study of homosexuality, these anomalous
persons have remained overlooked by anthropologists and historians. Still less attention has been devoted to the deeper question
of whether two sexes or genders are in the nature of things, be
they defined as biological or social, whether in our species or others. But with humans in particular, as one looks across time and
space, in history and culture, we should perhaps ask: Is sexual
dimorphism inevitable in human affairs? This book is devoted to
that question.

Today, many in the Western tradition, including scholars in
the field of sex and gender, assume without reflection the "naturalism" of sexual dimorphism. And their faith in this "commonsense" view is such that we must wonder – first with Michel
Foucault, in his writings on the prominence of the hermaphrodite in European sexual history, and more recently with the historian Thomas Laqueur, in his work on transformations in the
perception of the gendered body – just how things got to be
this way.[1] One might have thought that this domain of culture
formed a historically closed system; but then, from time to time,
we find thinkers such as Georg Simmel who are exceptional: he

11

complained as early as the turn of the century that there were too many categories and too few sexes to explain the immense varieties of human experience.[2]

In anthropology's encounter with the traditional societies – especially the exotic cultures of the non-Western world – myriad examples of divergent sexualities and gendered classifications have emerged over the past century. For example, studies of the North American Indian berdache have played a significant part in the Western conceptualization of these societies, even if the more radical implications of the phenomenon have been ignored, as Will Roscoe demonstrates in his essay here. In general, these cross-cultural variations in sexual and gender patterns have been downplayed when it comes to discussions of "normal" reproductive sexuality and kinship; that is, when it comes to thinking about whether there are only two sexes and genders in the nature of human groups. This neglect is largely due to the intellectual, social and morally defined strictures of sexual dimorphism. In my reinterpretation of the Mohave berdache third gender, for instance, I discuss the hidden ideology of sexual dimorphism that permeated the work of the early anthropologist George Devereux. Devereux's interpretation leaned heavily on Freudian ideas that viewed the berdache as a psychologically flawed homosexual and as a biologically abnormal invert.[3]

In addition to this general prejudice of our dimorphic classification system, our difficulties in dealing with divergent categories may be due to the long neglect of sexuality, not only in anthropology but in the social sciences at large. Until quite recently, the social sciences remained preoccupied with gender but had scarcely begun to conceptualize desire, notwithstanding the prodding of Foucault. And while social reproduction continues to charm much of social theory, our understanding of pleasure in ideas of sexuality and the erotic aspects of social relations remains nascent. In my Introduction, I review the efforts of recent scholars who are rethinking the basis on which social theorists reject or accept the existence of an alternative sex/gender classification scheme in other cultures. In the fine case studies in this volume, the authors demonstrate repeatedly why we must not reduce the richness and significance of divergent sex/gender categories and roles to a one-dimensional ideology of sexual dimorphism or to the residual category of homosexuality.

A few recent studies have anticipated a new approach to the question of a third sex and gender; among these one thinks immediately of Foucault's 1980 publication of the diary of Herculine Barbin, an early-nineteenth-century French hermaphrodite. The book reveals the growing crisis in the modern period's ideology of sexual dimorphism as this pressed upon one person's sense of being neither male or female. As Foucault puts it, Herculine, a "boy-girl, this never eternal masculine–feminine," committed suicide after being forced to change from one sex to the other, because he/she "was incapable of adapting himself to a new identity."[4] Notice here that Foucault's use of the concept of identity, unusual for him, suggests a special problem in ontology and the epistemology of desire that remains very much with us today. A century and a half later, the inability and unwillingness to fit the normative assignments of sex and gender would plague American transsexuals. As the sociologist Harold Garfinkel wrote, criticizing the essentialism of Western ideas of sexual dimorphism: "This composition is rigorously dichotomized into the 'natural,' i.e., moral, entities of male and female...and provides for persons who are 'naturally,' 'in the first place,' 'in the beginning,' 'all along' and 'forever' *one or the other*."[5]

Before the nineteenth century, predating the work of Darwin, Marx, Freud, Durkheim and the later social theorists examined in this book, it was widely believed that there were but two sexes. It was "natural" to be one or the other, no matter what the individual desired. Yet one had only to look to classical and archaic society to realize the recent nature of this "commonsense" assumption. Nature and desire could differ; and while nature would have its way – as the epigraph from Clement of Alexandria (third century A.D.) so eloquently describes – it could not deny the desires of others, including the gods. The Greeks and the early Romans seem to have shared in folk beliefs and practices that were more open in their epistemology of sexual nature and sexual culture. Their acceptance of sexual and gender variations emerged from fundamental sources: the variety of life forms and genders that Zeus could temporarily inhabit, at one time desiring a woman and later a boy; the significance of the god Hermaphroditus in Greek thought; the acceptance of the legendary Tiresias, who changed from male to female to male again in one lifetime, and whose soothsaying powers hark back to such pansexuality. All of these Greek forms showed a lively attention to anatomical differences and sexual options, but with more fluidity permitted in states of being and ways of acting human.

The historical studies described in this book reveal new images of sex and gender variations on the dimorphic model. During the centuries of the Byzantine Empire, as Kathryn M. Ringrose demonstrates in her essay, the palace eunuch was to fill a significant role that was at first ambivalently regarded, then largely tolerated and later even celebrated among those who aspired to it. In certain respects this epistemological tolerance was to endure until the Enlightenment. At that juncture, and under the influence of new historical forces and psychocultural conditions, especially the rise of state formations, a belief in one sex became ideologically marked. In the time that followed, early premodern society and economy would highlight the prominence of a two-sex model and the emergence of the intermediate same-sex-desiring category that fell in between. The benign and open-ended attitudes regarding gendered roles thus gave way to a sharper folk ideology of male and female, with a harsher code of intolerance pivoting on the role of the molly or the sodomite. With the approach of the modern period, as Randolph Trumbach and Theo van der Meer show in their essays here, a strong ideology of sexual dimorphism had emerged alongside the categories of same-sex desire. Since the late nineteenth century, sexual nature has been thought to divide along the lines of what we would today call sex and gender, culminating in the ineluctable dualisms of male and female, masculine and feminine, which, as Gert Hekma shows in his essay on sexology, medicine and the social sciences, anticipated a reductionist worldview of sexual dimorphism that reached its peak in late-twentieth-century popular culture.

We should not attribute these classification systems or their transformations to the structure of the mind, as sexologists and contemporary psychologists have been prone to do, but rather to culture. Although the key theorists, such as Freud, might agree with Nietzsche's dictum that all categorization involves treating dissimilar things as similar, they were not to refigure their own classifications of sex and gendered things in this light. According to the views of Darwin and many late Victorian social theorists, including Freud (at least the early Freud), there were but two categories of "normal" nature, male and female, whose essences and anatomies placed them in opposition, even at the level of the mind. The question of a third sex may not have ever occurred to Darwin; if it had, it was not assigned a role in his theory of evolution. Certainly the issue of anomalous individuals became prominent at this time, although it seems not to have significantly altered the thinking of major theorists, such as Freud, regarding what was "normal" and "natural" in humankind. The nineteenth-century sexologists and sexual reformers, however, were preoccupied with this problem, having created many classificatory schemas, including Uranians, homosexuals, the intermediate sex, psychic hermaphrodites and other such quaint notions, to identify persons whose minds or bodies or actions seemed to defy sexual dimorphism. Once again, in the mid-twentieth century, Alfred Kinsey – that great quantifier of American sexuality, who was trained in zoology – could well understand the difficulties involved in the classification of acts, as we see when he remarked that it is the human mind, not nature, that categorizes.[6] Yet he was an unerring dimorphic thinker, who never questioned the idea of male and female as a fundamental classification of humans, even as he helped to deconstruct the received biologism of homosexual and heterosexual in sexual study.

None of these evolving ideas was able to successfully challenge the extraordinary power of society and culture to lump together things regarded as equal and split others apart, marginalizing what is unclassifiable to residual categories, such as the deviant or the hermaphrodite. Male and female were a fundamental duality of human nature in the time of Freud and Kinsey and are still largely regarded as such today. Only now in the late-twentieth-century postindustrial society are we able to look afresh at the historical and anthropological evidence for an understanding of a fundamental issue of human existence: Is it possible, indeed inevitable, for alternate genders and sexual categories to emerge in certain times and places, transcending sexual dimorphism?

The question of a third sex first drew my attention in the early 1970s, through fieldwork among the Sambia of Papua New Guinea. The Sambia have long recognized the existence of what they call *kwolu-aatmwol*, a person of transformation, a "female thing changing into a male thing." Westerners would classify these persons anatomically as hermaphrodites. These rare individuals, whose bodies, especially their genitals, distinguish them from the mass, also make them distinctive in Sambia mythology and ritual — the focus of special beliefs regarding hermaphroditic ancestors. I have studied one of these persons, the shaman Sakulambei, in depth over many years. It was not until long after the study had begun, however, that I challenged my own American views and began to wonder whether the Sambia observed a three-sex system in their attributions of nature, culture and humans. Indeed, they did.

In biomedical sex research, these *kwolu-aatmwol* constitute a rare form of hermaphroditism (5-alpha reductase deficiency) known only in a few other places in the world. The phenomenon was first studied by American biomedical researchers in the Dominican Republic in the late 1960s, and their research has proven to be controversial because of their claim that it demonstrates the greater influence of prenatal hormones over culture in the development of male gender roles and sexual identity.[7] In my reinterpretation of their research, I have joined others, such as John Money and Anke Ehrhardt, who have pointed to the dangers of biological reductionism that lurk in the essentialist biomedical view of such extraordinary persons and their hermaphroditic bodies. As in the nineteenth century, some scholars have taken this biological reductionism to its logical conclusion of believing in some timeless verity of dimorphic human nature — a scientific positivism that we may trace from Darwin to Simon LeVay and what we might call the "gay brain" controversy of late – a kind of psychic dimorphism that would have made even Freud blush.

We are dealing with multiple cultural and historical worlds in which people of divergent gender and sexual desires exist on the margins or borders of society and may "pass" as normal to remain hidden in the official ideology and everyday commerce of social life. For this reason, on their discovery and representation in history and contemporary culture, they may become icons of what is deemed "normal" male or female nature and iconic of "matter out of place," to follow the well-trodden path of Mary Douglas's conception of symbolic classification. The hermaphrodite, for instance, may become a symbol of boundary blurring: of the anomalous, the unclean, the tainted, the morally inept or corrupt, indeed, the "monsters" of the cultural imagination of modern Americans, as Clifford Geertz has written of such fanciful creatures. The third sex or gender, to paraphrase Lévi-Strauss's famous notion of totemism, may not be much "good to think," but it has proven resilient in objectifying the hegemonic "first" and "second" categories of all Western culture.

Classification systems of sexual and gendered things thus need to be taken apart and put back together again in the conceptual exercise of thinking about sexual nature and sexual culture. This idea permeates a good deal of postmodern anthropology and history, where an enormous burden is placed on the representation of the Other. Thus, we are often led to question how representations of the third sex and gender, loaded with our prejudices about what is "natural" and "normal," are objectified to "create" or "think" the "homosexual," "transsexual" or "hermaphrodite." There is much of value in this line of work, although one has the sense that too often it is based on a weak or insignificant body of observations, with the impetus being too strongly borne by the study of representations alone. By contrast, the studies in this book begin from the other direction, in which a phenomenon has been studied for a considerable period of time, leading into questions of representation and symbolic interpretation of a higher order. For instance, Serena Nanda's essay on the hijras of India raises profound questions about the historicity and cultural reality of the "third sex" in the Indian tradition on the basis of long-term field study. It is through such rich case studies that we are able to question both the ontology and the epistemology for understanding Otherness in the larger and more profound comparative manner of the social sciences. Thus, one of the significant interpretative points that arises repeatedly in this book is not only what we know but how anthropologists and historians claim to know it. It does matter, I think, what the third sex/gender "looks like" and "acts like" – whether they are the eunuchs of the Byzantine Empire, the sodomites of eighteenth-century Holland, the hijras of India or women who dress in men's clothes in the Balkans, to name but several critical instances studied in this book. Whether the two sexes are viewed as constructed or naturalized or as social entities in a particular historical society and the extent to which the third sex or gender is included in cultural reality and common sense has to do with classification systems and the evidence we collect to understand them. In short, we want to understand how, in particular places and times, people construe not only the classification of the natural body but what Garfinkel has called the "cultural genitals."

To the best of our knowledge, this volume is the first of its kind to address these issues from the complementary perspectives of anthropology and social history. The contributors are attempting to create a new cross-disciplinary dialogue to deconstruct sex and gender dimorphism and reconstruct divergent codes and roles for representing and experiencing sexual and gendered natures, ontologies and epistemologies in human relations across time and space. We have organized these essays on the basis of their historicity; both the Introduction and the cross-cultural and historical studies that follow address three critical areas:

First, *third sex/gender categories and roles* are described and elucidated, a central descriptive task of exploration and documentation. This requires a basic understanding of the cultural and historical contexts in which the sex/gender schemata under question have evolved, become institutionalized, changed and matured. What, for instance, is a hijra? What criteria exist for the recruitment and legitimation of hijras as individuals and as a category? How long have the hijras been defined as such in the Indian tradition?

Second, studies of sex and gender in general and of the "third sex" in particular have typically omitted the description of *sexual conduct, erotic experience and codes of sexual comportment.* In this book we provide new and substantial material to understand how sexual action may influence the construction of third-sex categories and social relations. One clue is that the erotic experiences or actions of such persons may validate their own inclusion into the category.

Third, few studies have considered the relationship between *cultural processes and the historical reproduction of third-sex roles* and categories. Was the third-sex/gender category historically fragile or robust? For instance, were a certain number of individuals necessary to constitute the third-sex category in local folk theories of biology and their attendant social relations? Was there a stable population of such persons? Alternatively, symbolic reproduction of the third category may have occurred through such processes as mythology (e.g., Hermaphroditus) in the absence of individual exemplars in the world. What were the social, historical and cultural processes, such as socialization practices, religious rites, mythologies and political movements, that have constituted and reproduced third categories?

Some readers may question why we have focused on "three" entities. Why not four or five or myriad other categories of sex and gender? The presence of only two categories – the dyad – creates an inherent relationship of potential conflict, that is, inevitable oppositionality (the anthropologist Gregory Bateson once referred to this structural relationship as "symmetrical schismogenesis"). When, however, a third category or class is introduced, a new dynamic enters between the dyadic agents or entities, as Simmel's classic essay on the "triad" points out: "The dyad represents both the first social synthesis and unification, and the first separation and antithesis. The appearance of the third party indicates transition, conciliation, and abandonment of absolute contrast."[8] The code of "thirdness" should not be taken literally to mean that in all times and places there are only three categories possible in human classification; along with such writers as Lévi-Strauss, who is inconsistent on the matter, we should want to entertain the possibility of multiple categories in the nature of things in human traditions. The emphasis in the Introduction is in this regard heuristic; the third is emblematic of other possible combinations that transcend dimorphism. However, as the reader will also see, many historical and cultural examples seem to pivot around the question of a third category, which impinges on characteristics of the "deep structure" of the ontology and epistemology of how humans categorize things into twos, threes or other structures of the mind. For analytical purposes, then, the book emphasizes those traditions in which a male, female and third category are posited as part of the reality of nature and culture or the attempt to construct an alternate symbolic reality, in competition with the hegemonic order of a historical social tradition.

We wish to acknowledge the support and friendship of Michel Feher in his capacity as editor of Zone Books for his encouragement of this project. For sabbatical support that made possible the completion of this book, I am very grateful to the University of Chicago, Division of Social Science, and especially to its former dean and now provost, Edward Laumann. I am also grateful to the Anthropological Institute of the University of Amsterdam for its kindness during this time. For discussions related to the issues of this book, I am indebted to my friend Theo van der Meer, and for comments on the Introduction, I would like to thank Serena Nanda, Gert Hekma and Michel Feher.

Finally, this book is dedicated to the memory of my dear friend Martin P. Levine, who passed away in early 1993 in New York from complications due to AIDS. Marty visited Amsterdam in 1991 and was deeply struck by the national homosexual monument erected to gays and lesbians around the corner from the Anne Frank House. Today, when I pass by this monument and see the inscription from the famous Dutch homosexual poet Jacob Israel de Haan, I am reminded of the importance of friendship to Marty, and of his importance to me.

Gilbert Herdt
Amsterdam, The Netherlands, March 1993

Introduction:

Third Sexes and Third Genders

Gilbert Herdt

Purpose and Aims

Certain individuals in certain times and places transcend the categories of male and female, masculine and feminine, as these have been understood in Western culture since at least the later nineteenth century. The bodies and ontology of such persons diverge from the sexual dimorphism model found in science and society – in the way they conceive their being and/or their social conduct. Furthermore, in some traditions – cultures and/or historical formations – these persons are collectively classified by others in third or multiple cultural-historical categories. As the essays in this volume demonstrate, such persons and categories are more common in the human condition than was once thought.

This perspective on the transcendence of sexual dimorphism guides the anthropological and historical analyses that follow in several ways. First, we reexamine and redefine studies of sex and gender in light of critiques of sexual dimorphism, which generally suggest the limitations of a reproductive paradigm. Of course, there are conceptual dangers involved in breaking precipitously with the past convention of distinguishing arbitrarily between sex (as biology and nature) and gender (as culture and nurture). However, we aim in this volume to renew the study of sexual and gender variation across time and space, critically looking at the pitfalls of continuing to objectify the dichotomy of sex and gender, which is probably culturally bound and scientifically misleading. Second, we show that, in some places and times, individuals are grouped into divergent ontological categories, identities, tasks, roles, practices and institutions that have resulted in more than two kinds of persons, that is, what Westerners would classify as two sexes (male and female) or genders (masculine and feminine).[1] Studies of sexual "deviance" or "third genders" have typically conflated these two categories. Generally, sexual conduct has been ignored as a constitutive criterion leading to the formation of a divergent sex/gender category or the inclusion of individuals within it. Thus, to reassess these conceptual links, we examine historical and cultural associations among sexual dimorphism, social science theory and folk classifications of anatomy, erotic conduct and social relations.

Finally, while third sexes and genders are enduring categories and roles in some cultures, they are not present at all times and places, which has implications for the creation and maintenance of third sexes and third genders. On the one hand, such a non-universal status suggests an inherent tension between individual desires to *create* a third sex or gender and verities of the adaptation of human cultures to the phylogeny of *H. homo sapiens*, our species-specific "nature." On the other hand, although anatomy, sexual action and special social relations are common denominators – cultural signs – of classification into third-sex or third-gender categories in some traditions, they are neither necessary nor sufficient to *maintain* them. In short, there is no ready-made formula that will produce divergent sex or gender categories and roles, suggesting that special conditions – demographic, symbolic and historical – combine to create the necessary and sufficient basis for the conventionalization and historical transmission of the third sex or gender.

Historical Evidence and Cross-cultural Conjectures
A revolution in social-historical studies of sexuality and gender has created enormous interest in analyzing historical categories from a cross-cultural perspective.[2] What we are learning from these studies, and from the work of scholars influenced by them, is that a one-sex paradigm composed of a canonical male with a female body inside was predominant in Western texts until quite recently. Some time later, a three-sex system gave rise to a classi-

fication schema of four genders, evolving out of the eighteenth-century English "molly" and the Dutch "sodomite," for example, which led to a new and more complex classification of sexual natures and beings in the modern period.[3]

The extraordinary influence of the hermaphrodite in Western culture and art bears witness to the long-emerging tension between systems of sexual and/or gender classification and definitions of "nature" and "society." The representation of the erotic in Western art played with the dictates of sexual dimorphism in its pictorial androgyny, often heavily portrayed with the tabooed depiction of the homoerotic; this representation was later mediated, particularly after the Renaissance, through androgynous imagery in such works as Michelangelo's *Bacchus*.[4] Such pictorial androgyny is transformed into the later imagery of the monster, in which androgyny moves closer to the sexualized human being, especially the figure of the deviant. Hence, although a significant discourse on monsters and hermaphrodites had abounded for centuries, this approach was replaced with the modern period's conception of the homosexual as a hermaphrodite of the soul.[5] This development in turn anticipated the construction of the homosexual/heterosexual dualism with which we still live. Among the more interesting and enduring icons of the twentieth-century forms of this dualism in science and mass culture are the gender-transforming transsexual in American culture and the gay and lesbian body, especially in its biologically essentialist image.[6]

These powerful transformations in historical ideas suggest two critiques of both the cross-cultural and historical record on sexual dimorphism and multiple systems of sex and gender. First, many earlier scholars of history and culture predicated their work on the assumption of sexual dimorphism, so common in the literature since before Darwin's influence. Thus, when anthropologists first encountered individuals classified as "berdache" in the cultures of Native North America, these persons were often misinterpreted as biologically abnormal hermaphrodites or "degenerates" and, later, as deviant homosexuals, both of which categories run counter to the cultural phenomenology of berdache roles in these cultures.[7] Likewise, a similar process of misinterpretation and labeling in the third-gender roles of Polynesia from the time of Captain Cook to the present can be witnessed.[8] Second, a healthy skepticism about cross-cultural and historical claims of inclusion in dimorphic or divergent categories is justified when it comes to sex and gender; as Margaret Mead and Kenneth Read once warned, the cross-cultural record is fragmentary and inconclusive on these matters.[9] As the history of sexuality has repeatedly shown, claims made for the absence or essence of some entity, whether for homosexuality in other cultures or innate desires in our own, must always be *interpreted* on the basis of further study rather than treated as literal realities since such claims have often proved false, exaggerated or incomplete.[10]

The collection of evidence on sexuality from other cultures and historical documents is thus considerably complicated by the taboo against intruding into relations that are culturally defined as inherently private, or intimate or sexual, as Mead and later Michel Foucault warned.[11] It does make a difference to the practicing anthropologist and historian, for instance, whether a society approves or disapproves of sexual activity in general; these strictures (e.g., the negative attitudes of erotophobia, misogyny or homophobia) influence the data-collection process through what is revealed or hidden of sexuality.[12] Cultures that institutionalize intense ideologies of sexual dimorphism, as, for instance, in cases of religious fundamentalism, raise methodological issues in social analysis.[13] As the study of AIDS and sexuality has repeatedly shown, the investigation of alternative, marginal, illicit or illegal forms of sexual practice and social realities requires a different lens of inquiry from that of normative social science.[14]

Identifying individuals who diverge from the male and female categories can prove to be difficult even in cultures in which a third sex or gender role is present, because the condition may nonetheless be somewhat disparaged or considered deviant.[15] Because of laws and implicit rules, divergent individuals to whom these categories of being and action apply – sodomites, berdache, women dressed in men's clothes, hermaphrodites in New Guinea and so on – may slip between male and female roles. They may engage in the act of "passing" as normatively male or female or masculine or feminine (best understood through Erving Goffman's still-significant study of "the natural cycle of passing").[16] Through behaviors and practices that either set them apart from others or enable them to conform and to pass as normative, such persons carve out a special niche in their societies.

Thus, if the hermaphrodite bears a secret nature, there is not necessarily any reason to confess this nature, for it may offend sensibilities or spiritual and social rules. As Foucault remarked of nineteenth-century France, what the hermaphrodite Herculine Barbin "evokes in her past is the happy limbo of a non-identity, which was paradoxically protected by the life of those closed, narrow, and intimate societies where one has the strange happiness, which is at the same time obligatory and forbidden, of being acquainted with only one sex."[17] Indeed, as I will argue later, the historical and cultural phenomenon of passing marks a significant entry into the field of identities and identity theory, whereby the conventionalized male or female is masked and re-presented as something new in cultural representations.[18] Let the reader be forewarned, then, that we are dealing with matters of inherent difficulty when it comes to studying the third sex and gender.

Darwinian Sexual Dimorphism and Sexology

Over the past century it has been widely assumed, following Darwin, that sexual behavior served the purposes of reproduction and selective fitness of individuals in evolution above all. Darwin reasoned that natural selection affected males and females as a function of their roles in reproduction and/or from resource competition (especially for food), leading to dimorphism.[19] By *sexual dimorphism* is typically meant a phylogenetically inherited structure of two types of human and sexual nature, male and female, present in all human groups. Although we will not be able to examine its full implications in this review, much of the historical and anthropological literature suggests that this emphasis on dimorphism reveals a deeper stress on "reproduction" as a paradigm of science and society.[20] The reproductive paradigm remains prominent today in studies that go far beyond evolutionary thinking, to such an extent that I will refer to this as a "principle of sexual dimorphism," since it is represented as if it were a uniform law of nature like gravity. That is, it is believed canonical that, everywhere and at all times, sex and/or gender exist for reproduction of individuals and species. In short, reproduction, as suggested in the critiques formulated by feminist and gay and lesbian scholars for a generation, has been the "real object" of normative science, both in biology and social science, for much of the past century.[21]

This cultural achievement is all the more remarkable when we consider the many clues that suggested that dimorphism was an invention of modernism. Indeed, if one is to accept Thomas Laqueur's brilliant interpretations, from the time of Antiquity until the late eighteenth century popular culture and medical theory suggested that there was but one sex: a kind of signified male/masculine body and mind, inscribed on the incomplete and subordinate female body.[22] From the book of Genesis as well – an origin myth of the Judeo-Christian tradition – we are told how Adam created a second sex from his own loin. But as Laqueur has commented, "Two sexes are not the necessary, natural consequence of corporeal difference. Nor, for that matter, is one sex."[23] This paradigm was to change by the time of the Renaissance, after which the two-sex model gained in prominence – although without completely destroying the preceding ideas of nature and desire for expressing sex and gender.

Theorists who followed Darwin's consistent emphasis on reproduction typically viewed sexual selection as an innate and natural property of our own species as well. In the social-evolutionary theories of Victorian anthropology, the Darwinian revolution was enormously influential in how it "permanently redefine[d] not only 'man's place in nature,' but also his place in time – as well as the relationship of God both to nature and to humankind."[24] Sexuality is problematical in this context, since it was seldom explicitly discussed, and the study of kinship and marriage as social institutions was often reduced to matters of the biological selection of mates.[25] Following Darwinian thought and its popular manifestations in various fields, we find many permutations of what might be called an unmarked principle of sexual dimorphism: the differences between male and female were innate, as supposedly demonstrated in factors as diverse as morphology, brain size, tool use and the evolution of speech. Within nineteenth-century evolutionary anthropology and anthropometry, research reports on the measurement of sexual dimorphism in human groups were legion, extending from the time of Frances Galton (Darwin's cousin) through Franz Boas, the founder of American anthropology. Racial differences and racism (including the eugenics movement) figured prominently in some corners. Well into the twentieth century we find anthropometry stressing sexually dimorphic differences between the so-called biological races, with clear implications for Social Darwinism. Today, the continued emphasis on kin selection and sexual dimorphism in vulgar sociobiology (less so than in the field's more sophisticated renditions today) must surely be seen as a continuation of the early Darwinian fascination with sexual differentiation and survival.[26]

Human paleontology has been embroiled in debate over the past few years regarding the relation between such a reproductive paradigm and sexual dimorphism in the human fossil record. Evolutionary writers have typically followed Darwin in seeing a continuum of sexual dimorphism in lower to higher animal forms. For instance, some specialists argue that "in all human groups males average almost 1.1 times as tall as females and are correspondingly more massive."[27] However, paleontologists continue to question the significance of size variations in species and individuals for sexual dimorphism. Some authorities suggest that primate sexual dimorphism "corresponds closely to the degree of male competition for mates" and "human sexual dimorphism is clearly not typical."[28] Differences occur anatomically in fossil humans in the greater size of males and larger pelvic opening of females. But while its relevance has been projected into prehistory, as if this "followed the same pattern as today," many have questioned the uniformity of such a prehistoric dimorphism, since one trait might recede in prehistoric human beings (e.g., teeth) while another trait (e.g., epigamy) might increase.[29] "Sexual dimorphism can only evolve if there is dimorphism in selection

27

and/or dimorphism in genetic variances."[30] Comparative study of species suggests that primates vary according to whether their ancestors were more dimorphic than average, the size of the species and its ecological traits.[31] In short, sexual dimorphism may be significant for indexing matters of individual and species-specific variation, but its overall significance for sexual and gender differentiation has probably been exaggerated.

One can see in the development of later Darwinian thought and natural selection theory the elements that prodded the positive science of sexology toward an essentialism of both gender and sexual ideas. In this respect, sexology is a child of the nineteenth-century Darwinian tradition.[32] It follows that the emergence of sexology forged a social and political reform movement in reaction against antiquated ideas of sexuality. Many have seen in these developments the birth of modernism, or at least its lynchpin, for its modernist practitioners, especially Havelock Ellis and Freud, were adamant "sexual enthusiasts."[33] Concurrently, the coinage of *homosexuality* around 1870 and *heterosexuality* around 1890 had far-reaching implications for the principle of dimorphism in medical sexology.[34]

Quite simply, sexology was to propound two powerful ideas: that "male" and "female" are innate structures in all forms of life, including human beings, and that heterosexuality is the teleologically necessary and highest form of sexual evolution. For example, Iwan Bloch, a notable German scholar and ethnological writer in the sexological tradition, argued that evolution had driven men and women into different "thought worlds." Moreover, "heterosexuality becomes increasingly marked in the evolutionary scale of mammals and man." Furthermore, Bloch "was convinced that the greatest cultural and creative achievements came from 'normal,' not homosexual people.... He firmly believed that the 'normal' woman and not the lesbian would advance the feminist movement."[35] Freud was to struggle with these essentialist ideas and to reify many of them in his own developmental theory, including many of those that dealt with gender and sexuality. As Peter Gay writes of the sexological position of Freud in his later writings:

28

Freud's anti-feminist stance was not the product of his feeling old or wishing to be outrageous. Rather, he had come to see it as an inescapable consequence of men's and women's diverging sexual histories: anatomy is destiny. His comparative history of sexual development may be less than wholly compelling, but it calls on the logic of human growth as he defined it in the 1920s. The psychological and ethical distinctions between the sexes, he argued, emerge naturally from the biology of the human animal and from the kind of mental work that this implies for each sex.[36]

The two distinctive sexes and the imperative for reproduction thus combined to impel the biomedical sexological tradition toward what we might call an essentialist legacy of the paradigm.

Many of the progenitors of sexology, such as Karl Ulrichs and Magnus Hirschfeld, could not have foreseen the outcome of their efforts to establish a sexual science. They were themselves "homosexuals" and formed a hidden network of communicants throughout this period. Along with others, they began to formulate their texts on the basis of the ultimate aims of social reform, such as the liberalization of sexual laws.[37] They had agreed to innatist or biological positions, only to find these theories exploited by those quintessential biological reductionists, the Nazis. Hirschfeld's favorite motto, "Justice through Knowledge," was ultimately a defeated axiom after the Nazis' rise to power following the collapse of the Weimar Republic.[38] By this time much harm was already done; but this would not do away with the powerful intellectual program of medicalized sexology, which reemerged ever more strongly after the war. Indeed, it is especially after World War II and the founding of the modern sexual clinic that we find two key expressions of essentialized dimorphism:[39] sex assignment at birth and the evolutionary theory of the emergence of gender identity.

Sexological writing in the nineteenth century had begun to make an implicit distinction between nature and nurture, heredity and environment, biology and society. Under the influence of Darwinian thought and the putative mechanisms of natural selection, sexual dimorphism emerged in the language of developmentalism. Ultimately such dimorphism has fed into the contemporary paradigms of essentialism/constructionism, often wrongly reduced to mean biology/culture. An explicit individualism, or, more precisely, an ideology of Western individualism, strongly influences many of these early formulations of sexological writing.[40] For example, in the biomedical discourse on homosexuality and the "intermediate sex" in the late nineteenth century, the distinction between innate and acquired inversion is strongly marked between such scholars as Hirschfeld, Ellis and Freud.[41] More than half a century later, this distinction, still in combination with ideological individualism, results in a new form of dualistic definition: between sex as biological elements (genes, gonads, etc.) and gender as learned cultural elements (masculinity and femininity), as formulated by John Money and Robert Stoller, respectively. Thus continues an implicit contrast between environmentalism (forces outside the organism) and innatism or naturalism (forces inside the organism) in the literature of the mid-twentieth century, reasserted in sex research by Alfred Kinsey et al. in their survey study of sexual behavior of American males. Hence, what emerges is an approach that sees the inner biological elements of sexual development, among which is the male/female dichotomy, as innate and unchangeable. Although this is not without conceptual controversies and dilemmas, its force continues to the present.[42]

According to the canonical view in sexology, it follows that all human beings are classifiable as either male or female types at birth, through standard clinical and sexological practice.[43] This is accepted by all those who work both with normal and abnormal biological sexual differentiation, as is noted in my contribution to this volume. Male and female are differentiated at many different levels of biological development. Ultimately, this idea rests on the assumption of a generalized mammalian pattern of primary femaleness, out of which maleness emerges, which in his early writing Freud referred to as the "bedrock of biological bisexuality."[44] However, in modern parlance, for instance, consider these four components of standard Western clinical practice: chromosomal sex; gonadal sex; morphological sex and related secondary sex traits; and psychosocial sex or gender identity. Notice that these criteria do not include sociocultural classification systems; instead, Money and Ehrhardt, for example, assume a strong parallelism between sexual dimorphism in anatomy and gender dimorphism in cultural traditions.[45] It remains problematic whether these biological universals are always present.[46] As I discuss in my essay on 5-alpha reductase deficiency syndrome, medical practitioners assume in all cases that a two-sex system is in operation, never questioning whether the presence of a third sex might influence sexual and gender development. This is especially puzzling since some classical clinical case studies in Western countries such as the United States refer to hermaphrodites' subjective development not as male or female identity but as "hermaphroditic identity."[47]

"Critical learning theory" emerged as a potential antidote to essentialism at this time. A powerful and enduring perspective on the role of culture and society in influencing gender and sexuality, critical learning theory suggests a seeming alignment with the social construction of gender. However, this appearance is, like all varieties of essentialist and constructionist ideas, in part illusory because it assumes that learning gender identities takes place only with respect to the dimorphic two-sex system of male and female. Gendered identity as masculine or feminine is thus analogous to the imprinting phase of innate development in animals and in human phylogeny, with the effect that all human beings are either male or female in biological sex and feminine or masculine in gender identity.[48] This theory suggests that, early in development, sex assignment into either the male or female categories affects most learning in the areas of gender identity and sex role performance.[49] Sex assignment into either the male or female category is of such general importance that, after a child is approximately two and a half years old, the clinical advice for the doctor is never to suggest changing the child's sexual classification, no matter what information comes to light – even information that the original sex assignment at birth was in error and should have been to the opposite sex – because such a change will do great psychic violence to the mental health of the child.[50]

31

The epistemology of the approach owes much to Freud's theory of psychosexual development. Thus, the putative effect of early experience in infancy molds or "imprints" a gendered identity on the child.[51] A congruence of biological sex identity and social learning is assumed to create a harmonious effect in "normal and natural" child development in all cultures – notwithstanding transsexuals and hermaphrodites, who suggest a divergent or intermediate identity.[52]

The totalizing effect of the Darwinian heritage was to represent sexual dimorphism through time and space as a binary principle of social structure. The idea of applying the male/female dyad to domains of society and culture, including the sexual division of labor, promoted by turn-of-the-century social theorists such as the French sociologist Emile Durkheim, thus became an assumptive core of social theory.[53] Many anthropologists, for example, began their analyses of social structure with the observation that men and women were, everywhere, not only physically distinctive but also an "objective" basis for society and the economic division of labor.[54] A fine illustration of the trend in sexology comes from Money and Ehrhardt's classic text on sex and gender, *Man and Woman, Boy and Girl*, in which they reify sexual dimorphism as an essential structure of individual development in simple societies, operationalized as what they called "gender dimorphic behavior." They thus assume the existence of a two-sex and two-gender system in all times and places and argue, for instance, that in Australian Aborigine and New Guinea societies all economic and social tasks and roles are gender dimorphic; not only cooking and child care, but rituals and ceremonial practices as well. This dimorphic schema is then mapped onto social structure, culture and ecology, so that Money and Ehrhardt objectified ten quantitative "variables" (idealized culture traits) to be checked off in assessing the relative degree of dimorphism in the practices of native peoples.[55] This approach suggests in general that the biological dimorphism of male and female is projected into culture and symbolically reflected in its institutions, especially primary or objective institutions.[56]

In short, the question of divergent sex and gender roles and

categories cannot be considered apart from the evolutionary perspective on sexual dimorphism. This paradigm strongly influenced
sexology and generally expanded into classical social theory in the
late nineteenth and early twentieth centuries.

Classical Social Theory and Third-Sex Categories

It was not only sexology that was affected by nineteenth-century
ideas of sexual dimorphism. Anthropologists and historians have
emphasized reproductive functionalism in their studies of kinship,
family, gender roles, sexual practices and the regulation and reproduction of society. Over the past century, the theme of sexual
dimorphism has recurred throughout social theory, with the con-
sequent relegation of the third sex to the clinical laboratory of
"biological deviance" and the third gender to quaint textbooks
of anthropology.

Such a marginalizing emphasis is present in major thinkers
since the time of Darwin and Freud in evolutionary and sexual
theory, as well as in central anthropological writings by such figures as Durkheim, Mauss and Lévi-Strauss. Today, sexual dimorphism remains central to social-scientific thought and is regarded
by many anthropologists as an axiom of cultural classification.
Mead formalized this position in a classic essay in the early 1960s:
"In all known societies sexual dimorphism is treated as a major
differentiating factor of any human being, of the same order as
difference in age, the other universal of the same kind."[57] More
recently, the American anthropologist Robert Edgerton, who
contributed a significant early study of transsexualism in a non-
Western culture, has written:

> It is probably a universal assumption that the world consists of only
> two biological sexes and that this is the natural and necessary way
> of things.... It is expected that people will be born with male *or*
> female bodies and that, despite a lifetime of acts that compromise
> or even reverse normal sex-role expectations, everyone will continue
> to live in the body of either a man or a woman.[58]

Because male and female are tantamount to natural categories in

33

social classification, it follows that the intermediate is unnatural, inverted or perverse.[59] In short, to quote Clifford Geertz on the matter: "What falls between [male and female] is a darkness, an offense against reason."[60]

In general, anthropological studies of sex and gender since the early classics of Mead and Bronislaw Malinowski have assumed a two-sex system as the "normal and natural" structure of "human nature."[61] Mead suggests that the ultimate purpose of sex is for "mating and reproduction by physically mature, child-rearing human beings."[62] Reproduction in this model was problematic only in its social regulation: "Every human society," she said, must deal with two problems: "the need for reducing reproductivity in particular areas, as among unmarried women," and the aim of "ensuring or increasing reproductivity in other areas, among certain classes in the population." This model is still prominent in anthropology, and as Carole Vance has remarked of anthropological models of sex and gender, "The core of sexuality is reproduction."[63]

However much social historians have thought to evade the imperatives of Darwinian biology, biological sexology and essentialist ideas in gender study, it has remained difficult to operate outside sexual dimorphism as a conceptual system.[64] Consciously or unconsciously, some scholars of sexuality still cling to the modernist view that nature restricts culture, that male and female are the inalienable products of biology. These scholars tend to project back into the historical and anthropological records not only the current cultural categories of identity but also the preconceptions of social relations that operated and structurally supported the categories of the past.[65] As Theo van der Meer reveals in his essay on the eighteenth-century history of the Dutch sodomite, however, while male and female were powerful categories of representation and action, they were not so encompassing as to circumscribe desire for or romantic infatuations with the same sex or the emergence of a subculture of sodomites that evaded the sexual dimorphism of the times through a hidden network of signals and spaces.

But culture is both more diverse than nature and more insidious in its potential to "play" symbolically with the classifications

34

of human bodies and minds. And yet, while Lévi-Strauss demonstrated this point admirably, he failed to explore and understand the result of the critique against his own work, which, in kinship studies, proposed four, not three, sexes.[66] In his *mythologiques* project as well, the binary structure of the unconscious mind was invoked to situate the dimorphic categories of male and female at a level of "deep" culture akin to Freud's unconscious.[67] To take a clue from Foucault, the very notion of human sexual types – male and female, homosexual and heterosexual – is a survival of the realist zoological penchant of nineteenth-century thought in twentieth-century thinkers – including Freud and certainly Kinsey, and recently Lévi-Strauss – who have not reflected on the received dimorphic categories of Western culture in light of the immense variability of human groups. A fuller historical answer to why this is so rests with Foucault, of course;[68] we will examine several historical texts here and consider later the implications for anthropology.

With the beginnings of the early modern period and the importance of the French Revolution in redrawing the boundaries around the individual self, the discourse on sexual dimorphism begins to shape social theory.[69] A new thematic of individualism emerges to compete with the aristocratic order, a thematic of boundaries redrawn around an autonomous body and self in an age of new cults of the self in the context of struggles for class and sexual equality.[70] Here, the work of Rousseau is critical, for his texts contain some of the earliest indications of the debate in social theory over constructs and essences in sexuality. In Rousseau's famous disquisition on education, *Emile*, the child "does not feel himself to be of any sex, of any species. Man and woman are equally alien to him... it is nature's ignorance (*Emile*, IV, p. 219)."[71] Prior to sexual desire, Emile treats all humans instrumentally; they serve as a means to an end. But with sexual maturation, his desires become "essential" and he can no longer avoid treating others "as a means to his own end."[72] Because it is "essential," Rousseau suggests that it is best to postpone sexual gratification in the interest of creating a moral and friendly position and for cultivating reason instead of debauchery.[73] Thus, "Rousseau makes Emile moral by delaying his first sexual experience; thus he 'delays the progress of nature to the advance of reason' (*Emile*, IV, p. 316)." He states: "For the object of his desire is at first very unclear to the desirer, who 'desires without knowing what' (*Emile*, IV, p. 220)." "The first act of his nascent imagination is to teach him that he has fellows; and the species affects him before the female sex (*Emile*, IV, p. 220)." Joel Schwartz, in *The Sexual Politics of Jean-Jacques Rousseau*, adds, "One wants to obtain the preference that one grants. Love must be reciprocal. To be loved, one has to make oneself lovable. . . . The object of one's love must be a subject as well, for whom one is oneself in turn an object. For these responses Rousseau contends that 'a young man must either love or be debauched' (*Emile*, IV, p. 214, see also *Dialogues*, I, p. 688)." Thus we see the boundaries of a one-sex system being redrawn around notions of sexual equality in culture and romantic love in the shift to the modern period.

In the nineteenth century a powerful idea of the "divine savage" in a "natural" state profoundly linked the French Enlightenment thinkers, such as Rousseau and Diderot, with the formation of modernist discourse on sexuality. The notions of archaism and primitivism are obviously related to these representational systems.[74] Late Victorian anthropology was to serve as a significant intellectual link with the later sexology. As social historians such as Randolph Trumbach have written, forms of third sex and gender, first hermaphroditic and later homosexual, bridged modern versus premodern categories. For instance, Sir James Frazer's *Golden Bough*, Ellis's comparative study of sexology, Freud's armchair anthropology in *Totem and Taboo* and even the early writings of Malinowski and Mead continued to labor under the illusion of a primitive human nature in which sexuality was more simple and unrestricted than that of modern civilization.[75] This in turn hinted at the probability that sexual variations across human groups were small (despite Freud's and other sexologists' references to divergent erotic practices of archaic and non-Western societies, such as homoerotic relations among the ancient Greeks), while sexual dimorphism and reproductive heterosexuality loomed large in such "primitive" groups (i.e., those defined as having less compromised, more elementary "human nature").[76] Moreover, it is still widely held that sexual dimorphism is more prominent in simple societies, especially hunting-and-gathering band societies, than in technologically complex or modern societies.[77]

But twentieth-century anthropology has resisted monolithic theories that explain human nature through universal mechanisms of a common trait or characteristic, largely because such reductionism tends to explain away culture as a mere residue or frill of human life. The notion that sex might organize culture, as Freud consistently suggested, is particularly problematic, since it placed the burden of causation on biological phylogeny rather than on current social practice or function. Freud's famous thesis in *Totem and Taboo* was that a primordial group condition – a ruling tyrant father who was killed and devoured by his sons, who in turn incestuously took women from him – was a mythic/historical event, the Oedipal complex, that has unconsciously ruled over the phylogeny of human evolution ever since. In short, the Oedipal complex and incest taboos separated nature from culture and animal world from human society. The evidence for such a theory was of course nil, but Freud's genius lay in his speculative account that linked past and present in an unbroken chain. It is ironic that the two best-known anthropologists of sexuality and indeed of culture writ large (at least to an earlier generation), Malinowski and Mead, both were influenced by their attraction to and reaction against Freud's theory.

In Freud's *Three Essays on the Theory of Sexuality*, we find the view that male and female constitute the fundamental structure of society and human development. This is surprising for a number of reasons having to do with Freud's theory of the primacy of the male sex (the phallus), his theory of sexual orientation and his acceptance of hermaphroditism in human nature, as in the nineteenth-century concept of psychic hermaphroditism.[78] Freud's work is of great interest because of his presumption of innate biological bisexuality and the openness with which the fetishistic erotic interest may be attached in early human development to any social stimulus, creating possibilities for divergent sexual and gendered relations, such as the homosexual as an intermediate sex. Thus Freud deploys physicalist metaphors of how erotic interests are "split apart" and then "soldered together" again in new combinations.[79] Although sexual orientation vis-à-vis the sexual object is not viewed as purely innate or learned, Freud nonetheless leans toward the biological determination of developmental subjectivities, as, for instance, in three key areas: anatomy, mental attitudes regarding maleness and femaleness in society and the development of choice of sex object. Nonetheless, the possibilities of an open-ended construction of a third sex and/or gender are muted by the presumption of sexual dimorphism in human phylogeny, including the dimorphism of acquired and innate traits, which Freud borrowed from ideas of Jean-Baptiste Lamarck, Darwin, Karl Westphal and Ellis, supposedly manifested both at the phenotypic level (anatomy) and the genotypic level (the unconscious). German philosophical essentialism strongly influenced these ideas as well.[80]

Curiously, while Freud thought of the infantile human mind as "polymorphous perverse," the natural structure of development in the body was typically skewed to the male sex. Freud generally saw hermaphrodites as abnormal in mind and body, as interstitial between male and female.[81] Freud could never escape the essentialist view that humans have an innate biological bisexuality that inclines society to impose a definite structure of gender roles to regulate and direct its expression toward "normal" outcomes. Freud would have probably been surprised to learn that for centuries in the Byzantine Empire there were biologically normal males who became eunuchs not from an essential desire to have a female body or from a need for sexual relations with males; instead, they sought the prestige and privilege of the eunuch's position in the Byzantine court.[82] Thus, we see that Freud's view was too biologically driven and culturally bound to accommodate the range of variations in sex and gender development across time and space. When Freud's disciples, such as the psychoanalytic anthropologist Géza Roheim, were encouraged to study the most "primitive" of groups, such as Australian Aborigine society, it was to confirm more than to discover that the innate structures of a biologically driven Oedipal complex were to be found in all places, albeit in a more elementary way in rude societies.[83]

The later efforts of psychoanalysts – such as Erikson on European and non-Western societies and Sudhir Kakar on India – to "relativize" this model have met with only limited success.[84] Stages of development are seen as linear, as biologically founded, creating continuity between the drives and wishes of childhood and adulthood when in fact it is the marked discontinuities resulting from historical and cultural formations that are striking.[85] The innate structure is usually assumed to be a given; the cultural experiences are added on to it but without modification of what came before. Freud and his followers' naïveté is one thing, having come from decades past; but the contemporary ethnocentrism of psychology is startling. Witness, for instance, the continuing naïveté of some Western psychologists' stage models of sex and gender development, typically constructed without the benefit of historical and cross-cultural evidence or non-Western theories of the human condition, and the particular analysis of adolescence through assumptive structures of dimorphism.[86]

Ultimately, the exigencies of biology were made into the very substance, the phenomenology and cultural ontology, of the psychic determinism according to Freud. Freud always felt that, at the bottom of human nature – which he sometimes alluded to as the biological "bedrock" of sexuality – our species could not evade the "force" of anatomy and unknown chemical and brain factors.[87] This is why Freud's last great piece, "Analysis Terminable and Interminable," ends with the dour view that "unconscious resistance to insight," that is, the revelation of deep biological sexual drives and desires through psychoanalysis, was beyond the patient and the doctor because of its biological origins; hence, the Oedipal complex and differences between the sexes to which these neuroses correspond are likewise outside society's reach.[88] It is no wonder Freud clung to a dimorphic model of sex and gender despite the evidence to the contrary.[89]

With the emergence of French sociology and anthropology, we find further reflections of the nineteenth-century influence of dimorphism being worked out in social theory. Beginning with

39

Durkheim's classic statement of primitive society, *The Elementary Forms of Religious Life*, we find the argument that male and female are so fundamental to the structure of human society that they should be treated as equivalent to the dichotomy of the sacred and the profane.[90] I doubt whether Durkheim ever questioned the innateness of dimorphism in humans; sexual dimorphism and the duality of male and female symbolism in social action and its collective representations were central to his studies of economy, religion and society. However, we might predict that Durkheim would have subordinated the needs of the individual to the greater good of the collective, as suggested in the following quotation from his famous essay on the dualism of human social life:

> Society has its own nature, and, consequently, its requirements are quite different from those of our nature as individuals: the interests of the whole are not necessarily those of the part. Therefore, society cannot be formed or maintained without our being required to make perpetual and costly sacrifices.... We must, in a word, do violence to certain of our strongest inclinations.[91]

By suggesting that the nature of social existence forced the individual always to confront the duality of being both social actor and unique individual, Durkheim added to the significant commentaries on the problem of the imperfect fit between collective categories and individual bodies, what Roland Barthes once referred to as the problem of "unclassified feelings." Durkheim the utopian socialist thinker was concerned with the moral crisis of late-nineteenth-century liberal democracy – the sense in which modern society was failing to achieve the higher dictates of providing a sound communal existence. Given such a worldview, we might speculate that the anatomically ambiguous hermaphrodite would have been treated as an anomaly that should be fitted into the general social classification of male and female for the greater good.

Faced with the relationship between individual life crises and the social rites and ceremonies for fitting individuals into collective systems, it is not surprising that Arnold van Gennep, the French ethnologist writing in the same period, strongly reified sexual dimorphism. Van Gennep's *The Rites of Passage* suggests in general that the two sexes are the fundamental division of society: that in "all societies and all social groups" there is a classification of the "group confined to persons of one sex or the other." Thus, we find in his argument that coitus is an act both of union and identification, such that rituals function as a "separation from the world of the asexual to the sexual."[92] His dimorphism is even more far-reaching when he suggests that the situation is "simpler" for girls than for boys, since "the social activity of a woman is much simpler than that of a man," even in the case of puberty, where "first emission" does not automatically and intrinsically signify a change in status. There is always a distinction between male and female in these regards, he states, although a contrast must be made between physical and social maturity.[93]

Some scholars from this period, Georg Simmel in particular, lent a different perspective to sexual dimorphism and social classification by arguing that dyads and triads are instrumental to the structure of social action. Simmel's sociology is especially notable in its insistence that dyads and triads create different phenomenologies or thought worlds.[94] In the tradition of French anthropology, Mauss hinted at the possible basis of unclassifiable sensibilities and feelings posed by the third sex or gender in his statement that "Any society will find some individuals off system – or between two or more irreducible systems."[95] Likewise, Gregory Bateson's significant study of logical types of social relations in the Iatmul *naven* ceremony (Sepik River, New Guinea) was to demonstrate how symmetrical and asymmetrical dyadic relations may teleologically create and maintain systems of social classification and action.[96] Decades later, anthropologist Francis L.K. Hsu theorized that one or another of the kin dyads, such as the husband/wife dyad, form the basis of all fundamental value orientations in kin-based social relations, an approach that causes us to question whether there is an essential structure of dyadic or symmetrical relations that underlies the conceptual representation of sexual dimorphism in social theory.[97]

41

Sexuality poses a special case for the tribe of anthropologists; and while some ethnographies since the time of Malinowski's great book, *The Sexual Life of Savages*, have taken a critical perspective on sexuality, rarely has this been extended to the question of whether there are but two sexes. Malinowski's work shows the problems with which early anthropology was faced in conceptualizing beyond sexual dimorphism. Coming from Prussia with an aristocratic doctoral training in physics and a strong reaction against conventionalism that expressed itself in his love of the avant-garde, Malinowski pioneered field study in anthropology, beginning with his early study of the family in aboriginal Australia, followed by his famous work on the Trobriand Islands off the coast of New Guinea around the time of World War I.[98] Malinowski emerged with a functional theory of culture based on individual needs: culture exists almost as a direct expression of needs on the level of the individual to survive and reproduce across time. To his credit, Malinowski more than any other anthropologist of his generation discussed the role of pleasure in traditional society, in large part because of the kind of society in which he worked.[99] Many human customs, such as kinship practices, seem to meet no direct biological need, however; and the more symbolic such practices were, such as religious ritual or myth, the less his theory worked to explain Trobriand society, let alone the total human condition.

Consider, for example, the limitations imposed on culture theory by the Western concept of the incest taboos based on the idea of an essential nuclear family prominent in Western culture. The Trobriands became the first test of Freud's theory of the Oedipal complex applied to other cultures. At the time of Freud's great effort to popularize psychoanalysis and the theory of the Oedipal complex, anthropologists were among the first to chastise him for his insensitivity to cultural differences and his speculative reading of the early human record.[100] By the mid-1920s Malinowski had composed *Sex and Repression in Savage Society*, a critique of the Oedipus complex as being always shaped by cultural setting; in fact he did not eliminate Oedipal development but only suggested that in a matrilineal society the object of desire was the sister more than the mother, with the rival being the maternal uncle rather than the father. By the end of the 1920s, Malinowski's *Sexual Life of Savages*, a remarkable description of love, sexuality and kinship in the Trobriands, was making news for its rejection of the idea that "primitives" were sexually restricted.[101] In a sense, Malinowski's great work not only justified the notion of sexual liberation in the age of flappers by suggesting that "primitives" valued pleasure; his book also implicitly attacked the received gender-dimorphic categories of masculine and feminine. Yet Malinowski (like Mead) was unable to escape the historical influence of sexual dimorphism and procreation, returning always to the reproduction ideas of the family and sex as essential needs for human society.[102]

During the same period, Mead's work on gender and sexuality from Samoa was extraordinarily influential in recasting the discourse toward environmental relativism and away from the biological bases of gender and sexuality. Mead's position, as noted above, clearly rested on biological sexual dimorphism, however; in her Samoan work, this was constructed in the area of erotic and emotional differences between the sexes, reinforced by Samoan customs. In her triculture study in the Sepik River area of New Guinea, it was manifested more strongly in her social-development description of sexual "temperament" and "personality" differences, in which a biological force, much like Freud's libido, was suggested to differentiate and mold the sexes, although the baseline starting point of development was provided by culture rather than biology.[103] (The temperamental exceptions to this point, however, suggested that Mead did not move so fully away from innate biological structures as is often believed; see below.) Critiques of this work have shown the significance of neglected colonial change in the demography and political economy of gendered status and the naive ideology of American individualism that underlay it.[104] Thus, Mead finds that the personality traits denoted as masculine and feminine are "instrumental" but only "lightly linked" to sex differences.[105] Following her teacher, Ruth Benedict,[106] Mead consistently advocated that human nature is "unbelievably malleable" in response to culture and environ-

43

ment. Nonetheless, Mead, like her contemporaries, never challenged the preconception of biological sexual dimorphism. She
explained instances of alternate sex and gender roles, such as the
North American berdache, as signs of the "raw potential" of individual biological human nature to circumvent culture in "extreme
cases."[107] This model of functional anthropology in the American school of the 1930s suggested plainly that the raw potentials
of individuals must be biologically deviant or abnormal, with
the biological inversion of the berdache a classic example. Such
examples of third sex or gender were thus lumped into a vague
category of congenital homosexuality that ratified the nineteenth-century sexological discourse of "natural" dimorphism
and heterosexuality.[108]

The critique of sexual dimorphism and the incorporation of
nonreproductive sexuality into the cross-cultural and cross-historical record have been slow and precarious, as scholars since the
emergence of feminist anthropology have suggested. Gendered
analyses of kinship have been helpful: "One of the most conspicuous features of kinship is that it has been systematically stripped
of its functions...it has been reduced to its barest bones – sex and
gender."[109] But because gendered analyses have typically ignored
sexual conduct and practices, they have also tended to marginalize
third-sex and/or third-gender categories and representations in
culture and society.[110] More generally, Carole Vance states:

> Ethnographic and survey accounts almost always follow a reporting
> format that deals first with "real sex" and then moves on to the "var-
> iations." Some accounts supposedly about sexuality are noticeably
> short on details about non-reproductive behavior; Margaret Mead's
> article about the cultural determinants of sexual behaviors...travels
> a dizzying trail which includes pregnancy, menstruation, meno-
> pause, and lactation but very little about non-reproductive sexual-
> ity or eroticism.[111]

Studies of sex and gender variation across cultures and individual differences within cultures form the basis for the analysis
not only of social categories inherited from the nineteenth cen-

tury but also of a twentieth-century invention: the concept of "identity." After World War II, the concept of identity emerged in contexts of new social and political formations, both in popular culture and in science. Particularly in studies of national character, child-rearing and personality in the psychoanalytic work of Erikson, the notion of identity became increasingly influential for a generation of psychological, cultural and gender theorists.[112]

Concurrent with this movement was the emergence of a new "social constructionist" approach that split sex and gender from biology. For instance, in gender-role study, identity research signified an emerging social science constructionism in the United States, a society that is perhaps notable for the uneasy coexistence of multiple identities of gendered relations and essentialist ideas of sexual dimorphism.[113] This new constructionism was later to become "postmodernist" in character in a variety of fields, but especially in sex and gender and gay and lesbian studies. Feminist writers in the social sciences, in critiques of patriarchal society and male supremacy, have consistently attacked the imagery of sexual dimorphism without always challenging its preconceptions, at least until recently.[114] Today, however, scholars such as Theresa de Laurentis are critical of any attempt to construct experience, especially women's experience, while others, such as Gayle Rubin and Carole Vance, are reconsidering the place of sociocultural influences in models of gender and sexuality.[115] Much attention is directed to the analytic category of gender and how it is derived or differentiated from sexual difference.[116] Feminist writers such as Judith Butler and lesbian theorists such as Sarah Lucia Hoagland are skeptical of notions of identity, as in the constructions of sexual identity and especially of gender identity, since these limit the enterprise of reinterpreting male, female and a third sex as historically bound entities.[117]

In sum, by emphasizing both biological and symbolic reproduction, scholars have continued a theoretical emphasis on sexual dimorphism in human life, which has marginalized the study of sexual and gendered variations in human history and society. In a parallel way, Foucault has argued persuasively the extent to which sexual and social theory has promoted reproduction over pleasure as ultimate aims, from Attic Greece to the modern period of Freud.[118] Many studies that assumed "male" and "female" to be the fundamental dualism of human nature and culture fan out to incorporate the assumption that two genders, masculine and feminine, are inherent building blocks in human institutions, social roles, family relations, gender and sexuality. Ultimately this imagery is based on a worldview that imagines sexual differentiation in human development to strive ultimately for biological reproduction, while the purpose of gender differentiation is to further the symbolic regeneration of society through the division of labor, social productivity, kinship and family structure and, of course, sexual relations.

Sexual Orientation: What Is a "Third Sex" Not?
Of the various forms of preconceptions that undermine the study of sexual and gender variations, we have so far ignored one that is surprisingly tenacious and often overlooked: the idea that a third sex is simply a deviant sexual orientation.

The Western debate on two- and three-sex systems has long been entangled with discussions about the dichotomous nature of heterosexuality and homosexuality. In recent years, it has fallen to gay and lesbian theorists, in particular, to question the assumption that classifications of divergent sexes and genders should be based on or explained by reference to the heterosexual/homosexual dichotomy of Western culture.[119] Whereas anthropologists once believed that the berdache or *māhū* and other forms of alternate sexes or genders were the product of temperamental variations directed into the social "niches" of deviant sexuality for social adaptation, scholars such as Barry Adam, Stephen O. Murray, David Greenberg and Walter Williams have shown that we cannot interpret these social and historical forms as biological or accidental variations of some universal "it entity" like the Western homosexual that is purported to be in the very make-up of deviant human nature.[120] Hence, while the cross-cultural forms of same-sex practice and ontology are of great importance in understanding third-sex or third-gender matters both in Western and non-Western traditions, the latter are by no means reducible to

46

the former, any more than the nineteenth-century homosexual can be equated with the berdache.[121] Thus, I urge in this section that we not confuse desire for the same sex with a third sex per se, that gender-reversed roles are not the sole basis for recruitment into a third gender role, at least not in all social traditions; and that sexual orientation and identity are not the keys to conceptualizing a third sex and gender across time and space.

It is no mystery why sexual orientation has been lumped with the question of a third gender. As we have already noted, sexologists since the mid-nineteenth century assumed that the third sex typified a person attracted to the same sex. Sexological writers following Ulrichs and Hirschfeld (and here I would include Freud) and sexual reformers such as Edward Carpenter appealed for empathy and support of the "intermediate sex," who "suffer a great deal from their own temperament."[122] In particular, writers in the tradition of of the "congenital" theory of sexual inversion, following Richard Krafft-Ebing, tended to emphasize the supposed universals of shared hermaphroditic condition among humans, especially males, which explained how such a "temperament" was to be found in many times and places.[123] Twentieth-century scholars working in this tradition have sought physical and biological bases for sexual orientation, including sexual dimorphism of anatomy or brain functions, as in Simon LeVay's recent "gay brain" study.[124] Rather, the mystery is why scholars still regard homosexuality as the true or real or hidden cause of instances of third sex or gender in time and space. Surely the situation is not so simple. Recent conceptual schemas link same-sex desires to their social classification and expression by age, gender, class and egalitarian modes of social ideas and relationships.

Neither are the categories hermaphrodite or transsexual the same as third-sex and third-gender variations around the world, notwithstanding the enormous confusion surrounding the use of such terms. One is tempted, for instance, to think of the hijras of India as hermaphrodites (or homosexuals), when in fact they constitute a different kind of social person and cultural reality.[125] Likewise, the abuse of the term *hermaphrodite* in cross-cultural sexological research shows the failure of this biologically oriented

47

field to take seriously sex and gender variations.[126] In the category of the eunuch, there is a difference between someone who is castrated and someone who castrates himself, as Kathryn M. Ringrose shows in her essay below, and there is a further classification, such as in classical and Late Antique society, in Babylonia, China and kindred places, of men who castrated themselves in a ritualistic way.[127] These and other examples of "castrati" up to the nineteenth century in European society may constitute a potential third-sex category in such places.[128]

A continuing problem in the literature is the conflation of same-sex acts with identities and thus a confusion of a third sex with a third gender. "Third gender" in this logic means a reversal of gendered relations, with males performing female roles. Attraction to the same sex, therefore, essentially reflects abnormal parenting, social learning and other forms of role behaviors that can be corrected with enough gender-typical role modeling to reverse the resulting "gender dysphoria" (the current American sexological and psychiatric nosological classification of atypical or nonconformist gender behavior).[129] But how is same-sex behavior related to third-sex traits or identity? Here a deeper biological matter is involved, usually a function of temperament or another state variable that cannot be changed. Sexologists have typically explained third-sex identity with male and female as one essential dualism linked with the other dualism of heterosexual and homosexual. By the mid-nineteenth century, Eve Sedgewick argues, this symbolic equation was so powerful that it colored virtually every domain of male sociality and masculine-defined homosocial space, such as the famous ship cabins of Melville's "Billy Budd," with the result that the threat of the homoerotic was constant enough to require an effort to suppress any sign of femaleness or desire for the same sex.[130]

When categories of homosexuality have failed to fit an alternative historical or cultural tradition, bisexuality has been invoked. Beginning with the nineteenth century, as Gert Hekma suggests, sexologists (most notably Freud) began to explain the special fit between same-sex desire and social role with the putative category of biological bisexuality.[131] Sexologists such as Money and

Ehrhardt continue this conceptual line, suggesting, for instance, that New Guinea men must be bisexual since the "overlap between homosexual and heterosexual phases of life" through "exclusive or obligatory homosexuality is lacking."[132] Recently, Money also used the language of (an implicitly biological) bisexuality to describe the Sambia of New Guinea and the concept of the "Western transsexual" to compare with the hijras of India.[133] Such accounts are limited, relying on imported cultural schemas that bend and distort same- and opposite-sex practices in such traditions or see in such practices the essential biological desires of supposedly identical Western forms.[134] Such a textual bisexuality is at its core dogmatically biological and rests on an assumptive sexual dimorphism. Seldom have writers in the sexological tradition questioned whether, by comparison, the sexual dimorphism or the homosexual/heterosexual duality of Western culture applied to non-Western traditions.[135] Scholarly reviews over the past decade have generally agreed that, while these traditions share certain elements, they cannot in such simple ways be equated.

Neither is the endurable "androgyny" – the "confusion or conflation of the concepts of and terminology for hermaphroditism and homosexuality" so ancient, as Boswell has well remarked – the core of a universal third sex or gender.[136] Although gender transformation and symbolic inversion are at the heart of Western camp and thematic variations on men dressing as women from the onset of the early modern period to the present, cross-dressing has taken on new meanings from its earlier gendered basis.[137] Surely cross-dressing in its myriad forms is not simply another variant of homosexuality or third genders, although many scholars have viewed it this way; anthropologists after World War II, for instance, followed the authoritative lead of Clelland Ford and Frank Beach that "institutionalized homosexuality" is crossdressing or transvestism; that is, gender-inverted homosexuality equated with a third gender.[138] It is now widely agreed that crossgendered practices are but one form of same-sex conduct across time and space, with many variations on the theme.[139] Attraction to the same sex in many social traditions is a basis for inclusion into a category of persons who may be treated as special, marginal

49

or deviant, as criminals or sinners, as the case may be; but these may or may not be classified as a third category of sex or gender. The point is that there is no absolute link between sexual orientation and a third sex or gender. But if the characteristics of a third sex or gender are not dependent on a sexual orientation for the same sex, how are we to anchor anthropological and historical models?

Sex and Gender Dichotomies

How many sexes and genders have there been? By addressing this question, the essays below are of use in thinking beyond social constructionism and essentialism, dichotomies of dimorphism that remain widely polarized in scholarly discourse.[140] Indeed, in view of this critique of Darwinian thought and biomedical sexology, it remains to be seen whether we must continue the conventionalized distinctions between sex as biology (sexual nature) and gender as culture (gendered society) from the past. It seems clear that, in their cultural ideals, many societies continue to reproduce dimorphic systems. However, these must not be confused with analytic concepts, and we need not accept such a dualistic system at all, for it perpetuates the false past dichotomies of nature and culture. Typically, cognitive psychological jargon regards sex as biological and "clearer," and gender as cultural and "fuzzier."[141] But cognitive boundaries are not all that matter in establishing the existence of enduring third-sex and third-gender systems, particularly in non-Western and premodern societies.[142] The question raises the issue of whether sex and gender are different entities or things, how we might identify them if so and how we might find them situated in bodies or cultural persons or social relations in the world.

To question the number of sexes and genders is to reconsider the perceptions and interpretations of the history of Western sexuality, with the relevant period of time currently still under dispute.[143] It is widely agreed that Western nations, especially social elites and later the nineteenth-century bourgeois class, based their understanding of sex and gender on the existence of only two biological (and especially morphological) entities that we categorize as natural sexes: male and female. Sexology, as we have seen, split apart sex as biology and gender as culture in the last century, with the "homosexual" or "Uranian" or "intermediate" sex a symbolic go-between.[144]

Heuristically, Western social theorists and sexologists continue to divide their observations of human action into two distinct categories, one signified by anatomical sexual characteristics, usually the genitals, and the other signified by cultural, psychic or behavioral characteristics, usually instantiated in social relations. Traditionally, the former have been represented as sex factors, while the latter have been encoded as gender factors. Using these signs, the evidence reviewed here and presented in subsequent essays suggests that creating and maintaining a *third-gender* category is difficult, tenuous and problematic; yet clear examples of it are found in other times and places. Conversely, the creation of a *third-sex* category is more problematic and rarer; fewer cases have been identified in cultures and individual life-course histories.

The Darwinian revolution, as we noted, institutionalized a reproductive paradigm of sex and gender, body and mind, that – although contested by puzzling cases on the margins of normative science – remains at the center of biological and social inquiry. Nor has the paradigm of reproductive dimorphism dissipated through its failure to explain such phenomena as the forms of hermaphroditism or the gender-transforming roles of the berdache and, more recently, the Western transsexual. These "cultural objects" – previously marginalized by science – have increasingly come to the fore and pushed "normal science" into a more critical mode.[145] Moreover, since the 1960s – the second sexual revolution in the United States – a large measure of sex and gender research has tried to criticize and reinvent the categories of investigation, particularly by feminist and gay scholars on the periphery of such fields.[146]

For more than fifty years a canonical view proposed that culture and nature were distinct categories of structural analysis: in symbolic structures, sex was to nature and to "female," as culture was to gender and to "male."[147] Sex and gender as ultimate causes were typically dualized as nature and nurture and traced to correlates with social practices.[148] Later, critiques of such dualisms – implicitly critiques of sexual dimorphism – led to feminist gender analyses, such as the critique of Lévi-Strauss's theory of kinship.[149] Moreover, to circumvent the sex-equals-biology, gender-equals-society dichotomy, anthropologist Gayle Rubin once suggested combining the two: "A 'sex/gender system' is the set of arrangements by which a society transforms biological sexuality into products of human activity, and in which these transformed sexual needs are satisfied."[150] Building on these earlier critiques, scholars such as Donna Haraway argue that the models are themselves "cultural constructions," amalgams of Western science and folk belief.[151]

The "reality status" of the sex/gender dichotomy can never be one of a pure physical reality, for its meanings invoke particular social realities too. As anthropologists have been insisting for some time, these entities are symbolic as well as material, thus requiring interpretation according to the systems of meaning in which they emerge and are expressed. (Why do so many of these essentialist vs. constructionist discussions continue to be centered around the issue of homosexuality? The answer lies, in part, with the long challenge to reproductive ideology posed by same-sex desire.)[152] This point helps us to elucidate the chronic confusion between medical and social science models and the folk theories of local traditions in many nations. As Stephen Murray (following Ernst Mayr) has reminded us, the history of Western biological theory is replete with examples of essentialism versus constructionism in the understanding and classification of nature.[153] Thus, Murray writes of the "recurring clash between essentialism (doctrines that maintain there are a limited, readily conceivable number of species characterized by essential, distinct features) and nominalism (doctrines positing an inter-breeding population of individual organisms grouped more or less arbitrarily by species names)."[154] The essentialist assumes that reality refers to the timeless condition of the body, its phylogeny and ontogeny, whereas the constructionist interprets reality as situated in social roles and lives, with knowledge and desire creating existence not in the abstract but in particular social surroundings.

Neither anthropology nor history has succeeded very well in displacing or replacing these ideas of sexual dimorphism in human culture and development, despite the long-term existence of these critiques. In large measure this is because the perspective of cultural or historical variations on a two-sex model is relatively recent and radically new, and these variations are only beginning to shape the central conceptual tendencies in these fields. For example, scholars sometimes assume that anthropologists question the epistemology of all analytical categories, at least in the sense of contextualizing them (through cross-cultural study), if not in fact deconstructing them in line with postmodern critiques of colonial and world-system factors of socioeconomic change.[155] However, such a critical perspective on sexual categories and practices is new and partial in the field.[156] In recent decades, a division of labor has resulted in the promotion of "social construction" accounts of gender in anthropology and history and the biological components of sexuality in sexology. As this paradigm breaks up, studies from all sides are challenging the assumptive structure of sexual dimorphism and the hegemony of the scientific paradigm.[157]

The efforts of anthropologists and historians to refigure this dichotomy have been largely unsuccessful, including Rubin's (1975) essay, because of the powerful hegemony of the reproductive-dimorphism paradigm in the biomedical sciences.[158] However, a different perspective on the possibility of a third sex versus a third gender has emerged from the reinterpretation of sex and gender. Kessler and McKenna, for instance, in a widely cited text from the period, suggested that the categories of male and female – based on anatomical criteria – are neither universal nor valid concepts for a gendered classification system.[159] Instead of morphology, they suggest that, for some cultures, gender role becomes the central constituent of gender. Thus, they suggest that the berdache is "a third gender category, separate from male and female."[160] Not only do "they contend that a dual gender classification system is merely a cultural construction," as Bolin has noted, but they leave aside the question of whether sexual desire or practice enters in.[161] This is significant because, in the arena of sexuality, social pressures and power relations are never far from the expression of third-sex and third-gender roles.

Competing Cultural Systems

Anthropologists have long known that two distinct, even competing, cultural ideas may simultaneously coexist to explain how society works in everyday practice. For instance, as Edmund Leach demonstrated in his famous study of the political systems of Highland Burma, two ideologies of social relations and power may coexist as competing models or idioms for the organization of social interests: the one predominant, the other subordinate, for a time; but they may oscillate and reverse historically, changing social action "on the ground."[162] Again, we know that Muslim male religious ideals of male and female roles sometimes diverge from their folk understandings, especially in domestic life.[163] In each culture, local conceptions of "human nature" are woven in and around stories about gendered social relations and desires that get expressed in practice, although open contradictions between cultural ideals and social practice sometimes prevail.[164]

Systems of ideas about reproduction may come directly from folk or popular culture, although they are clearly influenced in the modern period by sexological science and medical notions of sex, reproduction, gender and the psychology of development.[165] Between science and popular culture or folk ideas, we have the basis for understanding a new moral discourse of classification relevant to the third sex and gender.[166] Such issues in relation to philosophy have been well studied in classical Attic culture following Socrates, wherein the rising social formation resulted in newly engendered roles and the eventual privatization of the psyche as individual self.[167] In short, the emergence of a historical category of the gendered self was gradually attached to sex roles, leading to more explicit sexual-dimorphic ideas crystallized in the scientific and technological (in Foucault's sense) discourse of ancient Greece.

But how do such ideas and practices influence the creation and reproduction of alternate sex and gender practices? Clearly, power is a key factor in deciding which ideas get played out in which arenas and by which actors. Rubin once suggested that Western institutions continue to oppress and subordinate the Western "subject" to heterosexual forms and women to patriarchal forms.[168] This occurs, she argued, through the exaggeration of sex differences in order to suppress equality between the sexes. "The division of labor by sex can therefore be seen as a 'taboo': a taboo against the sameness of men and women, a taboo dividing the sexes into two mutually exclusive categories, a taboo which exacerbates the biological differences between the sexes and thereby *creates* gender."[169] Such an analysis links conceptions of sex and gender with the need, in systems of inequality, to maintain through ideas or social relations these same forms of inequality.

Power structures must be seen not only in relation to their ability to coerce and force persons into the social classification of the sexes and genders but also as systems of ideas through which such power is manifested. The role of an elite or its discourse can critically influence the maintenance of a sex and gender system, namely, in its attitude regarding symbolically potent third-sex/gender figures, such as the hijras of India or the *māhū* of Polynesia. Such responses within a hegemonic situation include how cultural ideas of male and female are related to gendered relations and sexual practice and whether there might be two or more cultural idea systems (or mythologies) for reproducing sexual and gendered relations present within the same culture during the same historical period.[170] Historical and social formations create for cultural actors what we might call mainstreams and margins, social arenas which cultural spaces and social places define by who does what with whom and under what normative circumstances their actions are approved or disapproved.[171] Their actions and roles thus reflect the structure of power relations through dominant versus subordinate ideas of sexual relations during the historical period.

Certain cultures go to extreme lengths to exaggerate the differences between male and female. For example, among the peoples of New Guinea, such as the Sambia or the Bimin-Kuskusmin, sex and gender differences are prominent in myth and cultural

55

organization.[172] Reproduction is central to all of these, but what
is defined as "reproductive" varies greatly, as, for instance, in the
case of Sambia men who inseminate boys to complete their "biological masculinization," enabling the boys ultimately to become
reproductively competent.[173] Such a view underlines the importance of recognizing the inherently cultural nature of the definition of reproductive processes and the fallacy of opposing real and
symbolic forms of procreation.[174]

Consider the competing idea systems within the history and
sexual culture of urban Brazil.[175] Over several centuries, Richard
Parker suggests, the local beliefs of perceived anatomical differences were transformed into culturally defined ontologies of gender, with distilled ideas about appropriate sexual action. The
marked sexual dimorphism of this patriarchal system relates the
local concept of same-sex desire to "a kind of symbolic equivalent of the biological female."[176] However, sharply opposed idealized anatomical types produce defined realities of masculine and
feminine encoded into a collective system of sexual classification
that symbolically constructs social reality. Thus, what is sexually
exciting to Brazilians is also forbidden or taboo, so that the violation of the taboo creates a significant subordinate ideology of
state and church formations.[177] The classification system facilitates domination through the acceptance of sexual and gender
hierarchy, because the public ideology of institutions and discourse is highly dimorphic.

In the accounts collected below these "reproductive" factors
of power are expressed in variations on what might be called idea
systems of human sexual nature and human sexual culture. In our
own Western tradition, such conventionalized cultural definitions
of human nature confront us with moral systems of the classification of bodies, persons and acts that go well beyond Darwin's
nineteenth-century sexual dimorphism, as Foucault repeatedly
showed in his discussions of the "incorporation of perversions"
that inverted the masculine and feminine, making the sodomite
into the permanent "species" of the homosexual.[178] They represent a distillation of folk ideas; or, alternatively, ideologies of collective ideas of human nature crystallized into codes which tell

what a human being is and should be and that prescribe behavior in ways that create a full person across the life course.[179] In most traditions these pivot on male and female as fundamental types of human nature. But the fact that they are pivotal does not preclude the existence of alternate sex and gender ideas or social roles.

For example, the Bimin-Kuskusmin speak of hermaphroditic individuals and have a category for them; their autochthonous ancestor is hermaphroditic as well. Yet their sex and gender system is strongly marked for sexual dimorphism, seemingly unable to circumvent the powerful institutions that instill and reproduce male and female differences rather than blend them. (The Indonesian community studied by Cora DuBois is comparable to the Bimin-Kuskusmin in this respect; categories for hermaphrodites are not lumped together or confused with transvestite third-gender roles in these Indonesian societies, such as the *waria* role reported by Dede Oetomo.)[180] Cultural ideas of a third sex or gender are not to be interpreted automatically as manifestations of social reality, nor must they be confused with the schemas and practices of such peoples (a comparative principle reiterated by Mead in this context).[181] In short, the mere existence of an idea system that exaggerates sex differences does not preclude the institutionalization of a third sex in such cultures (indeed, among both the Sambia and Bimin-Kuskusmin these coexist).[182]

Power and Sexual "Passing"

Why, Goffman once asked in his influential book *Stigma* (1963) – a study of how social actors managed "spoiled" identities – does someone attempt to pass as "normal," a categorical Other, unless it is to avoid discredit and the loss of social status?[183] In the more extreme cases, sociologists have long suggested, the deviant or forbidden third sex or gender leads individuals to avoid being identified; that is, they are forced to adapt the appearances and accoutrements of hegemonic social roles and practices.[184] Alternate or "deviant" third-sex and third-gender roles are thus typically displaced to the illicit, immoral or illegal margins of society.[185] Those who are "passing" seek to hide their sexuality and be defined as normatively male and masculine or female and feminine (or heterosexual, e.g.; not gay or lesbian), objectifying the very categories (male and female) that stand in opposition to their hidden being and desires.[186] Such matters require an analysis of the embedded concepts that define and express cultural reality and how power manipulates realities and persons, as these impinge on the creation and presentation of an individual's sense of belonging to third-sex/gender categories, either overtly in public or covertly in private discourse and thought.[187]

The key to understanding the recombination of ideas about culture and nature here rests in the relationship between social status, power and the secrecy of passing as normatively male and female and heterosexual/homosexual in the Western tradition.[188] However, in American culture, unlike that of India or Native North America, we do not recognize sexual or gendered transformation in categories; change may occur in the person but not in the categories of male and female. The transsexual is thus required to hide and pass under threat of punishment, which is sometimes severe.[189] There is a cultural logic in the emergence of these categories and identities, a structural trend that relies on hierarchy and status differences. When males have more privileged positions, so the logic goes, when their relations derive in part from principles of subordination, then males who opt out of their "biologically based" sex roles lose status and are disparaged. No one would desire a decrease in status, or so goes the rational choice theory; therefore the change and loss of status can only be motivated by biological drives beyond the conscious intentions or free will of the person.[190]

Passing is a cultural performance but it is also a power play. With passing we come to a different problem in the creation and maintenance of a third sex or gender: the sense in which secrecy, lying, cheating and other tactics of opportunistic adaptation apply to the situation of the individual who cannot or will not conform to particular sex and gender conventions. The categorical distinctions at the cultural level are blurred or transcended at the level of social interaction, as with the cases of hermaphrodites and transsexuals. As Harold Garfinkel once insisted in his classic study of heterosexual passing among American transsexuals, the power of conformity in American culture is great enough to create the idea of "cultural genitals":

> From the standpoint of an adult member of our society, the perceived environment of "normally sexed persons" is populated by two sexes and only two sexes, "male" and "female." [Thus, it follows that] certain insignia are regarded by normals as essential in their identifying function.... The possession of a penis or a vagina as a biological event is to be distinguished from the possession of one or the other or both as a cultural event...[thus suggesting] the differences between biological and cultural penises and vaginas as socially employed evidences of "natural sexuality."[191]

One of the most powerful case studies of passing ever conducted is Garfinkel's remarkable ethnomethodological investigation of a biologically normal Southern California male changing to the social role of a female. His detailed study of "Agnes," a UCLA transsexual patient who successfully passed as female in every sphere of her life (including living with female roommates in a small apartment for two years), offers many cues for thinking about the social and moral pressures to conform to two-sex systems.[192] "Passing was not her [Agnes's] desire...it was necessity," he says. Garfinkel insightfully reveals the meaning of passing by intersexed persons as either male or female in contemporary society. He shows how they are moral ascriptions and recognizes that the status, social legitimacy and freedom of the actors are constantly in peril.[193]

In other times and places as well, avoidance of being forced into a cultural classification of normative sex or gender roles may require circumventing direct challenges to the authority system. Here the cultural actor may exercise the radical option of passing as a normative member of the sex or gender dyads of the hegemonic majority of the historical society in question. Biological females who dressed in men's clothes throughout Europe for centuries and females in the Balkans, especially those who aspire to the warrior role, who successfully pass as the empowered sex/gendered man are exercising such options.[194] They are surprisingly greater in number than we might have once thought.[195] The social possibilities of passing offer status enhancement or decline. Hence, as power and prestige are at stake, societies may go to some lengths to survey and control social transitions between these liminal positions; indeed, the third sex and gender is a state "betwixt and between" par excellence.[196] Similar social and political implications apply to biological males who castrate themselves to become palace eunuchs, the male sodomites of the seventeenth century, mollies of the eighteenth century, "inverts" and "intermediate-sexed" homosexuals of the nineteenth century and other categories in which aspects of the male actor are viewed as immoral, illegal or illicit in the classification of the social order. Conversely, the logic goes, women who opt for third roles and identities are opting "up": that is, moving socially and symbolically upward in the status hierarchy system. For example, female berdache, like women who take on manly roles, especially the admired position of the Balkan warrior males, are then reared as men and gender-identified as males. They remind us of the *kwolu-aatmwol* among the Sambia of New Guinea.[197] This raises questions regarding the instability of third-sex/gender categories,[198] a matter to which I will return in the conclusion.

Cultural Reality and Ontologies of the Third Sex

To create the meaningful conditions and agency of self-motivating social actors, every culture constructs its own ontology. For a collective ontology to emerge and be transmitted across time, there must be a social condition, eventually a stable social role, that can be inhabited – marking off a clear social status position, rights and duties, with indications for the transmission of corporeal and incorporeal property and status. We have already seen the power exerted to conform to reproductive and dimorphic structures that results in passing behavior. For an individual to express sex and gender being is not in itself always sufficient to sustain the beliefs, accoutrements and social structure of third sexes or genders. Ideally, categories of being acquire greater force the longer they exist historically and are eventually transformed into social roles and practices, as hinted by the cultural ontologies of the berdache, the hijra, the *māhū*, the Sambian *turnim-man* and other examples in this volume.

The work of culture in these famous traditions is to create ontologies that link the inside and outside of the person as a whole system.[199] By cultural ontologies, I mean local theories of being and the metaphysics of the world; of having a certain kind of body and being in a certain kind of social world, which creates a certain cultural reality; and of being and knowledge combined in the practice of living as a third sex or gender. Local models of ontology are concerned with the nature of being a person and of being in the world with such a nature. Such local theories implicitly ask: What drives, intentions, desires and developmental pathways characterize the nature of a person?[200] Are these characteristics found also in other persons or in entities (such as spirits) and the social and physical surroundings? By contrast, the Western folk ontology of sexuality takes as its intentional subject the lone individual, whose sexual nature is borne in the flesh of one sex or the other, but not in both, and who is viewed quite apart from other entities of a social and spiritual sort.

In short, the third sex has, in some places and times, emerged as an ontological entity, that is, a distinctive "subject" with its own moral voice. When people identify with a category, they endow it with a meaning beyond themselves. Thus, to say, "I am berdache," is to suggest an "I" (subject) in active identification with "berdache" (categorical object); and again that the subject and categorical object are in a stable formation across time.[201] That is not the case, of course, in a culture that lacks a third-sex category, such as France of the nineteenth century, in which the sorrowful hermaphrodite Herculine Barbin ultimately destroyed himself.[202] In the modern period, such persons seek a shifting target, a divergent and eclectic set of people who identify with ambiguous persons but not categories and who also feel the pull of other factors of social classification, such as class.[203] This is why the presence of androgynous figures, of ontological beings and entities, especially gods and spirits, is critical in understanding the emergence of culturally constituted third-sex and third-gender roles.

To take the textbook case of the ancient Greeks as a prominent starting point: it is not what you *are*, they might have said;
it is what you *do* that counts in the reckoning of gender and sexuality. Thus, the erotic relations between men and boys were not
a challenge to strongly dimorphic gendered roles, with masculine honor and feminine nature distinct, a view that was at once
ontological and instrumental in its everyday practice of differentiating nature from desire in their view.[204] The Greek system
of desires and appetites, their taxonomy of forms of love, was
indeed a curious combination of what would, in the later modern period, be referred to as social constructionism (impression-
ism) and essentialism (realism).[205] Whatever the exigencies of
one's body, especially the visible anatomy, we can ask: What social
role does the person take, or what position do they claim: that
of the first sex (male), second sex (female) or third sex (e.g., hermaphrodite)? Certainly the example of Tiresius the soothsayer
was widely known, signifying mythological indications of gender
transformation throughout the ancient world.[206]

Clearly, the Greek cultural signifiers of human nature were
characteristically gendered as masculine or feminine, but their sex
system was open to other signifiers.[207] Plato's idea of three sexes
as a part of an original human nature was prominent in the *Symposium*, and this no doubt bears to some extent on the concept
of *psyche* in Greek and the very different notions of culture and
human nature in the Greek tradition, which allowed a greater latitude of exceptions to the later historical gendered self that was
to emerge.[208] The god Hermaphroditus held a special meaning,
often equated historically with what we would today label the
folk ideology of homosexuality; and hermaphroditic images are
common in Greek art (and before that, in Egyptian statuary).[209]
Here too we see the ineluctable tendency of the modern period
to dimorphize classical culture.[210] This is why the example of
Tiresius, the epitome of a prophet, is telling: according to myth,
he was born of one sex, changed form to another, but later in life
changed back again, suggesting that the soothsayer should embody
both male and female qualities for greater magical power.[211]

Thus, the phenomenological force of the idealized form grows the longer it exists within the traditions of a culture, which is one of the aspects of the third sex and gender hitherto ignored by anthropologists.[212] Through time and the contextual routines and social habits of growing up, of constructing social relations around a certain identity, presentations of person and self are distilled, habituated and made into a rather enduring system of being of a third sex and/or gender.

Changing Genders and Transforming Sexes

Virtually all known forms of third sex or gender suggest transformation of being and practice: the alteration of qualities or essences of the body and person with time. This may have occurred in the womb, in early childhood or in later life. Of course, examples of alternate sex and gender categories are also known in which being of a different nature, that is, neither male or female nor masculine or feminine, is also known; but what marks the Western conception of these matters is the quality of transformation. Why this seems not at issue is that Western ontology and epistemology suggest that, while much about the individual may change, one's sex and gender (and nowadays their sexual orientation) should remain fixed and unchanging throughout the individual's life course. One indication of this comes in the context of the 1960s and what was at that time a new awareness of transsexualism. In this context, Mead once warned about the preoccupation of Americans with differentiating male from female, of placing too much emphasis on initial sex assignment rather than on subsequent gendered achievements that altered gender-role assignments, suggesting the very basis for mediating forms of sex and gender to emerge in the future. Her worry has been taken to its furthest reaches in the modern technological context, with the use of genetic screening to identify and restrict entrance of male and female athletes in competitions, especially the Olympics.[213]

What does such change indicate for non-Western ontologies? The Western view since the time of colonial expansion has been strongly influenced by reproductive assumptions about the ultimate and unchangeable nature of gender and sexuality. These attitudes were in turn mapped onto the interpretations of sexual activity and social roles among colonial peoples, which is evident from the responses to all forms of sodomy (here, "unnatural sexual practice") among colonized peoples from before the modern period, especially in the New World.[214]

It is fitting that we consider the issues of changing genders by first referring to the congeries of roles known as "berdache" in Native North America.[215] Here the person did not remove his or her genitals but moved into the other gendered role. Some berdache were of extraordinary influence in their own local communities, as Will Roscoe has shown from a recent biographical study. Among the Zunis, Roscoe notes, the death of a berdache such as We'wha elicited "universal regret and distress."[216] But for the Spanish and Anglo-Americans who overran the Southwest, berdache often evoked dismay, disgust, anger or, at the least, ridicule. Berdache were viewed as more than anomalies; they were monsters, freaks of nature, demons, deviants, perverts, sinners, corrupters. They committed the "nefarious vice," the "abominable sin." We can now see why, in the colonial period, it is reported that the perfect berdache would pass as a person of the opposite sex in order never to be detected.[217]

Notice the early tendency to identify berdache with biological abnormalities or to wonder whether there was a biological basis for their behavior.[218] Such a bias is in keeping with Western ontology, which ascribes sex and gender to biology and permits no transformation after birth, except in the recent case of transsexuals, through radical surgery. Berdache, in general, were changing genders, not sexes. The biological bias continues to the present.[219] In many such traditions, a strong inclination existed to attribute change to biological factors. This is often regarded in a negative light, although with many exceptions, as we will see. In the case of the palace eunuch, many negative qualities were attributed to the eunuch; eunuchs were anomalous, being unable to suckle but also unable to impregnate. Their association with the female world, with harems and slaves, seems to have lent them certain negative connotations, as Ringrose suggests.

The berdache was of course not singular but of many tribal forms, with different beliefs and social practices, as Roscoe shows.

The cultural ontology was legitimized by social practices, such as an initiation, folklore, a variety of social attitudes, generally approving sexual attitudes and higher-status positions for women and berdache. We will use the Mohave case as representative of selected issues here, although it is distinctive, and Roscoe's essay below illustrates more general trends.[220]

Several cultural and ontological features qualify the candidacy of Mohave berdache to a third-gender role.[221] First, Mohave recognized a distinctive ontology of the berdache, expressed in heartfelt desires, task preferences and cultural transformation, both at the level of the genitals and of personal pronouns. Second, they legitimized the role by spiritual power, an attribute lacking in our Western conception of these variations of sex and gender. Third, Mohave did not stigmatize the condition: they did not reduce the whole person to the sex act; the condition of the berdache was not illegal or immoral, only atypical; and in general social privileges were not withheld from the berdache. Nor did Mohave stigmatize the partners or lovers of the berdache, a point to which Greenberg has drawn special attention in viewing the general social support and acceptance of the third sex and gender among Native Americans.[222] Finally, they recognized that the sexual excitement of the berdache depended on being in a sexual and social formation with someone of the same biological sex but of the opposite gender. Their excitement (for "male" berdache, of being penetrated anally by their partners and having an orgasm in this way) suggests a significant basis for the personal ontology and commitment to the role throughout the life of the individual.

Furthermore, anthropological authorities tended to be reductionistic in reducing the berdache as a category to "abnormal" aspects of homosexuality or to gender inversion. Both Benedict's and A.L. Kroeber's functional theories suggested the biological abnormality of the berdache, who was unable to fulfill the warrior ideals of Native American cultures.[223] When bravery in warfare is expected, some will not by temperament be able to produce it, they reckoned: hence, the berdache. Abnormal individuals need a social niche, just like everyone else in a culture, Kroeber argued. The berdache was no different, just a special case of fitting a constitutional type to a cultural type. Kroeber expected that in any population there would be a certain number of abnormal individuals who could not fit the norm, and customs would evolve to accommodate the personal needs of the deviant nature to culture. George Devereux added the intellectual baggage of the Freudian "invert," which had its own representation of the homosexual as constitutional invert.[224] Mead also epitomized this position by suggesting that homosexuality and transvestism of the berdache type were inevitable mismatches between individual temperaments and the social requirements of particular cultures.[225] Bolin finds in general that the berdache category has been variously referred to as cross-cultural homosexuality, transvestism and transsexualism, with major disagreements on whether the focus of study was "sexual object choice, dress, gender role, or even identity."[226]

The spiritual aspects of the berdache are significant in interpreting the third sex and gender. In the case of the Mohave, for instance, the institution was sanctified by two sorts of symbols: a widespread origin myth; and dream theory, suggesting that Mohave women's dreams would influence the fetus in the womb.[227] Devereux shows connections between the dream theory and uterine fantasies of the mother of the berdache; but he goes further to regard all Mohave shamans as "crazy" and as "inverts," inversion as a biological defect and homosexuality in all tribes as neurotic.[228] Nor is this view entirely defunct. We find in Gisela Bleibtreu-Ehrenberg the functional notion that, where strong sexual dimorphism occurs, without the possibility of individual exceptions, "transvestism offers an institutionalized way of compensating for lack of success in a male role by assuming a female social role."[229]

Yet other authors have gone to the extreme of treating the berdache's capacity to change genders as a special case by virtue of its association with the role of the shaman or of magical power in general in these cultures. We know, of course, that not all shamans are berdache, any more than all berdache are shamans. Yet Mircea Eliade makes this generalization: "The majority of shamans are inverts and sometimes even take husbands; but even when they are sexually normal their spirit guides oblige them to

66

dress as women."[230] Still, in its strongest form, as in the writings of Bleibtreu-Ehrenberg, we find a general equation in which homosexuality in shamanism is viewed as the outcome and ultimate form, if not in fact the cause, of transvestism in all simple societies.[231] Obviously there are myriad examples of shamans who are not gender transformed.[232] There are also societies in which the prescription to change genders is a requirement of the role.[233]

One of the most curious cases is that of the Inuit Eskimo of Canada, in which is posited a complete theory of the ontology of the third sex, wherein the individual becomes a shaman as a fetus in the mother.[234] Thus, the "third-sex" Inuit shaman is perceived as changing genders by reincarnating from the opposite sex or having a spiritual past life that suggests gender transformation as an intermediate form of human being.

As Devereux interpreted it, the berdache provides a fine example of how custom defined desire: by virtue of being a berdache the social actor would want to act as the opposite sex, the biologically male berdache acting as female, for example, cutting himself to bleed as though he menstruated and simulating pregnancy by being bloated from constipation. But why would the person take the role on in the first place?[235] Devereux believed the reason had to do with biology, an innatism of inversion, and he used the ideal of nineteenth-century Western homosexuality through which to represent it. This was an unfortunate categorization; it violated more than it illuminated of the berdache role. Walter Williams has suggested that three Western norms were most violated by "male" berdache roles: gender reversal, passivity (male berdache in passive sexual relations with other males) and the subversion of nature by the "unnatural practices."[236]

But what about the cases of changing sex? Here, more radical ideas come into play, involving notions of transforming the body, its organs, fluids and reproductive capacities. The cases to consider in this book are those of the New Guinea hermaphrodites, the hijras of India and American transsexuals.

The 5-alpha reductase hermaphrodite is a rare species of biologically intersexed individuals that results in delayed anatomical maleness, with absent or tiny male genitals sometimes mistaken for female ones.[237] In the Dominican Republic, the study of such persons was conducted in the absence of a proper understanding of local ontological categories, especially the *guevedoche* ("penis at twelve"), which permits a kind of delayed third-sex or third-gender nature to emerge around the time of puberty.[238] Such persons have a folk classification that permits them the flexibility to change dress and tasks, names and decorative motif, with alterations in sexual partners, albeit those of the "appropriate" sex object at that stage of their lives. My analysis rejects the biological reductionism of the biomedical interpretation of this case.[239] Among the New Guinea Sambia, several criteria constitute the categorical *kwolu-aatmwol* ("female thing changing into male"). These traits include, for instance, anatomical ambiguity at birth; assignment of the infant to neither the male nor female categories but rather to the *kwolu-aatmwol* category; the existence of a lexeme and noun of the same name; a cluster of social attitudes about personal development and change; the existence of moral and social practices that constitute a different means of handling social life after puberty; and the autochthonous myth of parthenogenesis in the ancestors, whose first anatomical condition was hermaphroditic.

These criteria define a symbolic niche and a social pathway of development into later adult life distinctly different from the cultural life plan set out by a model based on male/female duality. Note again how the *kwolu-aatmwol* exists in a culture of extraordinary gender differentiation, with sexual dimorphism marked in humans and in nature, according to the Sambia worldview.[240] That such a categorical alternative exists at all is a true accomplishment, a partial victory of nature over culture – not as complete as the American transsexual who uses the wonders of medical technology to do so, but still rather impressive – such that we might be inclined to see it as a triumph of the third sex. And yet, in the Sambia scheme of things, no classificatory distinction is tenable that separates sexual nature from sexual culture when it comes to these persons. "Thirdness" in nature exacts its social cost; like the hijras, this form of thirdness is not admired, and any evidence that persons would cling to the categorical position must cause us to take notice. The Sambia evidence suggests that socialization into the role of a mistaken female produces such a strong learning effect that these cultural females would happily live as biological females their whole lives and never transform into the male sex, were it possible to do so. In this sense, cultural socialization of sex and gender triumphs over anatomical nature.

Certain kinds of characteristics serve to differentiate sex and gender categories in other cultures, and these are not confined to those of Western distinctions in any simple sense. For example, the forms of *bayot* and *lakin-on* reveal alternate-sex and alternate-gender persons from Cebuan society in the Philippines.[241] These two categories are synonymous for many things in local language, including homosexuality, transvestism, hermaphroditism and so on. Yet the ethnographer tells us that the

> Cebuan vocabulary...distinguishes between degrees of "*bayotness*." A slightly effeminate man is *dalopap* or *binabaye*.... When these terms are used in reference to a chicken, they describe a rooster with henlike plumage...[whereas] *bayot-babyot* are more effeminate males, who do not cross-dress and who usually are not considered active sexual inverts. [But] male transvestites, who normally regard members of their sex as erotic objects, are "real" or "true" *bayot*.... Identification of a person as a bayot or lakin-on...is based on both physical fetuses and behavioral characteristics. Cross-dressing is not essential for such classification.[242]

Indeed, we learn that it is dangerous to cross-dress "in public"; cross-dressing occurs only in private or in the anonymous circumstances of large cities for migrants.[243]

Here again, power and passing enter the picture; but the point is that significant local traits distinguish the development of alternate-sex and alternate-gender relations in such a small society. Compare this to the account of the Indonesian "third-sex" role of *waria*, as reported by Oetomo, or the *māhū* of Tahiti, known for centuries, analyzed by Levy and here reported anew by Niko Besnier, which provides important comparisons to the Cebuan and *waria* traditions.[244]

The hijras of India are another case of changing sexes, or, to be more precise, of being ritually invested into a third sex. In India sex/gender-role pressures are sufficiently great as to have generated variations of a third kind. The best-known form is that of the hijras, hermaphroditic or castrated males, who assume a ritual caste role that we may interpret as a third sex and gender. However, another lesser-known alternate category – in this case a third gender, not a third sex – is opted for by certain women. This occurs in the case of the unmarried celibate female who visibly dresses and acts as a man in many contexts in the Kangra fringe area of the Himalayas.[245] Although the hijra is constituted on anatomical grounds and the Indian women who dress as men are rare and created from gender-role distinctions only, the two types are significant variations on male/female dimorphism in one of the world's oldest and largest civilizations.

The hijras seek the protection and blessings of the Mother Goddess and in turn have the ritual power to bless and curse. As Serena Nanda notes, cutting off the penis defines the "ideal marker" of the hijra's role. Hijras can bless children, and curse adults, to earn a living; their powers exercise symbolic control over life and death. They legitimately claim as their own caste all children who are anatomically hermaphroditic or have a strong desire to become a hijra; that is, children who are neither male nor female and who may, as adults, be perceived either as hijra or, when apart from the caste, "pass" as biologically and socially normative females. The existence of a lower caste embodied by hijras completes the social reproduction of these persons in the collective of the social body as well. In fact, the hijra is not an entirely esteemed social category; it is perceived as somewhat discredited, as associated with fallen women, prostitutes, marginals and ritually dangerous underclasses that threaten the upper castes, from whom, incidentally, the hijras seem not to be drawn. Both sex and gender criteria help culturally to define the hijra, and we can identify the category as rather markedly "third" in nature and culture. In her extant analysis of the hijra, Nanda tends to see the dilemma and construct an account of the cultural reality of hijra; she compares the hijras with transsexuals.[246]

This analytic move, as she herself has noted and as she explores in new ways in this volume, is a problematic classification in two respects: there is no Western category of thirdness in general, and transsexuals experience an existential crisis in the definition of what Garfinkel has called their "cultural genitals."

The American transsexual displays very different ideas and social relations compared with the Indian hijras, a cultural instance that seems more fully inscribed as both a third sex and a third gender. American culture is heavily dimorphic in its sex and gender roles and institutions.[247] Transsexuals are driven – in the nineteenth-century biological sense of the term – to the radical surgical step of altering their morphology through medical technology to conform to their ontology. Notice that the hijra, too, undergoes castration, healing and bodily and spiritual rebirth to be more like the opposite sex, but in the Indian context, a cultural reality shared in public life extends beyond the doctor's office. Thus, a mismatch between transsexuals' anatomical nature and their inner, desired being moves them, much like the berdache, to sexual bonding with the opposite sex, but opposition is here based not on the morphology but on private reality that lacks a cultural seal of approval.

Notice that, as we move closer in historical time, we find increasing numbers of historical examples of cross-dressing and of women who dress in men's clothes. Perhaps this is an artifact of a better historical record. However, these are aspects of the transition not only to modernism but possibly also to the advent of increasing sex and gender hierarchies through the gender reversals and transvestism of the early homosexual role and of the transsexual in modern times. As noted by René Grémaux, the historical formation of women who dressed in men's clothes bears a relationship to gender passing for status enhancement.[248] In the twentieth century, one of the more remarkable examples of this genre was Jack Bee Garland (1869-1936), an American female who lived as a man. Jack claimed to enjoy the company of men more than that of women; and the biographer sees in this the evidence for Jack's being a female-to-male transsexual, although one wonders about the symbolic power and enticements of being and living as a man in such a strongly dimorphic and patriarchal society at the time.[249] Clearly, this leads to issues of seeing the transsexual not only as someone who senses the self to be in the wrong body and who desires to pass as the opposite sex, but of a problematical ontology of the self that has no matching social and historical category and role in which to anchor itself.[250]

Desire and the Transition to Modernism
The missing key to much study of third sexes and genders is the understanding of the desires and attractions of the individual and the role in which these influence the establishment of a social status as a third sex or the effort to pass as normative and live secretly as such. Especially in those instances of recruitment or advancement to a new position, of the Mohave child becoming a berdache or a young Indian male electing to have himself castrated, we are woefully ignorant of the reasons the individual desired such a transformation. How much of it is the product of ontology, of a sense of being that identifies with the category; and how much comes from social and sexual practices that direct individuals from the position of normative sex and gender roles and hierarchies? From anthropology and history our knowledge of these matters is limited, although the essays in this book are a notable advance.

By focusing on the concept of desire we face the challenge of linking these cross-cultural forms to the transition to modernism in our own Western tradition since the Renaissance. If my intuition is correct, this is exactly the missing element in understanding the creation and maintenance of the third sex and gender across time and space. What role do choice, free will and voluntarism play in discriminating individual and group social practices with respect to the third sex? Why, that is, does a ten-year-old Mohave select to undergo the ceremony to become a berdache, which his parents must arrange although not necessarily encourage?[251] Whatever the answers to such questions, the transition to modernism identifies the emergence of individual and private desire with the creation of third-sex and third-gender categories in culture and history.

To take a paradigmatic example from anthropology and social history, the emergence of same-sex desire and the creation of new third-sex and third-gender categories and roles are proving to be an area of immense interdisciplinary overlap in the study of the variety of "homosexualities." Where homosexuality was thought to occur in tribal societies, in the sense of same-sex desire coupled with gender transformation of social role and dress, it has been seen as the manifestation of something basic, primitive, biological: a certain kind of essential nature forcing its way out of the body.[252] We now see how naive such a view was.[253] It is well known from the research of Trumbach that a series of emergent sex and gender forms of social role and desire were prominent by the eighteenth century in England.[254] Later, as Hekma shows, sexologists who inherited these distinctions expressed a worldview that compressed all sex and gender variation into a two-sex-system equation of "perverse implantations," to use Foucault's term. And so often these linked biological forms to gender change as located in individual minds or bodies rather than examine any aspect of the historical or social conditions of their lives.

When might one legitimately see sexual desire or practice as a signifier of a third sex, as neither a male/female nor masculine/feminine signification? Some, such as Foucault, have wondered whether desire for the same sex creates these bases in society and psyche for the third sex (i.e., in his famous discussion of the nineteenth-century closet homosexual's "compulsion" to confess and the desires that emanate from this). As we are learning from the earliest reaches of the modern period, same-sex desires seem fundamental to the nature of some sodomites during the golden age in Holland and later to the mollies in England. While these developments were important in the formation of social classifications and hierarchy in the modern period, they also have profound implications for the emergence of moral ontological categories of sex and gender.

The moral ideology of dimorphic reproduction and its dualism of heterosexual and homosexual has changed greatly over historical time. Nearly three centuries ago same-sex desire was punished by death in many Western countries. For example, in Holland between the late seventeenth and early eighteenth centuries, the "sodomite" was tried and condemned to death, initially in secret and then in public execution, as Theo van der Meer demonstrates. Many people were executed during this 150-year period. The evidence from love letters and confessions suggests that some of these sodomites had a clear sense of desiring the same sex. Why were the early executions secret? Because sodomy was loathsome, such a crime against God and nature that it should not be discussed in public, a truly silent discourse.[255] The gender hierarchy of the time included the manifestations of patrician power of men over women and then over the "whore." As the sodomite network of the seventeenth century came into existence, this sex and gender system began to change, with the introduction of a new fourth category, the "he-whore," as a third-sex/gender role. By 1811 the worst abuses were over, and eventually the Netherlands went on to become not only the most enlightened of countries, but with increasing secularization, the most progressive in the area of same-sex rights. By contrast, in Germany this change did not occur; and with the fall of the Weimer Republic, the Nazis enforced a naive "naturalist" ideology of reproduction that made men superior to women, abortion a crime against the state and homosexuality a moral drain and threat to the reproductive virility of the fatherland.[256] These moralisms propped up a totalitarian order that required procreation to sustain its expanding engine.

In addition to looking at the issues of a third sex and gender from the perspective of a reproductive ideology or "technology," we might consider how desire and pleasure influence the emergence of the third sex or gender. Social history also teaches that the construction of the sexual as a morally based normative category of being and action was tantamount to the invention of sexual or gendered "normality" – especially through nineteenth-century medicine. Historically, as Foucault has detailed, the invention of normality as a social category of the nineteenth century had the greatest of consequences for emerging forms.[257] It led to a new sexual/cultural ontology, to the production of private desires and their hidden expression in power relations.

The construction of the homosexual in the modern period

becomes an important clue to understanding the emergence of sexual and gender dimorphism in this period. As sexology creates a zoological classification of sexual types, including the "intermediate sex" or "psychic hermaphrodite" prominent in the works of such figures as Ulrichs, Ellis, Hirschfeld, Carpenter and Freud, we see the beginning of a new form of evolutionary thinking. Krafft-Ebing incorporated many of Ulrichs's ideas into his sexological works. It was to Ulrichs perhaps that the notion of the intermediate sex as a "female soul enclosed in a male body" (*anima muliebris in corpore virili inclusa*) – or at least its popular form – must be credited. It was believed by some medical practitioners and popular authorities that one could identify the male homosexual immediately by physical examination; he would have a large or small penis, a lopsided mouth or another anatomical mark that signified his status as a "monster" of nature, an intermediate sex.[258] The "victims" of masturbation as a "disease" were similarly classified. Ulrichs believed that same-sex desires exist in everyone; but in the third or intermediate sex, the Uranian, these take a more intense dualistic form. From a letter of December 23, 1862, he states: "Sexual dualism, which is universally present in embryonic form in every human individual, simply reaches a higher degree of expression in hermaphrodites and Uranians than in the ordinary man and woman. With Uranians, their level of expression merely takes a different form than with hermaphrodites."[259]

The nineteenth century is an odd mixture of sexual libertarianism and excessive social classification and conformity, as historians such as Paul Robinson and Jeffrey Weeks have noted.[260] On the one hand, we might note how theories of heritable versus acquired theories of sexual inversion, especially those forms of same-sex desire, were increasingly contested and politicized. These were considered part of the intermediate third sex. Again, Ellis argued for biologically heritable conditions, while Krafft-Ebing suggested that acquired inversion, such as from the practice of "excessive masturbation," could lead to sexual inversion.[261] On the other hand, this was the age of Oscar Wilde and sexual progressivism; "boy worship" was "conspicuous at Oxford"; John Addington Symonds advocated the ethics of the homoerotic Greeks while himself serving as anonymous informant in Ellis's 1894 case study of homosexuality; and the British socialist activist Carpenter pleaded (in 1907) for the rights of the "intermediate sex."[262] Perhaps this cultural emphasis on both sexual libertarianism and social-conforming classification is to be explained as the product of a society itself divided over the role of gender and sexuality in the modernizing family and state. Whatever the case, these controversies have continued the preconceptions of the past, such as in the nature-versus-nurture arguments regarding sexual orientation.[263]

Hence, by the late nineteenth century, the third sex and gender were increasingly regarded as the product of sexual dimorphism and a definite degradation of reproductive evolution. For instance, while Hirschfeld advocated an innate conception of homosexuality as a third sex, the prominent intellectual savant of the era, Iwan Bloch, admired by Freud, held another view. Both Freud and Bloch shared the idea that bisexuality was in the state of nature and a regressive feature of mammals and humans. As Wolff writes in her biography of Hirschfeld: "Bloch shared Freud's view that heterosexuality was the truer aim of human sexuality. He wrote: 'Only the differences between man and woman represent the perfect state of sexual evolution. The "third sex" is a regressive phenomenon.' "[264]

As many nineteenth-century writers, such as Ulrichs, Hirschfeld and Freud, argued, there were obviously individuals inclined to actions that suggested they were neither purely male nor masculine. Freud's biologically based idea of a "psychic hermaphrodite" perhaps bears as much of the imprint of Aristotelian sexual-difference exaggeration as it does the late Victorian obsession with the definition of what was natural and unnatural in the highly individualistic bourgeois ethic of turn-of-the-century capitalism that then dominated.[265] We find encoded in the Freudian view in particular a consistent and strongly marked differentiation of classification on the basis of activity and passivity.[266] Changes in the structure of society and the cultural field of sexuality were to bring about increasingly rigid forms of social classifications of functions, drives, desires, sexual objects and sexual relationships.

Here, we should cite Foucault's by-now-famous comment on this change: "Homosexuality appeared as one of the forms of sexuality when it was transposed from the practice of sodomy onto a kind of interior androgyny, a hermaphroditism of the soul. The sodomite had been a temporary aberration; the homosexual was now a species."[267]

Third-sex/third-gender desires are more than matters of erotic arousal and more than the commitment to the social functions of gendered roles or sexual hierarchies, although they may include these matters. Desire represents a mode of being, a way of linking personal reality to cultural ontology; it represents the creation of an ontological space, situated halfway between the private and the public, between the individual and the secret side of the social person – especially one who inhabits a capitalist society with its marked ideology of individualism; and it represents a publicly defined cultural standard or institutional norm, with its symbolic expressions time honored as tradition and presented to the person and self as immutable cultural reality.[268] With desires writ large we are dealing, then, with the more inclusive desire to be and become a third-sex and third-gendered person. It is toward this end that a new history and anthropology is required to uncover those hidden forms from other times and places that elucidate larger meanings of being and becoming an alternate-sex and alternate-gendered being.

Endings and Beginnings

One of the critical points of this review has been to show that, with the emergence of modernism, the cultural elaboration of and attention to desire as new subject/object relationship and individual desires as a content of being and action became critical to understanding the emergence of a third sex and gender. This suggests that new elements of individualism, of oscillations of conformity to and rebellion against sex and gender hierarchies, increasingly entered into the discourse of interpreting what is normative and aberrant in transcending sexual dimorphism as we come closer in historical time to the present. Passing must also be underscored as a critical, emergent concept; it implicates normal and abnormal identity and the strategies of power avoidance in the effort to live and survive as a third-sex and third-gendered being. This too may be a product of the modern period and of modernist culture in general.

I have been critical above of biologically oriented sexology and sex and gender research that slights historical and cultural factors or reduces them to the fabled pigeonhole of a blackbox. As I have made repeatedly clear, however, these problems of folk categories and scientific essentialism of sexual dimorphism are roadblocks in anthropology and history as well, in part because of the overemphasis on gender and the underdevelopment of sexuality as a subject in anthropology.[269] But these fields, biology included, are changing. Recent biological thinking is more flexible on the question of sexual dimorphism and the possibility of a third sex "in nature." Thus we find the so-called hard-wired science investigators, those who watch birds and salamanders, and their collaborators who have made certain "hermaphroditic" fishes and "bisexual" frogs their specialities, suggesting phylogenetic plasticity instead of sexual dimorphism or heterosexual/homosexual dualism in species.[270]

All categorization involves treating dissimilar things as similar, to repeat Nietzsche's words, and such treatment is endemic in the areas of sex and gender. We are reminded of Susanne Langer's advice regarding the biological world: "The difficulty of drawing a sharp line between animate and inanimate things reflects a principle which runs through the whole domain of biology; namely, that all categories tend to have imperfect boundaries. Not only do genera or species merge into each other, but classifications made by one criterion do not cover the cases grouped together by another, so that almost all general attributions have exceptions, some of which are really mystifying."[271] A critical perspective that results from this review is that Darwin probably exaggerated the influence of sexual dimorphism in evolution. Certainly many who followed him, including sexologists, have done so; and while those of us in cultural and historical theory cannot do without these significant factors of sex and gender formation, we must be skeptical of their application to social life.

78

With the proposition of third sexes and genders we are dealing also with problems of duality, in Durkheim's sense, and with
the problem of thirdness, as denoted by such scholars as Simmel
and Mauss. But the problem is not merely one of irregular boundaries and scientific ineptitude in handling nature, as Langer implies: there is also the social and political threat of the marginal,
the rebel – the person who is beyond the margins; and the problem of passing is essential to an interpretation of deviance and
adaptation here. When someone is discredited, a degree of hiding is always required; and the fact that passing occurs in many
instances of third sex and gender suggests that power commonly
sanctions reproductive ideas and dimorphic roles.[272]

Such "problems" posed by the third sex and gender for an epistemology of sexual dimorphism and reproductive ideologies will
not go away. In social and historical traditions of multiple-sex
and multiple-gendered beings we are dealing with biological,
cultural and moral classification systems of humanity. The range
of cases reviewed here suggests only a small number of those
available in the extant literature, and these suggest a critical need
to rethink the distinction between sex and gender and between
sexual nature and gendered culture. Variations in sex and gender,
including the formation of third-sex and third-gender categories, roles and ontological identities are not universal; they vary
across time and space: And yet it is clear that these patterns are
more pervasive and significant in some cultures than in others.
Why is this?

One of the findings of my own comparative work on culture,
sexuality and historical change has been to demonstrate that the
intentional actor in search of a new identity requires a separate
social space; it is within this liminal space that culture is created
and transformed.[273] Secrecy is a special case of this sort.[274] It thus
follows that, for the liminal being of the third-sex or third-gendered person, categories create the possibilities of social relations;
but passing as normative may be required unless the social spaces
and cultural places for thirdness are structured across the course
of life. Only a few societies around the world have provided this,
such as the hijras of India; and these offer prime examples of the

institutionalization of third sex and gender into the social fabric of human groups.

The existence of a dualistic ontology, such as sexual dimorphism, as a principle in our worldview often predicates its antithesis and brings into being its mediators, whether at the level of ideology or social practice. Is the two-sex system of Western culture, male/female, heterosexual/homosexual, a universal or a local condition of human nature? If it is universal, why does it not occur everywhere? Yet, if it is local, why do we find so many examples of it distributed around the world? Does biological reproduction force humans to work around if not to invoke the two-sex system? My hunch is that, where reproduction is considered the sine qua non of sexuality, as in the United States during the past century, we should expect to find the most disapproving attitudes toward the third sex. Indeed, these attitudes might be characterized as representing the horror of sexual ambiguity, noted in the early 1960s by Garfinkel in his study of transsexuals, hermaphrodites and other odd sorts who passed as "normal."[275] We thus come to have instantiated within and on us the very signs of a two- or three-sex/gender system – onto our private parts and in the whispers of the self.

We must conclude that it is indeed rather difficult to create and maintain third-sex and third-gender categories; and perhaps the imperfect fit between personal and sexual desire and social duty or customary roles helps us to explain the reason. And yet, nonetheless, this achievement is by no means rare and is, indeed, to be expected as part of the historical, social and psychic landscape in a good number of times and places, as we have seen.

Conversely, sexual dimorphism is not inevitable, a universal structure. Certainly it is celebrated in many places but it is not privileged at all times and places. An insight that emerges from Bateson's study of the structural relations between roles and categories is the difficulty of maintaining balance between symmetrical dyadic systems.[276] That things come in twos and not threes, and that a third category tends to mediate the other two, has long been noted by social thinkers and those in exchange theory, perhaps iterated by Simmel's classic essay.[277] Many postmodern writers have critiqued the biological reductionism of past models of sexuality and gender. Many, such as Kessler and McKenna, for instance, treat the berdache and similar examples apart from male and female as universal categories of gender dichotomies.[278] They see the "dual-gender classification system" of our culture as a "cultural construction." It is obvious from my critiques that I am sympathetic with this view. However, in saying this, we must return to issues of desire, of pleasure, of being, which are transformed into doing, that is, into social and historical practice. Here, it seems to me in closing, we still have much to learn and a good deal of research ahead.

As I have shown elsewhere, the sexual ontology of the berdache is remarkable, because it posits a clear form of preferred sexual excitement, which may be one basis for attraction to the role.[279] No anthropologist has ever explained why these particular forms of social and sexual desire created the perfect fit between individual and culture among the berdache, or, indeed, why this form of sexual excitement would be attractive to them. Many of us are interested in how and why the hijra, the *māhū*, the transsexual, the *kwolu-aatmwol* and so on have become what they are and committed to their social positions. But we would like to know more about their cultural ontologies and personal realities as well as their appearances. We are in great need, therefore, of a new historical ethnography that reveals the everyday life of sexuality and power relations, including the conditions under which passing and emergence occur, as they have been revealed, for instance, in the context of gay- or lesbian-identified people who "come out" by declaring their same-sex desires to create new social relations rather than continue to pass and remain secret. We need an anthropology and social history of desire that will lead us to closer approximations of understanding the lived realities of peoples themselves.[280] It is toward this end that this book has modestly contributed a beginning.

PART ONE

Historical Contributions

CHAPTER ONE

Living in the Shadows:

Eunuchs and Gender in Byzantium

Kathryn M. Ringrose

Introduction

For almost a thousand years a loosely defined group of castrated men played key roles in Byzantine society, performing courtly, ceremonial, religious and other, less elevated functions. In an apparent paradox the practice of castrating men within the confines of the empire was forbidden under Roman law.[1] Christian teachings disapproved of the practice while applauding its outcome – permanent celibacy. Sources often notice and discuss eunuchs, but frequently hide them in the shadows in a way that belies their importance to society. Careful analysis of these references can provide access to societal attitudes about a wide range of matters involving sexuality and gender. Previous work on eunuchs in the Byzantine Empire has centered on their political and social roles at court, but little has been said about how they actually fitted into other parts of society. Most studies of eunuchs have been colored by the pejorative language used about them in the sources and by modern abhorrence of the practice of castration. This interesting antipathy toward eunuchs has deep and complex roots, roots that lie in definitions of gender that can be examined by a study of language and verbal imagery.

This essay explores the social and cultural placement of eunuchs in Byzantine society, going beyond a simple catalog of the positions they held to discuss several aspects of their sexual and gender identities. It attempts to show how they were perceived by the society in which they lived and worked. In the process it also demonstrates that sexual and gender definitions changed over time as Byzantine society changed. Finally, it raises issues regarding sex and gender as defined in current social science. A better understanding of the ways in which eunuchs were integrated into Byzantine society, in the cultural and anthropological sense as well as in political and institutional terms, will tell us more not only about the eunuchs themselves but also about the roles of men and women in Byzantine culture.[2]

Men, Women and Eunuchs: Some Definitions of Sex and Gender

The term *eunuch* as used in Late Antique and Byzantine sources was broader and more nuanced than the simple phrase "castrated male" seems to imply. Moreover, its definition changed within Byzantine society between the third and twelfth century. In its broadest sense the word *eunuch* refers not only to an individual who is physiologically incapable of engendering an offspring but also to one who has chosen to withdraw from worldly activities and thus refuses to procreate. Thus, until the ninth century the term encompassed anyone who did not as well as could not produce children, including men who were born sterile, men who became sterile through illness, accident or birth defect, men who were lacking in sexual desire and men and women who embraced the celibate life for religious reasons. It also encompassed men who had had themselves castrated voluntarily for personal reasons, including Christian priests who wanted to have easier contact with women parishioners, intellectuals who wanted to preserve their vital body fluids to increase their intellectual powers and men who wanted to have intercourse with women without fear of pregnancy. The term also encompassed men who had been castrated, or whose families had them castrated as children, so that they could qualify for positions at court traditionally reserved for eunuchs. Also included were castrated male slaves from the outer reaches of the empire (e.g., Cappadocia, Armenia, the Caucasus Mountains) who were castrated as young children and then brought to the empire and sold, and, finally, illegitimate offspring of the imperial house – such as Romanos's illegitimate son, Basil – who were often castrated and reared as part of the household staff.[3]

Thus, such a broadly used term is not very useful without a brief look at the way in which the Roman and Byzantine world conceptualized views of sex and gender.[4]

Aristotle and Galen, while taking for granted that men and women constituted polar opposites, conceptualized sexuality in terms of ascending ladders reaching toward perfection. The rungs of these ladders, some "biological" and others socially determined, were derived from theories of the humors prevalent in medical thought, ideal norms for the education and acculturation of young men and women, ideas about appropriate social behavior for the sexes and assumptions about the intellectual and moral potential of men and women. At the bottom of the ladder were women and girls, who were associated with coldness and dampness. Part of the way up the ladder were boys and adolescent males, who, having left the socialization of the women's quarters, were learning to be aristocratic men. At the top of the ladder were those men who possessed the ultimate masculine attributes – heat, dryness, activity, fertility and training in aristocratic male behavior. As they matured and were acculturated into appropriate aristocratic male behavior, young males gradually moved up the ladder.[5] Men who were castrated before puberty were "stuck" in a kind of arrested development. They certainly were more manly than women or young male children, but they could not reach the status of sexually mature men and thus could never attain the culturally defined attributes of full masculinity.

The ladder image implies not only a hierarchy of gender but also a male and female polarity. Thomas Laqueur argues in favor of a single-sex model for antiquity in which gender was more important than biological sexuality and then goes on to suggest that the female body is therefore always culturally constructed relative to a male reference point.[6] His argument has many merits, but it has to be reconciled with two other issues. In the Byzantine world male bodies were both culturally *and* physiologically constituted into individuals who were referenced positively toward men and negatively toward women. That is, when sources wanted to speak well of an individual they used positive attributes traditionally ascribed to men. When they wanted to be critical they employed negative values traditionally ascribed to women.

Moreover, despite this orientation to the ideal male, both Aristotle and Galen are also tied to language that leads them to express themselves in terms of sexual polarities. Thus, Aristotle says that eunuchs are changed into women, or, as he puts it, into a female state.[7] Galen, in discussing castration, says that it makes eunuchs similar to women, that is, they are lacking in heat.[8] Thus, he tends to class eunuchs with women and boys, perhaps implying that eunuchs are changed into women. The language used seems to imply that maleness and femaleness are polar opposites.

Galen actually presents a theory that goes beyond defining the female in terms of a lack of male attributes. He suggests that biological sexuality is related to the testes and argues that both men and women have testes and produce seed. Then, in an argument that runs parallel to the modern medical understanding of hormones, he says that it is the male testes that give men their masculine attributes and the female testes that give women their feminine attributes. Galen then speculates about the existence of a third group of mature animals, once either male or female, that have been surgically altered so that they lack testes.[9] The two types of altered animals develop similar physical traits and are "neither male nor female, but a third being different from both of the two." This passage comes close to describing a third sex, but it is one of the few sources to do so explicitly and uses pigs as the illustrative example. It is important to remember that Galen is talking here about animals, and he does not speculate directly in this way about human beings. But note, however, the underlying assumption of male/female polarity in the way that Galen presents the idea.

Following in the tradition of Aristotle and Galen, Alexander Trallianus and Aetius Amidensus Medicus, medical writers of the sixth century C.E., also discussed these issues. Using classifications based on the texture of human flesh, the appearance of the complexion in different individuals and their physical strength or hardness as opposed to bodily softness, these authors follow the earlier writings of Aristotle and Galen and classify women, children and eunuchs together while setting men aside as a separate group, lending support to Laqueur's conceptual model.[10]

Other authors classify the world in terms of generative powers. Clement of Alexandria separates men, women and eunuchs.
For him eunuchs constitute a broad category similar to the one
given at the beginning of this section. It includes those who are
born sterile, those who are castrated and those who choose not
to be sexual, including celibate men and women.[11] Eustratius the
Philosopher says that a eunuch, in his lack of fertility, is to a man
as a dead man is to a living man. Fertility, like life, is essential to
the definition of manliness; therefore eunuchs are not fully men.
Here, of course, the gender alternative is referenced to the "normal" man. Eunapios of Sardis clearly implies that eunuchs are not
really men when he says, "Since he was a eunuch he passed his
life as a man" or "since he was a eunuch he used force to make
himself a man."[12] Gregory Nazianzos seems to accept a male-
female polarity and places eunuchs in a nebulous third category
as women/men, individuals who are "womanlike and, among men,
are not manly, of dubious sex."[13] Similarly John of Damascus,
quoting Saint Basil, points out that a eunuch cannot suckle and
therefore is not a woman and yet is also not a man.[14]

What we see here are several intellectual traditions occurring
side by side. The medical/scientific tradition of Aristotle and
Galen certainly supports a vertical continuum that attempts to
explain physiological differences among men, women, children
and eunuchs as a progression toward masculinity. It also offers
convenient explanations for old age – elderly men move down
the physiological ladder in the direction of women, children
and eunuchs.

Yet despite the tidiness of this single-sex structure, a bipolar
model was clearly also lurking in the language available to Late
Antique and Byzantine authors.[15] The very structure of the Greek
language demands that individuals be either masculine or feminine. In this linguistic context eunuchs invariably took the masculine gender and were never associated with feminine or neuter
grammatical forms. Greek society reflexively placed individuals
in fixed masculine or feminine categories. Its language did not
readily allow for a definition of individuals of indeterminate sexual categories. Aristotle, however, did use the adjective ἀμφίβολος,

meaning an individual of indeterminate gender, for eunuchs. This term continues to be applied to eunuchs throughout the Late Antique and Byzantine period. Whether the conceptualization of gender was bipolar or single-sex-oriented, however, it remained difficult to define individuals who neither conformed to accepted polarities nor progressed along the ladder that bridged the sexual polarities and led to the male ideal.

The ability to procreate was important in defining gender. Byzantine society, like the Roman society from which it grew, was patriarchal in structure. Maintenance of the family was central, and loss of the generative function placed an individual outside of the logic of conventional, family-derived social categories. All of our texts acknowledge this and set eunuchs apart from this patriarchal schema, citing their lack of procreative ability, their origins outside the empire and their servile origins.[16] Yet none of them expressly states that eunuchs are a specific "third sex" or "third gender." The patterns of thought that involved sexual polarities were much too strong.

Children, because they also do not procreate, constituted a similar anomaly. But for them the condition was not permanent, and with proper societal conditioning boys became men and girls became women. Thus, while preadolescent boys were often seen as magically or spiritually distinct from adult men, they could be accommodated into the system. Ultimately the language and logic of polarity that was derived from procreation left eunuchs in limbo.

At the same time Byzantine society apparently did not rigidly link sexual activity with procreation. While eunuchs could not procreate, they could be sexually active. Eunuchs are often portrayed as engaging in sexual activity with both men and women. Since this sex act was not seen as a procreative activity and since procreation rather than sexual activity was the critical component of gender, the sexuality of eunuchs did not help place them in a clearly defined gender.

Constructing a Gender: Castration and Physiology
The inclusiveness of the term *eunuch* in the early Byzantine centuries reflects the ambiguities of definition regarding their sex-

ual status found in our sources. It also reflects the many ways in which the eunuchs who appear in our sources were castrated. The type of mutilation carried out, and the age at which it was done, varied greatly and affected the physiological outcome in ways that were evident to a society in which external appearances were important in establishing rank, status and moral worth as well as gender. We can make only educated guesses about some of the technical details of this complex problem, but in part the variety of people defined as eunuchs reflects the variety of ways in which castration could be performed and the fact that it could be done at almost any age.[17]

Medical texts indicate that surgeons understood the function of the *vas deferens* and knew how to cut off the supply of semen while retaining normal masculinity.[18] Michael Psellus tells us that eunuchs were made by mothers and nurses crushing infants' testicles.[19] Tying off of the testicles in infancy was also practiced. From about the tenth century the term for mutilated eunuchs becomes "cut," a term that probably refers to the surgical removal of the testicles, usually in childhood.[20] More extreme castrations, in which the penis was removed along with other genitalia, were also known, but this type of mutilation was rare in Byzantium.[21]

Late Antique and Byzantine authors speculated about the physical nature of eunuchs and their sexuality. They recognized that men castrated as adults retained most secondary male sexual characteristics and continued to be sexually active, while those castrated in infancy or childhood developed a distinctive skeletal structure, lacked full masculine musculature, body hair and beards, had an elevated voice range and rarely went bald. These physical traits came to be associated with eunuchs and provided part of the stereotypes that were ascribed to them. These authors also assumed that eunuchs, like women, could not control their sexual desires and were available as passive sexual partners for men while being, themselves, attracted to either men or women. Whatever their object of sexual choice, eunuchs were assumed to be frustrated and were objects of pity because they could not enjoy full masculine sexuality. Eunuchs in Byzantine society, at least those castrated as young children, were unique in being indi-

91

viduals who were physiologically altered and acculturated into a new gender role before they were old enough to have developed an idea of what their sexual object choice might be.

The physiological effects of castration were also believed to cause changes in a eunuch's temperament and moral fiber. Thus, eunuchs were thought to lack mental stability, to anger quickly and easily and to lack self-control. These societal attitudes about the moral worth of eunuchs date from the time of the Roman Empire and continue to appear in Late Antique and Byzantine sources. A common descriptive adjective used of eunuchs through-out this thousand-year period is ποικίλος, "changeable." Perhaps this is the psychological parallel to ἀμφίβολος, "ambiguous," men-tioned earlier in the discussions of the physiology of eunuchs. For example, Michael Psellus comments on the changeable nature of the eunuch John the Orphanotrophos. He says that he admires John's shrewdness, his cleverness in managing money and the way he can look at people and frighten them. He acknowledges that John is hard working and devoted to the emperor, yet he finds that John's moods are changeable. He finds him a complicated, intricate man, difficult to understand.[22] In an aristocratic soci-ety in which gender was strictly determined and affect was rigidly prescribed, eunuchs were believed to be able to change their psy-chological affect and share attributes of two genders. This per-ception probably contributed to the belief that eunuchs possessed special magical powers. In fact the term ποικίλος is often used for magicians.

Possibly because they retained some traits of prepubescent boys, possibly because they were incapable of wasting their vital essence in procreation and most certainly because they were often well educated and engaged in professions and activities that outsiders did not understand, eunuchs were regarded with awe and suspicion. The question of the degree to which a eunuch might represent a prepubescent boy is of great interest and is almost certainly related to the recurrent imagery in which boys, eunuchs and angels are mistaken for one another. All have a sim-ilar physical appearance and are incapable of generating offspring. I suspect that they all share similar magical powers, a topic of great interest that I will not be able to cover in this essay.[23]

Many of the traits ascribed to eunuchs also reflect the gendered polarities of language, attributing to eunuchs the opposite of behaviors and appearances that were the markers of aristocratic men and suggesting a lack of a fixed third category to which eunuchs might belong. The list of adjectives beginning with "α-" ("not") and describing eunuchs is strikingly long. To cite only a few examples, whole men are endowed with θῡμός (spirit, strength, courage, heart, desire). They are καρπός (fruitful), μέτριος (measured in their actions), ἀνδρεῖος (manly), προσηνής (gentle, kindly), μεταδότης (generous) and σθένος (strong). Eunuchs are ἄθῡμος (fainthearted), ἄκαρπος (unfruitful), ἄμετρος (immoderate), ἀνάνδρος (unmanly) or even, using the diminutive, ἀνδράριον (little men). They are ἀπηνές (unkind), ἀμετάδοτες (ungenerous), and they suffer from ασθένεια (weakness). There is also a shorter list that begins with "δυσ" ("un"). Men are easy, agreeable, "cool" (used in its modern rather than Galenic sense), popular. They have εὐχείρεια. Eunuchs are harsh, offensive, hard to manage, difficult, unpopular and unpleasant. They are characterized by δυσχερεία. Similar pejorative language is also used about women. All of this is summed up especially well in an early medical text: "Stiff, sickly, shrill-voiced, beardless, boyish, womanlike, these traits describe eunuchs. The traits of a man are his production of semen, warmth, strength, hairiness, pleasant voice, cheerfulness, strength of intellect and accomplishment.[24] One early commentator even suggests that a specific personality change accompanies castration: "To eunuchs there is, by nature, a mark more evil than among other men. So they are very savage minded, deceitful, evil doers, some more than others. Some of the cut eunuchs undergo a sudden change together with the mark of the cut. Most of them retain the nature of their kind."[25]

Thus, the sexual definitions of eunuchs in Byzantine culture were neither very consistent nor unambiguous, and most writers who referred to them left eunuchs in a nebulous place outside a conceptual scheme that linked gender and procreation and was male oriented. This did not, however, prevent society from constructing eunuchs as a distinct gender. We have already seen that they were believed to be physically of both a male and female nature and psychologically "changeable" and that these attributes were thought to be directly related to their castration.

Constructing a Gender: Acculturation and Social Roles
Despite the linguistic constraints connected with defining them as such, Byzantine eunuchs constituted a "third gender." They were excluded from male and female procreative roles and thus could not be recognized as either. They were assigned many social roles that were accepted as necessary but that had come to be considered inappropriate for either men or women as they were gendered. They also lived with a convention that attributed to them provincial, servile and nonaristocratic origins.

Distinctive and exclusive roles were linked not only to distinctive physiology but also to learned behaviors, mannerisms and a distinctive sexual status, all adding to the construct that helps us define them as a distinct gender. This can be seen most clearly in the case of the eunuch servants and household functionaries found both at court and in aristocratic homes. Maude Gleason, in a fascinating study of Late Antique physiognomic texts, offers a catalog of traits that were believed to characterize individuals who were neither fully masculine nor fully feminine.[26] These traits are almost identical to those later ascribed to eunuchs and include characteristics of voice, gait, raised eyebrows, mincing steps, slack limbs, a shrill weepy voice, upturned hands, shifty eyes and inappropriately loud laughter.

The acculturation to distinctive bearing and mannerisms is attested by a number of sources. Young castrated slaves were raised in the women's quarters under the supervision of older eunuchs. They were then educated at court for career paths open only to eunuchs. A common derogatory phrase was that eunuchs were "reared in the shade."[27] This phrase carries a number of different and charged meanings, including the assumption that eunuchs were reared under the same circumstances as women. Men live in light and brightness, the *palaestra*; women live in the *gynaecaeum*, enclosed, secluded. Ruddy, suntanned skin is a sign of masculinity; white, soft skin, femininity.[28] Similar distinctions were apparent in speech patterns. The eunuchs at court were conditioned to use characteristic speech patterns, and various texts discuss the "chattering" of eunuchs. This acculturation included facial expressions and body language. For example, the eunuch Joseph raised his eyebrows and looked haughty when he spoke to people.[29]

Byzantine sources regularly tell us that eunuchs must be graceful and well made, a trait that Danelides was aware of when he made a gift of one hundred eunuchs to the court. "For he knew they needed eunuchs and they are like flies among them, caring for them like sheep in the fold in the spring."[30] Eunuchs flock, hover, swarm. They act together as a group and, in political crisis, support one another, a stereotype borne out by shadowy but unmistakable evidence of an interconnected network of eunuchs serving at court and in the great houses of the city.[31] At least at court eunuchs also wore a distinctive costume.[32]

The stereotyping of eunuchs is illustrated clearly in one of the foundation legends associated with Hagia Sophia. In the course of the story Saint Michael, the archangel, appears at the building site. Because he is beardless, youthful and wearing a long white robe, it is assumed that he is a court eunuch.[33] The prescribed costume of eunuchs also included minor adornments, especially earrings, an identifying feature of both eunuchs and women.[34] Thus, distinctive roles and sexual status were linked with dress, mannerisms, speech and body language in a way that identified eunuchs as a separate gender. Society had well-defined expectations about them, and it had institutionalized the process of selection and acculturation that fulfilled these expectations. Although Western society tends to establish gender categories based on choice of sexual object, many other societies, including Byzantine society, emphasize occupation and appearance in determinations of gender status while rarely mentioning sexual object choice.[35]

Gendering also involves the assignment of specific and often exclusive roles in society. The acculturation of eunuchs prepared them for the tasks that Byzantine culture assigned to them. Many of these roles were considered to be unmasculine or else involved tasks that were performed by women outside an aristocratic society. At court eunuchs acted as "masters of ceremonies," controlling access to the emperor; as doorkeepers; as servants in charge of traditionally female activities like cooking, serving and care of the wardrobe. Court eunuchs were also trained for tasks that aristocratic males traditionally avoided, such as bookkeeping, managing money and speculating in real estate.[36] Certain positions at court were reserved specifically for eunuchs. They served as go-betweens in transactions between men and women of the court and between the court and the outside world. They acted as trusted secretaries. They served as singers at court. They were very much involved in marital transactions and prepared the dead for burial.[37] They regularly appear in our sources as barbers, bloodletters and doctors.[38]

Traditionally the emperor and the empress each had his or her own corps of household eunuchs. In the emperor's household they fulfilled female roles as caregivers, and sources, especially those hostile to eunuchs, often hint that they were sexual partners for the emperor.[39] Michael Psellus reports that the emperor Constantine VII's household was "most of all made up of those chamberlains and eunuchs of the bedchamber that he had procured. They were not among the well born nor those who are freedmen, but were provincials and foreigners. Since they owed their education to the emperor and adopted his nature, they were judged more worthy of honors than others. And they concealed the shame of their fate from people's opinion. They spoke and acted like freedmen and they were lavish with their wealth and abundant in their good works, and showed other gentlemanly qualities." Psellus, who is generally well disposed toward eunuchs, nevertheless finds them demeaned by their condition. When he talks about Michael V's actions in castrating John the Orphanotrophos's male relatives, for example, he says that their lives were made a "half death."[40]

Yet in the imperial household, especially during those periods when a woman held the throne, eunuchs became trusted political advisers and powerful administrators. Well before the tenth century they had acquired roles far beyond their much older functions as guardians of the harem. Nevertheless, because of

their gendered status, eunuchs could never pose a direct threat
to the crown.[41]

Eunuchs as Intermediaries and as Protagonists

Many of the roles and functions ascribed primarily to eunuchs
involved mediations and transactions across boundaries. These
roles often required that eunuchs supervise boundaries, especially
those charged with religious or supernatural elements. Regulat-
ing access to the emperor also meant protecting the sacred space
around him.[42] Mediating, brokering and transmitting messages
between persons who were constrained by etiquette from meeting directly all carried the same charge. Medical work and caring for the dead also required that eunuchs mediate between
this world and the powers of the supernatural. Finally, there are
numerous parallels between eunuchs as go-betweens and angels
as messengers that suggest that eunuchs mediated between the
world of immediate reality and the world of the imagination. Just
as women are engendered in many cultures as the monitors of
birth and death, so also eunuchs had an analogous terrain assumed
to be exclusively theirs. While individual eunuchs often occupied
powerful positions typically held by whole men in other cultures,
their success (or failure) had to be explained with reference to
their distinctive gender.

Court eunuchs also frequently appeared in important positions normally held by males in the army and the navy. The most
famous of these, of course, was Narses, Justinian's great general.
Procopius believed that the removal of the testicles destroyed
the seat of a man's natural powers, yet he was lavish in his praise
of Narses.[43] He marveled that a eunuch raised in the women's
quarters and accustomed to a soft life could overcome his inherent traits and command so successfully. Agathias chuckles at the
naïveté of the Goths, who assumed that Narses was just a feeble
caricature of a man who had set his masculinity aside and thus
were unprepared for his military prowess.[44] Both of these authors
stress the intelligence and skill of Narses, citing his planning and
execution of a large operation. Neither, however, attributes his
success to traditional, courageous manliness. In a different mili-

97

tary context, Leo the Deacon notes that the Scyths assumed that the eunuch Peter the Patrician was a "little woman raised in the shade." Leo then tells us how Peter surpassed everyone's expectations by killing a Scythian general in hand-to-hand combat. Despite that example of manliness, however, eunuchs were normally assumed to be successful commanders because they were clever, they were good at organizing campaigns and they understood strategy.[45]

By the eleventh century, as the power of the great aristocratic families grew and aristocratic male values that applauded individual courage and personal military skill increasingly colored historical accounts, we find eunuch commanders subjected to open ridicule. Nikephoros Bryennius, for example, admittedly a source prejudiced toward the Comneni dynasty, describes the events that took place when Alexius Comnenus was forced to turn his military command over to John the Eunuch, who had been sent out from court to replace Alexius. Alexius first rides out to review his troops and dazzles them with a riding display. John the Eunuch attempts to duplicate his feat and falls off his horse, at which the soldiers all shout "klu, klu," a derogatory phrase "which is customarily said to eunuchs."[46]

Outside the world of the court, eunuchs occupied a number of traditional niches, some of which were associated with marginality, pollution or outcast status. Eunuch singers in the church and actors in the theater both appear in Byzantine sources, part of a long tradition in which men played female roles in the theater and castrato singers were important in musical performances. The latter tradition would last until the nineteenth century. Eunuchs were often male prostitutes, and eunuch actors and prostitutes were often criticized for "talking dirty," for dressing in a "disorderly" manner and for pretending to be men. Eunuchs also frequently appear as physicians or teachers, professions occupied by educated slaves in the Roman world and requiring intimacy with men, women and children. In an echo of the logic that reflexively links eunuchs with the harem and the care of women and children, castration has traditionally facilitated this intimacy.

98

Parallel Definitions of Gender and Status: Lay Society and the Church

Some Religious Views of Eunuchs

The relatively tidy and straightforward vision of the creation and engendering of eunuchs as a self-perpetuating institution is only part of the story. It is a static picture that hides important changes in the attitudes about and status assigned to eunuchs by Byzantine culture and society over time. Christianity and the Church constituted a central force in this dynamic process. Thus far this discussion of the construction of a gender for eunuchs has explored the process in the secular society of Byzantium before the tenth century. Over time, however, lay society changed the way it defined eunuchs, giving the concept a narrower and more physiologically specific connotation. At the same time, religious rationales and practices created an alternative hierarchy of status for men, one in which moral worth and celibacy, in the context of the rejection of sexual desire, replaced procreative ability as standards for masculinity. Within this alternative gender hierarchy the sexual ambiguity of eunuchs became a serious issue only in the most conservative monastic circles.[47]

Throughout the history of Byzantium eunuchs occupied places at all levels of the ecclesiastical hierarchy. They were monks, priests, bishops and church officials.[48] Churchmen reflected secular society in their ambivalence about eunuchs, but they focused on different issues. Rather than a preoccupation with the male ideal and procreation as points of reference, clerical discussion of eunuchs tended to focus on their relationship to the ideal of celibacy. Because of their physical castration, eunuchs in the Church were assumed to be celibate. Yet ecclesiastical sources frequently suggest that, in the struggle for ascetic virtue, eunuchs had "cheated" and were not able to attain fully the celibate ideal. That is, celibacy was too easy for them because they did not have to struggle to attain it. Rather, they had achieved celibacy through the outside intervention of castration.[49]

Ecclesiastical opinions about this issue varied substantially, as is illustrated by the numerous Late Antique and Byzantine

99

glosses on Matthew 19.12, "For while some are eunuchs from birth, others are made eunuchs by men, and others have made themselves eunuchs for the sake of the kingdom of Heaven."[50] Some commentators, like Gregory Nazianzos, assume that this passage should be interpreted allegorically and thus applied to all men.[51] Most Late Antique and Byzantine commentators, however, assumed that it should be interpreted literally. In their interpretation, the passage is assumed to apply to three categories of men, those who are born without sexual desire, those who have been castrated and those who choose to remain celibate. When the passage is interpreted in this way those who become eunuchs through physical mutilation are often connected with the powers of evil. Epiphanius, in the *Panarion*, sets up his categories in a slightly different way when he says that the passage refers to three groups of people, those castrated by others, those who have castrated themselves, something he sees as a wicked act that is contrary to the power of Christ, and celibate men who "imitate the angels."[52] In the same vein, Clement of Alexandria offers an elaborate classification system for eunuchs. Using the term *eunuchs* in its broad definition, he distinguishes between those men born without desire for women, those born without fully functioning sexual organs, those who are made eunuchs "of necessity" by others and those who conquer their own bodies through the practice of celibacy.[53] Eusebius comments that Origen took Matthew 19.12 too literally when he castrated himself as a way of achieving celibacy.[54]

Athanasius glosses the passage by dividing eunuchs into two groups, those castrated by other men "for the sake of the kingdom of women, to guard them and be conspicuous over others," a worldly goal of which Athanasius disapproves, and those who castrated themselves.[55] In this context, when Athanasius talks about men castrating themselves, he is using the phrase in its metaphorical sense and saying that these individuals are electing to ignore their sexual natures and live the celibate life for the sake of the kingdom of heaven. For Athanasius this is the highest goal to which a man can aspire. Similarly, John Chrysostom divides eunuchs into two groups, those castrated by other men and those who castrate themselves, again metaphorically, and live the celibate life.[56] Those in the former group, he says, deserve no reward for their virtue, since their enforced celibacy comes from having their nature imposed on them, not from their own efforts. The latter group will be crowned in heaven because its members have practiced celibacy through their own efforts, for the sake of the kingdom of heaven. Chrysostom goes on to suggest that castration is the devil's work since it injures God's creation and allows men to fall into sin.

It is clear, just from this brief survey, that the ecclesiastical community of Late Antiquity and the early Byzantine period was uneasy about members who were castrated and thus had not had to struggle with their own sexuality. The Church was very uncomfortable with the fact of castration, especially self-imposed castration to ensure celibacy.

At the same time, however, there is never any suggestion that castrated men lacked the qualities of gender necessary for sanctity, priesthood or high office in the ecclesiastical hierarchy. Nor are castrated churchmen ever presented as members of a third sex or gender category.[57] If eunuchs fall into any stereotypical category in the world of the Church, it is one that presents castrated men as individuals for whom salvation can be more difficult than for other men but not impossible. This reflects the popular assumption that achieving celibacy is easy for castrated men and the assumed association of eunuchs with sin and worldliness, an extension of the social reality that eunuchs were associated with professions perceived as immoral, outcast or sinful by both the Church and society. Eunuchs were also associated with women in various ways that involved physical proximity, physical nature and social roles, and thus were suspect in masculine arenas. Finally, they were also associated with the courtly and aristocratic world of luxury, sexuality and earthliness.

In the end, however, the religious world of Byzantium, with its orientation toward celibacy and the ascetic, did not place eunuchs in the sort of limbo that was part of their distinctive gender in secular society. While facing some special obstacles, eunuchs could aspire to the same spiritual and celibate ideal and high position as could whole men. Since the Church was a world that excluded procreation from its concerns, the factors at work in constructing the gender status of eunuchs in the Church were different from those constructing the gender of secular eunuchs. We can see this clearly through a remarkable twelfth-century tract discussed below and by looking at how definitions of *eunuch* evolved over time in the secular and religious contexts of Byzantium.

A Twelfth-Century Dialogue about Eunuchs

We can perceive the status of Byzantine eunuchs in the twelfth century and detect some of the changes that had accumulated over eight centuries thanks to the fascinating early-twelfth-century *Defense of Eunuchs* by Theophylaktos, archbishop of Ohrid.[58] In this document we see that secular attitudes regarding eunuchs had hardened even as the Church was developing its own definition of the male ideal, one that undermined the distinct gendering of eunuchs.

Theophylaktos was a churchman educated in Constantinople. He wrote this work as a gift to his brother, who was probably a castrated cleric at Hagia Sophia, seat of the Byzantine patriarchate. The tract is cast in the form of a dialogue between a eunuch and a whole man on the occasion of the baptism of the eunuch's nephew, who had been castrated. The author begins by establishing that, in his mind, eunuchism is a well-defined, socially sanctioned institutional entity.[59] He divides adult males into two categories, those who are testiculated, or whole, and those who are eunuchs, and each group is represented by a participant in the discussion.[60]

The Critique of Eunuchs

The whole man speaks first. Echoing ideas I have discusssed earlier in this essay, he lists his charges against eunuchism. He points out that castration is wrong because it is forbidden under Mosaic and Roman law and that it is illegal because it destroys something that God has made. Castration spoils a child's character because it produces moral weakness. This charge is followed by the familiar litany of eunuchs' faults: they yield to passions; they are greedy, avaricious, miserly and unsociable in their behavior; they are self-

102

centered, licentious, ambitious, envious, quarrelsome and deceitful. Eunuchs also have bad dispositions, are easily irritated by
trifling things and are generally irascible. The whole man then
proceeds to a discussion of palace eunuchs, suggesting that their
position of power in the palace accentuates the above faults and
claiming that a predisposition to these faults is accentuated by
the fact that palace eunuchs are reared by women rather than by
"real" men. Thus young eunuchs lack proper role models. Women
teach them to be dissembling and slothful, while their weaker
moral faculties render palace eunuchs vulnerable to their passions
and prone to adopting effeminate traits.

The critic then moves on to theater eunuchs, who offend by
warbling and trilling. They sing pornographic songs and have even
introduced them into the church service. Some eunuchs behave
publicly like actors, eating dainties and drinking too much, affect-
ing a disorderly appearance, engaging in immoral behavior and
talking dirty. They even pretend to be men and attempt to achieve
sexual pleasure. In a quick aside the whole man comments that
the last offense was especially true of eunuchs who guarded the
harem. Eunuch actors, he says, are condemned by the company
they keep (other theater folk) and the dirty words they speak,
since words are the shadows of deeds. Viewers are aroused by
the sight of them rubbing themselves against women and this is
wrong. Finally, he charges that everyone knows that eunuchs are
ill omened. This cryptic remark is one of the most interesting in
the tract. Many of our earlier sources have contained veiled hints
that eunuchs are unlucky, in league with the forces of evil and
darkness, perhaps magical. This is an interesting problem that
needs further study.

In Defense of Eunuchs
Theophylaktos then gives the floor to the eunuch in his dialogue,
allowing him to present a defense of the institution. The eunuch
employs a number of standard rhetorical devices, for example,
deflecting his opponent's criticisms by suggesting that he is re-
tailing stereotypes that might be true of Persian and Arabian
eunuchs but not Byzantine eunuchs. He reminds his critic that

many churchmen are good and holy castrated men, suggesting that his opponent does not really know what he is talking about and is deliberately presenting only negative images of eunuchs. Here Theophylaktos seems to suggest that whole men cannot easily understand eunuchs because eunuchs have their own personal experience, which whole men cannot share.

The defender of eunuchs then proceeds to ask why those who practice voluntary celibacy are less evil than eunuchs, who were given no choice in the matter. Moreover, if the genitals are not to be used for procreation, why not just get rid of them? This question is raised in the context of a discussion of natural law. Critics of eunuchs say that castration is against nature, but what is "natural"? After all, if a child is born with a sixth finger, it is cut off. The function of the testicles is to produce sperm for procreation, but the higher goal of celibacy establishes that sperm is not needed for procreation. Why not, therefore, cut the testicles off, pruning the body just as a good farmer prunes his fruit trees to make them more productive? The eunuch goes on to ask how mutilation is different from the act of the ascetic who starves his body and thus destroys it. If the laws of God decree that the body should not be harmed, is this law not equally violated by the ascetic?

Next Theophylaktos, speaking through the eunuch, attacks the validity of traditional legislation against castration, suggesting that such controls are no longer relevant for Christians. The laws of Moses, he says, were written for another time and place and should not be applied literally. After all, the Hebrews thought that an individual's moral worth was reflected in his fertility, a value system now at odds with that of the Church. The long-standing Roman laws forbidding castration date from before Justinian, when procreation was thought necessary to make soldiers "men of blood." Such laws, he suggests, were created for a society that is very different from the world of the early twelfth century and the laws of Christianity. Roman law, after all, also punished those who did not marry. Christian ideals rendered Tribonian anachronistic when he included such legislation in the Justinian Code.[61] Here the author is suggesting that laws of all kinds can become outmoded and that we must look behind the law at real intent.

Theophylaktos then provides a careful definition of the term *eunuch*, one that is much narrower than its meaning in earlier centuries. He confines the term to individuals who have had their testicles either crushed or removed surgically, thus clearly limiting his use of the term to men who have been mutilated and excluding people who were "born lacking in desire," those born with defective genitalia and those who practice voluntary celibacy. To reduce the importance society places on worldly procreation, underscore the importance of celibacy and prove that eunuchs can achieve holiness, he catalogs important Old Testament figures who were eunuchs. He quotes scripture to show that, although eunuchs cannot have descendants on earth, they can have descendants in heaven, and they can achieve salvation like any other men.

Elsewhere he argues that church law must be understood in terms of time and place and should not be applied literally. It should be honored, but we must recognize that it was written for other times and conditions. Theophylaktos then summarizes his own position regarding eunuchs and castration, perhaps expressing the opinion of the Church of his time. He says that it is wrong for young men to have themselves castrated as a contraceptive measure, in order to seduce women, because in doing so they fail to respect the purpose of ejaculation and coitus. Adult castration is also sinful because it endangers the body.

The castration of children, however, is presented differently. When castration is done to preserve a child's virginity, it is an act of legitimate parental concern. The argument Theophylaktos makes here is interesting. He suggests that there are two sorts of men in society, those who live in the world and procreate children and those who adopt the celibate life and abandon their procreative function. In either case the path toward aristocratic manliness or ecclesiastical manliness (i.e., successful celibacy) must be established while the individual is still young. Here Theophylaktos is specifically advocating two different ladders, each leading to a different conception of full masculine perfection. It is clear that the older pattern of classical Graeco-Roman society, in which young aristocratic males were acculturated with great care to ensure that they would become proper men, has now been adapted to an ecclesiastical context that emphasizes early childhood rearing and may include physical mutilation to ensure celibacy. Theophylaktos answers the charges of those who say that castration is "against nature" by saying that "a Greek [i.e., a secular individual] lives according to nature and its laws are his goal, but ascetics choose a life beyond nature."[62]

Theophylaktos thus turns both civil and ecclesiastical legislation on its head. He accepts that castration is wrong if its goal is to allow unregulated sexuality, but it is good if it ensures celibacy. Consequently he advocates the abandonment of outdated laws designed to protect and encourage reproduction.

Theophylaktos's defender of eunuchs also argues that those who legislate against castration have not bothered to explore the origins of eunuchism. As a result those who perform castrations are forced to evade the law by pretending that they are performing this surgery to cure a disease. If the institution were evil, why would it continue to exist? If it were truly sinful to castrate, the law would not be ignored. Therefore, he continues, there must be a reason for having eunuchs, and he proceeds to explain why they are needed in society. Yet the only examples he then cites involve the eunuchs of the palace. The palace, he says, is entrusted to eunuchs because they are capable of receiving instruction, they think for themselves, in contrast to slaves, and they are not coarse and stupid as are slaves. Clearly the author has observed that palace eunuchs are educated and are acculturated into modes of behavior and personal appearance that are considered by society to be elegant and suitable for the court.

Next the apologist proceeds to answer his antagonist's specific charges about the vices of eunuchs. "You have testified to the many passions of eunuchs, which comes from their being totally crushed, reducing them to the feminine state. I will not dignify this with a reply."[63] His opponent's charges have angered the apologist, and yet the complexity and ambiguity of the problem of gender are such that he is reluctant to deal with it. At the same time he is offended at the suggestion that eunuchs might be classed with women.

The defender of eunuchs then proceeds to logical arguments, confronting stereotypes with real examples. How can eunuchs be described as physically and morally weak and at the same time wielding too much power in the state? After all, he says, there are historical examples of eunuchs who have been pirates and robbers, and they were certainly not physically weak. Eunuchs, he says, are accused of being niggardly and unsocial. How can this be the case when so many have acted as the protectors of widows and orphans? Eunuchs and whole men are alike in that some are good and some bad, but when eunuchs are bad it is noticed and commented on. This is especially true of palace eunuchs, yet the best of them model themselves on the imperial family.

Theophylaktos's critique of the use of stereotypes also extends to the religious world. How can eunuchs as a group be bad when so many of them hold important positions in churches and monasteries? They are good priests and bishops. Even if some eunuchs corrupt the singing in church with bawdy songs, other amateur singers who are whole men do the same thing. Why should the example of a few bad individuals create a stereotype about all of them? Moreover, since eunuchism is a "vessel of chastity" people should be predisposed to have a favorable impression of eunuchs. Finally, regarding the charge that eunuchs are ill omened, dull-witted men say the same thing about monks.[64]

Redefining Manliness: An Alternative Construction of Gender

Throughout *The Defense of Eunuchs* the author argues that eunuchs are men and that the presence or absence of reproductive organs should not be the measure of manliness. He suggests that society has recognized two complementary paths, or ladders, to male perfection. He is acknowledging the traditional ladder that referenced gender definition to an aristocratic male ideal, but at the same time he is articulating the premise that there is an equally valid path referenced to the ideal of the celibate and spiritual male. In such a mental world reproductive organs simply have a generative function, and if that function is irrelevant or unwanted then the useless material can be removed like a superfluous digit or branch on a fruit tree.

In this way Christianity and the Church created a ladder of status and perfection that, while it remained oriented to a male ideal (only men could be priests, after all), had rendered procreation irrelevant. Thus, a key component (the ability to procreate) of the complex of factors that led to the construction of a distinct gender for eunuchs in secular and court society had been eliminated in the religious realm.

The ecclesiastical community, at least as reflected in Theophylaktos, is defining manliness in a new way – in terms of spiritual perfection rather than physical or reproductive ability. For this part of society, at least, eunuchs are neither a third sex nor a third gender; they are simply men. For the rest of society eunuchs continue to be defined as incomplete men, although not necessarily as women. They have a place in society that is based on the presence or absence of sexual organs, the degree of development of the secondary sexual characteristics and cultural conditioning based on assumed gender.

We have also seen a gradual change in definitions of both male sexuality and gender, a change that is rooted in Christian thought, evolving philosophical traditions of Late Antiquity and social change. During the classical period masculinity was determined by procreative ability and active sexual roles. Eunuchs, especially those who lacked masculine biological traits, were despised. Some people may have seen them as a third sex, and they obviously constituted a third gender. With the development of the ascetic life and the rejection, at least in ecclesiastical circles, of sexuality and procreation as defining elements in society, eunuchs became less ambiguous sexually, although those who had been gendered into behaviors negatively perceived by the Church continued to be treated as outsiders by churchmen and laymen alike. Within the Church, however, a man who was castrated as a child and reared within the Church could achieve a high degree of social acceptance.

Byzantine eunuchs were thus a feature of Byzantine culture and society that reflected much more than the castration of men who could then safely function in the intimacy of the imperial household. If one looks past the polarity of language and male-oriented definitions of gender that are attached to eunuchs, it becomes apparent that they acquired the main attributes of a distinctive, socially constructed gender. Aside from their physical condition, they were embedded in a self-sustaining web of assumptions about their intrinsic nature and the gendered nature of their specific roles in society, external appearances, acculturation to sustain those appearances and the importance of procreation.

CHAPTER TWO

London's Sapphists: From Three Sexes to Four Genders in the Making of Modern Culture

Randolph Trumbach

In almost all modern Western discussions of the relationship of biological sex to gender and of the female gender to the male, the presumption is made that there are two biological sexes, man and woman, and two genders, female and male. But this is not so in all cultures, and it has not always been so even in Western culture. The paradigm of two genders founded on two biological sexes began to predominate in Western culture only in the early eighteenth century. It was a product of the modern Western gender system, which makes it peculiarly difficult for Westerners to see that this paradigm is not inherent in the empirical observation of the world. The paradigm of two sexes and two genders can be tied to the beginnings of modern equality between the two legitimated genders. It appeared probably throughout the modernizing societies of northwestern Europe, in France and the Netherlands, for example, and certainly in England, as this essay shows. But the new paradigm of the early eighteenth century was not really one of two genders. There was a third illegitimate gender, namely, the adult, passive, transvestite and effeminate male, or "molly," who was supposed to desire men exclusively.

This third gender marked the limits of desire in the majority of men who, in this new paradigm, were not supposed to know what it was like to desire males, although in practice they sometimes did. The desire of one male for another when it did occur was taken to be the result of the corruption of an individual's mind that had occurred in his early experience. It was not held to arise from the biological structure of his body. By the end of the

eighteenth century there is some evidence that there was beginning to appear a role for women which was parallel to that of the
molly for men. Such women were sometimes called "tommies,"
but the more usual term was "sapphist" – with sapphist and
tommy being the high and low terms for women, as "sodomite"
and "molly" were for men. But it is likely that, in the public
mind, women were not fully incorporated into the new gender
paradigm until the late nineteenth and the early twentieth centuries, since women continued to be given legitimate feminine
status more as a result of their sexual relations with men than
because of their avoidance of sex with women. At the point that
the lesbian role became crucial for women, Western societies
would have come to have a gender system divided into the four
roles of man, woman, homosexual man and lesbian woman. These
four roles were supposed to rest on the existence of simply two
biological sexes, since all attempts either to find a biological
basis for homosexual behavior or to characterize some homosexual persons as transsexuals have never been accorded the
standing in either popular or elite culture that childhood and
adolescent experience has been given as the supposed cause of
homosexual behavior.

For the most part, especially in the early eighteenth century,
women lived under an older paradigm as to the nature of the relation of biology to gender and sexual behavior. In the seventeenth
century, this paradigm had been applied to both women and men.
In this paradigm there were two genders – male and female – but
three biological sexes – man, woman and hermaphrodite. All three
biological sexes were supposed to be capable of having sexual relations with both males and females. But they were presumed, of
course, to have sex ordinarily with the opposite gender only, and
then only in marriage, so as to uphold the Christian teaching that
sexual relations were supposed to be primarily procreative.

Men and women had no difficulty in ascertaining their opposite genders. Hermaphrodites, on the other hand, were obliged
to permanently choose one gender or the other for themselves
and then to take sexual partners only from the remaining opposite gender. If hermaphrodites moved back and forth in their gen-

der, their sexual relations could then be stigmatized as the crime of sodomy. Men who had sex with males and women who had sex with females were also guilty of sodomy; but they were not (unlike the eighteenth-century molly) assigned to a third illegitimate gender because of these sexual relations.

In the seventeenth century, these relations between members of the same gender did not violate the gender code for two reasons. First, all persons were thought to be capable of desiring both genders. Furthermore, the minority who illegally acted on this universal human desire ordinarily had sexual relations with both genders and usually enacted their sodomitical desires within the rules of patriarchal domination. That is, adult men had sex with adolescent boys whom they penetrated and whose bodies tended to be smooth and small like women's. Women had sex with females, but without penetration. Sodomitical acts contravened the gender system only when they violated the patriarchal code, that is, when adult men allowed themselves to be penetrated and when women penetrated women. Because there was no third gender to which to assign individuals who thus inverted the patriarchal order in their sexual acts by penetrating or being penetrated in violation of their gender status, such persons were likely to be classified as hermaphrodites and, thus, as biologically deviant. In men, this classification was sometimes understood to be symbolic, but in the case of women, they were likely to be examined by doctors for signs of actual clitoral enlargement.

In the early eighteenth century there were two systematic transitions for males. The first transition was from a system of two genders and three bodies to one of three genders and two bodies. The second involved a change from a system in which active adult males had sexual relations with passive adolescent boys with neither party losing his masculine status to a system in which the minority of adult males who desired other males (whether adult or adolescent) were likely to try to transform themselves into women by moving, speaking and dressing as women. These two transitions in England, France and the Netherlands have been adequately described elsewhere.[1] What I wish to do in this essay is to consider the extent to which women in the eighteenth century – and specifically in London – were affected by the new paradigm regarding the relationships of bodies and genders to sexual acts between persons of sexually similar bodies. I look at three things: first, the standing of women as hermaphrodites, especially in the early eighteenth century; second, cross-dressing by women; and finally, what male contemporaries would have considered to be actual sexual relations between women.

It will appear that, for women, the development of the sapphist role began slowly after midcentury and could be seen very clearly enacted by some individuals in the last quarter of the century. In the first half of the eighteenth century, however, women who had sex with women also had sexual relations with men and were likely to use their hands for stimulation and to avoid penetration. At that time, men speculated that women who did penetrate other women must do so either because their clitorises were enlarged or by using an artificial penis. It is likely that some women did in fact use dildos and that some of these women dressed as men and married women. But it is also likely that most women who dressed and passed as men for any length of time did not seek to have sexual relations with women; this is probably true even of those who married women. Some women (like the actresses who took male roles on stage) cross-dressed in order to be sexually appealing to men, not women. But the appeal of such women lay in the knowledge of the beholder that they were women. Women who passed as men, on the other hand, did their best to conceal their body's sex. Only at the end of the century did there appear women who sought to be sexually desirable by dressing in part as men, but who wished the eye of the knowing beholder to be a woman's and not a man's. These women dressed partly as men and partly as women, and their appeal lay in this ambiguity. They therefore differed considerably from the occasional passing woman who lived entirely as a man and may have married women and perhaps used an artificial penis. These new ambiguously gendered women were London's first modern sapphists, and their sexual taste was conceived to be the perversion of a minority and not a wicked sin to which any woman might be brought by the effects of great debauchery.[2]

Hermaphrodites and Women

Men who had sexual relations with other men were sometimes still classified as hermaphrodites in the early eighteenth century even after the new role of the molly had appeared. In the late seventeenth century "hermaphrodite" seems to have been used as a term for men who were both active and passive in the sexual act. "There are likewise hermaphrodites," the *Wandering Whore* (1660) had said, "effeminate men, men given to much luxury, idleness, and wanton pleasures, and to that abominable sin of sodomy, wherein they are both active and passive in it, whose vicious actions are only to be whispered amongst us." But the same work had earlier described in a more matter-of-fact way those men who desired sodomy either with female prostitutes or with beardless, apprentice boys. When, however, Joseph Addison in 1716 referred to an ambiguous wizard as "one of your hermaphrodites, as they call them," he was probably not yet using the term to refer to the new species of the molly, who was characterized as a kind of male whore. This is clearer in Jonathan Wild's exchange in 1714 with William Hitchen, the corrupt Under Marshal of the City of London. Hitchen said he wanted to introduce Wild (the leader of the underground of thieves) "to a company of he-whores." But Wild, "not apprehending rightly his meaning, asked if they were hermaphrodites: No, ye fool, said the M[arsha]l, they are sodomites, such as deal with their own sex instead of females."

By 1731, William Pulteney's employment of the term against Lord Hervey shows that *hermaphrodite*, when used of a man, had quite clearly come to mean an effeminate man who desired sex with other men and had no reference to the biological condition of his body. Pulteney called Hervey "such a delicate hermaphrodite" who "you know...is a lady himself; or at least such a nice composition of the two sexes, that it is difficult to distinguish which is more predominant." Pulteney also made no distinction as to the roles taken in the act: "It is well known that there must be two parties in this crime; the pathick and the agent; both equally guilty." Both the active and the passive role in sodomy now made a man into this kind of hermaphrodite. About the same time Alexander Pope wrote his character of Hervey as being "one vile

115

antithesis. Amphibious thing! that acting either part...now trips a lady and now struts a lord." This sort of hermaphrodite was characterized not only by the sexual acts performed but also by the public combination of behaviors taken from both of the two legitimate genders, and it was this combination of behaviors, not the structure of his body, that made him hermaphroditic. Later, in 1739, Pope used the term hermaphrodite of Addison and Richard Steele themselves when he told Joseph Spence that both men were "a couple of H——s. I am sorry to say so, and there are not twelve people in the world that I would say it to at all." But it was *molly*, not hermaphrodite, that was the term most commonly used to describe the effeminate sodomite. And *molly* had originated not as a description of a type of body but as a term for a female whore. Male sodomites were, as William Hitchen had said, "he-whores."[3]

The term *hermaphrodite* was also sometimes used of women in a metaphorical way in the early eighteenth century, but its purpose was usually to stigmatize female clothing that seemed to impinge on the male domain. Women's riding habits especially brought out these comments. In 1713 John Gay wrote in the *Guardian* of a riding habit "which some have not injudiciously stiled the hermaphroditical, by reason of its masculine and feminine composition." In the previous year Addison had similarly complained of these "hermaphrodites" and their "amphibious dress" and had said that it was "absolutely necessary to keep up the partition between the two sexes." But Addison did not imply that these clothes (which were usually masculine only from the waist up since they were worn with skirts) signaled any female desire for sex between women. There may, however, have been some anxiety on his part in this regard. Certainly in the previous year when he had written to commend Sappho's great lyric of desire for a young woman whom she observed speaking to a man, Addison had taken care to say that "whatever might have been the occasion of this ode, the English reader will enter into the beauties of it, if he supposes it to have been written in the person of a [male] lover sitting by his mistress." But by and large, many eighteenth-century readers were able to ignore the lesbian

116

dimension of Sappho's work, and by a similar procedure, the term *hermaphrodite* could be used to stigmatize gender infractions in women without implying (as it did when used of men) any accompanying form of sexual desire between women.[4]

The woman who desired women, however, and accompanied this with overt masculine characteristics was in the eighteenth century often supposed to be an actual physical hermaphrodite. Her clitoris was likely to be examined by physicians for signs of an enlargement that might be the first stage in its transformation into a penis. There was even a tendency to think of all hermaphrodites as female, as seen in *The Treatise of Hermaphrodites*, published by Edmund Curll in 1718. The anonymous author of this work acknowledged that there were male hermaphrodites as well as female and even presumed there were more male hermaphrodites than female ones. Nonetheless, almost all of his discussion was about female hermaphrodites, demonstrating the popular tendency to think of all hermaphrodites as female. This author also thought of female hermaphrodites as women with enlarged clitorises. He did not insist that they all desired women, but he did claim that "the intrigues of my hermaphrodites are indeed very amazing and monstrous as their natures; but that many lascivious females divert themselves one with another at this time in this city, is not to be disputed." Women were more likely than men to desire to be hermaphrodites because of their lascivious irrationality. Pregnant women, as a result of their longings, were more likely to seek out a female hermaphrodite – an opinion shared by the author of *The History of the Human Heart* (1749). Women in hot places like Italy and France were more likely than those in cool England to seek such pleasures. But despite this libertine author's similarities to a more scientific writer like James Parsons (who wrote in 1741), it is apparent that he did not yet share Parsons's view that there were only two anatomies on which there were founded two genders. He still presumed that in women there were three anatomical sexes and that the desire of one woman to dominate another woman in a masculine fashion was likely to be the result of an anatomical, hermaphroditic condition.[5]

Young girls who engaged in mutual masturbation were warned

that their actions would result in the enlargement of the clitoris and that this might eventually cause them to be classified as hermaphrodites. In 1725 a girl of eighteen supposedly wrote to the author of the *Onania* (the most famous of antimasturbatory tracts) that for seven years she had practiced mutual masturbation with an older girl who shared her bed and served as her mother's chambermaid. The first girl said that she now found that "for above half a year past, I have had a swelling that thrusts out from my body, as big and almost as hard, and as long or longer than my thumb, which inclines me to excessive lustful desires, and from it there issues a moisture or slipperiness to that degree that I am almost continually wet, and sometimes have such a forcing, as if something of a large substance was coming from me." Her periods had stopped, and she wondered whether it was all tied to her masturbation or came "from anything in nature more in my make than is customary to the sex."[6]

In reply the author of *Onania* cited the case of two nuns in Rome that Dr. Carr had discussed in his *Medical Epistles*. These two women had changed their anatomical sex as a result of masturbation; they were expelled from their convent and took up male dress and occupations. Carr had said that this transformation did not have to be explained as magical. He argued that the genitalia of women were exactly like those of men, except that "by a defect in that respect they are only to be perceived inwardly," for women's bodies were conceived as being exactly like men's, only defective. The clitoris, uterus and ovaries in women were equivalent to the penis, scrotum and testes in men. What had occurred in the two nuns was that what was ordinarily hidden inwardly in a woman's body had by manipulation been brought outside of the body, thereby transforming them into men.[7]

The response of the author of the *Onania* also cited Dr. Drake's work on anatomy, which reflected a later point of view. Drake did not believe in the possibility of anatomical transformation, whether by magic or physical manipulation. Hermaphrodites were for him simply girls who had large clitorises and were consequently assigned to the wrong gender at birth. He had seen a three-year-old mistaken for a boy and christened as such by her parents: the neighbors had called her a hermaphrodite. James Parsons in 1741 took the same view, claiming that he was promoting scientific enlightenment against traditional superstition and cruelty. He cited the case of a London girl whom he had been told of by the surgeon John Douglas. She had been mistaken for a boy by her parents because of an enlarged clitoris. They dressed her as a boy and put her to serve as drawer or waiter at the King's Arms tavern in Fleet Street. There she shared a bed with a fellow servant who made her pregnant. She was turned away in shame and obliged to put on women's clothes. "The rumor," Parsons wrote, "of the drawer's being changed into a woman made a great noise all over the neighbourhood, and very likely would have been recorded for truth, if it had happened in any age a little earlier."[8]

Reports of hermaphrodites continued to be made. Dr. William Cadogan was said to have "seen many cases of confirmed hermaphrodites" in the course of his London practice. In some cases they apparently changed gender, to the confused disgust of some contemporaries who wished them to be one gender or the other. In 1771 it was asserted that there was "living in the East part of the town an hermaphrodite, who appeared about twelve years since in men's clothes, and was married to a woman with whom it lived till her death. After her decease, it dressed in women's apparel, and about four or five years since was married to a man, with whom it now lives."[9]

Parsons would have insisted that such an individual must be either a male or a female who had moved from one gender to another. Human beings, he explained, could not go back and forth between sexes like earthworms. But in the early seventeenth century, physiological and legal theory had presumed otherwise. Sir Edward Coke in his great commentary on the common law had said that "every heir is either a male, or female, or an hermaphrodite, that is both male and female." But Coke had also said that hermaphrodites could not live as both males and females: they were obliged to pick one gender and adhere to it forever. This was customary European law. If individuals went back and forth, they were guilty of sodomy. Some individuals, however, actually did go back and forth in Coke's day. For example, Thomasine Hall was christened as a girl. At twenty-two, however, she dressed as a man and joined the army. Hall went to America, where once again she became a woman. But when searched, he proved to have fully developed male genitalia. Hall was probably a male pseudo-hermaphrodite whose male genitalia had descended in late adolescence but who had been assigned to the female gender at birth. The American court in 1629 could not encompass such complications and sentenced Hall to dress partly as a man and partly as a woman.[10]

Parsons did mention briefly that some hermaphrodites could be males who had been wrongly assigned at birth. But in most of his discussion he presumed that most hermaphrodites were female. The 1710 translation of Nicholas Venette's *Mysteries of Conjugal Love Revealed* had distinguished five types of hermaphrodites. Parsons really had only one. He was interested in the women he called *Macroclitorideae* – the women with large clitorises. He intended to defend them against prejudice and cruelty by denying that they were different in nature from other people; they were not a separate race, and they were not capable of "exercising the functions of either sex with regard to generation." To tell such women that they were obliged under penalty to choose one sex and to stick with it was not to the point. Such "poor women" could not "exercise the part of any other sex but their own." And their sexual desire must presumably have been for men, not women. Parsons's position marked the beginning of the argument that biologically there are only two sexes, that on these anatomical differences are founded two gender roles but that both genders sexually desire only the opposite gender. No individual was able to perform the role of a gender that was not a reflection of that individual's sexual anatomy.[11]

It is apparent, then, that for Parsons hermaphrodites were not a third biological category (as had been traditionally held) but bodily defective males or females who were given, like all human beings, a male or female gender identity founded on the biology of their bodies and which they were not psychologically able to change. But there were still others who held the traditional view that hermaphrodites were a third biological category. These authorities now tended to fill this category with women since the passive sodomites who went back and forth between being male and female were supposed to behave as they did not because of a physical condition of their bodies but as a result of the corruption of their minds. Parsons himself must have felt the influence of the role of the molly since he limited his discussion to those hermaphroditic bodies that were to him fundamentally female. Both the new and old-fashioned views of hermaphrodites probably had been encouraged to see hermaphrodites as female by the long-standing view that the female body was an imperfect version of the perfect male body; hermaphroditic bodies, being imperfect, were therefore likely to be female. In the early eighteenth century the woman with the large clitoris did provide a biological category into which those women who were sexually active with other women could be placed by a society that had not yet conceived a social role for such women paralleling that of the molly among men. It was likely, however, that Parsons's view was becoming the dominant one in the middle of the century. This was no doubt in part a result of scientific observation, but it is also likely to have been linked to the beginning of the construction of a social role for women who had sex with women. By the end of the century there would be no need for a separate biological category in which to place such women. It would become possible to stigmatize them as tommies or sapphists, that is, as individuals whose minds had been corrupted from the normal desires of their female bodies.

Women and Cross-Dressing
In his discussion of the case of Catherine Vizzani, John Cleland suggested that women who dressed and passed as men were likely to be involved in sexual relations with other women, but this was not the case with most cross-dressing women in eighteenth-century London. For most of the century, sexual relations between women were not yet tied to cross-dressing, as sexual relations between men had come to be. Mollies, everyone knew, dressed as women. Most cross-dressing women did not dress as they did in order to attract other women. Some sapphists began to

cross-dress as a way of attracting women only at the end of the eighteenth century.[12]

There were women who married or courted other women in eighteenth-century London and who may have tried to use a dildo, as did Mary Hamilton and Vizzani (see below); but the use of a dildo in eighteenth-century cases cannot be proved. These marriages were prosecuted as frauds. Some of them were clearly intended to defraud women of their money. Sarah Ketson, for example, posed as a man called John in 1720 and tried to defraud Ann Hutchinson by courting her in marriage. Constantine Boone in the previous year had also been convicted of a fraudulent marriage; in her case there may have been an anatomical basis for her behavior, since she was also exhibited as a hermaphrodite at Southwark Fair. One young woman married an older one in 1773 for her £100, and another woman was convicted in 1777 of marrying three different women. But some of these marriages, no matter how they may have originally begun, eventually became acceptable to both women. Sarah Paul (who went by the name of Samuel Bundy) was debauched at thirteen by a man. To avoid Paul's mother, the man dressed her as a boy and adopted her as his son. Paul left him and went to sea for a year. When she returned, she bound herself to a painter (the trade of her seducer). She was there attracted to a young woman, Mary Parlour, and married her. Paul's wife soon discovered her husband's true identity but at first decided not to expose the affair. Eventually, however, Parlour had her arrested for fraud. But the bond between the two had become too strong. The wife kept the arrested husband company in prison and failed to appear at the trial. The magistrate burned Paul's male clothes and ordered her never to appear again as a man.[13]

Some marriages lasted most of a lifetime. John Chivy always dressed as a man and was married to a woman for nearly twenty years; Chivy separated from her a few years before his death. His identity as a woman was discovered only at his death. The most complicated, best reported and hardest to interpret of these long marriages is that of Mary East. At the death of her wife in 1766, it came out that for thirty-six years she had passed as the husband of the couple; she had successfully run a public house at Poplar and had creditably held many of the parish offices. The question that is most difficult to resolve is the nature of their sexual relation or, at least, whether there had been one at all. Had they posed as man and woman for economic convenience? A girl who was discovered to have dressed as a boy when she was hired at a public house in Duke's Place in London explained that she had done so because "boys could shift better for themselves than girls." It is possible, though, that East and her wife had carried on some sort of sexual relationship. East was very frightened by the men who tried to blackmail her after her friend's death by threatening to take her to the magistrate for passing as a man. These threats sound very similar to those directed against some men who paid a blackmailer threatening them with charges of sodomy. This latter kind of blackmail was a widespread practice and must have been known to a woman like East who had moved so successfully in the world of men. Her blackmailers may themselves have seen a parallel between East's behavior and that of sodomites. But her blackmail case is the only one that possibly involved the question of sexual relations between two women.[14]

The magistrate sometimes did arrest women for cross-dressing. Elizabeth Morris was arrested, whipped and put to hard labor in 1704 because she had dressed as a man and enlisted as a soldier in Lieutenant General Steward's regiment. At the end of the century Mary Jones, who was probably a prostitute, was arrested for dressing as a man and making a disturbance in Turmmill Street. Five years later, Ann Lewis was arrested for dressing as a sailor.[15] But it is impossible to say why these women were arrested when others who dressed and passed as soldiers and sailors were treated indulgently and sometimes even made into popular heroines. Christian Davies, Hannah Snell, Mary Knowles and Mary Talbot were the best-known eighteenth-century heroines of this kind, but many other cases appeared in the newspapers. These women usually joined the army or the navy either to be with their male lovers or husbands or to search for them. The writers of their stories occasionally displayed a certain prurient interest in how these women had hidden their anatomy or proved their sexual interest in women to their male companions. Snell had had to show that she was as interested as her fellow sailors in women, since they had begun to call her Miss Molly, implying that she was an effeminate sodomite; and she had had to explain away the appearance of her breasts when she was stripped and whipped. Davies had a silver tube made so that she could stand up in public and urinate. This act was one of the tests of manhood, as Dryden knew when he mocked the Amazonian whore who could otherwise pass for a man; Dryden told his male audience that they should

> ...laugh to see her tyr'd with many a bout,
> Call for the Pot, and like a Man Piss Out.

But none of these women were ever arrested for passing as men.[16]

Other women dressed as men because it facilitated their libertine life with men. Sally Salisbury dressed as a beautiful youth and went out into the streets with her young aristocratic male friends to attack passersby in the street. Three men drank together in a public house in Gateshead. When they tried to leave without paying, there was a scuffle and one of the men was discovered to be a woman. Lady Ann Harvey's coachman of sixteen years' service bore a child. She had been married to another servant in the family in the days when masters did not care for their servants to be married and had dressed and worked as a man to hide the marriage. Catherine Meadwell frequently dressed in men's clothes and used the name of Captain Clark. It probably helped her to get past suspicious landladies with the lover on whose account she was divorced. Charlotte Charke also probably started to dress in public en cavalier because it facilitated her secret, second marriage to John Sacheverell in 1746.[17]

Charke's Narrative can serve as a final demonstration of the complications that arise in interpreting a cross-dressing woman's life. On the one hand, Charke seemed to put on men's clothes for convenience and under special circumstances: it hid her secret marriage, and it was perhaps safer for her and her actress friend to stroll the provinces as a male actor and his wife ("Mr. and Mrs. Brown") than as two women. On the other hand, on a number of occasions, she courted women who were marriageable and with-drew from the situation only at the last moment. She enjoyed her popularity among the Covent Garden whores with whom she passed as Sir Charles. She stressed that she was not adept at female occupations like sewing and preferred those that were male. She remembered dressing in her father's clothes when she was four. All of this seems to suggest what Cleland would have called a secret bias. But she also liked men to some degree and bore a daughter. It has been suggested that, because she drew a hostile portrait of an effeminate male sodomite in her novel, she could not have had sexual relations with any of the women with whom she flirted. But this does not necessarily follow. It is likely that one could disapprove of the new role of the exclusive sodomite and yet practice a traditional bisexual libertinism – especially if one were a woman. This (as we shall see) was certainly the position of John Cleland in *Fanny Hill*, where the two women were approved of but the two male sodomites were very harshly condemned.

Such libertinism did not, however, make a woman respect-able. Charke's family was always uneasy over the possibilities that her life seemed to imply, and they broke with her over the ques-tion of her cross-dressing. It was one thing for Charke to take male roles on the stage where the audience knew the actress was a woman – but it was another to try to pass as a man in the street. Still Charke did not hesitate to publish her memoirs. But it is impossible in the end to say whether she ever experienced what would have seemed to her to be sexual intercourse with another woman. The majority of women who cross-dressed did so either because it made it easier for them to make a living or because it allowed them to move safely in a hostile environment. But a few women seem to have done so because it allowed them to enact a dominating sexual attraction with other women. A woman like Charke could cross-dress for both reasons. But throughout most of the century, the majority of women who had sexual relations with other women – and they must have been a very small liber-tine minority of all women – did not cross-dress and did not even take on masculine airs.[18]

Sexual Relations Between Women

Sexual relations between women were not illegal in England. Coke in the seventeenth century had defined sodomy to mean either sexual intercourse between a woman and a beast or anal intercourse by a man with either a male or a female.[19] But sexual relations between two women did not come under the sodomy statute. As a consequence there are no detailed descriptions of sex between women in the legal sources that parallel those for sodomy between men. There are, however, some imaginary descriptions – one by a woman, Delariviere Manley, and the rest by men.

Married women and prostitutes figure most prominently in these descriptions, but there are also descriptions of sex between young unmarried girls. In the case of the married women and the prostitutes, it is apparent that the women usually also have sex with men, even if in some cases their preference may be for women. Mrs. Manley in her 1709 *Secret Memoirs...from the New Atalantis* (vol. 2) described a "new cabal" or "sect" (p. 43) of aristocratic women who "have all of happiness in themselves." They kiss and embrace and are suspected by others of taking these things a little too far. The older women lament to the young "the custom of the world that has made it convenient (nay, almost indispensable) for all ladies once to marry," but their intention was "to reserve their heart, their tender amity for their fair friend" (p. 47). Occasionally one of the two women in a couple was described as having "something so robust in her air and mien, that the other sex would have certainly claimed her for one of theirs" but for the fact that she dressed as a woman (p. 48). The Marchioness of Sandomire (who was identified as the actual Lady Popham) dressed as a man and wandered through the prostitutes' quarter with her female favorite. Together they had sex with the prostitutes (p. 49). Another woman in the novel, Zara (or Catherine Portmore), grew discouraged with her male lovers and took a female lover, Daphne, who herself had affairs with men. Both women were part of the theatrical world. Financial necessity obliged Daphne to look for a husband, though she continued to live only for her female friend (pp. 50–56).[20]

The two prostitutes who have sex with each other in Cleland's

Memoirs of a Woman of Pleasure (1748) do not of course have husbands. But they do have sex with many men, and they clearly prefer men to women. In addition, neither of them seems to display any of the masculine characteristics that aristocratic women in fiction and in life sometimes displayed as part of their taste for women. Phoebe Ayres prepared Fanny Hill to have sex with men by enjoying the girl herself. Cleland described it as "one of those arbitrary tastes for which there is no accounting." It was "not that she hated men, or did not even prefer them to her own sex; but when she met with such occasions as this was, a satiety of enjoyments in the common road, perhaps too a secret bias, inclined her to make the most of pleasure, wherever she could find it, without distinction of sexes" (p. 12). Cleland, however, made it clear that his heroine Fanny has no real interest in this direction. She eventually says that she "pin'd for more solid food, and promis'd tacitly to myself that I would not be put off much longer with this foolery from woman to woman" (p. 34). In the actual world of prostitution, libertine men sometimes did take two women to bed at the same time – a practice known as "lying in state" (i.e., like a king) – but it is impossible to say to what degree the two women in such situations became involved with each other. It was, in any case, not a widespread practice. Of six hundred men arrested for being with prostitutes in London in the 1720s, only twenty-seven men (4.5 percent) were found with two women at once. Phoebe Ayres's taste for women may have been one that developed in prostitutes: it was claimed that there was unnatural wickedness in the Magdalen Hospital for repentant prostitutes when one girl put her hand into the bosom of another.[21]

The fashionable London world was able to talk of actual examples of these relations throughout the century – the women with shock, the men with delight. The Duchess of Marlborough told Queen Anne that Mrs. Manley's novel contained (among other scandal) "stuff not fit to be mentioned of passions between women." Horace Walpole reported that Lady Pomfret went traveling not with her husband but with Miss Shelly, "whom Winnington used to call *filial piety*, for imitating her father, in bearing affection to her own sex." He observed that Mrs. Cavendish was *"in-cun-sole-able"* on the death of Lady Dysart. This married woman had also openly displayed her tastes: "Gilly" Williams said that she seemed "by the heat of the waters, and the natural richness of her constitution" to be "more wickedly inclined than any young fellow here, and if Lady Betty Spencer is not sent away, I believe she will by force go in unto her and know her."[22]

Such stories, and the material from the novels, are distinctly parallel to the late-seventeenth- and early-eighteenth-century attitude toward sodomy between males that could be found among male rakes before the development of the role of the adult passive, effeminate sodomite, or molly. Such a rake was prepared to have sexual relations with both women and boys because he took the dominant role in both kinds of acts. Others might view his behavior as very wicked, but they did not think of him as effeminate. Sexual relations with a younger male did not lessen the masculine status of a rake; if anything, it reinforced the image of his power. The rake certainly did not go in for any degree of cross-dressing as part of his dominant sodomitical behavior. There were, however, a few adult males who took the passive role in sodomy. They were likely to be classified as hermaphrodites since they had changed, in effect, from being men to being women.

The women so far described were also likely to have sex with both women and men. It is true that in some cases marriage and sex with men were forced on them by economic necessity. But in most cases they are described as genuinely desiring both men and women, although they sometimes preferred one or the other. They were of course wicked because they were not chaste. But they are for the most part not described as losing feminine status because of their bisexual behavior. The one woman who cross-dresses in Mrs. Manley's novel does so probably as a means of passing unmolested in the prostitutes' quarter. In a few more cases, one of the two women in a relationship is described as having masculine airs but not as cross-dressing. It is these women alone who were deviant. It is they who were likely to be described as hermaphrodites. In this, these unusually active women directly paralleled the late-seventeenth-century adult males who were also characterized as hermaphrodites because of their unusual passivity in sodomy.

The author of the 1718 *Treatise of Hermaphrodites* had mentioned that some women used dildos. This was an alternative explanation of aggressive female sexuality that was likely to appeal to such male writers as Henry Fielding and Cleland. These writers belonged to a minority who, in the middle of the century, held that one woman's desire for another was founded on a corruption of the mind and was therefore similar to the adult, effeminate, male sodomite's desire for another male. Fielding, in his heavily fictionalized account of Mary Hamilton (who married several women), stressed again and again the problem that Hamilton had faced because she did not have a penis. She was brought to trial when her last wife's relatives found in her trunk "something of too vile, wicked, and scandalous a nature." That this was in fact a dildo is confirmed in the periphrastic language of the legal depositions and the newspaper reports. Fielding concluded that "unnatural affections are equally vicious and equally detestable in both sexes." He also tried to show that Hamilton had acted as she did after being corrupted by an older woman and not because of the structure of her body.[23]

Cleland translated and commented on the case of Vizzani that Giovanni Bianchi had reported from Italy. Vizzani had seduced several young women, including nuns. At her death Bianchi investigated her body to see whether it was anatomically different. He reported that her clitoris was not "of any extraordinary size" as it was supposed to be with women "who followed the practices of Sappho." It was indeed smaller than middle size. Vizzani, instead, had used as her penis a leather cylinder stuffed with rags and fastened below her abdomen. Cleland commented that her behavior must have proceeded "from some error in nature, or from some disorder or perversion in the imagination." The autopsy had proved that her body was normal. Therefore, he reasoned, her imagination must have been "corrupted early in her youth" by lascivious tales. In the course of time, her vicious practices might have caused "a preternatural change in the animal spirits and a kind of venereal fury." Cleland's tone here was very different from the way he had described the sexual encounters between Phoebe Ayres and Fanny Hill three years earlier. It may be that, having been once prosecuted, Cleland was simply being careful. But there is perhaps another explanation. Vizzani had died a virgin with her hymen intact. She had never submitted to a man. She had used a penis and dressed as a man. In all these ways she differed from Cleland's fictional heroines. Vizzani had become a sort of hermaphrodite, undergoing a "preternatural" change – she had deviated from the acceptable libertine norm of the bisexual woman and had become a monster. Because she had been exclusively interested in women, in Cleland's mind she had lost her status as a woman. Cleland added that women should be more severely punished when they appeared in public places in men's clothes. This should not be done for the sake of a silly diversion. For him cross-dressing was likely to become a part of a more serious sexual deviation.[24]

Men like Cleland and Fielding sometimes tried to fit the woman who actively sought women into a category parallel to that of the passive male sodomite: they consequently denied that such women had enlarged clitorises and said that they were motivated by the corruption of their minds – and by the end of the century could call them tommies, as men were called mollies. But such men were never consistent in their view about women who desired women. They used both the old and the new models to describe them. It is likely that they did so for two reasons. First, women, unlike men, had not in the eighteenth century yet come to be consistently classified into what by the late nineteenth century would be called a heterosexual majority and a homosexual minority. And second, women, again unlike men, did not yet define their gender identities in terms of their relationship to other women, as men defined theirs in relation to other men. Women were still given conventional female status because of the way they behaved with men.

The best evidence for both the emergence of the tommy's role and its relative unimportance for women's gender status can be found in a single source after 1770 – the diary of Mrs. Hester Thrale Piozzi. Mrs. Piozzi made many comments about male sodomy in the thirty years after she began keeping her diary in 1776. It might even be described as one of her great interests. She noticed the difference between Italian tolerance and English ostracism, and she usually approved of the latter, except when she found the poor man personally sympathetic. She wondered about the dynamics of personality that were involved. She was frequently convinced that she could detect sodomitical inclinations in men who had otherwise sought to hide them. And she felt that sodomy was on the increase, along with adultery and most other sexual vices.

Sexual relations between women, especially in Bath and in London, also caught Mrs. Piozzi's attention, if not to the same extent that male sodomy did. She comprehended it less and was more likely (in her mind) to be taken in by the vicious content of seemingly innocent female friendship. At Bath she found Dr. Dobson's wife "so odd" and "odious" and wrote that "this nasty Bath is a cage of unclean birds" – a phrase she fondly repeated ten years later. In 1789 she noted the charges that Marie Antoinette had been at the head of a set of monsters called by each other "Sapphists." In 1792 she praised Miss Trefusis's poems in honor of her female friends, Miss Weston and Miss Powell. But a year later she discovered that Miss Rathbone's house where these women had lived was "supposed to have been a cage of unclean birds, living in a sinful celibàt." She wondered why Miss Weston had been so averse to marriage, and why she had made "such ado" about Sally Siddons, the actress's daughter; but she explained to herself that "Miss Weston did use to like *every girl* so." Mrs. Siddons had told her that Siddons's "sister was in personal danger once from a female fiend of this kind." Mrs. Piozzi went so far as to say in 1795 that "whenever two ladies live too much together," they were suspected of "what has a Greek name now and is called Sapphism." But to Mrs. Piozzi, what these women did with each other were "impossibilities" – "such I think 'em." Or in other words, it was not clear to her phallocratic mind what two women could do sexually with each other. For Mrs. Piozzi, the point of sexual honor among men was the avoidance of sodomy: "no sin but one seems punished by the world's disapprobation – that crime is still discountenanced, no gentleman will speak to Doctor William Wynne" who was suspected of sodomy. But for women, honor flowed from their correct behavior with men; and to show this Mrs. Piozzi immediately followed her comments on Wynne by writing that there was "*some* idea – a *faint* one – about the point of honor amongst women too; Helena Williams's friends are all shamed of *her*" for running away with a married man.[25]

Among the sapphists Mrs. Piozzi knew of, one stood out. This was Mrs. Damer, whose tastes became the subject of widespread gossip. She was a sculptress and the daughter of General Seymour Conway. She was also a great favorite of Horace Walpole, who left her his house when he died and who had been in love with her father, who was Walpole's cousin. Damer had married at eighteen, but nine years later her libertine husband had blown out his brains after dismissing the blind fiddler and the four whores he had taken to a tavern. Within six years of her husband's death, her taste for women was well enough known to become the subject of *A Sapphic Epistle from Jack Cavendish to Mrs. D***** (1782). By 1795, when she was a woman of forty-seven, she had become so notorious that Mrs. Piozzi wrote that it was "a joke in London now to say such a one visits Mrs. Damer." Lord Derby insisted that Mrs. Farren, a comic actress who was his mistress, should stay away from Damer, who was fond of her. Five years earlier the affection between the two women had produced a quatrain that ran:

> Her little stock of private fame
> Will fall a wreck to public clamour,
> If Farren leagues with one whose name
> Comes near – Aye very near – to Damn her.

By the end of the decade, according to Joseph Farrington, Mrs. Damer had adopted some articles of men's clothes: "she wears a man's hat, and shoes – and a jacket also like a man's – thus she walks about the fields with a hooking stick." But she evidently still wore a woman's skirt. She was not a passing woman who dressed entirely as a man, but instead she combined female and male characteristics in order to attract women. She was courting Mary Berry (Berry was thirty-five and Damer fifty). Farrington thought their ecstasies "on meeting and tender leave on separating…whimsical"; their servants described one such separation when Miss Berry went to Cheltenham, "as if it had been parting before death." All that was lacking to make Mrs. Damer the female equivalent of a molly was a name. This the *Sapphic Epistle* of 1782 had given her when it wrote that Sappho was said to have been "the first Tommy the world has upon record." *Tommy* was probably the popular libertine term for a sapphic woman. But whereas "molly" has an extensive history from the early eighteenth century, this late-eighteenth-century poem seems to make one of the first recorded uses of "tommy."[26]

The partial social ostracism that Mrs. Damer suffered was, however, quite different from society's reaction to Eleanor Butler and Sarah Ponsonby, and it is important to ask why this was so. These two friends first met when Butler was twenty-nine and Ponsonby thirteen. Eight years later in 1778 (after a first unsuccessful attempt) they eloped together, and two years later they leased a house in the beautiful Welsh vale of Llangollen. There they spent the remainder of their lives in dedicated friendship. The world eventually came to visit them, including Mrs. Piozzi, who found them charming, corresponded with them and never made any negative judgment of them. Butler was handsome and looked rather like her own nephew; Ponsonby was pretty. They both seemed always to have dressed in riding habits, and from the 1790s onward they cropped their hair. As they aged in the early nineteenth century, it became impossible for strangers to tell them from old men, at least when they were seated, since they continued to wear skirts. Elizabeth Mavor suggested in her biography of them that it would be incorrect to categorize them as sapphists since their affection for each other was part of a pattern of romantic friendships between women. Mrs. Piozzi, for instance, had such a friendship with Mrs. Siddons. Mavor also said that the clothes and hair of Butler and Ponsonby might be explained by the custom among Irish gentlewomen (which they were) of wearing riding habits indoors and by their conservatism in keeping a hairstyle that had been popular among many women in the 1790s. It is certainly true that Mrs. Piozzi, who was very attuned to the issue of sapphism, does not seem to have suspected them in the teeth of the apparent evidence. It is clear that they did not project their relationship as an erotic one; and it is probable that if there had been erotic feelings between them, they themselves would have been unable to think of their feelings in such a way.[27]

Nevertheless, it is also true that some of their contemporaries did classify them as sapphists. In the summer of 1790 a column describing them appeared in a number of the London newspapers. It was sympathetic, but it left no doubt as to its meaning. Butler was described as "tall and masculine – always wears a riding habit"; Ponsonby was said to be "polite and effeminate, fair and beautiful." Ponsonby, in typical female fashion, oversaw the house, and Butler, in masculine fashion, superintended the grounds. It is likely that whoever wrote the column had only heard of the ladies and not seen them: Butler, at any rate, was short and fat. But the writer had a category in which to place them, and the ladies and their friends understood the meaning and were outraged. They wrote, significantly enough, to Edmund Burke to ask advice about legal action. Burke in 1780 and 1784 had sued two different papers for suggesting that he was at least sympathetic toward sodomy because he had protested in the House of Commons against the treatment that was meted out to sodomites in the pillory. He won both cases. In the year after the appearance of the column against the ladies, Burke also defended the honor of the Queen of France against the revolutionaries, aware, no doubt (as was Mrs. Piozzi), that she had been charged with being a sapphist. But his own experience with the libel cases had been unsatisfactory. He advised the two ladies not to act; he told them that he trusted "that the piety, good sense, and fortitude that hitherto have distinguished you and make you the mark of envy in your retreat" would allow them to despise the scandal; and he reassured them that it made no impression on those who valued them.[28]

The romantic friendship of Butler and Ponsonby does seem to have approached sapphism in some regards. They never married men, they lived together and they dressed, both of them, in a hermaphroditic manner. The relationship between them also seems to have had elements of traditional male-female differentiation, because of the sixteen years difference in age, as well as the difference to be seen in the handsomeness of one and the prettiness of the other. But they apparently did not experience their relationship as sexual. They did not project it as sexual. And consequently those who knew them did not perceive it as sexual. Mrs. Damer, on the other hand, not only dressed in a hermaphroditic fashion and liked younger pretty women; she clearly projected her affection for women as sexual. It was certainly perceived that way, and she was stigmatized consequently as a tommy and a sapphist. It is likely, therefore, that women attracted to women after 1770, when the new sapphist role had emerged, could either know or not know the sexual content of their feelings. Those who knew were likely to be those who were stigmatized. But those who did not know were still likely (like Butler and Ponsonby) to adopt some of the external characteristics of the sapphist role.

The stigmatization, however, was never as great as that experienced by male sodomites. Women's lives were never as public as men's. There is no evidence of a female sexual subculture of taverns or public places of assignation like those for male sodomites. There were some social nexus organized around prostitution and the meeting places of the fashionable and the theatrical worlds. But more important, most women felt they were female because of their relationship to men and not because they had avoided contamination by the sapphist's role. It is likely on the other hand that for men the avoidance of contact with sodomites was at least as important as their relationship with women in defining themselves as masculine. But the new sapphist's role probably did begin to affect women's consciousness to some degree, as the changing attitudes toward female cross-dressing show. By the late eighteenth century, actresses who took male roles and dressed as men on stage were found less exciting than they had been earlier in the century, as Kristina Straub's book shows. And by the early nineteenth century (as Dianne Dugaw, and Rudolf M. Dekker and Lotte C. van de Pol suggest), women had greater difficulty in passing in real life as men and the public became less interested in their stories. Women's bodies had even more certainly been transformed and made more similar to men's, since no one was likely to explain the behavior of a sapphist by examining the size of her clitoris. Her clothes might be hermaphroditic but not her body. By 1800, it was conceived in discussion both of men and women that there were only two types of bodies, male and female. But the variety of sexual acts in which human bodies might engage guaranteed that there were four genders, two of them legitimated, and two stigmatized. Consequently, in the modern Western world, there were men and women, and sodomites and sapphists. This system of four genders has been obscured, however, by the tendency to distinguish gender from sexual orientation in modern Western thought. It has become conventional to imagine a linked system of two sexes, two genders and two sexual orientations. But it is as appropriate to see sex and sexual orientation as aspects of the gender system rather than separate from it. Once that reorientation is made, the six-part system of sex, gender and sexual orientation can be reshuffled into a four-part gender system. It produces a more parsimonious and coherent system, and one in which it is never presumed that there is a biological reality that exists outside of the culture produced by our minds.

CHAPTER THREE

Sodomy and the Pursuit of a Third Sex in the Early Modern Period

Theo van der Meer

Introduction

In 1862 the German jurist Karl Heinrich Ulrichs proclaimed the existence of a third sex: "*anima muliebris virile corpore inclusa.*" Men who desired other men did so because they harbored a female soul in a male body, which originated in embryological developments, Ulrichs argued. The congenital origins of "Uranism," as he called it, were the best argument that homosexuality was part and parcel of nature, not contrary to it as it had been considered for centuries. Therefore, those who engaged in such behavior should be set free from persecution.[1] About the same time, Berlin's first professor of psychiatry, Karl Westphal, coined the phrase "*contrāre Sexualempfindung*" – contrary sexual feeling – for the same phenomenon, although in his opinion its origins were to be found in a congenital reversal of sexual feeling, itself the result of degeneration, in short, of moral insanity.[2]

Ulrichs and Westphal are just two of the men who participated in a discussion that raged in the second half of the nineteenth century and the early part of the twentieth regarding the nature and origins of homosexuality: whether it was acquired or innate and whether it was to be excused or lamented. The names of other scientists, such as Ambroise Tardieu, Johann Ludwig Casper, Karl Maria Kertbeny, Richard von Krafft-Ebing, Havelock Ellis, Magnus Hirschfeld and John Addington Symonds, have been added to a historiography dealing with (homo)sexuality in the nineteenth and early twentieth centuries. Willingly or unwillingly, these scholars have contributed to the emergence of third- or intermediate-sex notions in the science of that time, thus providing a safe ideological and psychological haven for those who desired people of their own sex. In fact, this historiography, which has gained momentum especially since 1976, when Michel Foucault published his first volume on the history of sexuality, has heralded the works of people such as Ulrichs and Westphal as the beginning of a new era. Indeed Foucault claimed a caesura in history that not only changed previously held opinions about same-sex behavior but by and large created the social roles and behaviors that accompanied the notions of a third sex. Sodomy, the "*crimen nefandum*," the "unmentionable vice" – common terms before Ulrichs coined his "Urning" and Kertbeny his "homosexuality" – according to Foucault simply referred to an act, whereas in later times it referred to a condition, a personality.[3] Despite the fact that these scientists derived their conclusions on the basis of case studies, they are historically presented as if they invented categories that were then nonexistent. According to this historiography, most homosexual behavior during most of the nineteenth century was still casual.[4]

In this essay I will show that same-sex roles came into being in a period of transition – the late seventeenth century to the second half of the nineteenth century. Furthermore, I will show that from very early in this period on, homosexual behavior was not considered spontaneous or casual, even if for the people involved it had been. I also want to show that, during the time Ulrichs and Westphal came to their ideas about the existence of a third sex and to the view that homosexuality was moral insanity, these ideas, however unarticulated, had their roots in popular belief both among people engaging in homosexual behavior and among their adversaries. I focus especially in this context on the Netherlands, which together with England and northern France, according to Randolph Trumbach, were at the core of an emerging modernity in terms of social, sexual and gendered relationships.[5] I deal especially with the prosecution, social organization and perceptions of homosexual behavior before and after the late seventeenth century.

More so than in France or England, "sodomites," men who

engaged in same-sex behavior, in the Netherlands were prone to persecution, at least in the eighteenth century. In 1730 the first major wave of sodomy trials hit the country, and such waves recurred well into the nineteenth century. From 1730 to 1811 between eight hundred and one thousand sodomy trials were held in the Republic of the United Provinces and its successors, the Batavian Republic (1795–1804) and the Kingdom of Holland (1804–10).[6] Extensive court records were kept, especially from 1730 on, and if used cautiously and together with printed sources, they allow not only for insight into actual prosecutions but also for a detailed reconstruction of the social organization and perceptions of sodomy as well as official and popular attitudes toward same-sex behavior. Such perceptions and attitudes were not isolated responses to homosexual behavior: they were anchored in the total culture of the time. Yet, as students of popular cultures have stressed, one should differentiate between these and elite cultures; not because they were totally isolated from one another – indeed they were often interrelated – but because for social and political reasons they could oppose one another or at least emphasize different cultural aspects.[7] It is in these cultural contexts that I will look at perceptions of homosexual behavior, paying attention to those of ecclesiastical and legal authorities, of people who engaged in such behavior and of the public at large. Some aspects I will describe here were no doubt peculiar to the Low Countries; however, others were shared with France and England.

Prosecutions

Before 1730

Ever since the twelfth century sodomy – anal intercourse either between males or between men and women, as well as intercourse with animals – had been a crime *mixti fori*, that is, a crime punishable by both ecclesiastical and secular authorities. Until the final quarter of the seventeenth century, however, sodomy trials remained a rare phenomenon in the Low Countries. Between 1300 and 1450 seven men were tried on sodomy charges in the city of Utrecht, less than 0.01 percent of all criminal cases in the city during that period.[8] In Amsterdam two sodomy trials are known from the sixteenth century and only one from the first half of the next century.[9] Five sodomy trials in the sixteenth and seventeenth centuries are known from Leiden, six from Middelburg, two from Delft and one from Breda.[10]

The provincial Court of Holland was exceptional. Between 1400 and 1550 it tried twenty-three men on sodomy charges.[11] However, two of these men were probably the victims of political rather than sexual controversies. In 1447 the president of the High Council of Holland came into conflict with the prosecutor-general of Holland and Sealand, and when the latter accused him of sodomy, he had to pay with his life. Half a century later the son of this prosecutor fell victim to the same kind of charge.[12] Ten of the sodomy trials of the Court of Holland were exceptional in yet another way. Held between 1463 and 1465, they were the only ones prior to the early modern period that were clearly linked to each other, whereas other sodomy trials until 1675 were incidental in the sense that they involved only one or two culprits. One man was convicted by the Court of Holland to be burned at the stake in 1463. A year later, an accomplice had his hair burned off his head and was whipped along the streets of The Hague. In 1465 eight others who had been sexually involved with the two just mentioned were tried in their absence and permanently exiled.[13] Only two sodomy trials are known to have been held in the seventeenth century by the Court of Holland, both resulting in a conditional acquittal.[14]

It was only after 1675 that sodomy trials were more often held by Dutch courts or that references to sodomy began to show up more or less regularly in Dutch court records. In 1676 three men – including a *burgomaster* (mayor) – were prosecuted on sodomy charges in Utrecht, which resulted in one death penalty.[15] In 1721 a man was also put to death in Utrecht on the same charges and, at the same time, the legal authorities received information about other men.[16] Between 1682 and 1684 four sodomites were executed in Rotterdam, and at least one in The Hague.[17] Several others were sentenced in absentia. In the next few decades, especially in Rotterdam, such trials became recurrent affairs. In 1702 two men were put to death there because they had perpetrated sodomy in an almoner's house.[18] In 1717, eight men who had been arrested at public toilets were sent into permanent exile by the court of Rotterdam.[19] Two men may have been drowned in a barrel because of sodomy in 1686 in Amsterdam, and in 1689 and 1715 the court in this city became aware of same-sex practices at public places through blackmail cases.[20] The same had happened with the Court of Holland in The Hague in 1702. Probably in connection with this last blackmail case, several men were prosecuted by the local court in that city.[21]

From 1730 On
In 1730, "the most extraordinary and accidental discovery of a tangle of ungodlinesses"[22] – a nationwide network of sodomites, including men from all social strata – triggered a series of prosecutions of sodomites that was unprecedented in the history of the country. As the provincial Court of Holland expressed that year, it was necessary "to exterminate this vice to the bottom."[23] Indeed, in terms of penalties meted out to the culprits, they were among the harshest of their kind in early modern Europe. Between 1730 and 1732, at least seventy-five men were put to death. Over a hundred men who had fled the country were sentenced in absentia and permanently exiled. Until 1811, the year in which the French penal code was enforced in the Netherlands, a series of such prosecutions as well as incidental sodomy trials occurred, most notoriously in 1764 in Amsterdam, in 1776 in several cities in the province of Holland and in 1797 in the cities of Dordrecht, The Hague and Utrecht.

From 1791 to 1810, sodomy trials were virtually annual occasions in Amsterdam. Between 1795 and 1798, the court in Amsterdam tried some forty people on charges of same-sex activities.[24] In these years women were prosecuted for the first time as well, solely on the basis that they had had sex with one another. Until that time, only women who belonged to the notorious transvestites and who usually had become soldiers or sailors had been tried for "unnatural" behavior when they had married other women.[25]

With the enforcement of the French penal code in 1811, sodomy no longer constituted a crime. But "public indecency," according to article 330 of the penal code, was a misdemeanor, and by stretching the notion of what was public to the limit, men who had engaged in same-sex activities were still prosecuted. In particular, in the first decades after 1811, soliciting – or the fact that two men had sex in a public space without being seen by anyone – was sufficient to sentence those who were arrested to the maximum penalty of one year of incarceration and a fine of 100 guilders.[26] In cases of repeat offenders – which regularly occurred – the penalty was doubled.[27]

Although most of these trials were incidental, accusations of "public indecency" unleashed waves of trials as in the eighteenth century. On a single day in 1816, twenty-nine men were convicted in Utrecht on the basis of this article.[28] And since it was much less difficult to prove public indecency than definite sexual acts, men who were accused of public indecency were more easily convicted than were their predecessors. If the courts so desired, it was quite simple to find other reasons to sentence a suspect. For example, article 331 of the penal code, dealing with violent assaults on the honor of a person, sometimes was used against sodomites. As late as 1845, a man who was charged with such an assault on another man was sentenced to a severe whipping and eight years incarceration. The evidence in this case had been so flimsy – even police officers expressed their doubts – that the prosecutor had demanded an acquittal, but he did so in vain.[29]

Prosecutions Restrained

For an appraisal of the prosecutions, especially from 1730 on, one should consider the intention expressed by the Court of Holland in that year to exterminate the vice of sodomy. It is obvious that, with the numbers of sodomy trials involved, Dutch courts saw only the tip of the iceberg as far as same-sex activities were concerned. Despite the Court of Holland's expressed intention, one may well doubt whether legal authorities in the Republic, at least during most of the eighteenth century, really wanted to unleash a relentless witch-hunt against people who engaged in homosexual behavior. Paradoxically, the reasons the prosecutions in the

Netherlands were so harsh were to a large extent the very reasons only a limited number of people were prosecuted. The explanation lies in the political structure of the country.

The Republic of the Seven United Provinces, as it had emerged during the Eighty Years' War (1568–1648) against the Spanish Habsburg Empire, was at best a loosely held federation. Each of the provinces was by and large independent in matters of taxation, administration and legislation. Their administrative and legislative bodies, the so-called states (*staten*), which in each of the provinces were constituted in a different manner, were almost sovereign. The Catholic provinces Brabant and Limburg were more or less regarded as occupied territories and were governed by the States-General. Furthermore, the States-General held only limited power over the army, the navy and foreign affairs. The prerogatives of the prince-stadtholders of the House of Orange were even more limited and were the subject of constant negotiations and fights. Until 1748 it was not a heritable office, and the states of each of the provinces had to appoint the stadtholder separately, or – as twice they did – refuse to do so, resulting in a so-called stadtholderless era (1652–72 and 1702–48). By the beginning of the early modern period, the nobility, at least in the west of the country, had already ceased to be a major political and social force. The Reformed (Calvinist) Church in the Netherlands got no further than becoming "the privileged church" and never became a state church. Although the church was a major social influence, its political powers were tightly controlled by secular authorities. It had no influence on the sodomite prosecutions.

Power in the Republic rested most prominently with an urban merchant and financial oligarchy that had also emerged during the years of war against Spain in the most economically prosperous and consequently most powerful province of Holland. Yet attitudes here, especially toward legal matters, were also parochial at best. The judicial system in this province was a quagmire of more than two hundred courts and jurisdictions, and each of them guarded its independence jealously, especially against the provincial Court of Holland, often on the basis of century-old prerogatives.[30] This provincial court was only in a very limited sense a court of appeal. On the other hand, it held jurisdiction over those parts of The Hague in which it and other institutes of government held office, as well as personal jurisdiction over officers of provincial or local government and their siblings.[31] On virtually every occasion – including the sodomite prosecutions – the Court of Holland tried to surpass its jurisdiction or at least was accused of doing so by local courts, usually resulting in bitter fights. Ironically, the extreme competitiveness between these courts sometimes provided suspects the time to escape.[32]

Legislation, including that regarding sodomy, was until the late eighteenth century even more of a patchwork. Some provinces had sodomy statutes, while others, such as the province of Holland until 1730, did not. However, from medieval times Amsterdam had such a statute, as did some rural areas.[33] In addition, legal tradition, often laid down in legal comments, as well as Mosaic and Roman law could also be applied. As far as sodomy was concerned the law pointed in one direction – or so it was believed: sodomy deserved the death penalty. The Constitio Criminalis Carolina from 1532, which was authoritative in most provinces, had also set the death penalty for sodomy between men, between men and women and between men and animals.[34] Perhaps one of the most remarkable things about these laws was that in general they did not necessarily lead to arbitrary verdicts. The reception of Roman law and the influence of jurists who were usually consulted in matters of capital offenses generally resulted in a *communis opionio* about the kind of penalty that was to be applied.[35]

After a decade of "democratic" or "patriot" uprisings, a French invasion in 1795 brought an end to the existence of the old republic, exile for the House of Orange and the rise of the Batavian Republic. An "enlightened" rudimentary democracy emerged that tried to abolish medieval political structures and to unify and centralize administration, legislation and civil and criminal justice. Napoleon in 1804 turned this republic into one of his satellite kingdoms under his brother Louis. When the latter tried to carry on an independent policy, Napoleon annexed the country in 1810. The end of the Napoleonic era in 1813 and the Vienna Conference brought a short-lived unification of the northern and southern

(Belgium) Netherlands, known as the Kingdom of the Netherlands under the restored House of Orange.

Waves of sodomite prosecutions such as those that occurred
in 1730 could have severe social, economic and political reper-
cussions. The sudden arrest or disappearance of people (often
whom nobody suspected) caused an enormous upheaval. It was
persistently rumored that the courts either let men from the
upper classes escape or tried them in secret, whereas men from
the lower classes were executed in public. Despite the fact that
the courts tried to make a show of prosecuting members of the
upper classes, most of these suspects either got away or were not
prosecuted at all.[36] For the oligarchy, which by its very nature
consisted of family factions, cabals and coalitions, it was neither
an attractive nor a likely option to prosecute its peers. Doing so
might have upset a delicate balance within its own ranks, not least
of all because until 1732 courts could confiscate the possessions
of people who were put to death or fled the country, and one
faction might have enriched itself at the cost of another. It is characteristic that in 1732 confiscation of goods was abolished after
legal fights over the possessions of a patrician from Delft who had
escaped in 1730.[37] The abolition of confiscation "was definitely
in the interest of some," Jan Wagenaar, Holland's eighteenth-
century historian par excellence, dryly commented some ten
years later.[38]

The handling of upper-class people was like a thread running
through the actions of the courts, as well as through the responses
of the common people, because it could and sometimes did upset
another delicate balance, that between rulers and the people they
ruled. All through the eighteenth century the credibility of courts
in such matters was at stake, and, as in 1730, the special treatment of upper-class people caused social unrest.[39]

In 1730 authorities faced with the fact that some very wealthy
merchants from Amsterdam had disappeared expressed their fear
that prosecuting them might "cause several inconveniences in a
land of trade."[40] On the one hand they felt that the reputation of
the country as a whole or of individual merchants could damage
international trade, considered the basis of Holland's prosperity.

On the other hand the flight of such merchants resulted in financial damage for their creditors and sometimes in bankruptcies.[41]

Political damage could become much worse, as the series of arrests in 1731 in a rural area near the city of Groningen showed. A local country squire, Rudolph de Mepsche, had more than thirty farm men and boys arrested in that year on sodomy charges, and twenty-two of them were executed on one day. According to many observers, these men were arrested either randomly or on the basis of their affiliation with de Mepsche's political opponent in that area. Whatever the case, those who were arrested had nothing to do with the network that had come to light elsewhere in the country.[42] Siblings, neighbors and local authorities tried to stop de Mepsche and to prevent the executions by calling on the provincial court and the states of Groningen as well as the States-General in The Hague. This was in vain, however, because these bodies had neither the power nor the wish to interfere. As a result, the administrative machinery in this province came to a complete standstill for no less than two decades.[43]

It may have been the absence of a central power that made the prosecution of sodomites in the Netherlands much more severe than in England or France, where a man like de Mepsche probably would not have had the opportunity to inflict such damage on the body politic. Only in 1749, shortly after the prince-stadtholder William IV took office with many more prerogatives than any of his predecessors, following a period of intense social and political upheaval, was what might have become a new wave of prosecutions stopped.[44] Clearly, it was not in his interest to begin his government – which because of his untimely death in 1754 lasted only for a short period – amid more social unrest.

But if parochialism – the basis of the political structure of the Republic – could be held responsible for the harshness of the sodomite prosecutions in the Netherlands, so too did it set limits on them so as not to damage the very fragile structure.

The legal system, moreover, lacked the professional apparatus to track down more than a few of the culprits. Hence, most verdicts were by default.[45] At the same time one should not overlook the distress such prosecutions levied on the courts' finances.

On the basis of bills of the prison warden, the torturer, the hang-man and other servants of justice, I have been able to make a rough estimate of how much the bailiff of Amsterdam spent in 1764 on prosecuting sodomites. These expenses accounted for approximately 30 percent of his total budget in that year (which was similar to the spending in other years).[46] Probably, as today, policing one kind of criminal behavior occurred at the cost of policing others. Even if sodomy evoked hair-raising fears – which to a certain extent it did (see below) – the consequences of crimes such as theft, burglary or manslaughter were probably perceived as a more acute problem to the citizenry.

Finally, sodomy, along with incest and adultery, belonged to the *crimina excepta*: crimes that were difficult to prove, since they left no *corpus delicti*. Despite attempts in 1730 to favor circum-stantial evidence in sodomy cases,[47] not least of all because of the delicate balance between the elite and the commoners, most judges acted as staunch legalists who demanded what they con-sidered definite evidence of illicit sexual practices. Scaffolding required a confession of the culprit. To obtain such a confession torture was allowed, but only if there was enough evidence to indicate that a capital offense had taken place and a confession was the only thing missing. Aside from a growing reluctance to apply torture[48] – it was abolished altogether in 1798 – accusa-tions of its unrelented application, as occurred in the trials led by de Mepsche in 1731, could undermine the credibility of the courts. Nonetheless, because sodomy belonged to the *crimina excepta*, prosecutors set out to gather as much information as pos-sible about the culprits and much of that was used to "convince" a suspect of his guilt. It is such information that gives extraordi-nary richness to the eighteenth-century sources. Even if they are sometimes distorted, they provide for a detailed reconstruction. For that reason, if nothing else, one might regret the ease with which courts after 1811 came to a verdict in public indecency trials! The documents that are left of such trials often give no information beyond the fact that such an indecency had taken place. Moreover, whereas eighteenth-century documents often give a detailed account of the sexual habits of those who were prosecuted, those of the nineteenth century often say that decency forbade it to be put down on paper.[49]

Despite the expressed intention to exterminate sodomy, no one could hope or even wish to police same-sex behavior to the fullest extent. The occasional waves of persecutions might then be appreciated as purges – the meanings of which were in the end highly symbolic. It is to such symbolism that I will turn in the final section.

Several other points must be observed as far as sodomite prosecutions are concerned. First, many of the trials before 1675 involved adult men who had had sex with adolescents, while those in later years generally involved adult men who had had sex with one another. Second, on rare occasions up to the early seventeenth century when men were found guilty of sodomy, at least those who had been "agens," inserters, were usually burned at the stake. Later in that century, until 1730, when they were found guilty of anal intercourse, sodomites were generally garroted, and whereas burning occurred almost by definition in public, garroting was usually carried out in secret in the cellars of city halls, "so that it might not be known that sodomy was perpetrated in this country."[50] The year 1730 not only was a watershed in terms of the sheer number of people prosecuted but also was marked because executions – again usually by garroting – were carried out (at least in the province of Holland) at the scaffold in front of large audiences. The particular consequences of this will also be discussed in the final section.

Social Organization

Before 1730
Until the late seventeenth century, according to Trumbach, most homosexual behavior in Europe occurred between adult men and adolescent boys. Active and passive roles, those of inserter and insertee, were strictly structured by age: adult men would penetrate boys. Such an adult, especially an aristocratic libertine like the "rake," would not lose his masculine status. This was not only because he penetrated the boy but also because he could keep

his mistress on one arm and his "catamite" on the other. He served as inserter to both boys and women. An effeminate man, the aristocratic "fop," however, was a womanizer, but this was to change. The late seventeenth century brought a marked transformation in northwestern Europe: some adult men began to desire other adult men; they would reverse active and passive roles and become effeminate. Thus effeminacy became the historical hallmark of the culturally marked sodomite. At the same time, for that very reason men in general became more and more anxious to avoid effeminacy so as not to be suspected or accused of engaging in unnatural behavior. Hence, the sodomite came to represent a third gender, according to Trumbach.[51]

The history of the Netherlands from the fifteenth century to the final quarter of the seventeenth century does not lead to such a clear conclusion in this regard for the data are insufficient on this matter. From this period, unfortunately, by and large only summary verdicts remain, which sometimes do not provide more than names. For example, of the eight men who were sentenced in absentia by the Court of Holland in 1465, the records say only that they were "notorious of sodomy."[52] At about the same time Coman Claes from Utrecht was burned because he had sexually used men many times as "women." Jan Belle Wambooys and Gijsbrecht Dirxks some time later suffered the same penalty because they had "done and completed this unclean work, that is against nature, with one another and with many other male persons."[53]

"Male persons" does not reveal very much. Because "such others" were not prosecuted, however, this suggests they were considered less guilty or not guilty, and this usually was the case with adolescents. On other occasions age or generational differences were explicitly mentioned. In 1444, a man was burned at the stake in Utrecht for sodomizing a boy.[54] In 1459 a certain Jacob Hanneman was burned in The Hague because he had sexually abused his natural son. As court punishment, the son was whipped till bleeding from head to toe because he had not resisted his father or called for any help.[55] Three out of the six men prosecuted in Middelburg between 1545 and 1655 were adult men who had engaged in sexual relations with "handsome" minor boys.[56] In 1620, another man was burned in Delft for sodomizing young mates.[57] In 1648 an Italian was banished from Amsterdam for buggering young girls and for attempting to do the same with a boy.[58] This sentence did not keep him from continuing his habits elsewhere: later he was punished for the same offense in Utrecht and The Hague.[59] Trials at the Court of Holland in the seventeenth century that resulted in an acquittal showed much the same pattern. In 1654, Litius Wielandt, a private tutor, was accused of abusing his young students.[60] In a second case, Captain Sigismundus Pape was supposed to have buggered a ten- or twelve-year-old boy, while also having repeatedly masturbated a twenty-one-year-old private.[61]

The case against the burgomaster Dirk de Goyer in Utrecht in 1676 set several landmarks. He had seduced two prepubescent boys and carried on his activities with them into their young adulthood. He had started with caresses, continued with sodomizing them and – one of the few cases of flagellantism in sodomy trials – had also whipped the boys. Lawyers gave extensive legal advice about the application of torture on one of these boys (the burgomaster himself had fled the city). It is the earliest testimony of its kind and was printed shortly thereafter in a collection of legal advice concerning concrete legal cases.[62] Furthermore, one of the boys said during the trial that the burgomaster had shown him an alley "to point out the places of her meetings." (The same alley was mentioned during the trials of 1730.) The boy's words are the first reference to public "cruising" sites in the records. The word *cruising*, according to the *The Queens' Vernacular*, is derived from the Dutch *kruisen*, a word used by eighteenth-century sodomites.[63] From that time on more such references appear until such sites were exposed in the persecutions of 1730.

Although many of the cases mentioned here show a clear pattern of intergenerational same-sex contacts, one must show restraint in drawing conclusions. Hierarchy – eventually between different age groups – may have been a more distinctive feature in such contacts, especially since hierarchy between different classes, sexes and age groups was of such general importance in early modern society. Nevertheless, Trumbach is probably right to assert that the roles of inserter and insertee were strictly exclusive. It was the older man or at least the social superior who penetrated the younger or the inferior. After 1675 this pattern would change rapidly. From that year on, references were made time and again to cruising sites. Even more, a new pattern in the archival records suggests an emerging subculture absent in the previous period. Of course, one cannot exclude the possibility that some of these cultural characteristics had existed long before: the ten sodomy trials before the Court of Holland between 1463 and 1465 hint at the existence of a rudimentary, hidden social network. But, in general, if such subcultural phenomena existed they went unnoticed, and the discovery of the sodomite network in 1730 caused deep surprise and, at first, disbelief among the Dutch authorities.

Cruising Sites
From 1682 on, cases in Rotterdam show that men were arrested who had met at public toilets. From 1689 until the 1760s, the city hall in Amsterdam was mentioned as a cruising place time and again in sodomy trials. Moreover, as four blackmailers who had found their victims in the city hall as well as at the commodity exchange explained after being arrested that year, men who wanted to get in touch with one another came to understand definite signs, one of which was to step on one another's toes.[64] In 1702, another blackmailer told the Court of Holland that men who cruised other men in a wooded area near The Hague would pat the back of one hand with the fingers of the other or wave their handkerchiefs. One of the peculiarities of this case was that this blackmailer, a soldier, knew of such habits in London as well; he had suggested to another man that they go to England to make money out of lords and gentlemen who engaged in homosexual behavior. In the same case witnesses mentioned a particular house in the city where these men gathered.[65] In 1717, men arrested in Rotterdam at public toilets talked about such an inn, Het Dolfijntje ("The Little Dolphin"), in The Hague.[66] The persecutions of 1730 and those of later years exposed these meeting

sites as well as more private parlors to public scrutiny. Among the common cruising places were public toilets, some of which earned female nicknames among sodomites, city ramparts, parks and gardens, public buildings like the city hall and several churches in Amsterdam, the tower of the cathedral in Utrecht, the very grounds where the Court of Holland held office in The Hague (nicknamed "the little hall" among sodomites), and theaters, as well as specific streets, squares and alleys where these people used to stroll.[67] In The Hague until 1730 at least four semibrothels existed that catered to sodomites.[68] Men from the upper echelons often brought along their own servants when they visited these houses; or, such visitors would request "a cute young fellow," whom the owners of the brothel would send for.[69] Often the owners provided gentlemen with servants who under cover of an employee/employer relationship actually entered into an illicit sexual relationship. In the 1720s many men would gather at the house of one of the higher clerks of the states of Holland. In Amsterdam there were at least two pubs where sodomites met until the persecutions of 1730, and one of them, The Serpent, drew a clientele from all over the country.[70] Although the prosecutions brought an end to these pubs, others emerged, it was discovered in 1764 when a new wave of arrests hit the city and again in the closing decade of that century. Some men would gather in specific shops that were owned by people who themselves engaged in such behavior.[71]

Often men who cruised other men had to share the public sites with another group: female street prostitutes. In the eighteenth century, authorities more or less routinely rounded up such women at the very places that were mentioned by men who were arrested on sodomy charges. Since authorities in Amsterdam in the 1760s once and for all cleaned the surroundings of the city hall of "street whores," the place was no longer mentioned as a sodomite hunting ground.[72] Even some less public places may have been common ground for prostitutes and sodomites alike. In 1751 a suspect told of a brothel in Amsterdam where "sodomy was done as well."[73] At about the same time, both in The Hague and Amsterdam, several men who had been arrested on sodomy charges were eventually convicted because they had kept female prostitutes.[74]

Signals
Sodomites, in fact, had much in common with these women. From the late seventeenth century on, courts became increasingly suspicious about the secret signals sodomites supposedly used at public sites. Some suspects were eager to satisfy their interrogators; the signs they described – stepping on one another's toes, waving handkerchiefs, nudging each other with their elbows – were gestures that could be understood as invitations for sexual encounters because everyone knew them to be obscene or, at least, to signal certain attractions. Together with a specific sodomite lingo these gestures formed a kind of vulgar *ars amandi* that whores and sodomites shared.[75] It was not by accident that a man in 1702 – not a suspect himself – who had been confronted with another man who tapped the back of one hand with the fingers of the other misunderstood it to be an invitation to go to the whores. As said before, sodomites described their activities at the public sites with the word *kruisen*. The same word was applied to street prostitutes (*kruishoeren*) and their walking to and fro at such sites.

The way interrogators interpreted gestures and lingo as cognitive behavior may well reflect their suspicions about the secret societies sodomites were thought to compose, much like the Freemasons. Yet it seems that much of this behavior, like most culturally meaningful gestures, was hardly cognizant; rather, it reflected certain skills acquired through a process of socialization. Some men were extremely capable of applying such skills, while others were not. Some men said that they were not familiar with any signals whatsoever. Others referred to the exchange of glances, not only at the sites mentioned but at virtually every place where people used to gather, especially in churches during sermons or in the so-called citizens hall in the Amsterdam city hall, where people went to learn about the latest news at home and abroad or to gossip. Many would simply stand next to another man at a urinal and stare the other in the face or look at the other's genitals. At public toilets under bridges – available for defe-

153

cation – some would wait long enough to ascertain that others who did so were of the same intention and grab their genitalia through the stalls.[76]

Sodomite Networks

A sodomite arrested in 1717 in Rotterdam told the court of others who used public toilets for their sexual encounters to such an extent that it was "as if together they formed a gang."[77] What this "gang" was like was brought to light by the prosecutions of 1730. The court of Utrecht rather by accident discovered the existence of a network of sodomites that ramified in many cities and garrisons throughout the Republic. This network included such prominent men as Baron Frederik Adriaan van Reede van Renswoude, president of the knighthood in the province of Utrecht and representative of the province in the States-General, as well as other members of the nobility; members of patrician families like the bailiff and a judge from Delft, a member of the city council of Haarlem, and the brother of the bailiff of Amsterdam; and rich merchants, army officers, solicitors, notaries and important clerks of the states of Holland. Yet these men were only a minority within the network. Most participants were petty shopkeepers, street vendors, privates or, especially, house servants.[78] Craftsmen were much less prominent in this and in later networks. This may have been due to a tighter social control of such people in their workshops and guilds, or to their professions' restrictions on their physical and social mobility, which by contrast seemed to characterize many of the other participants.[79]

Some of the men involved in these networks engaged in other antisocial activities: petty – and sometimes not so petty – crime, often seemingly connected to blackmail. For some, their criminal activities clearly were the result of poverty; for others they seem to have been related to their marginal existence as sodomites. It is telling, both of such an existence and of the way in which same-sex behavior was policed, that many of the incidental trials as well as the waves of prosecutions in 1764, 1776, 1797 and 1816 followed arrests for other reasons.[80]

Waves of prosecutions such as those in 1764 and 1776 revealed

the discovery of likewise hidden networks, although these included few upper-class people. It was only after the arrests made in
Dordrecht in 1797 that members of the oligarchy and aristocracy
were mentioned again. This time the networks included people
from the innermost circle of the former stadtholder William V,
whose government had come to an end two years earlier when
the French invaded the Netherlands to put an end to the ancien
régime. However, not only Orangists were involved; one participant was the "patriot" Willem Anne Lestevenon, curator of the
University of Leiden and member of the newly formed National
Assembly.[81] At the time the arrests were made he was representing
the Netherlands at negotiations in Paris. According to a biographer, he never returned because of a "scandal."[82]

Sodomite networks such as these were far from monolithic
in the sense that they were restricted to sexual contacts or that
everyone involved would participate to the same degree and with
the same expectations. One might say that these networks had a
core and a periphery. The peripheral men would most likely only
know each other's faces from public cruising sites. Of course there
were many sexual rendezvous between men from the core and
men from the periphery. Although the networks were indeed basically a form of organization of sexuality, men who were at the
core did not necessarily have sex with one another. Some maintained intense friendships or even shared social activities along
with their spouses, such as cardplaying and sitting at dinners. On
some occasions they provided one another with loans or stood
bail for one another, as the clerk Floris Reindert Husson used to
do in the 1770s.[83] He and his friend Hendrik Nederveen, a house
servant, were the darlings of their circle. Their friends described
fondly how the two of them often romped and acted as if they
were dueling, waving their arms like swords, or how, sitting in
an inn, they put cookies in one another's mouth.[84] When Husson
and Nederveen fled The Hague in early 1776 after Husson had
robbed the treasury of cash and bonds, perhaps to escape blackmail, some of their friends wrote them affectionate letters, expressing how much they feared for their safety and how much they
missed them. "Thou might appreciate, my sweet brothers, that

the condition I was in after so leaving two of my sweet friends to Providence left me with little to laugh about.... I went to sit alone and had a good cry because I needed to be relieved of my grief," Gerrit van Amerongen said in one of his letters to Husson. Another of their friends, Jan Mulder, related that he wished he had never known them, "so that my heart would not have been so tender about thy folks." Halfway through his letter, he hardly could go any further: "I have to finish here because my mind is overwhelmed by the circumstances thou folks art in right now; support then one another with a tender heart as long as it pleases the Lord."[85] Van Amerongen and Mulder had only been slightly involved sexually with the playful couple.

Life among those in the network was not always so peaceful. There were men who lost little love over one another, and disagreements easily turned into rows. Some men were avoided because they were thought to be too talkative. Francois Voogt, a visitor of a bookshop in Amsterdam where around 1760 some sodomites used to gather, was not well liked. Voogt had been the court torturer in the city since 1730; he began the job only a few days before the first arrests of sodomites that year. During his long career, at the court's orders, he had put several men on the rack who were accused of sodomy until he finally was arrested himself on such charges in 1762.[86] If that and his acquaintance with the court were not enough reason to keep him at a distance, there was the fact that the professions of torturer and hangman since the old days were thought to be dishonest and that their very touch – slight as it might be – could transform someone into a person whose own honor had been lost.[87]

Contrary to the pattern apparent in trials before 1675, most of the men who were involved in later trials and who participated in sexual networks were adults. In general, the age of such participants was between twenty and sixty. For some men initiation into same-sex practices coincided with their recruitment into the sodomite networks. Many others, however, had been initiated at an early age. While sex between adults may have become common, adolescents had not left the stage altogether. Some men claimed to have been seduced by age fifteen or sixteen and others to have been virtually raped by teachers or officers or by older brothers.[88] In 1731 three young men who at the age of twelve had started to play sexual games with one another were arrested in Utrecht. One of them had stopped after a while, but two of them had continued and eventually found their way into the networks.[89] Jan Kemmer, executed in Amsterdam in 1765, had gone through his initiation in an orphanage in Utrecht and included some fifteen boys in his confessions. After fleeing the orphanage he also found his way into the networks after an encounter in the citizens' hall of the Amsterdam town hall.[90]

Whereas some of these participants' lives seemed to have evolved mainly around their sexual habits and others were said to travel all over the country just for that purpose, there were men who moved in and out of the networks. Some sodomites did not participate in them at all. It was discovered that the notary public and solicitor Daniel van den Burch, who escaped the Court of Holland in 1730, had for years assaulted young clerks. On one occasion he had tried to grab the crotch of a man who worked in front of his house, and on another he masturbated in front of men who worked on board a towboat that was to bring him to Amsterdam. Yet he was not known by any of the men arrested that year.[91] Nevertheless, one of his former clerks, who himself had become a notary public and solicitor and whom van den Burch had married to his sister, used to have sexual encounters with some of those who were convicted.[92]

Many people traveled a good deal, since an extensive network of canals and rivers and a well-developed public transport system existed in the Netherlands. Some men, by nature of their profession, such as merchants, used to travel around the country and obviously knew their way around the sodomite scene. This was also true of street vendors and hawkers, who went from one local fair or market to another. Especially in the 1730 prosecutions, many of these men's names appear in the records of virtually every city where sodomy trials were held. Fairs, local festivities and ceremonial occasions, which usually were times of (hetero)sexual permissiveness, drew people from all over the country,[93] including men who looked for illicit sexual encounters with one another.

It is useful here to quote an observation from 1730 that sodomy was first introduced in the Netherlands by foreign – read Catholic – ambassadors during peace negotiations to end the Spanish War of Succession in 1712 and 1713 in Utrecht, "when the citizens of this country received the filthy sin of sodomy in her lap."[94] The presence of many foreign dignitaries would attract crowds and everything that went along with them. Even if the aforementioned observation was obvious nonsense (though in a way meaningful for the Dutch, as I will show in the final section), it was not by accident that some of the elderly people who were arrested in 1730 referred to "the ambassadorial times" in Utrecht.[95] One man in particular who had prostituted himself mainly with "the great" (i.e., upper-class people) was said to have made a lot of money in those days.[96]

Prostitution
Financial rewards for sex were a common phenomenon throughout the period described here. Adolescents who sexually obliged adult men before 1675 usually received money for what they did. Later, house servants or soldiers – usually young men in their twenties – who through mediators or via brothels were provided to wealthier men were sometimes "kept" or received gifts or currency for their sexual services. Especially after 1810, conscripts (a practice introduced in 1809) were probably eager to add to their meager incomes in this way. The sheer number of public indecency trials after 1811, which derived from the complaints of conscripts about being cruised while standing watch at public buildings and at city gates at night, suggests the large risks taken by many men looking for such sexual encounters.[97]

Yet the term *prostitution* used to refer to activities in this period is somewhat problematic. It suggests a kind of professionalism that most of the recipients of payment lacked. Early modern society was in every sense marked by inequality; financial and other transactions for all services, including sexual ones, endorsed the inequality and hierarchy between men of different classes and ages. Depending on his place in society, a man who was paid for sex with one man might himself pay to have sex with another. A young embroiderer, Pieter van Steijn, arrested in The Hague in 1730, clearly had let himself be recruited for financial reasons.[98] It is difficult to ascertain what other desires he might have had. Other men definitely acted on same-sex desires that they fulfilled with their clients or with one another. A number of these young men not only had sex for money with people from other social strata. They also paid in turn for sex with one Zacharias Wilsma, a former soldier and footman, who had obliged so many men that he became the principal witness in the trials of 1730.[99] Mainly on the basis of his confessions the authorities in Utrecht had put together a list of more than 140 names.[100] A final example comes from 1798. In Amsterdam Hendrik Herderschee – an eighteen-year-old who had been paid for sexual encounters since he was thirteen – frequently forced himself on other men. On one such occasion he let himself be buggered and then complained when the man ejaculated onto the ground, saying that it ruined his fun. Almost thirty years later, more than half of which he had spent in jail and despite a much-acclaimed religious conversion while in prison, Herderschee was convicted again for "public indecency." He had offered some boys money to go with him to a privy.[101]

Sex
It is probably safe to assume that *in sexualibus* there is little new under the sun. Yet from what has already been said about hierarchical features of early modern society, who does what with whom can be seen as a reflection of social and even political structures; and in the end it is a commentary on the relations within and between the sexes.

Mutual masturbation and sodomy – anal intercourse – were the most common practices among the sodomites of the eighteenth century. Because of the insuffiency of the sources from before 1730, little can be ascertained about mutual masturbation. Later it was not only a common practice among sodomites but also the one that was least burdened with social meanings, although already in 1684 the court of Rotterdam had said that it would always result in actual sodomy.[102] If "active" and "passive" roles in sodomy were strictly segregated in the previous historical period,

Trumbach is absolutely right in his conclusion that from the late seventeenth century on, such roles became reversible. Many of the men who were arrested in the eighteenth century admitted that they had been both *agens* and *patience*, often on the same occasion with the same partner. If one had buggered the other, then, immediately after, they reversed the roles. "Are you stallion or mare?" one man asked another whom he solicited. "I am both," he then added. Although in cases in which one man was paying another, the one who was paid was perhaps more likely to be the insertee, this was surely not the rule in all cases. Age or class seemed to make little difference.[103]

If some men had a definite preference for a certain role, particularly from the second half of the eighteenth century on, it was to be insertee rather than inserter. None of the men arrested said they had rejected being sodomized on any principle of dominance and subordination. A man might have trouble being penetrated, but this was for physical reasons. On several occasions men reported that they had been unsuccessful with sodomy because the penetrator was too well endowed. Yet several men told the courts that they simply had never had any interest in an active role. One man who was arrested in 1764 in Groningen and who had only been passive said he had a female constitution, a claim that medical investigation could not confirm.[104] "So far we have only arrested passive dabbers," the prosecutor of Amsterdam wrote in 1797 to a colleague, two years after he assumed office.[105] One of these had said he had been too old to become *agens*.[106] Perhaps, after a historical period of reversible roles among adult men, some felt that active or passive roles should complement one another, as in heterosexual relationships.

Noticeably absent from many if not most of these men's sexual habits – or skills – was fellatio. It was so uncommon that, despite the courts' prurient inquiries into the sexual experiences of the men they arrested, interrogations never hinted in that direction. References to oral intercourse showed up mostly when a man under arrest volunteered such information, and, when he did, this sometimes caused legal confusion. *Sodomia perfecta* meant an ejaculation in a body, yet no law or legal comment said exactly *where* in the body. Thus, for those in judgment of offenders, the question arose whether fellatio was "sodomy" in the legal sense as well.[107] They decided it was not. Besides, whereas sodomites had a wide range of expressions and colloquialisms to refer to masturbation or anal intercourse, "sucking" was about the only one they had for fellatio.

The reason fellatio was far less common may have been due to the lack of sexual sophistication among the lower classes. Female prostitutes, for instance, would not even masturbate their clients, let alone fellate them.[108] Sex for most people meant penetration: no more, no less. Little wonder that oral intercourse throughout Europe was considered to be an upper-class or at least the libertine's vice. Some cases I have found indeed suggest that fellatio was practiced mostly by upper-class people fellating lower-class men. The habits of the patrician Jacob Backer, brother of the bailiff of Amsterdam, caused wonder if not outright shock even among sodomites. He used to fellate young footmen, spit their semen into a glass and swallow it with wine. They talked about this with one another, and when on trial several men referred to these habits though they had not experienced the practices themselves.[109]

The sodomite Hendrik Eelders used to fellate his friend as well, though he definitely came from the lower strata of society. However, he seemed to have learned the practice from his well-to-do doctor, a man "who practiced [medicine] amongst many of the first people."[110] The doctor had fellated Eelders when he consulted him about an ailment. To indicate how unusual he himself thought it to be, the doctor remarked on that occasion, "Oh boy, I swallowed it!"[111] Yet, if many of Eelders's class were prepared to be fellated – some indeed considered it to be a special treat – they generally would not follow his example and become fellators as well.

To anticipate what I will say later on meanings, it is necessary to comment on notions of "active" and "passive" here, especially in regard to fellatio. For sodomy it was clear enough, as frequently used terms like *agens* and *patience* or "active" and "passive" suggest. The latter two terms were used by judges and suspects alike and referred unequivocally to inserting and being inserted, respectively. There could be no misunderstanding when a suspect was asked whether he had "perpetrated" or "suffered" the "crime." That did not exclude confusion about the intentions of the one who had "suffered" sodomy. Traditionally, an adolescent who had been sodomized could to a certain extent be excused because of his lack of knowledge or because he was supposed to have fallen victim to others. When the prosecutor from Amsterdam wrote about "passive dabbers," he added that in Amsterdam only those who had been both "active" and "passive" were put to death. That was an error, and it clearly contradicted Mosaic law, which said that both were to be given the death penalty. Aside from such ambiguity, active and passive roles were equated with masculine and feminine roles. Sodomites and prosecutors alike would refer, using a gender metaphor, to the passive role as "being used as woman." But what about fellatio? Who was considered active and who passive? Even more to the point, how did the fellators and the fellated feel about it? Who was regarded as masculine and who was not? Today, the fellator is considered a passive role, and in societies in which active and passive roles are rigidly upheld it might even be regarded as inferior. From what has been said before about fellatio among sodomites, the reverse seems to be true. The fellator was perceived as "active" and perhaps even imposed his social superiority or at least his libertinism on an inferior. Yet it adds to the confusion that the patrician Jacob Backer was nicknamed "*de zuigster*" (a female derivation of "the sucker") among sodomites.[112]

Love Affairs
So far the historical picture is one of a rampant promiscuity among sodomites, and rightly so. Most of the people who were arrested had had many sexual partners. Some included more than forty "accomplices" in their confessions. That, of course, did not exclude the possibility of love affairs, although there seems to be no way to determine how common they were. Court records, after all, deal with criminal activities of those who were arrested. Affection between men was not a crime, unless it resulted in sexual activities. References to such an affection could sometimes

help "to convince" a suspect, but in itself affection was not something the prosecutors looked for; in fact, one might suspect these prosecutors ignored it because it did not fit their stereotype of sodomites as insatiable sexual beasts. Personal papers, such as letters confiscated from suspects, suggest that such relationships in the course of the eighteenth century became increasingly common, more romantic and perhaps more a reflection of opposite-sex relationships. For example, in a conversation with some young men in 1800 a man matter-of-factly alternated between calling his lover "his husband" and "his wife."[113]

Affection may have played a role in the intergenerational contacts that came to light before the final quarter of the seventeenth century. However, the records do not show it, at least not in a straightforward manner. Yet, whatever may have been true about the accusations against the aforementioned tutor, Litius Wielandt, and the army captain Sigismundus Pape in the seventeenth century, their cases betray the complexities of relationships in a society that rigorously upheld social boundaries, allowing them under some circumstances to be broken, only to reinforce them. Wielandt was supposed to have sodomized at least one of his pupils when he slept with him in the same bed. The tutor did not make much of a point about sharing a bed with his pupils. He said he used to invite them to his bed as a reward for studying well.[114] The private who was supposedly abused by Captain Pape, according to the latter, had despite his accusations against the captain complained about the fact that he had lost the honor of sleeping with him.[115] Of course, for a long time it was common to share a bed with others, even strangers, and obviously many had not much choice in such matters. Yet, as Alan Bray has shown, with whom one slept could be of enormous social and sometimes even political importance.[116] To bestow on a person the honor of sleeping with a superior, particularly if this were publicly known, enhanced the social status of the underling because it showed the superior's affection for him. Moreover it did so without raising doubts about sexual orthodoxy.

Patriarchal attitudes did not totally disappear when adult men began to desire one another. Indeed, the cases of the more well-

163

to-do, who for some time kept a footman or another lower-class man, reflect such attitudes. Even relationships among men from the lower classes sometimes betrayed patriarchalism. In a number of them there was still a considerable difference of age, as between Hendrik Eelders and Jan Kemmer. Eelders, a vendor of broadsides, was some fifteen years older than Kemmer, a goldsmith. Kemmer had lived for a while with Eelders, and together they fled Amsterdam in 1764, when the city became the scene for new waves of prosecutions. A year later both men were arrested in Dutch Flanders. Here Kemmer revealed that occasionally they had sex while fleeing south, but this was only because Eelders violently forced him to do so.[117]

Despite or even because of a general promiscuity among these men, some obvious love affairs were jealously guarded. Two men who had an affair with one another, arrested independently in 1730 in The Hague and in Amsterdam, were said to have drawn up a kind of affidavit, which they were supposed to have called a "contract of marriage," that promised that they would have sex with others only when they had each other's consent.[118]

Letters found in the luggage of Jan Beeldemaker when he was arrested in 1797 testified of the jealousy and despair of his former lover, Samuel Rijnhart, who shortly thereafter found himself on trial in The Hague. Their relationship had run aground because of their promiscuity. Samuel begged Jan to come back:

> Sometimes I think that I hear you coming, but then again I think, he won't. Oh, might I one day enjoy that happiness once more, but oh I won't.

> Oh, how unhappy is this, sweet Jan forgive me once more, I promise and God is my witness, that I won't hurt or grieve you anymore. To live as in those earlier days; I would let you free if I only could be with you.... Oh, let this letter not be in vain, if we were to be together again, our friendship would be greater than ever.

> You know that I could never stand it when you were involved

with somebody else. You know why I do that, because I would like to have you all for myself.

Gave God that you changed your mind, I would not know what to do. I would kiss your feet. Oh, could I see you once more, but if not, may God take me out of this world.

Samuel suspected that Jan's new friend Willem prevented him from returning and inspired him to write nasty responses.

My request is that you won't write such letters again. You would not do such things, but you have someone with you who incites you. That is nothing, fare thee well with your friend Willem and do what you like.[119]

Some twenty-five years later Jan van Zaanen, a servant at weddings and parties in Leiden, fell in love with a man in Amsterdam, despite the fact that both of them already had lovers. Jan entertained sweet memories of their recent encounter:

I thank you for the good and sweet friendship I spent with you. Oh sweet friend, it has only been for a short while that I have been with you. I hope that it may last for a long time and that I may be in your arms once more. Oh the last kiss which I got from you and which I gave to you is still on my soul. Until now dear, I have been thinking of you. The last two nights and three days have hanged more heavily on my hands than the twelve days that I was in Amsterdam in the midst of you.

In one of his letters he referred to their lovers with a still-common Dutch colloquialism – "*vaste vriend*" – for a male lover in a same-sex relationship. Neither seems to have been very happy with his respective *vaste vriend*, yet to have one was obviously something of a conspicuous goal in life. With unrelenting logic Jan van Zaanen commented on such relationships:

It is true, I do not believe that there are friends or they have grieve with one another. The one more than the other. The one takes it more to heart than the other. I, for one, can take it to heart very heavily sometimes. And then I think again, come on, I won't lose courage.

His own lover was very suspicious of his contacts with others.

> Friday, I stayed with De Rooy until half past nine. My friend had been at my house twice that evening and then kicked up a row because he did not know where I had been walking. Then Piet and Jakob came Saturday morning with me to have a drink. My friend has also come and has not said anything to me and has gone again.... Saturday afternoon, when I was to dress myself to go to the wedding party to serve, there he came in high dudgeon and asked me with what kind of acquaintances I walked since I stayed out so late at night, and that I made up everything to get rid of him, but that thunder would strike damnation. It became very heavy with him. He had had a drink and, luckily, I did not, because otherwise there would have been blows. After he had vented his bile, he asked me to drink a drop with him and then he left again in good spirits.[120]

Effeminacy

Trumbach has written that from the late seventeenth century on effeminacy became the hallmark of the sodomite and of its successors in England. Before this period, effeminacy had characterized the womanizer, the fop.

Such notions existed in the Netherlands as well, and in fact they did not disappear in the eighteenth century, at least not in literature. For example, in his 1612 farce, *De Klucht van de Koe* (The farce of the cow), Gerardus Brederode wrote of young men who preferred the company of girls and would rather clean pans with them than engage in male pursuits. These men talked in an effeminate manner, yet nowhere was it suggested that they were sexually attracted to men. Justus van Effen, who in the eighteenth century published his own satirical paper, wrote in 1732 (while some of the sodomy trials had not yet concluded) a lengthy chapter on "effeminate men" wearing long curly wigs. He called them "hermaphrodites in mind," yet he said these men were out to make an impression on women.[121] The late-eighteenth-century predecessor of the dandy, the *petit-maître*, as he appeared in Holland's most famous epistolary novel, *Sara Burgerhart* (1782), was a prinked up, fatuous young man who tried to impress women. Aside from that, effeminate dress throughout the eighteenth century was considered one of the many vices of the upper classes. It was seen as one of the causes rather than one of the effects of sodomy, as will be shown later.

Whatever existed in the eye of the beholder in such matters, effeminacy in terms of dress, finery, speech, gesture and not least of all as a kind of "camp style" was widespread among the men who participated in sodomite networks, as had come to light from the eighteenth century on. A man who owned a notorious sodomite haunt in Utrecht recommended some of his visitors to Zacharias Wilsma, the witness who became all important in the 1730 trials, saying that they would suit him much better than those who were too prinked up.[122] He may have meant that they wore some outfit – effeminate and not in accordance with their social status – that made them easy to recognize or at least not very attractive in his eyes.

The owner of the sodomite pub The Serpent in Amsterdam, who had managed to escape in 1730, was said to speak in a "Johnny girlish" way.[123] Years later, Jan Mulder, who wrote such affectionate letters to Floris Husson, according to a description sent around by the Court of Holland, had (aside from stinking breath) a slimy speech and "in the way he expressed himself and in his gestures much affectation."[124] A man arrested in Utrecht in 1798 wore "a light frock with brown stripes, a white vest with red little dots, dark trousers, white stockings and shoes with ribbons [and] a triangular black shining hat with a black little rose, a black lus with a yellow button attached to it."[125] Even if eighteenth-century dress does not look very masculine from a twentieth-century perspective, for a man selling rags at fairs such an outfit seems outrageous. Another man, arrested in 1810, had been painted with make-up the night he was taken in, although it had already faded by the next morning, his captors said.[126]

Transvestism, though not often reported, did occur. Even the blackmailer who was arrested in 1702 in The Hague occasionally strolled around cruising sites dressed as a woman "for fun," he said.[127] A prebendary of one of the major churches in Utrecht before his arrest in 1730 had once been thrown out by his landlord after he had been seen dressed as a shepherdess.[128] A patrician from Hoorn who before that year used to roam every sodomite haunt with his cousin was reported to have dressed as a woman when he was a student in Leiden.[129] Later in the eighteenth century, a Frenchman in female dress with some others in Rotterdam was mugged by street boys. The boys — according to their new division of the sexes — shouted, "It is not a bitch, it is a Frenchman!"[130]

As early as 1717 it was reported that sodomites used to refer to one another as "*nicht*" ("niece" — a derogatory term today for an effeminate homosexual). "Thou behave like girls and speak if thou were girls," whores had commented to their hosts, men who in 1749 were arrested in The Hague on sodomy charges. The men used to address one another as "pussy and puppy dear."[131] "There goes Miss van de Pol," some who had gathered in a bookshop in Amsterdam in the 1760s said to one another when they saw the doctor, a notorious sodomite, pass in his carriage.[132] So as to indicate the kind of effeminate atmosphere he had found, a police spy who had forced his way into a sodomite circle in 1809 described how these men used to address one another with the affectionate term "my child."[133]

Many were known in their circle by female nicknames, often derivations from their own names. For example, Floris could become Florentina, Jacob became Jacoba and Jan was Johanna. Some nicknames seemed to refer to specific qualities. A certain Pieter was called "Petronella Roundabout Beautiful" and a certain Jan was nicknamed "Johanna Nightglass in the Ass."[134]

Of course, not everybody involved in the networks was effeminate. Some were said to have stout figures, and at least some of those who engaged in certain criminal activities — one man was a member of the most notorious gang that terrorized the countryside in the late eighteenth century — probably were not effeminate.[135] Francois Voogt, the torturer, was described in 1762 by a victim he had sexually assaulted as frightfully strong.[136]

I referred earlier to the difference in the quality of sources in the sodomy trials until 1811 and in the public indecency trials after that date. Indeed, there are hardly any references to effeminacy in the latter or to other pecularities of sodomite life for that matter.[137] Could it mean that men who engaged in same-sex activities became less effeminate, or was effeminacy no longer of concern to authorities? If the first were true, it would explain the second. One of the likely reasons that such references disappeared from the records is that they no longer had much relevance for the progress of indecency trials. Of course, it may also be that men who were interested in other men tried to hide effeminacy because public responses – about which more will be given later – by this time had become much more violent. It is at least striking that, in special registers that held standardized personal descriptions of everybody who was arrested, no references were made to effeminacy of those arrested on public indecency charges. (Yet again, this might be the result of the very standardization of such descriptions.)

Attractions
We have already seen how matters of physical attraction were relevant to sodomites: upper-class men coming to a brothel in The Hague and asking for a "cute young fellow"; a pub owner who did not like men who were too prinked up. Yet there remains the question of what attraction these men held for one another. What was thought to be attractive at a time when stinking breath was probably common and most faces were pockmarked, a time in Dutch historiography known as the "wigs era" to mark its supposedly widespread effeminacy?[138] Much of human experience is of course beyond generalization by historians. It is almost impossible to ascertain what fatal attraction Jan Beeldemaker held for Samuel Rijnhart, yet fatal it was, and not only for Rijnhart. While awaiting his verdict Beeldemaker managed to escape from prison with the help of the maid who served him refreshments; he had promised to marry her if she helped him. Despite the fact that he had never shown any interest in her sexually, she later stated, she had fallen in love with him. He had told her to follow him to

Prussia (he actually went to Brussels). The girl had to pay for her folly with a few years of incarceration.[139] Whatever Beeldemaker's physical attractions were – and probably they were considerable since he also obliged men from the court of the prince-stadtholder Willem V – he must have also been quite a character. Hendrik Eelders (arrested in 1765), when asked why he had picked the much younger Jan Kemmer, said that the young man "was so particularly acquainted with the Truths,"[140] meaning "biblical truths." As we shall see later in the perceptions of sodomites themselves, these "truths" are in fact crucial. For now it must suffice to say that Beeldemaker and Rijnhart probably got to know one another when they took confirmation classes in the Reformed Church in The Hague in the early 1790s.[141]

Some men, like the cobbler Arnoldus Menschen in 1763, stated clearly that they would have grabbed anybody indiscriminately at a public toilet. Obviously it was often too dark at such places to see very much. However, some were explicitly said to be "fair of face," which probably meant they were not pockmarked and were of a fair complexion, akin to a kind of feminine beauty. Other material – for example, the comment on men who were too prinked up – suggests that attractiveness was related to matters of masculinity. The long curly wigs that were so popular among the upper classes during much of the eighteenth century were even at that time considered "effeminate," and other wigs probably were as well. It is striking that descriptions of the young men who seem to have been most popular always mention that they wore their own hair. The patrician Willem Six before 1730 had several times expressed his interest in Pieter van Steijn, "that young fellow with his long hair."[142] Jan Beeldemaker wore his own hair in a pony tail.[143] Aside from haircuts, a stout figure or a certain posture represented masculinity. A solicitor in The Hague was described as "very good looking, being a stout and handsome man."[144] Corpulence may not only have been an expression of somebody's well being but of masculinity as well. Johannes van Solmus, a former soldier who had had many homosexual contacts, seems to have represented the ideal virtue of masculinity. He did not wear a wig, and he was "decently corpulent" and had "an alert or smart gait, keeping his breast high and his head straight."[145]

While age differences did not seem to interfere with attraction, there were other features that did. Pieter van Steijn had refused a certain Belgrado, "being such an ugly jew."[146] Bodily cleanliness was important. Floris Husson used to have sex with a beggar but decided against it when the man's looks and clothes began to appear more and more "desperate."[147] Even one beggar could say about another that he never had sex with him because "he was such a stinking scalliwag, always full of vermin and always drunk."[148] While for many, especially at dark cruising sites, it did not matter with whom they were dealing, for some the destitution in dress and lack of cleanliness of others set limits to their desires. Yet, in general those who radiated masculinity were thought to be the most attractive.

The Sodomite Role Revisited
So what of "the" sodomite role and the sodomite's sex or gender? It seems that an infinite variety of behavior patterns existed for which role theories can hardly account. The subculture described here surely could only have developed in an urban area. That such phenomena emerged not only within the metropolises of France and England but also in the Netherlands is not surprising. After all, Amsterdam with its 200,000 inhabitants was still the third largest city in Europe. It would take less than a day to travel by boat from Amsterdam to cities like Haarlem, Leiden, The Hague and Utrecht. The western part of the country, especially the province of Holland, was extremely urbanized. A majority of the country's two-and-a-half-million inhabitants lived there.

Yet homosexual behavior itself was of course not just an urban phenomenon. It occurred in rural areas, sometimes in the form of bands of vagrants that roamed the countryside, in homosocial institutes like orphanages and in particular on board ships that sailed to East India. No less than 5 percent of all the criminal trials held at the Cape of Good Hope, the baiting place of such ships, dealt with homosexual behavior on board, compared with much less than 1 percent in the cities back home.[149] As mentioned earlier, Jan Kemmer had his first homosexual experiences in an

orphanage in Utrecht before entering the subculture. In his confessions in 1765 he included more than ten other boys from that
orphanage. The same orphanage suffered a kind of purge during
the 1730 trials, and in the 1740s three young boys, including
an eleven-year-old, from an orphanage in Amsterdam were sentenced to long-term imprisonments. Two young adults who still
lived in the same house were put to death at the scaffold in 1743
for sodomy.[150]

Same-sex behavior in such settings differed considerably, however, from such behavior in cities. Usually it was either casual or
traditional in the sense that it would include an adult and a minor.
In rural areas it might indeed come about in a casual way, especially between boys playing games. Four sixteen-year-old farm
boys arrested in 1751 saw little difference between what they had
done and the sex play they had seen between their older brothers and sisters.[151] However, even in orphanages and between boys
of the same age group, hierarchy (or at least attempts to establish it) could play a role. The eleven-year-old boy was virtually
raped by a fourteen-year-old.[152] Age differences were the most
important feature of homosexual contacts on board ships. Usually, men higher in the ship's hierarchy sodomized younger cabin
boys.[153] However flimsy the empirical evidence about sex among
vagrants in Barry Richard Burg's book *Sodomy and the Pirate Tradition*, I have found one such case in the Netherlands. In 1737 two
obvious vagrants were arrested in Utrecht. They had had sex with
one another, and the youngest related that, when he slept with a
group in a barn one night, he was victim to a gang rape.[154]

Yet, what I said earlier about the core and the periphery of
the networks overlapping one another could be true for the networks and other forms of homosexual behavior as well. Sailors
sometimes engaged in sex in the subcultures on shore. The very
victim of the gang rape admitted that he had prostituted himself in different cities. On the other hand, Baron Van Reede van
Renswoude, a prominent member of the network that had come
to light in 1730, also used to "handle" farm boys.[155]

Some of the men described here were fully socialized into the
sodomite subcultures, while others were much less so or not at

all. There were those who could pick and choose from a whole range of behaviors or act out other roles as well. The situation becomes even more complex when a closer look is taken into these men's desires by turning to their marital status. Role theories, it seems, dismally fail to understand or to include desires. At best they assume that desire and role are one and the same and that somebody with a same-sex role is generally exclusive in his or her preference. Did a man such as the embroiderer Pieter van Steijn, who was recruited by one of the brothel owners in The Hague with the argument that he could make much more money through prostitution, desire other men or not? Shortly before his arrest he married, but this did not stop him from his other activities; in terms of behavior, he was perfectly socialized into the subculture. In an anonymous (religious) confession from 1730 in the records of sodomite trials of the Court of Holland – which could well have been his – the writer said that he had often verbally abused his wife, had masturbated other men at least forty times, had committed sodomy and had often looked in a dishonest way at his neighbor's wife.[156] It may well be that, despite his obvious skills within the subculture, van Steijn preferred women; at the very least he was ambivalent. Nonetheless, the marital status of others tells about the complexity of desires in a disturbing way.

All through the eighteenth century, many of the men who were arrested on sodomy charges were or had been married, sometimes more than once.[157] A considerable number married women who were older than they were, generally by only a few years, but sometimes by ten or more years. One man in Leiden was younger by no less then nineteen years.[158] The opposite situation occurred less frequently. It is tempting to come to easy conclusions about these men's intentions. One has to take into account, however, that in the eighteenth century in about 30 percent of the marriages men were younger than their spouses.[159] Even the number of children offers few clues. Obviously, those who had married barren women would have none. Some men whose spouses were still in their child-bearing years had no children, either, yet others – about the same number – did have children, and some had five or six. The wife of the high clerk of the states of Holland, Carel Aloth, bore him eleven children before he fled The Hague in 1730.[160]

Some men who had married barren women may have done so for material reasons, but what do we make of the broadside vendor Hendrik Eelders's marital situation? His wife was ten years older than he and they had no children.[161] After his execution in 1765, his wife begged the bailiff of Amsterdam for her husband's linen.[162] Before Eelders was arrested in the south of the country, and while he still wandered there with his partner, his wife had written him letters to warn him about what was happening in the city.[163] In 1816, a woman who was some five years older than her husband – a point a prosecutor did not fail to notice in very suggestive terms[164] – begged King Willem I for mercy on her husband. He was sentenced to death because he had killed a sixteen-year-old who blackmailed him with his sexual activities. The woman wrote that she did not believe her husband to have engaged in unnatural behavior because she had fully enjoyed all the pleasures of marriage.[165] Two years before, a woman who forcefully protested her husband's innocence to the king – he had been in prison since 1810 – claimed such pleasures as well and wrote that he had always been a deeply affectionate father to their children.[166]

Affection for spouse and children appears in other cases. Barend Blomsaet, one of the first men to be arrested in 1730, managed to smuggle little notes to his wife while he was on trial, giving her a detailed account of his confessions. They not only show that she must have been fully aware of his sexual behavior but also tell of his love for her and his children. For quite some time he had resisted his interrogators, but then, when beaten by torture and intimidation, he wrote a note saying that he had little need for food; he only got some salad and oil, in quantity "enough for our little girl." In a final note he commanded his wife and children to God. His wife, in a most moving letter to the court, begged for a mercy sentence for her husband and for permission – which was denied – to dress him in a clean shirt once he was executed and to bury him in a decent manner.[167] Jan Mulder, who was described by the court as an extremely effeminate man, in one

174

of his affectionate letters to Floris Husson referred in equally affectionate terms to his children and said how dear they were to him.[168] His testament mentioned that he was to be buried next to his wife.[169] Several men who fled The Hague between 1774 and 1776 and went to the county of Kleef in Germany were later joined by their wives.[170]

Of course not all of these men shared such affection for their spouses. There were extremely bad marriages as well. Litius Wielandt, who was acquitted by the Court of Holland in 1654, beat his wife in such a manner that she applied for the dissolution of their marriage and indeed divorced him.[171] The wife of Nicolaas Ockerse had divorced him *miserabilis personae* before he was arrested in 1730.[172] Shortly after their wedding he had removed her from their bed to replace her with a male servant whom he showered with affection and presents. Other women were left by their husbands, and some were abused both verbally and physically. Indeed, one was reported to have been sodomized by her husband. Especially after 1790, women petitioned the courts to be divorced from their incarcerated husbands. Courts usually granted such divorces, and in particular the court of Amsterdam explicitly referred to "sodomy" in such cases. That was an obvious error, because sodomy was not grounds for divorce, nor did it ever become one. Marriages like these could be dissolved only when, after the husbands were imprisoned, they were practically null and void.[173]

While many men were indeed married, a majority were not. Yet again, it is difficult to ascertain the meaning of this fact, since through the eighteenth century a considerable percentage of the population did not marry. Among the sodomites there were, no doubt, single people who had no desire for women. Yet for most of them during much of the eighteenth century, it remains unclear whether they did not marry out of choice or for less conscious reasons. It was only after 1750 that some men explicitly stated that they had no interest in women whatsoever. "I never had any genius for women," one sodomite said.[174] One of the most astounding cases is that of a minister of the Reformed Church, Andreas Klink, from 1757. His ideas about himself, as will be shown later, were most sophisticated. According to a witness talking about the minister's sexual appetites, the man would not stop even if the gallows were standing in front of his door. This witness and others had repeatedly advised their shepherd to find himself a wife, but they reported that he said he had no interest in marriage. He contested this at trial and said he had courted a young woman. That may have been true, but even the mother of this supposedly prospective bride said that the courtship had been halfhearted at best.[175]

Even if affection for spouse or children does not reveal one's sexual desires, it is obvious that many of these men wanted more than the notion of a sodomite role would allow for. Moreover, it seems that if many of these men acted out a role, it did not necessarily have to do with desires. On the other hand, even conscious desires and same-sex behavior did not necessarily result in the adaptation of a sodomite role. The just-mentioned Klink was minister successively in two different rural areas, one of them extremely parochial. His encounters were usually with young farmhands, whom he had invited to stay with him and sleep with him in his bed. Yet he never adopted the sodomite role as it existed in the cities.

Such individual differences and the accompanying anecdotes may seem trivial, yet it is in such details that human experience exceeds social theories and their generalization, be they about roles, sex, gender or sexual dimorphism. Nonetheless, one has to account for the social change that indeed occurred: from the strictly hierarchical sexual encounters of the period before the late seventeenth century to the more egalitarian encounters after, as well as the emergence of subcultural phenomena; from the reversible roles of the early eighteenth century to a more diversified situation from the second half of that century on; and – as I will show later – in the ideas sodomites held about themselves and those others held about them.

As Trumbach suggests, the hierarchical or intergenerational encounters that were dominant until the late seventeenth century mirrored the patriarchal relationships between the sexes in marriage. With the rise of what he called the "egalitarian marriage" or what Lawrence Stone termed "affective individualism," which also occurred in the late seventeenth century and which at least to a certain extent narrowed the gap between the sexes, came a growing appreciation of differences in sex roles, including the role of woman as mother, educator and guardian of domesticity. It is at such a diversification of sex roles and the growing equality between the sexes, according to Trumbach, that one has to look to understand why adult men with same-sex desires began to desire other adult men instead of adolescents.[176]

Dutch family historians claim that family life in the Netherlands largely resembled that of England and northern France. In these parts of Western Europe, patriarchal attitudes in regard to the choice of a spouse that were still dominant in the seventeenth century – though mostly held in check by local orders – dissipated around 1680. They were replaced by ideas about mutual love as a condition for marriage.[177] Along with it came an emphasis on domesticity at the cost of women's economic independence. Despite the patriarchalism of the previous period, widows and unmarried women could under some circumstances lead an economically independent life. In the second half of the eighteenth century there were fewer such independent women in the Netherlands than a hundred years before.

Changes in homosexual behavior in the late seventeenth century in the Republic coincided with changes in the relationships between the genders, as Trumbach argues for England. If opposite-sex relations were until that time generally characterized by patriarchal attitudes, so were same-sex relations (and perhaps even more). With the growing complexities of different sex roles for men and women in the course of the eighteenth century, same-sex relations seemed to grow more complex as well. This is suggested by attitudes about "active" and "passive" sodomy and love affairs between people of the same sex.

The question that remains to be answered – both in light of my opening remarks and Trumbach's assertion that sodomites came to represent a third sex or gender – is whether this was true for the Netherlands as well. Thomas Laqueur has made it abundantly clear that what seems to be the most obvious fact of life –

the existence of two sexes – was for centuries not a fact at all.[178] Only when sex roles changed in the eighteenth century did the eye of the beholder perceive two sexes that were in biological terms fundamentally different from one another. Up to that point it had seen only one: the male sex. Woman's body was the inverted and incomplete version of man's body. "Complete" and "incomplete" bodies explained the existence of two genders. Nature itself ordained that they were related in a hierarchical way to one another. If indeed the sodomite came to represent a third gender in the eighteenth century – taking into account the differences in behavior, in intensity of that behavior, in desires these men held and in the way in which human experience exceeds such a concept of gender – it is also in the eye of the eighteenth-century beholder that one has to look for the sodomite's gender. It is toward such a solution that the final part of this essay will take me.

Perceptions

Before 1730
Previously I noted that from 1730 on some people believed that homosexual behavior had been introduced in the Netherlands by foreign ambasssadors two decades before, during peace talks in Utrecht. Despite the fact that this was not true, the idea was not sheer propaganda. Many official comments in 1730 suggested that homosexual behavior so far was little known in the Netherlands and that in the country's history only a few people had been prosecuted on sodomy charges.

Such ideas originated in the very notion of the *crimen nefandum*, the crime not to be mentioned among Christians. It may have been Dutch idiosyncrasy, but the notion of "the unmentionable vice" was taken very literally until 1730. Perhaps most striking was the silence of the Dutch Reformed Church on the subject, at least so far as its own flock was concerned. Until 1730, sodomy had been mentioned only once at the many hundreds of provincial synods the church had held since the days of the Reformation, although the records of these synods show time and again

178

that participants lamented the sinful times that had swept the country.[179] Research into minutes of church councils from the seventeenth century, which otherwise deal with all kinds of carnal sins committed by members of the church, have not brought to light a single case of sodomy.[180] The late-seventeenth-century *Swart Register van Duysent Sonden* (Black register of a thousand sins), published by a church minister, did not contain a single word on same-sex behavior.[181]

There was only one noteworthy exception: if sodomy was mentioned at all, it was referred to as a "Catholic crime." Many Protestant theologians described the carnal sins of popes and other prelates. Rome was "the *catamitorum mater*," mother of catamites, as Josephus Scaliger wrote in the seventeenth century.[182] Pope Sixtus IV was persistently rumored to have given his cardinals special permission to indulge in sodomy during the hottest months of the year. The fifteenth-century bishop Giovanni Della Casa had written a laudate on sodomy, according to an even more persistent story (the poem, "Il Forno," was about heterosexual sodomy).[183]

What was true for the Church was with few exceptions true for literature as well. A sixteenth-century chronicle related the execution of the president of the High Council of Holland, Gooswijn de Wilde, in 1447, and the wildly popular seventeenth century *De Wintersche Avonden of Nederlandtsche Vertellingen* (Winter evenings or Dutch narratives), despite its arcadian title, gave a sensational account of the burning at the stake of a sodomite in Middelburg in 1605.[184] Unlike those in England and France, seventeenth-century libertine novels of Dutch origin did not mention sodomy.[185] Like the Protestant theologians, Dutch authors would refer to sodomy only as an "Italian" or more particularly "Catholic" habit.

If ever there was a conspiracy of silence, the Netherlands virtually invented it. In the first section of this essay I mentioned that, in the course of the seventeenth century, executions of sodomites were carried out in secret. On many though not all occasions seventeenth-century records of sodomy cases were destroyed and only summary verdicts were left (and sometimes not even that) so as not only to deny that sodomy did occur in this country but in effect to deny judges any practical knowledge of the subject.[186] In the end only jurists in their legal commentaries wrote about sodomy, and this was for a very limited audience.[187]

"The unmentionable vice" in the Netherlands was until 1730 not just a vice not mentioned: it was a vice that was not supposed to exist. This was not mere "propaganda": ecclesiastical and secular authorities alike participated in a process of denial that affected them psychologically as well. They were rudely brought back to reality – with great surprise – in 1730 on the discovery of the sodomite networks. The origins of this state of mind are to be found in what were presumed to be the causes of homosexual behavior, as well as in the body politic of the republic itself and in the special place the country was understood to hold in the world.

Before going into any detail about this it is necessary to stress the fact that these same authorities in 1730 made a complete volte-face once the networks were discovered. Whereas the very notion of the *crimen nefandum* rested in part on the idea that withholding knowledge about homosexual behavior would also block people from engaging in it, from 1730 on it was such knowledge, not ignorance, that was to deter people. As one church minister wrote a year later, there was a time to be silent and a time to speak out, and the latter had begun.[188] Within weeks after the first arrests, a stream of publications commenced; they included pamphlets, poems and songs, especially for the occasions of executions. Articles in literary and "scientific" journals as well as books written by vicars dealt with sodomy from a theological perspective and the question of what sodomy was all about: its nature, its origins and causes and its effects on mankind and society.[189]

Although later prosecutions sparked similar publications, in the second half of the eighteenth century sodomy became once again a subject for jurists. After Cesare Beccaria had published his famous *Dei Delitti e Delle Pene* in 1764, in which he lamented among other things the fact that convictions for sodomy often came about as a result of torture, Dutch jurists discussed not only whether sodomy was to be punished at all but also how best to prevent people from engaging in same-sex behavior. As in the publications from 1730, much of the discussion dealt with the nature, causes and effects of sodomy, yet in a more secular way that also implied further developments in ideas about sodomy.[190]

From 1730 on, extensive court records were kept; even if they were dealt with in a secretive way (they often were kept in secret drawers), they became a source of knowledge for future generations of judges. After the prosecutions had begun, the states of Holland issued a bill on July 21, 1730; its particular importance was not so much that it called for the death penalty for sodomy but that it ordered courts in this province to carry out death penalties in public. Such executions were, in the words of Dutch anthropologist Anton Blok, theatrical dramas in which everybody – from the judges, the hangman and the convict to the public – played a role.[191] The very way in which a person was executed conveyed meanings into the public domain. It sent a powerful message about what a sodomite was or was supposed to be to the public, which in the end would also affect sodomites' perceptions of themselves, although not always in the way authorities expected.

In short, a discourse, to use a Foucaultian term, on homosexual behavior began as early as 1730 in the Netherlands that contributed to the development of a popular belief about such behavior, on which – as stated in the Introduction – nineteenth-century medical discourse was built. I will now explore the particularities of this eighteenth-century discourse.

Discourse
Only one obvious source existed for an explanation of what sodomy was all about and for an answer to the acute question of why it had suddenly – as many felt – affected the country: the Bible, and more particularly its chapter on the destruction of Sodom and Gomorrah. That chapter had not been ignored in the previous period – on the contrary – but until 1730 it was never used to talk about same-sex behavior, at least not as far as the Dutch vicars' own flock was concerned. Yet in the seventeenth century the story of Sodom was crucial in providing a social and political the-

ory, and sometimes a social and political critique, that in 1730 could explain the "sudden" emergence of same-sex behavior in the republic. It also provided a kind of folk psychology that at an individual level could explain people's behavior.

Sodom and Gomorrah and the other three cities of Pentapolis had, according to the Bible, gathered great wealth because of the fertility of the plain they were settled on. Wealth and fertility had led the plain's inhabitants into indulgence in pride, "excess of diet" and contempt for the poor. Such gluttony had resulted in all kinds of debauchery and finally in same-sex practices and the appalling behavior of the inhabitants toward the angels visiting Lot. Therefore, they were punished with the total destruction of the Pentapolis.

The very fact that the republic had emerged victoriously from the Eighty Years' War against Spain (1568-1648) and had become one of the most prosperous and powerful countries in the Western hemisphere in the seventeenth century was considered proof of the special place the Republic and its people had in God's schemes. The Dutch had become His new chosen people after both the Jews and the Catholics had failed Him. Prosperity and power were God's rewards for sobriety, modesty and generosity toward the less fortunate, which, according to ministers and popular writers in both the seventeenth and eighteenth centuries, characterized the behavior of the inhabitants and rulers of the Republic in its early days. For that reason, same-sex behavior simply had not existed before the early eighteenth century. Prosperity, however, was also a mixed blessing. It was God's continuous test of man to resist temptation: How easily he could fall prey to gluttonous behavior with wealth, food and power! Despite the continuous warnings of its shepherds, so it was explained in 1730, the Dutch people had given in to hedonism. The trend had started with lesser sins, such as cardplaying and gambling, indulgence in food and drink and excessive dressing, and ended up with debauchery and finally sodomy. Sodomy was the result of the "surpassing steps of sinfulness," most authors agreed in 1730, which had affected the country's inhabitants. This explained the "sudden" emergence of same-sex practices in the Republic.[192]

It is obvious that an etiology in which homosexual behavior could be the result of cardplaying is not compatible with modern taxonomies of sexuality. Besides, where modern concepts have divided mankind into fixed categories of sexual human beings, eighteenth-century concepts implied that every human being could indulge in homosexual behavior.

Modern concepts of sexuality, homosexuality and sexual identities have set their very subjects – at least as objects of knowledge – apart from all other spheres of life. They are assumed to be intrinsic unities made up of physical, psychological and social elements; they are assumed to be universal and recognizable and as such they can presumably be studied throughout history and in different cultures. Yet these concepts find their roots in others, like those of "nature," "sex," "body," "psyche" and eroticism in general, that themselves are in constant flux and that, despite contradictions, create and re-create integrated and apparently seamless unities. To study past concepts of sexuality in general or same-sex behavior in particular requires that the historian abandon modern concepts and raise questions about categories such as nature, psyche and body and how they related to one another: for instance, if homosexual behavior was unnatural, then what was nature? What kind of unity existed between these categories, or, in other words, how did sexual life relate to other spheres?[193] How did (homo)sexuality relate to concepts of sex and sexual differences and to concepts of masculinity and femininity, and what actually constituted masculinity and femininity?

From its very beginnings, Calvinism was much less hostile toward "lust" than Catholicism was, at least up to the time of the Counter-Reformation. Catholicism had for a long time questioned whether carnal desires themselves were the result of the fall from paradise; it had preached celibacy as being closest to the original blissful state and had discussed whether or to what extent sex even within the confines of marriage and procreation was sinful.[194] Calvinism, on the other hand, not only rejected celibacy as unnatural but also did not consider procreation as the sole or prime purpose of sex between spouses. Indeed, procreation was divine command, but sex as a means to create companionship

183

between married partners contributed to the creation of a good environment in which to raise offspring.[195] Carnal desires and pleasure were both a prerequisite for procreation and a reward for spouses whose marriage was according to a celestial plan.

If such desires were a necessity for the survival of mankind, hunger and thirst, cold and warmth, and fatigue were necessary tools to sustain the body and individual existence through feeding, refreshment, dress and leisure. Yet there was a dangerous side to fulfillment of such needs, which could easily result in excess and hedonism. This was also true for emotions like love, grief and anger, which could result in mindless passion, doubts about the divine plan, fights, murder and manslaughter. Indulgence in one's emotions and needs ultimately led to debauchery and finally to unnatural behavior. It is small wonder one author could write that the seed of sodomy hid in each and everyone.[196] Sexuality did not represent a unity within itself but was part of a dichotomy according to which human needs could either be fulfilled with restraint or result in insatiability and gluttony. With the discovery of the sodomite networks in 1730 it was made plain that sodomy itself was the ultimate form of hedonism, resulting from "lesser sins" that over a number of years, despite the warnings of its teachers, had affected the country.[197]

Whether sex served procreation or companionship between spouses, it could only mean that the purpose of physical differences was to unite male and female, the vicar van Byler stated in 1731 in his book about sodomy. After all, woman was flesh of "his" flesh, bone of "his" bone, and "they knew one another as one flesh." As such, males were alien to each other, van Byler said, and therefore between them there could be no love but just "filthy greed."[198] In marriage man and wife owned each other's bodies; indulging in sodomy meant that man stole his body from his wife. Besides, as Saint Paul had taught the Corinthians (6.13), the body was not for fornication but for God; as the courts also stated in reference to people who had committed suicide, the body was the temple of the Holy Spirit. Hedonism, debauchery and ultimately sodomy polluted this temple and turned it into "a synagogue of the prince of darkness." The sodomite committed a terrible crime by taking his body – which was not rightfully his – away from God. [199]

"The flesh of his flesh" and "the bone of his bone" implied not only that woman derived her body from man but, as medical teaching until well into the eighteenth century also made clear, that the female body was an incomplete version of the male body and that there was in fact only one real sex. [200] Complete and incomplete bodies implied hierarchy between male and female as well as different capacities. If the body was a temple to be kept clean from hedonism, man was by nature better equipped for restraint than woman was and the latter could well be the insatiable being, as she was so often described in popular literature of the seventeenth century, unless she submitted herself to the hierarchy between male and female that was set by her body and by nature.

By showing restraint and controlling his emotions at every level a man respected his manliness. By giving in to hedonism and in particular to sodomy, a man violated his body, over which he was not sovereign but only reigned as God's steward, and which he was ordained to keep clean; he also violated the natural hierarchy between male and female that ordained him to sobriety. In short, he would become like a woman, insatiable, that is, unmanly. In that sense we can understand a seventeenth-century observation that men who engaged in same-sex behavior suffered from an "effeminate disease." [201] However much a sodomite became like a woman, in none of these commentaries was a single word written on the effeminate behavior among sodomites I described in the previous section.

In nineteenth-century evolutionary thinking, nature – though created by God – became a goal in itself. Through regeneration and degeneration and extravagant waste nature became an eternal experiment in selection. With concepts of an innate homosexuality nature also segregated individuals by the natural and the unnatural. Some were homosexuals, and most were not. However, for centuries nature had been where God had revealed Himself and His purpose, which, as one judge in a sodomy trial in 1797 put it, for all living beings meant a continuation of the existence

185

of their species. Where animals could only obey their natural instincts, human beings also possessed reason and free will. Animals did not and could not perpetrate same-sex acts – so the judge said – whereas human beings with their free will could give in to boundless desires. Through reason and the study of nature man could behold the divine plan and through his free will either live in accordance with this plan or place himself outside its boundaries. Homosexual behavior did not fit in with this plan; it was not part of creation and was therefore unnatural.

Nature in this scheme was a source of moral rather than an object of "scientific" knowledge and more an entity that was affected by man's moral behavior than an unchangeable one. It set the example for human behavior and human society, its rules and its laws, its hierarchy between the sexes and its boundaries between the rulers and the ruled. In this sense the body politic reflected nature. God had endowed some – the patricians – with the intellectual and moral superiority to become rulers, to keep order and to prevent chaos.[202] When individuals crossed the boundaries between classes – as the trials of 1730 so clearly showed some patricians had done – the body politic itself was threatened. Sodomy, being outside the divine plan and nature, threatened to destroy human society. Sodomy was the absolute contradiction: it turned the natural hierarchy upside down and turned men into women; it could undo creation itself. It would turn the world back to the chaos that had existed that very first day when it was still "a formless void."

Sodomy even threatened eternity. Many writers in 1730 addressed the issue of whether sodomites could be forgiven, whether they could still be taken into God's grace. The answer was that they could only if they showed genuine remorse and received their due penalties from the hands of judges. Sodomy by its very nature could easily spread, and with so many escapees who were not sentenced, all living souls and, for that matter, eternity itself could be destroyed.[203]

The Bible text of Sodom and Gomorrah provided a coherent, universal social theory, and in that sense there was little new in what was said in 1730. The only new element was that in its ultimate form – in which it included the mention of sodomy – this theory applied to the Republic as well, whereas formerly it applied only to other, Catholic countries.

As I said earlier, this theory could also serve as social and political critique. Although in cautious terms, theologians who wrote their treatises in 1730 lay the blame for the emergence of same-sex behavior in the Republic on the upper classes. After all, the rich and the powerful were the ones who had given in to excess, be it in dress or food or drink, who had betrayed the sobriety and restraint of their ancestors and who had failed the moral responsiblities of their class. They were the ones who were responsible for the seduction of lower-class young men by showering them with money, gifts and favors and had lured them into a kind of contact with the upper class which they otherwise would never have had.[204]

The Sodom text also provided a kind of folk psychology. Sodomy had been considered merely an incidental, spontaneous or casual act, as Foucault and Hekma argued two centuries later. But by 1684 a verdict of a sodomite in Rotterdam had already mentioned that mutual masturbation would undeniably result in anal intercourse. The general public and sodomites themselves in the eighteenth century agreed that, once a same-sex act was perpetrated, the culprit would hold on to this kind of behavior. At trials it was a common question to ask a suspect how long he had held on to this behavior and many of the suspects volunteered such information even when the question did not come up. Because people would hold on to it, even those who had perpetrated sodomy only once in an accidental, casual way were considered to be lost causes. The same was true for adolescents or, according to some, even for prepubescent boys.[205] The Dutch eighteenth-century satirist and pamphletist Jakob Campo Weyerman, whom I describe elsewhere as a mediator between elite and folk culture, was explicit in 1730 about this psychology. He also pointed to lesser sins like greed and gluttony as the sources from which sodomy sprang. However horrible and disgusting a sin might be, he wrote, it is easy to understand "that once she has been tasted, man usually will crave for its repetition." The new sin "boils" in

187

"our soul to singe all our senses.... What was only curiosity at first, degenerates into avidity and into a furious desire to diversions already perpetrated." "It is an absolute truth," according to Weyerman, "that evil dispositions and lusts can come of something that originally was natural."[206]

As folk psychology this theory would last well into a major part of the eighteenth century; it shows up as well in some texts in the early nineteenth century and might perhaps still find adherents among orthodox Protestants. As a social theory, even at the time it was put on paper, it fell desperately short. How many people could recognize in such a theory their neighbors, their husbands, sons or friends whom they had often known as affectionate fathers, obedient children or faithful churchgoers and whose arrest or flight deeply shocked them? It was equally unlikely that they would consider insatiable and brawling gamblers, drinkers, eaters and whoremongers as effeminate in any sense, let alone as easy preys for sodomites, as this theory held. The church minister van Byler anticipated this by saying that many of the sodomites were hypocrites. After a scholarly exposition of the theory, he said that these hypocrites could often not be recognized because they acted as devout people and as virtuous in citizenship and modesty. That was why every woman had to fear for her husband, every parent for his or her sons, every household for its domestics.

Aside from being a social theory, the explanation represented a symbolic universe in which every part had to do with the others. As such, it better explains the state of denial that so many ecclesiastical and secular authorities shared before 1730, as well as the hair-raising fears sodomy caused in that year, than it explains the origins of actual human behavior.

Nonetheless, this theory or symbolic universe found its counterpart in legal practice and in particular in the public executions of the culprits. Public executions were extensive rituals that served more than one purpose. They were highly stylized ceremonies and theatrical dramas. They were, of course, meant not only to punish and to exorcise the culprits but also to bring harmony back to a blemished universe, reconcile God with man, or, in this case, with Dutchmen, so that He would not withhold His blessing from the country or destroy it as He once destroyed Sodom. Yet, since nobody could hope to prosecute or execute all those involved, the convict became an expiatory sacrifice who suffered his life for all. As Mary Douglas has written about cleansing rituals that are meant to reconcile a polluted universe, the ritual of executions was also a double-edged sword: it was meant to exorcise the culprit, but also, given the fact that everybody was thought to harbor "the seed of sodomy" in himself, to exorcise potential same-sex desires.

Executions
The very form of public executions, in which everybody played a role, was replete with meaning, and executions contributed to the discourse on sodomy that began in 1730.

The execution ritual lasted three days. It began with an almost religious ceremony in which the prosecutor delivered his requisition, followed the next day by the announcement of the death penalty to those who were to be executed as well as by prayers in the churches. On the final day came the apotheosis at the scaffold. Much of the ceremony that day – such as the guards of honor and the blood-colored robes and other paraphernalia the judges wore – was meant to underline the god-given nature of the power and majesty of the authorities, who presided over justice in full regalia. Next to them and to the hangman, the convict was the most important actor in this drama. The drama's success – a victorious justice – depended to a large extent on the skills of the executioner and on how the convict behaved at the scaffold. Those who accepted their verdicts as rightful punishment for their behavior, who showed an appropriate remorse and prayed to God for forgiveness, were the darlings of their judges and of the public. In the days before the execution church ministers spent much of their time with the culprit to teach him about the Bible, to tell him why he was to be punished and to prepare him for his encounter with God. Obviously, these church ministers were often successful.[207] Samuel Rijnhart, the man who wrote the desperate love letters to Jan Beeldemaker, suffered such a severe attack of asthma when he learned that an appeal that was to save him from the gallows was rejected that a doctor had to bleed him twice. His judges decided therefore to hasten the execution to prevent him from escaping them through a natural death. When he had recovered a day later and received the announcement that he was to be executed the following morning, Rijnhart told his judges that they had given him the right penalty, and that, if they had decided otherwise, they would have committed a great sin in the eyes of God.[208] The next day, according to the prosecutor, "with exemplary tranquillity he stepped into eternity."[209]

Justice was victorious when the convict dutifully played his role, which was to convince the public that justice was done and that the judges had made the right decision. It was the approval of the public that confirmed and legitimated the powers that were. That was exactly what was lacking in 1731 in the executions carried out by the local judge de Mepsche, whom I have described earlier. De Mepsche had feared an outright revolt and had encamped an entire regiment of soldiers in his jurisdiction. Although protests by the inhabitants were muddled, many of those who were convicted, according to eyewitnesses, protested their innocence on their way to the gallows. It won de Mepsche neither love nor authority, and even during his life legends were spun around his evil personality, some of which survived well into this century.[210]

There were many ways to carry out a death penalty. In the eighteenth century the most common forms were hanging, garroting, decapitation, breaking on a wheel and drowning in a barrel of water. Burning at the stake – a common punishment for sodomites until the second half of the seventeenth century – was thought to be too cruel. Even when it was still done, a little bag of gunpowder was placed on the victim's chest to hasten his end. The disfigurement of corpses, common practice in parts of Europe in the early modern period, quietly disappeared. As a reminder of burning at the stake, the faces of some people who in 1730 were executed because of sodomy were scorched with burning straw after they had died (and sometimes before).[211] When the prosecutor in Amsterdam demanded that this be done as well to two young sodomites in 1743 it was rejected without much ado by the judges.[212]

Each kind of execution was given meaning both in regard to the perpetrator's crime and to the perpetrator's standing in life as well as his or her sex. So-called mirror penalties were meant to reflect the kind of crime the convict had committed. A woman who had committed infanticide could be executed with a doll above her head, and likewise a murderer could be hanged with a knife above his head.[213] Burning at the stake or drowning in a barrel was meant to wipe out or wash away the sins that had been committed.[214] Different kinds of executions implied different degrees to which a person was robbed of his or her honor. Decapitation, regarded as carrying the least dishonor and therefore generally applied to upper-class people who had committed a capital offense, was in 1730 explicitly rejected in cases of sodomy.[215] Hanging was the most common form of punishment for men, whereas breaking on the wheel was reserved for the most atrocious cases of manslaughter. Women were usually garroted, as were sodomites, aside from a few exceptions – in 1730 two men were drowned in a barrel in Amsterdam because of sodomy. Garroting could also be applied to men who had committed a crime that was considered cowardly, such as killing somebody in his sleep. In 1677 in Rotterdam a man suffered this penalty because he had supposedly attempted to set the Dutch fleet afire two years earlier, while the country was at war with most of its neighbors. His verdict explicitly said that, had he succeeded, he would have ruined the country.[216] The same was true of sodomites, who would evoke God's punishment in the way Sodom and Gomorrah had. It was thus that a sodomite was presented at the scaffold and that his punishment became part of a public discourse: a sodomite was like a woman, he was a coward and he had committed high treason; in short he had betrayed every aspect of an honorable manhood. Combined with the social theory that was derived from the Sodom text and according to which a sodomite as an insatiable being was like a woman, the sodomite at the scaffold came to represent a third gender: a man who with his free will had given up his male status, who had betrayed what his body ordained and thus had lost the prerogatives of his sex.

The Pursuit of a Third Sex

After an era that knew only one sex and two genders, because of the emergence of a sodomite subculture and what was thought to be a definite sodomite role the first half of the eighteenth-century witnessed the emergence of a third gender. This third gender was represented by an effeminate man, who was still different from a man who engaged in same-sex activities and was thought to be effeminate in speech, dress or other habits. A man who was arrested in 1736 in female dress in Amsterdam obviously was not thought to be a sodomite, since he settled his case with the prosecutor out of court.[217] A sodomite was effeminate in the sense that he had given in to lascivious behavior. But the sodomite's effeminacy, in terms of his physical appearance, as I described earlier, was to turn him into an altogether different being and category in the course of the eighteenth century, at least in the eyes of secular authorities, judges and jurists.

In 1750 a man was arrested in the city of Delft and charged with burglaries and robberies. While awaiting his death sentence, he confessed to having prostituted himself in a number of cities in the Republic. During one of the court hearings, he made a comment on sodomites that, albeit in different wording, recurred in many of the writings of the second half of that century. "One could recognize those folks," he said, "because there does not grow a beard on their cheeks, that their eyes are whorish, their speech is drawling and their movement wriggling."[218] A decade later, the jurist Franciscus Lievens Kersteman put it this way: sodomy resulted in "that effeminate posture, that drawsy eye, those whorish cheeks which one clearly observes in all those inhuman humans and which in some even affects their speech."[219] In 1777 an anonymous writer held that "men who are in the habit of perpetrating this evil are usually cowards, effeminate and, as is said, naggy."[220]

From the mid-eighteenth century on, the sodomite was like a woman because of his physical appearance. Yet he was not like just any woman, but like a whore, as these comments suggest. The sodomite was a "he-whore," eighteenth-century English authors wrote.[221] The word *whore* (*hoer*) in eighteenth-century Dutch could apply not only to a female prostitute but also to any woman who did not live in accordance with the chastity of her sex. The sodomite and the whore (and in this case the prostitute) had much in common, as I described earlier, not least of all the sites they both cruised, their gestures and their ways of finding partners. Now also their physical appearance, at least in the perceptions of some observers, had become alike. In Kersteman's experience their appearance turned sodomites into a recognizable species: "if the eye is the mirror of the soul and inner emotions intimate outwardly inner proclivities in the face, so are those who without prejudice pay attention to physiognomy not to be blamed." He himself had known such an effeminate person, Kersteman said, without knowing anything about his behavior. Yet in the end the man had been arrested and found guilty of sodomy.[222]

The sodomite's condition as a whore was not considered to be innate. His physical condition was the result of his behavior, not the other way around. Saint Paul, in his letter to the Church of Rome, had written that men burning in lust for other men would receive their appropriate punishment in themselves. According to Kersteman, the apostle had meant that sodomites were punished with an effeminate appearance.

In the second half of the eighteenth century an effeminate appearance had indeed become the hallmark of the sodomite in the eye of the beholder. In the debate about penal reform in the Netherlands that was sparked by writings such as Montesquieu's *L'Esprit des lois* (1750) and Cesare Beccaria's *Dei Delitti et delle Pene* (1764), effeminacy became a central issue when the debate addressed sodomy. As such it had an almost Malthusian accent. Montesquieu had considered the negative effects of this effeminacy on the strength of the state and the army. The anonymous tract from 1777 said that sodomites "are people who themselves are already lost to the state. The male sex becomes weak, effeminate and incapable of doing great things."[223]

In accordance with the ideas of Beccaria, penal reformers in the republic felt that the death penalty should no longer be applied to sodomites, primarily because it was not very effective in deterring others. Some were even afraid that the death penalty might encourage the young to engage in such behavior. After all, if they saw that the culprits who suffered this sentence had taken such enormous risks, they might think that the pleasures of sodomy must be worthwhile. Yet, since in these reformers' opinion the penal system and the scaffold as means to deter or "to educate" people in general were becoming more important, they pondered penalties for sodomy that were more humiliating. They emphasized the fact that sodomy was a gender-deviant act, and with an obvious consensus among them – some of their tracts were published at around the same time – most of the reformers wanted such culprits to be scaffolded in female dress, to be incarcerated in a women's prison, to carry out the meanest of female tasks like cleaning toilets and occasionally to be shown around in the streets in their infamous clothes.[224]

In the perceptions of secular authorities, sodomites became a more and more distinct category. In the early part of the eighteenth century, the language the authorities used was rather ambiguous. In 1731 the prosecutor of the Court of Holland in a requisition could speak of "those sodomitical people" as well as "perpetrators of such atrocious crimes";[225] occasionally people with more compassion used terms such as "those poor sinners."[226] In 1797, the language had changed considerably: independent of one another the prosecutors of The Hague and Amsterdam talked about "those monsters" who had to be chased out of their holes.[227]

Laqueur has shown that, in the course of the eighteenth century, following the growing appreciation of different sex roles for males and females, the awareness of the existence of two different sexes grew. Male and female had biologically different and, each in its own way, complete bodies. Yet, there were those men and women who failed the commands of their sex: effeminate sodomites and lewd women. The latter were those who abandoned their tasks as spouses, mothers and guardians of domesticity. These women became adulterers and prostitutes and indeed engaged in sexual activities with one another. As Trumbach made clear, by the end of the eighteenth century, one could speak of four sexes: male, female, the effeminate sodomite and what I would prefer to call the lewd woman. However, I want to stress what I said earlier: the condition of the sodomite and the lewd woman was acquired, not innate. As early as 1762 the prosecutor of Utrecht spoke of "people who were diseased with this default."[228] In 1820 another prosecutor used exactly the same phrase and added that these people could not be cured.[229] Most likely, when they used the word "diseased," the prosecutors had not a medical condition in mind but a moral one. (The distinction is not always clear: a medical condition could be the result of immorality.)

I now recall here what I said in the Introduction about Karl Westphal, his concept of "contrary sexual feeling," and "moral insanity" as far as the origins of homosexuality were concerned and my hypothesis that such a concept already had roots in popular belief at the time he articulated it as part of a medical discourse. Moral deprivation, from early on, was considered to be the cause of same-sex behavior. Over time, this notion became related to ideas about gender deviancy and finally sexual deviancy. As recent publications of sociobiologists and their opponents make clear, the question of whether this deviancy is innate or acquired has not been settled and has once again become the center of a sometimes fierce dispute. In the late nineteenth century, men and women with same-sex desires found a safe ideological and psychological haven in scientific concepts of a third sex. As I show in the next section, eighteenth-century sodomites who resisted the moral imperatives that transformed them into moral monsters with a condition for which they themselves were to be blamed developed a legitimacy for their behavior that paved the way for the open resistance of people such as Karl Heinrich Uhlrichs in the nineteenth century.

Resistance and Self-Perception
There was at least one thing sodomites and their prosecutors in the first half of the eighteenth century generally agreed on: that

at some point the culprits had been seduced into same-sex behavior, and that from that moment on they had retained this behavior. If not directly confronted with questions about this belief, many sodomites volunteered such information once they began to confess. As I pointed out earlier, this notion originated in a kind of popular psychology. Even those for whom a same-sex act had clearly been a casual one were lost causes. In 1774, the Court of Holland was told about a man who had related to his wife that he had been seduced at the age of fourteen and that he damned the day it had happened, but that afterward he could not stop indulging in such behavior.[230] Such a notion may explain the anxieties of Pieter Didding, a twenty-two-year-old who still resided in an orphanage in Amsterdam. One night in 1743, he had committed sodomy with another young man in a toilet in the orphanage. About a month later, he turned himself in to the fathers of the house. In court he said that he had "committed it this one time and never again and also had not given any thought of doing it again, but that after the committed act, he had become very sad and that his conscience could not rest about it, and...that he had since prayed day and night to the Lord to prevent him from such sins."[231]

According to Gert Hekma, most homosexual behavior in the nineteenth century was "still casual."[232] Court records in general show otherwise. While for some who were prosecuted the experience had no doubt been a casual one, for most of those prosecuted there was precious little that was casual about their behavior. That was as true for men who before the late seventeenth century engaged in same-sex acts with adolescents as it was for men in the eighteenth and nineteenth centuries. There were quite a few cases of – in criminal justice terms – recidivism. Paulus Hikken was acquitted in 1757 by the Court of Friesland and escaped arrest in 1764 in Amsterdam. A man like Hendrik Beun was twice prosecuted by default: first in 1764 in Amsterdam and second in 1776 in The Hague.[233] Hendrik Herderschee, after his conviction in 1798 and despite the fact that he had spent seventeen years in jail, become a devout man and claimed that his "natural feelings had inflamed" while being in prison, was arrested once again in 1826 because of a public indecency.[234] In the first few decades after 1811 some sodomites suffered several convictions for committing such indecencies repeatedly.[235]

Many of those who were arrested clearly hoped that a story about being seduced into same-sex behavior would somehow work as an excuse, but the courts saw this as no reason for absolving the behavior. It did, however, sometimes present the judges with an embarrassing situation.

Shortly after the first arrests of sodomites were made in Utrecht in 1730, two men who had not been taken into custody yet were talking in an inn in the city about what was happening around them and about their chances of escaping prosecution. One of them complained that the judges were behaving as if they were gods. "So what about it," the other responded. "The gentlemen who are sitting on the cushions participate in it sometimes as well." He added: "If they arrest me, I will tell everything I know."[236] This response must not be read as a lack of courage but as a challenge to the moral authority of the court. The speaker, Zacharias Wilsma, who after his arrest would become the court's primary source of information, knew all about gentlemen participating in the sodomite network. As a former soldier and footman he had sexually obliged many men all through the country, including officers and patricians. After being taken into custody, he testified in almost every city where sodomy trials were held against people he had either had sex with or whose reputation he knew. The court in Utrecht had good reason to keep him alive as the main source of information for a while, as other courts encouraged it to do. But once the trials had passed, the judges could easily have sentenced him to death. After all, from their perspective he was about the worst case one could imagine, being sodomized by so many and having himself sodomized so many others. Yet they did not give him the death penalty but decided to keep Wilsma in jail provisionally. In 1755, while he was still incarcerated, the judges in Utrecht told him that their predecessors had meant this to be a lifelong imprisonment.[237]

Was it a reward for his cooperation that the judges kept him alive, or could it be that Zacharias Wilsma had indeed successfully challenged their moral authority, which they themselves considered to be the natural and god-given basis of their power? In the previous sections, I pointed out that patricians in the Republic were all too aware of the delicate balance between them and the people they ruled and the fact that many in the country believed – for good reasons – that the courts would not prosecute people from the upper echelons. I also referred to the publications of the church ministers in which, in cautious terms, they blamed the upper classes for seducing young men from the lower classes. In fact this was part of a popular belief among these classes as well as among many sodomites, and perhaps even among the patricians themselves. An upper-class doctor, Hugo van de Poll, had told Hendrik Eelders in the early 1760s not to worry when they were talking about the risks they were taking: "there are too many among the great and they seduce the small."[238] The popular satirist and pamphleteer Jakob Campo Weyerman in two pamphlets he published in 1730 placed all blame on the rich and the powerful for luring their young footmen into same-sex behavior with money and presents. In fact, the picture he drew was a traditional one, based partly on seventeenth-century English literature about the so-called aristocratic rake.[239]

Samuel Rijnhart died in 1797 completely convinced of his guilt. As happened so often, secular and ecclesiastical authorities had succeeded in gaining control over his soul, one might say. But how would they have ever succeeded with a man like Zacharias Wilsma? Despite the fact that the courts were indeed often successful in "convincing" (the term was explicitly used in court records) a suspect, they also sometimes failed to do so. Barend Blomsaet, the man who in 1730 managed to smuggle notes to his wife in which he informed her about his confessions, wrote to her that after his death she should make public all the names he had mentioned in court. He could not accept that he was to suffer while the rich with whom he had dealt were to escape penalty. For weeks he denied all the charges that were brought against him, and at first he even withstood torture, only to give in after the pain became too much to bear. He wrote his wife that he could hardly sit anymore and his handwriting changed into almost unreadable hieroglyphs. In the end, he let his wife know, he wanted it all to be over and to die. "May God feed my soul," he wrote to her, shortly before he was executed.[240] Yet neither in his notes nor in his confessions was there a single shred of remorse toward his worldly judges.

In a society that was imbued with hierarchy, some found a personal legitimation for their behavior in the idea that men like them had been seduced by men from the upper classes. Except in the case of Wilsma, it was too shallow a defense to survive a trial; nor would any other defense do. Yet at the level of self-perception resistance against the moral judgment of sodomites grew during the eighteenth century. The idea of blaming upper-class men for their seduction did little to help sodomites, since it did not absolve anybody from personal responsibilities. But by the mid-eighteenth century some sodomites began turning to a different, unexpected source for their legitimation: the Bible.

In the Protestant provinces in the eighteenth-century Republic, about one-third of the adult population were confirmed members of the Reformed Church. For most Church members being confirmed was not an empty ritual but meant becoming part of a community that celebrated its unity with God through the holy meal.[241] It also meant firm demands made on one's public and private life and submission to the scrutiny of Church councils. Transgressing the boundaries set by the Church could mean the temporary exclusion from the holy meal; if the culprit refused to give up his sinful behavior – which often was of a carnal nature – he could become a social outcast.[242] As far as I could tell, the percentage of sodomites arrested who were confirmed members of the Reformed Church did not differ from that of the population at large.[243] For some sodomites being confirmed may have become void of meaning during their life, yet many others were devout people. Floris Husson, at the moment of his arrest in 1776, owned a small religious library. Most of the books were of recent origin, and he must have acquired them himself.[244] In one of his affectionate letters to Husson while Husson was still in flight in Germany with stolen bonds and money, his friend Jan Mulder wrote that he hoped Husson, despite the fact that he was in a strange country that professed another religion, had observed Thanksgiving Day. He himself had spent that whole day in church, he said, and had "laid himself down before God's throne." He had carefully listened to the sermons, which had filled him with "a tender heart" and had made him realize "that the Lord was so good to save us for this moment" and that he could still hope for salvation.[245]

Men like Floris Husson and Jan Mulder considered themselves to be morally responsible human beings. Despite the fact that official Church teaching prophesied the most horrible damnation for men like them, they found consolation in their religion. Because they were devout people, they were the ones who were most in need of legitimation. The church minister, Andreas Klink, who held very sophisticated ideas about himself, was the clearest exponent of this attitude, which also caused him many a hard battle with himself. He must have been a charismatic preacher who drew a large audience in his rural church; many in his audience would cry during his sermons, and he was held to be a deeply pious man. All during his trial, which lasted from 1757 to 1759, riots occurred among the people in the area where he came from because most did not believe the charges brought against him, attributing them to the jealousy of his fellow preachers. For years, those who testified against him even lived under constant threat of being murdered.

Klink had a habit of inviting young farmhands into his bed and sexually assaulting them once they were asleep. Ugly rows followed many such attempts, which usually ended with Klink kneeling down, praying and crying. Once, when he had made such an attempt on a fellow minister of the Church, the man had called him a hypocrite, saying that piety and such sin could not go together. Klink had answered that they could, while referring to David and other "great men" in the Bible. It was not his only defense. A servant of Klink related how the vicar had told him "that it was proper to his nature, while his mother, when pregnant with him and while his father not being at home, had had such a strong mind and desire for her husband, which he had inherited from her."[246]

Klink had phrased his ideas about what he thought to be his innate desires in terms of the (pre)scientific notions of his time: strong impressions on pregnant women affected the fetus and could result in giving birth to disformed children, even monsters. While on trial Klink never stood up for his opinions – he denied all charges – but nonetheless they caused fury among his prosecutors, probably because they were such a serious threat to their belief systems.

The prosecutor of the Court of Holland in his requisition went to considerable length to prove that Klink's religious legitimations were based on blasphemy. Pieter Loens, a lawyer who assisted the prosecutor, published a book in 1760 about this trial, which resulted in Klink's banishment from most of the provinces of the republic. Furiously, Loens wrote that sodomy was now "excused and apologized by cowardly, brainless creatures."[247] Nevertheless, he felt obliged to consider whether same-sex behavior could be the result of an inherited condition. It shows the threat Klink's opinions held for these authorities, particularly since he was such a charismatic man, that the only response Loens could muster was that it could not be true because he had not found any example of it in literature. But in order not to denounce the theory of the effects of a shock on pregnant women, he provided many examples of such women who had given birth to monsters.

In the second half of the eighteenth century, Klink was not the only one who held such ideas. Gerrit van Amerongen, who belonged to the circle of Floris Husson and Jan Mulder, after being forced to confess his "crimes" in 1776, suddenly stated at the end of his trial that "men who held on to it [sodomy] were like being born with it and they can be as amorous to one another as man and wife can be."[248] Since the men in this circle, according to Husson, talked among one another about their activities,[249] van Amerongen's statement probably reflects opinions that they shared.

Whereas Klink had developed his ideas in isolation – he was not part of a network, nor did he participate in any way in the urban subcultures – men like van Amerongen, Husson and Mulder had worked out their ideas with one another, not least of all

201

because they were devout people. Earlier I wrote that Hendrik Eelders said he had chosen his partner, Jan Kemmer, because he was so well acquainted with the biblical truths. A similar explanation may apply to Samuel Rijnhart's fatal attraction to Jan Beeldemakers, since they had taken confirmation classes together in The Hague. "It is a weakness that is innate and God has created no human being for his damnation," the servant Jan van Zaanen from Leiden wrote in 1826 to his newly found lover in Amsterdam.[250]

Van Zaanen's use of the word "weakness" represents a new awareness on the part of sodomites. Not only did these men think their desires innate; from the final quarter of the eighteenth century on, some sodomites began to use terms that reflected what they thought to be their gender. "Weakness," as opposed to "strength," seems to indicate a lack of (mental) masculinity that they shared with one another and that had created in them desires that set them off as a distinct category. Whereas in the early part of the eighteenth century sodomites would refer to others like them as men who "also existed in a filthy manner" or "a gentleman whose cart does not go straight either,"[251] Mulder in 1776 wrote to Husson (with a still-common Dutch colloquialism) about a man "who was also a member of the family."[252] "It is a weakness you and I share with thousands of others," one sodomite said to another in 1797.[253] "Are these people like us?" a group of sodomites asked in 1809 when a few men, who later turned out to be police spies, entered their circle.[254] "One cannot rely on any human being, but those who are of the family are the greatest bitches of all," Jan van Zaanen wrote to his lover in 1826.[255]

It would be wrong to suggest that all sodomites held such strong opinions about themselves and others in their circles. Yet, from the man in Groningen who in 1764 said that he had the constitution of a woman to the young Hendrik Herderschee, who had prostituted himself until his arrest in 1798 at age eighteen, many questioned their sex, gender or male status. Herderschee had first told the prosecutor that he had been seduced at the age of thirteen by an Italian, no less. Then he suddenly claimed to have a physical defect, about which he dared not speak outright. He asked permission to write it down. The prosecutor read "that the cause of my behavior is to be found in that those monsters [women] do not want me, because I lack a ball."[256] His comment implied that it was not the lack of a testicle that had made him engage in same-sex activities but his rejection by women. This may have caused him to doubt his male status, or, considering the misogynist expression he used, to attribute such doubts to women.[257] A man with whom Herderschee had had sex and who also used to have sex with female prostitutes seemed to have had such doubts about himself as well. He referred to the fact that he suffered from hypochondria and that he was often mentally troubled – which was confirmed by his neighbors and his doctor – and attributed this to his failure to win the love of a married woman. Obviously, he thought himself to have failed as a man.[258]

From the second half of the eighteenth century on, a group of sodomites emerged who considered themselves a distinct category with desires that were innate and based on a masculine defect. When Ulrichs in the second half of the nineteenth century proclaimed the existence of a female soul in a male body, he of course gave a much more positive twist to these ideas, but there can be little doubt that he articulated what already existed in popular belief. He and other authors who debated the existence of a third sex also gave such ideas a scientific status that must have been extremely appealing to many who held desires for their own sex. After all, it meant that there was no rationale for prosecuting people who engaged in same-sex behavior and that – as they themselves felt – in nature they had a room of their own.

Public Attitudes and Perceptions
In 1654, when the tutor Litius Wielandt was confronted after his arrest with accusations by his former maid that he had sodomized some of his pupils, he came up with a perfect defense, at least in terms of what the very notion of *crimen nefandum* was all about. He defied her testimony because she could not be a reliable witness: "Honest daughters," he said, "would not know about such things."[259] "Honest daughters" indeed may have been ignorant about sodomy for a long time, but after the emergence of the sub-

203

cultures in the late seventeenth century, it would often have been difficult for them not to know about such behavior. Despite the fact that sodomy was hardly talked about in official terms before 1730 and despite the surprise secular and ecclesiastical authorities showed in that year, especially in the neighborhoods where it occurred, people knew what was going on long before then. In 1702 several women who testified before the Court of Holland in a blackmail case spoke of a male brothel in The Hague and of young blackmailers they knew who probably also prostituted themselves. One of these women talked about a man who engaged in same-sex activities and who, according to her – in perfect harmony with current notions about sodomy – had picked up his habits when on a trip to Italy.[260]

When in 1730 arrests started to avalanche in the city, market women wondered out loud why "Red Tony had not been taken away yet." Long before that year, the children of one of the men arrested used to sing "here are the folks again" when their father received his male visitors. "No more Godless house nowadays than that of Meerman in the Wage street...many are seduced and spoiled there," an anonymous person wrote to the Court of Holland once prosecutions had started.[261] Both in Utrecht and The Hague men who were arrested in 1730 had long before been thrown out by their landlords or chased away from pubs because of their lewd life. For years the notary public Daniel van den Burch, who fled The Hague in 1730, had sexually assaulted young clerks who worked in his office and, when problems arose, always managed to settle them with their parents.[262]

The people in the streets had known of these activities for a long time, although few may have perceived the extent of them. What seems surprising is that these people did nothing with their knowledge: only a few complaints to the authorities are known before 1730.[263] The same seems to have been true for most of the eighteenth century. When in 1749 in Amsterdam a man named Christiaan Kip was caught in the act and beaten, bystanders commented, "Oh, that is that scalliwag, that is no wonder, he has had that name for so long."[264] Some years before, a riot had occurred in front of a house where two sodomites lived in the city. No police action had followed, and the men had moved to The Hague.[265]

It was generally at times when prosecutions were already ongoing that people showed a greater sensitivity to the subject and sometimes turned others in, although it usually followed a sexual assault. Yet even then, as in the case of the torturer of the Amsterdam court who was arrested in 1762 after such an assault on a young German man, witnesses appeared who had had similar experiences with him long before. In this case a witness related to the court how ten years earlier he had been warned about this man.[266]

Aside from blackmail and (mob) violence against sodomites – the latter becoming more frequent from the second half of the eighteenth century on – did the people in the streets have so little response to what was happening around them? Was it true that sodomites before 1730 were fully integrated into a city such as Leiden, as one Dutch historian has claimed?[267] The latter hardly seems likely, given the annoyance sodomites caused in their surroundings. An answer to this apparent indifference is to be found in the social cohesion in neighborhoods in the cities.

City neighborhoods throughout most of early modern Europe were tightly organized. They had their own annual festivities and neighborhood meals. Many had a kind of judiciary system according to which inhabitants could be fined for breaking certain rules, and neighborhood masters could arbitrate in conflicts in their judiciary. Neighbors often interfered in what we would consider private life, for instance, in marital problems and conflicts. In terms of social control and imposing discipline, such neighborhoods were much more effective than a city's administration or court could ever be.[268] In fact, one might suspect that they were competing with more official institutions and that people in the streets often preferred to settle problems – sometimes violently so – without the interference of official authorities. As some testimonies and confessions in 1730 show, people in the neighborhoods had effective means to isolate those who were a nuisance. Several of the men who were arrested that year in The Hague described how they had been warned of the company of certain men who had the reputation of being sodomites in their neighborhood. They also described not wanting to be seen with such men or visiting them only when it was dark.[269]

The other side of this coin was that to indict a neighbor or, indeed, turn him in to the authorities would have disrupted the neighborhood's cohesion. It was one thing to avoid a neighbor but another to see him hang on the gallows. Even if the public showed up in great numbers for public executions, people probably experienced such executions as dramatic events in the community about which one would not think lightly. Some neighborhood people even helped wanted men to escape. In 1764 Hendrik Eelders was warned that servants of the bailiff in Amsterdam had made inquiries about him, and he and his partner left the city in a hurry.[270] When in 1775 a bailiff of the Court of Holland and some of his helpers were seen sneaking around the house of Frans Hengstenberg, a sodomite, he was warned by a neighbor and managed to get away in time.[271]

Those who were family had particularly good reason to help a relative escape. At the same time the bailiff tried to arrest Hengstenberg, a colleague failed to do so with another suspect, whose relatives violently resisted his arrest.[272] Aside from the sometimes obvious affection they felt for such a relative, which would be reason enough to help him escape, it could also be in the interest of the family to do so: the defamation of a scaffolding or imprisonment of a brother, son or husband was felt by the family as well and could threaten their livelihood, as any loss of honor could. In 1732, a man in Utrecht complained that his neighbors constantly pestered him with the fact that his brother had been executed for sodomy.[273]

Whatever members of the public knew before 1730 about how courts dealt with sodomites, many obviously did not expect much good from it, as is to be seen from some of the early blackmail cases. As early as the late 1680s, four young blackmailers had for some years successfully extorted men whom they accused of sodomy. As one of those blackmailers said in court, he had learned from a friend that one need only make such accusations, regardless of whether they were true.[274] The victims would not dare to go to the authorities. When in 1735 several men were arrested

in Amsterdam, it was discovered that for ten years they had conducted such activities.[275] As the citizen Jacob Bicker Raije noted
in his diary after one of these blackmailers was hanged, they often
had made their accusations on "a loose foot."[276]

Especially after the second half of the eighteenth century, violence against sodomites became more frequent when they were
caught in the act (like Christiaan Kip in 1749) or when they had
made a pass at the wrong people. In 1774, neighbors who knew
about his whereabouts spoke of a man in The Hague who often
came home "picked and battered."[277] By the end of the eighteenth
century, it was often mentioned during trials that men who had
the reputation of sodomites had been beaten up, sometimes by
gangs of youngsters and, as it turned out, sometimes by constables.
In 1826 in Amsterdam a man charged with public indecency was
brought all battered into court. When asked why he looked this
way, he said that the police officers who had brought him to
court had purposely taken him through crowded streets. The
man, who had suffered convictions on the same charges before,
also complained about being maltreated by fellow inmates while
in prison.[278] Ten men, convicted in the same year in Amsterdam, mustered the courage to appeal their verdicts, which meant
that they were chained to other prisoners and taken by foot
to The Hague amid the abuse of the public.[279] Half of the way
there, at their arrival in Leiden, two of these men were wounded
by bystanders.[280]

It was also at the end of the eighteenth century that some
moral entrepreneurs set out to find out on their own account
about sodomites and the places they gathered. In 1809 a few such
entrepreneurs were responsible for the arrest of six men, who
with many others were known to gather in the house of a cobbler
in Amsterdam. The leader of the group who set out to explore
these gatherings used to visit them each time in the presence of
another witness, so that, once the arrests were made, several men
could give testimony against the culprits. Whether it was just
moral indignation that inspired him remains unclear. Several times
he had been convicted for violence, and it may well be that he
wanted to flatter the court or hoped for a reward.[281]

Despite what has been said before about the apparent indifference of the public and about the way in which the public settled their scores with sodomites in the neighborhoods where they lived, the prosecutions in general would find the support of the public, even if the public did not have a hand in them. Especially in 1730, many poems were composed praising judicial authorities for their pursuit of sodomites. Although most of these poems were written by hack writers who had an interest in flattering the authorities, like the more scholarly publications they found a ready market. Yet as I pointed out earlier, this support was not unconditional. If the public was not convinced of the convicts' guilt, people could turn violently, either against the judges, as happened in 1731 with the trials that were held by Rudolph de Mepsche, or against those who made the accusations. The latter occurred in 1757 when the Church minister Andreas Klink was arrested. The public also complained when it felt that equal justice was not given to all. In 1733 an anonymous letter to the Court of Holland claimed that a man who had fled Amsterdam in 1730 and returned a year later (only to be arrested) was murdered while on trial because he knew too much about gentlemen in the city council.[282] The official reading was that the man had committed suicide.[283] When one of the most important soap boilers in Amsterdam, who was also related to several patrician families in the city, was "only" sent into permanent exile from the city on same-sex charges in 1776, many of the citizens grumbled that his sentence was too light. This public attitude worried the court considerably, as the diary of one of the judges shows.[284]

By the end of the eighteenth century public support for the prosecutions presumably grew, as the gap between the courts and the people became less pronounced. In most of that century, patricians who sat in the courts administered justice on no account but their own. Usually their verdicts read that the behavior of the culprit "was not to be suffered in a city of justice." After the founding of the Batavian Republic in 1795, a more democratic system arose, and from then on judges, who often came from the middle classes and who for a decade had played an active role in the democratic uprisings, administered justice on behalf of the people and the republic.

All through the period described here the public had its own strategies toward sodomites that sometimes coincided with those of the authorities but just as often could differ considerably. Such a condition raises the final questions to be answered here: Did the public not share in the fears that were avowed by ecclesiastical and secular authorities, and did it endorse the meanings that these authorities applied to sodomites? In other words, did the public have a concept of a third gender or sex?

Fears over God's imminent wrath may have flared when in 1730 the extent of the sodomite network became known to the public. Yet, since divine interference was constantly felt in life and society, as the Church ministers always emphasized, and probably often in an incomprehensible way, a certain fatalism may have prevailed. On the other hand, since the destruction of the country often predicted by these shepherds had never occurred, many people may have felt that things would not take such a dramatic turn, as the Church minister van Byler astutely observed in his book in 1731. Fears flared, indeed, but not exactly as the ecclesiastics wanted. Many may have certainly felt that the country was invaded by a kind of fifth column, but the fears had more to do with rumors about secret trials and executions – which caused the states of Holland to issue the bill about public executions – and with rumors about the way in which upper-class people escaped prosecution than with a deeply felt fear of the imminent ruin of the country. After all, if rumors about secret executions were true, how could one be sure that the accusations against those who were tried were reliable? Couldn't anyone be the next to be arrested?

Everyone who had ever witnessed a public execution knew that the garroting of a sodomite meant that he was treated as a woman and as a coward. Nonetheless, it took time before the public would endorse such ideas. The poems that were published in 1730 on the occasion of the executions did not speak of effeminacy. Sodomites, in this folk literature, were presented as men who kept their seed from their wives, as women haters.[285] It was probably a notion that prevailed in these parts of Europe, as suggested by the title of a late-seventeenth-century English tract about sodomy, *The Women Hater's Lamentation*.[286] The introduction of a Dutch panegyric from 1730 on the beauty and virtues of women, a response to another book in which women were described as idle, crabby and fickle, said that the author of the latter "must belong to that damned seed, about which one to his grief, has heard so much in these sad days."[287] The pamphleteer Jakob Campo Weyerman, a mediator between elite and folk cultures, presented the only exception in folk literature. His opinion in these matters even anticipated those of official authorities by several decades, though he seemed to have had trouble phrasing it accurately: "everyone knows that this scum never has a masculine glance, nor a harsh voice; it is as cowardly as an incarcerated whore, and as cajoling as an impoverished nobleman who toadies a rich farmer for a midday or an evening meal."[288] In general, however, effeminacy in the public mind in the early part of the eighteenth century was probably still the hallmark of the womanizer, not the sodomite.

The folk literature of 1730 hardly dealt with the causes of same-sex behavior. References to a general sinfulness were enough. For most hack writers who wanted to flatter the authories, it would not have been wise to suggest what Church ministers said in cautious terms, and Weyerman said explicitly: that the rich and the powerful were most to blame because they had seduced their social inferiors.[289] Nevertheless, the public at large, including Weyerman, seems to have shared what I described earlier as a folk psychology: excess in eating, drinking and dress lead to all kinds of debauchery and ultimately to sodomy, and once someone had a taste of it, he would burn in lust for more. Curiously enough, the public did not apply this to the sodomites they knew about but rather to others, such as Freemasons. Freemasons, with their secret societies, were supposed to indulge in orgies of food and drink and therefore were thought to be or to become sodomites.[290] Yet while in official culture and in the symbolic universe indulgence, excess and hedonism constituted "an effeminate disease," in the public mind, at least in the first half of the eighteenth century, they were unrelated.

However, the discourse that began in 1730 and in which the public executions played such an important role had its effect on public opinion. As I said earlier, by the mid-eighteenth century the sodomite was considered a whore. When the burglar, thief and prostitute Jan ten Engel in 1750 said among other things that one could recognize "those folks" by their effeminate behavior and "the whorish looks in their eyes," he distanced his own desires from those whom he sexually obliged as much as he seems to have given expression to culturally recognizable features. The effeminate man by now was a he-whore, and a he-whore was a sodomite. In 1764 the Amsterdam bookseller Hermanus van Werkhoven, when tried for sodomy, related how once in the neighborhood of the city hall, one of the sites shared by sodomites and female prostitutes, he had been chased by street boys – much as they might pester whores – while they shouted "Hendrijn, Hendrijn" (a female derivative of his own name).[291] The effeminate man, as a sodomite, had become a recognizable species who as an official outcast had to face public violence, not for his acts per se but for what he was understood to be.

Conclusion

After a long era in which same-sex behavior predominantly occurred in hierarchical relationships, such as between adults and adolescents, which determined sexual roles, at the end of the seventeenth century this pattern rapidly changed. Same-sex behavior occurred more and more on an equal footing between adults who often would reverse "active" and "passive" roles in the same session. This change was probably due to what Trumbach called a gender revolution that took place in the same period. Patriarchal relationships between the sexes in northwestern Europe – northern France, England and Holland – gave way to egalitarian relationships and marriages based on mutual love and a growing appreciation of women's roles as spouse, mother and guardian of domesticity.

Along with the change in same-sex behavior came the emergence in this part of Europe of sodomite subcultures – networks, meeting sites, a sodomite parlance, body language and, without overlooking personal variety, a sodomite role – in which men from all strata of society participated.

When the extent of these subcultures was discovered in the Netherlands in 1730, it resulted in sometimes fierce persecutions that were to last well into the nineteenth century, even when sodomy itself no longer constituted a crime. Moreover, after several centuries of an official silence on the subject of same-sex behavior that was to prevent people from taking part in such behavior, with the persecution of sodomites a discourse about this behavior began that was to both educate and deter people. In this discourse sodomites at first became represented as a third gender in the society, which conceptualized the existence of only one sex, of complete male and incomplete female bodies. Popular psychology held that men who had given in to excess and gluttony and who (like women) had become insatiable would turn to sodomy, and once they had committed a same-sex act would continue the behavior. Gradually, when notions about the existence of two different biological sexes grew, the sodomite, as an effeminate man and a "he-whore," became a third sex, although in official discourse he blamed this condition on his lewd behavior. Sodomites themselves, who were able to consider themselves morally responsible beings – often devout men – despite the eternal damnation called upon them, started to offer resistance in the sense that they claimed the innateness of their condition, which was increasingly expressed in gendered terms. The public at large was the least articulate on this matter: by the mid-eighteenth century sodomites were indeed considered whores, a despicable species, which they remained well into this century. With different nuances the discourse that began in 1730 in the Netherlands contributed to the emergence of a popular belief about a third sex that eventually found a "scientific" articulation in the nineteenth-century medical discourse on homosexuality by people like Karl Westphal and Karl Heinrich Ulrichs.

212

CHAPTER FOUR

"A Female Soul in a Male Body":

Sexual Inversion as Gender Inversion

in Nineteenth-Century Sexology

Gert Hekma

Introduction

Theories of homosexuality as a third sex gained ground in the second half of the nineteenth century, culminating with the *sexuelle Zwischenstufen* ("intermediate sexual types") of Magnus Hirschfeld around 1900.[1] Hirschfeld, who was central in the debate over the nature of homosexuality, also coined the term *Transvestiten*.[2] Since the turn of the century, the emerging received opinion had come to hold that "homosexuals" indeed belonged to a third sex of feminine men and masculine women. Representatives of "Uranians" or "homosexuals," such as Karl Heinrich Ulrichs, began to speak of themselves as feminine and belonging to a third sex and to transform this idea into a biological theory – which built on certain modes of behavior developed in the cultures of the "sodomites" and "mollies" of those and earlier days – on the origins of homosexuality. In the wake of Ulrichs, physicians followed suit and reframed his theory for medical use.

With the burgeoning of sexology in the second half of the nineteenth century, many new concepts and explanations were brought forth. New terms for same-sex preferences were constructed: *"philopédie," "Urninge," "homosexual," "conträre Sexual-empfindung,"* which was translated into French and English as "sexual inversion."[3] Most sexual concepts that have shaped our consciousness date from this period: exhibitionism, fetishism, sadomasochism and pedophilia as well as heterosexuality. Similarly, the terms *sexual* and *sexuality* achieved their present meaning around this time.

Homosexuality was most often explained as a kind of inborn gender inversion and was called a "hermaphrodisy of the mind." But to what extent may one view the sexual inversion of that period as a third gender?[4] To explore this question, I shall review the development of theories of same-sex preferences from the 1840s through around World War I. Further, I shall discuss specific features of the "pederasts'" worlds in relation to the new theories of homosexuality and the third-sex traits attributed to homosexuals, or Uranians.

Early Medical Theories of "Philopédie"

In 1848, the French sergeant Bertrand raped and mutilated the corpses of women he exhumed from their graves. It was a scandalous and widely publicized case, but its notoriety was even further prolonged by physicians who discussed his case in terms of an autonomous psychiatric disease, namely, an "erotic monomania." Sexual aberrations had long since been considered in terms of either cultural defects or the results of insanity, but with Bertrand, ideas about deviant sexual forms began to change dramatically.

Previously, psychiatrists had never shown much interest in sexuality. Since the time of S.A.D. Tissot, the predominant belief was that masturbation led to all kinds of physical and psychic defects, while the "heinous sin" itself resulted from failures in child development and rearing.[5] Further, physicians often indicated that varying types of mental diseases were due to "excesses in drinking and sex." This in itself may have been an accurate assumption, for many inmates of the asylums did in fact suffer from advanced cases of syphilis, generally identified as "*dementia paralytica*," a recognized malady whose origin from venereal diseases was as yet unknown. As venereal diseases were mostly attributed to unrespectable behaviors, physicians paid very little attention to their causes. For similar reasons, masturbation was less a topic for respectable doctors than for educators or quacks. Physicians belonged to a rising profession that did not want to sully its image by discussing sexuality. For example, in *La Médecine des passions* (1841) J.B.F. Descuret discussed the passions of drinking and playing cards for money and fame, but he had little to say about the sexual passions.[6] When sexuality was discussed by psychiatrists in their systems of insanity, it was only in terms of erotomania, nymphomania and satyriasis. Erotomania referred to an excessive erotic imagination, mostly attributed to women who supposed certain men to be in love with them. Nymphomania and satyriasis referred to excessive sexual desire in women and men, respectively.

The only medical arena in which sexuality received attention (other than ideas on masturbation and insanity) was in forensic medicine. Sexual crimes received some attention in important textbooks, which discussed rape and problems regarding childbirth and sodomy. The major text of the 1840s on sodomy was Heinrich Kaan's dissertation, which bore the promising title *Psychopathia sexualis*.[7] Following Tissot, he believed that masturbation was the origin of all perversions and was itself the result of excessive fantasy. A vast array of secondary factors were also considered significant, including lustful parents, a sanguine temperament, the wrong living environment, bad food and a poor education. Kaan's theory, however, was very traditional, and the contents of his book did not fulfill the prospects of its precocious title.

In 1849, Claude François Michéa wrote an article on the case of Bertrand and thus became the first to modernize the theory of perversions. Even though Michéa's classification was traditional and based on the listings of forensic medicine, his explanation was completely new. Perversions, he stated, were inborn and, as such, were to be considered physiological failings. His primary example was not Bertrand's necrophilia but the Parisian pederast subculture. He spoke about *philopédie* ("love of boys") and defined its practitioners as effeminate men looking for same-sex relations.[8] Given the recent findings of remnants of a uterus in men by the German doctor E.H. Weber – whose research was cited but whose name was not mentioned in the article – Michéa hypothesized that the feminine habits and preferences of same-sex lovers were perhaps rooted in biology. The effeminacy of the sodomites had of course been known for some time, and Honoré de Balzac had even called them a third sex.[9] Michéa was the first, however, to

develop fully the theory that *philopédie* was an inborn phenomenon, and he thereby provided the basis of an identity and physiologically explained the effeminacy of these odd males.

Following Michéa, the medical literature on homosexuality
grew quickly, and many authors supported and sustained his biological theory. In the 1850s, Johann Ludwig Casper, for instance,
renewed discussion about the hermaphrodisy of the pederast's
mind, which could explain a minority of the cases of same-sex
behavior. He first wrote about pederasty in the inaugural issue
of his journal *Vierteljahrsschrift für gerichtliche und öffentliche Medicin*
(Quarterly for forensic and public medicine) and later in the second volume of his influential *Handbuch der gerichtlichen Medicin*
(Handbook of forensic medicine).[10] In the former, he discusses
eleven cases of pederasty, three of which are characterized by
effeminacy. According to Casper, this sexual inclination (*"geschlechtliche Hinneigung"*) is in only a few of the cases inborn and
in most a result of "saturation" by normal sex, a traditional view
of lewdness. Received opinion held that men who indulged in
lustful behavior outside marriage stumbled from one perversion
to another. Thus, for example, Kaan defined onanism as the *pars
pro toto* of perversions, meaning that persons who began with masturbation went on to more extreme sexual outrages.[11]

Before Casper discussed pederasty in his handbook as a possible
hermaphrodisy of the mind, many other physicians had already
addressed sodomy. To detect the act of sodomy they relied on traditional evidence, for example the injuries it caused to the passive partner's anus.[12] Such damage was, however, not considered
definitive proof of sodomy, because the same results could derive
from other causes, such as constipation. Casper's Parisian colleague Ambroise Tardieu opposed the theory of pederasty as a psychic hermaphrodisy in his *Etude médico-légale sur les attentats aux
moeurs*; he was convinced that proofs of "the passive habits of pederasty and sodomy" were to be found, among others, in the relax-
ation of the sphincter of the anus and the effacement of the folds
surrounding it.[13]

The old theory of sodomy concerned sexual acts and effects;
the new theory of homosexuality was about identities and causes.

Tardieu was a man of the past, remaining in the tradition of forensic medicine; Michéa and Casper, on the other hand, marked the beginnings of forensic psychiatry, for they were interested in mental causes of criminal behavior, just as Tardieu was interested in the consequences of crimes. The power system underlying law and medicine was changing, and medical theory mirrored these changes. Traditionally, forensic medicine was an auxiliary science for judges; now forensic psychiatry took the initiative. Discussions ensued about the "personality of the criminal," as in Cesare Lombroso's theory of the "born criminal," and later about the "sex pervert," as was found in Richard von Krafft-Ebing's *Psychopathia sexualis* (1886).[14] In earlier theories, masturbation and other forms of lewdness led to diseases of the neural system and the brain; according to the new theories, inborn brain deformations led to same-sex preferences. For a brief period, in the 1850s, the two theories clashed, but the forensic discussion of the signs of sodomy soon became outdated and the psychiatric debate on sexual perversions came to the fore.[15]

Thus, in the 1850s theories of sexual behavior and preference changed as did the medical practice related to them. For the first time, forensic experts based their knowledge on real cases of pederasty. Most prior literature had done without practical examples, but both Casper and Tardieu cited the many men they had seen on trial. The new theories seem to have been the consequence of a more active pursuit of deviants on the part of the police; the number of cases of pederasty reported in medical journals grew quickly.

The earliest texts on *philopédie* and pederasty by Michéa and Casper underlined the effeminacy of some same-sex practitioners. For example, the *homo mollis* ("soft man") described by Hieronymus Fränkel in 1853 would today be called a transvestite as well as a homosexual: Süsskind (Friederike) Blank was a man who dressed as a woman and seduced young men. Although he was convicted for unnatural fornication, he nevertheless continued to infect youngsters with venereal diseases. Fränkel's report on Blank was empirically grounded, in the tradition of forensic medicine. His explanation for the gender inversion was simple: as a tailor

Blank became addicted to the habits and sexual role of the female sex. There was nothing in his report about physiological predestination or inborn preferences.[16]

The next important article, which appeared in 1855 in Casper's journal, was written by F. Dohrn about a sixty-seven-year-old pederast who lived in a home for the destitute. He sexually abused five boys between the ages of seven and sixteen years with whom he had been allowed to sleep. The article focused on the evidence of sodomy. Regarding this man's personal history, mention was made that his former neighbors called him a *Zwitter* ("hermaphrodite"). After noticing that his home was regularly visited by a young man and discovering from his wife that she was not the one who entertained adulterous relations with this visitor, their distrust was directed toward the husband, whom they presumed to be a hermaphrodite as well as a pederast. But neither Dohrn nor Casper made the connection between same-sex behavior and hermaphroditism as the neighbors had. In his afterword to the article, Casper discusses three new cases of pederasty that have nothing to do with effeminacy.[17]

Physicians were the first to write about sexual aberrations, albeit reluctantly. Although the authors said they did not like to soil their pens with dirty topics, they knew that, as heirs to the Enlightenment, scientists were obligated to discuss every topic, even the filthiest of crimes. However, same-sex practitioners soon began to reject the charge of sin and abomination made against them. To break the spell of crime and folly, they invented new and more appropriate names for themselves, such as Uranian and homosexual.

Ulrichs and Uranism
In the 1860s, the lawyer Karl Heinrich Ulrichs began to publish on same-sex preferences. His work was essential to the innovative theory of same-sex attraction and the emancipation of homosexuality, which he called "Uranism." Ulrichs described Uranians as a third sex whose gender traits were inverted; a Uranian himself, he defended his preferences as being inborn. Uranism was his neologism, and he also spoke of the third sex ("*das dritte Geschlecht*").

Ulrichs began to explain his preferences in letters to his family, which date from the end of 1862.[18] In these letters, he compared his attraction to men with that felt by heterosexual women. According to Ulrichs, men were endowed with specifically male features, and he mentioned nine: male organs, lack of breasts, Adam's apple, male body and voice, beard, manly habitus, male inclinations and "sexual love drive" (*"geschlechtliche Liebestrieb"*) for women; he explained further that some of these features were absent in Uranians.[19] The idea of two completely different sexes was mistaken: there had always been not only hermaphrodites but also male persons who lacked some or most of these traits. Uranians definitely lacked the final attribute but also many other male qualities, as was clear for Ulrichs from his own case as well as from the six other Uranians he knew at this time. For him, Uranians formed a third sex.

The Uranian sex drive, according to Ulrichs, was inborn, since it developed early, before a child could decide on his sexual predilections.[20] He strongly claimed his right to such a drive: "The Dionian [heterosexual] majority has no right to construct the human society as exclusively Dionian; such construction of it is only scandalous abuse, because we have as much rights as you in the human society."[21] Uranians certainly had the right to sexual expression, but Ulrichs was not sure under what circumstances and in what form.[22] When he asked his family whether he should publish his ideas anonymously, they answered decidedly and unanimously in the negative. Nevertheless, within two years he started to publish his work, and after some years he even wrote under his own name.

Because of his writings, Ulrichs's formula of Uranism became world famous. The Uranian, he said, was an *"anima muliebris in corpore virili inclusa"* – a female soul enclosed in a male body. Ulrichs primarily discussed the male Uranian, although he later paid some attention to the lesbian, the *"Urninde."* His goal was to contribute not to sexual physiology but to legal reform:[23] "unnatural fornication" was a heavily penalized crime in the leading German state, Prussia, although not in others, such as Bavaria. Ulrichs feared that impending German unification would lead to the extension of Prussian law to all of Germany, and he developed his theory to fight the introduction of the "unnatural fornication" provision in a new law. He did not, however, succeed: in 1871, "unnatural fornication" became a crime throughout Germany, under the infamous paragraph 175, which still exists today, albeit in changed form.[24]

The physiological theory of Uranism had many aspects, the most interesting of which was the definition of Uranism as same-sex attraction combined with gender inversion. But compared with other third-gender forms, the inversion was limited: only the soul, not the body, belonged to the other sex. Of course, the dichotomy of body and soul was problematic, and this aspect of Ulrichs's theory was ridiculed by one of his critics.[25] Ulrichs took it for granted that the male body also showed some feminine qualities; his successor, Magnus Hirschfeld, believed this more firmly. For Ulrichs, the most important sign of gender inversion was sexual preference. This, however, was not very visible in signs of the body or of the mind. Ulrichs defended his theory with recent claims that hermaphrodisy originated in the first three months of pregnancy, positing that Uranism had a similar origin. The soul rather than the body became hermaphroditic in the case of the Uranian fetus.[26]

The most remarkable thing about the Uranian soul may well have been its hidden quality. A female soul was not a visible sign of gender inversion, and the male body did not indicate anything either. Clearly different from other third-gender forms such as the berdache or the hijra, the Uranian may have been effeminate but did not necessarily show any signs of it. To the contrary, he had good reason to hide his presumed female qualities. There was no institutional recognition of the third gender in Western Europe, and effeminacy could cause problems in employment, housing and family relations.

In this respect, the case of Carl Ernst Wilhelm von Zastrow is particularly noteworthy. A contemporary of Ulrichs, Zastrow had served a long prison sentence for sexual attacks on two boys. The main proof of his guilt was his same-sex preference. During the trial, many young working-class men, who were certainly much older than the assaulted boys, testified that the accused had had or tried to have sex with them. These testimonies provided crucial circumstantial evidence for establishing the guilt of the accused. Zastrow's pride in his acquaintance with Ulrichs's work was seen as a supplementary indication of his culpability by the police and the judges. He died in prison for crimes he probably had not committed. Zastrow's case clearly illustrates the contempt that existed for men who loved men and the utter lack of understanding of their desires.[27]

The next step Ulrichs dared to take in his theoretical work was to defend the moral rightness of sexual relations between Uranian men and Dionian young men.[28] As female prostitution was allowed and even medically regulated in many places in Europe, Ulrichs thought comparable relations between Uranians and Dionian youngsters should be permitted. He insisted not only on decriminalization of Uranism but also on the legality of such sexual relations, because he believed most Uranians desired sex with Dionians. Since sexual desire was then defined as attraction between opposites (male and female), Ulrichs believed that it was impossible for two Uranian men with preferences for men to fall in love with each other: "Is a Uranian sexually attracted to a Uranian? A little or not at all." They were as little attracted to each other as they were to women, for whom they felt abhorrence in sexual matters. The Uranian's object of desire was a person who was male in body and soul, that is, a Dionian.[29] Ulrichs recast the dichotomy of female and male desire into a theory of the Uranian lover and his Dionian beloved. This part of his theory attracted strong criticism from, for example, Rudolf Virchow and Alois Geigel, who were scandalized by such a suggestion.[30]

The rich sexual reality of Uranian lives undermined Ulrichs's dogmatic theory. As he relied on his experience more than on the classical examples he cited profusely (he was also the editor of the last European journal in Latin), he was obliged to adapt his theory to the diversity of same-sex experiences. Both the female appearance of Uranians and the sexual availability of straight boys may have been prominent and visible aspects of the underworlds during the time when same-sex relations flourished in the German states. But neither prominence nor visibility is a good guide for a complete picture of such attachments, whether in the nineteenth or twentieth century. With his growing knowledge of Uranian lives and the information he received in many letters from Uranians all over the world, Ulrichs was forced to adapt his theory. He made a place for *Uranodioninge* ("bisexuals") and *Uraniaster* ("circumstantial homosexuals"), and he further distinguished three kinds of Uranism. "*Männlinge*," more masculine Uranians, fell in love with younger feminine boys, contrasted with "*Weiblinge*," the effeminate Uranians, who loved masculine (young) men; in between was a group, part masculine and part feminine, whose sexual object was young males.[31] Especially in this last example, Ulrichs goes beyond the theory of sexual desire as opposition, because the difference between the Uranian (halfway between *Männlinge* and *Weiblinge*) and the young adult (between the state of boy and man) is not as sharp as it is in Ulrichs's other examples.[32]

After Ulrichs: Sexual Psychopathy
In 1869 and 1870, the novelist Karl Maria Kertbeny wrote two leaflets against the prospect of renewed criminalization of "unnatural fornication," for which he coined the term "homosexual." His approach was similar to Ulrichs's, his most important contribution being the new term.[33] While the theory was seductive, the social consequences were not. Since 1870, many psychiatrists had started to write on sexual perversions in line with Ulrichs's theory, but few endorsed wholeheartedly his plea for decriminalization. Rudolf Virchow, the leading German professor of medicine, advised (along with other physicians) the minister of justice to do away with the criminalization of sodomy and masturbation – because these acts did no harm from a medical point of view.[34] But medical doctors were much more interested in pathologizing perversions than in decriminalizing sodomy. Ulrichs's emancipatory policy was not at all successful, and it was not until 1900 that it received wide recognition, well after Ulrichs had died in exile in Italy. But his natural theory of Uranism became very popular among psychiatrists, much to his distress.

In the 1870s in Germany, the 1880s in France and soon after throughout Europe, sexual psychopathy became fashionable in psychiatric circles. Every important figure in French psychiatry published articles and books on it in the 1880s: Alexander Lacassagne, Lombroso's main opponent in criminal anthropology; Lacassagne's student Julien Chevalier, who wrote the first dissertation on sexual inversion in 1885; Alfred Binet, the inventor of both the intelligence test and fetishism as a sexual category; Valentin Magnan, the main theoretician of degeneration; Jean-Martin Charcot, the specialist on hysteria and Freud's teacher; Benjamin Ball, the first professor of psychiatry in Paris; and Paul Moreau of Tours, who was the first to publish a book on the topic, *Des aberrations du sens génésique* (Aberrations of the reproductive sense).[35] Krafft-Ebing was of course the main proponent of the new science of sexual aberrations; he began his research at Ulrichs's suggestion. Lombroso, the senator Paolo Mantegazza and Arrigo Tamassia in Italy; Benjamin M. Tarnowsky in Russia; Havelock Ellis and John Addington Symonds in England; and Nicolaas Bernard Donkersloot and Arnold Aletrino in the Netherlands were other specialists who began to work on sexual perversions.[36]

The discussion on prostitution also paved the way for sexology. After this, the debate on sexual variations, which had been taboo until then, became public and political. And because of the increasing prosecution of sexual crimes in the main cities of Europe, cases of sexual perversion were brought before doctors, who thus played an increasingly important role in the criminal process. The first cases of sexual aberration came to the attention of psychiatrists who were asked by the police or by the courts to give expert opinions. At the same time, medical science developed an interest in social and thus sexual issues, and new specializations such as public hygiene or medical policy were established. It was this growing attention to sexual variations that made it possible for someone like Ulrichs to speak out in the first person on Uranism.

Until 1890 sexology was a German and French discipline, but thereafter it became an international discipline, with Germany leading in the field. The term *Sexualwissenschaft* ("sexology") was introduced in 1908,[37] while the generic term until that time, "sexual psychopathy," was derived from the title of Krafft-Ebing's book. The main subject of this science was initially sexual inversion, as the subtitle of this same book indicated, "with special attention to the contrary sexual feeling." In what follows I shall untangle how this interest in sexual inversion developed in psychiatric circles.

Sexual Inversion in Sexual Psychopathy

Ulrichs's books of the 1860s, in which he propagated his ideas on Uranism, were crucial in the emerging discussion on homosexuality, and his formula of a "female soul in a male body" was cited by most subsequent authors. The first important case study following Ulrichs's work was an article about "*conträre Sexualempfindung*" (usually translated as "sexual inversion," but translated literally as "contrary sexual feeling") by Karl Friedrich Otto Westphal, which appeared in 1869 in the second volume of the influential *Archiv für Psychiatrie und Nervenkrankheiten*. Westphal, the first professor of psychiatry in Berlin and editor of the journal, discussed two examples: a woman attracted to other women, and a male cross-dresser. The lesbian was, according to Westphal, a normal female in her physiognomy and habitus. Her only abnormality was her sexual inclination (*Neigung*) for women. The male cross-dresser walked the streets to get money from men, but never admitted to "unnatural" behavior, either to the police or to the doctors. He was often apprehended for minor crimes, mostly thefts. The only effeminate characteristic of the cross-dresser, aside from his clothing, was his voice; otherwise he showed no signs of gender inversion.

Westphal discussed the lesbian and the cross-dresser as cases of contrary sexual feeling, even though the male cross-dresser was apparently heterosexual. While Westphal often cited the works of Ulrichs – especially his remarks on the Uranian's feeling of gender inversion – neither of his cases could be explained by the theory of sexual inversion, for the lesbian was a normal female biologically and the cross-dresser was a heterosexual man. Westphal insisted that both cases revealed a neuro- or psychopathic condition, but, in the absence of other signs of pathology, he could not prove that the contrary sexual feeling existed as "a completely isolated phenomenon."[38] If, in fact, the contrary sexual feeling was independent of other pathologies, an assumption that Ulrichs himself had made, then the Uranian's struggle for emancipation would have been a much easier task. But with these innovations, same-sex behavior could now be medicalized and pathologized. Westphal's text is pivotal in its discussion of homosexuality because it poses the question of the pathology of these feelings. In later discussions, physicians refuted the importance of this question, taking the pathological character of the "contrary sexual feeling" for granted. After this, Uranians like Ulrichs had to struggle not only against the criminalization of same-sex behavior but also against the pathologization of homosexual desires.

The main points of the debate ensuing after Westphal's article were as follows: First, the doctors discussed the explanation of sexual inversion, alternating between Westphal's neuropathology and psychopathology. F. Servaes considered inversion a neuropathic condition, caused by insufficient nutrition.[39] Second, all physicians considered these cases to be contaminated by feeble-mindedness. There seems to be a simple explanation for this. In the beginning, only the more ignorant and awkward practitioners were arrested by the police and were thus caught in the psychiatric web. No one discussed Westphal's question as to whether this abnormality was an independent phenomenon, thus the pathology of all cases of sexual inversion was confirmed by omission and consensus. This made it more difficult to defend Uranism and implied the beginning of the medicalization of homosexuality. Third, while gender inversion was always discussed, and psychiatrists claimed to have found gender-inverted behavior, the bodies of the men and women never showed clear signs of the other sex. Practices, not bodies, betrayed the contrary sexual feelings. All of this seemed to confirm Ulrichs's statement that only the soul of the Uranian showed gender inversion.[40]

Krafft-Ebing's first article on sexual anomalies appeared in 1877. In it he discussed all published cases and claimed that sexual inversion was both a neuro- and psychopathic condition, both hereditary and coexistent with other insanities. In his list of "remarkable features" of sexual inversion, attraction to the same sex figured only as the sixth item; he assumed that men were attracted to men as if they were women, while women attracted to women should feel like men. Homosexual preference and gender inversion were completely intertwined, a combination that Krafft-Ebing did not leave open to discussion. The cross-dresser of Westphal was the only case that did not exhibit a combination of the two. Krafft-Ebing added three nondistinct cases of his own to the repertory of sexual inverts in psychiatry.[41]

Although gender inversion was central to the theories of Uranism proposed by most psychiatrists, they had to acknowledge, as Ulrichs had, that there were more types of same-sex attraction than that described by the typical effeminacy of the Uranian. In *Psychopathia sexualis*, Krafft-Ebing distinguished four types of inborn homosexuality, from "psychosexual hermaphrodisy" (bisexuality) to androgyny, and three varieties of learned homosexuality, of which "*metamorphosis sexualis paranoica*" (something like transsexuality) was the extreme form. Most but not all varieties were characterized by femininity. The learned-behavior types were strongly colored by effeminacy, but the four innate types were not. Of those, bisexuality and homosexuality (an inclination only to the same sex) were not defined by the prevalence of femininity, unlike Krafft-Ebing's "effeminate" and "androgynous" types. Krafft-Ebing stated that the "homosexual anomaly" was restricted to the domain of sexual life and had no further influence on gender identity. Although this subtype was only one of seven, in his book it took up a third of the space devoted to sexual inversion.[42]

Krafft-Ebing's *Psychopathia sexualis* became the handbook of the new science of sexology, which took form in the last decades of the nineteenth century. Krafft-Ebing's model of sexual perversion and "contrary sexual feeling" was very influential, and many psychiatrists followed in his footsteps as he himself had followed in the footsteps of Ulrichs. Although not everybody accepted his mixture of gender and sexual inversion, it has nevertheless distinctly influenced the discussion on homosexuality to this day.

Sexual Inversion and the Homosexual Movement

The very first homosexual movement started in 1897 under the aegis of Magnus Hirschfeld with the Wissenschaftlich-Humanitäre Komitee (WHK). In 1899 Hirschfeld began publishing his famous *Jahrbuch für sexuelle Zwischenstufen* (Annual for sexual intermediaries), which ran until 1923. Hirschfeld was the main defender of homosexuality as a third sex, claiming that it was a natural and normal variation of sexuality. He argued, from the time of his first leaflet, published pseudonymously, that it should not be pathologized or criminalized.[43] Three years later he began his life-long struggle for homosexual emancipation under his own name, although he never "came out," or admitted that he himself was homosexual. In 1899, he sent a petition to the German Reichstag requesting the withdrawal of paragraph 175 from the criminal law.[44] In 1901, his *Jahrbuch* published an article by Krafft-Ebing in which the leading scholar of sexology – who died the next year – admitted homosexuality was always inborn and not pathological per se, as he had earlier claimed.[45]

Although Hirschfeld succeeded in gaining the support of many well-known Germans from the sciences, arts and politics for his struggle against the oppression of homosexuals, his efforts met with no success in terms of criminal reform prior to Hitler's rise to power; thereafter the situation grew only worse. Proposals both for stricter laws – the suggestion, for example, to include lesbianism under paragraph 175 – and for more lenient laws were discussed before 1933 but not enacted.

In 1899 Hirschfeld's struggle for legal reform was joined by a second journal, *Der Eigene*, which also became the title of an official movement in 1903. Adolf Brand was the leader of *"die Gemeinschaft der Eigenen"* (the community of self-owners) and the editor of the journal until its end in 1933 with Hitler's accession. This group promoted a theory of homosexuality opposed to that of Hirschfeld. For one of the early issues of *Der Eigene*, the poet and painter Elisar von Kupffer submitted a furious invective against the physicians' third-sex theory; in it he attacked the influence of medical authorities on the theory of homosexuality and their idea that homosexuals were always effeminate.[46] Inspired by the

227

Greek ideals of pederastic love and the German Romantic tradition of friendship, he stressed the masculinity of the followers of the *Lieblingsminne* and saw male homosexuals as masculine ideals for young men instead of pathological, pitiable cripples. This essay would serve as the introduction to a collection of homoerotic poetry von Kupffer published a year later, an anthology of the literary work of Greeks such as Theognis, Pindar and Plato, Romans such as Catullus and the German luminaries Goethe and Schiller.[47]

Kupffer was not alone in criticizing Hirschfeld and his theory. Other proponents of the "movement for masculine culture" eagerly joined him in opposing the theory of the third gender. The intellectual force of this group came from the biologist Benedict Friedländer, who contributed not only to *Der Eigene* but also to the *Jahrbuch*, and who collaborated with both Hirschfeld and Brand. In his *Renaissance des Eros Uranios* (1904), which became the bible of the movement, he outlined his biological theory of a virile homosexuality.[48] In an article for the *Jahrbuch*, he stressed the masculine and military capacities of male lovers and used the example of the Japanese generals who conquered the Russians in the war of 1905 to prove his theory.[49] He discerned three kinds of love: married love between men and women, the motherly love of women for children and same-sex love in friendship and pedagogics that was in general not sexual. Friedländer saw the last form of love as the foundation of social and political life, and he was critical of the emancipation of women, which he saw as undermining the beneficial impact of male love on society.[50] Priests, Jews and American culture were scolded for their tolerance of the female influences that might destroy the magnificent male culture.

Friedländer combined being Jewish and agitating against Jewish culture, defending at the same time homosexuality, masculinity and male bonding while opposing women's emancipation.[51] Not all defenders of male love were as antifeminist as Friedländer though: Edwin Bab, for example, suggested blending male and female culture while allowing space for separate male and female bonding.[52] The main argument, however, was clear: Brand's circle defended a virile, pederastic form of homosexuality, which was far removed from Hirschfeld's third gender and sexual intermediaries.

228

The split between the two movements concerned for the most part the different contents and meanings given to homosexuality. Although the views of Hirschfeld and many other "heterosexual" physicians may have had the strongest social impact, attitudes within the homosexual movement were not clearly in favor of the third sex. In the Dutch chapter of the WHK, which was founded in 1912 and survived until 1940, Hirschfeld's theory was certainly most influential,[53] but in England, John Addington Symonds and the other poets of Uranian love were inspired by classical examples and came nearer to ideals of friendship and Greek eros than to those of the third sex.[54] Edward Carpenter's "love of comrades" was rather close to the position of *Die Gemeinschaft*, although he later endorsed the theory of the third sex and set high hopes on the female qualities of men. Both Symonds and Carpenter were strongly influenced by the American poet Walt Whitman, whose poetry on love among comrades was widely acclaimed by homosexual writers and readers.[55] In France, Marc André Raffalovich had already emphasized the masculinity of the Uranians in 1895, and in the good Catholic tradition, he urged them to live in sexual abstinence.[56] André Gide developed a frankly biological theory of pederasty and beauty but discussed the effeminate homosexual, the "invert," mostly in a negative vein.[57] It appears that many homosexuals themselves were not too fond of the theory of the third sex and were rather more inclined toward ideals of friendship and pederasty.

Homosexual Worlds

The spokesmen for homosexuals may have been divided on the question of whether homosexuality should be considered a third sex or a sign of virility, but what ideas and practices existed in the worlds in which homosexuals enjoyed their pleasures? The material at our disposal has some important flaws, coming mostly from the police and psychiatrists, although some details come from autobiographies of homosexual men. It becomes clear in all these sources that there were a great variety of ways to enjoy homosexual pleasures, notwithstanding the social repression of such diversions all over Europe.

Of course, the more outlandish features of homosexual worlds were the most visible, and they thus regularly appeared in the descriptions of police officers and psychiatrists. For example, in 1862, the Parisian police officer L. Canler devoted a chapter in his memoirs to "*antiphysiques et chanteurs*" ("counternaturals and blackmailers"). His information dated from the second quarter of the nineteenth century, before the start of the large-scale persecution of sexual lewdness. Blackmail was the central topic of this chapter and perhaps one of this police officer's main activities. Canler discerned four groups of counternaturals, all with feminized names. The "*honteuses*" ("ashamed") and the "*rivettes*" ("screwers") were not discernible from normal men. The only remarkable thing about the "ashamed" was their feminine voice; similarly, the pederastic inclinations of the "screwers" made them the preferred victims of blackmailers. The two other groups were male prostitutes, the "*persilleuses*," flamboyant and effeminate mollies, and the "*travailleuses*" ("female workers"), male prostitutes with a slightly feminine style.[58] Canler's book offers a varied picture of the homosexual world with his four rather imprecise specifications, in which the effeminacy of the *antiphysiques* does play a part but is not dominant.

Twenty-five years later, Canler's colleague François Carlier published his memoirs on the "two prostitutions" in the 1860s, a large part of the book being devoted to the "*prostitution antiphysique*." His terminology of pederastic follies was completely derived from the underworlds in which these pleasures were taken up. He mentioned Canler's *rivettes, honteuses, persilleuses* and *travailleuses* but reworked his system and added some new categories, such as "*petits jésus*" for young prostitute boys and "*renifleurs*" ("smellers") for men who especially liked sex in public toilets. His definitions were a bit different; the *honteuses*, for example, now belonged under the rubric of the prostitute. Carlier's main types were the beginners, the *petits jésus*, and the older maids, often decrepit older men, *persilleuses* who had to use all their charms or even violence to earn a living from male prostitution.

Most remarkable are the stories he reported of same-sex pleasures in Paris. A normal part of this life was the masquerade balls that took place during carnival and on other occasions, when dressing in costume was allowed. These balls attracted many same-sex couples, where one of the partners would dress in drag. At one such ball police officers and the hotelier who had rented his ballroom were unable to detect, to their great astonishment, which among the veiled participants were men, although they kept close watch on this specific ball because it was rumored that it would be a pederasts' masquerade. Only because the party attracted the attention of many jealous *jésus* and their pimps did they finally learn that the "women" were excellent performers of feminine roles but pederasts nonetheless. Not all *antiphysiques* were interested in female attire. Carlier also reported that certain Parisian bars catered to men who liked to have sex with soldiers. He gave the example of a man whose entire life was devoted to the pursuit of soldiers in uniform. Another pederast's taste for violence was satisfied by enacting scenes of robbery on himself in the back alleys of Paris; he liked to have athletic men beat him up.

The examples of Canler and Carlier indicate that female clothing and styles were an important part of nineteenth-century Parisian pederasts' pleasures, but there were many other styles and desires equally present. Jeffrey Weeks confirms this fact in his article on male prostitution in London during the same period.[59] Feminine behavior was an integral part of same-sex worlds, but other modes existed simultaneously. The working-class boys and soldiers who made up a large part of male prostitution were not likely to cross-dress, nor were their clients. Flamboyant female dress would have been imprudent for homosexual men or male prostitutes in any European city; most had to hide their sexual behavior at all costs.

Hirschfeld's *Berlins dritte Geschlecht* (1905) contributed immensely to our knowledge of the world of the third sex in turn-of-the-century Berlin. Although he was a prisoner of his theory of *Zwischenstufen* and posed as an outsider to this world, he gave some interesting insights into Berlin's homosexual life. He frequented private parties, bars and restaurants, masked balls and places of male prostitution. He stressed the importance of male couples in order to emphasize homosexual respectability while ignoring the sexual side of their lives, since homosexual conduct was considered unrespectable, even criminal. Everywhere he found either happy couples or unhappy singles who were on the verge of committing suicide. Couples usually consisted of a masculine and a feminine homosexual, the latter often going in drag to private parties or masked balls. The balls were a daily occurrence in Berlin at this time.[60]

Male prostitution had three forms: "sexually normal" young men who represented a risk to homosexuals because of possible blackmail;[61] soldiers who were to be found in half a dozen bars around Berlin's military barracks and in the famous Tiergarten park; and young homosexual men who frequently came in drag to the cruising places. Similar to homosexuals who cruised soldiers were those who looked for working-class athletes in gymnastic clubs. Bathhouses were not as important to the gay world in Berlin as they were in Saint Petersburg or Vienna. Outdoor cruising seemed to be nonexistent apart from male prostitution, according to Hirschfeld's report on homosexual life in Berlin, which, however, is not a very reliable source on this point.

Although Hirschfeld was a strict defender of the theory of the third sex, it becomes clear from his own account in *Berlins dritte Geschlecht* that many Uranians did not adopt female clothing or feminine styles. All evidence points to the fact that the most important objects of sexual desire in the homosexual world of this time were masculine young men, for example, soldiers and athletes. But being attracted to virile young men did not oblige the desiring subject (the homosexual) to adopt a feminine position. There were men who enjoyed homosexual pleasures but were not "intermediate sexual types," for example, the members of *Die Gemeinschaft*. As in the case of Ulrichs, the social realities of the third-sex world did not comply with Hirschfeld's theories.

From my research in the archives of the courts in Amsterdam and The Hague and of the military court in Haarlem, most men who stood trial for same-sex offenses were of the lower class.[62] They were arrested for outdoor cruising, sex with minors or making unwelcome advances on other males. In only a few cases were these men reported to be effeminate or to have a homosexual identity. It is also clear that these cases represented only a small portion of what was going on around public toilets and in parks. Of course, homosexual acts were not criminal offenses in the Netherlands at the end of the nineteenth century, except in cases of public indecency or the seduction of minors under the age of sixteen. Nevertheless, according to my findings from these and other sources, effeminacy in men who practiced homosexuality was a rare occurrence in the Netherlands in this period. Most homosexual behavior seems to have been incidental – that is, between men and boys who had no special homosexual preferences and who came together because women were not readily available for their straight desires. Other men had pederastic desires but no feminine attributes, and some men indeed exhibited feminine qualities.[63] A survey of the archives of the Dutch asylums of Meerenberg (1880–1908) and Medemblik (1884–95) reveals that most of the approximately forty-five cases in which same-sex acts or desires were mentioned concerned the debauched; in only two cases was gender inversion suggested.[64] Such feminine men were only a small minority of the men looking for same-sex opportunities or love, according to all available information.

Even when homosexual men exhibited effete traits, as did Oscar Wilde in England, Paul Verlaine in France and Louis Couperus in the Netherlands, to give some examples from literature, their gender behavior was only partially inverted. All three were married, and although they were perhaps dandyish in their behaviors and clothing, they were rarely or never seen in drag. Their manners may have been considered effeminate by a large part of the public and attracted malicious jokes from the press, but it was clear that they were men.[65] Inversion of gender was a rare occurrence in nineteenth-century Western Europe; very few men led life in the manner described by the German physicians Fränkel and Westphal.

Conclusion
Uranian men were considered by many physicians and some of their own spokesmen to constitute a third sex. All the material

on homosexual lives, desires and acts makes clear that they were found in a bewildering variety. There were virile Uranians, there were Dionian men who ventured into the worlds of same-sex relations, where they found easier sexual satisfaction, and indeed there were effeminate Uranians. Given this variety, I shall examine four points: First, how to evaluate the contradictory information on the supposed feminine qualities of the Uranians; second, why such femininity was so stressed by doctors and by many Uranians themselves; third, what being represented as a third gender meant in regard to homosexuals; and fourth, what the importance was of effeminate habits in homosexual lives.

It is clear that the theory of the third sex had an important place among theories of homosexuality. Two leading figures of the emerging homosexual movement invented and disseminated it, and many psychiatrists contributed to its popularity. The theory was further disseminated in medical accounts and in novels, to such a degree that this model of homosexuality has influenced popular dramatic genres to this day. In this century, it has produced the most influential image of homosexual men. But there were important countercurrents, especially among homosexual intellectuals who disliked being conceptually emasculated and recast as quasi-feminine or who did not feel effeminate at all. Nevertheless, the model of the homosexual as a third sex gained ground because it was a nonthreatening representation of homosexuals for heterosexuals.

Removing the threatening representation of homosexuality seems to be the most important reason so many doctors and homosexuals endorsed this theory. It made the heinous sin of sodomy – a thought to which everyone was subject – into something harmless, transforming sodomites into nonmasculine men who could not endanger the virility of "normal" men. They were given a fixed and paltry place in the gender system, and the lustful and powerful seducers they had always been seen as faded into an image of pitiful effeminates. At a time when new models of masculinity were developing everywhere in Europe – in sports and the military, among colonialists, nationalists, socialists and Zionists – the Uranians were pushed out of the male world because of their supposed femininity.[66] At the same time, new models of sexuality developed, and it soon became clear that masculinity and homosexuality were incompatible, and that a real man thus had to be heterosexual. More and more, manliness was defined as *non*homosexual, and heterosexuality for men came to mean being masculine.

The strategies Ulrichs and Hirschfeld developed to emancipate homosexuals worked to a certain extent. Homosexuals were indeed able to find a place in society, but it was a position no other man envied. The criticisms of the theory of the third gender by the "movement for male culture" were to the point but without social effect, since most straight people preferred the idea of Uranians as effeminate cripples. In the turmoil of new definitions of sexuality and gender, homosexuals won in respectability what they lost in masculinity. Theirs was a pyrrhic victory that brought at best an equivocal identity. The sexual theories of Ulrichs, Krafft-Ebing, Hirschfeld, Carpenter and others opened the eyes of many men who discovered a new name and a new identity for themselves, which may have been the most lasting – and ambiguous – success of all the new theories on sexuality.

But what did it mean for homosexuals to belong to the third sex? It was something quite different from what the third gender elsewhere, such as the berdache or the hijra, denoted in other cultures. If we want to see the Uranians as a third gender, the best comparison would be the American Indian berdaches a half a century ago who were forced to hide their gender identity to prevent officials of the American government from discovering their status. By showing only one not very conspicuous gender attribute, they could make clear within their own culture that they were berdaches, whereas outsiders easily missed this sign.[67]

The gender inversion of homosexuals was very partial and seldom ostentatious. It was something attributed to them, but rarely taken up by them. These feminine qualities were not fixed. It could be the voice, an effete theme in clothing or a nonmasculine style in self-presentation. Uranians could to a certain extent move in and out of the role requirements of both genders. The feminine style was only for nightlife and for homosexual meeting places; neither during work nor at home would homosexuals ever show their female side. But the female soul was something that could always filter through the "normal" appearance of gay men. Belonging to the third gender brought the permanent danger of being exposed as a degenerate pervert. Male lovers were thus reluctant to show their feminine qualities, because they pointed after all to their sexual desires. Being known as effeminate was a nuisance; being known as homosexual was scandalous. The third gender was a style of life that usually inspired contempt and in special circumstances, perhaps, desire, but few people would take this position eagerly in public. Ulrichs did so, but Hirschfeld and most homosexuals publicly distanced themselves from their homosexuality. The best performers succeeded in playing with female roles.

The social endorsement of the theory of the third sex, by psychiatrists, for example, also had another effect. It made the process of "coming out" much more difficult for young men. To choose the option of homosexuality has always been very difficult: young men who were homosexually inclined not only had to defy the social opprobrium of homosexuality but also to position themselves in relation to the supposed femininity of homosexuals. Some feminine youngsters were perhaps pushed by their peers and parents into a homosexual role, which suited them perfectly. But more masculine boys had additional problems and hesitations in coming out as homosexuals, having to spurn two stigmas: the homosexual and the feminine. Even if they made the choice to come out, they continued to have good reason to hide their homosexual preference and to feel ashamed about it. In this way, the theory of sexual inversion as gender inversion helped to restrain the expression of homosexual identities and behaviors.[68]

The theory of the third sex was based on historic experiences in the subcultures of sodomites or mollies. Many sources indicate that femininity played a central role.[69] Perhaps sodomites adopted feminine styles, habits and clothes as an expression of their deep desires, but it is more likely that it was either a pose to attract the sexual attention of men from outside the subculture or a mimicry of male-female relations.

236

To understand the feminine styles of the mollies, it is important to distinguish between behavior in public and private spaces. In private places, such as molly houses, sodomites were among themselves, and the gender inversion mimicked marriage, sometimes jokingly with male prostitutes in the masculine roles, but also more seriously in expressing the wish to be a certified couple of loving men. In public places, men who desired sexual contacts with adult men probably best succeeded by taking a female position, using feminine charms, suggesting passivity. Although the goal was not to communicate their effeminacy, they did play a female role when it came to sexual encounters. Sodomites had the best chance of meeting men who were not sodomites but who quite often did not object to such sexual adventures in the streets, public toilets, bars and parks, where contacts of this sort were most often made. The reasons why men made themselves available for these encounters varied. Sometimes they did so for money or because it was the easiest way for them to obtain sexual satisfaction. Often they were foreigners (soldiers, sailors or travelers) who did not incur the same risk as locals when venturing into these places. In such dangerous encounters, the safest strategy for homosexuals was not to question the masculinity and activity of their partners. Thus, they often took a more passive and feminine position as an effective and safe strategy of seduction.

If the dichotomy of objects and subjects of sexual desire was a successful strategy, this did not mean that homosexuals were under all circumstances effeminate or that all encounters between homosexuals and heterosexuals followed this model. There were certainly homosexuals who posed as masculine, and more rarely "normally sexual" male prostitutes who posed as feminine. In research on the Amsterdam homosexual and lesbian bar culture since the 1930s, it appears that most men and women did not think of themselves as "*nichten*" or "*potten*" (comparable to "queers" and "butches"), but they nevertheless knew and sometimes exploited the system of gender and sexual inversion. The system worked as long as sex with females was difficult for men to obtain because of the imperative of virginity for girls and the monetary cost of prostitution. As contraceptive methods became more widely available and their use increased at the end of the 1950s, heterosexual men became less likely to indulge in same-sex relations. At the same time, homosexuals started to give up their feminine styles and to develop an interest in their own. The system of what in these times was called "queer" and "trade," and "butch" and "femme," was based on the model of prostitution. From the 1960s on, gay men did not want to degrade themselves in relations with "normal" men.[70] The new model of gay life and sex was that of friendship and marriage. This change in homosexual self-image and style made it possible to discuss legal reform, medical depathologization of homosexuality and, later, gay and lesbian parenthood and marriage.

The masculinization of homosexual styles since the 1950s does not necessarily mean that gay men have become virile. Since homosexuals dispensed with the exclusivity of feminine styles and habits, the spectrum of gender possibilities has broadened to include different options, making it easier for men with homosexual preferences and masculine styles to come out of the closet and proclaim their homosexuality. Gay men began to adopt a "macho" style of sex and gender, and although many outsiders doubted the masculine qualities of the style, it caused a revolution in models of gay desire. The idea that sexual attraction existed only between opposites began to disappear as "macho" men and "clones" had sex with each other, disregarding the older model of queen and trade that governed the homosexual world until the 1950s. Gay couples no longer exclusively consisted of a male and a female partner. To find masculine men, gay men could now look among themselves in their own worlds and no longer depended on sexual border traffic with "normal" youngsters.[71]

On the other hand, the effeminate homosexuals or queens did not disappear but became a minority in the gay world. Much of the social support for feminine styles foundered. Nowadays, such styles are part of the diversity of the gay world. The revolution in forms of desires and identities that has occurred since the 1950s has meant not a transition from one style to another but the addition of new models to the older ones that were already evolving themselves.[72] The young queen of the 1950s may still

238

be living in the 1990s, but he is quite a different figure from the young queen of the 1990s who may have adopted a punk or Madonna style.

The third sex has been a powerful metaphor, virtually monopolizing the image of homosexuals in social life for the last hundred years. Because it was considered a shameful identity, it posed a major obstacle for many young people to identify themselves as homosexuals. The suggested effeminacy of gays was a forceful social strategy that marginalized homosexual desires and thus prevented the development of gay identities. As an impediment it worked well, but it also provoked a powerful strategy of seduction that made sexual border traffic between gay and straight men possible and satisfactory. The "camp" tradition of gay men would have been unthinkable without their supposed effeminacy.[73] For a century, men with same-sex desires were pushed into the role of a third gender. Many of them enjoyed this role, but others resisted it and felt compelled to deny their desires. Now we have come to a new epoch in which most gays are able to play with and joke about their gender roles. But how long will it take before straight men are capable of the same?

CHAPTER FIVE

Woman Becomes Man in the Balkans

René Grémaux

Introduction

Biological females wearing men's garb and often men's weaponry, performing men's jobs and enjoying, at least to some extent, public recognition as men have been reported from time to time in the western Balkans since the first half of the 1800s. The custom was until quite recently found in the Dinaric range of mountains stretching from Bosnia-Herzegovina to central Albania. This cultural practice, to which this essay is devoted, was found predominantly among the rural/pastoral population, rarely in the region's few urban centers.

Most descriptions of the practice date from the beginning of the twentieth century, and they pertain to the south Slav and north Albanian frontier zone – the barren and often inaccessible mountainous area through which the present-day border between Albania and Yugoslavia runs. The local population has derived its meager living in part from some agriculture of the small fertile plots, but primarily from keeping small livestock. Whereas agricultural activities have been concentrated in the lower regions near the permanent winter hamlets, cattle-breeding and dairy production has taken place predominantly on the higher-situated summer pastures. In such a context, these persons often aroused the astonishment of foreigners, since their mere existence defied the fundamental human division of men and women, a dimorphism commonly conceived of as being rooted in the unchangeable facts of nature.

The existence of female cross-dressing in early modern times has recently been shown by Rudolf Dekker and Lotte van de Pol.[1] Drawing mainly on Dutch historical archives and other written sources, they have traced a large number of instances from the mid-sixteenth to the early nineteenth century. Often these cross-dressers were females who disguised themselves as men to become sailors or soldiers. Their hidden nature was eventually discovered, upon which dismissal followed. In fact, many of these cross-dressers were tried, since their "deceit" was usually accompanied by other illicit activities, such as marrying another woman. These "females in breeches" were commonly despised for subverting the "normal" gender order by political and ecclesiastical authorities and, seemingly, by the general public as well.

Female cross-dressing was not exclusive to Holland or the Balkans, though; it apparently existed across Europe and in European settlements elsewhere. European tradition abounds in hagiographies, folk songs, myths, fairy tales and legends with the theme of the female who dresses and lives as a man. Julie Wheelwright has portrayed some of these instances, from the American West to the former Soviet Russia.[2] These "amazons and military maids," as she calls them, wore masculine attire for various reasons – some to conceal their female identity altogether for considerable periods of time, others to indulge in cross-dressing during military exploits, on the stage and so forth, only occasionally and unlawfully.

Balkan examples, however, differed greatly from such long-standing and widespread female cross-dressing in Europe. Much more was at stake here than the mere donning of male garb to attain certain short-term goals. In the Balkans the practice enabled a more permanent and institutionalized social crossing or "passing" than elsewhere. It concerned crossing gender identities rather than merely cross-dressing, since the individuals assumed the male social identity with the tacit approval of the family and the larger community.

In exploring the vast, mainly Serbo-Croatian ethnographic literature for this region of southeast Europe, I have come across some 120 cases of biological females who lived their lives, or most of their lives, as social men. In my fieldwork in Yugoslavia during the summers of 1985 through 1988, I had the opportunity to meet and work with two of these few surviving masculine "sworn virgins." I gathered direct and indirect information from those who knew them well, and I conducted interviews with relatives, friends and acquaintances of those who are now deceased.

Time and Space: The Ethnographic Context
The south Slavs (i.e., Montenegrins) and Albanians (i.e., Ghegs) speak mutually unintelligible languages belonging to two separate branches of the Indo-European language tradition. In this region the Slavic population is predominantly Serbian Orthodox, and only a minority professes to be Islamic. The Albanian population of the north is almost equally divided between Roman Catholicism and Islam. Nothwithstanding these linguistic and religious differences, the people inhabiting the core area shared, until recently, a harsh warrior culture constructed along the lines of a corporate lineage organization.[3] These exogamous lineages were based on patrilocal (virilocal) marriage arrangements, patrilineal descent and inheritance of real estate. This society of localized patrilineages typically failed to provide women with full social rights. In a sense, women remained, throughout their lives, social outsiders.

Another important characteristic of local social life was the flourishing patriarchal mentality encompassing and penetrating virtually every sphere of life, a consciousness that still prevails. Intergroup killing in the form of feuding and blood revenge was rampant, halting only in the face of a communal threat from abroad. The clannish and tribal appearance of this region in the late nineteenth and early twentieth centuries contributed to its anachronistic image. In this period, the apparent heyday of female cross-dressing, it is clear that, along with kinship, gender was decisive in the ascription of social role and legal status. Gender segregation ruled throughout the public domain. Household chores and tasks in the peasant and pastoral economy were usually strictly gendered. As a rule, females were unarmed and hence considered inviolable. According to indigenous common law, they

enjoyed immunity and remained under men's tutelage throughout their lives. This male-female dichotomy of rights and duties
left little room to maneuver freely, and, as one might expect, the
conditions for a distinctive "third gender" came about.

Virginity and Masculinity: Some Preliminary Considerations
Within this context, the social male was one of many cultural
traits Montenegrins and Ghegs formerly shared. Apart from minor
cultural differences across time and place, as well as less significant dissimilarities consistent with religion and ethnicity, two
main types of social males should be distinguished. The first type
comprises the biological female person who is raised as a son from
infancy or early childhood; the second type embraces the biological female who, later in life, after having been socialized as a
woman for many years, reconstructs herself as a "social man." Outstanding in this transformation was the commitment to abstain
from matrimony and motherhood. By virtue of their vow to lead
a virginal life, such persons were referred to as *zavjetovana djevojka*,
in the local Slavic vernacular, and as *vajzë e betuar*, in the Albanian
counterpart, both meaning "sworn virgin." More often, however,
these individuals are designated *tobelija* ("person bound by a vow")
or *virgjinéshë* ("female committed to virginity"). The latter term is
used by Albanians only, whereas the former concept is employed
both by Albanians and by the neighboring Slavs. All of these terms
imply a kind of nonfeminine behavioral pattern as determined by
matrimony and maternity. Other nouns, such as the South Slavic
muskobanja ("manlike woman"), stress overt masculinity.

The alleged virginal quality – an issue to be substantiated
later – needs attention here. Mary Douglas, in particular, demonstrated how the human body might serve as a primordial natural symbol.[4] With its orifices, discharges and functions, the body
constitutes a rich source of metaphoric imagery and discourse.
The female body, with its distinctive reproductive and sexual
states, is easily deployed as a marker of discrete social spaces and
identities. Of the subsequent stadia of a woman's life – maiden,
mother and matron (postmenopausal woman) – the first is chosen to represent the fertile, undamaged integrity of the social

whole. In such a representation, the untouched, impermeable virgin's body is a first-class metaphor for Balkan society.

The anthropological interest in virginity which has emerged in recent decades is chiefly directed at this condition's social function and the cultural meaning as a temporary state. That is, it stipulates how the young girl, who has not yet become "specified" as woman, is altered by the triplet of marriage, sexual intercourse and motherhood.[5] Comparatively little scholarly attention, however, has been directed to sustained virginity and celibacy in females. Moreover, when this subject is addressed, its cultic and monastic forms typically receive the most scrutiny. The more secular and downright profane forms of virginity rarely ever come to the fore.

Feminist scholarship has produced fine and innovative studies on females defying ordinary systems of classification, such as virgins, viragos, barren women, prostitutes, widows and other postmenopausal women.[6] Virginity is inherently an extremely ambiguous and ambivalent human condition, for it is considered to be neither a masculine nor a feminine quality, but rather a peculiar combination of both. Virginity extending into adulthood constitutes an anomaly within the universe of fecund adults that is divided into men and women. Furthermore, one cannot easily fit adult virgins into another binary pair, that of girl/woman. With the young girl the adult virgin shares the assumed sexual purity, while at the same time she has the potential, like a woman, of giving birth. As Kirsten Hastrup proposes, virgins can also be perceived as a "third sex" (see n.5). In any case, they are commonly regarded as being betwixt and between several important conceptual categories expressed as binary pairs: woman/man, natural/supernatural and profane/sacred. Those who hedge the boundaries of such vital concepts as these are most "dangerous" or "polluting" in Douglas's sense. For this reason such persons are, potentially, both very vulnerable and very powerful at the same time. The purity of the *virgo intacta* and the corruption of the *demi-vièrge* are treacherously close to one another. Likewise, the virginal roles of saint and witch are equally potent in symbolic media. Virgins not only straddle the two genders, but they also

245

mediate in the other binary oppositions mentioned above. Like all other mediators, they can perform their function only as long as the dividing lines exist and no merging of categories occurs. With regard to the virgins' role in the prevalent man/woman division, it must be stressed that its impact is not merely affirmative. Virgins challenge common concepts of femininity, of which motherhood and dependence on men are basic traits, and moreover they threaten the clear-cut demarcation of both genders. In transvestite Balkan virgins, we see this inherent ambiguity and ambivalence substantially reduced by their classification as "social men," as well as by prescriptions and restrictions concerning their sexual behavior.

In the following description, I have selected four typical case histories to illustrate ethnographically those females who became males. The material presented here derives in part from my own field research. Among other things, it reveals the gradual extinction of this phenomenon as a social institution during the course of the twentieth century. This presentation is followed by a discussion of the sexuality and gender identity of the persons under study, focusing on two interconnected questions: How do they relate sexually to men and women? And to what extent do they actually identify themselves with the male gender? I conclude this essay by considering whether one can properly speak of the Balkan "social men" as a third gender.

Case Histories

Case 1: Mikas

In 1885, the Serbian doctor Milan Jovanovic-Batut reported his strange encounter with Mikas Milicev Karadzic, a twenty-two-year-old soldier in the Montenegrin village of Zabljak. Before examining the assembled soldiers, the doctor was told that Mikas was a "wonder of the world," but in the course of a superficial open-air examination of the cohort he was unable to discover anything special about him. To his great surprise, the doctor was afterward informed by the commander and the captain that Mikas, whom he considered a "strong lad," was in fact a girl who had originally been called Milica. The father, a celebrated hero, had been killed in a battle when Milica, his only child, was still very small.

The commander explained the situation as follows:

> What could the poor widow do without a male head of the household? Out of sorrow and consolation she dressed Milica as a man and gave her the new name Mikas. The child got used to it, and later even did not wish it otherwise. With the boys she played, with the boys she tended the sheep, and nobody was allowed to mention that she was not a boy. When her comrades put on a belt with arms, she did not want to remain deprived of them either. Riding horseback, jumping, shooting a rifle and throwing stones at targets...all with them and all like them as well.

Asked whether the mother and the nearest kin approved of this, the commander answered affirmatively. Their initial expectation that Mikas's tomboyish behavior would end with adulthood proved false. When he grew up, Mikas did not turn to skirts and distaffs but continued to work and enjoy the company of males. To the Karadzic clan, however, Mikas was a great embarrassment. The clan advised and reprimanded him but in vain: "The more strongly they did so, the more stubborn he became: instead of becoming a woman he would rather lose his head." After listening with disbelief, the doctor sent for Mikas. Behind closed doors and with only the two present, Mikas admitted to being a girl. His comrades, he said, treated him as their equal, and obtrusive boys had long since stopped being a nuisance. No one dared to mock him. Such a person, he declared convincingly, "pays with his head."

Questioned by the doctor about the way he hid the menses, *zenski cvijet,* the "women's flower," in the company of men, he denied having them: "I do not have that. At the age of thirteen, for some months, but afterward never." "Hearing this," the doctor wrote, "was enough for me. I realized that her entire nature had changed." He added, "Has this occurred by strong will, or has it come about by force of habit?" Because he thought Mikas faced much personal trouble ahead, the doctor admonished him in a fatherly way to change his life. But Mikas turned a deaf ear to his words and expressed his determination to stick with the masculine way of life. Saying farewell to Mikas, the doctor cried a little out of sorrow for this "wretched creature."[7]

Mikas continued his way of life and was observed toward the end of the 1920s by Marijana Gusic, an ethnographer from Croatia. Arriving at Mikas's log cabin, Gusic was given anything but a kind welcome by the aged inhabitant. He refused to receive her and reproached a fellow tribesman thus: "Why are you bringing me this stranger-woman?" The ethnographer's husband, however, was not sent away. As a male he was allowed to sit with Mikas in front of the little cabin and to take pictures (figure 5.1). Local people still recall Mikas as a person who greatly distrusted strangers, and who allowed only kinsmen and neighbors to enter his dwelling.

Unable to interview Mikas, Gusic had to rely on information provided by relatives and neighbors. According to them, the young Milica was "masculinized out of sorrow," not so much by his young widowed mother, as Jovanovic-Batut's informants claimed, as by his deceased father's mother. My own informants agreed on the decisive role played by Mikas's grandmother. Gusic also heard that Milica was proclaimed a boy and renamed Mikas (a masculine form of Milica) "in order to prevent the house, the hearth and the candle from being extinguished." In this way Mikas could succeed his famous father.

Probably around 1880, the chieftains of three clans of Jezera (a division of the Drobnjak tribe) put the problem of Mikas to the Orthodox bishop Visarion Ljubisa when he visited Zabljak. This traditional high authority in both religious and secular matters, according to Gusic, talked with Mikas and instructed that no one should ever insult him in any way. Although the bishop approved of Mikas's masculinity, he still limited his male prerogatives by saying: "Mikas, never drink brandy, because it might bring shame to you and your house." Jovanovic-Batut, too, was informed about the bishop's intervention on the request of the "poor" Karadzic clan in this case. Yet, according to his information, it was ineffective, since Mikas avoided every possible confrontation

FIGURE 5.1. Mikas Milicev Karadzic,
1929.

with this authority. However, oral tradition today claims that Mikas's special status was sanctioned by the three clans of the Jezera at the intercession of a bishop whom Mikas met personally. In the local vernacular, Gusic goes on to inform us, Mikas was labeled either *ostajnica* ("she who stays," that is, an unwed female who replaces the lacking male heir in her father's house) or *muskobanja* ("manlike woman"). His status required everlasting virginity; violation of this taboo would have called for his death by stoning. Toward the end of the 1920s, at the time of Gusic's unfortunate visit, Mikas was living alone. Despite his considerable age, Mikas still performed all the hard tasks of a man, such as mowing, stacking hay, ploughing and harvesting. He also prepared and cooked his own meals but refrained from exclusively female tasks like handiwork. Female relatives and neighbors performed these tasks for him out of charity or for a small fee. Mikas was addressed by females with terms such as *djever* ("husband's brother"), *svekar* ("father-in-law") and *kum* ("godfather" or "elderly man").[8] Every November, Mikas celebrated as a genuine son of his clan the feast of the Archangel Michael. As master of the house, Mikas received numerous guests, in whose presence he lighted the ceremonial candle and performed other ritual acts that were normally reserved for males. By visiting and congratulating Mikas on this occasion, the community paid tribute to him as the descendant of Milic Karadzic. In official documents Mikas was registered under the male name Mikas Milicev Karadzic, which enabled him, for instance, to vote in parliamentary elections at a time when female suffrage was nonexistent.

In the late 1920s Mikas was living under reduced circumstances, owing to several successive years of drought. Three cows and some land was all that was left of his initially much larger patrimony. I was told that Mikas in his younger years owned a good deal of fertile land and a flock of fifty sheep of the highest quality. Cattle breeding and cattle trading occupied him so much that he was forced to lease out his arable land for sharecropping. Gusic describes the aged Mikas as an unhappy, mentally deranged person with clearly visible misogynistic and misanthropic traits. In her opinion, the enforced celibacy and male role were to blame for this. The high status Mikas enjoyed in the local community was too small a compensation for his "unnatural" way of life.[9]

When I visited Jezera, I learned that several old people still have a vivid memory of Mikas, who died more than half a century ago. All my informants stressed Mikas's striking masculinity in spirit, appearance and behavior, as well as his fierce insistence on being treated and respected as a genuine male, which seems to have been his main task in life. Although they doubted Mikas's claim of not having monthly periods, women – including the one who washed him during his final illness – had noticed extremely ill-developed breasts, a condition caused, they said, by tying them up. Mikas is said to have always used the male gender when talking about himself, and his voice and manner of speaking were also quite manlike.[10] Talking about Mikas, my informants alternately used "he" and "she," as was also observed by Gusic when Mikas was still alive. In his presence, however, nobody would have had the insolence to call him a woman, although everyone in Jezera knew that he was a biological female; feelings of reverence, but also of fear, prevented them from doing so. Mikas's utmost sensitivity to even the slightest defilement of his much-cherished manliness was well known, as was his resoluteness to avenge such indecency. Being called by female names like Milica or Mika outraged him and induced him to throw stones at the evildoer or to hit the offender in the head with his *cibuk* (a long Turkish pipe). One expression in particular stirred his fury beyond all limits: "*Mika-puklaca*," which related his original (female) name to an obscene word for female genitals. Such an insult made Mikas draw his pistol and fire without compassion. It was above all young people, fond of teasing, who nicknamed him "*Mika-puklaca*," but if this insult reached his ears they had to reckon with his bullets. Interestingly enough, while the word *puklaca* has since become obsolete in Jezera, the combination *Mika-puklaca* is still used by youngsters today, even among those who have never heard Mikas's story.

Mikas did not use his masculinity opportunistically, as is shown by the tragicomic event that occurred in 1916, when the tiny kingdom of Montenegro was occupied by the Austrian army. Mikas, one of numerous soldiers who fell into the hands of the Austrians, awaited with resignation his deportation with the other prisoners of war. However, this was prevented by the intervention of Vasilije Pipovic, his neighbor, who was fully aware that Mikas would never disclose his secret in order to be released. He applied to the Wachtmeister on duty and informed him about Mikas's true sex, at which time he was promptly released. According to one version of the story, the Austrians refused to believe that Mikas was a woman until he was forced to show what his clothes hid.

Females used to kiss Mikas's hand submissively, as they were expected to do whenever they met a venerable elderly male. Friends presented him with coffee and tobacco, since Mikas loved both. He used to smoke the *cibuk* and drink coffee without sugar, luxuries usually reserved for men. His favorite pastime was to sit in one of the Zabljak inns. Although he was referred to as a *pasalija*, that is, one who enjoys life like men in the company of a Turkish pasha, he is said to have spent his lifetime without having sexual intercourse – in this respect he wanted nothing to do with males. In his younger days, it is said, a reckless youth made an attempt to assault Mikas indecently when he was asleep, at which time he immediately reacted by drawing his ever-present pistol. With women too – whom Mikas treated with overt contempt – he did not have intimate relations, although he was not totally indifferent to their beauty. Mikas is said to have expressed among men his eagerness to touch females lasciviously. Once, a woman told me, Mikas passionately grasped the legs of a girl sitting next to him and paid the girl compliments on her charm. According to this informant, Mikas was physically attracted to females but had never been able to have a woman at his side like ordinary males. "Poor Mikas!" she concluded. The local shoemaker told me cheerfully that the aged Mikas, referring to his youth, once sighed, "When we were boys...."

In June 1933, the sick and weakened Mikas was carried on the back of an ox from his home to the house of Muso (Milutin) Baranin to spend his last days in the care of Jelena Simicevic, Muso's young bride. As Mikas's paternal aunt's grandson, Muso was the heir-apparent. I was told by the widowed Jelena that she used to call Mikas *svekar* ("father-in-law") or *strika* (from *stric*: "father's brother" or "elderly man") and that she herself was called *snaha* ("daughter-in-law" or "sister-in-law") by him. Feeling the end drawing near, Mikas called Jelena, whom he seemed to have loved despite his general attitude toward women, and said in a deep masculine voice, "*Snaha*, please do not disgrace me!" for he was deathly afraid of being buried in female dress. Mikas gave her money and sent her to the tailor in Zabljak to buy a proper outfit for his burial costume. Jelena did what she was asked and bought Mikas a new outfit consisting of white socks, woolen trousers, a vest and a cap. When Mikas died in the autumn of 1934, he was dressed in this manly costume and, with the approval of the Orthodox priest, was buried like a man at the Zabljak churchyard.

Case 2: Tonë
On June 17, 1971, the cemetery of Tuzi, close to the Albanian border in Montenegro, was the setting for the funeral of Tonë Bikaj, a *virgjinéshë* in male dress born seventy years earlier. Fifteen years later I paid a visit to the village where he had spent the last decades of his life with Gjelosh, his much younger brother. On that occasion, Gjelosh proudly told me the fascinating story of Tonë's life.[11]

Tonë was born in the predominantly Catholic Kelmënd tribe of the highlands of adjacent north Albania. Tonë was the first child of Tom Lule Bikaj and his wife Katarinë. His parents' wedding had been delayed by twelve years, since Tom was arrested for taking part in the armed struggle against Turkish rule in Albania. The death sentence originally imposed on him was commuted to long-term penal servitude in faraway Anatolia.

Tonë's birth was followed by the birth of two sons and two daughters. However, both sons – the pride and joy of every patriarchal family – died at an early age from the much-feared endemic malaria. Left without brothers, Tonë decided, when she was about nine years old, to become the son and brother the parents and sisters needed so much. Tonë promised never to marry and exchanged girls' clothes for boys'. Instead of the female tasks he used to perform at his mother's side, he started to help his father with

253

male tasks. This radical change, however, was not completed by the adoption of a masculine name.[12]

The decision to behave like a boy pleased his parents very much. When he visited peasants in the neighborhood, his father proudly introduced them to his "new son." Like all other sons in these unsafe mountains, Tonë received weapons from his father at the age of fifteen. When Tonë was twenty years old, a happy event occurred in the Bikaj family: the forty-nine-year-old mother gave birth to a son, who was named Gjelosh. For little Gjelosh, Tonë performed the role of the older brother who looked after him and protected him in times of trouble – all the more necessary because of the advancing age of the parents. As the years passed, Tonë succeeded in changing his voice, way of speaking, posture and manners to such a degree that it was hard to distinguish him from a biological male. His tribe recognized and honored Tonë as a man. When his sisters reached the age of marriage, they were handed over to their grooms by Tonë, who acted in this respect just like an older brother.

The attitude Tonë displayed at the end of World War II, when the Communist victory was near in Albania, may serve as proof of his fighting spirit. Together with his brother, he joined the nationalist guerrilla movement in his native area. Tonë, who commanded an all-male resistance fighters' unit, was forced to surrender after a three-month struggle, as was his brother. In the meantime their mother, who had actively supported the resistance by providing food, was shot by a people's commissar for refusing to cooperate in persuading the guerrillas to agree to a cease-fire.

Tonë's surrender was followed by an imprisonment that lasted more than a year. During this confinement, he was deeply upset at being treated as a woman and being separated from his comrades-in-arms. When Gjelosh was finally released in 1951, both he and Tonë – their father had died immediately after the war – ventured to cross the Albanian border illegally. This hazardous enterprise turned out well, and both arrived on Yugoslav territory safe and sound. Completely destitute, they settled in Grudë, a Catholic Albanian enclave in Montenegro, close to the Albanian border. In this new environment they founded a communal household headed by Tonë. In his capacity as *zot shtëpie* ("master of the house") he received guests and participated in traditional all-male gatherings. At his brother's wedding in 1953 he acted as *vëllam*, the male (commonly the groom's father, uncle or brother) who leads the bride to the groom. Tonë continued to live with Gjelosh and his wife, and the couple's children used to call Tonë *babá* ("father"). The acceptance of Tonë as a male within the family seems to have been so complete that at least some family members were ignorant of his female sex. "It was only after his death that I realized Uncle Tonë had in fact been a woman," a young man about twenty-five years old told me.

Gjelosh's earnings as a carpenter in nearby Podgorica (Tito-grad) allowed them to buy some land and build a house. Tonë stayed mainly in the village during the years that his brother commuted. Outdoors he performed only those tasks that corresponded with his male status, like the heavy and prestigious work of mowing and stacking hay. Indoors Tonë occupied himself with cooking and the preparation of meals but not with womanly handicraft. Initially the house and land were registered in the name of Tonë, but by the late 1950s his brother Gjelosh received this honor. His retreat from the position of master of the house, however, was just a formality: in reality, nothing changed. Tonë remained in charge of the house and continued to participate in the gatherings of the male heads of households. Gjelosh, who had gradually become a successful farmer and all-around craftsman, always escorted Tonë to these meetings with pride.

Among the Albanians living on the Montenegrin side of the border Tonë gained considerable popularity as a singer and musician, and many people I met remember him as such. Like a genuine male he used to sing "mountaineer songs," holding one hand behind the ear, and he performed other traditional songs accompanying himself on the *lahutë* or *gusle*, a bow-and-string instrument. In addition, he was known to be a good player of the *fyell*, an end-blown flute. Singing and making music for an audience that included males, activities traditionally considered improper for local women, was a kind of specialty of many Albanian sworn virgins.[13]

Unlike her experience with Mikas, Gusic was given a warm welcome by Tonë when she visited him in 1960. In her opinion, Tonë was a pleasant and satisfied person who enjoyed the high esteem accorded him by both the family and the wider community. Gusic found no trace of the mental derangement that she discerned in Mikas.[14] Tonë's death in 1971 was preceded by three years of serious illness, during which people often paid him visits. Among those who stood at his bedside were several Franciscan nuns, with whom he felt a strong bond both as a pious Catholic and as a virgin.[15] In accordance with his will, he was buried in the antiquated male costume he had worn on special occasions. At the funeral a photo of Tonë wearing that costume, taken some years before, was placed atop the coffin (figures 5.2, 5.3, 5.4). At the cemetery some men – relatives and friends of the deceased – wanted to start the *vajtim*, a traditional impromptu lamentation or funeral oration in verse, but were prevented from performing it. The custom of the local Grudë tribe allegedly did not allow a biological female to be publicly lamented by males. Gjelosh still feels sorry that Tonë was deprived of the last honors of a man, to which he was said to be entitled according to the customs of his natal Kelmënd tribe.

Case 3: Stana
In a small mountain village in central Montenegro lives Stana Cerovic, who dresses and behaves like a man.[16] Although everyone there knows that he was not born a male, he counts as a distinguished *domacin* ("master of the house"). After having heard that Stana, who is now about fifty years old, appreciates well-intended interest in his special position, of which he is proud, I visited his house twice, in 1986 and 1987. On both occasions I was kindly received by Stana's eldest sister Borika, while Stana was away with the cattle in the summer pastures. The first time I could not go out into the vast highland pastures to look for Stana, for I neither had the time nor was prepared; the second time I had to refrain from going to see him out of respect, since he had recently lost his most beloved sister, Vukosava. In the accompanying drawing (figure 5.5) Stana is depicted by an artist with this sister. A

tie was added to his costume to emphasize the masculinity of his appearance (in the original photograph, it was lacking).

Stana is the youngest of the five children – all female – of Milivoj Cerovic and his spouse. Two of them married, and the others – Borika, Vukosava and Stana – remained unwed and continued to live together in the parental home after the deaths of their father in 1953 and their mother in 1958. As is usual in this region during the cold season, the family occupies a house made of stone in a village in the valley where the arable meadowland is situated; during the warm season they live in log cabins in the upland pastures. In the past, when Borika was still a good walker, each of the three unwed sisters lived in these pastures, where Borika and Vukosava occupied themselves with female tasks such as dairy production and raking, while Stana performed male tasks like mowing, stacking hay and protecting their cattle. In recent years, it was always Stana and Vukosava working as brother and sister in the summer pastures, but now a sudden death has deprived Stana of his dedicated companion Vukosava, his dear "Koka" (hypocoristic of *kokoska*, "hen").

Stana's family is well known for its heroism. His father was the grandson of a renowned captain of the Montenegrin army and a close relative of the legendary Novica Cerovic, who was famous throughout the Orthodox South Slavic lands for his share in the killing of the detested Turkish (i.e., Muslim) lord Smailaga Cengic in 1840. Father Milivoj was overtaken by disaster when, after the death of Borika's twin brother, Milos, at the age of two months, no more sons were born to him. Without a male child, Milivoj's house, for all its glorious history, would suffer a humiliating decline. To avert still more daughters from being born, the fifth was called Stana, a name signifying something like "stay!" or "stop!" But despite all their hopes, no son was born to prevent the extinction of the house, and Stana remained the last born. In order to delay the inevitable fate by one generation, the young Stana was encouraged by the parents to adopt the male role. Stana's father used to call the child coaxingly "my son!" (she was his favorite) and at the age of five Stana was already smoking the leftovers of his tobacco. Borika watched with sorrow how Stana,

FIGURE 5.2. (left) Tonë, 1960. Tonë was famous for playing the *lahutë*, a privilege normally reserved for men.

FIGURE 5.3. (right) Tonë carrying a pistol as a reminder of his wartime exploits, ca. 1968.

FIGURE 5.4. View of Tonë's funeral, 1971. To the right of the coffin stands
Tonë's brother Gjelosh. A photograph on top of the coffin shows Tonë dressed
in the clothes in which he was buried.

FIGURE 5.5. A drawing depicting Stana Cerovic with his beloved sister
Vukosava, ca. 1960.

twelve years younger than she, gradually came to resemble boys in dress and behavior. "I considered it unnatural," Borika confided to me, "and I have told my parents this time and again, but on every occasion I was given to understand: let Stana dress and behave as she pleases." Once it became fully clear that Stana would never marry or retreat from his male way of life, Borika and Vukosava decided not to leave their sister alone at home, and thus they stayed single too.[17]

Stana's formal education consisted of eight years of primary school in a nearby village, where he excelled in mathematics and ball games as well as in boyish pranks. The grown-up Stana is praised by his eldest sister for his keen mind, diligence and strength but is also characterized as being "furious." When it comes to alcohol, Stana holds his own and can drink male comrades under the table. Even though he has never adopted a male name himself, he is sometimes jokingly called "Stancane," a peculiar masculine adaptation of Stana.

As a true son of the Montenegrin highlands, Stana displays a passion for hunting and shooting. He usually joins the men in the wolf hunt, although he has no hunting license. He has been trying for years to obtain one, citing the menace that the increasing number of wolves presents to the livestock. As soon as a shooting club was founded in a neighboring village, Stana applied for membership, but his request was turned down. Stana is nevertheless an excellent marksman, as he showed at a tournament organized about nine years ago by the club: seeing all the male competitors missing the mark, he abandoned the passive role of spectator and grabbed a rifle. Much to the dishonor of the competitors, Stana's first shot hit the mark.

Toward the end of 1985 the journalist Petar Milatovic managed to interview Stana. From this interview, in which Stana consistently used the masculine grammatical gender while talking about himself, I quote the following revealing statements:

"When I grew up I told my father that I would be his son. I took an oath never to marry or to abandon his house as long as I live." And he added, as if he were looking for approval, "Do I really have to let it happen that after him there won't be anyone

in this house to light the fire?" The reporter, pointing at a sewing machine, provocatively questioned Stana if he was perhaps the
one in the house who used it; he indignantly replied, "No, really,
and it doesn't suit me either...I am the master of the house!...
That is for these two sisters, they potter around it.... And they
do the milking, of course.... That's not for a man. I plough,
mow, gather wood." Remarking on his rejected request for membership in the shooting club, he asserted, "most of all I detest
being a female...nature is mistaken." He clearly expressed misogyny and denounced women for their chatter and preoccupation
with clothing. Instead of "wasting" his time in female company
he preferred to go "with the men, to have a conversation, to play
cards." After the interview the reporter was informed by an insider
about Stana's frequent attendance at the dance in the local cultural center, where he associates and drinks with the men. On
one such occasion he is reported to have said, chuckling to his
companions, "Oh, if I could somehow drive that daughter of
Milovan into a corner.... Come across her in seclusion."[18]

Case 4: Durgjane
In Prizren in the Kosovo-Metohija area of Serbia resides Durgjane
Gllavolla, who until recently taught Albanian (her native language)
in one of the city's primary schools. In August 1985, at the head-
master's recommendation, I made my way to a tearoom – an outstanding example of a men's space – where Durgjane kills time.
When I arrived there, Durgjane seemed not to be present, but
she showed up as soon as she was informed that a stranger was
looking for her. At first glance, it was not easy to discern that
Durgjane was female, since she was sporting gray trousers, a white
shirt and a short hairstyle. Her voice, bearing and movements further strengthened the masculine image. This impression changed
when I perceived the curve of the chest and a certain expression
of the eyes. The sole unusual features about Durgjane were big
reddish birthmarks on the face and neck. She said hello to me
kindly but decisively, and after a short while proposed to leave the
tearoom for her uncle's house on the same street. In the lengthy
conversation that ensued she responded in a friendly but quite

pompous way to my questions. Answering in fluent Serbo-Croatian she consistently made use of the female gender while talking about herself (see n.10). She was fully aware of the fact that, by apparel, behavior, profession and way of thinking, she was a rare exception among the local female population, in particular among her Islamic Albanian contemporaries. This exceptional position, as she clearly stated, did not displease her; it filled her with a certain pride.

Durgjane was born in 1937 in the same town where she now lives, the last child of poor and simple parents. Before she was born, her father Ibush (Ibi) and mother Lutvijë had lost eight of nine children to disease and malnutrition, including all four of their sons. To prevent the newborn child from meeting the same fate, the desperate parents turned to a wise Muslim priest for advice. He recommended calling the child Durgjane, a curious Turkic-Arabic name with the magical meaning, "Stay, my soul!" On his advice the parents also searched in trees for a stone. In the end their efforts were rewarded. According to the priest's instructions, the precious stone was put in the child's bath and afterward safely stored in a high place of the room, where it remained for some decades until the old house was deserted. "Lest no evil fall upon the child," so the explanation of the magic ran. Describing her parents' "superstition" in this matter, Durgjane smiled scornfully.

Her father, it is claimed by usually reliable sources, secretly declared the small Durgjane a *virgjinéshë* or *tybelí* (the local form of *tobelija*), that is, a sworn virgin, so that she could be his fictitious son.[19] Yet another authority relates this case to a folk belief according to which infants could be prevented from dying by dressing them up as members of the opposite sex.[20] To me Durgjane vehemently denied becoming a sworn virgin at the instigation of her father during infancy. Claiming to be averse to everything that smells of tradition, Durgjane does not consider herself to be a sworn virgin and utterly dislikes being compared to those virgins of the "backward" countryside. "Not incited by my parents' wish, but because *I* wanted it that way I started to dress and behave like a boy. As far as I remember I have always felt myself

FIGURE 5.6. A sworn virgin photo-
graphed by an English woman traveler
in 1908. Smoking, wearing threadbare
clothing and going barefoot emphasized
her masculine persona.

more like a male than a female." On the subject of her parents, Durgjane added, "At my birth it was of secondary importance to them whether I was a boy or a girl; the only thing that really did matter was saving my life." This insistence on her own responsibility, I presume, originated in the need to clear her parents of the charge of having pursued an "unnatural" procedure, which is now increasingly vilified as a manifestation of sheer traditionalism. Durgjane even considered it necessary to take the entire Albanian population, which is in general heavily stigmatized for its alleged backwardness, under her wings by stating, "I can't imagine that our parents could have done such a thing to their children." By claiming all responsibility herself, Durgjane emphasizes her manliness since, according to today's standards, more honor is derived from a chosen rather than an imposed "deviant" way of life.

In her youth many people took her to be a boy, and since she did not mind it at all she tried not to spoil their illusions. She used to join the boys in their horseplay and attended school with them when it was still unusual for Albanian Muslim girls to follow formal education. At the teachers' college, where she was enrolled after the technical school she had originally attended was transferred to a distant city, a certain event occurred that still fills her with malicious pleasure. The teacher would begin statements with "As there are no girls in our class..." when he wanted to treat a subject he considered to be unfit for female ears. To his great surprise, he was told by one of the pupils that Durgjane was not a boy but a girl. "Oh, how stupid I have been. Am *I* supposed to be a teacher?" While uttering these words the teacher is reported to have beaten himself upon the head.

In the early 1950s the young Durgjane was appointed to a teaching post in a village close to her native town. Originally she was registered as a schoolmaster. As I was assured by the primary school inspector of those days, Mehdi Bardhi, Durgjane was appointed as a male teacher, even though it was known to him and others that she was in fact female. They let her pass as a male, assuming she had good reasons to do so. I do not know exactly when Durgjane was officially redesignated as a schoolmistress instead of schoolmaster, but by 1957 she was already designated as a female teacher at a village school.[21] In 1966 Durgjane was working as a schoolmistress in her native town, as was observed by Mirko Barjaktarovic.[22] Notwithstanding her downright masculine behavior and appearance, Barjaktarovic wrote, she used to refer to herself as a female. When I visited the teachers' room, my attention was drawn to a framed color photograph of the assembled men and women of the staff. Wearing a two-piece man's suit, Durgjane's figure looms large in the foreground, surrounded by her junior female colleagues in dresses and with long hair.

Durgjane likes to show off as a sports enthusiast. In her youth she played soccer with boys; later she played handball. She played on a women's handball team that went almost undefeated in 1957–58. Her fame spread throughout the country, and she was given the opportunity to join the Belgrade team. Since she did not want to leave her family she had to reject this attractive offer. Looking back now, Durgjane regrets not having employed her talents by becoming a trainer.

As noted, Durgjane claims to be the sole person responsible for her way of life. Above all, she is protective of her mother, who died in 1979 and whose ring she wears as a loving souvenir: "Though she didn't know how to read or write she certainly was not a conservative person. After my father's death in 1950 she tried together with my father's brother to prevail on me to behave and dress as a woman. Both of them preferred me to marry." As Durgjane confided to me, she had by then already grown much too attached to her masculine behavior to be able to comply with their wishes. Nor could she give up her manliness – which she seems to consider her second nature – when males courted her. When Barjaktarovic asked the twenty-eight-year-old Durgjane why she did not adopt female attire and get married, she responded in a resigned way that such a thing would be "very difficult" to do at that time. Her only sister had recently died, and Durgjane had decided to raise the deceased's children "like her own," yet "differently" from the way she herself had been raised.

Today Durgjane lives alone in an apartment, but she still spends a lot of time with her foster children, who respect her and call her *této* ("aunt") Dan. She is fond of doing the housework and boasts of her cleanliness. According to her, the only good thing about marriage is having children. Although she would have liked to have had a child, she never would have sacrificed her independence to a male solely for this reason. Durgjane finds the traditional submissive role of married women abhorrent. Fortunately her job enables her to be in close contact with children. "Year after year," she boasted, "my class receives many more applications than there are places."

Durgjane's favorite way of passing time is a good, serious conversation with males, in the course of which alcohol is often enjoyed. She heartily dislikes stupidity and garrulousness in women, even more so when it is found in men. Durgjane is a popular customer of the tearoom where I met her. In this all-male meeting place she is respected and treated as an equal, as the manager and some of his habitués told me.

Durgjane likes to promote herself as a worldly person who is free from the prejudices of tradition. Unlike most women of her generation and ethnic background, who never leave the horizon of their native area, Durgjane is well traveled. In her small car she has made trips to metropolises like Istanbul and Paris, where "curiosity" drove her to visit gay bars and hangouts. Without expressing her sexual preference or tendencies clearly, Durgjane declared herself disappointed by what she observed in those establishments.

At least some of her fellow townsmen appear to consider her hermaphroditic, that is, combining physical characteristics of both sexes. A middle-aged Serbian woman who was convinced of this herself, however, frankly admitted she was completely ignorant of Durgjane's antecedents. Durgjane's "unnatural" appearance evokes so much aversion in this woman that she cannot even stand to face Durgjane while shopping or walking. This avoidance does not seem to be restricted to the informant. To me Durgjane repeatedly and emphatically declared that she had a perfectly normal female physique. The obvious psychological predilection for masculinity and the alleged biological femaleness seem to have found a livable balance in her personality. Anyway, she let me know, "I'm really satisfied with my life."

267

Discussion and Some Comparative Perspectives

All four individuals described in the previous section "crossed over" in their youth to the male gender on the initiative of, or at least by the consent of, their (grand)parents as a substitute for a male heir. A structural precondition of this gender-crossing was the extremely high appreciation of males and masculinity in the culture. The house – a unit combining social, economic, moral and cultic functions – was doomed to disappear in the absence of a male heir. The extinction of a house, symbolized by the quenching of fire, caused profound distress to its members and was much feared by them. In everyday life, parents who failed to produce a son suffered a loss of status or downright ostracism.

In the traditional context these masculinized individuals were in principle bound to perpetual virginity, normally by oath. Virginity was thought in the patriarchal culture to be synonymous with "masculine" virtues like purity and strength. Outside of its symbolic value, as indicated in the Introduction, virginity also performed an important practical function: it prevented non-nubile females from bringing forth children who would a priori be considered "bastards" and have no legitimate place within the system of patrilineages. According to the indigenous cosmology, children spring from the "blood" of the father; the mother's part in procreation is confined to that of incubating: "The woman is a sack for carrying," as a costumier of tribal north Albania put it.[23]

There is much uncertainty and dissension concerning the meaning of "virginity" as applied to the individuals in question. Did these virgins always have to refrain from sexual contacts with males, or did they rather enjoy some kind of freedom in the realm of (hetero)sexuality?[24] Or, using a distinction common in classical Antiquity, should such a person be labeled *virgo intacta* or simply *virgo*, the latter term denoting "unattached, unwed female"?[25] The case histories known to me all seem to point in the direction of complete heterosexual abstinence; yet some general statements on those who became sworn virgins in order to escape an arranged marriage – a type of sworn virginity almost exclusively found among north Albanians – indicate the opposite in relation to their itinerant life-styles. Statements of this kind date back to the turn of the century. Spiridion Gopcevic informs us generally about girls in the Catholic tribes of Mirditë who crossed over to the male gender: "On his travels this new man only has to take care not to become pregnant, for that would cause his death."[26] And concerning the wandering sworn virgins of the tribes of Malësí, an all-but-chaste behavior is mentioned by Karl Steinmetz.[27] However, with regard to these statements made by foreigners the question arises whether they are based on actual evidence or just on impressions.[28] It is possible, after all, that they were deluded by the "nonvirginlike" audacious manners in male company. Rude language was often heard from the mouths of sworn virgins, especially in public drinking places, and sometimes they even publicly flirted with males.[29]

Sworn virgins among Catholic Albanian tribes are reported not to have taken the oath of chastity. According to Ernesto Cozzi, an Italian missionary working in Malësí, only the (very few) nuns of this area were really bound to perpetual chastity.[30] And his contemporary, the Czech traveler Viktor Dvorsky, noted that, at Zatrijebac on the Montenegrin side of the border, "A 'virgin' promises only not to enter matrimony, but does not promise to remain a chaste maiden."[31] In any case, the alleged heterosexual liberty of these "virgins," assuming normal fertility and lack of prophylactics, must have been severely restricted by the danger of pregnancy. Capital punishment (by stoning in Montenegro and by fire in northern Albania) was prescribed by customary law for pregnant nubile girls and sworn virgins. My material, however, does not include a single enactment of this Draconian punishment on the latter.[32] Pelja Osman mentions an alternative procedure allegedly pursued by Albanians at the Montenegrin border: "Should a *tombelija* accidentally become pregnant (which is a very rare event), then she has to denounce that man (the father) and marry him. If he disagrees, a blood feud arises between the lineage of the *tombelija* and the lineage of that man." The need to avenge a sworn virgin's honor could cause a bloodbath: "In 1894," Osman continues, "Boca Preljina became pregnant, and because of her seventy-two men were killed."[33] Although we remain ignorant of Boca's own destiny, her case perfectly shows how risky illicit relations with sworn virgins could be.

Of the very few persons I know of who returned to the female gender and married after having lived for a considerable time as sworn virgins in male disguise, one case in particular appeals to the imagination – a case that clearly reflects the waning influence of tradition on the individual's life. The person concerned was born in 1926 in Nisor, a village near Suva Reka in Kosovo-Metohija, the fourth daughter of a simple Muslim Albanian peasant family named Ejupi. Since the parents lacked a son, they decided to let the newborn girl pass as a boy and to conceal her true sex from the outside world. The father forbade the girl to be called by her original female name Fatime and gave her the male name Fetah. Widowed at an early age, the mother was charged with the difficult task of guiding Fetah undetected through the first stages of life. Proceeding cunningly she managed to bypass the *synét* (circumcision) of her "son" and postponed the search for a future bride indefinitely. To have a son was of great importance since a childless widow or a widow with only daughters had no customary right to occupy her deceased husband's homestead; she had either to return to the house of her birth or to be married off once again.

Perhaps the mother's success would have continued had Fetah not been recruited in 1944 by the conquering Yugoslav partisans. Only after she had been in the army for two years was she exposed as a female in a medical checkup, at which time she was promptly discharged from military service. Or returning to her native village, she continued to dress and behave as a man. She was appointed a member of the revolutionary community council, in which capacity she participated actively in the struggle for equal rights for Muslim women. Seclusion and veiling were the main targets of Fetah's campaign. In the following years, the local community grew more and more aware of the fact that Fetah was a female. The final unmasking occurred in 1951 when, much to the discontent of her mother, Fetah married Asllan Asllani. Her husband once declared that he had to "seize" the resisting Fetah, who was at that time still wearing male clothing, in order to make her his bride. At marriage, her female name Fatime was reinstated and her

270

tight manly trousers were changed to the wide harem trousers. It was far from easy for her to get used to the role of housewife. In retrospect, Fatime claims to be content with having become a woman. She recently declared to a journalist, "I'm happy with my son and two daughters." To conclude this story a moving detail ought to be mentioned: Her mother never accepted the loss of her only "son" and died without granting Fatime forgiveness.[34]

Belonging primarily to the man's world, the transvestite sworn virgins often openly disdained women. Their degree of misogyny sometimes rivaled even that of biological males, as Gusic's above-mentioned experiences with Mikas showed. At the beginning of the twentieth century, Mary Edith Durham reported a similar example of overacting on the part of an Albanian virgin in male dress she happened to meet among the Hot, a tribe of Malësí. "She treated me with the contempt she appeared to think all petticoats deserved – and turned her back to me," wrote an annoyed Durham.[35] As a matter of fact, this independent, unmarried English woman, sporting a short hairstyle, was more or less considered a sworn virgin by male natives during her extensive travels through highland Albania, and thus was treated respectfully.[36]

Sexual tendencies toward females seem to be present in the cases of Mikas and Stana, albeit in a rather limited and repressed way. Although I found absolutely no trace of liaisons with women, cohabitation of masculine sworn virgins with female partners is not completely unknown. I know of three such couples, in two of which a sexual relationship is actually indicated. At least two of these three couples were bound by "blood-sisterhood," a kind of ritual or spiritual kinship that, however, does not usually include living together.[37] According to Tatomir Vukanovic, sworn virgins were in some places ill reputed for "certain abnormal sexual relations" with their blood-sisters.[38]

The first of these couples belonged to the Kuci, a mixed Montenegrin-Albanian tribe, and consisted of the Orthodox Montenegrin Djurdja Popovic and her *posestrima* (blood-sister) and fellow sworn virgin Curë Prenk Rexhinaj, a Catholic Albanian. Stevan Ducic, a fellow tribesman and contemporary, depicted this "interesting pair of blood-sisters" briefly in a book probably written around 1910. Coming from the neighboring village of Koce and bringing along the paternal inheritance, Curë had settled down fifteen years earlier in the house of Djurja's father, a former captain in Medun. They formed a joint household and lived together "in the greatest harmony." "Only very seldom are they apart; they are always working together," Ducic wrote.[39] His words leave us guessing at the nature of this relationship, and no other known source provides information about it. In 1939 Barjaktarovic met Djurdja but did not report anything about this relationship.

Betrothed at the age of eighteen, Djurdja had begun preparing the wedding gifts. She noticed that her mother, who still had two other younger daughters, sadly watched her doing the needlework for the presents. "Mother, it looks as if you're not glad that I'm getting married." Her mother replied affirmatively, saying, "If you get married I'll be left alone, but if you stay with me, I'll have a son." On hearing these words Djurdja threw down her embroidery. She decided to stay in her parents' home and changed her appearance by cutting off her hair, taking a shepherd's crook and putting on a black cap and a coat; however, she kept the skirt. From then on she devoted herself to tending cattle. She started to smoke and mixed increasingly with males. Barjaktarovic goes on to recount how Djurdja lost her father shortly after her decision not to marry her fiancé; her mother, however, lived until 1937. As long as the mother was alive, Djurdja's means of subsistence were satisfactory because of the father's pension, but afterward she suffered material deprivation.[40]

The second couple consisted of Shefkije Rexhepi Cur and her companion Rukë, who both belonged to the Madjup (sedentary Muslim Romany) community of Djakovica, a small town in Metohija near the Albanian border. Vukanovic called on the manly dressed Shefkije in 1958, who was at that time about forty-seven years old. Shefkije's earnings as a singer and player of the *dajre* (tambourine) were insufficient to support her and, accordingly, she had to rely on social assistance. After having become a sworn virgin at the age of fifteen, she at first lived with her brother, but in 1938 she left him to found a joint household with her friend

Rukë, with whom she concluded the solemn bonds of blood-sisterhood.[41] From neighbors in the Romany quarter Vukanovic understood that this relationship apparently also had a sexual component.[42] When I made inquiries in 1985 I discovered that Shefkije and Rukë had died several years earlier. Some local informants had a vivid memory of the small Shefkije with her masculine clothes and cap and the feminine-looking Rukë, famous for their performances at wedding parties: this eccentric couple had left an indelible memory.

The third couple is a contemporary one among the Orthodox population of northern Montenegro. Curious about the vicissitudes of "N.N.," who was recognized in 1955 during a medical screening of the population, I paid a visit to his native village in 1986. According to Gusic, whose husband took part in the screening, this person was born in 1941 to a poor peasant family and at the age of ten was declared *ostajnica* ("she who stays behind," that is, not to be given in marriage) out of the nine daughters by the widowed mother. Ever since, he wore boy's clothes, except for special occasions such as the medical checkup, at which he arrived dressed as a girl.[43] Villagers told me that this person, who is still dressed as a man, is now living and working in a town. He is said to live with a "beautiful" and "feminine" friend from a good family. They are inseparable and cause quite a stir. In modern usage they are referred to as *lesbeke* ("lesbians").

When discussing this kind of relationship it is difficult to ignore a tradition from Bosnia-Herzegovina published toward the end of the last century by Ivan Zovko. Among the phenomena discussed by Zovko is that of the *muskobaracas*, which, according to him, means "mannish women" (German *Mannweiber*). In translation the German text offers the following description of these women:

> They fight like males and are crazy about doing everything in the way males do. Unfortunately, our Lord has created them as women! They dress themselves like males, talk like males; in brief, do everything like males. *Several* muskobaracas *are even claimed to have fallen in love with other girls and married them*, but are said to have treated

them roughly, as if God hadn't created them for that purpose. They hate every woman's adornment as the devil hates the baptized soul [emphasis added].[44]

The original Serbo-Croatian text, however, indicates that these marriages were brought about by *deception*; the brides were apparently under the illusion that the grooms were male.[45] Marital deceit of this type is occasionally reported in early modern Western Europe, but as far as the Balkans are concerned it is very hard to find actual proof of its occurrence;[46] I know of only one instance, badly documented at that. Immediately after World War II, two Muslim Bosnians got married, but later their marriage was annulled because the bride found out that she was married to a female. This case, which is mentioned by Vukanovic in passing, is all the more mysterious since both partners were subsequently hospitalized for months in Belgrade for an unspecified disease.[47]

It is not inconceivable that in the earlier history of the Balkans women could be classified as men to the extent of acting as husbands without hindrance. In fact, an institutionalized "woman marriage" is known in some parts of the non-Western world, most notably Africa, where it is predominantly found in patrilineal and patrilocal tribes. There the custom enables rich widows without heirs to obtain a wife, for instance. By paying the customary bride-price the female husband is the father (*pater*) to the children, who result from a liaison with some male (*genitor*). Alternative strategies to provide heirs are also to be found in tribal Africa, such as the "ghost marriage" in which a girl is married to a deceased male and the "marriage with the house" in which a girl is not given in marriage but remains in the paternal home; in both cases sexual encounters with males occur in order to secure offspring.[48]

In view of the eye-catching similarities among the classificatory fictions that enable strict observance of the principles of patrilineality and patrilocality, one would expect to find in the tribal part of the Balkans ingenious emergency measures like those mentioned above. According to the particular logic intrinsic to this Balkan culture, though, it appears rather unsatisfactory to induce females to embrace the male gender role when it is threatened with extinction if they are not also granted the right to ensure progeny themselves.[49] Viewed from this perspective, the Balkan institution of sworn virgins who administer the parental homestead until death, when it is transferred to kinsmen, seems to be merely rudimentary. Much research into the historical development of this institution will be needed to test this conjecture.

The four individuals described in the case studies differ to a considerable extent in claiming masculinity. Mikas, whose intense claim is perhaps connected with a hormonal disorder, constitutes one extreme, and Durgjane, who seems to have totally adandoned this claim, the other. Some, such as Stana and Durgjane, are not secretive about their female physique, although they respond to it in different ways: to Stana it seems to be a matter of regret; to Durgjane, one of indifference. Others renounce their femaleness completely and are hypersensitive about allusions to it, as Mikas was. It stands to reason that the latter are almost inaccessible to research, since they consider every kind of special attention paid to them a manifestation of doubt concerning their cherished masculinity.

In such a case the researcher might try a white lie, as I did in 1985 when visiting a large Muslim village in the Sandzak, the area around the city of Novi Pazar in southwestern Serbia. To meet the retired local photographer, so far unapproachable to other researchers, I pretended to be interested in old photographs of local buildings, costumes and the like. In this way I managed to be introduced to and admitted by him. Referring to information provided by a relative of the person concerned, the Serbian legal ethnologist Ljiljana Gavrilovic states that the person was raised as a man since infancy because the well-to-do parents were without a son. Later a son was born, but this happy event did not change the status of the appointed son. Only the oldest and closest relatives seem to know that this person was born a girl, but they try to hush it up as much as they can.[50] During the hours I spent at his place I noticed that the members of the household, as well as the visitors on the occasion of the *Kurban-bajram* (a Muslim festival), all treated the person as a man. "Uncle" and "brother" were the words used by relatives when referring to this individual in his absence. I had to take care not to reveal my fore-knowledge by slips of the tongue that would have offended the photographer. In both the domestic circle and the village I found no trace of skepticism regarding this person's male sex, but older men from surrounding villages told me they had once heard the person referred to as *hadum* ("eunuch") and as *ni zensko ni musko* ("neither female nor male").

Apart from those socialized as male since infancy, individuals who were brought up as girls sometimes also laid claim to masculine prerogatives, as is shown by the following two examples. A case probably dating from the mid-nineteenth century is mentioned by Dervis Korkut. In Gora near the river Lasva in Bosnia lived a "very pretty" Muslim girl of an aristocratic family, about whom we learn the following:

> When her lover died, she put on a man's suit and started to live entirely like a man, she rode horseback, smoked, carried arms, and even went to girls under the window and knew the art of *asikovati* [courting by means of reciting poems]. She adopted a male name and allowed nobody to mention her girl's name, or to make an allusion to her sex in general.[51]

The next case, reported by Vukanovic, originates from the turn of the century and concerns not a girl but a widow. Badë, a Muslim Albanian from the village of Spiljanije at the river Ibar, had become a sworn virgin after her husband died. Costumed and armed accordingly, with the typical ponytail on top of her otherwise smooth-shaven head, this new "he" must have had quite a manly appearance. Once a man "mocked" him for being a female, and the widow thought it necessary to avenge the masculine honor by killing him. For this crime the Turkish authorities of the day – who did not recognize female impunity as local custom did – sentenced the widow to several years of hard labor, after which she returned to the house of her deceased husband to continue living as a sworn virgin.[52]

A Third Gender? Notes on Ambiguities and Contradictions
Notwithstanding the often convincing masculine image of these
individuals and their smooth passing as men in everyday life and
despite the high esteem they often received as honorable males
by the local communities, there are several indicators that their
gendered role and identity were not altogether clear to others.
The nouns mentioned in the Introduction that comembers of the
communities used in referring to them are of feminine grammatical gender. Nevertheless, in addressing these persons, especially
those who vehemently insisted on being male, any allusion to
femininity was usually omitted out of reverence or fear. Yet one
comes across local equivalents of "maiden" and "virgin" used as
terms of self-reference. Such words were especially employed in
private encounters with authorities from the world beyond the
local community – a doctor, ruler, priest, officer or civil servant,
that is, someone to whom an explanation was thought necessary
or appropriate. Sometimes we also hear a "social man" declare
self-assuredly, "I am a maiden with a man's heart in my chest."[53]
The combination of both genders is also apparent in a term of
reference such as *momak djevojka* ("boy-girl")[54] and in nicknames
like *muska Nevena* ("male Nevena," Nevena being a female name).[55]
Significantly, no recourse was made to the neuter gender in referring to these persons. Instead of the available Slavic personal pro-
noun *ono* ("it"), local folks commonly alternated between *on*
("he") and *ona* ("she") in referring to them, thus expressing the
power of the binary gender concept. In such instances, a certain
validity is granted to the notion of an intermediate or "third"
gendered status.

The traveler Durham, discussed earlier, is one such example.
Given her automomy as an unwed bluestocking with rather unfeminine behavior and looks, she was often treated by local men as if
she were one of their sworn virgins: "I was treated with great
honour and classed with the buck-herd. No woman was allowed
to eat with me in a tribesman's house. I ate with the men, but as
they had to draw the line somewhere, they often helped my horse-
boy first."[56]

Ambivalence of this kind is more often encountered in social interaction, and we also find it reflected in the realm of common law. Unlike nubile females, the female who was brought up as a son to become heir to a sonless father was able to inherit real estate. Such a social male enjoyed usufruct of the paternal property until his dying day, a right shared by marriageable females until their wedding and by returning widows and divorcées. By marrying, to wit, by becoming a wife and mother, a female lost all rights to real estate (and often to any property at all) in her natal family. The *tobelija* was expected to safeguard the property until his final hour, as it was to be handed down to the legal male heirs, preferably agnatic relatives. This means that a social male was merely inheriting without being entitled to act as testator, as neither alienating real estate during one's lifetime nor bequeathing it at will was allowed.[57] This limits the possibility of a third gender having transmissible material property, which limits transmission of the social status.

According to customary law, women were not eligible to pledge or act as jurors in native juridical proceedings. Hence, the girl who refused an arranged marriage had to take the vow of celibacy in the presence of males, close kinsmen and tribal chiefs, who acted in this respect as cojurors. If the virgin in the end breached her vow, it was not this person but rather the male cojurors who were held responsible by the rejected groom's family.

Nor in the realm of violence was the original, biological femaleness completely disregarded. Unlike ordinary females, who were unarmed, the female who became a social male could be completely armed and actively take part in feuds, raids and the like. Yet intentionally killing or wounding such a person while in full awareness of the fact that he was a female by nature was considered shameful and unworthy for a genuine hero. "True men," according to Balkan ideas, would not dare disgrace themselves and their kin by hurting a female. Although the sources are inconsistent on this point, I have the impression that in general these social males retained the immunity conferred by their female sex or their former gender.[58] This allowed them to kill males without having to fear being killed in retaliation. This gives some social advantage to the idea of a third-gender role. It would be wrong, however, to consider this a deliberate attempt to run with the hares and hunt with the hounds. *Tobelijas* sometimes escaped retaliation against their will, as their often cherished masculine vocation and their experienced solidarity with their comrades-in-arms called for a treatment like that received by any other man, instead of being publicly set back in the female place, a sort of *noblesse oblige*.

The following case exemplifies nicely the consequences of a female taking the role of revenger. The virgin Emin from Orenjë in Çermenikë (central Albania) had lost her father in the course of feuding when she herself was still in the cradle. As she grew older, she realized that her four cousins, the only males in her family, displayed very little eagerness to retaliate. At the age of fifteen Emin secretly bought a rifle and used the first opportunity to kill the evildoer. By this (killing) the accounts were squared. "But the enemy refused to make peace, saying that a kill by a woman did not count, and they were not yet therefore 'one for one.'" Yet this case is interesting not only because the enemy did not reckon this killing in settling the account: the reactions of her own kinsmen speak volumes. "Her cousins were trebly annoyed. She, a woman, had proved herself their superior in courage; for her crime one of their lives was forfeit; and they had hoped to compound the feud without further bloodshed, a hope she had destroyed. In fact, she had embittered the feud by putting the enemy to the shame of losing a relative at a woman's hands."⁵⁹

In the domain of tribal politics the position of the sworn virgin was also fraught with ambiguity. As a rule, females had no right to participate in the all-male gatherings of the group. The codex of north Albanian traditional legal rules states that the virgins who behave like men are allowed to sit with them during gatherings, but it exempts them from discussion, and certainly from voting.⁶⁰ Yet individual *tobelijas* from the Albanian Malisor community on the contested Montenegrin border inform us that they took active part in such meetings.⁶¹ Likewise, scattered instances of capable widows representing the household to the outside world are reported.⁶² In a sense, then, gender intermediates were thus able to make the best of both worlds, for sometimes they cunningly took advantage of the existing lack of consequences. In the final analysis they were females, inasmuch as their biology was never entirely overlooked, and by this very fact it was most dishonorable for a man to harm them in retaliation.

Belonging to an intermediate gender category may have caused much inconvenience to the individual's psyche, yet being betwixt and between also opened new perspectives and brought about opportunities. It would be an exaggeration to state that the ambiguity between the sexual nature and the gendered culture of the individuals was completely resolved; yet the sex reassignment as male, which stressed the importance of "cultural genitalia,"[63] was surely instrumental in reducing the inherent ambiguity to manageable proportions, as were the proclaimed sexual taboos of a virginal, asexual life. This applies both to these individuals, for the phenomenon limited their feelings of gender dysphoria, and to this part of Balkan society as a whole. Perhaps the fear and uneasiness experienced by normally gendered persons in dealing with these extraordinary persons were thus kept in check. Yet the message of Balkan cross-dressing is mixed: only in cases of necessity, when survival is at stake or when bloodshed is to be averted, are transgressions of innate human nature acceptable (or even prescribed).

Within the universe of adults, the few virgins lined up with the males inasmuch as they also remained in their natal villages, whereas women moved in with their in-laws. This important spatial aspect of gender should not be overlooked, as we have seen in the case of *tobelija* Djurdja Popovic from the Kuci tribe.

Can these individuals indeed be considered to belong to a category beyond the standard division of male/female and masculine/feminine? In other words, do they constitute a third gender? With this I imply something other than a mere copying of the gender role opposite of one's original ascribed gender (i.e., gender-crossing) or simple mixing of male and female gender traits (i.e., gender-mixing). The designation *third gender* should, I think, be reserved to creative bricolage, resulting in an authentically new, genuine, alternative form of human existence outside the realm of mainstream gendered roles, a form of life beyond the two stereotypical gender categories (dualistic gender coding) and including much more than mere erotic preference or sexual behavior (object choice). The inherent ambivalence of virgins, or people considered virginal, is of crucial importance here.

Cross-culturally we find such individuals either classed with women or with men (for example, gender categories in Polynesia), although in both instances they constitute a distinctive subcategory because of their potential, though not fully realized, femininity. In Balkan culture virgins were seen as a relatively unclassified category, clearly set apart from those who have become "women" through matrimony and motherhood, and somehow more akin to the male gender – which serves more or less as the marked prestige gender. Prolonged virginity, that is, virginity continued throughout adulthood, met with the same ambiguity. In local symbolic discourse, the semantic difference between "woman" and "virgin" is still large. Women and virgins are to some degree still subjected to differing behavioral standards. Masculine behavior may be deemed most improper for women, but not for virgins. One can add, concerning women, that when their reproductive age is over, when they are widowed or when they are otherwise believed to have stopped having intimate contact with men, declassification occurs. They retreat from the status of women and return to a more primordial state close to that of men. In postmenopausal women we encounter "unfeminine" traits such as smoking, drinking and speaking in male company. Elder females are sometimes treated by males as their peers or even their superiors. In this manner, so it seems, socially expressed and accomplished femininity (the self-effacing life of wife and mother) is rewarded.

As a final remark, I would restate how informants in the field were sometimes surprised to find me investigating the lives of local females who had never wed and had led a man's life: "What is so exceptional about them that you have come all this way? After all, they are not women but virgins!"

PART TWO

Anthropological Contributions

CHAPTER SIX

Polynesian Gender Liminality

Through Time and Space

Niko Besnier

This essay focuses on the "intermediate" gender categories of the islands of Polynesia, an aspect of Polynesian culture that has captivated Westerners' curiosity since the beginning of sustained contact over two centuries ago. Conspicuously prevalent throughout the region, the adoption by certain individuals of attributes associated with a gender other than their own is deeply embedded in dynamics of Polynesian cultures and societies.[1] In this essay, I address the complex ways in which the phenomenon articulates with social and cultural processes, particularly the politics of sex, gender and sexual orientation, the meaning of power and prestige and the interface of structure and agency.

An underlying concern of this essay is the recognition that discourses of sex and gender are always saturated with morality in one or another of its manifestations. Morality becomes particularly central when these discourses penetrate the life of the Other in the context of intercultural contact. In the situation I focus on here, several discursive traditions can be identified. First are eighteenth- and early-nineteenth-century European seafarers' travelogues and missionaries' journals, which reflect the specific agendas of that period concerning sexuality and gender. (Eventually, North American travelers and religious figures would join their ranks, but nothing will be said here of these latter-day commentators.) In the early part of the twentieth century, the voices of anthropologists entered the discussion, although more through omission than description. The latter part of the century witnessed the emergence of modern anthropological accounts, which will form the core of this essay, along with results of my own field research. To these one must add journalistic and literary representations of a phenomenon that lends itself particularly well to cross-cultural sensationalism. Most recently, gender studies and lesbian and gay studies have added their voices to the chorus, basing themselves primarily on interpretations of the historical and ethnographic literature. In the course of the following discussion, I attempt to animate these various discourses and illustrate the moral agendas and specific priorities that underlie each one of them.

The phenomena on which this essay focuses raise particularly thorny categorical questions, and hence the choice of labels is problematic. Prefiguring the interpretation I will argue for here, I shy away from referring to the category under question as a "third gender." However, I will assert from the outset that the phenomenon is primarily an issue of *gender* rather than *sex*, because it is primarily defined in social and cultural terms. At the same time, I recognize that the distinction between gender and sex is anything but straightforward and will show that the category in question is also grounded in the problematics of sexuality.[2] Labeling is further complicated by the fact that words referring to the phenomenon differ across Polynesian languages. The best-known terms are the Tahitian and contemporary Hawaiian terms *māhū*,[3] which have no known etymology, and the Samoan term *fa'afafine* (pl. *fa'afāfine*), literally, "in the fashion of a woman," cognates of which are found in several other Polynesian languages. In contemporary Tonga, the category is called *fakaleitī* – the root *leitī* is borrowed from the English "lady" – or *fakafefine* (it is unclear whether there is a difference between the two terms), while Tuvaluans normally use the Gilbertese borrowing *pinapinaaine*. In all of these languages, these terms can function as nouns to refer to a person, as verbs to refer to demeanor or action and often also as adverbs to specify the manner in which an action is being performed; such patterns of linguistic multifunctionality are not specific to these terms. Whenever possible, I will use untranslated Polynesian terms when referring to particular island groups, despite the fact that these terms can be and often are used derogatorily.

286

When speaking generally, I avoid the term "berdache," which is strongly identified with Native North America, and the labels "transvestite," "transsexual," "homosexual" and "gay," which at best capture only one aspect of the category and at worst are completely miscontextualized. Rather, I use the expressions "gender liminality" and "gender-liminal person," which turn out to be much more than conveniently neutral labels. As I will demonstrate, the notion of liminality, first theorized by Arnold van Gennep and later elaborated by Victor Turner, captures many attributes of intermediate-gender status in Polynesia.[4] The three major characteristics of liminal events and persons that Turner identifies, namely, their "betwixt and between" locus, outsider status and social inferiority, will be shown to be relevant to Polynesian gender-liminal persons. Other common cross-cultural attributes of liminality, such as its affinity with performance and rituals of reversal, will also be discussed below.

This study has two limitations. First, it is impaired by the paucity of detailed treatments of gender liminality in specific Polynesian contexts. Reification and overgeneralization are thus real dangers in this enterprise, as they are in many works on related phenomena, like the berdache in Native North America.[5] There is some evidence that gender liminalities across the various cultures of the region share many features. As more information becomes available on contemporary gender liminality in various parts of Polynesia, particularly Samoa,[6] regional commonalities emerge, although significant differences also become evident, suggesting that the proliferation of descriptors across Polynesian languages is not just a linguistic phenomenon. However, the dearth of information on many island cultures suggests caution and leaves open the possibility that further research may reveal important and hitherto overlooked patterns of variation. Whenever possible, I will present ethnographic information about *particular* Polynesian settings, rather than pan-regional generalizations. Furthermore, as I will discuss, the characteristics of gender liminality are subject to much intracultural diversity across individuals and contexts. In the course of the following discussion, I will address the significance of this diversity, which I view as a crucial facet of gender liminality rather than mere deviations from a prototype.

Second, this essay focuses on liminal men, namely, persons with male sexual attributes who adopt certain social attributes normally associated with women. But the mirror-image situation is not unknown: in contemporary Polynesian contexts, one does find women who dress like men, perform certain tasks for which men are traditionally responsible, are sexually aggressive with women and are given labels that mirror terms referring to liminal men (e.g., Tongan *fakatangata* and Samoan *fa'atama*, "in the fashion of a man"). Liminal women are considerably fewer and less noticeable than liminal men; similar asymmetries are very common with gender-crossing across the world.[7] There is anecdotal evidence that female liminality may be of relatively recent origin, in contrast to historically well-established male liminality. What is clear is that liminal women embody a hidden discourse in both anthropological and local representations and that they are even more liminal than their male counterparts.[8] To date, no analysis of the phenomenon has been conducted, and my silence here is but a reflection of this ethnographic vacuum. Yet the importance of questions that liminal women pose for our understanding of gender and sexuality in Polynesian societies cannot be overstated: What are the meanings of female liminality? How does the phenomenon contrast with liminal men? Why is it considerably less frequent and salient than male liminality? Echoing Evelyn Blackwood's critique of the common socio-scientific assumption that lesbianism is simply the "mirror image" of male homosexuality, I suggest that an exploration of female liminality in Polynesia will open up a host of questions that do not arise in the ethnographic inquiry of male liminality.[9] Unfortunately, too little information is available at this time to warrant any coherent statement on the topic.

The Historical Construction of a Category

For Europeans of the Enlightenment and early Romantic era, Polynesia, one of the last frontiers of colonial expansionism, was the embodiment of a paradise that Westerners had left behind in their quest for civilization. Early contacts between Western explorers and Tahitians or Hawaiians were perfectly timed with the rise of post-Enlightenment Romanticism in Europe. On the other side of the world, explorers found what they thought was humankind in its primeval state, unencumbered by the proscriptions of civilized mores. And, of course, one of the most prominent features of the harmonious marriage of humankind and nature was the apparent straightforwardness with which islanders approached sexual matters, particularly in Tahiti and Hawaii. Witness Bougainville's description of his first acquaintance with Tahiti, a now-classic passage in the annals of history:

As we came nearer the shore, the number of islanders surrounding our ships encreased. The periaguas [i.e., canoes] were so numerous all about the ships, that we had much to do to warp in amidst the croud of boats and the noise.... The periaguas were full of females; who, for agreeable features, are not inferior to most European women; and who in point of beauty of the body might, with much reason, vie with them all. Most of these fair females were naked; for the men and the old women that accompanied them, had stripped them of the garments which they generally dress themselves in. The glances which they gave us from their periaguas, seemed to discover some degree of uneasiness, notwithstanding the innocent manner in which they were given; perhaps, because nature has every where embellished their sex with a natural timidity; or because even in those countries, where the ease of the golden age is still in use, women seem least to desire what they most wish for. The men, who were more plain, or rather more free, soon explained their meaning very clearly. They pressed us to choose a woman, and to come on shore with her: and their gestures, which were nothing less than equivocal, denoted in what manner we should form an acquaintance with her. It was very difficult, amidst such a sight, to keep at their work four hundred young French sailors, who had seen no women for six months. In spite of all our precautions, a young girl came on board, and placed herself upon the quarter-deck, near one of the hatchways, which was open, in order to give air to those who were heaving at the capstern below it. The girl carelessly dropt a cloth, which covered her, and appeared to the eyes of all beholders, such as Venus shewed herself to the Phrygian shepherd, having, indeed, the celestial form of that goddess. Both sailors and soldiers endeavoured to come to the hatch-way; and the capstern was never hove with more alacrity than on this occasion.[10]

With this description, Bougainville unwittingly heralded a new era for the Pacific, during which the politics of sex and gender would become inextricably interlocked with the politics of colonialism.[11]

But soon enough, European perceptions of Polynesia changed course. Particularly as the London Missionary Society was being established in Tahiti, vanguarding massive missionary endeavors throughout Polynesia for years to come, the island turned, in the eyes of the foreigners, from the New Cythera (the name that Bougainville bestowed upon it) to "the filthy Sodom of the South Seas":

> In these Islands all persons seem to think of scarcely anything but adultery and fornication. Little children hardly ever live to the age of seven ere they are deflowered. Children with children, often boys with boys. They are often on the mountains playing in wickedness together all the day long.[12]

As Neil Gunson aptly summarizes, "the Evangelical missionaries had little doubt that Satan, adversary of God and man, reigned as absolute sovereign over the South Sea islanders."[13] In the contrast between explorers' and missionaries' discourses, one can read the full text of Europeans' attitudinal discords toward the "uncivilized" at the turn of the eighteenth century: free of the shackles of civilizations, yet inclined toward unspeakable practices, Tahitians and other Polynesians were in their eyes at once noble and ignoble savages.[14]

Besides infanticide, human sacrifice and adultery (as well as cannibalism next door in the Marquesas), one feature of Tahitian society particularly captured the missionaries' attention:

Something that was seen among the people today shews these heathens, like the heathens of old, are given up to vile affections; the men leaving the natural use of the woman, burn in their lusts towards another, men with men working that which is unseemly. Indeed it is said that Otoo [Tū, paramount chief of Tahiti, later King Pōmare I] never cohabits with his wife but has a number of boys with whom he satiates his passion.[15]

The Tahitians' "predilection" for "sodomy" had already been amply described in seafarers' journals, in only slightly less morally condemning terms. George Hamilton, surgeon on the British frigate *Pandora*, who spent three weeks on the island, had remarked in 1791 that young men were kept "for abominable purposes."[16] In 1789, William Bligh described "a class of people common in Otaheite called Mahoo":

> These people...are particularly selected when Boys and kept with the Women solely for the carnesses [*sic*] of the men.... The Women treat him as one of their Sex, and he observed evry restriction that they do, and is equally respected and esteemed.[17]

With these observations began the Western construction of Polynesian gender liminality that, in the next two centuries to come, would take many different forms.

Recurrent in early testimonies is the theme of the horny European sailor mistaking a Polynesian gender-liminal person for a woman. The vignette appears in 1789 in one of the earliest mentions of a Tahitian *māhū*:

> I cannot help relating a very droll occurrence that happened in consequence of one of their nocturnal Heivas [i.e., dance performances]. Attracted by the sound of drums, and a great quantity of lights, I went on shore one night with two of our mates to one of these exhibitions. We seated ourselves among some of our friends, whom we found there; when one of the gentlemen who accompanied me on shore took it into his head to be very much smitten with a dancing girl, as he thought her; went up to her, made her a present of some

beads and other trifles, and rather interrupted the performance by his attentions; but what was his surprize when the performance was ended, and after he had been endeavouring to persuade her to go with him on board our ship, which she assented to, to find this supposed damsel, when stripped of her theatrical paraphanelia, a smart dapper lad. The Otaheiteans on their part enjoyed this mistake so much, that they followed us to the beach with shouts and repeated peals of laughter; and I dare say this event has served as a fine subject for one of their comedies.[18]

(The frequent association of gender liminality with dancing in historical records is significant, as will be discussed below.) A similar story surfaces in reference to New Zealand in a 1789 entry in the journal of a member of James Cook's crew on the *Endeavour*, one of the few (and not unequivocal) mentions of what may be gender liminality among the Maori at the time of contact:

One of our gentlemen came home to day abusing the Natives most heartily whoom he said he had found to be given to the detestable Vice of Sodomy. He, he said, had been with a family of Indians and paid a price for leave to make his addresses to any one young woman they should pitch upon for him; one was chose as he thought who willingly retird with him but on examination provd to be a boy; that on his returning and complaining of this another was sent who turnd out to be a boy likewise; that on his second complaint he could get no redress but was laught at by the Indians. Far be it for me to attempt saying that Vice is not practisd here, this however I must say that in my humble opinion this story proves no more than that our gentleman was fairly trickd out of his cloth, which none of the young ladies chose to accept of on his terms, and the master of the family did not chuse to part with.[19]

The slapstick nature of these equivocations were obviously humorous not just to European bystanders but, more importantly, to Tahitian and Maori witnesses as well.[20] While one should resist reading too much into these passages, they are nevertheless suggestive in light of the striking associations of gender liminality with satire and the burlesque in contemporary Polynesia.

British seamen and missionaries of the Georgian era evaluated the practices of which they caught glimpses in Tahiti through a specific framework of moral reference. In the late eighteenth century, "sodomy" had become the focus of particularly virulent revilement in England. As is well documented, sodomy was an "utterly confused category" into which fell many "unnatural practices," principally homosexual and heterosexual oral or anal intercourse and bestiality and which was closely affiliated in eighteenth-century thought with a broad panoply of nonsexual crimes.[21] However, at the close of the century, the meaning of sodomy was becoming more specifically focused on homosexual intercourse, an evolution that went hand in hand with changes in gender relations and the gradual emergence of a homosexual protosubculture.[22]

In England, these changes vere accompanied by increasingly severe persecution in the decades during which contacts with Polynesian societies were becoming more sustained. Legal sanctions against sodomitic crimes were considerably more serious there than in any other European country: while capital punishment for sodomy is last documented in 1784 for the rest of Europe, death sentences for "unnatural crimes" in Britain lasted until the third decade of the nineteenth century.[23] Although successful legal prosecution was commonly hindered by the vagueness of the legal definition of sodomy, the importance that the crime had acquired in the legal and social consciousness of turn-of-the-century England gave rise to a virulently repressive climate.[24] The repression became particularly intense in times of war, during which sodomy would be perceived as a "foreign infection" and an instrument of mutiny, and its witch-hunt-like prosecution as a patriotic act.[25] The repression did not affect all social classes equally: "Whereas aristocratic males accused of sodomy were allowed to escape to the Continent, the artisans, soldiers and unskilled workers (the men most often arrested for sodomy in Georgian England) could look forward to the pillory, a punishment that usually resulted in death."[26] Nowhere was repression more virulent than in the British Navy, particularly in times of war, where it targeted almost exclusively enlisted (hence working-class) men, in keeping with patterns of civilian prosecution. Court-martial records of the second half of the century indicate that sodomy was considered as serious as murder and mutiny; a whopping 31 percent of all executions resulted from sodomy convictions.[27] Ironically, it was the Royal Navy, the institution most fixated on sodomitic behavior, that reached the shores of Tahiti in the late 1700s.[28]

In contrast to the copious early accounts of *māhū* in Tahiti and, more equivocally, of comparable categories in Hawaii, the Marquesas and New Zealand, no mention is made of the phenomenon in Western Polynesia, despite the fact that it is equally conspicuous in all regions today. Yet contact between Europeans and islanders was sustained, if not more so, in Western as in Eastern Polynesia. For example, in 1805, a young British sailor, Will Mariner, was taken captive in Vava'u, Tonga, and subsequently spent four years as the adopted son of paramount chief Finau 'Ulukālala, on which he based an ethnographic account following his return to England;[29] nowhere in Mariner's otherwise meticulously detailed work is there any mention of gender liminality. Even though nineteenth-century missionaries and travelers to Samoa did not shy away from describing in great detail "sinful" Samoan practices, as Jeannette Mageo points out, *fa'afāfine* are not mentioned at all in their accounts.[30] A curious and unexplainable contrast thus emerges between early Euro-American descriptions of Eastern Polynesia, especially Tahiti, and Western Polynesia.

However, skepticism must be exerted in drawing inferences on the organization of social life and culture in the Polynesian past from the historical record.[31] The absence of historical documentation on gender liminality in Western Polynesia does not necessarily mean that it is a postcontact phenomenon. While the mention of a social category in the historical record is an indication that some form of it was present at the time of contact, little can be inferred from historical silence. Early cross-cultural contacts are complex events, and a multiplicity of factors can determine what one group will notice about the other.[32] These historical differences only suggest that caution must be exerted in generalizing about Polynesian gender liminality and that a re-construction of the history of gender liminality in the region is not possible. If anything, fragments of historical representations like missionaries' and seafarers' journals, which remained highly peripheral to the events they purported to describe, should be read as texts of perhaps greater relevance to European social his-tory than to early-contact Polynesian societies.

Contemporary Perspectives

The initial flurry of historical testimonies on Tahitian gender liminality in the early voyager and missionary literature was fol-lowed by a century and a half of relative silence on the subject. In particular, little was said about it in the large volume of eth-nographic descriptions generated in the first decades of the cen-tury.[33] For example, Ernest and Pearl Beaglehole do not mention gender liminality in rural Tonga, while the numerous ethno-graphic reports published by Honolulu's Bishop Museum contain only passing references to the category, usually under rubrics enti-tled "sexual aberrations" or "perverted instincts," alongside "adul-tery," "prostitution," "celibacy" and "sterility."[34] The reasons for this near-silence are difficult to ascertain. Were Tongan and Mar-quesan villagers, by then intimately familiar with what Western-ers disapproved of, careful to conceal from visitors' scrutiny what they knew should not be included in the "cover story" of their culture? Were *fakaleitī* simply absent in the Tonga of the late 1930s? Or were fieldworkers uneasy with the category and uncer-tain about its place in the procrustean ethnological checklists fashionable in those days? No simple scenario comes to mind. But its consequence for our purposes is that the historical record on sexuality and gender liminality in Polynesia is discontinuous.

Does discontinuity also characterize the historical evolution of the category itself? In light of the fundamental social and cul-tural transformations that Polynesia has experienced since the days of early contacts, prudence should be exerted in assuming a his-torical continuum between gender liminality as early European voyagers described it and its modern-day manifestations. Yet the overall resemblance between them is striking, suggesting at least some degree of historical continuity. Today, gender liminality is very much alive, at least in regions of Polynesia that have not been subjected to intensive colonization (as Hawaii and New Zealand have) and, if anything, has become increasingly salient. This state of affairs is remarkable when compared to the fate of other forms of liminal gendering or sexuality in the face of colonialism and social change. For example, neither "ritualized" homosexuality in Melanesia nor the Native North American berdache has survived the moral onslaught of colonial authorities and missionaries.[35] Probably no single explanation can account for the contrast between the vitality of Polynesian gender liminality and the fate of comparable phenomena in other parts of the world.[36]

The first detailed ethnographic investigation of Polynesian gender liminality was conducted by Robert Levy, who in the early 1960s focused on two Tahitian villages.[37] The composite description of Polynesian gender liminality provided in the rest of this section is based principally on Levy's Tahiti material, on descriptions of Samoan gender liminality and on my own field data from Tonga and Tuvalu.[38]

Gender-liminal persons are most fundamentally distinguished by the nature of their labor contribution. In most rural Polynesian contexts, men are primarily in charge of "heavy" work, such as fishing, gardening and harvesting green coconuts, while "lighter" tasks like everyday cooking, house cleaning, gathering firewood, doing the laundry, weaving mats and making tapa cloth are commonly the responsibility of women. In urbanized areas of Polynesia, nonelite men typically become laborers, while nonelite women take on clerical jobs in the best of circumstances or occupy menial positions in the service industry, working as chambermaids in hotels and "housegirls" for expatriate Westerners, for example. In both rural and urban settings, the gender-liminal person gravitates toward women's work. Like the berdache in Native North American societies, the gender-liminal person in Polynesia is commonly thought to excel in women's tasks: his mats are said to be particularly symmetrical and regular in shape, his domestic chores singularly thorough, and he is more resilient to tedium than the average woman. In urban settings, liminal men are superb secretaries and coveted domestic help. In this sense, liminal persons are more womanly than women, a theme that recurs elsewhere.

The Tahitian *māhū*'s presentation of self, like the Samoan *fa'afafine*'s and Tongan *fakaleitī*'s, typically includes some "feminine" characteristics. Some cross-dressing is evident, particularly in urban centers and on festive occasions like dances, although there is no report of any gender-liminal individual cross-dressing on a permanent basis anywhere in Polynesia. In Tonga, the typical *fakaleitī*'s demeanor includes a swishy gait and speech patterns and nonverbal communicative behavior normally associated with women, such as a fast tempo, verbosity and an animated face, which contrasts with men's generally laconic and impassive demeanor. Throughout Polynesia, liminal persons are coquettishly concerned with their physical appearance, as evidenced by a propensity to wear flowers, garlands and perfume and, in urban contexts, heavy makeup. (While both men and women commonly wear flowers and perfume in Polynesia, the practice is particularly associated with younger women, and only women use makeup where it is available.) Everywhere in the region, the gender-liminal person is principally associated with domestic social spheres, as are women. For example, the young *fakaleitī* in rural Tonga is noticeably less mobile than his nonliminal age-mates: at night, while the latter roam the village and "hang out" in the periphery of houses in which kava drinking is taking place, smoking, chatting in a blasé fashion and engaging in casual micro-displays of manly bravado, the *fakaleitī* confine themselves to well-lit domestic settings and to the company of women.

The friendship networks that younger gender-liminal persons partake in usually consist of their female age-mates, with whom they are commonly depicted as "walking arm-in-arm, . . . gossiping and visiting with them."[39] On Funafuti Atoll, Tuvalu, young women enjoy spending time with *pinapinaaine*, with whom they can nurture a friendship with someone other than another woman without the ever-present specter of sexual tension in interactions between unrelated women and men. They particularly savor their *pinapinaaine* friends' clownish performances at dances, where the latter make risqué comments on men's appearances and actions, which the younger women themselves would hesitate to make. However, while the carefree figure that the younger gender-liminal person cuts finds an appreciative audience, his aging counterpart, whose women friends have all married and now have "serious" matters to attend to, acquires an element of pathos in the public eye. Older *fakaleitī* in Tongan society socialize with women of their age, although they are generally somewhat more isolated than both younger *fakaleitī* and male age-mates.

In the more stratified societies of Polynesia, gender-liminal persons are drawn from all social backgrounds. Historical records often described Tahitian *māhū* as members of chiefly entourages, in which they acted as the confidantes of high-ranking women and men and as providers of sexual services for male chiefs. In these accounts, it is unclear whether these *māhū* gained access to chiefly circles by virtue of their birth rank or through upward mobility and whether they were more frequent or salient around chiefs than among commoners (early European travelers were considerably more concerned with the former than the latter). In contemporary Polynesia, gender-liminal persons of different social rank have differing characteristics, although what these distinctions are is a complex and ill-understood question. It is clear that liminality itself does not increase the individual's rank, power or prestige; in fact, the opposite scenario is usually the case. However, I will show below that certain secondary characteristics of gender liminality sometimes provide the opportunity for upward mobility.

There is no compelling evidence that gender-liminal persons were or are associated with religious life anywhere in Polynesia. In this respect, Polynesian liminality differs from the phenomenon of the Native North American berdache, whose connection to shamanism is generally recognized.[40] Particular liminal individuals can be medical practitioners, the category which most resembles that of the shaman in contemporary Polynesia, but there is no particular link between gender liminality and curing knowledge. Gender liminals may have been thought to have access to certain shamanistic powers in some aboriginal Polynesian societies, although no unequivocal historical record of this association exists. It is very unlikely that liminal persons ever had any close link to religious contexts associated with the maintenance of chiefly hegemony. The only possible exception to this generalization is contemporary Hawaii, where *māhū* are frequently represented as *kahuna*-like.[41] There may be some historical basis for this representation, in that *māhū* are closely linked to *hula* performance, which has always had certain ritual functions. However, it must be understood in the context of the reconstruction of Hawaiian ethnicity. In their efforts to rebuild an ethnic identity, modern-day Hawaiians deliberately seek inspiration from American Indians, with whom they share an oppressor, much more than from other Polynesian groups. I surmise that many of the shamanistic connotations of contemporary Hawaiian *māhū* identity are borrowed from Native North America.

Gender Liminality and Sexuality

An important aspect of Polynesian gender liminality is homosexuality, the very attribute that earned the fascinated scorn of European observers of eighteenth-century Tahiti.[42] In "traditional" Polynesian contexts, partaking in homosexual activities is neither a necessary nor a sufficient criterion for gender-liminal status. Engaging in same-sex erotic behavior does not brand one as a *fakaleitī* in Tonga, a *pinapinaaine* in Tuvalu, or a *fa'afafine* in Samoa: male adolescents and young adults are widely known and "expected" (in the "nonofficial" version of culture) to engage in mutual masturbation as part of sexual experimentation. In Tuvalu, where jail sentences are a liberally used method of controlling the behavior of men in their late teens and early twenties (there is a "boys will be boys" quality to being known as having spent a few months in prison), homosexual behavior is a well-known feature of prison life. In Fiji, homosexuality is also associated with British-style elite private schools. Adolescents and ex-prisoners are frequently chided about their homosexual encounters. In Tongan society, adolescents' homosexual play is viewed as less damaging to the social order than premarital heterosexual encounters; the latter always threatens an idealized brother-sister relationship and is overshadowed by the dreaded specter of a socially undesirable face-saving marriage if pregnancy ensues. Nor does one's identification as a *fakaleitī* presuppose a history of or identifiable "preference" for homosexual encounters. Indeed, *fakaleitī* status in Tonga, as in Samoa and perhaps Tahiti, can be "assigned" early in life, much before the awakening of sexual desires of any type.[43] The evidence thus suggests the following important point: sexual relations with men are seen as an optional *consequence* of gender liminality, rather than its determiner, prerequisite or primary attribute (as Charles Callender and Lee M. Kochems show, this pattern is cross-culturally widespread).[44] Thus, Polynesian gender liminality must be distinguished from lesbian and gay identity in Western societies, of which sexual orientation is the most important defining trait. The contrast is hardly surprising or new: as we know from Michel Foucault and others, lesbian and gay identities arose in the West, particularly among the middle classes, in the context of recent historical evolutions in the notion of personhood as a holistic and atomistic entity, a trend closely tied to the elaboration of individualism as a foundational value of capitalism.[45] Western-style lesbian and gay identities further differ from gender-liminal Polynesians in a fundamental way: if the latter engage in sexual relations, they always do so with nonliminal men, never with members of their own category.

Although sexuality is not deterministic of gender liminality, its centrality to the definition of gender liminality cannot be overlooked. Indeed, while not all gender-liminal individuals have sex with nonliminal men, they are always perceived as a possible sexual conquest by men in societies like Samoa and Tonga, in the same way that women who are not classificatory relatives always are the potential target of a man's sexual advances. Social relations between liminal and nonliminal men thus foreground potential sexuality in a way that cannot be ignored. In Tonga and to a lesser extent Tuvalu, the *fakaleitī* or *pinapinaaine* often sexually taunt nonliminal men in ways that resemble and often caricature the way that young women tease men, particularly when the *fakaleitī* or *pinapinaaine* is surrounded by young female friends; the performance is typically punctuated with squeals and giggles from female audiences. But even when the *fakaleitī* does not flirt with men, he is frequently the target of harassment and physical violence, particularly from men in various states of inebriation.[46] The gender-liminal individual is viewed as potential sexual "fair game" in a much broader sense than women are, in that no brother-sister relationship shields him from the all-out sexual advances of nonliminal men. In stratified Polynesian contexts, low-ranking liminals are most vulnerable to violence, while high-ranking gender-liminal persons are somewhat shielded, but not completely protected, from the consequences of this perception by their social position. Thus, understanding liminality purely as a gender phenomenon and excluding sexuality from its characterization is misleading. Even if the importance of homosexuality in the definition of gender liminality is a relatively recent development, as some have argued, the fact that it has become important must be accounted for.[47]

Little information is available on erotic aspects of gender liminality. Levy indicates that the Tahitian *māhū*'s sexual encounters consist in his performing fellatio on non-*māhū* men, who view the *māhū* as a convenient, pleasurable, relatively pressure-free alternative to women for the release of sexual tension.[48] In Tonga and Tuvalu, young men brag in private about anally penetrating gender-liminal men and having intercourse between their thighs. Sexual encounters in which a gender-liminal person plays the role of the inserter are commonly reported not to occur anywhere in Polynesia, although my own ethnographic data contradict this generalization. Throughout the region, no great stigma is associated with taking on the role of the inserter, although it has the potentially negative connotation of one not able to procure women for one's sexual gratification. This explains in part why sexual encounters with liminal persons are associated principally with younger men, who are thought to lack experience in obtaining female sexual partners. If a nonliminal man can secure ready access to a female sexual partner, through marriage for example, as commonly argued in Polynesia, there is no reason for him to seek out gender-liminal men. This reasoning is more than just an idealization: nowhere in the region does one witness men regularly seeking liminal sexual partners after marriage, in contrast to patterns evident in Melanesia.[49]

Generally speaking, intercourse with gender-liminal persons is patterned on heterosexual encounters, with the gender-liminal person taking on the sexual role of the woman. But sexual intercourse involving gender liminality differs in one significant way from idealized, socially sanctioned heterosexual contact: it is inherently viewed as promiscuous, transient and lacking in significance. For Tongan men, sex with a *fakaleitī* is akin to intercourse with a *fokisi*, "woman of loose virtue," although perhaps of slightly lower prestige.[50] It is a conquest with no implications beyond the encounter itself and of little consequence for the man other than as an opportunity to release sexual tension and an occasion to brag to one's peers. In addition to procuring sexual pleasure, intercourse with a *fakaleitī*, like intercourse with a *fokisi*, can increase one's prestige as a virile youth. Marriage or any other form of attachment bears no relevance to either situation, as it is reserved for high-prestige tokens of womanhood, namely, the exalted Western Polynesian virginal young woman of high rank and dignified demeanor (Tongan *tāupo'ou*, a less elaborated category than its Samoan cognate, the *tāupōu*). Unlike the *fokisi* or *fakaleitī*, the *tāupo'ou* only submits to sexual deflowering with reluctance and no signs of pleasure, and only within the bounds of socially sanctioned marriage. The gender-liminal sexual partner, like the woman of loose virtue, is an eminently discardable and exploitable object. In Fiji, the metaphorical term that was applied to gender-liminal men in the early 1980s was *wādua*, which refers literally to a simple, usually homemade string-band musical instrument whose hinged bow is moved to modify the tension of a single string. The basis for the metaphor was explained to me as follows: the gender-liminal person is akin to a musical instrument that can be easily manipulated to play any note its user desires. In Tonga again, sexual encounters with a *fakaleitī* are acts through which prestige is transferred like a commodity from the *fakaleitī* to his partner and in which the *fakaleitī*'s degraded social status is thereby foregrounded. The obligatory power asymmetry involved in sex with a *fakaleitī* is simply a manifestation of the asymmetry that characterizes all "illicit" sexual encounters. It explains in part why sex between nonliminal adult men is inconceivable (other than in prison and similarly bracketed circumstances), since it would require one man to subject himself to degradation, which no man in his right mind would consent to.[51]

The gender-liminal person's experience of sexuality is socially defined as falling outside of the realm of what is locally sanctioned as erotic, not unlike women's heterosexual experience in many cultures. In Tahiti and Western Polynesia, the gender-liminal person is pervasively represented by nonliminal persons as lacking the sexual anatomy of a normal adult man: they are often described as having penes that are "too small" for heterosexual contact and that are uncircumcised or unsupercised, despite the fact that this is normally not the case.[52] These perceptions, in their contemporary forms at least, are obvious naturalizations of the gender-liminal person's experience as extraneous to the erotic: like male children who have not reached the age of circumcision or supercision, they are deemed incapable of experiencing sexual desire, and, according to the received discourse, their contacts with nonliminal men are devoid of erotic meaning. The sole purpose of the encounter is to satisfy the sexual needs of the nonliminal man.

However, these representations are one side of a contested field of meaning. While little is known about the extent to which gender-liminal individuals' personal erotic experience diverges from the social definition of sexual desire, there is evidence that for liminal men sexual encounters are not devoid of erotic excitement, despite the society's denial of its existence.[53] Indeed, when boasting about their sexual conquests of *fakaleiti*, young Tongan men often provide graphic detail of the *fakaleiti*'s erotic excitement, which they ridicule mercilessly (this is also true of narratives of encounters with *fokisi*). In Samoa, many *fa'afāfine* bragged to the ethnographer Mageo about their sexual successes with men, thereby contesting the social boundary between legitimate and illegitimate sexual experiences.[54] Clearly, the hegemonic imposition of moral standards of legitimacy is subject to subversive opposition.

303

The contemporary situation in Polynesia is further complicated by the presence, particularly in the more acculturated areas
of the region, of gay identities and perhaps communities that differ from "traditional" gender liminality and resemble patterns
observable in Western contexts. This phenomenon is not new in
areas where the Western colonial presence is well established, as
in Hawaii and New Zealand.[55] In the early 1960s, Levy identified
a Tahitian neologism, *raerae*, referring to "somebody who does
not perform a female's village role and who dresses and acts like
a man, but who indulges in exclusive or preferred sexual behavior with other men," and further noted some confusion among
his informants over categories and their meaning.[56] In the early
1990s, Samoa is witnessing the emergence of individuals who
understand themselves as having a gay identity in the Western
sense of the term and position themselves in society differently
from *fa'afāfine*.[57] How these patterns are related to older patterns
and how society is responding to them are fascinating questions
that deserve further scrutiny. While some headway has been made
toward an understanding of the sociocultural value of gender
liminality, much remains to be learned about its relationship to
erotic life.

Liminality and Gender

As the above discussion makes clear, gender liminality in Polynesia
must be understood within the broader context of the culture and
politics of gender. However, how the phenomenon fits in this context is a complex question. Levy hypothesizes that liminal individuals in Tahiti function as negative images of gender identity: the
māhū shows non-*māhū* men what not to be. Tahitian men need
such negative images because their society offers little differentiation between women and men. For example, the Tahitian language lacks gender markers, personal names in Tahiti are gender
neutral, labor is not clearly divided across gender lines and gender boundaries are frequently crossed for metaphorical purposes,
as when men dance together if not enough women partners are
available.[58] The resulting androgyny that Levy sees in Tahitian
society fails to provide a strong mold in which men's gender iden-

tity can be shaped (it is unclear in Levy's account whether women are thought to be similarly handicapped). Thus Tahitian culture must offer institutions in which this identity can solidify. One is supercision, which marks passage into both adulthood and manhood; the other is the presence in every village of a *māhū*, who counterexemplifies male identity.

While suggestive when first advanced, Levy's functionalist account presents a number of problems, which become particularly glaring in light of the explosion of research in the anthropology of gender that postdates the publication of Levy's work. First, the depiction of Tahitian gender-blending is problematic. The linguistic evidence (lack of grammatical gender, neutrality of personal names, absence of gendered pronouns) is invalid: as sociolinguists have argued, grammatical gender is largely unrelated to social gender, and the presence or absence of the former says nothing about the nature of the latter.[59] A better argument could be made if linguistic praxis in Tahiti did not index gender identity as clearly as other aspects of social identity, such as rank, as Elinor Ochs suggests for Samoa;[60] however, even if this situation is true of Tahiti, its implication for the formation of a relatively "strong" or "weak" gender identity must be examined very critically.

Furthermore, the evidence that Tahitian society lacks a gender-based division of labor is equivocal at best, even if one assumes the relationship between social and psychological aspects of gender to be unproblematic. As an example of the lack of labor gendering, Levy invokes food preparation: "men take a leading part in festive and traditional cooking [while] women do most of the 'ordinary' non-festive cooking."[61] But feasts and ordinary meals belong to different social spheres in Polynesia, and lumping them together into a single social activity is a mistake. The ethnographic literature on contemporary Tahiti suggests that many men's tasks are not accessible to women and vice versa: for example, only Tahitian men slaughter pigs, engage in physically demanding forms of fishing and do the heavy work in gardening, while the laundry, housekeeping and fruit gathering are exclusively women's work.[62] Tahitians indeed have strong ideas about the gendering of certain forms of labor: even though most Tahitian women are physically capable of cutting firewood, their doing so is seen as "inappropriate."[63] It is the case that men occasionally do women's work and vice versa, as when a spouse is unable to perform his or her tasks because of illness. But occasional forays into some of the work activities of the other gender are likely to be bounded by norms of appropriateness, and they hardly imply that women's and men's work are not well distinguished. On the contrary, they can affirm the division of labor across gender lines rather than erase it, particularly if the contexts in which this situation takes place are clearly bracketed: men doing the laundry in exceptional circumstances can be interpreted as a negative example of what men should not do. It should also be noted that the lack of a clear division of labor does not necessarily give rise to the blurring of gender identities. Among the Weyéwa of the Sunda Archipelago, women and men share all labor. Yet women and men are very clearly distinguished in other ways: for example, women do not have access to certain high-prestige cultural knowledge, such as competence in poetic forms that give men access to ancestral spirits.[64] Clearly, gender identity is constructed in many different social and cultural arenas, which often convey contradictory messages.[65]

Second, Levy's characterization of the cultural function of the *māhū* rests on problematic presuppositions. The model assumes that the absence of clear gender differentiation is by definition a problem that needs to be "resolved." Even if it were, societies offer a wealth of possibilities for distinguishing between women and men, and indeed for creating asymmetries between gender groups, by restricting women's independent access to material resources and power, for example, or by institutionalizing kinship structures in which women are transacted entities while men act as the transactors.[66] It would be most surprising if a society like Tahiti needed to "invent" the *māhū* to provide what other cultures find so easy to provide through other, simpler means that can be justified as being already in place for other purposes.

Furthermore, the exact mechanisms through which the Tahitian *māhū* enacts a negative portrayal of masculinity are at best unclear. Indeed, the *māhū*'s role, behavior and identity are intermediate between those of women and men. For example, George Biddle remarks that, in the early 1960s, the *māhū* distinguished themselves from all other Tahitian men (with the exception of a few missionaries) by letting their beards grow.[67] Thus, if anything, the *māhū* blurs gender categories rather than affirms them. Levy's argument would be stronger if, like the Samoan *fa'afafine*, to which I will return presently, the Tahitian *māhū* regularly flaunted his sexuality in a flagrant, outrageous and exaggerated manner, not unlike Western drag queens.[68] As many authors have demonstrated for various purposes, exaggerated caricatures are much more powerful indicators of what not to be than depictions that resemble reality too closely.[69]

Third, Levy's account fares poorly when placed in historical and comparative perspective. As noted earlier, the presence of the *māhū* in early-contact Tahitian society is well documented. The extent to which history has altered the definition of the category is not known, but its persistence cannot be denied.[70] However, early-contact Tahitian culture offered a much clearer differentiation of gender than Levy's representation of contemporary Tahitian culture does, as he acknowledges.[71] While the grammar of gender in ancient Tahiti was as complex as in the rest of Eastern Polynesia, its articulation with power dynamics through the mediation of an elaborate *tapu* system provided a framework that permeated all aspects of life (e.g., by forbidding women and men from eating together and eating the same types of food) and a matrix through which gender differentiation was very clear. Yet, despite the fact that there was no need to resolve an unclear gender dimorphism, ancient Tahiti had its *māhū*.[72] What was then the meaning of the *māhū* in the eighteenth century?

Equally problematic is the presence of gender liminality in Polynesian societies in which gender boundaries are anything but blurred. For example, Bradd Shore analyzes Samoan culture as animated by an overarching system of oppositions in which the complementarity between maleness and femaleness figures prominently, particularly as manifested in the brother-sister relationship.[73] While the relationship between this system of complementarity and social praxis is very complicated, it is nev-

307

ertheless clear that Samoan culture offers a pervasive grid through which genders are differentiated.[74] Indeed, the androgyny that Levy observes in Tahiti cannot be easily applied to Samoa (nor, for that matter, to Tonga). Without necessarily implying that gender liminality should be accounted for in exactly the same terms across Polynesian societies, the extent to which Tahitian gender liminality resembles the phenomenon in other Polynesian contexts must somehow be explained. Levy's functionalism, being closely tied to the picture of Tahiti he depicts, provides little by way of an explanation for the regional prevalence of the phenomenon.

Despite the problems associated with it, Levy's account opens a potentially fruitful avenue, namely, understanding the gender-liminal person as a negative case. Mageo proposes that Samoan *fa'afāfine* are not representations of "femaleness" as a coherent and unitary category, but rather they align themselves with *specific instantiations* of womanhood in various contexts.[75] In some instances, the *fa'afafine* is a representation of mature nonvirgin womanhood, namely, the category labeled *fafine*, "mature woman"; in other contexts, he signifies the category labeled *teine*, "unmarried, and presumably virginal, girl," which he often parodies.[76] The highly visible parodic displays of female sexuality in public contexts that many (but not all) *fa'afāfine* engage in demonstrate how the ideal virginal young woman should *not* behave. Thus the *fa'afafine* is not so much a negative model for men, as Levy argues for the Tahitian *māhū*, but rather for younger women. I will return to the implications of Mageo's compelling analysis below.

Is Gender Liminality "Institutionalized"?

Gender liminality in Polynesia is frequently represented as an institution. This is particularly so in the secondary literature, where the topic has acquired, by force of conjecture, the quality of a textbook case. Witness its depiction in an encyclopedic work: "In contemporary Tahiti, males who adopt [a] transgender role are accepted in their same-sex orientation and are even granted a semi-institutionalized position of esteem."[77] Another author states that the *māhū* is institutionalized, "in the way a chief or a shaman is an institutionalized status with prescribed role requirements."[78] In these descriptions, the Polynesian gender-liminal individual is described as what Herdt calls an "it-entity," namely, an emically well defined and internally consistent category that fits in a sort of sociocultural niche preprepared by the social order.[79]

These characterizations call into question the exact nature of "institutionalization," a notion that George Devereux was the first to invoke with reference to "abnormal" sexual behavior.[80] In an analysis of the Native North American berdache, Whitehead demonstrates the difficulties of arriving at an exact definition of what an institution is, particularly when sexuality is involved.[81] The degree to which a particular practice or identity is institutionalized depends on many disparate factors, none of which are sufficient or necessary: its internal consistency, its moral evaluation, its ritual elaboration, the extent to which it answers a structural need, its centrality or marginalization in the political and economic life of society and in kinship systems and so on. While the characterization of a practice as "institutionalized" may be too vague, one still needs a tool to distinguish, among others, berdache identity in Native American societies, lesbian and gay identity in middle-class Western contexts and the identity of the hijra, North India's "third-gender" category.[82] In this section, I address some of the ways in which gender liminality in Polynesia can be thought of as "institutionalized" and evaluate the evidence accordingly.

A cursory glance at gender liminality in all Polynesian societies for which information is available quickly reveals that the category leaks at the seams. First, within each Polynesian context, who is and is not included in the category varies across contexts. Levy notes that in the Tahitian village where he conducted fieldwork several men were described as *huru māhū* or "*māhū*ish" because they exhibited certain effeminate traits.[83] While these individuals differ from prototypical *māhū* because they do not engage in homosexual behavior, as Levy points out, the fact that not all prototypical *māhū* do so casts some doubt on the distinction. Elsewhere, one finds a great deal of fuzziness at the boundaries of gender-liminal categories. In Tonga, for example, a young man who displays womanlike interactional mannerisms (such as a wider range of facial expressions than those expected of men) can be disparaged as a *ki'i fakaleitī*, "little *fakaleitī.*" Mothers and other caregivers often use comparable strategies in disciplining their male children, particularly when they fail to perform chores that are normally the responsibility of boys of their age. In other words, while some individuals consistently fall within the boundaries of gender liminality, every man or boy can be potentially qualified as gender liminal on the basis of personal features or behavior, even if metaphorically.

Second, the characteristics of gender-liminal persons vary greatly from one individual to the other. It is possible to describe, as I did earlier, a composite prototype for the referent of terms like *māhū*, *fa'afafine* and *fakaleitī*, which corresponds to the way that Polynesians themselves would describe these categories. Yet it is impossible to define a list of necessary and sufficient conditions, because one finds individuals in all societies who fail to conform to the prototype in one way or the other. It is useful to draw a comparison between Polynesian gender liminality and the hijra of North India. Like Polynesian liminals, hijras differ greatly from one another in self-presentation, role and identification with the hijra "ideals": some are primarily prostitutes, others are primarily religious gurus, while others emphasize their role as ritual performers.[84] Where the difference lies is in the fact that North Indian society has a clear normative notion of what hijra status consists of, the principal feature of which is ritualized emasculation. Indeed, many hijras have not subjected themselves to the operation, but the idealization of the hijra as emasculated is nevertheless a prominent "necessary" characteristic of hijra identity. Thus hijras who are not emasculated live under constant fear of "discovery" when they perform rituals expected of hijras, as when dancing in other people's households on the occasion of the birth of a male child. In contrast, no such ideological construct exists in Polynesia.

Third, one of the more puzzling aspects of Polynesian gender liminality is the fact that particular individuals may opt out of the category in the course of their lifetime, and frequently do so. The usual way out of gender-liminal status is heterosexual marriage, through which the gender-liminal person can prove his manhood, as is the case of the Omani *xanīth*, and hence his ability and willingness to answer the social expectations of a conventional man.[85] For example, in the early part of my Nukulaelae fieldwork, a man in his early twenties returned to the atoll for a brief holiday after studying overseas. While abroad, he had taken on the role of a *pinapinaaine*, particularly by cross-dressing, rumor of which had not taken long to reach the atoll. On his return, his family instructed him to put an end to his nonsensical behavior and to get married and have children, which he promptly did. The implications that such midlife changes have from the perspective of the individual is a complex question: heterosexual marriage does not erase liminality from one's biography, nor does it always ensure one's exit out of liminal status, as some individuals continue to be labeled as liminal men even after marriage. But midlife changes demonstrate that gender-liminal identity can be transient. It thus cannot be understood as solely located in the individual in the same fashion as lesbian and gay identity in middle-class Western societies, and it should not be thought of as an immanent social institution.

Arguably the most important parameter of intracultural variation is the fact that gender-liminal identity "blooms" in a particularly elaborated fashion in certain social contexts while it is subdued in others. For example, the gender-liminal features of the Samoan *fa'afāfine* are most foregrounded in performances of various types, particularly when a comic and clownish component is involved.[86] "Traditional" dances, including fund-raising performances for church-related activities, and modern-day heirs of traditional forms, like Saturday-night floor shows at Pago Pago discotheques, are prime loci for the display of *fa'afafine* regalia and behavior. In many Polynesian societies, one encounters more or less formalized comedic genres, from clowning performances that arise spontaneously during dancing to culturally elaborated forms like the Samoan *fale aitu* (literally, "house of spirits"), theatrical events that are rehearsed and plot driven. The gender-liminal person is particularly associated with spontaneous clowning in many Polynesian contexts. But even in more formal genres like the Samoan *fale aitu*, the male lead comedian apes gender liminality (e.g., effeminate demeanor, simulated sexual interest in other male actors) even though he is usually not otherwise identified as a *fa'afafine*.

A particularly telling feature of the association of gender liminality with performance on the one hand and comedy on the other is its resilience and adaptability to social change. In Nuku'alofa, Tonga's main urban center, the ultimate setting for the elaboration of *fakaleitī* identity is the *fakaleitī* beauty contest, a mirthful but important occasion held once a year in the city's best hotel. Notably, the cultural bond between performance and gender liminality is evident throughout Polynesia, from the most tradition-oriented island or village to the most acculturated areas. In very tradition-oriented societies like Nukulaelae atoll, the gender-liminal person is often the community's most accomplished and innovative composer and choreographer; at the other extreme, in a highly acculturated area like Hawaii, where chanting and *hula*-dancing feature prominently in efforts to reconstitute a Hawaiian heritage, both art forms are in large part controlled by *māhū*. But in Tonga, Samoa and probably elsewhere, the very individuals who don heavy makeup and outrageous costumes for performances commonly return to considerably less marked styles of self-presentation in everyday contexts. Thus, gender-liminal identity is foregrounded or backgrounded depending on the nature of the social context.

The problem of the interconnection of gender liminality, social context and individual identity is more complex and must be contextualized in Polynesian notions of personhood. Throughout Polynesia, personhood is viewed as lacking the consistent, atomistic and homogeneous character of Western middle-class notions of personhood but as capable of considerable malleability and adaptability to changing social contexts. For example, the person in Samoa is conceptualized as a complex system of more or less autonomous facets that are selectively foregrounded in different social contexts.[87] Each aspect of the person is related in complex ways to particular emotional experiences, interactional dynamics and social roles. While there are significant differences from one Polynesian culture to the other, the same basic pattern recurs throughout the region.[88] Of course, the plasticity of the person does not preclude the recognition of interpersonal differences. For example, Nukulaelae Islanders recognize individualities, character traits and interpersonal variations, which they talk about a great deal. Individuality in these cultures is viewed as deriving from the individual's propensity to foreground particular facets of her or his personhood.

This brief and necessarily oversimplified excursus into Polynesian ethnopsychology provides the necessary framework for an understanding of gender liminality. Rather than being grounded in the individual in an essentialist fashion, it is more crucially a characteristic of the relationship between the individual and the social context. Of course, not all attributes of gender liminality are equally context bound, in that some, such as womanlike facial movements, are less subject to overt control than others, such as campy demeanor. However, it is those aspects of the category that are most consciously controlled and that depend most on context that are perceived as most central to liminal status. In certain contexts, certain men display and elaborate on behaviors and attributes associated with femininity and are more adept at doing so than other men. Mageo notes that any Samoan man can ape femininity in performance contexts for comic effect; "the *fa'afafine* is a boy that jokes as most Samoan boys do, but does so more consistently rather than intermittently and acquires accompanying paraphernalia."[89] This analysis suggests a new twist to the relationship between gender liminality, social context and personhood: while personhood molds itself to social context, the relationship between structure and agency is constitutive, and particular contexts can become the "specialty" of certain individuals. Further evidence from my own fieldwork on Nukulaelae supports this analysis. Certain individuals on Nukulaelae are thought of as particularly adept gossips. This is explained in two ways: these individuals seek out contexts appropriate to gossip (e.g., by frequenting cooking huts, a common setting for gossip) in which the gossipy aspect of their personhood can be given full rein, but they are also constantly on the lookout to turn nongossip social interactions into gossip. In a similar fashion, the Nukulaelae *pinapinaaine* is a man who seeks out contexts in which he can *perform* his gender liminality (by socializing with young women, through active participation in dance performances, for example); in other social contexts, his slightly effeminate demeanor is a constant reminder of the possibility that the context may turn into one in which he can perform as a gender-liminal person, if the circumstances allow it. If the context is inappropriate for such a performance, as in the case of a formal meeting in which high-status individuals are present, he downplays his femininity.

The context boundedness of gender liminality has further implications. With the exception of modern-day Hawaii, where *māhū* status appears to be less closely connected to comedy, Polynesian societies view contexts in which displays of gender liminality are elaborated as antistructural, norm breaking and counterhegemonic, and the gender-liminal person plays a central role in bestowing these characteristics onto them. In Western Polynesia, gender liminality is closely associated with lack of restraint and decorum, as illustrated most strikingly by the gender-liminal person's association with a lack of sexual restraint. Recall the sexually charged jesting that Funafuti *pinapinaaine* delight their female companions with, the Samoan *fa'afafine*'s association with nonvirginal womanhood in certain contexts and Tongan men's perception of the *fakaleitī* as sexual "fair game" unguarded by a brother's protection.

In contexts with less overtly sexual connotations, gender liminality also emerges as antistructural through its association with clowning, particularly in Samoa.[90] Its noticeable elaboration in performance contexts, which is a beautiful example of the general associations that Turner describes, is easy to explain.[91] Performances in Polynesian cultures, particularly dancing, feature a strong antistructural component: in Samoa, traditional dance forms like the *pō ula* are based on a structural tension between *siva*, a graceful and dignified genre of dance movements, and *'aiuli*, namely, unrestrained and indecorous clowning.[92] The opposition between restraint and lack of it in Samoan dancing is a structured enactment of conflictual oppositions at play in all aspects of Samoan culture and social order, as Shore masterfully demonstrates. Thus, rather than enact the triumph of order against nonorder, the dance displays, in a stylized manner, an unresolved but balanced tension between them. Even though these dualistic structures are most elaborated in Samoan culture, similar patterns are in evidence elsewhere in Polynesia. In Nukulaelae dance performances (*faatele*), an opposition exists between the row of young women (or sometimes men) who, facing the "official" audience, dance in a highly controlled style, and the singers and drummers who sit in a tightly knit concentric circle behind the young women. The singers and drummers become increasingly "out of control" as the tempo and loudness of the singing increases; some may gesticulate wildly to encourage further *matagi* "trancelike displays" in the chorus, while groups of two or three spontaneously get up to their feet and dance in the background, often in a clownish fashion.[93] Crucially, Nukulaelae's *pinapinaaine* plays a central role in gesturing, clowning and engendering structured chaos in the chorus (he is, however, constrained by a physical handicap).

Rather than equate decorum, gravity and norm making with social order and view clowning, parody and norm breaking as a threat to it, social order is better understood as achieved through a balance of opposing forces.[94] This characteristic of Polynesian societies lends support to semiotically informed models of society and culture as more or less controlled heterogeneity.[95] However, in many respects, clowning is not on an equal footing with decorum with respect to the politics of power and prestige. Clowning, lack of restraint and norm-breaking action are inherently antihegemonic and as such are inappropriate, antithetical and unbecoming to high-profile power brokering. For the gender-liminal person, this has several implications. First, gender-liminal features must be downplayed in contexts in which power is explicitly reproduced and transformed and in which counterhegemonic action is particularly risky. Thus it befalls the Samoan *fa'afafine* constantly to evaluate social situations for their recep-

ANTHROPOLOGICAL CONTRIBUTIONS

tiveness to his antistructural femininity and to foreground and background his liminality accordingly. Second, gender liminality in its most overt forms is antithetical to sociopolitical ambition and is certainly not the most direct route to a socially "respectable" niche in society. The gender-liminal person may seek political power, but, as a precondition for his ambition to be taken seriously, he must shed his liminal status by entering in a heterosexual marriage and having children. In short, to hang on to one's gender liminality is to ensure that one remains outside of the race for political power and prestige in Polynesia. If there is a Polynesian equivalent of the Melanesian *rabisman* ("rubbish man"), the gender-liminal person is an excellent candidate.[96] (Indeed, among the Melanesian Hageners, the rubbish man is "like a woman," as Marilyn Strathern demonstrates.[97])

Serious doubt is thus shed on traditional representations of the social status of Polynesian gender liminality, in which it is typically depicted as "more than simply tolerated, [but] often highly respected."[98] It is not surprising that the social status of gender liminality in "non-Western" contexts is a central concern of recent cross-cultural literature stemming from gender studies and gay and lesbian studies. A common and more or less clearly articulated motivation in this corpus of work is to demonstrate that preindustrial societies are more "tolerant," "accepting," "approving" or "accommodating" of erotic diversity and gender variation than "the West."[99] While such moral and political agendas are perfectly understandable in the context of lesbians' and gays' struggle for a political voice in postindustrial societies, they result in gross oversimplifications of the issues and in reifications of such key categories as "non-Western societies," "acceptance" and social "tolerance." Furthermore, the very question of social tolerance (a term that Herdt aptly describes as "an invidious descriptor")[100] presupposes a highly specific model of structure and agency, according to which personhood is an essentially atomistic phenomenon rooted in the psychological biography of the individual, which varies little across time and social contexts. In this view, personhood and its characteristics, such as sexual orientation, are fundamental, unalterable and nature-given attributes that society at large may accept or reject. But much anthropological work has shown that this ethnopsychological model is deeply rooted in the middle-class ideology of postindustrial societies and is not universally applicable.[101] In addition, the golden mythology professed by Western gay scholarship on the fringe of anthropology clearly buys into a highly romanticized view of the "Other" comparable to those found in the multiculturalist movement, which bears only a remote relationship to the ethnographic evidence.[102] Little is even mentioned of the fact that the gender-liminal person is frequently the target of harassment and physical violence in societies like Samoa and Tonga, as noted earlier. Clearly, the relationship of gender liminality to social structures and cultural processes is much more complex than traditionally represented.

To be sure, there are forms of prestige outside of mainstream, hegemonic and high-profile social contexts. For example, I have demonstrated elsewhere that being accused of sorcery can be extremely damaging to one's reputation and social status in Nuku-laelae society. But sorcery accusations do not affect everyone equally. When they target a politically ambitious man who, in his mid-forties, is at an age and in a position where he is expected to partake in mainstream political life, rumors of sorcery can literally destroy his career.[103] In contrast, when directed at a twice-widowed woman of loose morals who is widely suspected to have instigated the death of both her husbands, gossip about sorcery can be overturned and used by its victim to increase the awe in which she is held because of the powers attributed to her.[104] In a similar fashion, gender-liminal persons may acquire certain forms of alternative prestige, the most obvious of which is recognition of their excellence in performance arts, the very contexts in which liminality can be most appropriately foregrounded. They can become esteemed repositories of artistic and cultural traditions, which in fact they frequently are throughout the Polynesian region. It is this association with the performance of culture that provides gender-liminal persons high visibility in tourism in many areas of Polynesia, to which many are also drawn by their frequent interest in innovation and change. In

317

the tourist industry, they frequently animate displays of (more or less invented) "cultural traditions" to outsiders, and often become mediators of the interface between island societies and foreigners. These roles sometimes open the door to upward mobility: well-known Tongan *fakaleitī* and Samoan *fa'afāfine* have become hoteliers and entertainers and have tapped into important founts of monetary and symbolic capital. Thus, to state that the person who foregrounds his gender liminality is excluded from partaking in the race for power and prestige does not mean that the role is completely devoid of rewards. But while areas of social life in which the gender-liminal person excels, like dance performances and tourist-oriented displays of cultural heritage, are symbolically related to power structures, they can also be dismissed as mere symbols that pale in importance when compared to domains in which preexisting power structures are explicitly reproduced, maintained and enacted. Crucially, these are the domains from which the gender-liminal person is excluded.

The gender-liminal person's prestige does not result directly from his liminal status, because liminality in and of itself is anything but prestigious; but prestige and power may result from certain secondary associations of liminality. It is particularly befitting of Polynesian contexts that certain facets of an individual's identity may be valued, while others are held in low esteem, given Polynesian notions of personhood as a multifaceted entity. In certain contexts, such as artistic performance, the liminal individual is esteemed and admired, while in other contexts his lack of social standing may be centralized. This situation can be usefully contrasted with Erving Goffman's depiction of stigmatized individuals in mainstream North American society, whose persona may be "spoiled," in the eyes of society, by a single stigmatized trait (alcoholism, physical handicap, homosexuality, etc.).[105] In contrast, prestige, esteem and social approbation in Polynesian society are better understood as characteristics of the relationship between persons and social contexts rather than immutable features of persons.

Does Polynesian Gender Liminality Constitute a Third Gender?

The foregoing discussion naturally leads to the question of the status of liminal persons in the Polynesian culture of gender. Should liminality be considered as a third gender separate from women and men but on par with them with regard to their status as social and cultural categories, as many have argued?[106] In the following discussion, I argue that, while gender liminality is a particularly striking illustration of the permeability and permutability of gender categories in Polynesia, there is no compelling evidence that Polynesian cultures accord it separate gender status.

First, no reference whatsoever is made to gender liminality in the social principles on which all Polynesian cultures base the organization of society and culture, namely, the grammar of kinship.[107] As in all societies,[108] kinship in Polynesia is structured on the basis of a fundamental opposition and asymmetrical complementarity between male and female entities, which leaves no room for an "in-between" category. The praxis of kinship, through the structuration of the family, the organization of political power and the generation of symbolic structures, is related to the structure of kinship in a complex manner, in Polynesia as everywhere else; but neither does one find any overt reference to gender liminality in praxis, as evidenced by the absence of a brother's protection of his liminal brother's chastity.

Second, from a different perspective, there are fundamental qualitative differences between gender liminality as a category and the categories constituted by women on the one hand and men on the other. As I demonstrated earlier, gender liminality is multifarious in the extreme. Its boundaries are porous, insofar as different degrees of gender liminality can be identified that can vary in form and intensity across contexts. While there is some variation in how manhood and womanhood manifest themselves, this variation is considerably less dramatic than variations across liminal persons. Similarly, the fact that particular men may retreat out of gender liminality in the course of their lives finds no counterpart in the grammar of gender: no boundary crossing ever takes place between men and women.

Third, the context boundedness of liminality presents a striking contrast with gender. It is true that, in keeping with Polynesian understandings of personhood as a multifaceted entity, both women and men can foreground or background signs of femaleness or maleness, as when high-ranking Samoan chiefs assume in certain ceremonial situations the sitting position of a woman, with one leg astride his opposite thigh in contrast to the normatively male tailor-fashion cross-legged posture.[109] Other examples abound in both generalities and details of social life, particularly those aspects of society and culture in which the ambiguous role of Polynesian women as high-status sisters and low-status childbearers becomes important.[110] But nowhere does one find in the structure of male and female genders the same degree of dependence on social context for the recognition of the category as one does with gender liminality. It is also significant that the domains in which gender liminality is most felicitously foregrounded, such as artistic performance, can also easily be dismissed as mere symbols of the more "serious" domains in which female and male identities are constituted, such as political and ceremonial domains.

In short, there is no compelling reason to treat gender liminality as a challenge to gender dimorphism. Of course, recognizing a dimorphism between women and men as social and cultural categories is not equivalent to dividing society into two watertight groups; as discussed earlier, female and male symbols are related to women's and men's identities in a complex manner in Polynesian societies. So characterizing gender liminality as something other than a third gender is not simply the result of the naturalization by Western ethnographers of gender as a uniquely dichotomous phenomenon, as is popularly maintained in many gender- and gay-studies circles.[111] Indeed, the insistence on viewing liminal individuals as forming a third-gender category can be equally criticized as a Western romantic construction of the "Other" as "different" from a reified "Western" view of sex and gender, which itself is in need of critical clarification. In the case of Polynesian gender liminality, all evidence suggests that gender liminality operates within the confines of this dimorphism. In the conclusion, I will elaborate on several alternatives to the third-gender hypothesis and suggest an account of the place of liminality in the structure of gender.

Gender Liminality on Nukulaelae

Nukulaelae is a small, isolated atoll of the Tuvalu group, on the boundary between Polynesia and Micronesia, with a population of 350. Like many other Polynesian societies, Nukulaelae society includes gender-liminal individuals, of whom one is a permanent resident of the atoll. In the following, in an effort to provide ethnographic information on particular forms of Polynesian gender liminality, I briefly describe the special problems that the Nukulaelae case presents, stressing the tentative nature of my investigation of this aspect of Nukulaelae society. Until now, I have hesitated to write up these materials because of what I perceived to be the idiosyncratic character of the Nukulaelae case. However, I now believe that the gender-liminal "norm" as it has been presented in the literature has reified a category that is anything but unified. By presenting information on a case that appears to deviate from a reified "norm," I argue for a more particularistic approach to the study of Polynesian gender liminalities.

On Nukulaelae and elsewhere in the group, Tuvaluans view gender liminality as a borrowing from the Micronesian Gilbert Islands to the north, where many other "undesirable" traits of Tuvaluan culture, like sorcery, are also thought to have originated.[112] The term *pinapinaaine*, or *pina* for short, is a loan word from the Gilbertese language (the Tuvaluan word *fakafafine* is also used, although more rarely). Tuvaluans assert that liminal men and women abound in Gilbertese society, although the phenomenon is not mentioned at all in the ethnographic literature.

During my four-odd years of fieldwork on Nukulaelae between 1979 and 1991, the one permanent resident of the atoll labeled *pinapinaaine* was a man in his mid-forties, whom I will call Founuku. All other Nukulaelae liminals reside on Funafuti, the capital atoll of the country, or abroad, and visit the atoll for brief periods of time. This fact is significant: Nukulaelae people, particularly younger ones, view outmigration as generally desirable, but gender-liminal persons actively seek opportunities to live away from the atoll. The prospect of cash-earning employment, which presupposes some educational achievements (usually a secondary-school diploma over which there is an enormous amount of competition), provides these opportunities, and it is not incidental that *pinapinaaine* are overrepresented in governmental offices on Funafuti, the government furnishing most of the salaried employment available in the country. Salaried employment does give liminal individuals some claim to prestige in light of the fact that only the privileged are involved in the monetized economy, although this prestige remains for the most part marginal to life on Nukulaelae (the principal beneficiaries of this prestige are not the wage earner himself but the liminal individual's nonliminal older relatives in residence on the atoll whom the wage earner supports through remittances). At the same time, migration allows gender-liminal individuals to put some distance between themselves and the strictures of "tradition" and the concomitant Christian-based morality. Although religious discourse is largely silent on the topic, being considerably more concerned with issues like sorcery, adultery, conversions to other religions and liquor consumption, religious morality can nevertheless inhibit those who follow less-than-orthodox paths in life.[113] In Founuku's case, however, migration is not an option because of a severe physical handicap, the result of an illness he contracted when he was a child. While he is mobile and even travels to Funafuti on occasion, negative Nukulaelae attitudes toward physical handicaps have severely curtailed his access to the regular range of opportunities in the course of his life.

The reasoning that Nukulaelae people consistently offer to account for Founuku's status as *pinapinaaine* is related to his handicap. Men, particularly younger men, are expected to make themselves "useful" (*aogaa*) to their kin groups and the community by "climbing [trees]" (*kake*); this activity functions as a synecdoche for men's role in food production, which also involves fishing, tending swamp-taro gardens and catching birds. But because Founuku is not physically capable of climbing trees, he displays his "usefulness" to the kin group and the community by excelling at skills that his physical condition allows him to perform, namely, weaving, cooking and washing clothes, all of which fall squarely within women's domain.[114] His industriousness and energy (*maalosi*) are widely recognized: his mats are particularly well executed, and he produces them with maximal efficiency. The appreciative recognition that Nukulaelae accord to Founuku's energy echoes the North American berdache's reputation as an "ultra-successful woman."[115] However, there is no evidence that Founuku's strength and industry is linked to semen ingestion, as Louis Joseph Bouge states in reference to the Tahitian *māhū* (but does not prove).[116] The connection between semen ingestion and virile energy widely attested in Melanesia appears to be essentially absent in Polynesia.[117] What is interesting about the causal link that Nukulaelae Islanders draw between Founuku's handicap and his liminality is that he is not the only handicapped man on the atoll, yet he is the only *pina*.

However, this is not perceived as a contradiction, in that other handicapped people are simply said to have "opted" to become "useful" to society in other ways. One man, for example, became an accomplished builder of canoes and tender of pigs, activities typically associated with male roles. Nukulaelae's highly sociocentric view of the person does not mean that biographies must conform to preset grooves over which the individual has no control. On the contrary, people are viewed as making rational choices in the face of different options and strategies.

Founuku also excels in at least two additional activities: singing and gossiping. While everyone sings and gossips, these activities, according to received assumptions, occupy a much more important role in women's lives than in men's. For example, men's gossip is defined as "chatting" (*sauttala*), and, even though it is as socially damaging of other people's reputations as women's talk, it is often contrasted with the latter, which is said to be more insidious, dramatic and socially disruptive than men's chatting. In contrast to men, Founuku speaks very fast, makes extensive use of pitch and volume contrasts for dramatic effect, has an animated nonverbal communicative style and can become quite excited in the narrative of a good scandal. In short, his gossiping style comes very close to the prototype of woman's talk in Nukulaelae interactional ideology. Founuku is also an accomplished composer of dancing songs and an innovative choreographer, and these skills earn him some prestige in the eyes of a society for whom dancing and singing are almost an obsession. In the early 1980s, he was instrumental in establishing a dancing group, which half of the island community eventually joined and which came to have considerable prominence not just as entertainment troupe but as a forum for fund-raising activities for the atoll's development projects. Founuku authored an entire repertoire of songs and dances for the group, designed costumes of impeccable taste by Nukulaelae standards and ran the entire venture with great expertise and authority. Through his gossip, songwriting and choreography, Founuku's presence in the community is anything but subdued. His hut is a social center for younger people, mostly younger women but also adolescent men.

Founuku differs from other men of his age in a number of other respects. First, he is not married. Although there are a few other older bachelors in the community, they are generally pitied as having been unable to secure a spouse when they were younger and are judged to be slightly morally deficient for having failed their responsibility to the community to produce children. The moral connotations of Founuku's situation are somewhat mitigated by his handicap, which impairs him in providing for a family and hence from attracting a suitable spouse. For example, it is not said of him that he is *maa i faafine* ("shy or ashamed in front of women"), a common rationalization for the behavior of visiting *pinapinaaine*.

Second, Founuku is widely rumored to engage in surreptitious sexual encounters with young men, who sometimes boast of having had sex with him (as "inserters," as usual). But more morally damaging is the rumor that a few years back Founuku had tried to coax an eight-year-old boy to fellate him. The picture is thus considerably more confused than common depictions of liminal men in other Polynesian contexts lead one to understand. Third, and most important, Founuku is excluded from the political arena for all intents and purposes because he is not the head of a family. Again, he is not alone in this situation and falls squarely under the social rubric of a low-prestige man with little political clout and aspiration. He does not partake in meetings of the Council of Elders, in contrast to most men of his age. However, he is very successful in claiming a strong covert voice in the affairs of the community through gossip.

In most consequential respects, Founuku is identified as a man. He does not cross-dress, he does not engage in overt, caricatured portrayals of femininity, he sits on the men's side in the gender-segregated church and is very much perceived as taking a male role in the micropolitics of kinship. If anything, his maleness in this respect is centralized: Nukulaelae people frequently refer to his *mafi* ("physical strength"), which he amply demonstrates when disciplining younger members of his kin group; and indeed he is a strapping fellow despite his handicap. He is particularly notorious for having ferociously beaten a twenty-year-old *tuaatina* ("classificatory sister's son") who had been behaving in an antisocial manner, thus fulfilling an eminently male duty.

The picture that this very brief sketch presents is therefore complex. In certain ways Founuku is identified with mature maleness, while in other ways he is associated with immaturity, lack of prestige and importance, and femininity. But Founuku does not behave in ways that are completely novel to the culture. There is indeed limited creativity in his presentation of self, and, far from devising a new identity that would lend support to a "third gender" analysis, his personal characteristics are well established in the community. It is equally important to stress that the Nukulaelae data are essentially based on a single member of the community. However, I question whether this fact should be viewed as a limitation. Indeed, Nukulaelae society in general, like other small atoll societies, is very much made up of "individual cases." As I have attempted to show elsewhere in my analyses of politics, gossip and sorcery on the atoll, an understanding of such categories as personhood, power and prestige must take into account the social biographies that each agent assembles through social action. For example, Nukulaelae lacks a clearly defined system of social stratification comparable to, say, neighboring Samoa's. Underlying the atoll's sociopolitical system, one finds conflicting yet coexisting ideologies, each of which calls for very different organizational structures.[118] It is not surprising that the political arena provides malleability, and the political structure in place at any given time can differ radically from structures in place at other times. Crucially, the exact nature of the political order at any given moment is shaped by the individuals in charge. Failing to recognize the particularism of political processes and attempting to arrive at faceless generalizations about life in small-scale communities like Nukulaelae miss a crucial facet of how life is locally understood and organized. Thus, while Founuku deviates in major ways from the "textbook" version of the Polynesian gender-liminal person, this brief case study suggests caution in identifying "textbook versions" of such multifarious categories.

Conclusion

This essay has analyzed the social and cultural context of gender liminality in various Polynesian settings and the relationship of the category to its context. I have described Polynesian gender liminality as a complex phenomenon grounded in several aspects of social life and symbolic structures, and its complexity derives in large part from its multifarious nature. Beginning with a review of historical representations of Polynesian gender liminality, I turned to functionalist accounts of the phenomenon, arguing that, while they do capture some of the cultural essence of gender liminality, they fail to account for its complexity. Through a more detailed inquiry into the relationship of gender liminality and sexuality, the culture and politics of gender and social inequality, I showed that a shift in focus from function to meaning provides a more fruitful stance from which the complexities of the phenomenon can be unraveled.

I then challenged common representations of gender liminality as a third-gender category by demonstrating that gender liminality operates within the confines of a dimorphic view of gender and its symbols. There are several alternatives to viewing Polynesian gender liminality as constituting a third gender. First, liminal persons can be thought of as "switching" gender identity, to become women who "happen" to be physiologically male. Many arguments militate against this account: liminal persons always keep some masculine traits, even at the most cosmetic level; in Western Polynesia, they do not have access to an important aspect of womanhood, namely, the status of the exalted virgin, to which even "fallen" young women at least can stake a claim; and they always retain the potential of returning to full male identity if the social context requires it. A second alternative is to conceptualize liminality as only incidentally related to gender and more pivotally defined by issues of power and economic status. Such an analysis was proposed in reference to the *xanīth* in Oman in the controversy that followed the publication of Unni Wikan's original analysis of the phenomenon.[119] According to this account, the *xanīth* acquires womanlike attributes because he is a prostitute, an occupation in which he engages because of economic necessity. In Polynesia, the gender-liminal person is associated with loose sexual conduct, but economic factors do not play a motivational role in this association, at least in the more traditionally oriented areas of the region.[120] Furthermore, while power and prestige certainly play a role in gender liminality, they do so in terms of the culture and politics of gender and not independently of them.

The last alternative, which in my view best captures the intricacies of the phenomenon, posits liminal individuals as men who borrow certain social and cultural attributes and symbols normatively associated with women. The nature and number of these attributes differ from one individual to the other; many can be foregrounded or backgrounded according to the social context; they can be shed if certain incompatible priorities emerge, such as the need or desire to partake in on-stage political processes. While liminality is best viewed as a borrowing process rather than as a role or identity, it does give rise secondarily to a rather loosely defined identity. Fundamentally counterhegemonic, it can be a means through which some individuals stake a claim on certain forms of prestige, but at some cost, as evidenced in the low status with which it is associated in the politics of sexual encounters, for example. This perspective on gender liminality provides a framework in which the variability of the category and its place in structures of power can be better accounted for than other models. It

327

also resonates well with our current understanding of Polynesian ethnopsychologies. Whatever its nature, gender liminality is the locus of a great deal of ambiguity, conflict and contestation in Polynesian societies. It is the site of conflicts between social demarcations of the boundaries of eroticism and person-based sexual desire, between social and personal understandings of gender and between the diverse definitions of morality, among others.

An important and related theme that has surfaced recurrently in this essay but which I have not addressed directly is the sensitivity of Polynesian gender liminality to social change. Mention was made of this sensitivity in reference to the development of Western-style gay identities in such societies as Samoa, whose relationship to more traditional patterns of gender liminality is still poorly documented. Social change was also represented as particularly problematic in highly acculturated areas like Hawaii and New Zealand: the association of shamanism with *māhū* identity in Hawaii, which I suggested to be a borrowing from Native North America, is a case in point. Gender-liminal individuals readily associate with tourists and other expatriates, as prostitutes, performers, or otherwise, and it is more than their dish-washing skills that give them privileged access to domestic positions in hotels and in the homes of Westerners. Questions raised by social change are especially important in light of the fact that Polynesian gender liminality is frequently represented as frozen in time,[121] while at the same time many descriptions are composite portraits made up of vignettes from radically divergent time periods, in which the question of cultural continuity is never raised. These questions are also consequential in that gender-liminal individuals are often innovators and are thus particularly receptive and adaptive to change (the parallel with Western gay men as trendsetters in middle-class North America is both puzzling and compelling). Finally, much of the intra- and intercultural diversity that the category exhibits can be attributed directly to the complexities of emergent modernity in the Pacific Islands. Further discussion of gender liminality in Polynesia cannot take place without locating the category in a specific historical context and must address its relationship to modernization and change.

CHAPTER SEVEN

How to Become a Berdache: Toward a Unified Analysis of Gender Diversity

Will Roscoe

> The men are strongly inclined to sodomy; but the boys
> that abandon themselves thus are excluded from the
> society of men and sent out to that of women as being
> effeminates. They are confused with the *Hermaphrodites*
> which they say are found in quantity in the country
> of the *Floridians*. I believe that these Hermaphrodites
> are none other than the effeminate boys, that in a
> sense truly are *Hermaphrodites*. Be that as it may, they
> employ them in all the diverse handiworks of women,
> in servile functions, and to carry the munitions and
> provisions of war. They are also distinguished from the
> men and the women by the color of the feathers that
> they put on their heads and for the scorn that they
> bring on to themselves.
>   — Francisco Coreal*

Introduction: The Problem of Translation
This was how the Spanish traveler Francisco Coreal, who visited
Florida in 1669, described the social role that anthropologists now
term *berdache*. The presence of berdaches had been well docu-

---

*Francisco Coreal, *Voyages de François Coreal aux Index Occidentales...* vol. 1
(Amsterdam: J. Frederic Bernard, 1722), pp. 33-34 (my trans.). Concerning the
authorship and reliability of this text, see Gabriel G. Jaramillo, "Francisco Coreal
y su Viaje a las Indias Occidentales," *Boletín de la Sociedad Geográfica de Colombia*
11.1 (1953), pp. 27-62.

mented by Coreal's time.[1] In fact, Coreal was clearly aware of these reports, for he devoted as many words to clarifying their discrepancies as he did to reporting his own observations. This pattern can be traced from the earliest accounts of the Spaniards to present-day ethnographies. What has been written about berdaches reflects more the influence of existing Western discourses on gender, sexuality and the Other than what observers actually witnessed.

Typically described, in the words of Matilda Stevenson, as men who "adopt woman's dress and do woman's work," male berdaches have been documented in nearly 150 North American societies.[2] In nearly half of these groups, a social status also has been documented for females who undertook a man's life-style, who were sometimes referred to in the native language with the same term applied to male berdaches and sometimes with a distinct term.[3] Although the existence of berdaches has long been known to specialists in North American anthropology, the subject has been consigned to footnotes and marginal references. In the past twenty years, however, berdaches have become a subject of growing interest. An expanding base of empirical data concerning the social, cultural and historical dimensions of berdache status has become available.

In this essay, I take advantage of this recent work to propose a theoretical model of berdache roles as distinct gender categories (e.g., third and fourth genders). I begin with a review of the history of the anthropological study of berdache roles and a summary of recent literature on the subject. Following this, I propose a new analytical program for theorizing berdache roles and demonstrate its utility by applying it to several of the outstanding questions in berdache studies.

Until quite recently, serious investigation of berdaches has been confined to the most basic problems of description and definition. Throughout five centuries of contact, a bewildering variety of terms has been employed by Europeans and Americans to name this status, with new ones introduced in almost every generation.[4] Such practices have created doubt not only about the nature of

330

berdache roles but also concerning their very presence in cases in which confusing terminology makes it difficult to know whether different writers were referring to the same phenomena. The difficulty is that Euro-American cultures lack social and linguistic categories that can translate the pattern of beliefs, behaviors and customs represented by North American berdaches. Instead, writers have chosen between mutually exclusive terms that emphasize either gender variation or sexual variation – "hermaphrodite" and "sodomite," for example, or, more recently, "transsexual" (gender) and "homosexual" (sexuality). *Berdache* was originally an Arabic and Persian term for the younger partner in a male homosexual relationship, synonymous with "catamite" or "Ganymede."[5] Used in North America since the seventeenth century, the term was not generally adopted until the nineteenth century, and only then by American anthropologists. The dissimulation effected by the use of all these different terms was so great that observers like Coreal arrived in the New World expecting to find two distinct classes of persons (i.e., *Hermaphrodites* and *garçons effeminés*).

Although the principle of cultural relativity has been central to twentieth-century anthropology, its application to differences in gender and sexuality has been slow. Perhaps this is because most discourse on sexuality and gender in Euro-American societies during this period has been dominated by psychology and sexology. Perceiving the relativity of sexuality and gender patterns requires the simultaneous perception of the cultural basis of the knowledge produced by these disciplines. Not recognizing the importance of culture in constructing the desires, roles, identities and practices that constitute gender and sexuality, anthropologists and other observers have paid little attention to local beliefs, focusing instead on a much grander story, one that holds enduring fascination for the Western imagination – how culture confronts nature (and the individual confronts society) and all the possible outcomes that these givens can produce.[6]

Above all, it took the emergence of feminist theory and its critique of biological determinism to make a serious reevaluation of the berdache role possible. This can be traced back to the work of Elsie Clews Parsons and Ruth Benedict, whose insightful, if

331

brief, discussions of berdaches in the early twentieth century were informed by a feminist understanding of the social construction of gender roles.[7] Between the 1920s and the 1960s, a similar perspective can be traced in references to berdaches by Ruth Landes, Ruth Underhill, Gladys Reichard, Nancy Lurie, Omer Stewart, Harry Hay and Sue-Ellen Jacobs.[8] A less direct but just as significant influence has come from the field of literary criticism and the methods of discourse analysis. The degree to which poststructuralist theory has sensitized scholars to the relativity of the categories and taxonomies they use cannot be underestimated. In the field of anthropology, analyzing the "rules of discourse" that shape the texts readers rely on, whether anthropological, historical, literary or native, has become a key tool of cultural analysis.

In the 1970s, these intellectual developments combined with a social climate in which gender and sexual differences had become topics of broad public interest to produce a fluorescence in berdache studies. In 1976, Jonathan N. Katz published a collection of original texts on berdaches in his popular book, *Gay American History*, which Harriet Whitehead cited extensively in her 1981 essay, "The Bow and the Burden Strap."[9] This was followed by a major article by Charles Callender and Lee Kochems in 1983 based on a thorough review of the anthropological literature; articles on female berdaches in 1983 and 1984 by Beatrice Medicine and Evelyn Blackwood, respectively; a series of articles by me; and two major book-length studies based on fieldwork and historical research by Walter Williams and me.[10]

As a result of these diverse contributions, a consensus on several points has begun to develop. The key features of male and female berdache roles were, in order of importance, *productive specialization* (crafts and domestic work for male berdaches and warfare, hunting and leadership roles in the case of female berdaches), *supernatural sanction* (in the form of an authorization and/or bestowal of powers from extrasocietal sources) and *gender variation* (in relation to normative cultural expectations for male and female genders). In the case of gender variation, cross-dressing was the most common and visible marker, but it has proven a more variable and less reliable indicator of berdache sta-

FIGURE 7.1. Charlie (Navajo), ca. 1895. Berdaches did not always cross-dress. In this photograph by A.C. Vroman, a Navajo berdache (on the right) wears a style of clothing distinct from that of both men and women. Note the amount of silver jewelry, which indicates wealth and prestige.

333

FIGURE 7.2. Finds-Them-and-Kills-Them (Crow), ca. 1877–78. Some berdaches actively participated in male pursuits. In 1876, the Crow berdache Osh-Tisch, or Finds-Them-and-Kills-Them (also known as "Squaw Jim"), adopted male dress for a day to join a Crow war party at the Battle of the Rosebud. This picture of "Squaw Jim" (on the left) and an unidentified female, taken by John Fouch, is the earliest known photograph of a berdache.

334

tus than previously assumed. As the passage from Coreal shows, in some tribes male berdaches dressed distinctly from both men and women. In other cases, berdaches did not cross-dress at all, or only partly. In the case of female berdaches, cross-dressing was even more variable. Often, female berdaches wore men's clothes only when hunting or participating in warfare.[11]

The sexual behavior of male and female berdaches was also variable. Where data exist, they indicate that the partners of berdaches were usually nonberdache members of the same sex – that is, berdaches were homosexual, if we define that term narrowly in terms of behavior and anatomy.[12] Some berdaches, however, appear to have been bisexual and heterosexual. This was most often the case when adult men entered berdache status primarily on the basis of visions or dreams (see discussion below). Berdaches participated in both casual encounters (reported for male berdaches) and long-term relationships (reported for both male and female berdaches). Unfortunately, little is known about what social norms and kinship rules might have governed these relationships. At least some reports suggest that berdaches observed the same incest regulations as other members of their tribes.[13]

In sum, the most reliable indicators of berdache status were its economic and religious attributes and not gender or sexual difference alone. Further, the variation of berdaches in terms of occupational and religious pursuits *surpassed* rather than fell short of social norms. Again and again one finds berdaches attributed with exceptional productivity, talent and originality. The careers of such male berdaches as We'wha (Zuni), Osh-Tisch (or "Finds-Them-and-Kills-Them") (Crow) (see figure 7.2) and Hastíin Klah (Navajo) (see figure 7.3), and female berdaches like Qánqon (Kutenai), Running Eagle (Blackfeet) and Woman Chief (Crow), suggest that this reputation was often deserved.[14]

A second point of agreement is that berdaches were accepted and integrated members of their communities, as their economic and religious reputations indeed suggest. In many cases, berdaches enjoyed special respect and honors. In a few cases they were feared because of the supernatural power they were believed to possess. If berdaches were scorned, hated or ridiculed by their

335

tribespeople, however, it was likely for individual reasons and not a function of their status as berdaches. In yet other cases, Indian joking relationships have been mistakenly interpreted as evidence of nonacceptance. In fact, in many tribes, individuals were subjected to teasing precisely *because* they enjoyed high status or prestige.[15] Finally, many reports attributing American natives with hostility toward berdaches have been shown to reflect the Euro-American author's values and not native judgments.[16] Indeed, what is missing at this point is an analysis of a confirmed case of a tribe *lacking* such a role or genuinely hostile to it.

A third area of consensus involves the abandonment of deterministic hypotheses concerning the "cause" of berdache behavior. Viewing berdaches as wholly determined products of social forces has a long history. The very language used to describe them has foreclosed the possibility of their agency. This is typically done through the repetitive use of passive, transitive and reflexive grammatical constructions. The passage from Coreal illustrates all three: "the boys that *abandon themselves* thus *are excluded* from the society of men.... *They employ them* in all the diverse handiworks of women" (emphasis mine). Such practices predetermine and overdetermine berdaches as the objects of action, never the subjects.[17] The anthropological version of these tropes takes the form of etiological theories that account for berdaches in terms of external forces alone – for example, the suggestion that the berdache role was a social status imposed on men too weak or cowardly to measure up to stringent tribal standards of masculinity. This suggestion has been convincingly disproved by evidence of males uninterested or unsuccessful in warfare who, nonetheless, do not become berdaches and by the actual participation of berdaches in warfare.[18] Indeed, a good part of the prestige of berdaches was due to the belief that they enjoyed the same kind of supernatural sanction as successful hunters and warriors. Consequently, most recent work on berdaches acknowledges the role of individual motivations, desires and talents in determining who became a berdache.[19] Berdaches are finally being recognized as historical subjects – individuals who actually desired to be berdaches because of the rewards that life-style offered.

FIGURE 7.3. Hastíín Klah (Navajo), ca. 1925. Klah, the famous Navajo berdache, combined the knowledge of a medicine man with the female skill of
weaving to create a new genre of Navajo textile with ceremonial designs.
Klah's sandpainting tapestries helped transform Navajo weaving from a craft
to a fine art.

337

A fourth area of emerging consensus addresses the problem of translation referred to above. Whereas berdaches have been traditionally conceptualized as crossing or exchanging genders, as the terms *transvestite* or *transsexual* imply (or exchanging object choice, as *homosexual* suggests), several investigators (including myself) have begun to argue that berdaches in fact occupied a third gender role, or, in the case of tribes with both male and female berdaches and distinct terms for each, third and fourth genders.[20] A multiple-gender paradigm was first proposed by M. Kay Martin and Barbara Voorhies, whose 1975 book, *Female of the Species*, included a chapter titled "Supernumerary Sexes." They noted that "physical sex differences need not necessarily be perceived as bipolar. It seems possible that human reproductive bisexuality establishes a minimal number of socially recognized physical sexes, but these need not be limited to two."[21] In her 1983 commentary on Callender and Kochems, Jacobs referred to berdache status as a third gender, a characterization she considers more inductive than the Western paradigm of gender-crossing.[22] The first definitive argument for a multiple-gender paradigm was put forward by Blackwood, who proposed the "rigorous identification and labeling of the berdache role as a separate gender." "The berdache gender...," she concluded, "is not a deviant role, nor a mixture of two genders, nor less a jumping from one gender to its opposite. Nor is it an alternative role behavior for nontraditional individuals who are still considered men or women. Rather, it comprises a separate gender within a multiple gender system."[23]

Both positive and negative evidence supports the argument that berdache status constituted a culturally acknowledged gender category. On the one hand, it can easily be shown that a dual-gender model fails to account for many of the behaviors and attributes reported for berdaches — for example, berdaches who did not cross-dress or attempt to mimic the behavior of the "opposite" sex or those who engaged in a combination of female, male and berdache-specific pursuits.[24] On the other hand, the consistent use of distinct terms to refer to berdaches, a practice that prevented their conceptual assimilation to an "opposite" sex, is positive evidence that berdache status was viewed as a separate category.[25] Such native terms have various translations, from the obvious "man-woman" (e.g., Shoshoni *tanowaip*) to "old woman-old man" (e.g., Tewa *kwidó*) to terms that bear no relation to the words for "man" or "woman" or simply cannot be etymologized (e.g., Zuni *lhamana*).[26]

In many tribes, the distinction of berdaches from men and women was reinforced by sartorial practices and the use of symbols, such as the distinct color of feathers worn by Floridian berdaches reported by Coreal. In other cases, as I have shown in *The Zuni Man-Woman*, the religious functions of berdaches and the life-cycle rites they underwent were specific to their status while paralleling the kind of functions and rites pertinent to men and women. Similarly, among such tribes as the Zunis, Navajos, Crows and others, myths accounting for the origin of berdache status placed that event in the same context in which male and female gender categories were defined (stating, in so many words, "when the spirit people made men and women, they also made berdaches").[27]

Although the points made so far apply equally to male and female berdaches, it is clear that female roles were not simply mirror opposites of male berdache roles. Unfortunately, the study of female berdaches lags behind that of male berdaches, and several features of this status await clarification. Medicine concluded that "warrior women," like male berdaches, occupied "socially sanctioned role alternatives." These were "normative statuses which permitted individuals to strive for self-actualization, excellence, and social recognition in areas outside their customary sex role assignments."[28] Some researchers, however, have concluded that female berdache roles were less viable and female berdaches less tolerated than were their male counterparts, and others have argued that the term *berdache* should not be applied to women at all.[29] Callender and Kochems found documentation of female berdaches in only thirty tribes.[30] Whitehead concluded that "when women did the equivalent of what men did to become berdaches, nothing happened."[31] On the other hand, Blackwood has argued that the female berdache role was socially and ontologically on par with male berdache status in the sense of being a distinct alterna-

339

FIGURE 7.4. Pine-Leaf (Crow), 1856. Whereas male berdaches elicited disgust from Euro-American observers, female berdaches often captured their imaginations. James Beckwourth and others wrote semifictionalized accounts of female berdaches – such as Pine-Leaf, modeled after Women Crow, a female berdache chief of the Crow tribe in the 1840s. These writers romanticized what seemed, from a white male perspective, an admirable but ultimately futile (and tragic) attempt to achieve equality with men. From T.D. Bonner (ed.), *The Life and Adventures of James P. Beckwourth* (New York: Harper and Bros., 1856).

tive identity.[32] At Zuni, I found that the female berdache role was less visibly marked than the male role (i.e., there are no reports of cross-dressing by women) and may have been more variable from individual to individual, but linguistic and religious practices still countenanced a distinct status for women who combined male and female pursuits, as evidenced by the use of the same term, *lhamana*, to refer to both male and female berdaches.[33]

Where Do Berdaches Come From?:
The Theoretical Challenge

Derived from the Latin *genus* – meaning "kind, sort, class" – "gender" has come to be used by researchers in several fields to distinguish socially constructed roles and cultural representations from biological sex.[34] Indeed, throughout Western history, popular belief and official discourse alike have acknowledged the role of social learning in sex-specific behavior, but biological sex has always been considered both the point of origin and natural limit of sex roles. What we call gender, in this view, *should* conform to sex, a belief that is rationalized alternately on moral and naturalistic grounds. The study of non-Western cultures, however, reveals not only variability in the sociocultural features of sex roles but also, as I argue below, wide variation in beliefs concerning the body and what constitutes sex.

If gender can be multiple, and potentially autonomous from sex, it becomes crucial to clarify exactly what it denotes. (In fact, definitions of *gender* are rare in the literature of "gender studies.") For the purposes of cross-cultural analysis, therefore, I define *gender* as a multidimensional category of personhood encompassing a distinct pattern of social and cultural differences. Gender categories often draw on perceptions of anatomical and physiological differences between bodies, but these perceptions are always mediated by cultural categories and meanings. Nor can we assume the relative importance of these perceptions in the overall definition of personhood in a given social context, or that these differences will be interpreted as dichotomous and fixed, or that they will be viewed as behavioral or social determinants (as opposed to, for example, a belief that behavior might deter-

341

mine anatomy).[35] Gender categories are not only "models of" difference (to borrow Clifford Geertz's terminology) but also "models for" difference. They convey gender-specific social expectations for behavior and temperament, sexuality, kinship and interpersonal roles, occupation, religious roles and other social patterns. Gender categories are "total social phenomena," in Marcel Mauss's terms; a wide range of institutions and beliefs find simultaneous expression through them, a characteristic that distinguishes gender from other social statuses.[36] In terms of this definition, the presence of multiple genders does not require belief in the existence of three or more physical sexes but, minimally, a view of physical differences as unfixed, or insufficient on their own to establish gender, or simply less important than individual and social factors, such as occupational preference, behavior and temperament, religious experiences and so forth.

Since the work of Ruth Benedict and Margaret Mead, anthropological studies of sex roles have focused on the relationship between sex and gender – a relationship that has been described as both motivated and arbitrary. A multiple-gender paradigm, however, leads us to analyze the relationship between the body and sex as well. Although morphological differences in infants may motivate a marking process, in a multiple-gender paradigm the markers of sex are viewed as no less arbitrary than the sociocultural elaborations of sex in the form of gender identities and roles. North American data, for example, make it clear that not all cultures recognize the same anatomical markers and not all recognize anatomical markers as "natural" and, therefore, counterposed to a distinct domain of the "cultural."

In traditional Zuni belief, for example, a series of interventions were considered necessary to ensure that a child has a "sex" at all. This began before birth, when the parents made offerings at various shrines to influence the sex of the developing fetus. In fact, the infant's sex was still not fixed at the time of birth. If a woman took a nap during labor, for example, the Zunis believed the sex of her child might change. After birth, interventions intended to influence physical sex continued. The midwife massaged and manipulated the infant's face, nose, eyes and genitals.

If the infant was male, she poured cold water over its penis to prevent overdevelopment. If the child was female, the midwife split a new gourd in half and rubbed it over the vulva to enlarge it.[37] In this context, knowing the kind of genitals an individual possesses is less important than knowing how bodies are culturally constructed and what particular features and processes (physiological and/or social) are believed to endow them with sex.

Previous theoretical work on berdache roles has taken the correspondence between sex and gender for granted, and this has skewed the resulting interpretation of berdaches in both subtle and fundamental ways. This is perhaps best illustrated by Whitehead's 1981 essay, "The Bow and the Burden Strap." As this essay remains the most sustained attempt to generate theory to account for berdache roles to date, it might be helpful to analyze its arguments and discursive strategies in some detail.

Following Henry Angelino and Charles Shedd, Whitehead defines berdaches as "gender-crossers," "person[s] of one anatomic sex assuming part or most of the attire, occupation, and social – including marital – status, of the opposite sex."[38] She links the presence of such roles to the widespread Native American belief in the power of dreams and visions. This "vision complex" had an implicit economic dimension in that random contact with the supernatural was believed to bestow skills and luck in activities that created wealth and prestige. Such beliefs served to rationalize differences in individual success within otherwise egalitarian communities. At the same time, the activities that generated prestige were also coded for gender, so that gender, like skills and good fortune, was viewed as somewhat random. It became a "status," in the sense of a rank or standing, something achieved rather than ascribed. The fact that Native American women had relatively equal access to this prestige system, through food and crafts production, childbearing and household administration, left open the possibility that some men might decide to pursue these activities as well. In fact, Whitehead credits berdaches with opportunistic motives: to gain the "material prosperity and cultural respect that accrued to the assiduous practitioner of female crafts." The berdache quits "the battlefront...of male prestige...

343

ANTHROPOLOGICAL CONTRIBUTIONS

to take up a respectable sort of lateral position – that of ultra-successful female."[39] His reputation for excellence, therefore, reflects an ideology of masculine supremacy: of course, he's better, he's a man!

The images of the military and the marketplace in these passages – evoked by terms like "battlefront," "lateral position" and "material prosperity" – signal an intertextual moment, a point at which Whitehead's text links up with other, master discourses, in particular that representing the encounter between feminism and the Western intellectual tradition. In this context, berdaches become figures in a feminist just-so story in which male exploitation and female resistance are portrayed as primordial/universal events. As Whitehead writes, "The culturally dominant American Indian male was confronted with a substantial female elite," which he found profoundly "disturbing." "It was into this unsettling breach that the berdache institution was hurled. In their social aspect, women were complimented by the berdache's imitation. In their anatomic aspect, they were subtly insulted by his vaunted superiority. Through him, ordinary men might reckon that they still held the advantage that was anatomically given and inalterable."[40]

The real problem with Whitehead's argument, however, is not its discursive moves but its reliance on two analytical dichotomies that from a multiple-gender paradigm must be questioned. The first, as suggested above, is the sex/gender binary, which opposes biological sex to sociocultural gender. Second is the opposition of economy and economic relations to ideology (the base/superstructure opposition of Marxist theory). Both dichotomies have an essentializing influence that undermines the attempt to understand berdache roles as cultural constructions.

As Whitehead argues, "A social gender dichotomy is present in all known societies in the sense that everywhere anatomic sexual differences observable at birth are used to start tracking the newborn into one or the other of two social role complexes. This minimal pegging of social roles and relationships to observable anatomic sex differences is what creates what we call a 'gender' dichotomy in the first place."[41] Callender and Kochems echo this when they state that gender "is less directly tied to this anatomical basis, although ultimately limited by it."[42] Unpacking these formulations reveals two propositions: social gender is based on the "natural facts" of sex, and, since there are only two sexes, there are only two genders. It follows that, if an individual is not one, then she must be the other. The only variation possible is an exchange of one gender for its "opposite" or some form of gender-mixing; but there are no possible variations that cannot be defined by reference to male or female. It also follows that in such a system there can be only one sexual orientation, namely, heterosexual.[43]

The assumptions of a dual-gender system have been criticized in recent years on both empirical and theoretical grounds. It may, indeed, be arguable that all societies have *at least* two genders and, as suggested above, that these two genders are linked to perceptions of physiological differences. What constitutes anatomical sex, however – which organs (or fluids or physiological processes) are considered the signs of maleness and femaleness – has been shown by scholars in several fields to be as much a social construction as what has been termed *gender*.[44]

Deconstructing the sex/gender binary reveals a hierarchical relationship between the two terms. That is, anatomy has primacy over gender, and gender is not an ontologically distinct category but merely a reiteration of sex. This is apparent in Whitehead's comments on female berdaches. "For someone whose anatomic starting point was female," she argues, "the infusion of an official opposite sex component into her identity was by no means so easily effected," because, "throughout the continent, the anatomic-physiological component of gender was more significant in the case of the female than in the case of the male, and was thus less easily counter-balanced by the occupational component."[45] But this raises the question: If gender differences are to be viewed as anchored to an "anatomic-physiological component," then on what grounds can we argue that gender roles are not, in fact, "natural" (i.e., mirroring and/or determined by biology)? And if we accept the contention that having a female body makes it more difficult to become a berdache, then have we not

345

conceded that the difference that defines women also makes them inferior?

In sum, if berdaches are to be understood as simply exchanging one gender for another, then they can indeed be interpreted as upholding a heterosexist gender system. If they are to be understood as entering a distinct gender status, however, neither male nor female, then something more complex is occurring. A multiple-gender paradigm makes it possible to see berdache status not as a compromise between nature and culture or a niche to accommodate "natural" variation but as an integral and predictable element of certain sociocultural systems, not a contradiction in Native American beliefs but a status fully consistent with them.

The second analytical dichotomy underlying Whitehead's thesis is the opposition of economic relations to cultural belief systems. This is yet another binary in which the relationship between the terms is hierarchical – that is, beliefs and cultural forms are the product of economic relations. The limitations of a purely economic model become clearer if we test it against specific cases from North America.[46]

Drawing on the hypothesis linking berdaches to prestige systems, for example, we might predict that as a given North American society increased its capacity to produce surpluses and support economic specialization (e.g., by adopting or intensifying horticultural production), both women and berdaches would take advantage of the new opportunities for acquiring prestige, and their status would increase accordingly. Expanding production would also support population increases and concentration and, therefore, the number of berdaches in a given community would increase as well. As this occurred, we might predict that berdaches would begin to function collectively, along the lines of a priesthood.

Evidence from North America does indeed suggest that berdaches enjoyed economic and religious prestige in sedentary, horticultural communities; and in some communities, it does appear that a berdache priesthood had developed.[47] In Florida, for example, Spanish and French colonizers encountered large settlements of sedentary farmers, organized into castes and ruled by

chieftains. As Coreal suggests, berdaches appear to have functioned collectively in carrying out their role of tending to the
sick and injured and burying the dead. The famous illustration
published by De Bry shows no less than six "hermaphrodites" –
two pairs carrying patients on stretchers and two individuals carrying full-grown men on their backs. The accompanying text
speaks of them acting as a group.[48] Other evidence comes from
the earth-lodge villages of the northern Plains. Among the Hidatsa,
according to Alfred Bowers, there were fifteen to twenty berdaches in a village. They were an "organized group," a "special
class of religious leaders," who collectively fulfilled various ceremonial functions.[49] Among the Crows, close relatives of the
Hidatsa, who had abandoned settled, village life for nomadic buffalo hunting in the eighteenth century, berdaches pitched their
tipis together and were recognized as a social group. Among the
Cheyenne, who had also lived in horticultural villages before the
contact period, berdaches functioned as a group in organizing the
scalp dance.[50]

At the same time, other North American horticultural societies
appear to have lacked berdache roles altogether – in particular,
the sedentary communities of Algonquian- and Iroquoian-speak-
ing tribes of the Northeast and Atlantic Coast regions.[51] Berdaches
are well attested among Algonquian speakers west of the Appala-
chians. Marquette, for example, wrote of Illinois berdaches that
"nothing can be decided without their advice."[52] Certainly the
prestige and economic status of women was high among both
Northern Iroquois and Coastal Algonquians. They produced durable trade goods and played key roles in food production and tribal
politics. Several historical cases of women chiefs and warriors
among New England Indians are known from the colonial period.[53] In fact, it may be that a careful review of seventeenth- and
eighteenth-century sources will reveal the existence of berdaches
in these eastern tribes. Nonetheless, a hypothesis based on economic factors alone would lead us to expect a prominence on the
part of berdaches that would have been more generally noted. At
the same time, when we examine the social organization of these
groups we find little in terms of mode of production or prestige

347

systems to distinguish them from comparable tribes with berdache roles.

In other cases, a prestige-based model fails to account for the
presence of berdache roles where they do occur. According to
Whitehead, North American societies lacked "full prestige differentiation," and to accommodate a fuller range of social specialization and individual variation, they simply elaborated gender
into multiple categories. The berdache role was a "cultural compromise formation founded on an incipient, though never fully
realized, collapse of the gender-stratification system."[54] Presumably, societies with more elaborate prestige systems would not
produce such a role.

Pacific Northwest Coast tribes, however, provide several examples of North American societies with elaborate systems of
prestige differentiation – including social ranking into classes of
nobility, commoners and slaves; ranking of lineages and tribes;
inherited titles, names, property and leadership roles; elaborate
displays of wealth and symbols; distinctions between prestigious
and lowly occupations; and so forth. Contrary to Whitehead's
hypothesis, male and female berdache roles have been documented in nearly half of the thirty-five societies in the coastal
region between northern California and southern Alaska.[55]

The most complete picture comes from reports of Franz Boas
and T.F. McIlwraith on the Bella Coola, which reveal well-developed male and female berdache roles with the same key features
found elsewhere in North America. Entry into berdache status was
based on preference for the work of the other gender, which was
credited to the influence of Skheents, the supernatural patron of
berdaches. In mythology, Skheents is the first picker of berries –
an important seasonal food item – and he guards a bevy of young
maidens. He was also portrayed in masked dances. According to
McIlwraith, "His face is that of a woman, his voice that of a
woman, but he has masculine characteristics as well."[56]

Berdache status appears to have been well integrated into the
Bella Coola system of social ranking. According to McIlwraith,
the profession of first berry picker, the woman who had the right
to decide when berry harvesting could begin, depended on the

ownership of an appropriate ancestral name. Occasionally, a male berdache was given one of these names. Again, we see that prestige, even in a system of ranking and inherited privileges, is still gender based. At the same time, gender is not seen as dichotomous and fixed and, as a result, a third category becomes viable.[57]

As this review has shown, efforts to develop theoretical models of berdache roles can no longer rely on the analytical dichotomies of sex/gender and economy/ideology. New analytical tools are needed to explain not only the occurrence of berdache roles but their similarities and differences across diverse societies as well.

How to Become a Berdache: Toward a Unified Analysis

In an earlier essay, I argued for the employment of multidimensional models in analyzing social and cultural differences in sexuality and gender.[58] I suggested that definitions based on single traits such as "gender identity" or "sexual object choice" be replaced with a multidimensional inventory of all the differences to be found in a given cultural context associated with a status such as "berdache" or "homosexual," whether in terms of social role, gender variation, economic specialization, religious roles, sexuality or subjectivity.[59] A counterpart to multidimensional description and cultural translation is now needed at the level of cultural analysis. Jane Collier and Sylvia Yanagisako offer such an approach in their program for a "unified analysis" of gender and kinship. They point to a growing recognition among theorists that the social phenomena of gender and kinship are manifestations of the same sociocultural processes. What is required at this point, they argue, is a methodology capable of analyzing these larger processes without relying on such analytical dichotomies as sex/ gender, nature/culture or domestic/public. They propose a three-part analytical program for this purpose.

The first phase entails the *cultural analysis of meaning*. In this phase the objective is to explicate the cultural meanings people realize through their practice of social relationships. At this stage of analysis, the investigator needs to ask, "What are the socially meaningful categories people employ in specific contexts, and what symbols and meanings underlie them?" In terms of gender

349

diversity, we would want to know what kind of beliefs are associated with and are necessary for the formulation of berdache gender categories. Were gender and sexuality viewed as natural, constructed, inborn or acquired traits? Was the berdache, therefore, an anomaly, a monster or a prodigy? How were berdaches conceptualized in terms of the categories and meanings associated with kinship, economics, politics, religion and other social systems?

The second phase of a unified analysis involves the construction of *systemic models of inequality*. This is accomplished by analyzing the structures that people create through their actions and tracing the "complex relationships between aspects of what – using conventional analytical categories – we might call gender, kinship, economy, polity and religion."[60] Such ideal-typical models of how power and social difference are organized in various societies are particularly valuable for comparative purposes. In the case of berdache roles we would want to know: What was the position of the berdache as a producer and a consumer within the larger system for creating and circulating power? What avenues of economic specialization were available to the role? What was the position of berdaches in relation to the organization of other genders and the division of labor between them (with special attention to the economic standing of women)?

Being synchronic in nature, systemic models have a built-in bias toward the persistence and continuity of social orders. For this reason Collier and Yanagisako include *historical analysis* as the third element of their program, pointing out that the ideas and practices that seem to reinforce and reproduce each other from a systemic perspective can be seen to undermine and destabilize each other from a historical perspective. Historical analysis also leads to the consideration of individual factors in social developments – the motivations, desires and self-generated meanings of the individuals who participate in "events" and occupy social "roles" – and to an analysis of the construction of subject positions.

In what follows, I hope to illustrate the utility of a unified analysis in generating a theoretical model of berdache roles that can help answer some of the key questions in berdache studies as illustrated by ethnographic data from the Pueblo, Navajo and Mohave Indians.

The Pueblos

As we have seen, the most widely shared features of berdache roles were in the areas of economic and religious specialization. Nonetheless, some key questions remain unanswered. What was the relative importance of economic and spiritual dimensions in determining whether an individual became a berdache? Was it possible to become a berdache based on spiritual qualifications alone? Is a "vision complex" the only kind of belief system in which alternative gender roles can arise? More generally, what is the relationship between division of labor and gender ideology?

Perhaps the clearest evidence of the degree to which beliefs functioned independently of economic factors were those cases of vision-induced entry into berdache status by adult men who had not previously manifested berdache traits. This occurred in vision-complex cultures, especially among Plains tribes, where following supernatural instructions was considered mandatory. Indeed, even successful warriors, if visited with dreams or visions considered specific to berdaches, assumed berdache identity.[61] In other words, even though the economic dimension of berdache roles was their most common feature, native beliefs concerning supernatural experience were sufficient to sanction entry into the status on their own. Future research should focus on the possibility that multiple gender statuses might exist in societies without any economic correlate or where such a correlate had lapsed.

This evidence leads us to ask whether a vision complex is the only kind of belief system in which berdache roles could occur. The Pueblo Indians, for example, in contrast to many Plains tribes, lack any manifestation of a vision complex, as Benedict pointed out in her classic study, *Patterns of Culture*. The cooperative values of Pueblo communities, arising from the collective nature of agricultural production and communal living, deemphasized all forms of individualism. Direct contact with the supernatural was not sought and not welcomed. As Benedict notes, "If a Zuñi Indian has by chance a visual or auditory hallucination it is regarded as a sign of death. It is an experience to avoid, not one to seek by fasting."[62] The very notion of individual contact with and use of supernatural power was suspect – this was the activity of witches. Instead, all dealings with the supernatural were invested in priesthoods and religious societies. Although Pueblo berdaches were often religious specialists and their supernatural counterparts were portrayed in ceremonies, if they were considered "holy" it was not because of their berdache status as such but because of their religious training, which required the mastery of complex oral literature and ceremonial procedures.

Despite the absence of a vision complex, berdaches have been documented in a majority of Pueblo communities.[63] The economic basis of their status was similar to that of Plains berdaches. Pueblo women produced and distributed both food and durable goods, and these products were coded as being female.[64] Specialization in these areas by males entailed no loss in social standing. Nonetheless, Pueblo and Plains belief systems were distinct in how they legitimated multiple genders. Among the Zunis, the berdache role was sanctioned not by individual contact with the supernatural but through tribal myths that relate the creation of berdache status as an autonomous cultural category, much as gender distinctions, kinship categories and other social statuses are accounted for.[65] Unfortunately, not enough data have been collected on Pueblo beliefs concerning the origins of berdache inclination in individual cases. According to Jacobs, the Northern Tewa believe that the exposure of an infant's genitals to the light of the moon will "cause" it to be a berdache.[66] The moon, among Plains tribes, is often associated with berdache status, but, significantly, Tewa belief involves not a dream or vision of the moon but merely accidental exposure.[67]

The examples of Plains and Pueblo societies provide evidence that berdache status can exist in conjunction with diverse subsistence patterns and belief systems. At the same time, despite these differences, neither Plains nor Pueblo economies produced significant inequalities of wealth, and both afforded a basis for berdache status in terms of economic specialization. Similarly, while Plains and Pueblo societies rationalized berdache roles in different ways, both groups shared a basically constructivist view of gender in that neither viewed gender as determined by sex or, for that matter, made a distinction between sex and gender.

We might go one step further and question the dichotomy between economic and spiritual domains altogether. As Collier and Yanagisako point out, social structures are realized through practices; they are part of one process. The practices related to the production and circulation of spiritual power create structures just as much as the production and exchange of material goods. The religious specialist transforms and redistributes "raw" spiritual energies to meet a variety of human needs. Spiritual power is constantly being transformed into material goods (and back again) through mechanisms such as feasting, fees for healing services, ceremonial giveaways and so forth. It can be accumulated and invested; it can be used to control other resources and bodies. In many cases it is possible to attach quantifiable values to spiritual power, depending on the importance and role attributed to it in the larger belief system.

Viewing "spiritual power" and "material goods" as differential products of a unified system, we can see that in both Plains and Pueblo societies "power" could be accrued through food production, crafts production and provision of religious services. The "mode of production" for spiritual power, however, differed. Among Plains societies, spiritual power was acquired through individual means, whereas among the Pueblos it was a strictly collective production. In sum, the Plains spiritual economy lent itself to the kind of development whereby berdaches could augment gender difference with spiritual power – both acquired in the same way. The Pueblo organization of spiritual power did not lend itself so readily to the linkage between berdache status and religious ability. But if the opportunities for accumulating spiritual power (as an individual) were fewer among the Pueblos, the economic opportunities for crafts specialization and food production were certainly just as great.

The Navajo Nádleehé
If one were to select the North American tribe in which ber-

FIGURE 7.5. Sarah Winnemucca (Northern Paiute), 1883. The failure to understand native definitions of female berdaches has led to many cases being overlooked. According to contemporary Pauites, Sarah Winnemucca, the Indian "princess" and advocate for Indian welfare in the late nineteenth century, cross-dressed when she traveled alone and for this reason was considered *duba's* or berdache. She appears here in a non-traditional "Indian" costume of her own design.

daches enjoyed the highest status on the basis of prestige system, one would be much more likely to select the Pueblos than their neighbors, the Navajos. Although one of the largest and most successful tribes today, the Navajos have been characterized in the anthropological literature as nomadic foragers and hunters whose culture was only slightly modified by the adoption of farming from the Pueblos and sheepherding from the Spaniards. Such a social system would not seem to be one capable of supporting the economic and religious specialization associated with berdache status. Yet to judge from reports from the past one hundred years, Navajo *nádleehé* may have enjoyed the greatest economic opportunities, prestige and respect of any berdaches in North America.

As Willard Hill reported, Navajo families welcomed a *nádleehé* in their midst.[68] Children with berdache tendencies were given special care and encouragement, and "as they grew older and assumed the character of *nadle*, this solicitude and respect increased, not only on the part of their families but from the community as a whole." Berdaches were often given control of family property and acted as the head of the household, supervising both agricultural and domestic work. They wove, made pottery, tanned leather, made baskets and did other female crafts, and they often became religious specialists, a male role. Certain ceremonials required their participation.[69] They also served as go-betweens in arranging affairs between women and men. In terms of sartorial practices, they might dress like men, women or neither.[70] Unfortunately, little is known about Navajo female berdaches, except that the same term was applied to them as to male berdaches, and, according to Hill, they were equal in number.

The comments of Navajo elders recorded by Hill in the early 1930s reveal the high status *nádleehé* enjoyed:

> If there were no *nadle*, the country would change. They are responsible for all the wealth in the country. If there were no more left, the horses, sheep, and Navaho would all go. They are leaders just like President Roosevelt.

355

A *nadle* around the hogan will bring good luck and riches.

You must respect a *nadle*. They are, somehow, sacred and holy.[71]

Gary Witherspoon's work on Navajo thought and language provides some suggestive insights into the Navajo conceptualization of third-gender status. All beings, including natural phenomena, were believed to have both an inner and outer form. Sometimes these forms were of different genders. Speech, for example, which is female, is the outer form of Thought, which is male.[72] Nor are inner and outer forms necessarily fixed; an inner form may have many different outer forms. Thus, we find that the term *nádleehé* literally translates as "one who changes continuously," suggesting that berdaches were seen not as crossing genders or entering a distinct category but as fluctuating between outer and inner dimensions of male and female forms – a third *process* rather than a third category.[73] This is consistent with Witherspoon's conclusion that the Navajos envision "a cosmos composed of processes and events, as opposed to a cosmos composed of facts and things."[74]

A synchronic model of the Navajo socioeconomic system, however, would not account for the social and cultural elaboration of the berdache role in that tribe. This is a case in which historical analysis, the third element of Collier and Yanagisako's program, is especially valuable.

For this purpose, three phases in the Navajo history need to be distinguished.[75] When the ancestors of the Navajos first arrived in the Four Corners area in late prehistoric times, they were hunter-gatherers, living in small nomadic bands. There is no reason to believe that a berdache role did not already exist among them, as it did among the historic Great Basin tribes, whose subsistence patterns were similar to those of the proto-historic Navajos. Even so, opportunities for economic specialization for either women or berdaches would have been limited. The encounter of the Navajos with the ancestors of the Pueblo Indians was a fateful one, however, for the Navajos acquired not only the means of growing their own food but new crafts and religious practices as well. Significantly, Navajo women seem to have been

both the vehicles and beneficiaries of many of these developments. Farming and weaving, male pursuits among the Pueblos,
became a joint activity of women and men in the first case and a
strictly female art in the second. It was during this phase of Navajo
history, before their first contact with Europeans, that a semi-
sedentary life-style replaced earlier nomadic patterns.

The acquisition of the horse and sheep by the end of the seventeenth century marked the beginning of a second phase in the
history of the Navajo economy. Sheep became the property of the
matrilocal household and in many cases the outright property of
women. This, together with their significant contributions to
food production, meant that women's labor alone could provide
families a basic subsistence. At the same time, women also produced textiles, pottery, basketry and other valuable exchange
goods. This freed men to engage in the lucrative if sometimes
risky practice of raiding Pueblo and Hispanic villages, an extension of their traditional pattern of traveling in bands to collect
resources and hunt. The potential now existed for surpluses and
the accumulation of real wealth sufficient to support talented
family members in various specializations, especially religious
practice. In this period, the role of the medicine man appears to
have grown accordingly in importance. But a key point is that
the changes in subsistence patterns fostered by these historical
events all tended to increase the social and economic autonomy
of Navajo women, or, rather, of the group of women who constituted the matrilocal household and managed the family's affairs
in the absence of men. At this point, the Navajos meet the conditions for the elaboration of alternative gender statuses predicted
by a prestige-based hypothesis.

A third stage in Navajo history was ushered in by their defeat
at the hands of the American military in 1863 and the onset of
the reservation period. The changes that this entailed, however,
tended to limit men's economic activities more than women's.
Whereas Navajo men could no longer engage in raiding, most of
the traditional economic pursuits of women remained open to
them, including gardening, sheepherding and weaving. Gradually,
Navajo men turned to large-scale sheepherding and the art of jew-

357

elry making. Our first documentation on Navajo berdaches dates from this period, and it reveals the extraordinarily high status they enjoyed.

The career of the famous Navajo *nádleehé* Hastíin Klah (1869–1939) provides a glimpse of how historical and structural factors interact in the formation of a status like that of the berdache (see figure 7.3).[76] Born at the onset of the reservation period, Klah was nonetheless raised by his family as a traditional berdache. He became an accomplished weaver and medicine man – prestigious female and male activities, respectively. By combining these skills, he was able to create an entirely new artifact – large weavings depicting ceremonial designs. Before this time (c. 1920), Navajo weaving was strictly secular and purchased primarily for use as floor coverings. Traders paid weavers for their work by the pound. Klah's tapestries, on the other hand, were purchased by wealthy art collectors and museums, whose interest eventually extended to traditional weaving styles, so that what was once a "craft" became a "fine art."

At the same time, Klah's skills as a medicine man were in high demand, as the Navajos turned to traditional religion in response to the stresses of reservation life. With income from his weaving, his medicine practice and the herds of sheep he owned with his female relatives, Klah had the ability to accumulate significant wealth in Navajo terms – except that he chose to give most of it away and devote his attention to spiritual pursuits. In the 1920s and 1930s he collaborated with several scholars and researchers to record his ceremonial knowledge. He also traveled extensively in the white world, extending the traditional function of Navajo berdaches as cultural and social mediators into the realm of intercultural relations.

Klah was equally innovative when it came to Navajo religion. Gladys Reichard credited him with the creation of a systematic synthesis of Navajo philosophy out of what had been a diffuse set of beliefs and practices. He also appears to have elaborated the role of the supernatural berdache known as Begochidiin. Accounts of this figure are complex. Karl Luckert traces Begochidiin back to ancient preagricultural hunting patterns.[77] He is the son of the sun and often linked with the moon. He is the patron god of hunters, but these associations are overlaid with features of a culture-bearer. He is credited with providing the first seeds for agriculture and inventing pottery. In myths told by Klah, Begochidiin is especially prominent. Indeed, in Klah's rendering, he becomes a transcendental figure who bridges not only gender and economic differences (hunting and farming) but age distinctions and racial differences as well (Klah described him as fair-haired with blue eyes).[78]

In sum, Klah flourished during the early reservation period because rapid changes in Navajo subsistence patterns provided unique social, economic and intellectual opportunities for individuals with the skills traditionally associated with his role. Being ambitious and talented, he took advantage of these opportunities and was undoubtedly not the only berdache to have done so. In the process, he contributed to the further elaboration of berdache status and an extension of its vitality into the twentieth century.

A synchronic analysis of Navajo social structure alone would not account for the high status of berdaches like Klah. The case of the Navajo *nádleehé* reveals how historical factors can be crucial in accounting for the development of multiple genders. In other cases, historical study may provide answers concerning the absence of berdaches in tribes in which we might expect to find them. In sum, a unified analysis that includes a historical dimension provides the best approach to accounting for the formation of gender roles and identities.[79]

The Mohave Alyha· *and* Hwame·
As long as berdaches are culturally recognized *as* berdaches (i.e., consistently referred to with a distinct term) and individuals and communities do not engage in a social fiction concerning their anatomy (by suppressing or "forgetting" the individual's actual anatomy or pretending that it had somehow been changed), cross-dressing alone is not necessarily indicative of a gender-crossing pattern. The sartorial practices of both male and female berdaches have been shown to be far more variable than previously assumed. Clothing and ornament in most North American societies con-

359

stituted a semiotic system for signaling not merely gender but social standing, kinship status, religious status, personal accomplishments, age and so forth. Cross-dressing itself often occurred in ritual and mythological contexts with little or no reference to berdache status. However, if male berdaches not only wore women's clothing but imitated women's reproductive processes and female berdaches did the reverse, then a sex/gender belief system would appear to be operative, with "berdaches" behaving according to the logic of dual and dichotomous sexes. Such an example appears to be provided by the Mohaves of the Colorado River area.

This case is worth examining because it seems to provide the strongest evidence *against* a multiple-gender paradigm of berdache roles and because the Mohave example is frequently cited in the secondary literature as illustrating North American berdaches in general. This is due largely to the vivid ethnographic account of Mohave male berdaches, or *alyha·*, and female berdaches, or *hwame·*, provided by the psychoanalytic anthropologist George Devereux in the 1930s.[80] Although the earliest Spanish explorers noted the presence of berdaches in this area, we are largely dependent on Devereux's report for our knowledge of them.[81]

According to Devereux, Mohave berdaches consistently, indeed rigorously, behaved according to the precepts of a cross-gender model – as individuals of one anatomical sex striving to become the "opposite sex." *Alyha·* insisted on being referred to by female names and with female gender references. They only practiced receptive anal and oral intercourse, and although they appeared to have achieved orgasm, they discouraged personal contact and even reference to their male genitals, using the Mohave word for clitoris to refer to their penises, the term for labia majora to describe their testes and the word for vagina to refer to their anuses. A special ceremony served to confirm male berdache status, during which clothes of the "opposite" sex were made and presented to them. They subsequently received female facial tatoos. Both *alyha·* and *hwame·* might enjoy casual or long-term relationships with nonberdache men and women. If in a partnership, according to Devereux, *alyha·* and *hwame·* were consistently referred to as a "wife" or "husband," respectively.

What has earned the *alyha·*, in particular, a permanent place in the ethnographic literature is Devereux's account of their elaborate mock pregnancies. These were carried out in excruciating detail, including the simulation of pregnancy through self-induced constipation followed by the "birth" of a stillborn fecal fetus. The whole production culminated with the burial of the "fetus" and the observance of the appropriate mourning rites, in which the *alyha·* required her husband to participate. *Alyha·* were also reported to simulate menstruation by scratching themselves until they bled.

Devereux's data on female berdaches are less consistent. *Hwame·* are not said to have employed male physiological terminology to refer to their genitals, and one informant told Devereux that *hwame·* did not necessarily take male names. Some women became *hwame·* after having children. They ignored their own menses but followed the taboos required of husbands when their wives menstruated or were pregnant. They did not necessarily cross-dress. Sex between a *hwame·* and a woman was performed in a variety of positions, without distinct active or passive role-playing. Like male berdaches, *hwame·* were often shamans.

Although Devereux's report provides convincing evidence of cross-gender beliefs and practices on the part of Mohave male berdaches, it poses some difficulties when used to make generalizations. The extreme gynemimetic behavior that Devereux attributes to the *alyha·* is unique in North America. There are one or two reports of berdaches taking measures to hide their male genitalia when appearing naked before women, but nothing remotely similar to the fake pregnancies of the *alyha·* has been reported elsewhere, not even among linguistically related neighboring tribes.[82] The challenge, therefore, is to account for this apparent discrepancy, and here, again, a unified analysis provides an effective approach, leading us to consider, in turn, cultural meanings, socioeconomic structures and historical factors.

The first test of whether Mohave berdaches represent a case of culturally patterned gender-crossing would be to determine whether the Mohaves believed gender to be dichotomous and fixed and whether, therefore, a third position was conceptually

ANTHROPOLOGICAL CONTRIBUTIONS

impossible. In fact, a close examination of evidence reported by Devereux and A.L. Kroeber reveals that the social labeling and conceptual patterns of the Mohave are more compatible with a multiple-gender paradigm than a cross-gender model. The use of distinct terms for male and female berdaches, for example, is not consistent with the maintenance of a social fiction of gender-crossing and transformation. In fact, although Devereux states that Mohaves consistently used "he" and "she" in referring to *hwame·* and *alyha·*, respectively, he later presents extensive quoted material from an informant who repeatedly uses "he" in referring to *alyha·*.[83] Perhaps the Mohaves' cross-gender references to berdaches were less literal than Devereux understood them. They may have been meant in the same sense conveyed when the pronouns "he" or "she" are placed in quotation marks in written texts.

Similarly, as the Mohave "emphatically stated" to Devereux, the purpose of the initiation ceremony for male berdaches was not to effect a transformation in their "personal habits" but merely to acknowledge them. This ceremony follows the common pattern of rites of passage as outlined by Victor Turner, with the phases of separation, liminality, and incorporation (the boy spends a night covered up while shamans sing over him; the next day he is led in a dance to the river where he publicly strips and enters the water; after four days his face is painted and he reenters the community as an *alyha·*).[84] The passage, however, is not from male to female, but from boy to *alyha·*, a transition of both gender status and age.

The full-length version of the origin myth of the *alyha·*, originally told to Kroeber in 1902 and summarized in his *Handbook of California Indians* (published in full in 1972), provides valuable evidence on this point.[85] The account begins in the house of the god Mastamho, where four women are seated in a directional circuit around him. Mastamho proceeds to assign each a particular identity or function, creating, in effect, female gender subcategories: one is to be a shaman (and not marry), one is to be a "loose" woman, the third is a mother about to give birth and the fourth woman is a midwife. With instructions from Mastamho, the infant is delivered. As the narrator relates:

FIGURE 7.6. Hé-é-é (Hopi). As in the case of male berdaches, female entry into otherwise male domains often enjoyed supernatural sanction. According to Hopi legend, the warrior maiden, Hé-é-é (on the left), defended her village against an attack when the Hopi men were absent. She wears her hair half up in a female style and half down in a male style, a common convention for the portrayal of male and female berdaches among the Western Pueblos. From Jesse W. Fewkes, "Hopi Katcinas," *Twenty-first Annual Report of the Bureau of American Ethnology, 1899–1900* (Washington, DC: Government Printing Office, 1903).

Now the baby lay there, looking around. "Sit back from him there," Mastamho said, "That boy knows much more than you all: he will be a leader." The baby was looking this way and that, its eyes winking. Then it said: "I want a name. What will you call me?" Mastamho said: "He is a boy, but I think we will give him not a boy's name, nor a man's but a girl's. I call him Hatshinye-hai-kwatsh'iδe."

Mastamho picked up the baby, held it in his hands, "I will tell you all about him. I want you to learn what I will teach about this child." Then he sang, swaying his hands from side to side with the child on them, and the four women danced to his motions.

When he laid the child down, the boy thought: "I am a boy; but shall I wear a breech-clout or not? Shall I wear girl's clothes or boy's?"[86]

The myth foregrounds the capriciousness of gender assignments.[87] In the next passage, Mastamho initiates a series of tests that reveal the boy's preference for girls' toys. Acknowledging these preferences, Mastamho instructs the boy in the skills of women's games and dancing, placing him in charge of both. He provides the boy with a dress and gives him a new (female) name.

Throughout the account, the boy is referred to as "he," and while he is instructed in certain manners and skills of women, he is also described as having traits unique to his status (e.g., leadership, skill in gambling and ability to cure venereal disease). There is no suggestion of anatomical change or the imitation of female reproductive functions. In fact, neither this account nor the briefer ones cited by Devereux provide mythological precedence for gynemimetic behavior. Mohave mythology presents *alyha·* status as a distinct and autonomous category of personhood, on par with other gender-based statuses such as the shaman, the chief, the midwife, the sexually active woman and so forth.

The account of the *alyha·* initiation ceremony collected by Kroeber is of particular interest because of the description of the face painting applied to the *alyha·* at the conclusion of the ceremony. Mohave men and women painted their faces with distinct male and female styles. The face painting described by Kroeber's informant consists of "a vertical stripe down from each eye and another down the nose to the mouth."[88] This design is illustrated in Kroeber's *Handbook* and in an article by Edith S. Taylor and William J. Wallace as a *male* style.[89] Similarly, although male berdaches assumed female personal names, they did not assume the clan name borne by all the women within a lineage.

In fact, various comments recorded by Devereux suggest that, in the minds of most Mohave, *alyha·* and *hwame·* retained qualities of their "original" gender and combined them with those of the "opposite" gender, and for this reason they were always thought of as distinct from both men and women. "You can tease an hwame·," one Mohave told Devereux, "because she is just a woman, but if you tease an alyha·, who has the strength of a man, he will run after you and beat you up."[90] *Alyha·* were not courted like ordinary girls; nor were they viewed as equivalent to female wives. "He must be awfully hard up to marry a womanly man," was a typical comment concerning a man who chose to marry an *alyha·*. According to Devereux, many Mohave wondered whether the husbands of *alyha·* "really thought they were having intercourse with a woman" — in other words, *they* knew that the *alyha·* was "really" a man; surely the husband of the *alyha·* knew as well.[91]

In explaining the development of berdache orientation in individual cases, Mohaves credited a combination of predestination, occupational preferences, social influences and, above all, dreams. As a contemporary Mohave explains, "Dreaming was the very core of Mohave life. It was the source of each individual's special skill, of his prowess as a warrior, and of his success in all his undertakings. A Great Dream might foretell the birth of a male child to his father. Later the dream would return to the child as he grew to manhood and listened to others tell of their dreams. Then he dreamed his own and became a man."[92] In other words, dreaming was key to acquiring gender identity, whether male, female or berdache. Although all dreams were believed to have originally occurred in the mother's womb, the dreams of *alyha·* and *hwame·* were not apparent until, as children, they began to express preferences for particular work activities. Devereux was told, "When there is a desire in a child's heart to become a transvestite [*sic*] that child will act different. It will let people become aware of that desire. They may insist on giving the child the toys and garments of its true sex, but the child will throw them away."[93] Although berdache identity is presented as predetermined and involuntary, this passage clearly points to a psychic and not a physiological point of origin.

In sum, Mohave beliefs combined the two modes of rationalizing berdache status described earlier: supernatural sanction similar to the Plains pattern *and* mythological precedence, as in the case of the Zunis and Navajos. Both rationales are more consistent with a multiple-gender paradigm than with the gender-crossing model.

If Mohave work activities were not gender coded, the markers of berdache status might be expected to shift to other areas, such as anatomy, but there is no evidence for this. We find the same correlates of berdache status, in terms of social, economic and religious specialization, in Mohave culture as in other North American groups. Overall, the division of agricultural and domestic work appears to have been fairly informal (as it was among the Pueblos and Navajos). Wives and husbands worked together in their fields, and, according to Devereux, *alyha·* were not the only males to perform housework: tribal heroes who take care of ailing families and middle-aged men who marry very young girls are also described as performing domestic tasks.[94] However, prestige was still gender based. For men, it was achieved through military exploits, leadership roles and religious specialization; for women, through food and crafts production and female forms of shamanism.

In sum, neither the belief system of the Mohave nor their socioeconomic patterns provide an explanation for the cross-gender behavior attributed to Mohave berdaches. The expectations and beliefs are those found in a multiple-gender paradigm. Although some berdaches may have insisted on a fiction of gender-crossing, the community as a whole did not go so far. This leaves the consideration of historical factors – or, more broadly stated, the possibility of nonstructural and nonpatterned sources for this behavior.

We might begin with a reexamination of Devereux's report. Gilbert Herdt has pointed out the extent to which Devereux's account of Mohave berdaches conformed to the Freudian theory of homosexuality as a phenomenon of sexual inversion.[95] This tended to lump together individuals now distinguished by such terms as "gay," "lesbian," "transvestite" and "transsexual." In fact, it would be tempting to define Mohave berdaches as an instance of transsexualism, but this would be misleading. The goal of modern transsexuals has been to appear so convincing as members of their chosen sex that others never suspect they had ever been anything but that sex.[96] As we have seen, the practice of holding public ceremonies to confirm *alyha·* status made any such fiction impossible among the Mohave. Further, the *alyha·* described by Devereux appear to have aspired specifically to the acquisition of female *reproductive* functions. Western male-to-female transsexuals, on the other hand, tend to be preoccuppied with the inappropriateness of their male genitalia in relation to their gender identification. They aspire more to female morphology than reproductive functions, with the acquisition of breasts taking priority over a vagina. If *alyha·* were identically motivated, we might expect not elaborate fake pregnancies and simulated menstruation but attempts to castrate themselves and/or enlarge their breasts (both of which are possible with methods available in a preindustrial society).

Although there is no reason to doubt the accuracy of his reporting, Devereux himself made no direct observations of berdaches, relying instead on the memories of informants recalling events of the late nineteenth century and often relying on second-hand information. Although referring to the existence of other informants, Devereux cites only three specific sources for his data on berdaches — Ñahwera, reputedly the last Mohave who knew the *alyha·* initiation songs (but not a berdache himself); an eighty-year-old woman who had heard about (but not seen) the *alyha·* ceremony when in her youth; and Hivsu· Tupoma, a male shaman who had known Kuwal, a Mohave who, in the late nineteenth century, had had more than one *alyha·* wife. It appears that most of Devereux's information concerning berdache pregnancies was

367

provided by Hivsu· Tupoma, based on stories he heard from Kuwal. Of course, it must be kept in mind that in a small community the behavior of two or three berdaches might constitute "tradition" for a given generation.

It seems possible, therefore, that the behavior Devereux described had its origins in individual factors more than in cultural expectations and may have been specific to the individuals known to (or heard of by) Devereux's informants, in particular Kuwal's wives and the dynamics of Kuwal's relationships with them. This leads us to ask which motives besides the desire to cross genders might underlie the imitation of pregnancy by Mohave berdaches. A comment Devereux recorded provides one clue: "Some men who had enough of it [marriage to an *alyha·*] tried to get rid of them politely, alleging barrenness of the alyha·. But no alyha· would admit such a thing. They would begin to fake pregnancy."[97] In other words, faking pregnancy may have been the somewhat desperate strategem of an individual threatened with the loss of a lover, not unlike cases of hysterical pregnancy in females. Getting the husband to participate in mourning rites for the still-born "infant" (and burial rites were serious business among the Mohave) amounted to his capitulation to the fantasy and, therefore, a victory for the *alyha·*.

In fact, the culturally patterned dimensions of the fake pregnancies attributed to Mohave berdaches can be discerned, but they are related less to beliefs concerning gender than to expectations concerning the behavior of shamans and a general anal preoccupation in Mohave culture. As Devereux reports elsewhere, any unusual manipulation of the genitals by children, such as hiding the penis between the legs or holding it backward to urinate like a mare, was considered typical behavior of future shamans.[98] Similarly, the fecal fetus of the *alyha·* is consistent with a pattern of anality evidenced in Mohave mythology, naming practices and individual fantasies.[99] The multilayered significance of the *alyha·*'s offspring becomes apparent when read in light of the mythological account of how the daughter of the culture-hero Matavilye is impregnated after swallowing her father's feces, an act that also causes his death.[100] All this suggests that the mimetic pregnancy of the *alyha·* was a symbolic, not a literal, enactment – a ritualistic manipulation of "dirt" (in Mary Douglas's sense of pollution) to mediate life and death – and therefore on an entirely different order than the behavior of modern transsexuals. There was no real possibility of "passing" as a woman in traditional Mohave society (after all, Mohave women were traditionally bare-breasted most of the year), but through magic one might at least approach the mystery of the creation of life.

Yet another line of investigation is suggested by a brief passage in Devereux's original article. Reporting on the contemporary (i.e., 1930s) status of homosexuality among the Mohave, Devereux describes three men "accused of" "active and passive homosexuality" – none of whom cross-dressed or had undergone the *alyha·* initiation. All three men lived together, and two were half-brothers. According to Devereux, "They are usually referred to as each other's wives and are said to indulge in rectal intercourse."[101] What is striking here is the indefiniteness of the role attributions. Devereux invokes the distinction between active and passive homosexuality, but he fails to indicate *who* is active and *who* is passive. In the rest of his article, these distinctions are crucial. One of these men would have to be a husband and another a "wife," and the "wife" would be expected to vehemently insist on the distinction.

Certainly traditional practices were lapsing by the 1930s, which would account for these nonberdache forms of homosexuality, but another possibility worth considering is that not only casual but committed homosexual relationships such as these were a viable option in traditional Mohave culture – alongside the option of being a berdache or a partner of a berdache. Because such a possibility does not fit Devereux's preconceived theory of "homosexuality" as sexual inversion, he does not explore it (although he does report that casual homosexual relations were "frequent" in traditional times). This would indeed distinguish the Mohave from other tribes, where the best evidence at present suggests that committed, sexual partnerships and cohabitation between members of the same gender were rare. If this were an option in Mohave culture, the only motivation for entering the berdache role would be to express a strong sense of gender difference.

As this analysis suggests, Mohave beliefs and practices are more complex than a gender-crossing model would predict. A review of Devereux's original report reveals how Western assumptions concerning gender and sexuality can powerfully shape ethnographic observations and even lead the ethnographer to overlook the presence of social patterns – in this case, the possibility of nonberdache homosexuality. The Mohave case also underscores the importance of allowing for the divergence of individual meanings and motivations from normative beliefs. In small-scale societies, idiosyncratic behavior can too easily be mistaken for a "traditional" cultural practice.

Conclusion

Berdache status was not a niche for occasional (and presumably "natural") variation in sexuality and gender, nor was it an accidental by-product of unresolved social contradictions. In the native view, berdaches occupied a distinct and autonomous social status on par with the status of men and women. Like male and female genders, the berdache gender entailed a pattern of differences encompassing behavior, temperament, social and economic roles and religious specialization – all the dimensions of a gender category, as I defined that term earlier, with the exception of the attribution of physical differences (the Navajos may be one exception; see n.74). But physical differences were constructed in various ways in Native American perception, and they were not accorded the same weight that they are in Western belief. Social learning and personal experiences (including ritual and supernatural experiences) were considered just as important in defining individual social identity as anatomy. Viewing female and male berdache roles as third and fourth genders, therefore, offers the best translation of native categories and the best fit with the range of behaviors and social traits reported for berdaches. Conversely, characterizations of berdaches as crossing genders or mixing genders, as men or women who "assume the role of the 'opposite' sex," are reductionist and inaccurate.

Given the presence of multiple genders, what are their social and cultural correlates? The three cases discussed here suggest that most of the variations in the berdache role among different North American societies were related to cultural systems of meaning and historical factors more than differences in prestige systems. Despite a wide variety of subsistence patterns, North American modes of production and division of labor did not in most cases produce significant or fixed differences in wealth and status. At the same time, they also afforded an economic dimension to berdache status in terms of productive specialization. Even so, economic potential alone does not predict the presence of multiple genders. Whereas sedentary horticultural communities may have provided more opportunities for specialization, it was among the Navajos, for historical reasons, that the berdache achieved highest status. Similarly, in terms of belief systems, although a vision complex can serve to rationalize alternative gender statuses and foster entry into the status by individuals who do not manifest the typical traits of berdaches, berdache roles can flourish within cultural systems lacking a vision complex altogether. Finally, as in the Mohave case, even with economic opportunities and beliefs similar to other North American groups, individual motivations, both psychological and situational, could powerfully shape the construction of what otherwise appear to be "traditional" features of social roles and the meanings surrounding them.

There are no definitive variables for predicting the presence of multiple genders, but I believe we can specify a set of minimal conditions for the possibility of such statuses. First is a division of labor and prestige system organized in terms of gender categories, so that the potential exists for female specialization in production and distribution of food or exchange goods. Second is a belief system in which gender is not viewed as determined by anatomical sex or in which anatomical sex is believed to be unstable, fluid and nondichotomous, and, therefore, an autonomous third category is viable. Third are the occurrence of historical events and individuals motivated to take advantage of them in creating and shaping gender identities. If these conditions are present, then multiple gender roles can develop – and it becomes possible to become a berdache. Conversely, I would hypothesize that, for a given society in which multiple genders were present, it would take not only the elimination of the economic dimension of such statuses but a lapse in the belief systems rationalizing them and the introduction of a dual-sex ideology to effect a full collapse of such roles.

The next step in berdache studies will be the recognition that gender diversity is not an isolated feature of North American societies but a worldwide phenomenon, represented in most culture areas as well as in certain historical periods of Western societies. Gender diversity will become one more part of the story of human culture and history that is anthropology's job to tell.[102]

CHAPTER EIGHT

Hijras: An Alternative Sex and Gender Role in India

Serena Nanda

The hijras of India pose a challenge to Western ideas of sex and gender. The cultural notions of hijras as "intersexed" and "eunuchs" emphasize that they are neither male nor female, man nor woman. At a more esoteric level, the hijras are also man *plus* woman, or erotic and sacred female men.[1] Hijras are devotees of Bahuchara Mata, one of the many versions of the Mother Goddess worshiped throughout India. It is by virtue of their sexual impotence (with women) that men are called on by Bahuchara Mata to dress and act like women and to undergo emasculation. This operation removes the male genitals, which are the main symbol of masculine sexuality, and endows hijras with the divine powers of the goddess (*shakti*) and of the ascetic (*tapas*). As vehicles of divine power, hijras engage in their traditional occupations of performing at the birth of a male child and at marriages and as servants of the goddess at her temple. Hijras also engage in prostitution with men, although this directly contradicts their culturally sanctioned ritual roles. Unlike other ascetics, hijras lead their daily lives within their own social communities, and their position in Indian society shares features of both a caste within society and renouncers outside it. As individuals, hijras exhibit a wide variety of personalities, abilities and gender characteristics and also vary widely in the relation of the private self to culturally defined roles.

In this essay, I approach an understanding of the hijra through both the public and private dimensions of the role. In the first part I look at the hijras as they are culturally conceptualized, particularly in relation to Hinduism, which provides a positive context for alternative sex and gender roles. In the second part, I discuss some individual dimensions of the hijra role, looking at variation among them in gender role and identity. Finally, I suggest two important factors that account for the maintenance of the hijra role over time and some directions of change in contemporary Indian society.

The Cultural Definition of the Hijras

In India, "male" and "female" are seen as natural categories in complementary opposition. The model of this opposition is biological, but it includes criteria ascribed in the West to gender: males and females are born with different sexual characteristics and reproductive organs, have different sexual natures and take different, and complementary, roles in marriage, sexual relations and reproduction. The biological, or "essential," nature of the dichotomy between male and female and man and woman is amply demonstrated in both the medical and ritual texts of classical Hinduism, in which bodily fluids and sexual organs are presented as both the major sources of the sex and gender dichotomy and its major symbols.[2] Each sex has its essential, innate nature, consisting of physical and moral qualities, although these are alterable. The essential opposition between men and women that is most relevant to the hijras is the different sexual natures of the two.

In Hinduism, the female principle is the more immanent and active, animating the male principle, which is more inert and latent. This active female principle has a positive, creative, life-giving aspect and a destructive, life-destroying aspect. The erotic aspect of female power is dangerous unless it is controlled by the male principle. Powerful women, whether deities or humans, must be restrained by male authority. Thus, the Hindu goddess subordinated to her male consort is beneficent, but when dominant the goddess is aggressive, devouring and destructive. This view of the danger of unrestrained female sexuality characterizes a more down-to-earth sexual ideology as well. In India, both in Hinduism and in Islam, women are believed to be more sexually

374

voracious than men; to prevent their sexual appetites from caus-
ing social chaos and distracting men from their higher spiritual
duties, women must be controlled. This opposition between male
and female sexuality is joined to other oppositions in the Hindu
classification system between hot and cold, erotic and ascetic.
It is the hot, erotic, aspects of female sexuality that the hijras partake of and display and that transform them into "sacred, erotic,
female men" embodying both the beneficent and destructive
potential of the goddess.

In Hinduism, the complementary opposition of male and female, man and woman, represents the most important sex and
gender roles in society but by no means the only ones. The inter-
change of male and female qualities, transformations of sex and
gender and alternative sex and gender roles, both among deities
and humans, are meaningful and positive themes in Hindu mythology, ritual and art.

As eunuch-transvestites, a major identification is made between the hijras and Arjun, hero of the Mahabharata, who lives
for a year in the guise of a eunuch, wearing bangles, braiding his
hair like a woman, dressing in female attire and teaching the
women of the king's court to sing and dance. In this disguise,
Arjun participates in weddings and births, providing legitimation
for the ritual contexts in which the hijras perform.[3] The portrayal
of Arjun in popular enactments of the Mahabharata in a vertically
divided half-man, half-woman form highlights this identification.

This form of Arjun reiterates the sexually ambivalent Siva, who
appears as Ardhanarisvara, also a vertically divided half-man, half-
woman, representing Siva united with his shakti. Ardhanarisvara
supports the identification of Arjun with Siva and of both with
the hijras. Siva is an important sexually ambivalent figure in Hinduism, incorporating both male and female characteristics. He is
an ascetic – one who renounces sex – and yet he appears in many
erotic and procreative roles.[4] His most powerful symbol and object
of worship is the *linga*, or phallus, but the phallus is almost always
set in the *yoni*, the symbol of the female genitals. The generative
power of the phallus severed from Siva's body is another important
point of identification between him and the hijras, as we will see.

375

Other Hindu deities are also sexually ambiguous or have dual gender manifestations. Vishnu and Krishna, an *avatar* or incarnation of Vishnu, are often presented as androgynous forms. In one myth, Vishnu transforms himself into Mohini, the most beautiful woman in the world, to take back the sacred nectar from the demons who have stolen it. In another well-known myth, Krishna takes on female form to destroy the demon, Araka, whose strength came from his chastity. Krishna is able to overcome Araka by transforming himself into a beautiful woman who seduces Araka into marriage and thus makes Araka vulnerable to destruction.

In yet another myth, the basis of a festival in South India attended by thousands of hijras, Krishna comes to earth as a woman to marry a king's son, who is, by this marriage, granted success in battle by the gods. The price the son must pay, however, is the sacrifice of his life when the battle is over. During the festival hijras enact the role of women who marry and later, as widows, mourn the death of their husbands, represented by the god Koothandavur, an incarnation of Krishna. And an important ritual at the Jagannatha temple in Orissa involves a sequence in which Balabhadra, the ascetic elder brother of the deity Jagannatha, who is identified with Siva, is seduced by a young man dressed as a female temple dancer.[5]

In some Hindu sects, worship involves male transvestism as a form of devotion. Among the Sakhibhava, a sect devoted to Krishna in which he may not be worshiped directly, the devotees impersonate Radha, Krishna's beloved, and through her devotion to Krishna indirectly worship him. In this impersonation, male devotees dress in women's clothing, simulate menstruation and have sexual relations with men, and some devotees even castrate themselves.[6]

The Hindu view that all persons contain within themselves both male and female principles is explicitly expressed in the Tantric sect, in which the Supreme Being is conceptualized as one complete sex, containing male and female sexual organs. Hermaphroditism is the ideal. In some of these sects, male transvestism is used as a way of transcending one's own sex, a prerequisite to achieving salvation. In other Tantric sects religious exercises involve the male devotee imitating a woman to realize the woman in himself; only in this way does the sect believe that true love can be realized.[7]

Ancient Hindu texts refer to alternative sexes and genders among humans as well as deities. Ancient Hindu texts mention a third sex divided into four categories: the "waterless" male eunuch who has desiccated testes; the "testicle voided" male eunuch who has been castrated; the hermaphrodite; and the "not woman," or female eunuch, that is, a woman who does not menstruate. The more feminine of these, whether male or female, wore false breasts and imitated the voice, gestures, dress, delicacy and timidity of women and provided alternative techniques of sexual gratification.[8] The Kama Sutra, the classical Hindu manual of love, also specifically refers to eunuchs and the particular sexual practices they should engage in.

Another ancient reference to a third sex is a prostitute named Sukumarika, "good little girl," who appears in a Sanskrit play. Like the depiction of a hijra in a recent popular Indian novel, Sukumarika is accused of being sexually insatiable.[9] As an individual of the third sex, Sukumarika "has no breasts to get in the way of a tight embrace, no monthly period to interrupt the enjoyment of passion, and no pregnancy to mar her beauty."[10] Like the hijras, Sukumarika was ambivalently regarded: she inspired both fear and mockery, and it was considered inauspicious to look upon her.

The ancient Hindu depiction of alternative genders among humans and deities is reinforced by the historical role of the eunuch in ancient Hindu and, in particular, Muslim court culture, which has a five-hundred-year history in India. This historical role has merged with those described in Hindu texts as a source of contemporary hijra identification. It is the cultural flexibility so characteristic of Indian society that permits it to accommodate sexual ambiguity and even accord it a measure of power. Although sometimes ambivalently regarded, these mythological, dramatic and historical roles nonetheless give positive meaning to the lives of the many individuals with a variety of mixed gender identifications, physical conditions and erotic preferences who join the

FIGURE 8.1. (above) Bahuchara Mata in a popular poster.

FIGURE 8.2. (right) A hijra serves at the temple of Bahuchara Mata.

hijra community. Where Western culture strenuously attempts to resolve, repress or dismiss as jokes or trivia sexual contradictions and ambiguities, in India the cultural anxiety relating to transgenderism has not given way to a culturally institutionalized phobia and repression. Despite the criminalization of many kinds of transgender behavior by the British and, after independence, the Indian government, Hinduism still appears content, as it has been traditionally, to allow opposites to confront each other without resolution, "celebrating the idea that the universe is boundlessly various, and...that all possibilities may exist without excluding each other."[11]

Hijras as a Third Sex and a Third Gender
The popular understanding of the hijra as an alternative sex and gender role is based on the model of the hermaphrodite, a person biologically intersexed. The linguistic evidence suggests that hijras are mainly thought of as more male than female, although females who do not menstruate can also become hijras. The word *hijra* is a masculine noun, most widely translated into English as either "eunuch" or "hermaphrodite (intersexed)." Both these glosses emphasize sexual impotence, which is understood in India to mean a *physical* defect impairing the male sexual function, both in intercourse (in the inserter role) and in reproductive ability. *Hijra* sometimes implies, but is not culturally equivalent to, *zenanna*, a term that literally means woman, and connotes a man who has sex with other men in the receptor role. It is widely believed in India that a man who has continued sexual relations in the receiver role will lose sexual vitality in his genitals and become impotent. It is sexual impotence (with women), then, and not sexual relations with men that defines the potential hijra. As hijras say, "We go into the house of all, and never has a eunuch looked upon a woman with a bad eye; we are like bullocks (castrated male cattle)."[12]

Hijras identify themselves as incomplete men in that they do not have the desires for women that other men do. They attribute this lack of desire to a defective male sexual organ. A child initially assigned to the male sex whose genitals are later noticed to be ambiguously male would be culturally defined as hijra, or potentially hijra. If a hijra is not born with a "defective" organ (and most are not), he must make it so by emasculation. Although all hijras say, "I was born this way," this cannot be taken literally to refer to a physical condition, although it *is* meant to refer to the innate essence of a person, which includes, as I noted previously and will discuss later, physical, psychological and moral qualities. Hijras differentiate between "real" or "born" hijras (a physical hermaphroditic condition) and "made hijras," namely, emasculated men. But, in both cases, the hijra role is defined biologically as a loss of virility, or as "man minus man."[13]

Thus, Indian emic sex and gender categories of hijra collapse the etic categories of (born) hermaphrodite and (made) eunuch. While ambiguous male genitalia serve as the most important culturally defined sign of the hijra, in practical terms any indication of a loss of masculinity, whether impotence, effeminate behavior or a desire for sexual relations with men in the receptor role, may be taken as a sign that one should join the hijras. Much less frequently, women who fail to menstruate take this as a sign that they should become hijras, but masculine (or nonfeminine) behavior in women is never to my knowledge associated with becoming a hijra.

The term *hijra* also collapses the two different analytical categories of sex and gender; the Western social scientific distinction between these two terms is not part of Indian discourse. While hijras talk about themselves as "neither man nor woman" in physical terms, defining themselves as "not men" because their male organ "does not work" and defining themselves as "not woman" because they cannot bear children, they go on to add criteria that are clearly also those of the feminine role in India, such as their preference for women's clothing and women's occupations, their liking for children, their gendered erotic fantasies and experiences, such as their desire for male sexual partners, their temperaments (i.e., they feel "shy" with men) and their gender identity, as either women or hijra.

The collapsing of the categories "intersexed" and "eunuch" as well as those of sex and gender is confusing to the Westerner who makes a distinction between these categories. Furthermore, while sexual impotence with women is a culturally defined sign of the hijra, it is only a necessary but not a sufficient condition for being a hijra. The *dharma* of the hijras – their religious obligation – is emasculation: hijras who are not hermaphrodites are in almost all cases impotent men *who undergo emasculation*. It is this irrevocable renunciation of male sexuality and virility that is at the heart of hijra identity as ascetics. This is true both for hijras and for the larger society.

Hijras as Woman and as Not Woman
While hijras, as eunuchs or hermaphrodites, are "man minus man," they are also, unlike eunuchs in other cultures, man *plus* woman. They imitate many aspects of the feminine gender role: they wear women's dress, hairstyles and accessories; they imitate women's walk, gestures, voice, facial expressions and language; they prefer male sexual partners and experience being sexual objects of men's desires; and many identify themselves as women. Hijras take feminine names when they join the community and use feminine kinship terms for each other such as "sister," "auntie" and "grandmother." In public transport or accommodations, they request "ladies only" seating and they periodically demand to be counted as women in the census.

But although hijras are "like" women, they are also "not women." Their feminine dress and manners are often exaggerations, particularly in their aggressive sexuality, and indeed are designed to contrast with the normative submissive demeanor of ordinary women. Hijra performances do not attempt a realistic imitation of women but rather a burlesque, and the very act of dancing in public is contrary to ordinary feminine behavior. Hijras use coarse and abusive speech, both among themselves and to their audiences, which is contrary to the ideal of womanhood in India. In Gujarat, hijras smoke the *hookah*, which is normally reserved only for men, and the many hijras who smoke cigarettes acknowledge this as masculine behavior.

The popular understanding of hijras as neither men nor women led to laws punishing their attempts to dress as women: some

Indian rulers in the eighteenth century required that hijras distinguish themselves by wearing a man's turban with their female clothing. A century later, hijras were also noted as wearing "a medley of male and female clothing," in this case wearing the female sari under the male coatlike, outer garment.[14]

The principal reason hijras are thought to be "not woman" is that they lack female reproductive organs and therefore cannot have children. One hijra story tells of a hijra who prayed for a child. Her wish was granted, but since she had not specifically prayed for the child to be born, she could not give birth. She remained pregnant until she could not stand the weight any more and slit her stomach open to deliver the baby. Both the hijra and the baby died. This story was told to me to illustrate that it is against the nature of hijras to reproduce like women, thereby denying them full identification as women. The small number of hijras who identify themselves as having been born as women, that is, assigned by sex as females at birth, joined the hijras only after it became clear that they would not menstruate and, consequently, could not bear children.

The Making of a Hijra: Emasculation

While the born hermaphrodite is the paradigm for the alternative sex, most hijras are "made" through emasculation, the surgical removal of the male genitals. This operation transforms an impotent man, a "useless creature," into a powerful person, a hijra, who now becomes a vehicle of the power of the Mother Goddess to bless and to curse. Emasculation links the hijras to two powerful procreative figures in Hinduism, Siva and the Mother Goddess, and it sanctions the hijras' ritual roles as performers at births and marriages. Emasculation is explicitly identified with the worship of Bahuchara Mata, whose main temple is near Ahmedabad, in Gujarat. Bahuchara is widely worshiped in Gujarat, particularly by women who wish to conceive a son. She is particularly associated with male transvestism and transgenderism and thus has a special relationship to the hijras, several of whom are always present at her temple to bless devotees and tell them of the power of the goddess. Many myths attest to

383

Bahuchara's special connection to the hijras. In one story, a king prayed to Bahuchara for a son. She granted him his wish, but his son, named Jetho, was born impotent. One night Bahuchara appeared in a dream and commanded Jetho to cut off his genitals, dress in women's clothing and become her servant. Jetho obeyed the goddess, and from that time on, it is said, impotent men get a call in their dreams from the goddess who commands them to undergo emasculation. It is said that an impotent man who resists this call will be born impotent for seven future births.

Hijras call the emasculation operation *nirvan*, defined in Hinduism as liberation from finite human consciousness and the dawn of a higher consciousness. The Hindu scriptures call the beginning of this experience the "opening of the eye of wisdom," or second birth. The hijras, too, translate *nirvan* as rebirth, and emasculation for them is a rite of passage containing many symbolic elements of childbirth. Through emasculation, the former impotent male person dies, and a new person, endowed with the sacred (female) power of the goddess, is reborn. Despite legal proscriptions against it, the emasculation operation continues among hijras throughout contemporary India, although it is done in secret, hidden from the public and the police.[15]

The operation is (ideally) performed by a hijra, called a "midwife," and includes the stages of a classic rite of passage. In the preparatory stage, the goddess is asked for permission to perform the operation, a sign that is conveyed by various omens. This stage allows for the resolution of ambivalence; that ambivalence exists is suggested by the fact that many hijras must try several times for the omens to be favorable. In the operation itself, all or part of the genitals (penis and testicles) are severed from the body with two diagonal cuts with a sharp knife. They are later buried in the earth under a living tree. In the liminal stage, after the operation, the *nirvan*, as the initiate is called, is subject to many of the same restrictions as a woman after childbirth. In the reintegration stage, the *nirvan* is dressed as a bride, signifying the active sexual potential in the marriage relationship. She wears *lac* (a red resinous substance) on her feet and hands and red powder on her forehead and is adorned with a fancy sari and jewelry (here the identifica-

384

tion is made with another set of Hindu symbols: red-hot-erotic-feminine). She is taken by a group of hijras in procession to a nearby body of water and performs a final ritual that completes the transformation from impotent man to hijra, or sacred, erotic, female man.

Hijras testify that only emasculation can transform an impotent man, who is "useless, an empty vessel, and fit for nothing" because he is unable to procreate, into a powerful figure. In Hinduism, impotence can be transformed into generative power through the ideal of *tapasya*, that is, the practice of asceticism, or the renunciation of sex. *Tapas*, the power that results from ascetic practices and sexual abstinence, becomes an essential feature in the process of creation.

Ascetics appear throughout Hindu mythology in procreative roles, and of these, Siva is the greatest creative ascetic. In one Hindu creation myth, Siva carries out an extreme, but legitimate, form of *tapasya*, that of self-castration. Brahma and Vishnu had asked Siva to create the world. Siva agreed and plunged into the water for a thousand years. Brahma and Vishnu became worried and Vishnu told Brahma that he, Brahma, must create, and gave him the female power to do so. So Brahma created all the gods and other beings. When Siva emerged from the water and was about to begin creation, he saw that the universe was already full. So Siva broke off his *linga*, saying "there is no use for this *linga*," and threw it into the earth. This act resulted in the fertility cult of *linga* worship, which expresses the paradoxical theme of creative asceticism.[16]

Consistent with the paradox of creative asceticism, it is the severed phallus that is the embodiment of *tapas* and is associated with Siva. The falling to earth of Siva's severed *linga* does not render him asexual but rather extends his sexual power to the universe. O'Flaherty's comment that Siva's *linga* "becomes a source of universal fertility as soon as it has ceased to be a source of individual fertility" bears directly on the status of the hijras, who as emasculated men (whose sex organs are buried in the earth) nevertheless have the power to bless others for fertility.[17]

The widespread association of the powers of asceticism with

self-castration in Hindu mythology, particularly as associated with Siva, provides the legitimacy for hijra emasculation, often conceptualized as self-castration. The identification of the hijras with the power of generativity concentrated on the male genitals separated from the body is clearly related to their ritual importance on "occasions when reproduction is manifest – at the birth of a child – or imminent – at marriages."[18] It is in these roles that the hijras are most well known, and for which they receive "respect" from society. It is also in these roles that they display the hot, erotic, female sexuality, which, rather than mere sexual ambiguity, is the source of their power.

Hijras as Ritual Performers
The most well-known role of the hijras is that of performing at a house where a male child has been born. The birth of a son is a cause for great celebration in India and, indeed, is viewed as the major purpose of marriage. On this happy and auspicious occasion hijras bless the child and the family and provide entertainment for friends, relatives and neighbors. The performances consist of both a traditional hijra dance and song repertoire and contemporary Indian folk and film music. These performances have comic aspects that mainly derive from the hijras' caricaturing of women's behavior, especially that of an aggressive sexuality. At some point in the performance, one hijra inspects the genitals of the newborn to ascertain its sex. Hijras claim that any baby born intersexed belongs to their community, and it is widely believed in India that this claim cannot be resisted. They then use their power as vehicles of the Mother Goddess to bless the child for what they themselves do not possess – the power of creating new life, of having many sons and of carrying on the continuity of a family line. When the performance is completed, the hijras claim their *badhai,* a traditional presentation of gifts of wheat flour, cane sugar, sweets, cloth and a sum of money.

Hijras also perform at marriages, before the ceremony at the home of the bride and afterward at the home of the groom. In these performances they bless the couple with fertility: the birth of a son is not only the desire of the family but also means more work for the hijras. These performances, like those for the birth of a son, are comic and contain flamboyant sexual displays and references to sexuality that break all rules of normal social intercourse in gender-mixed company. The humor is based on the ambivalence toward sexuality in India and parallels the ambivalence toward the hijras themselves. This is particularly true in North India, which has been influenced by Islamic sexual ideology. In this ideology, people (women in particular) are believed to have very strong sexual impulses that must be controlled to prevent social anarchy. Yet sexual impulses and activity are obviously necessary for the most important purpose in marriage, that of having a male child and continuing the lineage.[19]

This view of sexuality contributes to the North Indian cultural definition of the family of the bride as subordinate to the family of the groom: in giving the bride away, her family, specifically her male elders, is making her partake of sexual activity, which demeans her, and by extension, the family itself. In addition, there is a North Indian preference for the bride to "marry up," that is, into a family considered to be of a higher social and economic status than her own. This superiority of the groom's family is a lifelong aspect of the connections made by marriage and is expressed by a one-sided and perpetual gift giving.

Hijra performances comment on both the sexual and social aspects of the unequal relationship between the bride's and groom's families. The sexual innuendos, expressed both verbally and in dance, break the cardinal rule of North Indian culture in which reference to sexuality is avoided between people of unequal status. Much of the hilarity of these performances is contained in little skits and jokes in which the hijras make critical comments on various characteristics of the groom's family and on the relationships engendered by marriage that are a source of potential conflict, such as those between mother-in-law and daughter-in-law, or between sisters-in-law. Here the hijras fulfill a common role of liminal figures, that of identifying and diffusing tensions arising from social hierarchy.[20]

Hijra performances are surrounded by ambivalence, which parallels the ambivalence toward hijras themselves. The treat-

FIGURE 8.3. (above) A guru at a hijra gathering.

FIGURE 8.4. (right) Hijras bless a male child.

FIGURE 8.5. (over) A chela arranges the hair of her guru.

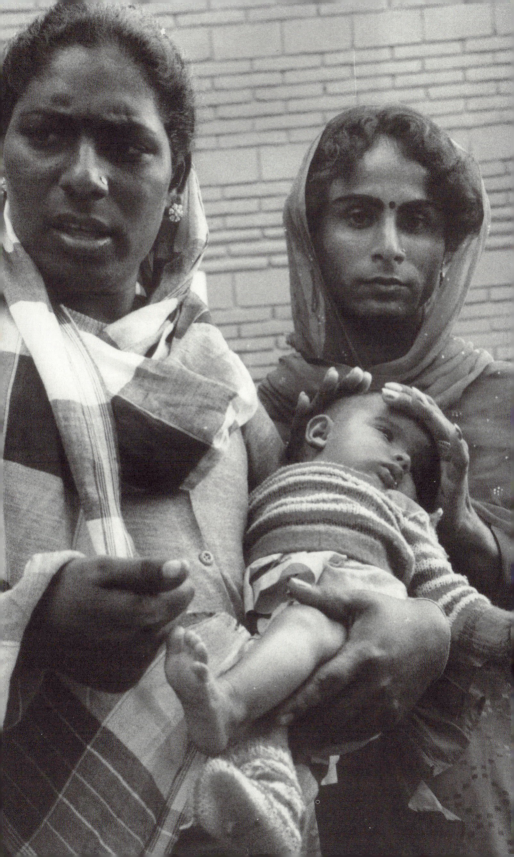

ment of the hijras rests on a combination of mockery, fear and respect. Although hijras have an auspicious presence, they also have an inauspicious potential. The loss of virility the hijras represent is a major specific source of the fear they inspire. The power of hijras to bless a family with fertility and fortune has an obverse side: they are also believed to have the power to curse a family with infertility and misfortune. And while their entertainments and requests for alms include praise, a refusal to pay leads to insults and curses. The ultimate weapon of a hijra is to raise her skirt and display her mutilated genitals, which is a source both of shame and insult for the audience, as well as a curse by which the hijras contaminate the potentially fertile with a loss of reproductivity.

As figures who serve and represent the goddess in her erotic aspects, hijras are both endowed with power and are also a focus of cultural anxiety. In India, eroticism and asceticism are regarded ambivalently: both have divine power, yet both can lead to social chaos. Hijras express this paradox with their bodies and their behavior. As "eunuchs" they embody the "cool," ascetic male quality of the renunciation of desire, while in their behavior, they display "hot," uncontrolled feminine sexuality. They are thus very much "creatures of the outside," powerful though they may be.[21] As persons who do not marry and who renounce family life (*samskara*), hijras are outside the social roles and relationships of caste and kinship that define the person in Hindu culture.[22] As individuals apart from these pervasive networks of social dependence and social control, hijras, like other ascetics, are regarded as potential threats to the social order.[23]

Hijras use this sexual and social liminality to manipulate and exploit the public to their own advantage. Having no social position to maintain *within* the hierarchy of caste and kinship, hijras are freed from the constraints of respectable behavior and nearly invulnerable to social control by those outside their community. Their audiences sense this and it makes them vulnerable to economic extortion, as they weigh the cost of giving in to the hijras' coercive demands for payment against the likelihood that, if they do not pay, they will be publicly abused, humiliated and cursed.

But just as hijras challenge their audiences, audiences, too, challenge the hijras. Ascetics have always been regarded with skepticism in Indian society, and the notion of the "false ascetic" – one who pretends to be an ascetic to satisfy his lust – abounds in Hinduism. Sometimes, people in the audience of a hijra performance will challenge the performers' authenticity by lifting their skirts to see whether they are emasculated and thus "real" hijras, or "fake hijras," men who have male genitals and are thus only impersonating hijras. If the performers are found to be "fakes" they are abused and chased away without payment.

The power of the hijras' performance lies in the potentiality of female sexuality, not in its actuality. Their power is compromised by the fact that hijras engage in prostitution, despite their many protestations to the contrary. Prostitution, which is not part of the cultural definition of the hijra role but which is widely, if covertly, acknowledged, undermines hijra credibility by running counter to the power they derive from *tapasya,* the ascetic practices that include the renunciation of sexual desire. Hijras recognize that their activities as sexual partners for men undermine their already tenuous hold on legitimacy as ritual performers and go contrary to the wish of Bahuchara Mata, who requires chastity from her hijra devotees. For this reason, hijras go to some length to distinguish themselves from male prostitutes. Despite the stigma on prostitution within the hijra community, it is important economically and the hijra community accommodates prostitutes rather easily.[24]

The Hijra Role and the Private Self

In Western society, in which sex and gender are viewed as dichotomous, anomalies, whether biological hermaphrodites, individuals whose erotic preferences are directed toward members of their own sex or persons with mixed psychological gender identifications, are made to fit into the category of either male or female, man or woman. Unless they fit into these dichotomous sex and gender categories, there is no place for them in society. In India, as we have seen, multiple sexes and genders are acknowledged as possibilities, albeit ambivalently regarded possibilities, among both human beings and deities. Individuals who do not fit into society's major categories may indeed be stigmatized (as the hijras are) but may also find a meaningful and positive way to pursue their life course because of the particular Hindu concept of the person.

In Hinduism, personhood is linked to participation in relations of caste and kinship, through which individuals become dependent on, and subject to, the control of others. It is through these group affiliations that human beings become persons, and it is the sacraments, or mandatory life-passage rites, that confer on human beings the cultural qualities of personhood.[25] Thus, being human is a necessary but not sufficient condition for being a person. Eligibility for full personhood is not equal for all: it is more available for men than for women, and for the three twice-born castes, who undergo a second birth, than for *shudras* (previously called untouchables), who cannot perform this rite.

Full personhood is built on the oppositional categories of male and female, who, through sexual intercourse in marriage, produce progeny, especially sons. Thus marriage, based on the expectation of fertile sexuality, is central to full personhood. An individual who dies without being married is considered an incomplete person. A man who is impotent, or a woman who does not menstruate, is thus disqualified from achieving full personhood.

But for the individual who is incapable of reproduction, as either a man or a woman, or does not wish to marry, there is a meaningful role available that transcends the categories of (married) man and (married) woman. This is the role of the ascetic, or renouncer. In identifying with the ascetic role, individuals who are sexually "betwixt and between" for any number of biological reasons or personal choices are able to transform an incomplete personhood into a transcendent one.[26]

This possibility is tied to the Hindu concept of the person as context specific and relational and the notion of *dharma,* or right action, as relative. All human beings are regarded as possessing different and unequal attributes of humanity. For all persons, depending on the specific historical and cultural context, the particular life stage and the innate traits carried over from previous lives, there is a particular moral obligation or life task that is right *for them*. As long as individuals follow their own particular life path, their *svadharma*, they are on the road to self-realization. In this philosophy, no action is right or wrong in itself, but only so in relation to the traditional patterns of the group to which individuals belong and their own nature. As the Bhagavad Gita says: Better one's own duty, even imperfect, than another's duty well performed.

The concept of *svadharma* leads to a tolerance of a wide diversity of occupations, behaviors and personal styles, as long as these are seen as the working out of a life path. This is particularly so when the behavior is sanctified by tradition, formalized in ritual and practiced within a group. Hinduism recognizes that human beings achieve their ultimate goals by following many different paths, because they differ in their innate essences, moral qualities and special abilities. Hinduism thus affords the individual personality much latitude in behavior, including that which Western society might label "criminal" or "pathological" and attempt to punish and cure.

The ethical relativism embodied in *svadharma* means that even impotent men, denied the possibility of full personhood through marriage and reproduction, nevertheless have their own life path, which is to undergo emasculation and become hijras, devotees of the Mother Goddess, when she calls them. Were these individuals to remain merely impotent men who could not marry and beget children, they would be nonpersons and, for failing to carry out their *svadharma* in response to the call of the goddess, would suffer the additional consequence of being born impotent for seven future births. But the concept of *svadharma* gives individuals a framework within which to find positive meaning in their lives. In their identification with ascetics, hijras – emasculated men, devotees of the goddess, renouncers of family and caste and the material concerns of this world – transform the dross of lost virility into the gold of divine power.

Hijra Gender Identity
Gender identity has been defined as the private experience of

gender role: the experience of one's sameness, unity and the persistence of one's individuality as male, female or androgynous, expressed in both self-awareness and in behavior. Gender role is everything that a person says and does to indicate to others or to the self the degree to which one is either male, female or androgynous. Gender role would thus include public presentations of self in dress and verbal and nonverbal communication; the economic and family roles one plays; the sexual feelings (desires) one has and the persons to whom such feelings are directed; the sexual roles one plays and emotions one experiences and displays; and the experiencing of one's body, as it is defined as masculine or feminine in any particular society. Gender identity and gender role are said to have a unity, like two sides of a coin.[27]

While gender identity, like all aspects of individuality, is shaped by an interaction of both prenatal and postnatal factors, Western psychologists generally hold that gender identity is generated primarily by sex assignment as male or female at birth, that it is established in a critical period in early childhood (from about eighteen months to three years) and that it is not subject to change after that point, or at least not very easily and without great psychic cost.[28] Displays of a mixed-gender role, an ambivalent gender identity or a gender identity that fluctuates over the life span would be generally regarded as problematic, if not pathological, in Western society.

This view is beginning to change, particularly among anthropologists. Although some anthropologists have been open to the idea that ambivalent and nonstable gender roles and identities are not necessarily pathological, and indeed, can be culturally patterned, the serious study of alternatives to dichotomous and stable gender role/identities, and how these alternatives are related to socialization in a variety of cultures, has only recently begun.

In this regard, Gilbert Herdt's work on gender role/identity among pseudohermaphrodites in the Dominican Republic and New Guinea raises interesting questions and suggestions for a new research agenda.[29] His reinterpretation of the *guevedoche* of the Dominican Republic and his study of some hermaphrodites among the Sambia suggest that, in certain cultural situations, ambiguous gender socialization in childhood does occur and results in ambivalent gender identity, or a gender identity that can be transformed at certain stages in the individual's life, as new social and sexual roles are adopted.

These insights are directly relevant for exploring gender identity among hijras. They confirm my own view that gender identity is neither so tied to sex assignment as psychologists seem to think nor so unchanging over a lifetime. On the contrary, my study of the hijras suggests that gender identity can continue to undergo change after childhood, even in some dramatic ways.

The possibility of changing gender identities is not immediately apparent from hijra personal narratives. Without exception, these narratives include assertions that the informant experienced a desire to be like a female since early childhood, engaging in such feminine role behavior as playing only with girls, dressing in girl's clothing, preferring domestic chores to boys' play, assuming a girl's name and later, as they got older, acting as sexual receptors for older boys and men. At first blush, hijra personal narratives seem to have the same insistence on the continuity of feminine gender identity as do narratives of transsexuals in the West.

Despite these common, even stereotypic, narrative elements, however, a deeper look indicates much variation among hijras in all aspects of their sex and gender identities and variable relationships between their gender roles and gender identities. With some hijras there seemed to be a strong and explicitly verbalized fit between their gender role and their expressed gender identity, as indicated above. This was most noticeable in the hijras who identified themselves as women. They experienced themselves as women, psychologically and emotionally, and, in all aspects of gender role, made strong efforts to present themselves as much like conventional Indian women as possible. They dressed modestly and imitated housewifish respectability, they had strong emotional attachments to their long-term male sexual partners whom they called their "husbands," they expressed strong desires to conceive and raise children, they underwent emasculation primarily to change their bodies to those approximating women's and they related the positive experience of emasculation to being able to "have sex like a woman," that is, sexual intercourse in a face-to-face position. Some of them took hormones to feminize their bodies, and had the medical technology of India permitted reconstructive surgery to create a vagina, they would probably wish to have it done. These hijra narratives show no sign of a faltering or ambivalent gender identity, like those of Western transsexual narratives.

Other hijras, who may currently define themselves as women or as "neither man nor woman," cite some of the common narrative themes of feminine childhood behavior, but display mixed-gender-role signals in clothing, public behavior, acceptance of emasculation, sexual interests and practices, talk about the self and reflections on the stages in their lives.

How can one explain the variation in gender role and gender identities among the hijras? It is impossible for me to know the extent to which ambivalent gender-role and identity in hijras I met is a result of ambivalent early-childhood socialization, taking on new gender roles, a lack of practice in feminine behavior or pressure and socialization from the hijra community.

The socialization of new hijras by community elders reinforces the gender-role contrasts between men and women. New hijras who act inappropriately in their new feminine roles are frequently admonished, "What, are you a man that you're behaving in such a way!" Despite many hijra complaints that the elders are "too strict," however, the process of gender transformation after joining the community is necessarily gradual and mixed gender-role behavior is accommodated. Some hijras, for example, continue to dress in men's clothing, have not adopted feminine names and keep delaying the emasculation operation. It is the ability of the hijra community to tolerate a wide range of gender-role behavior and gender identities, without losing its cultural meaning, that is one of its great strengths, accounting for the community's persistence over time.

The degree to which the hijra community recruits new members who already have a mixed-gender identity and the role that membership in the hijra community plays in either intensifying or creating such a gender identity are also only a matter for speculation. Certainly in the cases of the small number of hijras who were anatomically ambiguous at birth, it seems likely that they experienced socialization for a mixed-gender identity, although not necessarily at a conscious level. The personal narrative of one "born" hijra, Salima, suggests that ambivalent socialization in childhood does occur and that this may result in ambivalent gender role and identity reinforced by joining the hijra community (see figure 8.7).

Salima exhibited many aspects of the Indian feminine role: she had a long-term sexual relationship with a man she called her husband, and she had actually gone through a marriage ceremony with him. As both Salima and her husband were Muslims, she wore a *burkha* (a head-to-toe covering), as Muslim women do. While many elements of her personal narrative stressed feminine behavior in childhood, it seemed to me that Salima's gender identity was ambiguous. She always referred to herself as "neither man nor woman" and took pride in being a "born hijra." Although she always dressed in women's clothing when I knew her, she often, unlike any other hijra I met, had a several days' growth of beard. In addition, my taped interviews demonstrated that she always used grammatical terms indicating a masculine speaker when she spoke about herself, although she vociferously denied this.

Salima appears to have been assigned as a male at birth, although her genitals were ambiguous. Salima's mother tried many medical and religious methods to help them grow, without success. When Salima was about eight years old, a doctor told her mother, "There is nothing that can be done, your child is neither a male nor a female." Soon after this, her mother gave Salima permission to live with the hijras, who had been visiting her frequently. In remembering her childhood, Salima indicated what to me could be interpreted as ambivalent gender-role socialization. To begin with, Salima's condition was a source of tension between her mother and father, with her mother acting as an intermediary to protect Salima from her father's anger. But Salima's mother as well appeared to alternate between beating Salima for her feminine behavior and "letting her do as she liked," between trying everything to get her to be a boy and defending her against

FIGURE 8.6. (above) An elder conducts a hijra initiation.

FIGURE 8.7. (right) Salima, a born hijra.

ridicule from peers and neighbors. Ultimately Salima's mother resigned herself to Salima's ambiguous sex and let her go live with the hijras, a solution quite to Salima's satisfaction.

While ambivalent gender-role socialization in childhood might be most clear for those born visibly intersexed, like Salima, it may also operate in other, nonintersexed hijras as well, although at a less conscious level. Since most hijras are not, despite the widespread and deeply held belief to the contrary, identified as hijras at birth or in infancy, or even early childhood (up to two or three years old), and claimed and brought up by hijras, family and peer socialization must play a role in their gender ambivalence. The hijras I met and interviewed were brought up with their families and left their homes to join the hijras in early or late adolescence. In the absence of physically ambiguous genitals, they would have been assigned to the male sex and, given the importance of sons in India, raised as males. How then can their taking on an alternative gender role and their present ambivalent gender identity be explained?

Unconsciously ambivalent socialization may be one answer, joined in a seemingly large number of cases by early experience of acting as sexual receptors for men. Sushila, for example, is a hijra who displays a mixed-gender role and gives indications of a mixed identity. She dresses consistently as a woman, has long hair and always has a "husband." Indeed, at one point she adopted one of her husbands as her son, arranged his marriage and became a mother-in-law and later, when her son's wife gave birth, a grandmother. Despite this, however, Sushila has persistently delayed getting the emasculation operation, she is constantly getting into fistfights, with both men and hijras, and she smokes and drinks, sometimes to excess. She criticizes other hijras who are too attached to their husbands or too submissive to them and is vocal about her refusal to buckle under to a man. When she talks about sex, it is almost always in connection with earning a living as a prostitute rather than any emotional feelings.

Sushila's narrative has some clues about ambivalent socialization. She recalls that her mother often supported her when she fought with some schoolmates who had ridiculed her for her feminine behavior (dressing like a girl in school) and also said that her mother "liked my swaying [feminine] walk." Prominent in her narrative was acting as a sexual receptor for men (for which she received money) in her adolescence. I think it was only in retrospect that Sushila linked her effeminate behavior in childhood to becoming a hijra, and she was not knowledgeable about hijras until after her childhood. It was not until she ran away from home in her teens because her brother was harassing her for her sexual activities that she thought of joining the hijras. Her narrative suggests that joining the hijras may have provided her with a supportive environment and rationale for her sexual preferences and that only gradually, as she continued to stay with the hijras, did she reinterpret her feminine behavior as a sign that she was "neither man nor woman." Still another hijra, now in her mid-forties, who displays a completely feminine role, once pointed out to me a photograph of herself as a young adult dressed in male clothing. "That was when I was a boy," she said, "when I lived with a Christian family."

For many hijras like Sushila a key point in a changing gender identity may well be the self-acknowledgment of the pleasure they experience from being sexual receptors for men. This gradual recognition of the desires of the self may lead to interpreting oneself as an effeminate man, no longer capable of having sex with a woman. Thus, many hijras refer to these early sexual experiences as having "spoiled" them, in the sense of denying them the ability to take on the most important male roles in India, those of husband and father. With the recognition that this life path is denied them, the hijra community provides an opportunity for an alternative identity and an environment that is more emotionally and economically satisfying than life on the streets. It is at this point, perhaps around the time their parents are thinking of arranging their marriage, that they join the hijra community. Once there, strong pressure to drop masculine behavior and take on more aspects of feminine behavior would logically be accompanied, in varying degrees, by a gradual change in gender identity.

Membership in the hijra community means that individuals intensify their social interaction with other hijras and simultaneously distance themselves from their former friends and relatives. This effect adds to the explicit and informal socialization within the community to make a commitment to a hijra gender role and identity. Entry into the community through formal initiation is only the first step; a second significant point of transformation – or for some, a symbol of the completion of the gender identity transformation – is the decision to undergo emasculation.

Unlike transsexuals in the West, who must convince the medical establishment that they are indeed "a woman in a man's body" and have felt so since childhood, hijras express various motives for undergoing this sexual surgery, as well as ambivalence toward it. Some hijras view emasculation as transforming them into women (contrary to the hijra cultural definition) and wax enthusiastic on that account; other hijras, however, mention motivations unrelated to the gender transformation: as a way of "changing their luck," as primarily a religious experience or as a way to increase their prestige and their earnings. Several hijras I knew talked of the operation almost with indifference: they told me that the nerve in their male organ "has broken and it is no good for anything [i.e., having sex in the inserter role] anyway, so why not get rid of the useless thing."

It seems then that not all of those who undergo the sexual surgery wish to be, or feel themselves to be, transformed into women, at least at a level they are aware of. The cultural meaning of the emasculation operation is after all transformation into a hijra, not a woman. After the operation, however, it may be that an individual's gender identity might move more in the direction of the feminine. To the extent that gender identity even partially depends on how we experience our bodies, it would seem difficult to experience one's self as a man, without male genitals. Conversely, it would appear difficult to experience one's body as that of a woman merely because there are no male genitals. Those hijras for whom a feminine gender identity was very strong went beyond the operation, in the use of hormones, to make their bodies more feminine. Most hijras, even those who know about hormones, do not take them, however, and their masculine bodies are (perhaps must be) an important factor in their ambiguous gender identity.

Hijra personal narratives cast doubt on the Western idea that gender identity is always permanent over a lifetime. They also suggest that gender identities may vary among people occupying the same gender role. Hijras exhibited variety in the salience of different aspects of a feminine gender role for the individual's gender identity. Some hijras, when talking about themselves as women or as "neither man nor woman," emphasized their body image, others emphasized their role as mothers in adopting children, others emphasized their sexual desires for men, or their previous sexual experience with men, and still others emphasized the hijra identification with (male) ascetics.

The hijra role is remarkably successful in its capacity to incorporate individuals with a wide variety of gender characteristics, behaviors and identities. Supported by Hindu mythology and notions of *svadharma*, the hijra as an alternative sex and gender role has been maintained for well over a thousand years. In the next section I focus on two factors that may help explain the extraordinary continuity of this role: the psychodynamics of the Indian family and the socioeconomic adaptation the hijras have made within the Indian caste system.

The Hijra Role in Indian Society: Continuity and Change

Hindu Family Structure, the Mother Goddess Cult and the Hijra Role
The maintenance of the hijra role in Indian society may be explained in part by the interaction of the Indian cult of the Mother Goddess with psychodynamic factors in the Hindu family. Whereas at one level the hijras' claim to power is through the ritual sacrifice of the phallus, which identifies them with Siva, at a more conscious and culturally elaborated level it is the Mother Goddess that is the focus of hijra religious devotion and the most explicitly acknowledged source of their powers. Thus, the Mother Goddess cult is critical in understanding the hijras.

Success and salvation in Hindu India is equated with submission, particularly in regard to the Mother Goddess. The Mother Goddess is compelled to offer help when confronted with complete surrender of the devotee, but those who deny her wishes endanger themselves. Thus, underlying the surrender is fear. This simultaneously beneficent and destructive aspect, expressed in myth and ritual, represents the ambivalence toward the real mother that is perhaps universal. But the Hindu Mother Goddess is singularly intense in her destructive aspects, which, nevertheless, contain the seeds of salvation. This dual nature provides the powerful symbolic and psychological context necessary to understanding the continuity of the hijra role over time.

Hindu mythology and its hijra variants abound in images of the aggressive Mother Goddess as she devours, beheads and castrates, destructive acts that nevertheless contain symbolism of rebirth and initiation, as in the hijra emasculation ritual. A common expression of this theme is the many myths portraying the Mother Goddess as angry castrator of her mortal consort, who attempts to evade her sexual advances by explaining that she is like a mother to him. These myths suggest that the consort experiences the offering of the goddess's love as an incestuous confrontation, one from which he must free himself by transforming himself into a child, a form of emasculation, but one less severe than castration.[30]

While in some myths the goddess does the castrating, in others the devotee – son, consort, worshiper – castrates himself as a way of resolving the conflict presented by his anxiety over his inadequacy to fulfill the sexual needs of the mother. As noted earlier, self-castration is considered a sign of intense devotion to the goddess and elicits the highest respect among hijras.

The salience of these themes in varying forms in Hinduism suggests that the hijra cult, with its associated emasculation, is perhaps only one extreme of a more general continuum of ritual practices that derive their psychological effectiveness from the particular cultural and social context of Hindu India. Kakar sees the many mythopoetic and ritual manifestations of "bisexuality" (read sexual ambivalence or transgenderism) in India as "express[ing] powerful living forces in the individual unconscious – dark, ambivalent forces, repressed by most...that only the deviant, [because] of...intense mental anguish, dares to act out."[31]

Kakar locates these "ambivalent forces" in the particular form of the Indian "family drama." While in all societies the image of the "bad mother" combines aggressive destruction and a demanding sexuality, in India it is in the seductive, provocative presence that the mother extends, because of her own unsatisfied erotic needs, that the possibility of transgenderism most centrally lies. Several social factors in India combine to dispose a young mother to turn the full force of her eroticism toward an infant son, including the culturally required repression of a woman's erotic needs, her distance from her husband in the joint family, her increase in status and respect when she bears a son and the closeness between the mother and son for a prolonged period that is abruptly discontinued around the sixth or seventh year.

The young boy's ego cannot cope with the sexual demands of the mother, nor can he happily accept the separation from his mother that his rejection of her entails. The son's response to the mother's overpowering demands and his simultaneous desire to retain her protection result in a fear of the "devouring mother." This fear leads to a "vicious circle that spirals inward in the Indian unconscious: mature women are experienced as sexually threatening to men; this contributes to 'avoidance behavior' in marital sexual relations; this in turn causes women to extend a provocative sexual presence towards their sons, and this eventually produces adult men who fear the sexuality of mature women."[32]

The mother's overpowering incestuous demands on the son lead him to want to avoid them at all costs, even at the cost of his manhood. But although the rejected mother becomes dangerous, her presence is so necessary that abandonment by her is unthinkable – hence, the worship of the goddess as mother. For it is the goddess, dangerous though she is, who nevertheless brings blessings, salvation and rebirth – just as it is the mother, potentially dangerous as she is in the possibility of abandoning her son, who nevertheless is the object of the son's deepest longings for reconciliation. This fear of the devouring mother is an important psychodynamic factor in explaining the most extreme devotion and abject submission of the male devotee to the Mother Goddess – a devotion that prominently includes symbolic and, as with the hijras, actual castration.

The devotee's attempts at reconciliation with the mother through the worship of the goddess are expressed in many Hindu myths and rituals involving transgenderism, some of which I have noted earlier. In these myths and rituals, the male's attempt to remove his masculinity, which he vaguely perceives to be the basis of his conflict with his mother, is supreme. Longing for fusion with the mother that brings salvation, the male devotee – in rituals ranging from transvestism to emasculation – proves his submission and is thereby assured of the nurturing and life-giving presence of the desired mother. In the castration ritual, the hijra *nirvan* finds a way both to flee the sexually demanding mother and to be reconciled with her.

The hijra conceptualization of the emasculation ritual as rebirth illuminates the ritual as part of the struggle against death, which, because of the Hindu family drama, takes a characteristically Hindu form of a desire for fusion with the mother. It is this desire that gives Mother Goddess worship its power. As the hijras say, "The Mata gives us life and we live only in her power." Through emasculation, hijras, as devotees of the goddess, achieve the ultimate identification with the mother, thereby reducing their anxiety about separation from her. "The only unbearable harm that the Goddess can inflict on the worshiper is to abandon him. This, not mutilation, is the source of devastating grief."[33] The hijras' identification with the goddess through the sacrifice of their genitals assures them of her life-giving power, warding off death. In the particular sociocultural context of India the Mother Goddess cult resolves, by culturally patterned acting out, the culturally generated conflicts over the incestuous mother.

Cultural patterns of Hindu India are not merely a background hospitable to various kinds of gender ambiguities; they also generate psychodynamic processes strongly implicated in the maintenance of various forms of transgenderism, including extremes such as the hijra. These psychodynamic forces have helped enable the role to continue over time, attracting a wide variety of persons – those called transvestites, homosexuals and transsexuals in the West – without losing its cultural meaning.

Social Structure and Economics
The socioeconomic system of caste joins the psychodynamics of the Mother Goddess cult as the key factors supporting the maintenance of the hijra role over time. The caste system of India, with its corporate social units, occupational exclusivity, control over its members and hierarchically based group allocation of rights and privileges, accommodates many different kinds of peoples, such as Muslims and indigenous tribal peoples, who, though originally outside the Hindu system, become incorporated into it as castes or castelike groups. Although hijras claim to be ascetics, and thus outside the caste system, they are organized into a community which has many features of a caste (*jati*) or ethnic group (*quom*) and can therefore be incorporated into Indian social structure. References to hijras as "half a *quom*" indicate their somewhat anomalous position as both inside and outside caste society.

Hijras are drawn from many castes and from the Hindu, Muslim and Christian religious communities. Most hijras appear to be drawn from the lower, though not unclean, castes. I never met a hijra who claimed to come from a Brahman family, and the taint of disreputableness that attaches to them suggests that this is not an attractive option for upper-caste persons.[34] When a person joins the hijras, however, all former caste identities are disregarded, and no distinctions of purity and pollution are made within the community. Like other renouncers, their hijra identity transcends caste and kinship affiliations.

At the same time, it is the caste- and kinship-like features of the hijra community that are adaptive and have contributed to its social reproduction. Hijras function like a caste in their claim to a monopoly over their occupation as ritual performers on specific occasions. They also exercise control over their members like a caste, with outcasting the ultimate sanction. Also, like other castes, hijras have origin myths that justify their claimed place in society. The hijra community, like other *jatis*, successfully reproduce themselves, although through social rather than biological processes.

Hijra social organization also has the structural and psychological features of an (ideal) Hindu extended, joint family.[35] Hijras typically – and ideally – live in communes organized around a relatively permanent group of up to twenty individuals. Members contribute their earnings, whether from performing, begging for alms or prostitution, to the household, in return for which they are given clothes, shelter, food, perhaps jewelry and pocket money by the household leader. The household is the effective organization at the local level and may even hold property collectively, although property is more likely to be in the name of one elder.

Crosscutting the distribution of hijra households in space is a division of the hijra community into "houses." These are not local, domestic groups but rather symbolic descent groups, functionally equivalent to lineages. Each house has a *naik*, or chief, who is the leader of that house in a particular city or region. The *naik*s of a city collectively form a *jamat*, or meeting of the elders, which handles intracommunity disputes, sanctions hijras who violate community norms, including expulsion from the community, stakes out the territories within which each hijra household may work, makes decisions for the group, acts as the audience for the initiation of new recruits and mediates whenever necessary between the hijras and the larger society, such as in police cases brought against them.

Seniority is the major principle of social organization in the hijra community, expressed in a hierarchy of *guru*s (teachers) and *chela*s (disciples). Every hijra initiate must be sponsored by a particular *guru*. The *guru-chela* relationship combines aspects of those between parents and children, husbands and wives, and religious *guru*s and their disciples and thus has economic, affective and spiritual dimensions. *Guru*s provide guidance, work and support for their *chela*s, and *chela*s owe obedience and loyalty, and part or all of their earnings, to their *guru*s. This relationship is also the basis for a network of fictive kin, as a *guru*'s *guru* becomes a "grandmother" and *chela*s of the same *guru* are "like sisters."

The *guru-chela* organization is a very effective recruitment device, directly contributing to the persistence and expansion of the hijra community. Any hijra who wishes and can afford it (since the *guru* rather than the initiate usually pays the initiation fee) can become a *guru*, which immediately increases her prestige in the community, as well as her income, as *chelas* always give something – either cash or gifts – to their *gurus*. Thus, hijras are always on the lookout for new recruits. While most hijras join voluntarily under the sponsorship of a particular *guru*, there is a coercive nature also to the *guru-chela* relationship. *Gurus* are always trying to maintain their investments – economic and perhaps affective as well – in *chelas* that they have financially supported, and thus they pressure likely candidates to make a permanent commitment to the group.

Through adopting many features of castes and kin, particularly control over members through control over work, hijra community organization effectively adapts to the socioeconomic context in India. This castelike status of the hijras was recognized in the edicts of Indian states, which granted one hijra in each district hereditary rights to a parcel of land and rights to collect food and small sums of money from each agricultural household in a stipulated area. These rights were protected against other hijras and legitimately passed from *guru* to *chela*. This granting of rights was consistent with the Indian concept of the king's duty to ensure the ancient rights of his subjects.[36] Even today, although in a vague and somewhat confused way, hijras refer back to these rights as part of their claims to legitimacy; they insisted to me that the Indian government respected these rights as well, reserving certain housing blocks especially for hijras.

In addition to a culture hospitable to gender variance, culturally patterned psychodynamics that generate conflicts and resolutions open to transgenderism and an internal social structure that is economically adaptive and provides for social reproduction, demographic factors also play a role in the maintenance of the hijras as a community. India's large population provides the "critical mass" that is important in transforming any cultural category into a group and thereby leading to the development of a subculture. In the much smaller societies of Native America or New Guinea, where alternative sexes and/or gender roles appear, the relatively small populations would seem to preclude a community such as the hijras from developing.

Figure 8.8. (above) A hijra dances at a college event.

Figure 8.9. (right) A hijra prostitute dances at a party.

Change

With the advent of British rule, the position of the hijras began to lose traditional formal legitimacy. While the British initially recognized some of the traditional entitlements awarded the hijras as they assumed control over Indian states, ultimately the British government refused to lend its legal support to the hijras' "right of begging or extorting money, whether authorized by former governments or not."[37] They thereby hoped to discourage what they found to be "the abominable practices of the wretches." Through a law disallowing any land grant or entitlement from the state that "breach[ed] the laws of public decency," the British finally were able to remove the hijras' state protection.[38] In some British-influenced Indian states, such as the state of Baroda (in present-day Gujarat), laws criminalizing emasculation, aimed specifically at the hijras, were passed, and these laws were incorporated into the criminal code of independent India.

These laws appear to have had no deterrent effect.[39] Hijras continue to become emasculated, and few prosecutions are brought, partly because the practice is carried out secretly and partly perhaps because of the still-strong traditional Indian recognition of the validity of the many different ways of being human. Even a largely unenforced criminalization does, however, delegitimize the ritual practice central to the hijra cult, and in a recent case, several hijras were charged and punished under the section of the Indian penal code that makes emasculation a criminal offense.[40] These cases add the stigmatization of modern government authority to the traditional ambivalence toward the hijras.

In addition to government hostility, hijras complain that opportunities for their traditional work are declining as Indians are having fewer children under the pressure of family-planning programs and propaganda. In addition, new life-styles inhibit hijra performances. In modern blocks of apartments there are usually security guards, who increasingly act as gatekeepers to prohibit entry to various traditional street performers, including hijras. It is also likely that, as a result of increasing Westernization of values and culture, the role of many traditional ritual performers like the hijras becomes less compelling. Life-cycle ceremonies in India generally are becoming shorter, even when they continue to be performed, and many nonessential ritual features are dropping off. In response to these changes and to the economically competitive marketplace of contemporary India, the hijras seem to have successfully adapted through the exploitation of some new economic opportunities, such as establishing territories of shops from whose proprietors they ask for alms, and the expansion of some historical occupations, such as prostitution, which has become an increasingly important source of income. Although prostitution is stigmatized within the hijra community, it is widely engaged in. Historical sources have always associated hijras with prostitution, although these same sources cite hijra protestations to the contrary.[41] All the hijra prostitutes I met claimed they engaged in prostitution only because the decline in demand for their traditional occupations leaves them no alternative way to make a living. The survey of one hundred hijras in Delhi indicated clearly that the earnings of hijras from prostitution are far higher than the earnings of their families of origin, who mainly fell into the category of the economically impoverished.[42]

The expansion of prostitution is of major benefit to *gurus*, who can therefore be expected to encourage it. Individual prostitutes always work under the control of a hijra *guru* to whom they must give part or all of their earnings. Indeed, some *gurus* seem no different from "madams," living in style off the earnings of a household of hard-working hijra prostitutes, who in addition to giving their earnings to the *guru* are closely supervised by them to make sure they do not run off with the customers and thus deprive the *guru* of her income. In spite of this situation, however, few prostitutes work on their own. The community of *gurus* and prostitutes provides a working space, a steady source of customers, a minimum assurance of physical security in case customers get rowdy and someone to pay off the police so that they are not arrested, because prostitution is illegal in India. Not unimportantly, the group milieu also provides prostitutes with a social life.

But because prostitution is considered a low calling, offends the goddess and undermines the legitimacy of the hijra ritual role, special accommodations have to be made to incorporate it within the community. This is achieved by organizing prostitution in a structure parallel to that through which more traditional hijra work is organized but separating it in space. Thus, in large cities of more traditional hijra culture, such as Bombay or Delhi, hijra prostitutes live together in apartments separate from those hijras who maintain more respectable occupations. Hijra prostitutes do, however, maintain social ties with the community, and they participate in the networks of fictive kinship and the organization by "houses." Hijra prostitutes appear to be recruited from the *zenanna* class and pay an initiation fee to join the hijra community. In this way, the hijra community absorbs some of its own competition and benefits financially. While some of these hijras may have originally joined only to earn a living, they may be persuaded, by pressure from their *gurus*, to undergo emasculation and make a stronger commitment to the group, in time seeking their own *chelas* from whom they may earn.

In addition to prostitution, hijras have also tried to increase their earnings by broadening the definition of occasions on which they claim their performances are necessary or at least appropriate, for example, at the birth of a girl as well as a boy or at the opening of a public building or business. Certainly, the numbers of poor and emotionally lost children and teenagers who venture alone into the cities provide an ongoing source of recruits who can beg for alms and engage in prostitution, even if they cannot carry out ritual performances. For these persons, the economic security and the emotional comfort of the group life of the hijras can prove seductive, particularly if the individual has been rejected by his family for cross-dressing or engaging in sexual experimentation with men.

For the present, whatever the constraints operating on the hijras as a community, there seems to be no indication of the role dying out. Despite the stigma that may be attached to individual hijras, the power in the role still commands respect, or at least fear. The powerful psychological factors, joined with economic motivations, against a background in which culture and religion can still be marshaled to give meaning to alternative sex and gender roles, seems to indicate that the hijras, unlike alternative gender roles in many other societies, will be around for a long time to come.

Few systematic attempts have been made to correlate alternative gender roles with other aspects of culture, and this volume makes an important contribution to that effort. The continued salience of the alternative gender role of the hijra in contemporary Indian society raises questions about this relationship in a particularly insistent way. Although it has been suggested that gender differentiation may be a key factor in explaining the presence of alternative gender roles, the Indian context does not bear this out; for in India the hijra role functions in a culture in which male and female sex and gender roles are viewed as essential, sharply differentiated and hierarchical.[43]

What does seem to be an important explanatory key is the importance of the Mother Goddess in Hinduism. In India, the devotion to the Mother Goddess, and the corresponding significance of feminine creative powers, is still strong, unlike other cultures where Mother Goddess cults were submerged or effaced by the introduction and subsequent dominance of the Judeo-Christian tradition. Although this devotion is combined with ambivalence about the untamed sexuality of women, it nevertheless provides a context in which gender transpositions – from male to female – remain valid and meaningful.

The cultural significance of the feminine, when joined to the distinctive Hindu concept of *svadharma*, gives wide latitude to individuals whose gender roles and identities vary from the cultural norm. It is the genius of Hinduism that it allows for so many different ways of being human. The hijras will undoubtedly be viewed by many in the West as bizarre and pathological; yet their role becomes comprehensible when understood within the context of Indian culture. The hijra role is strong testimony that Western sex and gender dichotomies are not universal. As such, it provides a model of cultural diversity that may help Westerners reflect anew on their own culture and become more flexible in accommodating those individuals who do not fit into traditionally prescribed sex and gender categories.

CHAPTER NINE

Mistaken Sex: Culture, Biology and the Third Sex in New Guinea

Gilbert Herdt

Introduction

In the early 1970s, a time when issues of biological versus cultural origins of gender identity were emerging again in debates on sexuality, a group of American medical investigators published their account of a rare hermaphroditic disorder known as 5-alpha reductase deficiency syndrome. In brief, genetically normal males in the rural Dominican Republic were mistaken as females at birth and reared as completely "normal" girls. Then, at puberty, they were said to suddenly change gender roles, to act and identify as men. Julliane Imperato-McGinley et al. claimed not only that these individuals switched their identities and desires but that they did so without social or psychological influence from others.[1] Furthermore, it was claimed that this change in gender identity resulted from prenatal hormones that had "masculinized" their brains, compelling them spontaneously toward their "natural" sex. The study concluded:

In a laissez-faire environment, when the sex of rearing is contrary to the testosterone-mediated biological sex, the biological sex prevails if the normal testosterone-induced activation of puberty is permitted to occur. Thus, it appears that the extent of androgen (i.e., testosterone) exposure of the brain in utero, during the early postnatal period and at puberty has more effect in determining male-gender identity than does sex of rearing. This experiment of nature emphasizes the importance of androgens, which act as activators, in the evolution of male gender identity.[2]

Although supporters and critics of the Dominican Republic work have argued over many aspects of the study, the question of whether a third-sex category might exist, and how this would change the explanation of the issues, has been all but ignored. A recent study of 5-alpha reductase deficiency hermaphroditism among the Sambia of Papua New Guinea has opened an entirely different interpretation of "mistaken sex."[3]

Among the Sambia, a group of hermaphrodites similar to those in the Dominican Republic has been described in more anthropological and clinical detail (beginning with my 1981 study).[4] My initial work with the Sambia suggested that the construction of a third sex − the *kwolu-aatmwol* − was inexorable in their culture. Gradually, I have come to accept that the Sambia, at least, have created a historically divergent third-sex category, which is regarded as neither male nor female, based on the genitals and other characteristics necessary to differentiate among the three sexes.[5] However, continuing fieldwork, as well as intensive clinical interviews and detailed study of one *kwolu-aatmwol*, Sakulambei, a shaman, has led me to think that, while the Sambia recognize three sexes and at birth assign infants a sex, their worldview nevertheless systematically codes only two genders, masculine and feminine.[6] Hence, the inherent tension or even dialectical relationship between their three-sex and two-gender systems poses a continuing problematic in their own cultural history and representation of the hermaphrodite.

Contrary to the medical doctors' view of the Dominican Republic hermaphrodites, then, the Sambia study suggests that an indigenous third-sex category has been present all along but typically ignored by Western agents. Together with traditional pressures to conform to hierarchical gendered roles, these social facts are critical in explaining why individuals reared as biological females in both cultures might opt to "change" roles following puberty. However, the change is not from a female to a male role, and certainly not to a male identity; the change is from female to a third sex. Also ignored in the Dominican Republic study are the difficulties faced by hermaphrodites reared in the direction of masculinity; I will examine this among the Sambia. Finally, the review of these studies provides new perspectives for understanding why the biologically reductionist interpretation of this hermaphroditism has been so intriguing to Western science for the better part of two decades.

Anthropology and the Third Sex

The classification and meaning of hermaphroditism is a particularly challenging topic in the anthropology of sexuality. In the representation of the hermaphrodite, the order of culture seemingly clashes with the order of nature. Indeed, as Michel Foucault once noted, "For a long time hermaphrodites were criminals, or crime's offspring, since their anatomical disposition, their very being, confounded the law that distinguished the sexes and prescribed their union."[7] Many anthropologists believe that much of gender is "constructed," to use the prevailing textual metaphor, a paradigm that finds its foundations in the classics of Ruth Benedict, Bronislaw Malinowski and Margaret Mead, among others.[8] However, does this metaphor extend far enough to accept that an alternate sex/gender system of more than two statuses, male/masculine and female/feminine, may be created? In general, anthropologists have not been willing to go this far in their interpretation of the issues.

Much sex and gender research in sexology and later in anthropology assumes that sexual dimorphism is the innate and essential foundation of sex assignment and the modeling of gender-identity development across cultures. Not only is this order of nature thought to be an ontological preconception in natural species, but it is readily extended to gender antecedents of human nature across societies.[9] Sexual dimorphism is certainly prominent in Western biological and evolutionary thinking since Darwin, and it continues in recent work.[10] Perhaps sexual dimorphism seems so natural that our culture and – therefore – Western science have scarcely considered the absolutism that this piece of common sense exercises over sex research. Feminist and Marxist critiques have considered parallel issues in biologically reductionist interpretations of women's roles and the reproduction of motherhood.[11] Generally, however, reductionism continues in studies of males, where there appears to be a compelling match between the cultural expectations ascribed to males and the biological fact of their maleness.[12] Interpretations of hermaphroditism have likewise tended to obey a presumed natural law of dimorphism, encoded in cultural reasoning, that assigns all things sexual to biological types, male and female. Even Robert Edgerton, whose sensitive study on the Kopot of East Africa provided a primary text, recapitulates the Western essentialism of sexual dimorphism: "It is probably a universal assumption that the world consists of only two biological sexes and that this is the natural and necessary way of things."[13]

Why does the Western model of sex and gender remain so heavily indebted to an assumed sexual dimorphism in human nature and development? During the past century, as sexologists and later anthropologists and social historians encountered numerous instances of fuzzy sex and gender categories of individuals who seemed to be neither clearly male nor female, feminine nor masculine, the strong central tendency has been to reduce the variations to the male or female sex. This is because, in brief, these fields emphasize reproduction rather than cultural roles or personal desires as the focus of sexuality and gender.[14] In explaining why persons have seemingly failed to conform to the two-sex system of male or female roles, two interpretations have typically been advanced. First, these individuals were interpreted as biologically aberrant, usually in genetic or hormonal development. I call this the deficit model of human development; it has been popular in explaining, for instance, the existence of the berdache role among Native North American Indians for decades (in the functional accounts of A.L. Kroeber, George Devereux and Mead, among others[15]). A second interpretation, the social constructionist model, searched for social and historical factors that might explain the construction of an alternate identity or role but without challenging the underlying two-sex model of Western culture and science. In fact, these explanations do not neatly fall into these two categories, nor are they mutually exclusive, as indicated in the Introduction to this book.

But the relationship between cultural categories of sex and

gender-identity development remains problematic in two areas. First, does a society have a two-sex or three-sex (or more) code for sex assignment at birth? Those who argue for the biological primacy of sex assignment in the determination of gender identity are puzzled by ambiguous sex assignment, leading to the strong probability of hermaphroditic gender identity.[16] Second, does a society implement a two- or three-gender code developmentally to the gender-role socialization of individuals across the course of life? And does this coding apply as well to exceptional persons, such as hermaphrodites? Abundant cross-cultural evidence, as reviewed in the Introduction, suggests the existence of third-gender categories in other cultures and the inclusion of both normative and aberrant individuals in these categories, but it is unclear whether they are socialized as normatively male/female.[17]

A key problem concerns the ideological significance that a two-sex system such as ours places on sex assignment in childhood. As Mead once suggested, however, "sex assignment may be far more complex in other cultures than our own," largely because in subsequent "sex role assignments" there are stages at which gender status can change in the process of socialization during life (Mead listed eleven forms of these across cultures).[18] Gender-identity theorists have emphasized the difficulty of postnatal gender change, but recent critiques have challenged the primacy of early influences.[19]

In a remarkable essay, Clifford Geertz has argued that the Western dimorphic model is neither universally shared nor scientifically reliable when it comes to understanding hermaphroditism across cultures.[20] His conceptual position straddles the line between Benjamin Lee Whorf and Ludwig Wittgenstein and views gender categories as reflecting neither individual experience nor collective representations. Rather, he sees gendered categories as the workings of a cultural system of meanings and perceptions applied to "commonsense" formulations. Some peoples hold rather unhappy attitudes toward hermaphroditism, Geertz says, citing Edgerton's Pokot of East Africa, the ancient Romans, and, more extreme, contemporary America, whose natives express feelings of horror and nausea about hermaphroditism. Others, however, such as the Navajo of Native North America, hold a positive view of hermaphroditism, W.W. Hill tells us. Because of their curative powers, the Navajo berdache, or *nadle*, were "movers and shakers" who brought magical blessings to the community. The Navajo compared them to the American president Franklin D. Roosevelt. Thus, it seems that hermaphrodites were even "afforded a favoritism not shown to the other children in a family."[21] The Navajo categorize transvestites and hermaphrodites together as *nadle*, although Hill remarks that their hermaphrodites dressed and acted as women: an outcome suggested by a meaning of *nadle* as "being transformed."[22] How very different from Edgerton's Pokot, who, like Americans, look down on the hermaphrodite, although not with disgust. Rather, they see them as simple errors of God: like a botched clay pot, pathetic and useless.

The Greeks' mythic and ritual regard for the hermaphrodite was noteworthy, partly because of the divine precedent of Hermaphroditus.[23] Also famous in myth was Tiresias, the soothsayer, "who was born a boy, changed into a woman, and then back into a man."[24] These instances are especially remarkable because the Greeks, like the later Romans, usually destroyed hermaphrodites and other abnormal infants at birth. The Greeks apparently circumvented this taboo by "mistakenly" assigning a hermaphrodite to the female sex, a situation not unlike 5-alpha reductase hermaphroditism. These cultural variations in sex-assignment codes and socialization attitudes suggest an alternative approach to mistaken gender. While morphological sex is generally easy to classify, at least in a two-sex system, gender tasks and meanings are not. Category membership is harder to advance for gender; sex is a clearer and gender is a fuzzier set.[25] Cultures such as our own that overlay sexual dimorphism in nature on gender-identity development in humans tend to be essentialist and morally restrictive regarding conceptions of personhood and sexual conduct. Perhaps, then, the more gender is defined by the two-category classification of biological dimorphism, the more disgusting and stigmatized gender anomalies will seem. On the other hand, cultures with three-sex systems tend not to advance such an inexorable and seamless fit between gender identity and sexual classification.

Thus, they will tend to be less restrictive in socialization and more accepting of sexual variations, making androgyny a significant motif in cultural representations, even in the sacred.[26] Their permissiveness might be characterized, to use Freud's famous phrase, as "polymorphous perverse."[27]

Underlying these two ideal types of sex and gender coding are alternative ontologies of sexual being.[28] Each ideal type is pragmatically associated with different commonsense beliefs and empirical attributions about maleness, femaleness and hermaphroditeness in everyday discourse. Dimorphic cultures, such as that of the Euro-American tradition, define persons primarily by biological or deeper psychological essence, which is thought to be invariant through life.[29] Polymorphous cultures such as those of the Sambia of Papua New Guinea, by contrast, define persons as more fluid and as relatively male or female, according to social and developmental characteristics such as life-span stage, socioeconomic status and body ritual.

The Dominican Republic Case

The Dominican Republic syndrome (steroid 5-alpha reductase deficiency) is extremely rare; it occurs as a hormonal defect but only in males who seem otherwise biologically normal and is inherited as an autosomal recessive trait.[30] The hormonal defect in these male pseudohermaphrodites is caused by a genetic deficiency in the enzyme 4 steroid 5-alpha reductase, which impairs the metabolism of testosterone to dihydrotestosterone (DHT). Since DHT is the prenatal mediator of the masculinization of external genitalia, such persons are at birth sexually ambiguous, with a marked bifid scrotum that appears labialike, an absent or clitorislike penis, undescended testes and associated hermaphroditic traits. Some of these persons are recognized and assigned as males at birth, but in other cases the ambiguous characteristics cause the individual to be categorized as female in sex, with subsequent socialization as females.[31]

This "natural experiment" in mistaken sex assignment would be theoretically uninteresting for gender research were it not that subsequent virilization occurs in these persons at puberty.[32]

Because they are genetically normal males, with presumed prenatal exposure of the brain and central nervous system to testosterone, all 5-alpha reductase hermaphrodites begin to virilize
again at puberty through the peripheral timing effects of their
own plasma testosterone. Hence, the voice deepens, muscles
develop, the penis grows somewhat and testes descend. Erections
occur; sexual intromission is possible but without insemination,
because of abnormal urethral position. The Dominican Republic research established that thirty-eight hermaphrodites were
known from twenty-three extended families spanning four generations in three rural villages. The local condition is known as
guevedoche ("penis at twelve"). Of these subjects, nineteen were
supposedly reared "unambiguously" as girls; eighteen of these
nineteen were studied. "Of the 18 subjects, 17 had successfully
changed to a male-gender identity and 16 to a male gender role."[33]
These persons are said to have changed through stages of "no
longer feeling like girls, to feeling like men, and finally to the conscious awareness that they were indeed men." Change in sex role
from female to male occurred at around age sixteen. Their postpubertal masculinity was indicated by sexual interest in women,
with intercourse at ages fifteen to seventeen. Fifteen of sixteen
living subjects have since had common-law marriages with women.
As "men," these former "women" took social roles as farmers and
woodsmen, their wives being housewives and gardeners, which
are locally normative socioeconomic routines. The medical team
therefore concluded that "in a laissez-faire environment, when
the sex of rearing is contrary to the testosterone-mediated bio-
logic sex," the biological sex will prevail and "override" the social
environment's gender socialization.[34]

The Dominican Republic hermaphrodites posed a major challenge to the breakthrough theory of John Money, J.G. Hampson
and J.L. Hampson.[35] They argued that gender-identity development is determined by sex assignment and rearing, not by the
gonads, a conclusion that Albert Ellis had exhaustively presaged in
the literature on hermaphroditism.[36] In cases of ambiguous sexual
genitalia, they added a new criterion for standard clinical practice:
sex of assignment up to age two and a half is the best predictor of

nonpathological gender development.[37] Gender-identity change by clinical sex reassignment after this age is extremely risky for subsequent positive mental health.[38] Microscopic prenatal sex hormonal research since that time has not changed the picture.[39] These theorists had always claimed, in short, that the social environment was the key to the development of gender identity.

In retrospect the contested view that prenatal hormones caused identity development had wide-ranging effects on research and clinical treatment. The Dominican Republic study has been vigorously criticized by Money, Heino Meyer-Bahlburg and Anke Ehrhardt who chided the work because "clinicians have become insecure and now seriously suggest assigning males with 5-alpha reductase deficiency to the male sex, despite the fact that they will grow up severely diminished and with ambiguous genitalia."[40]

It is easy to prick holes in the study, as some critics have done. The ethnography is absent and interview data are sketchy; neither the interview schedule nor the exact psychosexual assessment procedures have ever been published.[41] Robert T. Rubin, J.M. Reinisch and R.F. Haskett have deconstructed the reported sample size on female-to-male sex-role change: of the eighteen subjects, two were dead, one continued to maintain an adult female identity and was married, another dressed as a female but reportedly considered himself male, while another lived alone as a "hermit" in the hills.[42] Thus, thirteen rather than the nineteen subjects were actually observed to make a clear-cut sex-role change.[43] These critiques raise two basic questions: Are Dominican Republic pseudohermaphrodites sex assigned and reared unambiguously as females? And is their postpubertal gender identity clearly male, so that "they consider themselves as males and have a libido directed toward the opposite sex," as claimed?[44]

A review of the Dominican Republic study reveals inadequate evidence for these developmental claims, before or after puberty, either behaviorally or mentally. We are told that villagers are aware of the existence of the hermaphroditic condition in local villages, even though the ontology of the *guevedoche* is never described. We are also told that the prepubertal subjects "showed self-concern over their true gender"; between the ages of seven

427

and twelve anatomical abnormality made them aware that they were "different."[45] Public bathing and crowded living conditions may expose their childhood genital oddity, which seems critical to their gender socialization.[46] Indeed, the *guevedoche* feel "insecurities because of their...genitalia.... They view themselves as incomplete persons...[which] saddens them. They fear ridicule by members of the opposite sex and initially feel anxious about forming sexual relations."[47] We must also wonder at the circumstances of the two *guevedoche* who did not convert to the male role despite the considerable reasons for doing so (see below). Finally, the fact that the sex-role change occurred as late as between ages fourteen and twenty-four, with a mean age of sixteen, seems inconsistent with the main effect, that is, the hormonally driven theory of gender-identity development.[48]

A critical reinterpretation of this study requires two new "insider" understandings of how the *guevedoche* cultural system works. First, their cultural system seems to code not two but three sexes. It is striking that neither the medical researchers nor their critics have noticed this simple yet profound social fact.[49] In the 1979 report it is noted, "The phallus enlarges to become a functional penis, and the change is so striking that these individuals are referred to by the townspeople as *guevedoches* – penis at 12."[50] Again, villagers' familiarity with the anatomical differences is noted, because subjects are ridiculed as *guevedoche* or *machihembra* ("first woman, then man").[51] This registers a cultural difference in the local system of commonsense sexual categories used in sex-assigning and socializing *guevedoche*. The villagers have more than a simple word for hermaphrodite; they have a triadic sexual code. That the village ontology includes a third-sex category – neither male nor female, but *guevedoche* – challenges the biological answers to the two developmental questions raised above.

The second understanding involves rethinking the cultural topography of the Dominican Republic. The researchers argued that the Dominican Republic works in a laissez-faire fashion with regard to gender-identity development, implying no social pressure on *guevedoche* to move to the male or female gender poles.

Here we are stymied by a hiatus of ethnographic information on the *guevedoche* category. Yet, existence of the *guevedoche* suggests that over generations villagers have historically responded to the presence of these persons through the construction of gender-related norms, rules and attitudes that served to mediate the normative male-female dichotomy widely occurring throughout the Dominican Republic. We cannot know whether the third-gender category was adopted elsewhere. In the absence of such local knowledge, we must rely on the distal ethnographic corpus to interpret the cultural meanings of the male-female dichotomy locally.[52] Caribbean images of gender inequality hardly constitute the neutrality evoked by "laissez-faire," and this seems generally true throughout the region.[53]

Anatomically ambiguous and stigmatized hermaphrodites have much to gain and little to lose by "switching" sex roles. Dominican males are better off than females, for men have wives as domestic workers, are preferred at birth and have higher political and economic status. To summarize from a recent Dominican ethnography: "*Machismo* also helps explain why power is in the hands of males."[54] In cases of an unbalanced sex ratio of children in a family, children may be "adopted" as inexpensive servants – which raises the question of the desired economic contribution of the *guevedoche* to families in rural Dominican Republic.[55] That *guevedoche* – either primarily female or male hermaphrodites in sex socialization – should aspire toward the ideal of *machismo* is understandable.

Contrary to the biomedical explanation, then, my hunch is that the Dominican *guevedoche* does not experience postpubertal developmental change as being from female to male. Instead, the transformation may be from female – possibly ambiguously reared – to male-aspiring third sex, who is, in certain social scenes, categorized with adult males. This is a very different view from that of Imperato-McGinley et al., who suggest that, as the result of (testosterone-induced) "serious self concern" over their sex, *guevedoche* began to "feel like men."[56] We are told almost nothing about the proximal social circumstances of this "feeling," which seems decontextualized. However, we know that cultural

429

influences were always developmentally present. *Guevedoche* are not so confused as to forget that by sex assignment they were not male: that is why villagers call them *guevedoche*!

Two important missing links in the Dominican Republic study are related to this symbolic interpretation. The first has to do with the absence of detailed clinical ethnography on the subjective identity states of those *guevedoche* reared in the male direction, a point to which I will return. The second missing link concerns the outcomes of those two female-assigned *guevedoche* who did not switch roles. Imperato-McGinley et al. provide anecdotal notes to fill this gap, and while their report is not ethnographically satisfying, it casts further doubt on their own biological interpretation.[57] Subjects 4 and 25 in the study did not make the switch to the male role. In particular, subject 4 "adopted a male gender identity" (the measure or index of this is not reported) but "continues to dress as a female."[58] This person has not had sex with women, denies sexual attraction to women, has worn false breasts for years and desires a sex change to become a "normal woman." Had they been reported ethnographically, the circumstances of gender resocialization of these female *guevedoche* could illuminate their mistaken gender and subsequent sex-role change. Suppose, for instance, that a person's sex assignment was unequivocally female, providing a stronger biological bias to femaleness or that any hint of ambiguity in sexual development was hidden from others.[59] Or suppose that her temperament was somehow better matched to the female identity or role than that of the others.[60] The possibilities are developmentally complex but not infinite.

Interventions by the medical research team in the Dominican Republic villages seem to have been dramatic. Various clinical specimens – blood and urine – were taken. The related psychosocial intrusions are hinted at in a statement on "materials and methods," although the full impact cannot be gleaned from the relevant reports.[61] We may have in these reports an example of "hospital culture" exported to the field and then withdrawn to the clinic, where the "clinical gaze" of sex surgery would further confound their interpretation and decontextualize gender identity and role even more.[62] Thus, too, cross-cultural sex research may directly alter the social field in which it takes place.[63] Did a two-sex Western folk model unwittingly color the Dominican Republic hermaphroditic study? From a letter in *Science* we learn that "the younger pseudohermaphrodites of the last generation are being raised as boys, and the townspeople therefore now recognize the condition."[64] If these researchers were ethnographically insensitive to the distinctions between two-sex and three-sex cultural codes and between normative males and *guevedoche*, they may have inadvertently interpreted or even cued cultural responses so that formerly naive actors came to label *guevedoche* as male or female, denying their own third-sex schema. This suggests that, all along, the presence of a third-sex category and role was ignored by the medical doctors, resulting in a biased interpretation of why and how individuals supposedly shifted from the female to the male sex after puberty.

The New Guinea Case
The island of New Guinea and its off-lying coastal societies is home to the most ethnically diverse social field in the world. Sexual and gendered roles and practices have long been known to be extremely varied along systematic lines in economy, society and culture.[65] Nonetheless, sexual dimorphism seems historically strongly marked in these societies; further, three-sex or three-gender variations in Melanesia are rare and controversial. Only recently has hermaphroditism been studied. D. Carleton Gajdusek first suggested that hermaphrodites reported from scattered parts of Melanesia might manifest 5-alpha reductase deficiency similar to that of the Dominican Republic study.[66] His guess has proven correct. Anthropological reports of hermaphroditism from New Guinea, such as those among the Hua and the Bimin-Kuskusmin (identified by Fitz Poole), are probable cases of 5-alpha reductase deficiency.[67] The presence of a third-sex category among the Bimin-Kuskusmin is particularly interesting in view of the marked androgyny motifs of their origin myths.[68] We may tentatively conclude that, in certain Melanesian cultures, the existence of a third sex, on the basis of the criteria of folk biology and anatomy, seems

definite, whereas the existence of third-gender categories and roles is doubtful.

The Sambia institutionalize a strident form of gender dimorphism in their beliefs and practices regarding nature and culture, and yet they also recognize in both human and nonhuman species the existence of a third sex. They do not, however, seem to offer any recognition of a third gender role or practices. Anthropological fieldwork beginning in 1974 made me dimly aware of a few slightly unusual persons, whom I at first misinterpreted as transvestites, only later to realize that, when Sambia referred to them as *turnim-man*, they meant some form of biological and anatomical transformation. In short, these persons, classified in local culture as *kwolu-aatmwol* ("changing into a male thing"), are what in the Western tradition would be called biological hermaphrodites or intersexed persons.[69] I have studied one of them in depth, a male pseudohermaphrodite named Sakulambei, over a ten-year period, originally because of his role as a powerful shaman and later because of his hermaphroditic gender identity.[70] I have recently published a fuller biographical and ethnographic clinical case study of Sakulambei, which discusses his sense of being a third sex.[71]

Ethnographic Setting
The Sambia are a hunting and horticultural tribe of some two thousand people who inhabit extremely rugged, isolated mountain valleys in the Eastern Highlands. Their atomistic communities – small simple hamlets – are built atop steep ridges formerly barricaded against enemy assault. The harsh beauty of the land belies the fierce, endemic warfare that pervaded Sambia life before pacification in 1964. Descent is patrilineal and residence is patrilocal; hamlets are composed of tiny exogamous patriclans that facilitate intrahamlet marriage. All marriage is arranged; courtship is unknown, and social relations between the sexes are not only ritually polarized but often hostile. Like other New Guinea Highland societies, Sambia segmentary descent groups are associated with a men's secret society that ideologically disparages women as inferior, dangerous creatures who can pollute men

and deplete them of their masculine substance.[72] The economic division of labor reflects this warrior ethos: women are confined to garden work and child-rearing. Although men fell trees and erect fences, the heavy, dirty work of gardening and domestic chores is left to women, while men spend more time hunting.

How do Sambia understand the nature and functioning of the sexes? The male sex is socially preferred and valued. The female sex is inferior in every way except in reproduction. Females are thought to be naturally fertile and are believed to mature naturally without external aid, for their bodies contain a menstrual blood organ (*tingu*) that hastens physical and mental development, puberty and eventually menarche – the key sign a woman is ready for marriage and procreation. At menarche a woman is initiated through secret ceremonies in the menstrual hut forbidden to males. Males, on the other hand, do not naturally mature as fast or as competently as females, Sambia believe. Womb blood and maternal care hold them back and even endanger their health. Males cannot attain puberty or other secondary sex traits (e.g., body hair, mature glans penis) without semen. And their bodies do not naturally produce semen, as Sambia see it. Therefore they require inseminations and magical ritual treatments of various kinds over many years to "catch up" with females and become strong men.

One aspect of Sambia beliefs and cosmology regarding the male body is critical to understanding their view of hermaphroditism. Males also possess a *tingu* organ, but it is believed to be "dry" and nonfunctional. Indeed, a mother's birth, menstrual and vaginal fluids – which a boy cannot help but take in – eventually impede masculine growth. Males possess a semen organ (*kerekukereku*), but unlike the female *tingu*, it is small, hard and empty at birth: it contains no semen of its own and cannot manufacture any. Although semen is believed to be the spark of human life and, moreover, the sole precipitant of biological maleness (strong bones and muscles and, later, male secondary sex traits), Sambia hold that the human body cannot naturally produce semen, so it must be artificially and externally introduced (like an androgen).[73] Hermaphrodites mistakenly assigned to the female sex are there-

433

fore deprived of semen and can never properly masculinize, even to the extent of the *kwolu-aatmwol*, who are reared in the direction of masculinity. The ritual function of homosexual fellatio, then, is to consume semen and thereby produce maleness. The excess sperm is stored in the semen organ for adult use. Biological maleness is distinct from the mere possession of male genitalia, and only repeated inseminations of the boy are thought to confer in him the reproductive competence that culminates in manliness and fatherhood. This also helps to explain why the *kwolu-aatmwol* who are reared in the context of male initiation seem to be more enthusiastic fellators and, because they are typically unmarried and show the signs of puberty later than do others, continue in the role for a longer time. In some obscure way, this may also influence the perception of their gendered relations.

Male development and masculinization after childhood are the responsibility of the men's secret society and its initiation system. Boys are initiated through harsh ordeals at seven to ten years of age. They are physically separated from their mothers, natal households and younger siblings. For years thereafter they must live in the men's house and shun all females. Avoidance taboos are rigidly enforced with shaming, beatings and death in circumstances where they believe a boy has told women ritual secrets. Over the next fifteen years, boys undergo six secret initiations in all, which correspond to age grades and ritual status. First-state initiation (*moku*) males are called *choowinuku*; second-stage initiation (*imbutu*) occurs between ages eleven and thirteen; and third-stage initiation (*ipmangwi*) bachelorhood puberty rites are for youths fourteen to sixteen years of age. All three of these initiations are done in sequence on large groups of boys who become an age-set cohort. These rites make boys and youths members of a warriorhood, the local unit of which is based in and responsible for defending its own hamlet. The final three initiations are organized for particular youths, underlining their individualized character as "life crisis" events for the young men and their brides. Fourth-stage initiation (*nuposha*) may occur anytime after the *ipmangwi*. It is a marriage ceremony, with secret rites and sexual teachings for individual youths, who have a woman assigned for their marriage. Fifth-stage initiation (*taiketnyi*) takes place when a man's wife has her menarche. Final, sixth-stage initiation (*moondangu*) is held when a man's wife bears her first child. Two children bring full adult personhood (*aatmwunu*) for man and woman alike.

Female development and feminine socialization take a very different course among the Sambia. Girls remain closely attached to their mothers and older sisters. They are key helpers and baby-sitters in ways their brothers are not. Girls are brought into gardening activity earlier and more comprehensively than boys. Girls remain with their parents for longer than their brothers too, for they do not leave their natal households until their late teens, usually after menarche. There are no initiation events for females until the marriage ceremony is performed. They are then secretly instructed in sexual and reproductive knowledge and tasks and female folklore and ceremonies. The menarche ceremony is their next main event. Formal "marriage" occurs prior to menarche, although genital intercourse is forbidden before menarche, which is typically later. In the minds of Sambia, the first-stage initiation of boys at ages seven to ten is in some fundamental ways equivalent to the menarche ceremony of females in their late teens – a cultural identification that attests to the very different status positions and development goals of the sexes, as well as to the prolonged "childhoods" of females. With motherhood, women assume increasingly important roles in the village and its social world, ultimately enabling them to become respected female elders.

These ritual systems of dimorphic gender socialization can be found throughout New Guinea. What is special about the Sambia, other neighboring Anga tribes, and related societies of the Papuan Gulf, such as the Keraki of the Fly River, is the widescale institutionalization of boy-inseminating rituals.[74] Sambia practice secret same-sex fellatio, which is taught and instituted in first-stage initiation. Boys learn to ingest semen from older youths through oral-sexual contacts. First- and second-stage initiates may serve only as fellators; they are situationally forbidden from reversing erotic roles. Third-stage pubescent bachelors and older youths act as recipients of fellatio, inseminating prepubescent boys. All males

435

pass through both social erotic stages, being first fellators, then serving as recipients: there are no exceptions, since all Sambia males are initiated and pressured to engage in homosexual fellatio. After marriage, they continue same-sex insemination of boys until the birth of their first child. Sixth-stage rites bring an end to homoerotic activities, although a few males, typically "stronger" and more in the mold of idealized war leaders, discreetly continue sexual relations with boys along with their marital relations.

The Sambia Third Sex
To summarize the ethnography of Sambia hermaphroditism: Sambia have three sexual categories, male, female and *kwolu-aatmwol*, a word that suggests a person's "transforming into a male thing." In popular discourse, however, Sambia use another term – *turnim-man* – from Neo-Melanesian Pidgin, which refers to "turning into a man." As a historical/symbolic category in their society, parents and midwives know that the condition causes anatomical ambiguity at birth and dramatic masculinization at puberty.[75] Hermaphroditic infants are sex assigned as *kwolu-aatmwol* and not as male. Those assigned as female are mistakenly reared as normal females. Yet because the phenomenon has existed for generations and the midwives and mothers go to some lengths to examine the infant's body for signs of the *kwolu-aatmwol*, it is unlikely that a mistake in sex assignment will occur, and only a few instances of such a mistaken assignment, as reported below, are historically known.

In their worldview, the Sambia regard hermaphroditism as a sad and mysterious quirk of nature. They see the signs of a third sex in species such as the pandanus tree and cassowary.[76] But in human beings, it has a more unfortunate connotation. The *kwolu-aatmwol*, unless distinguished as a shaman or war leader, is quietly disparaged. When discovered at birth, the child is reared in the direction of masculinity, but not unambiguously; rather, it is referred to as either *kwolu-aatmwol* or male, because parents know that their infant will not change into a female. Sometimes the *kwolu-aatmwol* is teased as a child and humiliated by peers for having "no penis." Nevertheless, several of these people assigned to the third-sex *kwolu-aatmwol* category are well known in local his-

436

tory. One of them, now deceased, was famous both as a shaman and a fight leader. The *kwolu-aatmwol* is not therefore rejected or frozen out of daily and normative social contacts and may indeed rise to distinction through special achievements, as Sakulambei has done. Nor do Sambia feel disgust toward these liminal beings. Still, theirs is a sexually polarized society, and parents do not want infants to be hermaphroditic: the men believe that intersexed infants are sometimes killed at birth by women.[77] If it passes as female, however, it is sure to survive. Consequently, at birth, women check the infant's sex carefully to ensure that it is not *kwolu-aatmwol.*

In 1983 I was visited in the field by Julian Davidson, an endocrinologist from Stanford University, who analyzed blood samples from the Sambia pseudohermaphrodites, confirming our hunch that 5-alpha reductase deficiency syndrome was present.[78] I have since identified fourteen male pseudohermaphrodites over three generations since 1910; they derive from eight villages having a total historical population of about 1,700. Of these fourteen subjects, six are living, and five have been studied in some depth.

Five of the total were reared as females. Nine of the fourteen *kwolu-aatmwol* were reared as males. Two of these are still alive. One late adolescent continues to live as a female, although she is unmarried, physically larger than a normal female and now known to be a *kwolu-aatmwol.* The other living subject is an older adult who was reportedly reared ambiguously as a female. Signs of anatomical peculiarity in this individual after puberty, such as the lack of breast development, were obvious but were ignored. However, she was married in a normative marriage arrangement at nineteen to a man who then discovered that she had a small penis. The outraged and shamed husband wanted to kill her, but their relatives intervened. After this traumatic incident, the mistaken female began wearing male clothes and, taking a male name, moved far away. Today this individual passes as a male in a distant Highland town. He is unmarried, and although he dates women, he seems uninterested erotically in them. In three other historical cases the same social outcome occurred: the switch from one sexual category to another took place only after marriage, humili-

437

ation and exposure.[79] In these instances, however, the psychosexual change was not from female to male but from putatively female to *kwolu-aatmwol*, sometimes opportunistically categorized with other men for symbolic purposes strategically useful to the men and/or the hermaphrodite.

In certain regards one could argue that the adolescent *kwolu-aatmwol* constitutes a third-sex category for Sambia. However, it can be noted that Sambia only very rarely initiate *kwolu-aatmwol* into third-stage *ipmangwi* status. Typically, they remain second-stage *imbutnuku*. One definite case, that of Sakulambei, is known in which initiation from second to third stage did occur.[80] The circumstances of this initation suggest that Sambia seem to recognize the importance of biological puberty as an antecedent condition of attaining social puberty. They deny social puberty to aberrant biological males because of their apparent "failure" to achieve physical maturation. One might have thought the force of consistency would influence the men's decision making, leading to a lumping together of the *kwolu-aatmwol* with normal males. But a remarkable feature of the Sambian response to the developmental course of male-identified *kwolu-aatmwol* is that no further initiations, including the collective third-stage *ipmangwi* ceremony, are normatively planned or sponsored for them.[81] Because by canonical male theory all males are fully initiated into the six stages of the men's secret society, this omission seems to violate the men's own idea of the same ritual treatment applied to all men. Indeed, the Sambia are so ideologically consistent regarding the uniformity of male ritual development that for some time I ignored asking about the subsequent initiations of the hermaphrodites.

Thus, I had observed Sakulambei initiated into the third stage in the 1970s, so my view was influenced by the apparent normative character of this event. Only later did I realize that the men, Sakulambei's father and clan brothers included, had excluded him for initiation with his own cohort in 1968. Subsequent work revealed that he had entrepreneurially engineered his own 1975 initiation in another phratry through a powerful relative's influence, an old male shaman invested in Sakulambei's career.[82] Later

438

interviews and ethnohistorical work showed that all other male-assigned hermaphrodites had likewise been bypassed for "pubertal" initiation. Moreover, all cases of female-to-male sex-changing occurred without any subsequent initiation into the men's society, an extraordinary outcome that again challenges the internal consistency of the view that all men are initiated, but one that the Sambia ignore. Sakulambei's history thus supports the interpretation of a three-sex code in subsequent socialization. Biological changes in the male body anticipate the subsequent social events of third-stage puberty rites. For the person sex assigned as *kwolu-aatmwol* they suggest that ritual initiation is not enough to "activate" complete masculinization.[83] The late-adolescent transformation of the mistakenly female-assigned *kwolu-aatmwol* comes long after this person's male age-set cohort has passed into advanced normative role-status positions. Sambia believe that it is too late to change the sexual status and related ritual knowledge in both types of late bloomers.

That the socialization of individuals such as Sakulambei is ambiguous can be seen both from their social behavior and their internal identity state. They show less aggressive and assertive action and more nurturing and deferential behavior than normative males. If parents feel ashamed of or reject the child, the mental health outcome is poorer.[84] The *kwolu-aatmwol*'s odd-looking genitals (small or abnormally shaped phallus and possible undescended testicles) make them fearful of revealing themselves. Thus, they avoid any situation in which they must serve as an inseminator in adolescence and they remain sexually timid as adults.[85] Because Sakulambei, for instance, was not properly initiated at puberty and could prolong his practice of the homoerotic recipient role in normative male ritual development, his history of sexual behavior is aberrant. There were other ambiguous features in Saku's ritual development: for instance, contrary to all other male Sambia, Sakulambei has never nosebled or felt the need to let "female" blood from his body.[86] He feels it is a part of his core identity. It is no surprise, then, that the *kwolu-aatmwol*'s gender-identity state is neither clearly male or female: they have a hermaphroditic psychosexual identity that is distinctly differ-

439

ent, and their phenomenology reveals them to feel unique or alone in the world.[87]

New Guinea systems would seem to manifest the strongest sexual dimorphism in their conceptions of the natural world and human nature. In fact, however, we find discordance between the order of nature and the order of culture. Perceptions of androgyny in species such as cassowary and the pandanus tree are coded into symbolic systems.[88] In other New Guinea contexts the husbandry of hermaphroditic pigs is popular and symbolically potent.[89] Hermaphroditism is encoded also in the primal ancestors of certain peoples.[90]

Among the Sambia, too, such a myth exists, and its hermaphroditic theme speaks both of what to be and not to be in male development. Its revelation comes to initiates at the completion of their final initiation into full manhood.[91] The myth tells of two persons, with small breasts and tiny penes, who began the world. The story causes concern among some men in the audience about whether males, females or hermaphrodites are sexually dominant. Their anxieties are played down, however, since the hermaphrodites are absent because *kwolu-aatmwol* never hear this story, since they are not initiated beyond the third stage. The myth of parthenogenesis does, therefore, "charter" Sambian hermaphroditism in a sacred sense. Its secrecy does not repair the psychological feelings of hermaphrodites, however. Nor does its existence preclude some derision of the third sex as a lower form in the order of nature. Here, then, the Sambia attitude toward the *kwolu-aatmwol* is ambivalent: its existence is sufficiently independent as an ontological and cultural category that, for Sambia men, and perhaps women, too, the hermaphrodite is sometimes a useful blessing, as the Navajo seem to feel, but a mixed one, because they fear their children being hermaphrodite. The *kwolu-aatmwol* category thus functions largely as a major albeit pejorative category in Sambia culture (see also Robert Levy's study of the Tahitian *māhū* third-gender role in the maintenance of normative Tahitian male identity).[92]

Like other New Guinea societies, the Sambia is a gender-preoccupied culture. Males have the upper hand in public affairs, their gender hierarchy supported by the men's ritual cult. In such a world, a rational choice would favor one being born male, in spite of its ritual contradictions and real-life dangers. Would we not, therefore, expect the hermaphrodite, belatedly discovered to be mistakenly female, opportunistically to change to "male"? And yet, this bit of common sense does not match the facts. In the four historical cases of change in sex roles, the female-defined *kwolu-aatmwol* did not convert to a different role until after their exposure and failure as females. One of them still lives as female. In other words, social catastrophe forced them either to change or to face an unbearable and ambiguous future as no longer clearly female but not yet male-associated pseudohermaphrodites.

It is hard to see in this forced outcome nearly twenty years after birth strong evidence for a hypothetical effect of male testosterone-exposed brains overcoming gender-role socialization. I am impressed much more by the continuity in gender development that was interrupted only by the ultimate failure of the female-assigned hermaphrodite's body sexually and reproductively to deliver what was necessary for her to fulfill her social destiny.

Obstacles to the Perpetuation of a Third Sex
In this essay I have reviewed two cultural cases and demonstrated the importance of a third-sex category and role in each. What began as a critique of universals and a search for factors of cross-cultural comparison has become instead a critical inquiry into the assumptions of Western scientific models of sexuality and folk ideologies of the classification of individuals. Far from being a curiosity from the cabinet of anthropological exoticism, the third sex and gender have become a way of understanding how normal science in biology and normative inquiry in anthropology may be reshaped in a different image.

In retrospect it seems obvious that these peoples in the Dominican Republic and New Guinea would have evolved a three-category sex code in living with male pseudohermaphrodites in their midst over generations. And these beleaguered souls, such as Sakulambei, are in turn spared much of the intolerable dilemma

441

of having to be what they are not: unambiguously male or fe-male.[93] The presence of a third-sex category, with sex assignment at birth and some differences in growing up, serves to mediate gender dimorphism, providing a different, perhaps anomalous or residual if not fuzzy set of responses to their bodies and, within themselves, to their own sense of their identities. Yet there are burdens to belonging to the third sex, as we have seen; and in a culture that is stridently misogynist and dimorphic in its thought system, as the Sambia indicate, there are formidable obstacles to the construction of such a permanent social category.

This interpretive study has provided two alternative critical developmental points for explaining how Dominican intersexed males, mistakenly reared as females, become the cultural beings "men" in local discourse. One is that what counts is not anatomical sex as an objective fact but the cultural meaning of sex assignment in the symbolic world and its treatment of the person. The infant's anatomical ambiguity creates a horrific deficit only in a two-sex cultural category system like ours. In a three-sex system, with its more indistinct boundaries, the person's sex and identity are reckoned in relation to a more complex sexual code and social field having three alternate socialization regimes and outcomes, each of which is known to be historically coherent: male, female and hermaphroditic. In this sense, these persons are not "mistaken females" but, rather, *guevedoche* and *kwolu-aatmwol*; that is, third genders. The second point derives from the developmentally later effect of how a three-category system provides for greater fluidity in postpubertal gender-identity transition into adult roles. It is to the inherent social advantage of the hermaphrodite to "switch" from a mistaken female-defined to a male-defined hermaphrodite, once the person enters an adult career, because the power dynamics of gender roles in both these cultures create such motivations. This interpretation suggests an entirely different hypothesis than that of the biomedical model.[94] Only a profound inner sense that one is inexorably female would inhibit such persons from making the structural sex transformation from exposed "female" to hermaphroditic male. This sense would be an identity state similar to that of the primary transsexual, one whose roots have been sewn by culture deep in the order of the nature of the person.[95]

The Dominican Republic study epitomizes the history of medicalized sex research, which focuses too much on the level of individual experience, taking a "lone child" model that ignores social context and ideology in gender development. In a wise and far-sighted conclusion, Mead once suggested a similar critique of the American folk model: "Early and absolute assignment of sex [and] continuous therapeutic interference with any anomalies are all highly congruent with this contemporary emphasis on the importance of every human being able to function in the same way."[96] However, the two studies examined here do not resolve the controversy over biological determinants of gender identity. The 5-alpha reductase deficiency syndrome clearly creates extraordinary prenatal hormonal effects in gender development. We cannot know for sure what is hormonally normal and abnormal in such cases or what the long-term effects of hormones on adult behavior will be.[97] No biopsychic "force" can be ruled out.[98] But neither has the existence of prenatal hormones as the ultimate cause of sex-role transformation been demonstrated, so it is false to think of the Dominican Republic case as a "natural experiment" for such reasons.[99]

Sufficient demographic instances in a local group make it plausible, and perhaps inevitable, that over time a third-sex category will symbolically emerge to classify and handle the hermaphrodite. As a cultural ideal this category may be perceived and projected into the order of nature. Feral animal species may be classified as third sex, for example, while other animal species may be domesticated to place them in the third sex as well. Because most hermaphroditism occurs in males who are competitive in public affairs and may be preoccupied with exaggerating their superiority over females anyway, this third category is inherently problematic and unstable in gender hierarchies. Where it applies purely to biologically normal males, it may be utilized as the antithesis of masculinity, as in the case of Tahitian *māhū*, where femininity is not the logical sign of what "not to be."[100] Its practical and material manifestations may be blurred in praxis, how-

443

ever, because cultural ideals of gender may be invoked or denied for strategic situational advantage. The point is that the third gender is a perishable category, and the historical consciousness and social practices related to it may suffer demise in encounters with Western Others, whose ideals and pragmatics are more strictly dimorphic.

A particular unconscious collusion between American folk biology and sexual ideology has evolved in gender-identity research, making it difficult to separate formal scientific from folk criteria in many cases. Beginning with Freud, it could be shown that each treatment of a gender-identity theme starts with an assumption of biological essence in or regulated by males. From this perspective, the deficit model of gender variations arises. Males are missing something inside: not enough genes, not enough hormones, not enough mother, not enough father – the cultural factors informing sex assignments and development are generally ignored.[101] Furthermore, folk models of human nature and culture are situated in the power structure of societies so as to produce unconscious structural variations in reaction to hermaphroditism.[102] The polymorphous culture of the Navajo seems to have achieved a remarkable zenith in its cultural praise of the blessed hermaphrodite. For the ancient Greeks, their polytheism and gender fluidity were associated with a model of sexual polymorphism; whereas the later Romans, increasingly exposed to diverse cultural standards imported from throughout the empire into Rome, became successively more orthodox in clinging to naturalisms and more restrictions on Roman citizenship.[103]

For the Dominican Republic and Sambia, the historical institutionalization of a third-sex category implies a cultural transcendence of human dimorphism by investing in a more "fluid," polymorphous conception of the person. In short, the gendered socialization of the hermaphrodite is not unambiguously male or female. And the cross-cultural variations reviewed in this essay attest to the importance of gendered signs of identity as cultural and historical achievements, with implications for the emergence, in certain times and places, of a third sex.

Gender identity is not entirely a social construction, and sexual variations are not merely an illusion of culture. The felt experiences of having a certain body, including the desires and strivings of the person socially identified with that body, combine to create a powerful ontology across the course of life. Surely, some elements of sex/gender development are internally motivated or hormonally time loaded in ways that can influence the outcome of such a life. However, we are reminded of the importance of social classification of sexual dimorphism and of the resistance to the creation of a third sex that is so enduring in Western culture. As Maccoby once countered: "It is not children who have critical periods with respect to gender assignments, but societies; that is, after a given age, too many people know a child, and their memories are too long to permit them to change the nature of their supportive behavior."[104] We do not have to alienate human culture and history from biology to accept that, in some places and times, a third sex has emerged as a part of human nature; and in this way, it is not merely an illusion of culture, although cultures may go to extreme lengths to make this seem so. However, an illusion it would be to imagine that the answer to the problems of mistaken sex in human affairs can ever be solved without recourse to the work of culture and the study of individual desires.

445

CHAPTER TEN

Transcending and Transgendering:

Male-to-Female Transsexuals,

Dichotomy and Diversity

Anne Bolin

> Fluidity and discontinuity are central to the reality in
> which we live.
> – Mary Catherine Bateson

Introduction

The berdache traditions documented globally have captured the
anthropological imagination as testimony to the complexity and
diversity of gender, offering serious challenges to scientific paradigms that conflate sex and gender. This complexity is reiterated
in Euro-American gender variance among those who have come
to identify themselves as preoperative, postoperative and nonsurgical transsexuals as well as male and female cross-dressers and
transvestites.

These individuals form a transgender community that is in the
process of creating not just a third gender but the possibility of
numerous genders and multiple social identities. As such, they
challenge the dominant American gender paradigm with its emphasis on reproduction and the biological sexual body as the sine
qua non of gender identity and role. As a political movement the
transgender community views gender and sex systems as relativis-
tic structures imposed by society and by the privileged controllers
of individual bodies, the medical professions. The transgenderist
is disquieting to the established gender system and unsettles the
boundaries of bipolarity and opposition in the gender schema by
suggesting a continuum of masculinity and femininity, renounc-
ing gender as aligned with genitals, body, social status and/or role.

447

Transgenderism reiterates what the cross-cultural record reveals: the independence of gender traits embodied in a Western bio-centric model of sex.

The purpose of this essay is to contribute to the deconstruction of the Euro-American gender paradigm by focusing on cultural change in gender-variant social identities with particular attention to the male-to-female transsexual. Gender-variant identities are analyzed as derivative yet transgressive of the wider gender schema. Ethnographic data from my research on male-to-female transsexual and male transvestite identities are provided as historical background to this undertaking as they situate the social construction of gender-variant identities of approximately ten years ago (data were collected from 1979 to 1981).[1] The question of cultural change in the social construction of the male-to-female transsexual identity is examined on the basis of information collected in 1992. Three sociocultural factors influencing this change are subsequently identified, followed by a discussion of their implications for the Euro-American gender paradigm.

Parameters and Methods
Several caveats are in order at the start. Because the ethnographic effort is labor intensive, there are limits placed on the parameters of research.[2] This essay concerns only those individuals born with the appearance of male genitals who are assigned and raised as males but who are gender transposed to varying degrees. The research and consulting population includes males who identify themselves as male-to-female transsexuals, cross-dressers (the term preferred by those in the transgender culture over transvestite) and those who label themselves "transgenderists." Member ("native") language usage is followed in referring to this community.[3]

Although physiological females are indeed part of the trans-gendered community, this study does not include female gender variation. Unfortunately, this exclusion inadvertently contributes to the silence of female-to-male preoperative, postoperative and nonsurgical transsexuals, female transvestites and "masculine"-appearing lesbians. In this regard, Jason Cromwell suggests that the invisibility of female-to-male transsexuals is directly related to the Western gender paradigm, just as the visibility and privileging of male-to-female postoperative transsexuals is dominant in clinical discourses.[4] As will be discussed, this paradigm is a biocentric one emphasizing the physiological insignia of gender.

My methodology is primarily qualitative. The ethnographic scope of this research spans ten years and includes investigation of male-to-female transsexualism and transgenderism locally, regionally and nationally. For two years I immersed myself in the daily lives of male-to-female transsexuals and to a lesser degree those of male cross-dressing consultants.[5] In 1992, I interviewed transgendered individuals using formal and informal methods, including content analysis of an open-ended, in-depth questionnaire as well as discourse analysis of various transgendered community newsletters, brochures and other texts.[6] In addition, I attended and collected data at two national conferences for the transgendered community, the "National Transgender Annual Meetings" (a fictive name) and a well-known and much-celebrated annual international event, the Fantasia Fair. This approach allowed for an in-depth focus on diversity.

Male-to-Female Transsexuals and Male Transvestites: Dichotomizing Diversity

In 1982, I concluded the intensive participant-observation phase of my research in the Berdache Society, a grass-roots organization of male-to-female transsexuals and male transvestites. My inquiry followed male-to-female transsexuals as they separated themselves from their former male lives after they found the social identity of transsexual and began a process of transformation that included hormonal treatment and psychotherapy, ideally culminating in sex-conversion surgery. Their transformation had the characteristics of a rite of passage in which men "became" women; their "becoming" involved the transmutation of personal identity, social identity and physiology. This approach suggested that transsexuals did not begin their transition with fully crystallized feminine personal identities, as is widely reported in the medical literature, but rather gradually acquired a feminine identity. Their transformation is summarized in Table 1.

Table 1

SCHEMATIC REPRESENTATION OF "BECOMING"

STAGE	INSIDE	OUTSIDE		
	PERSONAL IDENTITY TRANSFORMATION	SOCIAL IDENTITY TRANSFORMATION	PHENOTYPIC TRANSFORMATION	RITE OF TRANSFORMATION
1	Gender confusion and/or self-concept that one is more like girls than boys	Occupying male role, secretly dressing as a woman	Male	...
2	Transsexual primary identity, subidentity as woman	Dressing as woman more and more, dual role occupancy, passing in public, self-consciousness	Male, but feminization from hormonal reassignment	Separation and transition, liminality, disorder
3	Primary identity as woman, transsexual subidentity	Dual role occupancy, anticipating full-time status as woman, successful passing, less self-consciousness	Hormonal reassignment, increasing feminization and feminized	Separation and transition, liminality, out of disorder
4	Primary identity as woman, rejection of transsexual identity, a natural woman	Full-time status as woman (successful passing rejects notion of passing), role performance as woman, natural and unself-consciousness	Increasing feminization and feminized, anticipates, and undergoes, surgical construction of vagina	Incorporation, normalcy and order

The Berdache Society and the networks it spawned played a critical role in the creation of a transsexual identity among its members. This was in part enhanced by the approximately twenty-five self-identified heterosexual male transvestites (the term they used at the time to describe themselves) whose participation in the Berdache Society contributed to its identity-brokering functions by providing an identity counterpoint.[7] At the time of my fieldwork, there were only three gender options (social identities) available for physical males who cross-dressed among the group I worked with: the surgically oriented male-to-female transsexual, the male transvestite and the gay female impersonator/cross-dresser.

Transsexuals distinguished themselves from gay female impersonators and male transvestites. Gay female impersonators represented one kind of inside-outside dichotomy; the male is inside, beneath the outside sartorial system of female. The inner or "real" self is male and the social self is an illusion of presentation.[8] Transsexuals viewed themselves as the only authentic participants in the inside-outside dilemma, perceiving gay female impersonators as engaged in parody and play, "camping it up" with gender identity and role.[9] Transsexuals established a party line that polarized male-to-female transsexuals and gay female impersonators. In contrast to gay cross-dressers, the transsexual was not engaging in an illusion or an impersonation but rather in a true expression of a feminine gender identity. By extension, male-to-female transsexuals regarded themselves as heterosexual if erotically attracted to males, lesbian if attracted to women and bisexual if attracted to both. According to my informants, gay men did not understand the critical difference between gay female impersonators and male-to-female transsexuals.

Because gay cross-dressers were eliminated from the Berdache Society, male-to-female transsexualism and male transvestism emerged as two discrete social identity options with clearly defined attributes, associated life-styles and coping strategies. Male-to-female transsexuals defined themselves by a bottom-line criterion of desire for hormonal reassignment and surgery, privileging their status within the Berdache Society. If one was not

ANTHROPOLOGICAL CONTRIBUTIONS

absolutely committed to having the surgery, then one was de facto a transvestite. Transvestites were delineated as heterosexual men (men attracted to women) who had the urge to cross-dress but were not "really" women. If these individuals had a feminine identity, the reasoning went, they would be pursuing surgery – with no apologies.

While male-to-female transsexuals regarded these identities as qualitatively discrete, many transvestites did not agree. For them it was a distinction of degree rather than kind. However, the transsexual dichotomization came to dominate the Berdache Society in various subtle yet clearly visible ways. Newcomers were presented with only two mutually exclusive possibilities for experiencing cross-dressing. If one were transsexual, then pursuit of hormones and surgery accompanied one's transition. Desire for bodily reassignment became a mark of authenticity to male-to-female transsexuals. Identifying someone as "TS," member argot for a male-to-female transsexual, or "TV," member argot for a male transvestite, provided members with a script for relating to one another: what topics would be of interest, how they could be helpful, what common ground existed for associating outside the group meetings and so on. Members of the Berdache Society were more comfortable interacting with others who clearly identified themselves as either TV or TS. Neophytes were made aware of this expectation and learned that it facilitated their incorporation in the group.

Discourses of Destiny: Constructions of the Transsexual Identity

The previous discussion has focused on the social organization of gender-variant identities among a group of transsexuals and transvestites. In this section, I take the position that the social construction of these gender-variant identities reproduces the Euro-American gender paradigm. Furthermore, the biological bias of this paradigm has framed the emergence of the transsexual identity both as a clinical entity and as a member-constructed and member-experienced identity. Because gender is conflated with biological sex, it is no surprise that the transsexual identity has emerged as a medicalized one. This may be understood as part of a more generalized trend in which bodies, physiological sex and reproduction have been co-opted by the clinical sectors.[10] In this context, I emphasize the medicalization of the transsexual identity as a social-historical discourse reifying gender as biological. I then analyze the transsexual identity as it is constructed by the members of the Berdache Society. While the native construction reproduces the biologized and medicalized one in many ways, it is also resistant. This rebellion against the dominant gender schema is an important ideological element of the social changes in the cultural shaping of gender-variant identities presented in the final section of this essay.

Medicalization and Social Reproduction
The late 1960s spawned an era that may be characterized as the flourishing of the physiologically altered preoperative and post-surgical transsexual. During the 1970s and early 1980s more than forty North American gender clinics, many affiliated with medical schools and universities, were offering programs leading to surgical reassignments.[11] Male-to-female transsexualism was given form by such growing medicalization.

From its inception, the transsexual identity sustained the Western paradigm that the sexes are oppositional and differences in behavior, temperament, character, emotions and sexual orientation are constituted in biological polarity. This opposition is represented by the genitals, the symbols of reproductive differences and the primary basis for assigning biological sex. "Gender attribution is, for the most part, genital attribution," write Suzanne J. Kessler and Wendy McKenna.[12] However, despite the power of genitals in assigning sex, late-twentieth-century medicine has produced increasingly sophisticated methods for determining biological sex and identifying "invisible" physiological components such as chromosomes, hormones, internal gonads and reproductive structures. It is ironic that, the more scientific and complex the determinants of biological sex become, the less they can be relied on to indicate gender. The androgen insensitivity syndrome in women illustrates the preeminence of genitals in assigning and attributing sex, despite the presence of contradictory biological evidence.[13]

Androgen insensitivity syndrome (or testicular feminization syndrome) is a sex anomaly in which genital women are found to be chromosomal males with male levels of circulating testosterone.[14] They are, however, bodily females as a consequence of an inherited inability to utilize their own testosterone. Because they are born with a vagina, they are generally identified and raised as girls.[15] This anomaly, among others, clearly points to the segmentation of sex from gender and the complexity of determining sex from biology. Despite the bolstered scientific effort to locate the determinants of sex, it is no wonder that genitals emerge as a safer and seemingly more stable biological insignia than that which cannot be seen, the internal and invisible parameters of cells and hormones. In the final analysis, genital reductionism is the template for the medical construction of the transsexual identity since that which cannot be seen is not essential in the construction of identities for individuals.

In the Western paradigm women are people with vaginas; therefore, if a man believes himself to be a woman, he must look the part, down to the genitals. This paradigm has no room for the social woman with male genitals as is found elsewhere in the world.[16] Male-to-female transsexual surgery underscores the Euro-American principles of gender that are regarded as natural and inevitable: that is, that there are only two sexes and that these are inviolable and are determined by genitalia.[17] These principles are articulated in a legal postsurgical policy in which the male-to-female transsexual may be issued a new birth certificate or the existing one is altered to reflect the new status. This new gender status is justified on the biological grounds that the postsurgical male-to-female transsexual is a genital and bodily woman. This articulates with heterosexuality as a central component in the polarity of gender.[18] Male-to-female transsexuals are thus required to divorce their spouses before a surgeon may perform the conversion operation. Failing to do so would create a situation of legal lesbian marriage.

It is important to note that transsexualism, as a historical phenomenon, was defined by the development of two important medical technologies that made possible innovative alterations of the male body: hormonal reassignment therapies and sex-reassignment surgery. These treatments circumscribed the medical creation of male-to-female transsexualism. The newly developing field of endocrinology in the 1920s played an important part in the medicalization of transsexualism. However, Vern Bullough notes that the significance of this field has been neglected in the history of transsexualism.[19] It was during this era that Harry Benjamin, recognized as the parent of the discipline of transsexualism, first treated a male client experimentally with ProgynonRX (an estrogenic hormone) and was successful in promoting breast growth.[20] Although the first male-to-female transsexual surgical procedures may have been those performed on "Lilli Elbe" in the 1920s, it was not until 1953 that the male-to-female transsexual identity first gained widespread recognition through the work of Christian Hamburger, George Stürup and E. Dahl-Iverson, who made public the surgical conversion of George Jorgensen into the now-famous Christine.[21]

Surgical conversion and hormonal reassignment have come to dominate the medical designation and psychological diagnosis of transsexualism. An individual is judged to be transsexual on the basis of a cross-sex identity that is manifested by a sustained desire for surgery.[22] Although Benjamin proposed early on that male-to-female transsexualism and male transvestism represented a continuum and were really "symptoms or syndromes of the same underlying psychopathological conditions, that of sex or gender role disorientation and indecision," he still prioritized the desire for physical changes as the critical factor that distinguished the two syndromes.[23] In Benjamin's model fully developed transsexualism was diagnosed by the quest for surgery and the wish to live as a female, while the male transvestite "is contented with cross dressing alone."[24]

Both the surgical conversion of transsexuals and hormonal management reproduce the biological imperative of the Euro-American gender ideology. For example, among the variety of hormonal management regimens available to transsexuals, two primary strategies have dominated. One strategy involves daily and/ or regular intake of a consistent hormonal dosage. The other approach is one in which transsexuals are given a hormonal regimen in which estrogen, with or without progesterone, is cycled in order to simulate the fluctuation in estrogen in the reproductive woman's cycle. In a study of twenty gender clinics, five were found to subscribe to a cycling program of three weeks of daily intake of estrogen, followed by a week without hormonal therapy.[25] One endocrinologist in my area of research endorsed a program of two weeks of intake of oral estrogens, followed by seven to ten days of a progestational agent in conjunction with estrogen and finally a week free of hormones. Because there is evidence (although very controversial) that fluctuations in hormones may have side effects, I asked the endocrinologist how cycling might affect male-to-female transsexuals. He acknowledged the possibility of fluid retention and mood fluctuations but suggested that these could be treated with interventions, such as diuretics, used to treat premenstrual syndrome in women.

This cycling regimen may be viewed as a discourse that defines the "normal" woman as a reproductive one. Despite male-to-female transsexual infertility, this approach duplicates the menstruating woman's hormonal system. Such a regimen is based on a model of biological coherence between hormones, genitals and the salience of reproduction in medical accounts of women's biology.[26]

Transsexuals: Biological Reproduction and Rebellion
Transsexuals in the Berdache Society were culturally active in constituting their own self-definition. Nevertheless, this self-image was refracted through the medical construction of transsexualism. As previously discussed, this was embodied in surgical and hormonal reassignment. A few examples of transsexual discourses from my research follow to illustrate the impact of medicalization and the imperialism of biology in asserting gender.[27]

In support of the surgical solution was an "origin" story and ideology that male-to-female transsexuals were individuals on whom nature had played a cruel joke – they were females trapped in male bodies. Through surgery they were destined to escape their stigmatized status, unlike male transvestites, who would remain men in women's clothing. In this sense, conformity with the prevailing biocentric gender schema privileged male-to-female transsexuals through the potential to achieve "normalcy" and authenticity through genital and hormonal conversion. This belief facilitated the development of a personal identity as female rather than transsexual, a status that would eventually be discarded and replaced with the sense of lived "womanness" made surgically and legally legitimate.

Transsexual distinctions between male-to-female transsexuals and transvestites were girded by this model of potential transsexual authenticity and completeness as women. For transsexuals, the distinction between the two populations was a qualitative one based on the desire to become completely "natural," to have the surgery along with hormonal reassignment. The result was a biologically created female who was physiologically and cognitively concordant. As described in the words of one transsexual: "Because of my transsexualism I have suffered, but I have also learned many wonderful things about life and the human spirit. I have learned to accept my condition and to love myself. I think of myself as a woman whose condition can be corrected through surgery."[28]

From the transsexual's standpoint, being a male-to-female transsexual was only a temporary condition. Transsexualism was an identity to be outgrown as one eventually became a "whole" woman. Physical feminization was an important part of this process of personal and social identity transformation. Transsexual humor and folklore often played on the "natural" differences between transvestites and transsexuals. Transsexuals teased one another with remarks such as "Jane [a transsexual] certainly passes well for a TV." Although there were a number of transvestites who passed as well as transsexuals, the transsexual sentiment was that they were destined to be superior at passing because they were, after all, women inside who had the added advantage of hormonal therapy. This was carried even further in the comment of one transsexual, who joked: "I can always tell when one of the

TVs has visited because the toilet seat is always left up." Finally, the biological elitism of the transsexual was expressed by one who stated: "TVs will always be sick men."

As mentioned previously, it is important to note that transvestites did not view the difference between themselves and transsexuals as a qualitative one, but rather one of degree. From the transvestite's standpoint, there was a great deal more diversity among people who were male transvestites than was acknowledged by the member dichotomy of TV and TS. They regarded gender-variant identities as much more fluid and plural than did the transsexuals. They did not, for the most part, see transvestites and transsexuals as two distinct and static identities. In fact, they frequently stated that the context of a person's life was essential in determining how cross-dressing or one's "feminine" side was expressed. For example, how a man was situated in terms of career, family and age could make all the difference in whether he identified himself as TV or would actually take the step and begin taking hormones. One transvestite who was recently divorced with grown children stated, "I can make this change [begin taking female hormones] now where I couldn't before with the kids around and my wife against it." For some transvestites, life context was regarded as the feature that distinguished the two gender-variant identities, while for others the distinction was just a matter of degree of desire.

Transvestite members generally viewed gender-variant identities as shifting and nonunitary. For transvestites multiple motivations and psychic complexity characterized their lives. Some transvestites liked to cross-dress because it had an erotic element, yet others were driven by public passing as an exciting and risk-taking adventure. Many transvestites shared the view that cross-dressing provided relief from the stress of the male role. In such a way, cross-dressing allowed them to reveal a "feminine" inner side of themselves that they could not express as men. This was not unlike the transsexual self-view of an inner female self trapped in a male body. Despite this evidence, transsexuals maintained a view of distinctiveness based on motivation for surgical and hormonal reassignment. For transsexuals, any reason *not* to pursue

biological alteration was just an excuse and indicative of transvestite status.

Transsexuals relied on biological paradigms to enhance the
meaning of their process of transformation as well. As they went
through transition, the period of changing gender through the use
of hormones, electrolysis, intensifying passing efforts in public
and the like, they regarded themselves as reexperiencing the stage
of puberty. Hormonal changes in the body were a central defining feature of this period. Their bodies were changing just "as" a
genetic woman's had.[29] This distinguished them from male transvestites and gay cross-dressers who were impersonators of women,
both ersatz females. Their puberty was modeled on "natural" maturation, on authentic or "real" women's experience. The development of the female body shape (despite the penis) eventually
led transsexuals to reject the notion of passing and ultimately
their transsexualism, for their outward appearance was aligning
with their "true" inner selves, women. Transsexuals did not regard
permanent nonsurgical status as an option. There were no voices
for choices at this time, unless one wanted to acknowledge that
one was not "really" transsexual but rather transvestite. Transsexuals themselves were legitimized by the hope and desire for surgical conversion.[30]

While male-to-female transsexuals supported a premise that
equated biology with social gender through the quest for surgery
and genital legitimacy, they offered a nascent challenge to biological reductionism that gained impetus over the course of the next
decade. As a social identity, transsexualism posits the analytic
independence of the four gender markers – sex, gender identity,
gender role or social identity (including behaviors and appearance) and sexual orientation – that are embedded in the Western
gender schema as taken-for-granted premises and regarded in a
number of scientific discourses as "naturally" linked. Such categories of classification involve a binary gender paradigm that rever-
berates with the ideological underpinning of heterocentrism.

Male-to-female transsexuals rebelled openly and verbally
against the underlying heterocentrism of the dominant gender
paradigm. While supporting the polarization of genders on the

basis of genitals and body, transsexuals were quite adamant about segregating gender identity and sexual orientation as discrete, subverting the conflation of femininity and heterosexual eroticism. For the male-to-female transsexual, heterosexual eroticism was designated by an erotic attraction to physical males, while a lesbian erotic orientation was defined by attraction to physical females. A review of the professional literature revealed that heterosexuality was frequently cited as an intrinsic attribute and defining feature of transsexualism. Data from my research population on sexual orientation indicated far more diversity in sexual preference than was commonly reported in the literature. Of my sample, only one person was exclusively heterosexual, three of the six exclusive lesbians were living with women who themselves were not self-identified as lesbian,[31] one bisexual was living with a self-identified lesbian, and two male-to-female transsexuals were living with one another. This diversity contradicts a paradigm that equates gender identity with sexual preference. Lesbian or bisexual preoperative male-to-female transsexuals challenged the "natural" equation of gender identity, genitals, appearance and heterosexual orientation by presenting a rainbow of possible arrangements of these attributes.

The Transgendering of Identities: From Dichotomy to Continuity
In reiterating Western biologized gender through surgical reassignment, male-to-female transsexualism endorses a formula for gender constitution in which social woman is equated with genital woman. In addition, Berdache Society transsexuals proffered a categorization scheme in which transsexuals were polarized as "protowomen" and transvestites as men who dressed as women, a model that also sustained gender as genitally based. Yet transsexualism also offered a challenge to the biological basis of gender and consequently provided the opportunity for change from a polarized system in which transsexuals and transvestites were dichotomized as variant women and men, respectively, into one in which a continuum and multiplicity of social identities were recognized and encouraged. Through recent research, it has be-

come apparent that there has been a movement in which people of various gender-transposed identities have come to organize themselves as part of a greater community, a larger in-group, facing similar concerns of stigmatization, acceptance, treatment and so on. This recognition of similarity fostered by a growing political awareness of gender organizations has facilitated the burgeoning of new gender options, such as the "transgenderist." *Transgenderist* is a community term denoting kinship among those with gender-variant identities. It supplants the dichotomy of transsexual and transvestite with a concept of continuity.[32] Additionally, it highlights a growing acceptance over the past decade of nonsurgical options for physical males wishing to live as women. An emerging sense of collectivity has propelled the recognition of the multiplicity of gender-variant identities including transsexualism and transvestism but exceeding these as well. This sense of collective interests is important for understanding cultural-historical change in gender identities and in clarifying the relationship of individual experience to the social construction of gender variance.

Diversity in the personal identity of the male-to-female transsexual and male transvestite populations has been an important source of change in the social construction of identities over the last ten years. Heterogeneity in personal gender identity was the raw material for the creation of pluralism in social identities. Although diversity of gender identity was found among both transsexuals and transvestites in terms of personal identity, it was masked by a Berdache Society polarization into the two social identities of transvestite and transsexual, a distinction that was also supported by clinical segregation.[33] Underlying this dichotomy was a continuum of gender identities among those whom I researched. It included a pantheon of personal motives involved in wearing women's apparel described earlier: as sexual arousal, to relieve tension generated by male role strain, to express a "feminine" component of the personality and, for the surgically oriented, as a vehicle to express a cross-sex identity. This continuum of identities was artificially severed by the classificatory criterion of an extreme desire for physiological alteration by male-to-female transsexuals. Over time, the expression of heterogeneity in the subjective experience of individuals has been given voice in the social construction of gender variance. The polarization of transsexuals as women and transvestites as men is currently in a process of ideological revision in which continuity is emphasized and the dominant Western gender paradigm is challenged rather than cloned.

Pluralism in gender variation is both cause and consequence of at least three sociocultural influences intersecting with diversity in personal gender identity. These are (1) the closing of university-affiliated gender clinics,[34] (2) the grass-roots organizational adoption of a political agenda and (3) social alternatives to embodiments of femininity as somatic frailty.[35]

The Closing of University-affiliated Gender Clinics
The Berdache Society's polarization of transvestites and transsexuals was embodied in the surgical conversion of male-to-female transsexuals. Segregation emerged as a praxis within gender clinics where only the most extreme cases of cross-sex identity qualified for the surgery.[36] According to Dallas Denny:

> The clinics subscribed to "man trapped in a woman's body" notions of transsexualism (and vice-versa) [as did the Berdache Society transsexuals]. Transsexual people were considered to be homogeneous. Those men who had not played with dolls in childhood, who did not report feeling like a girl from the earliest age, or who had any history of enthusiasm or success at masculine activities were in trouble.[37]
>
> The directors and staff of the clinics tended to view SRS [sex reassignment surgery] as essential for satisfactory adjustment in the new gender. They did not seem to realize that it is possible to live as a woman or a man without the expected genitalia.... Those who were not accepted for SRS were not offered hormonal therapy.... Those who were not offered services were often told that they were not transsexual.[38]

Denny warns that this is not an indictment of all gender clinics or of the surgery itself but that it does reflect the experience of thousands of transsexual men and women.[39] A number of social rationales conspired to perpetuate this situation. By carefully controlling clients, the clinical personnel, particularly surgeons, was protected from possible malpractice litigation in the case of patients with regrets.[40] In addition, rigid "entrance" requirements for clinics ensured small populations so that intensive follow-up as well as research was possible.[41]

Just as clinics were partially responsible for the dichotomization of gender-variant identities through promoting the sex-reassignment surgery, their widespread closing in the 1980s facilitated sociocultural mutation in the social construction of transsexual and transvestite identities. The termination of the Johns Hopkins Gender Clinic as a result of political rifts in the professional treatment community was subsequently followed by the closing of university-affiliated clinics throughout the United States. Only about a dozen gender clinics remain and these are notably unaffiliated with the research interests of academia and are consequently more client centered.[42] Client-centered gender clinics may contribute to greater flexibility in the expression of gender identities. The research agenda of university-sponsored treatment programs may well have biased the selection of the male-to-female transsexual clinic population through the use of extreme and stereotypical entrance criteria, thereby denying treatment to more divergent individuals.

Sharon, a fifty-year-old postoperative transsexual, provides a classic profile of the male-to-female transsexual who would be considered a likely candidate for surgery in the traditional gender clinics.

> When I was a child my favorite pastime was playing dress-up. When I told people I wanted to be a girl, no one listened, or told me I could not because I was a boy.... In 1953, the Christine Jorgensen story became headlines. It confirmed my belief that I could be a female.... In 1954, I began to experience erotic sensations while dressed [as a woman]. I considered this to be negative. I did not understand the sensations, and an erection destroyed the appearance I wished to achieve.... 1962 was the first year I admitted to myself

that I was not a man, and never would be. I was a "God knows what," with a male anatomy. By 1979 my life-long dream was to be a legal and functional female.

In contrast, client-centered programs cater to the diverse interests and personal goals inherent in gender-variant peoples and populations, allowing for a pluralism in the expression of gender identities. The following three examples represent variations and revisions of the traditional dichotomy. These voices would not have been heard ten years ago. Without the availability of categories extending beyond and between those of transsexual and transvestite, such individuals have suffered great confusion and emotional stress over where to fit in. Joan, born a male thirty-nine years ago, offers another view of transsexualism:

> I'm a transsexual. I'm different from many in that I do not, at this time at least, feel a need to "fade into" society and hide my past. Rather, I have come out to all around me, family, friends and co-workers.... I am not yet living as a woman full time, but I am just starting a part-time job where I'll be doing a...job as Joan. On my regular job (three days a week), I'm still Jerry.... I don't really believe that I'm a "woman trapped in a man's body." I'm not sure what I am, only that making this transition is more important to me than anything else in my life.

Karen, who waited until she was forty-five to pursue full female attire, expresses self-identity in this way:

> To use the more common terminology, I would say I am transgendered. I cross-dress but not for sexual display or attraction. There is a feeling that is feminine, pretty and desirable. Yet, I don't change as a "person." My gestures and walk are compatible with a feminine appearance, but not exaggerated, my voice unchanged. I don't consider myself a different person, just another visage or aspect of the same person. My friends that observe me in both modes would substantiate this. In addition, passing is of no concern to me. I don't

really "do outreach" or "in your face" but only subject myself to situations in which people are aware of my maleness.

At times I prefer feminine gestures and expressions, but more often masculine responses. When societal binarism insists I choose one pole or the other, I choose masculine. I have been raised as a male, my sexual anatomy is male, etc. Nonetheless, I insist that I am "ambigenderal." I claim all gender space, if you will, and exist within this spectrum at different points at different times.

Pat expresses both a male and female self:

> I currently maintain a full-time androgynous persona, eliciting as many "ma'ams" as I do "sir" responses. My goal is to be free to present myself full female all the time, while still expressing a healthy degree of androgyny. Living as a woman gives me a much fuller range of expression than as a man. In time, I may feel more comfortable confronting the world with the unabashed ambiguity of total androgyny.

Public recognition and legitimacy of alternatives encourages multiple treatment options and the opportunity for the continued decoupling of gender and sex.

Grass-Roots Organizations, Political Action and Transgenderism
While there is not universal agreement on the term *transgendered*, there is an emerging generic semantic space that is inclusive of all people who cross-dress. It includes those who self-identify as male-to-female transsexuals, male transvestites and cross-dressers, and those who lie between the traditional identity of transsexual (as someone seeking hormonal and sex-reassignment surgery) and the male transvestite.

The transgender community is viewed here as a reflection of the expanding political concerns of the individuals involved who wanted a voice in treatment, in defining themselves and in offering activities, conferences, support groups and other events to further their interests and needs as a growing community. The social construction of identities has become the property of a community with a political agenda. Among the organizations I have investigated, efforts have been made to embrace diversity and recognize similarity amid the disparity. This may be regarded as a pan-gender trend reflected in the creation and public use of a new category, transgenderism.

Transgenderist may be used in a very specific sense to include persons such as nonsurgical or even presurgical male-to-female transsexuals who want to live permanently as female in gender.[43] According to Merissa Sherrill Lynn of the International Foundation for Gender Education (IFGE), "Most people who consider themselves to be transgenderists do not want or need sexual reassignment surgery, and do not identify with 'transvestite.' "[44] These individuals are also described as

> persons who change gender roles, but [who] do not plan to have reassignment surgery. They have alternatively been defined as persons who steer a middle course, living with the physical traits of both genders. Transgenderists may alter their anatomy with hormones or surgery, but they may purposefully retain many of the characteristics of the gender to which they were originally assigned. Many lead part-time lives in both genders; most cultivate an androgynous appearance.[45]

Transgenderism may therefore include the self-proclaimed androgyne, the individual who wishes to express both male and female identification through sartorial and bodily symbols of gender, appearing as a blend, sometimes of one gender more than the other. Ariadne Kane, director of the Human Achievement and Outreach Institute, has promoted this approach as an option for individuals. Kane has a variety of personal expressions of "felt" gender that vary from day to day or even within the day, and uses cultural symbols of gender to reveal inner felt dimensions of gender (figures 10.1 and 10.2).

Throughout my earlier research in the Berdache Society, nonsurgical male-to-female transsexuals remained invisible; I knew only one individual locally who, although claiming to be a transsexual, was going to live as a woman without having the sex-change surgery. Recently, I located a number of similar individuals with no great effort. The implications of this field research are substantiated by various other indicators as well, for example, community journals, newsletters and literature. It seems there has been a "coming out of the closet" of those who regard themselves as nonsurgically inclined and hence transgenderists. This transgendered social identity most likely includes a number of people who in the past would have considered themselves transvestites. Current transgenderism would likely incorporate people like the male transvestites of the Berdache Society who in my earlier research did not see the distinction between themselves and male-to-female transsexuals. Other candidates likely to self-identify as transgenderists are those who would have been rejected from the gender clinics.

"The Transgender Alternative," an article that appeared in the journals of two of the major organizations for the gender community, offers an excellent definition of this identity.[46] This article discussed nonsurgical solutions by a self-identified transgenderist, Holly Boswell:

> When a transsexual sister of mine observed that "so many of us simply stall out and fail to achieve our goals of sex reassignment surgery," I felt compelled to question her premise: "Maybe a lot of these people who apparently stall out have found a more comfortable and appropriate middle ground. Maybe there are not so many transsexual people after all." Cross-dressers may also have a sense of this, yet be equally unsure of this middle ground.
>
> The middle ground I am referring to is transgenderism. I realize this term (heretofore vague) also encompasses the entire spectrum: cross-dresser to transsexual person. But for the purpose of this article...I shall attempt to define transgender as a viable option between cross-dresser and transsexual person, which also happens to have a firm foundation in the ancient tradition of androgyny.[47]

Boswell promotes transgenderism as an alternative that may include transvestite men who cross-dress, nonsurgical male-to-female transsexuals who live as women full-time but choose not to have the surgery but who may or may not take female hor-

FIGURES 10.1, 10.2. The faces and figures of Ariadne Kane, director of the Human Achievement and Outreach Institute.

mones and even androgynes, persons who blend genders and do not try to pass. According to Boswell, "S/he is, perhaps, an harbinger of our future."[48]

The revisioning of gendered identities is reflected in national organizations for the transgender community such as the International Foundation for Gender Education and the American Educational Gender Information Service, two prominent organizations with political agendas. Such organizations have focused on bringing the diverse members of the transgender community together and providing information as well as influencing treatment issues such as classification in the *Diagnostic and Statistical Manual of Mental Disorders (DSM-IIIR)*, a document widely used by therapeutic professionals in the mental illness classification and diagnosis of clients, including those with gender-identity "disorders."[49]

A decade ago, organizations kept a low profile and focused on service to their particular gender identity group. The focus was inward and it lacked a political emphasis. In contrast, today the Congress of Representatives, an umbrella organization that encompasses all the transgender community organizations and groups in the United States, provides a community-based approach that emphasizes serving the needs of the various organizations and extant gender constituencies. This national network is a vehicle for the further blending and expansion of identity borders. Each organization has a representative in this congress:

> Despite its rough beginning, the Congress of Representatives is ready to offer a forum for extensive dialogue between support group rep's.... As we open ourselves to the ideas of others, let's keep in mind that these "labels" (CD [cross-dresser], TG [transgenderist], TS, etc.) need not be divisive. They're just a shorthand expression of individuality.
>
> Because the gender community was first organized mostly by members of focused [closed] groups, there has been a troubling lack of cohesiveness that has resulted in polarization [between TS's and heterosexual CD's]. With the new trend of open support groups, that foundation [of commonality] can be strengthened. And as open support groups begin to nurture more columns of non-hetero CD's,

TG's, female-to-male TS's, androgynes, etc., we may achieve a structure that can support a roof. With the spirit of unity and inclusiveness that is promoted by open minds, open hearts, and open groups, we may indeed create the temple of a community we can all call home.[50]

Ideally, the interests of no single group are privileged and the political focus can be kept on common concerns rather than differences. This realignment illustrates the shifting of identities as part of a strategy for empowerment and extends from the national level to the local level. It is expressed in support groups such as the Southern Janus Alliance, which "is open to people dealing with all gender issues: androgyny, cross dressing, transgenderism and transsexualism."

This recent strategy contrasts rather sharply with the early efforts of the Berdache Society. The male-to-female transsexual members who came to dominate the governing of Berdache Society felt that the less people knew about them the better. There was a consensus among both transsexuals and transvestites that education of the public at large could only result in making it more difficult for them to pass. The primary concerns of transsexuals centered on areas of contact, such as the medical and psychological sectors, the legal profession and significant others (who were also of concern to transvestites). Challenging media stereotypes was regarded as an impossible task, necessitating "outing" themselves as transsexuals or transvestites. The specific needs of the transvestite population were overshadowed by those of the transsexual group. The transvestite members were satisfied at that time with support, information and opportunities to cross-dress.

Sharon (a male-to-female transsexual) described the formation of an organization not unlike the Berdache Society in the Northeast in 1979 known as the Ephemeral Center, a pseudonym. By the fall of 1981, she reports,

A few cracks began to show up in my idealism ... to form an organization that would provide community such as housing, a strong financial base, a self-supporting organization by and for the community of TS's and TV's – a community for unity that would be an international organization with a political agenda.... The second generation of Ephemeral Center members had arrived, and they did not share my vision. For the most part, they were satisfied with the status quo, and were resistant to change.... [By 1982] the third generation had arrived and the resistance to change...became worse than ever.

In 1986, Sharon's goals were finally achieved, and with the help of friends the Ephemeral Center was renamed and reconstituted as an international organization dedicated to bringing the diverse segments of the community together. Sharon organized the first international convention in 1987 for the entire transgender community. This organization and convention served as an important model for fusing plurality. According to Sharon:

> This convention was the first time any effort was made...to bring our community's leaders together to tend to the business of our community as a whole. It was our community's first real convention.... I emerged as a leader just at the time our community was ripe to become a community, and society was ripe to allow that to happen.

The open organizations of today now seem to aim at integrating the interests of all the transgendered constituency. In the words of one organization advertising for a conference:

> Our intention is to bring our people and our friends together so we can learn how to better understand each other's needs and issues, learn how to respect each other's differences...and to work together for the benefit of all. The convention also exists to reach out to the general public, to help them better understand our issues, and to respect us as positive, constructive and contributing members of society and as human beings.

The agenda of valuing and respect has advanced the possibility of a permanent rather than temporary transsexual social identity, an "out" transvestism and a pride in one's past social history as gender-variant people. It is akin to a new kind of ethnicity. In this regard, Lydia, a middle-aged postoperative transsexual, argues that:

> Transsexual people must learn to come out. The closet for them is as real as it is for gay men and lesbians. But transsexualism has two closets.... That's where people go after their transitions to deny their pasts and their transsexualism. It makes them vulnerable to outing, just as it does the gay and lesbian community. In the past, there was little choice but to go into the closet at the end of the rainbow, for public identity as a transsexual person meant media attention, ridicule, loss of employment and employability, and even physical danger. As times have changed, it has become possible to have a public identity as transsexual and still have a reasonably normal life. The most important result of this is that it enables transsexuals to provide feedback about the treatment process.

Political efforts also include destigmatizing transvestism by divesting it of its association with fetishism and "sexual perversion." In this regard, Tracy, a self-identified transvestite, comments:

> Those of us who are transvestic and/or transgendered – but not transsexual – are most unhappy with the *DSM-IIIR* classification. There "we" are listed as transvestic fetishists, right there with the sado-masochists,...child molesters and...aggressive butt-rubbers. Considering we don't "do" anything to anybody, especially a nonconsenting person, the inclusion with this group makes us furious. We are summarily dismissed as deviants rather than variants in Western society.
>
> The alternative is to be transsexual or gender dysphoric – i.e., GIDAANT, gender identity disorder of adolescence and adulthood, non-transsexual type. Now is that a mouthful? An obviously exaggerated attempt to force people into a category. George Orwell would be delighted.

When identities go public and become the domain of organizations as image managers, then efforts at normalization will effect presentation of self and the social construction of gender identities.[51] For example, one organization that hosts a weekend of mingling and public cross-dressing stated in their brochure:

> We are going to enforce our dress and behavior policies.... Evidently there are a few uninformed who think hotels allow "real" women dressed as hookers to "troll" the lobby...*please* (for all our sakes) use the same taste in *attire* you would want your sister, mother, or your dad, (if he's one of us) to use. People in [————] have very definite ideas about what a *lady* should look like,...help us convince them we are no different from the average woman in style of dress.

Despite the recent political agenda supporting diversity, this policy represents a continuing conservative trend that discourages variant gender-identity presentations. It seems evident in this case that androgyny would not be welcomed either. Nor is it implied here that divisions within the transgendered community and the privileging of surgically oriented transsexuals no longer occur. For example, the New Woman's Caucus, an organization for male-to-female transsexuals, offers a special conference for the postsurgical transsexual population. The caucus recognizes the surgery as an "unambiguous rite of passage, which separates the *seeker* from the *changed*."[52] Lee, a postoperative male-to-female transsexual, has described herself this way: "I am a new woman. My identity is that of a female – mentally, spiritually, physically, legally and socially." Because Lee works for a nationally self-supporting transgendered organization employing members of the transgender community, she has represented the traditional dichotomy of transsexual and transvestite in a unique way:

> My problem now [since her recent surgery] is a little different than it has been...now I'm a female and still have to work with men. The only real difference between me and any other woman is most of the men I have to work with wear dresses [i.e., are male transvestites and transgenderists].

Lisa, a self-identified transvestite, remarked to me that the breach between transsexuals and transvestites still continues amid the change:

> Fetishistic TV's are generally closeted, or use prostitutes, but have no interest in organization or socialization. The TS community often protests that the TG's are not "real women" because there is no surgical orientation to their goals. For me, it is difficult to understand these divisive attitudes. Without tolerance or acceptance of gays, there is no tolerance of the cross-dresser, and the TS is considered a freak.

While division does continue to exist, the efforts of the national organizations have led to significant progress.[53] For example, one postoperative male-to-female transsexual asserted that "the greatest change is the ever increasing willingness of different groups and people to respect other people's differences and work together for the benefit of all. We're growing up." Another individual acknowledged that "one of the biggest changes I have seen in the transgender community is you no longer have to fit in a box. You do not have to be 'TS' or 'TV.' It is okay to be transgendered. You can now lay anywhere on the spectrum from non-gendered to full transsexual."

It is not surprising that the cross-cultural record and anthropology's relativism have been included in the social construction of gender-variant identities by the organizational gatekeepers of the gender community. At both the transgender community conferences I attended, symposia were organized that included historical and cross-cultural aspects of cross-dressing. This emphasis has continued as an interest of various organizations throughout the United States where anthropologists and historians are called on to present evidence of "traditions" of cross-dressing. At the National Transgender Annual Meetings, a community-based conference, I was invited as an anthropologist to present cross-cultural evidence of cross-dressing. Members of the audience were most interested in two topics: the kinds of data that identified the berdache as a high-status position and the question of how ber-

ANTHROPOLOGICAL CONTRIBUTIONS

dache are conceptualized as third or alternative genders mitigating against clinical typologies.[54]

It was apparent that various audience members were familiar with the recent anthropological works on this subject such as Serena Nanda's study of the hijras of India, Will Roscoe's *The Zuni Man-Woman* and Walter L. Williams's research on the Native American berdache.[55] All were mentioned by members of the audience at both the national transgender community conferences I attended.

Based on this recent foray and my previous experience, I've concluded that the plethora of anthropological works on the subject of gender variation have an eager market outside of academia. At the National Transgender Annual Meetings a handout written by Wendy Parker was distributed, entitled "Historical Facts of Interest to the Gender Community," containing two full pages of citations demonstrating (1) events and individuals involving the acceptance and toleration of cross-dressing, for example, "1530 A.D. Spanish explorer Cabeza de Vaca documents seeing 'soft and feminine' men doing 'women's' work among Florida Indian Tribes. First observation of Indian berdache by Western culture"; (2) events and explanations exploring the reasons cross-dressing was discriminated against, for example, "1200's – The beginning of church/state campaign against gender and sexual variations begin during Medieval period of Crusades. Brought in from Persia, sexual relations with young feminized boys was considered an accepted Islamic practice and therefore considered 'heresy' as it was a 'pagan' ritual"; (3) information concerning important figures in the history of cross-dressing, including the "invention" of various clinical terminologies, for example, "1900 – Julian Eltinge becomes big hit on Broadway performing in drag. Becomes America's first successful female impersonator"; and (4) important events in the organization of cross-dressing, for example, "1976 – Ariadne Kane founds the Outreach Institute and begins the first Fantasia Fair. This major cross-dressers convention has been given yearly uninterrupted to today."

Anthropological as well as historical data are reinterpreted as part of the "roots" and developing empowerment of the trans-

476

gendered community. Interestingly, what seems to be happening is an integration and valuing of the anthropological concept of relativism, that is, the recognition that culture is an important component in the construction of gender ideologies, identities and statuses. Cross-historical and cross-cultural education allows individuals, regardless of their self-identity, to employ this information as a "neutralization technique" or disclaimer. Because relativism is a "reflection on the process of interpretation itself," for transgendered people it facilitates the re-creation and reinvention of themselves as a gender community.[56]

This recently developing unity seems to be expanding to include the gay community, which has been previously excluded as a separate subculture based on oppression of sexuality rather than gender identity. Both the transgendered community and the gay community have shared a serendipitous interest in cross-cultural material.[57] According to Midnight Sun, "cross-cultural material is often used to support claims about contemporary Western homosexuality."[58] In *Living the Spirit: A Gay American Indian Anthology*, gay Native Americans have also found their roots in berdache traditions just as have transsexuals and transvestites. By being Other and seeking roots with Otherness, transgendered people and gay men and women can transform their status momentarily or more deeply. By using the berdache as a model, the transgender community and homosexual community become active participants in reshaping their culture and in finding affiliation where division existed.[59]

Such reconceptualizations are not just labeling theory in action but a complex process of revisioning. It may be likened to Roscoe's concept of lesbian and gay "cultur-ing" – defined as "the negotiation and formulation of homosexual desire into cultural forms and social identities."[60] The transgender community is perhaps involved in a project of "cultur-ing," creating new forms and seeing new relationships in social forms as identities. Diversity in personal identities are re-presented as social constructions through formal organizations that, in turn, affect personal identity by providing more flexibility in the ideological system of gender.

Femininity, Embodiment and Social Change
The growing transgender community has also been influenced by changes and challenges to embodiments of femininity. Conventional femininity in the late twentieth century is in a process of redefinition socially, economically and, especially important to this essay, somatically, as feminine fragility is contested by an empowered athletic soma. Women's bodies have undergone radical revision from the nineteenth-century hourglass and corsetted ideal to the very thin silhouette of the 1960s.[61]

The 1980s and 1990s have brought alternative somatic models for women. While the slenderness of the 1960s has continued to prevail, a worldwide movement toward health and fitness has resulted in a revised feminine body ideal that includes toned muscles and taut physiques.[62] Women bodybuilders' stout muscles, previously relegated as a trait reserved for men, have begun to undermine biocentric ideologies and equations of muscularity and manliness. Rachel McLish and Cory Everson have helped to usher in a new femininity that has subverted prevalent images of frailty. Feminism has opened new embodiments of womanhood that offer greater flexibility in appearance and somatic contours.[63] Since bodies in the Western gender paradigm were regarded as "naturally" constituted contours, this has implications for the social mapping of transgenderism. There may be backlashes against somatic revisioning, but it nevertheless continues to undermine biological sex as the determinant of bodily form.

Women bodybuilders in particular and other women athletes in general have contested the male equation of muscularity, strength and masculinity embedded in biologistic readings of bodies. The new muscular soma of women reinscribes other changes in women's position socially and economically. Women athletes' physiques may even appear androgynous. Sports like track, long-distance running, heptathlon and triathlon, mountain climbing and bodybuilding create new embodiments of femininity and defy the traditional soma of woman as soft and curvaceous. Women athletes have added significant muscularity and leanness, advancing a new contour that has little body fat and few curves.[64]

Have such widespread changes in the feminine body and its

478

implicit query to biology inspired changes in the transgender community? Has the broadening of body "shapes" and images for women perhaps reduced requests for surgery by making passing easier? Will the more androgynous woman's image and changes in gender roles contribute to a lessening of male cross-gender identification? While these questions cannot be answered at this time, it may be assumed that the relaxing of bodily gender rules and the undermining of the biological paradigm since the 1960s has undoubtedly contributed to the trend toward a transgendered community and the creation of nonsurgical transsexuals. Such transformations of the female body erode constructs of behaviors and bodies as natural by creating the possibility for a social woman with a penis.

The androgynous-appearing soma of some women athletes combines symbols of masculinity and femininity on a physical level. It could be argued that this external mixing of gender cues may also imply and reflect an internal blending of emotional, characterological and behavioral propensities previously segregated by gender.[65] The approach of Kathy, a petite middle-aged cross-dresser, to womanhood resonates such a blend of neo-femininity in which assertiveness is combined with an empowered body image (figures 10.3 and 10.4):

> The women I have always found attractive and try to emulate are assertive, self-sufficient, and emotionally and physically strong. This body type and personality type have become increasingly accepted. The image I portray is essentially that of an alert, athletic, highly trained female bodybuilder. Acceptance by society of this type of woman has benefitted me greatly. Ten years ago, there were no female body types such as mine thought to be attractive. Cory Everson, Florence Griffith Joyner, and others have broken new ground.

Lois, a forty-five-year-old preoperative transsexual, reiterates this new femininity:

> These changes in the wider societal gender roles have had an effect. I found that in today's society a woman can do anything she wants.

FIGURE 10.3. (left) A newly emerging bodily image in male cross-dressing.

FIGURE 10.4. (above) A more traditional image of femininity portrayed by a cross-dresser.

This means I did not have to give up my interest in economics or engineering. These changes meant that I did not have to be Susie homemaker if I did not want to. Also, these changes have made it easier for me to do a transition and pass. Being six feet tall and having big bones made for one big girl. In the past you would have stuck out like a sore thumb, but today there are a lot of big girls and also you don't have to be a Barbie doll in order to pass as a woman.

Implications for the Euro-American Gender Paradigm

Ten years ago male-to-female transsexualism supported the binary gender schema by dividing gender-dysphoric individuals into men and women where transvestites were considered "sick" or pathological men and transsexuals were women on whom nature had erred. In contrast, the recently emerging transgendered identity offers an account of gender as a social product by giving one the option of living as a woman or a "blend" without surgical reassignment. The transgenderist may or may not feminize: some appear androgynously, and others pass. The possible permutations within transgenderism are innumerable and lay bare the point that gender is not biology but is socially produced. Moreover, female gender identity as lived by male-to-female transsexuals, transgenderists and women is not necessarily framed or limited by an attraction to men. Transsexuals have contested this blatantly. Gender identity operated independently, thereby subverting the biocentric paradigm in which gender identity is "naturally" conjoined with heterosexuality.

In an analysis of the content of brochures and flyers from a number of support groups, it was common to find groups not limited to a particular gender identity advertise, for example, "a safe and caring atmosphere that is open to anyone male or female, gay, straight, bisexual or asexual, who wishes to explore their gender issues," or "a new club for cross dressers is [now] open to all CD's, regardless of sexual preference(s).... No Gay and/or Bi-men unless CD." Sexual orientation as a critical characteristic for identification is thus dismissed; or, as one preoperative transsexual stated, "When you're transsexual, every sex is the opposite sex." This view repeals the idea of polarity inherent in the biocentric model of gender, and it signifies sexuality as an unruly and potentially malleable construct that is independent of identity.

It is in the arena of sexual orientation where the unrealized potential for a third gender may be found. Out of deconstructed gender polarity arises the possibility of a social woman with a penis. This woman embraces the ineffable by eroding the coherence of heterosexuality and biological gender. The polyvocality of sexual and gender potentialities is illustrated by the following four examples in which the complexity and decoupling of physiological sex, gender identity and sexuality are explored.

Sharon is a fifty-year-old physiological male and lives as a transsexually inclined female:

> Although I'm capable of performing sexually as a male, I must fantasize myself as a women in order to do so. I'm basically asexual. Sex is not and never has been important. I've never really felt sexually attracted to anyone, male or female. However, my preference for sexual partners has always been female.

Roland, forty years old, was born a physiological female and offers another narrative in which sexual orientation is destabilized.

> I'm a female-to-male in transition on his way to becoming his true self – *male*. I am presently living with a post-op male-to-female [transsexual] who is my significant other. She is very successful – a professional woman. We plan to marry. [In my thirties] I began to sexually awaken – I had numerous lesbian relationships and kept it [transsexualism] hidden.... Most of my time has been spent in the gay community, as a lesbian, where transsexualism is rarely understood or accepted.

Clare, a forty-six-year-old male-to-female transsexual who has been taking female hormones for the last two years, also recorded a sexual history that defies the gender schema of heterosexuality. Clare has been involved with a bisexual man for twelve years:

> [My partner's] primary orientation is homosexual. He fell in love with my male person. I have been, until recently, a reluctant lover

for him because I'm not gay.... Two years ago he [left the country for employment] and when he returned, my body had undergone changes, considerable breast development, I'd removed the hair from my chest and legs. As I had feared, his passion for making love with me has waned, yet our bond of love is as strong as before. It's interesting how my desire for him has changed. I now crave his touch whereas before I did not.... Our love transcends our physical relationship which has become the stuff of bad fiction. When he was wildly hot for me, I was hesitant. Now, the roles are reversed. We laugh about it, though the pain of loss on both sides is real.... [He said] he was amazed upon seeing Clare for the first time. He said he found himself treating me differently, being more gentle with me.

Jane, a late-thirtyish transgenderist, lives as a woman with "her" wife Mary. They were married when Jane was John, and over the course of time John has become feminized with hormones, electrolysis and hairstyle. Although this has caused problems in the marriage, Mary has continued to try and accept these changes. John is still able to engage in penile intercourse, as the hormones have not as yet interfered with the capacity for erection, although this will eventually happen. This case illustrates how Western gender terminology, which is so reliant on biological insignia, becomes incoherent when the genitalism of the gender paradigm is revoked. From her perspective, Jane has a lesbian relationship with her wife (Mary). Yet she also uses her penis for pleasure. Mary does not identify herself as a lesbian, although she maintains love and attraction for Jane, whom she regards as the same person she fell in love with although this person has changed physically. Mary regards herself as heterosexual in orientation, although she defines sexual intimacy with her spouse Jane as somewhere between lesbian and heterosexual.

The rules for construction of heterosexuality as "natural" in the gender equation are impugned by these cases. In the Western paradigm, gender operates as "the central organizing principle of sexuality" and sexual orientation exists only in relationship to gender and physiology.[66] "Males are expected to be *men:* tough, strong behavior is not enough unless they are also attracted to women as sexual partners. Thus, heterosexuality is a major component of 'normal' gender expression."[67] When sexuality can no longer signify heterosexuality because biology no longer signifies gender, the disjunction of sex as reproduction is played out and the gender paradigm is unsettled.

Conclusion

In earlier research I analyzed the transformation of the male-to-female transsexual as a journey from gender disorder to order. The surgically oriented male-to-female transsexual rendered invisible the instability of gender through the quest for sex-reassignment surgery. A decade later, as a result of several socio-cultural factors previously described, transgenderism subverted rather than sustained the Euro-American gender paradigm. Transgenderism perpetrated the disassembling of gender. According to Jason Cromwell, "To acknowledge the validity of 'men with vaginas' (and 'women with penises') would be to admit that men as well as women could resist and thus, subvert the social order, by approximating the 'other' but never fully becoming the 'other.'"[68]

The transgenderist harbors great potential either to deactivate gender or to create in the future the possibility of "supernumerary" genders as social categories no longer based on biology.[69] The surgically oriented male-to-female transsexual has confirmed the independence of sexual orientation and gender identity through bisexual and lesbian orientations. The transgenderist has pushed the parameters of the gender paradigm even further by disputing the entire concept of consistency between sexual orientation and gender. If, indeed, "the paradigm that there are two genders founded on two biological sexes began to predominate in western culture only in the early eighteenth century,"[70] then perhaps the task of twenty-first-century scholars will be to deconstruct the social history of a trigender paradigm whose awakenings began in the 1990s.

Photo Credits:

5.1. Branimir Gusic.
5.2. Marijana Gusic.
5.3. Gjelosh Bikaj.
5.4. Gjelosh Bikaj.
5.5. Borika Cerovic.
5.6. Mary Edith Durham.
7.1. Seaver Center for Western History Research, Natural History Museum of Los Angeles County.
7.2. Jim Brust.
7.3. Dane Coolidge Collection, Bancroft Library, University of California, Berkeley.
7.5. Nevada Historical Society.
7.6. Smithsonian Institution.

Notes

PREFACE

1. Michel Foucault, *The History of Sexuality: Vol. 1*, trans. Robert Hurley (New York: Viking, 1980); Thomas Laqueur, *Making Sex: Body and Gender from the Greeks to Freud* (Cambridge, MA: Harvard University Press, 1990).

2. Quoted in Gordon A. Craig, "Demonic Democracy," *New York Review of Books*, February 13, 1992, p. 41.

3. George Devereux, "Institutionalized Homosexuality among the Mohave Indians," *Human Biology* 9 (1937); Gilbert Herdt, "Representations of Homosexuality in Traditional Societies: An Essay on Cultural Ontology and Historical Comparison, Part I," *Journal of the History of Sexuality* 2 (1991).

4. Foucault, "Introduction," in *Herculine Barbin: Being the Recently Discovered Memoirs of a Nineteenth-Century French Hermaphrodite*, trans. Richard McDougall (New York: Pantheon, 1980), pp. xi and xvi.

5. Harold Garfinkel, *Studies in Ethnomethodology* (Englewood Cliffs, NJ: Prentice-Hall, 1967), p. 116; emphasis mine.

6. Alfred Kinsey et al., *Human Sexual Behavior in the Human Male* (Philadelphia: Saunders, 1948), p. 639.

7. Julliane Imperato-McGinley et al., "Steroid 5-alpha Reductase Deficiency in Man: An Inherited Form of Male Pseudohermaphroditism," *Science* 186 (1974), and "Androgens and the Evolution of Male-Gender Identity among Male Pseudohermaphrodites with 5-alpha Reductase Deficiency," *New England Journal of Medicine* 300 (1979); Herdt and Julian Davidson, "The Sambia 'Turnimman': Sociocultural and Clinical Aspects of Gender Formation in Male Pseudohermaphrodites with 5-alpha Reductase Deficiency in Papua New Guinea," *Archives of Sexual Behavior* 17 (1988).

8. Kurt Wolff, ed. and trans., *The Sociology of Georg Simmel* (Glencoe, IL:

Free Press, 1951), p. 145. See also Jean Piaget, *Structuralism*, trans. C. Maschler (New York: Harper Torchbooks, 1970).

INTRODUCTION: THIRD SEXES AND THIRD GENDERS

1. I am indebted to several colleagues for comments on this chapter, including Gert Hekma, Serena Nanda, Kathryn M. Ringrose and Niels Teunis.

2. Michel Foucault, "Introduction," in *The History of Sexuality: Vol. 1*, trans. Robert Hurley (New York: Viking, 1980); John J. Winkler, *The Constraints of Desire* (New York: Routledge, 1990).

3. Thomas Laqueur, *Making Sex: Body and Gender from the Greeks to Freud* (Cambridge, MA: Harvard University Press, 1990); see chapters by Randolph Trumbach and Theo van der Meer, this volume.

4. Edward Lucie-Smith, *Sexuality in Western Art*, rev. ed. (New York: Thames & Hudson, 1991), p. 204.

5. Ann Rosalind Jones and Peter Stallybrass, "Fetishizing Gender: Constructing the Hermaphrodite in Renaissance Europe," in Julia Epstein and Kristina Straub (eds.), *Body Guards: The Cultural Politics of Gender Ambiguity* (New York: Routledge, 1991); Foucault, "Introduction," *Herculine Barbin: Being the Recently Discovered Memoirs of a Nineteenth-Century French Hermaphrodite*, trans. Richard McDougall (New York: Pantheon, 1980).

6. Gilbert Herdt and Andrew Boxer, "Introduction: Culture, History, and Life Course of Gay Men," in Herdt (ed.), *Gay Culture in America* (Boston: Beacon, 1992); see also Anne Bolin, this volume.

7. Compare Willard Williams Hill, "The Status of the Hermaphrodite and Transvestite in Navaho Culture," *American Anthropologist* 37 (1935); George Devereux, "Institutionalized Homosexuality among the Mohave Indians," *Human Biology* 9 (1937); Herdt, "Representations of Homosexuality in Traditional Societies: An Essay on Cultural Ontology and Historical Comparison. Part I," *Journal of the History of Sexuality* 2 (1991); Will Roscoe, *The Zuni Man-Woman* (Albuquerque: University of New Mexico Press, 1991); see also Roscoe, this volume.

8. Niko Besnier, this volume.

9. Margaret Mead, "Cultural Determinants of Sexual Behavior," in William C. Young (ed.), *Sex and Internal Secretions* (Baltimore: Williams & Wilkins, 1961); Kenneth Read, *Other Voices* (Novato, CA: Chandler and Sharp, 1980). See also Herdt and Robert J. Stoller, *Intimate Communications* (Berkeley and Los Angeles: University of California Press, 1990); Donald Tuzin, "Sex, Cul-

ture and the Anthropologist," *Social Science and Medicine* 35 (1991).

10. David Greenberg, *The Construction of Homosexuality* (Chicago: University of Chicago Press, 1988); Herdt, "Representations," parts 1 and 2; Trumbach, "London's Sodomites: Homosexual Behavior and Western Culture in the Eighteenth Century," *Journal of Social History* 11 (1977); van der Meer, this volume. See also Herdt, "Introduction," in Herdt (ed.), *Ritualized Homosexuality in Melanesia*, paperback ed. (Berkeley and Los Angeles: University of California Press, 1993); Hekma, this volume.

11. Mead, "Cultural Determinants"; Foucault, *History of Sexuality*. Of course, social scientists continue to struggle with the long-standing "taboo" on sexual investigation and the difficulty of collecting comparable data across time and space; see Herdt and Stoller, *Intimate Communications*; and Carole S. Vance, "Anthropology Rediscovers Sexuality: A Theoretical Comment," *Social Science and Medicine* 33 (1991).

12. See van der Meer, this volume. Reviewed in Herdt and Stoller, *Intimate Communications*.

13. See René Grémaux, "Franciscan Friars and the Sworn Virgins of the North Albanian Tribes," *Religion, State, and Society* 20 (1992), and this volume.

14. Reviewed in Herdt, "Introduction," in Herdt and Shirley Lindenbaum (eds.), *The Time of AIDS* (Newbury Park, CA: Sage, 1992).

15. Suzanne J. Kessler and Wendy McKenna, *Gender: An Ethnomethodological Approach* (New York: Wiley, 1978); Edward Sagarin, "Sex Rearing and Sexual Orientation: The Reconciliation of Apparently Contradictory Data," *Journal of Sex Research* 11 (1975).

16. Erving Goffman, *Stigma* (Englewood Cliffs, NJ: Prentice-Hall, 1963).

17. Foucault, "Introduction," in *Herculine Barbin*, p. xiii.

18. Eve K. Sedgewick, *Epistemology of the Closet* (Berkeley and Los Angeles: University of California Press, 1990).

19. Charles Darwin, *The Descent of Man, and Selection in Relation to Sex* (London: J. Murray, 1874). Reviewed in Russell Lande, "Sexual Dimorphism, Sexual Selection, and Adaptation in Polygenic Characters," *Evolution* 34 (1980).

20. See Foucault, *History of Sexuality: Vol. 1*; Jeffrey Weeks, *Sexuality and Its Discontents* (London: Routledge & Kegan Paul, 1985); for reviews of Victorian and Darwinian influences, see George Stocking, *Victorian Anthropology* (New York: Free Press, 1990); Vance, "Anthropology Rediscovers Sexuality."

21. See, for example, reviews in Michelle Z. Rosaldo and Louise Lamphere (eds.), *Woman, Culture and Society* (Stanford, CA: Stanford University Press,

1974); Emily Martin, *The Woman in the Body* (Boston: Beacon, 1987); Donna Haraway, *Primate Visions* (New York: Routledge, 1990); Edward Stein, "Conclusion: The Essentials of Constructions and the Constructions of Essentialism," in *Forms of Desire: Sexual Orientation and the Social Constuctionist Controversy* (New York: Garland, 1990); Vance, "Social Construction Theory: Problems in the History of Sexuality," in Dennis Altman et al., *Homosexuality, Which Homosexuality?* (Amsterdam and London: An Dekker/Schorer, 1989).

22. Laqueur, *Making Sex*.

23. *Ibid.*, p. 243.

24. Stocking, *Victorian Anthropology*, p. 325.

25. The question is raised whether a radical break or epistemic barrier was passed in the works of later theorists, such as Bronislaw Malinowski, who tried to reject certain of his own evolutionary principles, but also continued postulates of individual utilitarianism on which these were based, as Stocking, *Victorian Anthropology*, pp. 321–22, argues.

26. On biological determinism and cultural relativism, see Derek Freeman, *Margaret Mead and Samoa* (Cambridge, MA: Harvard University Press, 1983); on Social Darwinism, see Charles Benedict Davenport and Morris Steggerda, *Race Crossing in Jamaica* (Washington, DC: Carnegie Institution of Washington, 1929); on sociobiology, see Marshall Sahlins, *The Uses and Abuses of Sociobiology* (Chicago: University of Chicago Press, 1976); and Donald Symonds, *The Evolution of Human Sexuality* (New York: Oxford University Press, 1979); see also Haraway, *Primate Visions*; Anne Fausto-Sterling, "Society Writes Biology/Biology Constructs Gender," *Daedalus* 1987 (Fall); Bonnie B. Spanier, "'Lessons' from 'Nature': Gender Ideology and Sexual Ambiguity in Biology," in Epstein and Straub, *Body Guards*.

27. Grover S. Krantz, "The Fossil Record of Sex," in Roberta L. Hall (ed.), *Sexual Dimorphism in Homo Sapiens: A Question of Size* (New York: Praeger, 1982), p. 86.

28. C. Owen Lovejoy, "The Origin of Man," *Science* 211 (Jan. 23, 1981), p. 211.

29. Krantz, "Fossil Record," p. 86; see also Lovejoy, "Origin."

30. Walter Leutenegger and James M. Cheverud, "Sexual Dimorphism in Primates: The Effects of Size," in William L. Jungers (ed.), *Size and Scaling in Primate Biology* (New York: Plenum, 1985), p. 48.

31. Cheverud et al., "The Quantitative Assessment of Phylogenetic Constraints in Comparative Analyses: Sexual Dimorphism in Body Weight among Primates," *Evolution* 39 (1985).

32. Hekma, this volume.

33. Paul Robinson, *The Modernization of Sex* (New York: Harper & Row, 1976), p. 3; Robinson argues that Havelock Ellis (perhaps more than Freud) was the key to the invention of modern sexuality in its contemporary issues and dilemmas.

34. Foucault, *History of Sexuality: Vol. 1*; reviewed in Weeks, *Sexuality*; Herdt and Boxer, "Introduction."

35. Quoted in Deborah Wolff, *Magnus Hirschfeld: A Portrait of a Pioneer in Sexology* (London: Quartet, 1986), pp. 116–17.

36. Peter Gay, *Freud: A Life for Our Time* (New York: Doubleday Anchor, 1989), p. 516.

37. Robinson, *Modernization*; Weeks, *Sexuality*.

38. Richard Plant, *The Pink Triangle: The Nazi War Against Homosexuals* (New York: Holt, 1986), p. 29ff.

39. For a critique of the effects of the trend in the United States and the formation of a Cold War ideology, see John D'Emilio and Estelle Freedman, *Intimate Matters: A History of Sexuality in America* (New York: Harper & Row, 1988).

40. Weeks, *Sexuality*.

41. Wolff, *Hirschfeld*. See Robinson, *Modernization*; Weeks, *Sexuality*; Hekma, this volume.

42. Alfred Kinsey et al., *Sexual Behavior in the Human Male* (Philadelphia: Saunders, 1948); see, e.g., reviews in June M. Reinisch et al., *The New Kinsey Institute Report on Sex: Up-to-Date Answers to Questions About Sex* (New York: Pharos Books, 1990); critiques of John DeCecco, "Sex and More Sex: A Critique of the Kinsey Conception of Human Sexuality," in David P. McWhirter et al. (eds.), *Homosexuality-Heterosexuality: Concepts of Sexual Orientation* (New York: Oxford University Press, 1990); and Weeks, *Sexuality*.

43. John Money and Anke Ehrhardt, *Man and Woman, Boy and Girl* (Baltimore: Johns Hopkins University Press, 1972).

44. Stoller, *The Transsexual Experiment*, vol 2. *Sex and Gender* (New York: Aronson, 1975).

45. Money and Ehrhardt, *Man and Woman*. Compare Spanier, " 'Lessons' "; and the critiques in Ernestine Freidl, *Women and Men: An Anthropologist's View* (New York: Holt, Rinehart & Winston, 1975).

46. Stoller, *Transsexual*.

47. Stoller, *Sex and Gender* (New York: Science House, 1968).

48. Money, J.G. Hampson and J.L. Hampson, "Imprinting and the Estab-

lishment of Gender Roles," *Archives Neurology and Psychiatry* 77 (1957); Stoller, *Sex and Gender.*

49. Ehrhardt, "The Psychobiology of Gender," in Alice S. Rossi (ed.), *Gender and the Life Course* (New York: Aldine, 1985); Zelda Luria, "Psychosocial Determinants of Gender Identity, Role and Orientation," in Herant A. Katchadourian (ed.), *Human Sexuality: A Comparative and Developmental Perspective* (Berkeley: University of California Press, 1979).

50. Money et al., "Imprinting"; Heino F.L. Meyer-Bahlberg, "Hormones and Psychosexual Differentiation: Implications for the Management of Intersexuality, Homosexuality and Transsexuality," in John Bancroft (ed.), *Clinics in Endocrinology and Metabolism*, vol. 11 (London: Saunders, 1982).

51. Reviewed in Richard Green, *The "Sissy Boy Syndrome" and the Development of Homosexuality* (New Haven, CT: Yale University Press, 1987); see also Stoller, *Sex and Gender*, for an argument for "biological force" in sex and gender development.

52. Bolin, "Transsexualism and the Limits of Traditional Analysis," *American Behavioral Scientist* 31.1 (1987); Herdt and Julian Davidson, "The Sambia 'Turnimman': Sociocultural and Clinical Aspects of Gender Formation in Male Pseudohermaphrodites with 5-alpha Reductase Deficiency in Papua New Guinea," *Archives of Sexual Behavior* 11 (1988).

53. Emile Durkheim, *The Division of Labor* (Glencoe, IL: Free Press, 1895).

54. Roy D'Andrade, "Sex Differences and Cultural Institutions," in Eleanor E. Maccoby (ed.), *The Development of Sex Differences* (Stanford, CA: Stanford University Press, 1966), pp. 175–76; see the critique in Peggy R. Sanday, *Female Power and Male Dominance* (Cambridge: Cambridge University Press, 1981).

55. Money and Ehrhardt, *Man and Woman*, pp. 126–27.

56. See, for example, John Whiting, "Socialization Process and Personality," in Francis L.K. Hsu (ed.), *Psychological Anthropology: Approaches to Culture and Personality* (Homewood, IL: Dorsey, 1961).

57. Mead, "Cultural Determinants," p. 1451.

58. Robert B. Edgerton, *Rules, Exceptions, and Social Order* (Berkeley and Los Angeles: University of California Press, 1985), pp. 77–78. See also his "Pokot Intersexuality: An East African Example of the Resolution of Sexual Incongruity," *American Anthropologist* 66.6 (1964).

59. Words such as "unnatural" and "perverse" deserve to be placed in quotation marks because they carry a host of cultural and historical meanings – an intellectual baggage of considerable import for writing the history of cate-

gories of sexual representation, although Foucault, *History of Sexuality: Vol. 1,* does not do so, for reasons having to do with a reconstruction of the discourse in which they are embedded (see Herdt, "Representations"). Throughout this essay I usually place these terms in quotes but do not do so at all times, in part because of stylistic felicity, but in larger measure because I feel that we do not take seriously the social and political agenda hidden in such terms when we do bracket them – a point of political discourse to which Foucault, in, e.g., his "Introduction" to *Herculine Barbin,* directed attention elsewhere. Such stylistic gimmicks are the source of much prevarication and even intellectual dishonesty when it comes to the critical interpretation of third sexes and genders.

60. Clifford Geertz, "Common Sense as a Cultural System," in *Local Knowledge* (New York: Basic Books, 1984), p. 85.

61. Mead, *Coming of Age in Samoa* (New York: Morrow, 1928); Malinowski, *Sex and Repression in Savage Society* (Cleveland: Meridian, 1927).

62. Mead, "Cultural Determinants," p. 1457.

63. Vance, "Anthropology Rediscovers Sexuality," p. 878; for an example of the prevalence of this model, see, e.g., Alice Schlegel and Herbert Barry, *Adolescence: An Anthropological Inquiry* (New York: Free Press, 1991).

64. Laqueur, *Making Sex.*

65. See, e.g., John Boswell, *Christianity, Social Tolerance, and Homosexuality* (Chicago: University of Chicago Press, 1980); and the critiques in Greenberg, *Construction.*

66. Claude Lévi-Strauss, *Les Structures élémentaires de la parente* (Paris: Presses Universitaires de France, 1949), and *Totemism,* trans. Rodney Needham (Boston: Beacon, 1963).

67. Lévi-Strauss, *The Savage Mind* (Chicago: University of Chicago Press, 1966); see critique in Geertz, "The Cerebral Savage," *Encounter* 28 (1967), pp. 25–32; see also Gayle Rubin, "The Traffic in Women: Notes on the 'Political Economy' of Sex," in Rayna R. Reiter (ed.), *Toward an Anthropology of Women* (New York: Monthly Review Press, 1975).

68. Foucault, *History of Sexuality: Vol. 1*; see also Weeks, *Sexuality*; and Laqueur, *Making Sex.*

69. Laqueur, *Making Sex.*

70. Dorinda Outram, *The Body and the French Revolution* (New Haven, CT: Yale University Press, 1989).

71. Joel Schwartz, *The Sexual Politics of Jean-Jacques Rousseau* (Chicago: Uni-

versity of Chicago Press, 1984); the internal in-text citations to Rousseau's *Emile* are quoted from Schwartz's study.

72. *Ibid.*, p. 79.

73. *Ibid.*, pp. 79–80.

74. Marianna Torgovnick, *Gone Primitive: Savage Intellects, Modern Lives* (Chicago: University of Chicago Press, 1990), p. 185, reminds us that the "earliest meanings of the word primitive" are associated with the "original state of something . . . 'going home,' like 'going primitive,' is inescapably a metaphor for the return to origins."

75. Sir James Frazer, *The Golden Bough: A Study in Magic and Religion*, 12 vols., 3rd ed. (London: Macmillan, 1911–15); Havelock Ellis, *Studies in the Psychology of Sex*, 2 vols. (New York: Random House, 1936); Sigmund Freud, *Totem and Taboo*, vol. 13, *Standard Edition of the Complete Psychological Works of Sigmund Freud* (London: Hogarth, 1955); Malinowski, *The Family among Australian Aborigines* (London, UK: University of London Press, 1913); Mead, *Coming of Age*. See also Herdt, "Ritualized Homosexuality in the Male Cults of Melanesia, 1862–1982," in Herdt (ed.), *Ritualized Homosexuality in Melanesia* (Berkeley: University of California Press, 1984), pp. 1–80; Torgovnick, *Gone Primitive*. Of course, the earlier forms of the conceptual framework, and those by the sexologists rather than the anthropologists, were the more naive and reductionistic. For example, one may still read Alfred Irving Hallowell's informative critique (*Culture and Experience* [New York: Schocken, 1967]) of Freud's pseudoevolutionary notion that phylogeny recapitulates ontology in the simple societies studied by anthropologists to see the strong nineteenth-century influence here.

76. For his view on archaic and non-Western practices, see Freud, *Three Essays on the Theory of Sexuality*, vol. 8, *Standard Edition of the Complete Psychological Works of Sigmund Freud* (London: Hogarth, 1953). See also Robinson, *Modernization*; and for a popular view, Torgovnick, *Gone Primitive*.

77. See, e.g., Richard Lee and Irven DeVore (eds.), *Man the Hunter* (New York: Aldine and the Wenner-Gren Foundation for Anthropological Research, 1968); Lévi-Strauss, *Les Structures élémentaires*; Lovejoy, "Origin."

78. As late as 1967 we find Money discussing seriously the basis for "psychic hermaphroditism" in the human mind, especially in same-sex desire, largely (although not completely) rejecting the original notion.

79. Freud, *Three Essays*, pp. 11–12 and 15.

80. Evidence of an early German essentialism, as represented through Schopenhauer's ideas on men as the embodiment of "pure intellect" vs. women,

who represented "pure biology," is manifested in the Freud and Fleiss letters; see Gay, *Freud*.

81. Freud, *Three Essays*, pp. 7–8.

82. See Ringrose, this volume.

83. Géza Roheim, "Psycho-analysis of Primitive Cultural Types," *International Journal of Psycho-Analysis* 13 (1932), pp. 1–224; cf. Malinowski, *Sex and Repression*.

84. Erik Erikson, *Childhood and Society* (New York: Norton, 1963); Sudhir Kakar, *Intimate Relations* (Chicago: University of Chicago Press, 1990); reviewed in Stanley M. Kurtz, *All the Mothers Are One: Hindu India and the Cultural Reshaping of Psychoanalysis* (New York: Columbia University Press, 1992).

85. Lawrence Kohlberg et al., "Child Development as a Predictor of Adaptation in Adulthood," *Genetic Psychology Monographs* 110 (1984), pp. 91–172; Herdt, "Developmental Continuity as a Dimension of Sexual Orientation Across Cultures," in McWhirter, *Homosexuality-Heterosexuality*.

86. For example, Susan Gelman, Pamela Collman and Maccoby, "Inferring Properties from Categories versus Inferring Categories from Properties: The Case of Gender," *Child Development* 57 (1986); Jacquelynne S. Eccles, "Adolescence: Gateway to Gender-Role Transcendence," in D. Bruce Carter (ed.), *Current Conceptions of Sex Roles and Sex Typing: Theory and Research* (New York: Praeger, 1987).

87. Stoller, *Transsexual*; this was the view against which cultural relativists such as Mead launched their early cross-cultural gender studies; see Mead, *Sex and Temperament in Three Primitive Societies* (New York: Morrow, 1935).

88. Freud, *Analysis Terminable and Interminable*, vol. 23, *Standard Edition of the Complete Psychological Works of Sigmund Freud* (London: Hogarth, 1938).

89. Laqueur, *Making Sex*.

90. Durkheim, *The Elementary Forms of Religious Life* (Glencoe, IL: Free Press, 1965), pp. 161–62.

91. Durkheim, "The Dualism of Human Nature and Its Social Condition," trans. Charles Blend, in Kurt H. Wolff (ed.), *Essays on Sociology and Philosophy* (New York: Harper Torchbooks, 1964), p. 91.

92. Arnold van Gennep, *The Rites of Passage*, trans. Monika K. Vizedom and Gabrielle L. Caffee (Chicago: University of Chicago Press, 1960), pp. 34, 67, 171–72 and 189.

93. *Ibid.*, pp. 67–68.

94. Georg Simmel, *The Sociology of Georg Simmel*, trans. and ed. K.H. Wolff (Glencoe, IL: Free Press, 1951).

95. Quoted in Lévi-Strauss, *Introduction to the Work of Marcel Mauss*, trans. F. Baker (London: Routledge & Kegal Paul, 1987), p. 18.

96. Gregory Bateson, *Naven*, 2nd ed. (Stanford, CA: Stanford University Press, 1958).

97. Hsu (ed.), *Kinship and Culture* (Chicago: Aldine, 1971).

98. Malinowski, *The Sexual Life of Savages in North-Western Melanesia* (New York: Harcourt, Brace, 1929).

99. Herdt and Stoller, *Intimate Communications*.

100. Reviewed in Hallowell, *Culture and Experience*.

101. Malinowski, *Sexual Life*; Freud, *Three Essays*.

102. Compare Vance, "Anthropology Rediscovers Sexuality."

103. Mead, *Coming of Age*, and *Sex and Temperament*.

104. Deborah Gewertz, *Sepik River Societies* (New Haven, CT: Yale University Press, 1983).

105. Mead, *Sex and Temperament*, p. 280.

106. Ruth Benedict, "Continuities and Discontinuities in Cultural Conditioning," *Psychiatry* 1 (1938).

107. Mead (*Sex and Temperament*) tells us that she observed one berdache among the Omaha Indians during the fieldwork of her second husband, Reo Fortune.

108. Mead, *Sex and Temperament*, p. 283; Herdt, "Representations."

109. Rubin, "Traffic," p. 199. For comparative analyses, on the basis of sexual meanings of kinship, social exchange and reproduction in the context of boy-inseminating rituals in Melanesia, see Lindenbaum, "Variations on a Sociosexual Theme in Melanesia," in Herdt (ed.), *Ritualized Homosexuality* (1984); Marilyn Strathern, *The Gender of the Gift* (Berkeley and Los Angeles: University of California Press, 1988).

110. Evelyn Blackwood (ed.), *Anthropology and Homosexuality* (New York: Harrington Park, 1986).

111. Vance, "Anthropology Rediscovers Sexuality," pp. 878–79; Vance also chastises Suzanne G. Frayser's *Varieties of Sexual Experience: An Anthropological Perspective on Human Sexuality* (New Haven, CT: Yale University Press, 1985) for devoting "all but a few pages" to reproductive and family matters in spite of its inclusive title.

112. Erikson, *Childhood and Society*, and *The Life Cycle Completed: A Review*

(New York: Norton, 1982); cf. Robert Bellah et al., *Habits of the Heart* (Berkeley and Los Angeles: University of California Press, 1985); and Stein, "Conclusion."

113. See esp. the review of the literature in Herdt, "Introduction: Gay Youth, Emergent Identities, and Cultural Scenes at Home and Abroad," in *Gay and Lesbian Youth* (New York: Haworth Press, 1989); and Herdt and Boxer, "Introduction."

114. See e.g., Carol Gilligan, *In a Different Voice* (Cambridge, MA: Harvard University Press, 1982).

115. Theresa de Laurentis, *Technologies of Gender* (Bloomington: Indiana University Press, 1987); Rubin, "Thinking Sex," in Vance (ed.), *Pleasure and Danger: Exploring Female Sexuality* (London: Routledge & Kegan Paul, 1984); Vance, "Social Construction Theory."

116. See also Dorothy C. Holland and Margaret A. Eisenbach, *Educated in Romance: Women, Achievement and College Culture* (Chicago: University of Chicago Press, 1990), for their critique of "symbolic reproduction." In the view of writers such as de Laurentis (*Technologies*), the deployment of a concept of gender and sexual technology, following Foucault, is seen as but another form of knowledge for representing social practice (see also Strathern, *Gender*).

117. Judith Butler, *Gender Trouble: Feminism and the Subversion of Identity* (New York: Routledge, 1990); Sarah Lucia Hoagland, *Lesbian Ethics* (Palo Alto, CA: Institute of Lesbian Studies, 1988).

118. Foucault, *The History of Sexuality, Vol. 2: The Uses of Pleasure*, trans. Robert Hurley (New York: Random, 1986); see also Robinson, *Modernization*; Laqueur, *Making Sex*.

119. Stein, "Conclusion."

120. Barry Adam, "Age, Structure, and Sexuality: Reflections on the Anthropological Evidence on Homosexual Relations," *Journal of Homosexuality* 11 (1986); Stephen O. Murray, *Social Theory, Homosexual Realities* (New York: Gai Saber, 1984); Greenberg, *Construction*; Walter L. Williams, *The Spirit and the Flesh* (New York: Beacon, 1986).

121. Herdt, "Representations."

122. On Freud, see Herdt, "Developmental Continuity"; Edward Carpenter, *Edward Carpenter: Selected Writings*, vol. 1: *Sex* (London: GMP, 1984), p. 193. "After all, it is possible that they may have an important part to play in the evolution of the race." The essay on the "intermediate sex" is especially remarkable for its passionate plea for social acceptance of same-sex desire, its naive folk theory of gender characteristics combined with sexual "temperaments," and its

attempt to apply the ideas across cultures, expecially in simple societies where "hermaphrodites" are found to be present in the "gods and religions and conceptions of human nature" (p. 277ff).

123. Richard von Krafft-Ebing, *Psychopathia Sexualis: A Medico-Forensic Study*, trans. Harry E. Wedeck (New York: Putnam, 1965).

124. Simon LeVay, "A Difference in Hypothalamic Structure Between Heterosexual and Homosexual Men," *Science* 253 (1991); LeVay, a gay-identified biologist, claimed to find a morphological difference in the brains of gay men (using the corpses of purportedly homosexual men who died of HIV/AIDS) that makes them more like heterosexual women. The "gay brain" theory is but the latest form of anatomical reductionism, however well intentioned the theory. I am grateful to Carole Vance for suggesting the term "gay brain."

125. Nanda, this volume.

126. Herdt, this volume.

127. See also Greenberg, *Construction*, pp. 120–23.

128. "Until the early nineteenth century, the boy sopranos who sang in the Sistine Chapel were castrates" (*ibid.*, p. 123). While they could be classified as "hermaphrodites," they are more properly "castrati," although this term usually does not identify a third-sex category in history.

129. See Green, *"Sissy Boy Syndrome,"* for this kind of approach, and Stoller and Herdt, "Theories of Origins of Homosexuality," *Archives of General Psychiatry* 42 (1985), for a critique of it.

130. Sedgewick, *Epistemology*; Trumbach, this volume; David Halperin, *One Hundred Years of Homosexuality* (New York: Routledge, 1990).

131. See Hekma, this volume; Herdt, "Representations."

132. Money and Ehrhardt, *Man and Woman*, p. 135.

133. Money, "Sin, Sickness, or Society?" *American Psychologist* 42 (1987). On the Sambia, see Herdt, *Guardians of the Flutes* (New York: McGraw-Hill, 1981); in the case of the hijras, see Money, "Preface," in Nanda, *Neither Man nor Woman* (Belmont, CA: Wadsworth, 1990).

134. See Herdt, "Representations," for a critique of this model in the New Guinea study of William H. Davenport, "Sex in Cross-Cultural Perspective," in Frank A. Beach (ed.), *Human Sexuality in Four Perspectives* (New York: Wiley, 1977). In this view, boy-inseminating practices are for the purpose of creating masculinity out of femininity in the boys and in reproducing the patterns of dimorphism in culture and economy of these native peoples, a kind of tautology that depends on the teleology of Darwinian sexual dimorphism.

135. Herdt and Boxer, "Introduction."

136. Boswell, *Christianity*, p. 375.

137. Greenberg, *Construction*; Esther Newton, *Mother Camp: Female Impersonators in America* (Chicago: University of Chicago Press, 1979); for popular views, see Marjorie Garber, *Vested Interests: Cross-Dressing and Cultural Anxiety* (New York: Routledge, 1991); and Susan Sontag, "Notes on Camp," in *A Susan Sontag Reader* (New York: Routledge, 1982).

138. Clelland Ford and Beach, *Patterns of Sexual Behavior* (New York: Harper, 1951) state: "In 49 (64 percent) of the 76 societies other than our own for which information is available, homosexual activities of one sort or another are considered normal and acceptable.... The most common form of institutionalized homosexuality is that of the berdache or transvestite. The berdache is a male who dresses like a woman, performs women's tasks, and adopts some aspects of the feminine role in sexual behavior with male partners. Less frequently a woman dresses like a man and seeks to adopt the male sex role" (p. 137). There is no ready reason to agree with the view other than their opinions, however. Ford and Beach's review, though historically significant in its own right, most certainly dealt with only a small range of societies, biased by culture area, and by the paucity of sexual material contained within them, not to mention problems of the quantitative coding of sexual practices and similar material. There is no necessary reason to believe that the berdache is more frequent than other forms of same-sex desire and sexual practice cross-culturally; indeed, I suspect that age-structured same-sex practices or boy-inseminating rites are the more frequent of these across cultures and histories (reviewed in Herdt, "Representations," and "Introduction," *The Time of AIDS*). See Herdt, *Ritualized Homosexuality in Melanesia* (1984) for a similar methodological warning.

139. See, e.g., the critiques of Greenberg, *Construction*; Herdt, *Ritualized Homosexuality* and "Developmental Continuity"; Trumbach, "London's Sodomites"; Adam, "Age, Structure, and Sexuality"; and see Roscoe, this volume, who suggests that it is more productive to view age, gender, power and other aspects of third sexes and genders in the light of the analysis of gender writ large.

140. See Vance, "Anthropology Rediscovers Sexuality"; see also Herdt, "Representations"; Herdt and Boxer, "Introduction"; Richard Mohr, *Gay Ideas* (Boston: Beacon, 1992); Stein, "Conclusion."

141. Maccoby, "Gender Identity and Sex Role Adoption," in Katchadourian (ed.), *Human Sexuality*, pp. 194–203.

142. Murray, "Fuzzy Sets and Abominations," *Man* 18, n.s. (1983). We need

to attend rather self-consciously to the language and concepts we use in denoting and describing the entities and relationships to which categories of thirdness as well as sex and gender apply. We face some conceptual risks: one is to become jargony and lose a fresh perspective; another is to copy or mirror the clinical/biological sciences and their zoological language.

143. Foucault, *History of Sexuality: Vol. 1*; Jones and Stallybrass, "Fetishizing Gender"; Laqueur, *Making Sex*; Trumbach, this volume.

144. Hekma, this volume.

145. Compare Bolin, "Transsexualism," and this volume; Haraway, *Primate Visions*; Laqueur, *Making Sex*.

146. Vance, "Anthropology Rediscovers Sexuality."

147. Lévi-Strauss, *Savage Mind*.

148. For instance, D'Andrade, "Sex Differences," suggests that male initiation is associated with patrilocal societies, whereas couvade is associated with matrilocal societies. There are problems with such schemas, such as (1) one can usually find exceptions in the cross-cultural record; (2) the most extreme cases, e.g., berdache (or couvade), should occur in matrifocal societies but do not; and (3) although matrifocal and matriarchal societies (i.e., the Iroquois) should produce some extreme effect, this does not occur.

149. Lévi-Strauss, *Les Structures élémentaires*; Sherry Ortner, "Is Female and Male as Nature Is to Culture?" in *Woman, Culture, and Society* (Stanford, CA: Stanford University Press, 1974); Strathern, *Gender of the Gift*.

150. Rubin, "Traffic," p. 159.

151. Haraway, *Primate Visions*.

152. See Stein, "Conclusion." The answer, I believe, resides in the old problem – not of nature and nurture, and not merely of deviant or normative, but rather, again in critique of the Darwinian dimorphic approach, of what is pleasurable and nonreproductive, a point to which Vance, "Anthropology Rediscovers Sexuality," has drawn significant attention.

153. Murray, "Fuzzy Sets," and *Social Theory*.

154. Murray, "Fuzzy Sets," p. 396.

155. See, e.g., the important work of Halperin, *One Hundred Years,* and Winkler, *Constraints*; reviewed in Herdt, "Representations."

156. Herdt, "Representations"; Vance, "Anthropology Rediscovers Sexuality." Indeed, most of this work comes from newer ethnographies of sexuality and gender – especially those that take "homosexuality" and now "gay/lesbian" as their objects – wherein anthropologists, typically on the margins of the dis-

cipline, have questioned the two-sex model of human nature and symbolic form; see, e.g., Williams, *Spirit and Flesh*.

157. See, e.g., Rubin, "Thinking Sex"; Leonore Tiefer, "Social Constructionism and the Study of Human Sexuality," in Stein, *Forms*.

158. Rubin, "Traffic"; Vance, "Social Constructionist Theory."

159. Kessler and McKenna, *Gender*, pp. 29–30.

160. *Ibid.*, p. 29. Others were to follow – reviewed in Charles Callender and Lee M. Kochems, "The North American Indian Berdache," *Current Anthropology* 24 (1983), pp. 443–70; Nanda, *Neither Man nor Woman*.

161. Bolin, "Transsexualism," p. 51; Greenberg, *Construction*; Roscoe, this volume.

162. Edmund Leach, *Political Systems of Highland Burma* (London: G. Bell, 1954).

163. See Unni Wikkan, *Behind Hidden Veils* (Chicago: University of Chicago Press, 1982), esp. ch. 4.

164. Again, this has become apparent in the context of sexual research in the AIDS epidemic; see Herdt, "Introduction," *The Time of AIDS*.

165. Foucault, "Introduction," in *Herculine Barbin*; Geoffrey Ernest Richard Lloyd, *Science, Folklore and Ideology* (Cambridge, UK: Cambridge University Press, 1983); see also Haraway, *Primate Visions*; Laqueur, *Making Sex*; Martin, *Woman*.

166. Haraway, *Primate Visions*.

167. Lloyd, *Science, Folklore and Ideology*; Bennett Simon, *Mind and Madness in Ancient Greece* (Ithaca, NY: Cornell University Press, 1978); discussed in Herdt, "Self and Culture: Contexts of Religious Experience in Melanesia," in Herdt and Michele Stephen (eds.), *The Religious Imagination in New Guinea* (New Brunswick, NJ: Rutgers University Press, 1989).

168. Rubin, "Traffic."

169. *Ibid.*, p. 178.

170. See Trumbach, this volume, for his interpretation of the creation of four sex and gender systems in eighteenth-century England.

171. John Gagnon, "Disease and Desire," *Daedalus* 118 (1989), pp. 47–77.

172. On the Sambia, see Herdt, this volume; on the Bimin-Kuskusmin, see Fitz John P. Poole, "Transforming 'Natural' Woman: Female Ritual Leaders and Gender Ideology among Bimin-Kuskusmin," in Ortner and Harriet Whitehead (eds.), *Sexual Meanings* (Cambridge, UK: Cambridge University Press, 1981).

173. Herdt, *Guardians*, and this volume.

174. Brigitta Hauser-Schäublin, "The Fallacy of 'Real' and 'Pseudo' Procreation," *Zeitschrift für Ethnologie* 114 (1989).

175. Richard Parker, "Acquired Immunodeficiency Syndrome in Urban Brazil," *Medical Anthropology Quarterly* 1 (1987), and *Bodies, Pleasures, and Passions: Sexual Culture in Contemporary Brazil* (Boston: Beacon, 1990).

176. Parker, "Acquired Immunodeficiency Syndrome," p. 161.

177. Parker, *Bodies, Pleasures, and Passions.*

178. Foucault, "Introduction," in *Herculine Barbin*, p. 43.

179. Herdt and Boxer, "Introduction."

180. Cora DuBois, *The People of Alor: A Social-Psychological Study of an East Indian Island*, vol. 1 (New York: Harper Torchbooks, 1961); Dede Oetomo, "Patterns of Bisexuality in Indonesia," in Rob A.P. Tielman et al. (eds.), *Bisexuality and HIV/AIDS* (Buffalo, NY: Prometheus, 1991).

181. Mead, *Male and Female: A Study of the Sexes in a Changing World* (New York: Morrow, 1949).

182. Herdt, this volume.

183. American transsexuals and, at one time, closet homosexuals referred to such passing as an avoidance of a discarded social "self," with an appeal to a folk theory of dual, not triadic, sexual nature, conforming to the ideology of oppression within the hegemonic society of the times.

184. Howard S. Becker, *Outsiders: Studies in the Sociology of Deviance* (New York: Free Press, 1963); Goffman, *Stigma.*

185. Herdt, "Introduction," *The Time of AIDS*. One of the lessons of the AIDS epidemic is that the phenomenon of sexual risk is very difficult to study because typically these practices are defined as immoral, illegal or illicit and are pushed to the margins, even denied, by the members of a society; see Herdt and Lindenbaum, *The Time of AIDS.*

186. Herdt and Boxer, "Introduction."

187. See Roscoe and Nanda, this volume.

188. Herdt, "Introduction," *The Time of AIDS.*

189. Bolin, this volume.

190. Reviewed in Herdt and Boxer, "Introduction." Thus we see the problem that Freud faced in his *Three Essays*; he could not reconcile the facts of "natural" biology with the "perverse" desires of a masculine-acting male who desired sex with another (typically effeminate) male, making the masculinized male into a subjectified "sexual invert." This suggested that males would opt out of their privileged social roles in the patriarchy. In fact, in spite of Freud's knowledge

of Attic boy-inseminating practices, he found the "masculinized invert" to be the most puzzling of all third-sex/gender cases (see Herdt, "Introduction," in *Ritualized Homosexuality*). This popular Freudian view seems to have had a surprisingly tenacious effect on stereotypes of both male and female homosexuality in American culture (George Chauncey, Jr., "From Sexual Inversion to Homosexuality: Medicine and the Changing Conceptualization of Female Deviance," *Salmagundi* 58–59 [1982]).

191. Harold Garfinkel, *Studies in Ethnomethodology* (Englewood Cliffs, NJ: Prentice-Hall, 1967), pp. 122–23.

192. *Ibid.*, pp. 135–36.

193. Compare Bolin, "Transsexualism."

194. Julie Wheelwright, *Amazons and Military Maids: Women Who Dressed as Men in Pursuit of Life, Liberty, and Happiness* (London: Pandora, 1989); Grémaux, this volume.

195. Nanda, *Neither Man nor Woman.*

196. Van Gennep, *Rites of Passage.*

197. Herdt, this volume.

198. See Foucault, "Introduction," in *Herculine Barbin*, on this point.

199. See Herdt, "Representations."

200. Strathern, *Gender.*

201. Whitehead, "The Bow and the Burden Strap: A New Look at Institutionalized Homosexuality in Native North America," in Ortner and Whitehead, *Sexual Meanings*, pp. 80–115; Williams, *Spirit and Flesh.*

202. Foucault, "Introduction," in *Herculine Barbin.*

203. Compare Carpenter, *Selected Writings.*

204. Winkler, *Constraints*; Halperin, *One Hundred Years*; surveyed in Herdt, "Introduction," in *Ritualized Homosexuality.*

205. Foucault, *The Uses of Pleasure*; Laqueur, *Making History.*

206. Vern Bullough, *Sexual Variance in Society and History* (Chicago: University of Chicago Press, 1976); Greenberg, *Construction.*

207. Lloyd, *Science, Folklore and Ideology*; Winkler, *Constraints*; see also Greek Hippocratic theory. This theory "produces an elaborate theory of three kinds of men constituted by different combinations of male and female seed... and does the same for three kinds of women.... When female seed from the male is overpowered by male seed from the female...[These] are called 'androgynous.' The women are called 'manly' " (Lloyd, p. 91).

208. Herdt, "Self and Culture."

209. For instance, one can see three types of images in ancient Egyptian statues: males always wear beards; women always wear plaited hair; eunuchs are always men without beards. See the signifiers mentioned in Ringrose, this volume, as well.

210. We can see the early Christian influence of this from a classical text. Boswell, *Christianity*, pp. 375–76, supplies from Peter Cantor: "The church allows a hermaphrodite – that is, someone with the organs of both sexes, capable of either active or passive functions – to use the organ by which (s)he is most aroused or the one to which he is more susceptible."

211. Bullough, *Sexual Variance*.

212. See Geertz, *Local Knowledge*, for example.

213. Albert de la Chapelle, "The Use and Misuse of Sex Chromatin Screening for 'Gender Identification' of Female Athletes," *Journal of the American Medical Association* 256 (14).

214. D'Emilio and Freedman, *Intimate Matters*; Williams, *Spirit and Flesh*.

215. Reviewed in Callender and Kochems, *North American Indian Berdache*; Williams, *Spirit and Flesh*.

216. Roscoe, *Zuni Man-Woman*, p. 4.

217. Devereux, "Institutionalized Homosexuality."

218. *Ibid.*; Benedict, "Continuity and Discontinuity"; Hill, "Status"; A.L. Kroeber, "Psychosis or Social Sanction," *Character and Personality* 8 (1940).

219. Whitehead, "The Bow and the Burden Strap."

220. Devereux, "Institutionalized Homosexuality."

221. Herdt, "Representations."

222. Greenberg, *Construction*.

223. Benedict, *Patterns of Culture* (Boston: Houghton Mifflin, 1934); Kroeber, "Psychosis."

224. Reviewed in Herdt, "Representations."

225. Mead, *Sex and Temperament*, and "Cultural Determinants."

226. Bolin, "Transsexualism," p. 53. This is why prior efforts to refigure the study of third genders has met with only partial success. For example, Rubin's classical analysis ("Traffic") helped to break new ground but is now dated (as she recognizes in her "Thinking Sex") in its use of the assumptive categories of heterosexual and homosexual. When it comes to the berdache, indeed, many such works now appear in a similar light (e.g., Whitehead, "The Bow and Burden Strap") when, for instance, they view Mohave berdache and their marriages as "homosexual," although they clearly are much more complex rela-

tions, as Roscoe shows in his chapter in this volume (cf. Jane Collier and Sylvia Yanagisako [eds.], *Kinship and Gender* [Stanford, CA: Stanford University Press, 1987]). The lack of convincing evidence from field and historical study in support of the existence of multiple sexual and gender categories was also critical to the impasse at the time; see Saskia Wieringa, "An Anthropological Critique of Constructionism: Berdaches and Butches," in Altman et al., *Homosexuality, Which Homosexuality?*

227. Herdt, "Representations."

228. Devereux, "Institutionalized Homosexuality"; reviewed in Herdt, "Representations."

229. Gisela Bleibtreu-Ehrenberg, "Homosexualität und Transvestition im Schamanismus," *Anthropolos* 65 (1970).

230. Mircea Eliade, *Shamanism: Archaic Techniques of Ecstasy*, trans. W.R. Trask (Princeton, NJ: Princeton University Press, 1972), p. 125n.

231. Murray, *Social Theory.*

232. See, e.g., Larry G. Peters and Douglas Price-Williams, "Towards an Experimental Analysis of Shamanism," *American Ethnologist* 7 (1980).

233. Reviewed in Herdt, "Homosexuality," in *The Encyclopedia of Religion*, 15 vols. (New York: Macmillan, 1987), vol. 6, pp. 445–52.

234. Bernardin Saladin d'Anglure, "Du Foetus au chamane: La construction d'un 'troisieme sexe' Inuit," *Etudes Inuite* 10.1–2 (1986).

235. Devereux, "Instutionalized Homosexuality."

236. Williams, *Spirit and Flesh.*

237. Herdt and Davidson, "Sambia 'Turnim-man.' "

238. Julliane Imperato-McGinley et al., "Steroid 5-alpha Reductase Deficiency in Man: An Inherited Form of Male Pseuodohermaphroditism," *Science* 186, pp. 1213–15.

239. Reviewed in Herdt, this volume.

240. Herdt, *Guardians.*

241. Donn V. Hart, "Homosexuality and Transvestism in the Philippines: The Cebuan Filipino Bayot and Lakin-on," *Behavior Science Notes* 4 (1968), p. 214ff.

242. *Ibid.*, pp. 215–16.

243. *Ibid.*, p. 218.

244. Oetomo, "Patterns"; Levy, *Tahitians*; Besnier, this volume. Recently, Kris Poasa, "The Samoan Fa'afafine: One Case Study and Discussion of Transsexualism," *Journal of Psychology and Human Sexuality* 5 (1992), has described a

case of *māhū* that she interprets as transsexualism.

245. Peter Phillimore, "Unmarried Women of the Dahaula Dhar: Celibacy and Social Control in Northwest India," *Journal of Anthropological Research* 47 (1991).

246. Nanda, *Neither Man nor Woman*.

247. Bolin, this volume; Mead, "Cultural Determinants."

248. Grémaux, this volume; Wheelwright, *Amazons*.

249. Louis Sullivan, *From Female to Male: The Life of Jack Bee Garland* (Boston: Alyson, 1990).

250. Compare Foucault, "Introduction," in *Herculine Barbin*.

251. Devereux, "Institutionalized Homosexuality"; Herdt, "Representations"; cf. Roscoe, this volume.

252. See, e.g., Carpenter, *Selected Writings*, on the "intermediate sex."

253. Greenberg, *Construction*; Herdt, "Ritualized Homosexuality," "Representations," "Introduction," in *Ritualized Homosexuality*; see also Besnier, this volume.

254. Trumbach, "London's Sodomites."

255. Compare Foucault, *History of Sexuality: Vol. 1*, on the public "secret" of the homosexual in the nineteenth century.

256. Plant, *Pink Triangle*.

257. Foucault, *The Birth of the Clinic*, trans. A.M.S. Smith (New York: Pantheon, 1973), and "Introduction," in *Herculine Barbin*.

258. Other authorities disagreed with this notion (see Hekma, this volume). However, until recent times (and even up to today in some quarters) certain persons continued to believe that one could pick out homosexuals by their physical traits, most noticeably those conforming to the popular stereotypes that male homosexuals are effeminate and female homosexuals are masculine; see Henry L. Minton, "Femininity in Men and Masculinity in Women: American Psychiatry and Psychology Portray Homosexuality in the 1930s," *Journal of Homosexuality* 13 (1986), pp. 1–22.

259. Quoted from John Lauristen and David Thorstad, *The Early Homosexual Rights Movement (1864–1935)* (New York: Times Change Press, 1974), p. 47; cf. Carpenter, *Selected Writings*; reviewed in Robinson, *Modernization*, pp. 4–8.

260. Robinson, *Modernization*; Weeks, *Sexuality*.

261. Ellis, *Studies*; Krafft-Ebing, *Psychopathia Sexualis*.

262. On Wilde, see Richard Ellman, *Oscar Wilde* (New York: Knopf, 1988), p. 60; on Ellis, see Phyllis Grosskurth (ed.), *The Memoirs of John Addington*

Symonds: The Secret Homosexual Life of a Leading Nineteenth-Century Man of Letters (New York: Random House, 1984), p. 284ff; on Carpenter, see his *Selected Writings*.

263. Robinson, *Modernization*. Note how the very concept of Freud's "sexual preference" and Kinsey's "sexual orientation" are problematic here, being largely "internal" desires, but neither purely acquired nor learned, according to the dualistic developmental schema of Western culture (Herdt, "Developmental Continuity").

264. Wolff, *Hirschfeld*, p. 116.

265. Laqueur, *Making Sex*.

266. We find this represented as well in the later work of Helene Deutsch on women, *The Psychology of Women*, vol. 1. *Girlhood* (Toronto: Bantam, 1973), as, for example, in her commentary (p. 340): "No male-female contrast appeared in this [patient's] relationship; the essentialized contrast was that of activity and passivity."

267. Foucault, *History of Sexuality: Vol. 1*, p. 43.

268. Herdt, "Representations"; Herdt and Boxer, "Introduction."

269. Herdt and Stoller, *Intimate Communications*.

270. See Money, "Sin."

271. Susanne K. Langer, *Mind: An Essay on Human Feeling*, vol. 1 (Baltimore: Johns Hopkins University Press, 1967), p. 259.

272. Goffman, *Stigma*.

273. Herdt, "Self and Culture"; Herdt and Boxer, "Introduction."

274. Herdt, "Representations."

275. Garfinkel, *Ethnomethodology*.

276. Bateson, *Naven*.

277. Simmel, *Sociology of Georg Simmel*.

278. Kessler and McKenna, *Gender*, p. 30.

279. Herdt, "Representations."

280. Herdt and Boxer, "Introduction."

CHAPTER ONE: LIVING IN THE SHADOWS

1. Anne Hadjinicolaou-Marava, *Recherches sur la vie des esclaves dans le monde byzantin* (Athens: Collection de l'Institut français d'Athens 45, 1950), like many other scholars, notes the contradiction that Byzantine emperors pass legislation condemning castration while having eunuchs at their own courts. According to the canons of the early Church a man who was castrated accidentally or by

another person could become a priest, bishop or cleric. Those who castrated themselves were considered to be "homicides, hateful to God and unsuitable for church office," *Syntagma Canonum* in ed. Jacques Paul Migne, *Patrologiae Cursus Completus, Series Graeca* (Paris, 1857-87) (hereafter *P.G.*), vol. 105, col. 762. The canons of the Council of Nicaea repeat the above injunctions, then point out that civil law has traditionally punished those who castrate themselves with death, confiscation, exile or fines. Castrations were not allowed within the Roman state, but barbarians were permitted to castrate other barbarians outside the state. Any slave made a eunuch was to be freed. By the early tenth century the law code of the emperor Leo the Wise reflects the prevalence of castration in Byzantine society and the need to adjust the law to current practice. While Leo acknowledges that castration creates a creature "far different from what God intended," he objects to past punishment for those who performed castrations. It is wrong to castrate, he says, even as a punishment. The new law punishes imperial servants who castrate with removal from court and large fines. For those outside the court, punishments are reduced to fines, tonsuring, confiscation of goods and exile. Victims, if slaves, are compensated with their freedom; if free they receive no compensation (*Law Codes of Leo the Wise, P.G.*, vol. 107, cols. 886-910).

2. The Byzantine custom of making and having eunuchs has long fascinated historians. The most useful modern work on eunuchs has been done by Rodolphe Guilland, "Les eunuques dans l'empire byzantine," *Etudes Byzantines* 1 (1943), "Fonctions et dignites des eunuques," *Etudes Byzantines* 2-3 (1944-45), "Etudes de titulature byzantine; les titres auliques reserves aux eunuques," *Revue des Etudes Byzantines* 13-14 (1955-56), "Etudes sur l'histoire administrative de l'empire byzantine: les titres auliques des eunuques," *Byzantion* 25 and 27 (1955, 1957). His work is essentially a prosopographical study that identifies particular figures in Byzantine sources and concentrates on the offices of the eunuchs of the imperial court. In 1978 Keith Hopkins devoted two chapters of his book *Conquerors and Slaves* (Cambridge, UK: Cambridge University Press, 1978) to a sociological analysis of the eunuchs of the court. He offers a thoughtful analysis that seeks to demonstrate that eunuchs exercised real power, i.e., they were not simply scapegoats for emperors and hostile commentators. He dismisses the pejorative language used about them as "what we might expect." He notes the obvious comparison between Byzantine court eunuchs and court Jews in the German states in the seventeenth and eighteenth centuries. They were similarly reviled yet well rewarded and powerful. He points out the criti-

cal role eunuchs played in mediating between humanity and an increasingly unapproachable emperor and between the aristocracy and a growing bureaucratic structure. The importance of eunuchs at the Byzantine court correlates with the development of court ritual at the end of the third century. Michael McCormick, in his recent book, *Eternal Victory* (Cambridge, UK: Cambridge University Press, 1986), shows the ways in which the power of the eunuchs was illustrated in court ritual. More recently Peter Brown discusses eunuchs as part of his study of the body in early Christian society in his book *The Body and Society: Men, Women and Sexual Renunciation in Early Christianity* (New York: Columbia University Press, 1988). I am grateful to him for several lengthy conversations regarding my work.

3. Romanos's illegitimate son, Basil, born to a Scythian mother, was castrated and rose to prominence at court. Leo the Deacon, *Historiae libri X*, ed. C.B. Hase (Bonn, 1828), p. 46. Michael Psellus tells us that Constantine VIII relied heavily on court eunuchs who were provincials and foreigners, not born of freedmen or the well-born. They were reared and educated by the emperor and they "adopted the emperor's nature." Psellus, *Chronographia*, ed. E. Renauld, 2 vols. (Paris, 1926-28), p. 27.

4. See Kathryn M. Ringrose, "The Eunuchs of Byzantium, Language, Image and Gender," paper presented at the annual meeting of the American Ethnological Association, Memphis, TN, April, 1992.

5. Brown, *Body and Society*, pp. 10-12, points out the importance that was placed on the acculturation of young men and the need to develop them in accordance with socially determined ideals of masculine behavior, to move them along the ladder of masculine perfection.

6. Thomas Laqueur, *Making Sex: Body and Gender from the Greeks to Freud* (Cambridge, MA: Harvard University Press, 1990), p. 22.

7. Aristotle, *Generation of Animals* 4.1.766a 20-35. Aristotle goes on to suggest that women are also like eunuchs in that both lack beards and like children in that they do not make semen. For Aristotle, castration changes an individual from a male to a female condition, but he never says that a eunuch is a male who has become a female or any specific third category of being. Aristotle notes that eunuchs, because of their mutilation, are greatly altered in appearance and come to bear an appearance of effeminacy. This comes about because some of the parts of every individual are first principles. When a first principle has been removed, of necessity many of the parts that are associated with it are also removed. The male is ἄρσεν because of a certain ability, and the female is Θῆλυς

because of a certain inability. A eunuch is ἀμφίβολος, an individual of indeterminate gender.

In the Roman period this idea can be found in Lucian, "The Eunuch" in *Lucian*, Loeb Classical Library (1936), p. 341. Then, later in the text, Lucian humorously presents the opinions, which he doesn't necessarily share, of a part of society that is sufficiently offended by the "hybrid" nature of eunuchs as to find them monstrous and alien to human nature and suggests that they are unlucky and should be excluded from sacred space and places of public assembly. *Lucian*, p. 178. In this passage Lucian clearly sees eunuchs as a third category. Claudian, whose diatribe against Eutropius is a model of invective, and cannot be assumed to reflect general opinion, says that a eunuch is a *semivir* – a half-man. *Claudian*, Loeb Classical Library (1946), p. 151. "A eunuch can be neither a mother nor a father; the former nature hath denied thee, the latter the surgeon's knife" (p. 155). A eunuch is "one whom the male sex has discarded and the female will not adopt" (p. 173). He is *ambiguus*. In the tenth century Leo the Deacon continues to echo this rhetoric when he calls Joseph the eunuch γύναιος τεχνητός (an artificial woman) ἀμφίβολος (of indeterminate gender). Leo the Deacon, *Historiae libri X*, ed. C.B. Hase (Bonn, 1828), p. 39.

8. Galen, *Opera omnia*, ed. C.G. Kuhn, 20 vols. in 22 parts (Leipzig, 1821-33; reprint, Hildesheim, 1964-65), vol. 8, pt. 1, pp. 40-41. This also explains why eunuchs lack beards, do not go bald and do not suffer from gout, a disease that he believes to be caused by excessive body heat.

9. Galen, *Opera omnia*, vol. 4, pt. 5, p. 569, cites the obvious biological changes that men and animals experience after castration, then reports that he has heard that the Cappadocians castrate female pigs (presumably removing the ovaries, although Galen thinks they are the testes) and create a milder, more succulent-tasting animal. The castrated female pigs "come to resemble those male pigs who have been castrated, like them they are well nourished and rich (fatty) and have more desirable flesh than other female pigs even as castrated male pigs have sweeter flesh than other males." "And just as the attribute of strength and virility occurs in men, in women a feminine attribute exists and in a feminine animal, if its testicles are removed, it becomes similar to a castrated male. All the parts of the body have the same power in both. That which was removed in each case was that which was responsible for the masculine and feminine in each. When this operation had been completed the thing that was left had for itself a nature such as if it had been, from the beginning, neither male nor female but a third being different from both of the two." In each case,

he says, removing the testes of either a male or a female animal produces a third being that is different from either one, a being defined by its lack of testes.

10. Alexander Trallianus, *Therapeutica*, in ed. Puschmann, *Alexander von Tralles* 1 (Vienna: Braumuller, 1878; reprint, Amsterdam: Hakkert, 1963), p. 127, l. 13; Aetius Amidensus Medicus, *Aetii Amideni libri medicinales I–IV* in ed. A. Olivieri, *Corpus Medicorum Graecorum* 8,1 (Leipzig: Teubner, 1935), p. 92, l. 79.

11. Clement of Alexandria, *Stromata* 1-4, eds. Otto Stählin and Ludwig Früchtel (Berlin: Akademie, 1985), bk. 3, ch. 15, pp. 97–99.

12. Eunapios of Sardis, *Fragmenta Historiorum Graecorum*, ed. Carolus Müllerus (Paris, 1885), vol. 4, p. 44.

13. Gregory Nazianzos, *In Praise of Athanasius*, in *P.G.*, vol. 35, col. 1106.

14. Saint John of Damascus, in *P.G.*, vol. 95, col. 1564, in a discussion of eunuchs, gathers what he considers relevant earlier texts about eunuchs. These include Saint Basil's letter to Simplicia. In this harsh letter Saint Basil summarizes many of the earlier stereotypes about eunuchs. The invective language of Saint Basil is regularly repeated in later sources. It is interesting to note that Saint John of Damascus omits some elements of Saint Basil's letter, e.g., the observation that eunuchs will not be witnesses at the Last Judgment. For the letter of Saint Basil, see Saint Basil of Caesarea, *The Letters* (Cambridge, MA: Loeb Classical Library, 1961), p. 229.

15. These language problems are compounded when we try to translate Greek into English. For example, John Skylitzes, *Synopsis historiarum*, ed. A. Thurn (New York: de Gruyter, 1973), p. 335, l. 43, uses the term ἄνανδρος, "unmanly," for eunuchs. This is regularly translated as "effeminate," which is a modern English meaning imposed on the term when the real sense of the word is lack of masculine traits.

16. By the eleventh century, it is apparent that castrations were regularly performed within the Byzantine empire and that youths who were castrated were often drawn from free-born families within the empire. See, e.g., Ann Moffott, "The Byzantine Child," *Social Research* 53 (1986), p. 719.

17. The best medical description of castration that we have comes from the seventh-century physician Paul of Aegina, who says that it pains him to have to perform castrations, but that sometimes powerful people force him to do so. He then describes two forms of castration, the crushing of the testes in the infant and the excision of the testes in an older individual. He considers the latter method of castration to be preferable. See Paul of Aegina, *Epitomate medicae libri septem*, in ed. J.L. Heiberg, *Paulus Aegineta* (Corpus Medicorum

Graecorum, vols. 9.1 and 9.2) (Leipzig: Teubner, 1921, 1924), bk. 6, ch. 68, p. 111.

18. Aline Rouselle, *Pornea: On Desire and the Body in Antiquity* (Oxford: Basil Blackwell, 1988), pp. 120–28, deals with this difficult issue very well.

19. Psellus, *De Legum Nominibus*, in *P.G.*, vol. 122, col. 1027, l. 11.

20. Some authors (e.g., Theophanes Continuatus, Skylitzes, Nicephorus Bryennios) use both the term ἐκτομίας, "cut," and εὐνοῦχος, "eunuch," in the same text. It is unclear what distinguishes one from the other, although I suspect that eunuch is a more general term that covers a variety of mutilations, intended or accidental, while ἐκτομίας refers specifically to excision. Alexander Kazhdan, in his entry on "eunuchs" in the excellent *Oxford Dictionary of Byzantium*, implies that ἐκτομίας is the singular form of εὐνοῦχος. Yet εὐνοῦχος appears regularly in the singular as well as plural and ἐκτομίας appears, although rarely, in the plural form.

21. This is suggested by the well-known text of Liutprand of Cremona, which states that fully castrated eunuchs were rare in Byzantium, and by a fifteenth-century Italian text that suggests a change from partial to fully castrated eunuchs at court when the Turks took over the empire; Liutprand of Cremona, *Antapodoseos Libri Sex*, in ed. Migne, *Patrologiae Cursus Completus, Series Latina* (Paris, 1844–91), vol. 136, p. 896. When the Byzantine Empire was conquered by the Turks in the fifteenth century a comment in Théodore Spandounis suggests that, at least among the eunuch servants who served in the harem, complete castration was introduced. See C.N. Sathas, ed., *Documents inédits relatifs à l'histoire de la Grèce au Moyen Age* (Paris: Maisonneuve, 1890), vol. 9, p. 205.

22. See Psellus, *Chronographia*, vol. 2, p. 59.

23. In the Greek Magical Papyri the magician, using a prepubescent boy, who is sexually pure as a medium and assistant, casts a spell to summon an angel. See Hans Dieter Betz, ed., *The Greek Magical Papyri in Translation Including Demotic Spells* (Chicago: University of Chicago Press, 1986), p. 5.

24. Aretaeus Medicus, *De Causis et signis acutorum morborum*, in ed. K. Hude, *Aretaeus* (Corpus Medicorum Graecorum, vol. 2) (Berlin: Akademie, 1958), p. 71, l. 26.

25. Adamantius Judaeus, *Physiognomonica*, ed. R. Foerster, *Scriptores physiognomonici Graeci et Latini*, vol. 1 (Leipzig: Teubner, 1893), p. 351, l. 10.

26. Maude W. Gleason, "The Semiotics of Gender: Physiognomy and Self-Fashioning in the Second Century c.e.," in David M. Halperin, John J. Winkler and Froma I. Zeitlin (eds.), *Before Sexuality: The Construction of Erotic Experi-*

ence in the Ancient Greek World (Princeton, NJ: Princeton University Press, 1990), pp. 389–417.

27. Leo the Deacon, *Historiae libri X*, p. 7, l. 3; Skylitzes, *Synopsis historiarum*, p. 225, l. 40.

28. Aetius Amidensus Medicus, *Iatricorum liber XV*, ed. S. Zervos, "Aetiou Amede(eta)nou logos dekatos pemptos," *Athena* 21 (1909), p. 46, l. 12; Alexander Medicus, *Therapeutica*, p. 127, l. 13; and Galen, *Opera Omnia* 13.506, all discuss the differences between the flesh of men as a group and women, children and eunuchs. For example, Galen says, "Individuals with soft flesh and sensitive bodies suffer from bad humors. This group includes women, especially those with pale complexions, boys, eunuchs, men with fair skin, men who live in cold places, men whose bodies are cold and full of phlegm and men who are soft and white. Those who live in hot dry places, like Egypt and Arabia, are made strong by their dry bodies."

29. Leo the Deacon, *Historiae libri X*, p. 47, l. 11; Psellus, *Chronographia*, vol. 1, p. 60, regarding John the Orphanotrophos.

30. *Theophanis Continuatus*, ed. I. Bakker (Bonn, 1838), p. 318.

31. Skylitzes, *Synopsis historiarum*, p. 258, l. 37.

32. The eunuch protospathars, e.g., wore a special neck decoration which Philotheos tells us was decorated with pearls, so that their badge of office distinguished them from protospathars who were not eunuchs. They also wore a special uniform, a white tunic adorned with gold in a special pattern and a red doublet with gold facings. See J.B. Bury, *The Administration System in the Ninth Century with a Revised Text of the Kletorologion of Philotheos* (New York: Franklin, 1958), p. 121.

33. This legend can be found in the *Scriptores Originum Constantinopolitanorum* published in the Bonn Corpus in connection with the pseudo-Kodinus. We now know that it is a part of a collection of foundation legends probably dating from the tenth century. See *Scriptores Originum Constantinopolitanarum*, ed. Theodorus Preger, 2 vols. (Leipzig, 1901–07; reprint, New York, 1975), p. 86. For a later version of the legend see George P. Majeska, *Russian Travelers to Constantinople in the Fourteenth and Fifteenth Centuries* (Washington, DC: Dumbarton Oaks Research Library and Collection, 1984), p. 199.

34. There is a familiar hagiographical genre in which a woman dresses as a man in order either to enter a monastery and practice extremes of asceticism that would not be allowed in a convent or to escape from her husband or family. Because she wears earrings she is assumed to be a eunuch. In this genre the

earrings are a critical gender marker. For example, Sta. Matrona, in the tenth-century *vita* by Symeon Metaphraste, is one of the many holy women who pretend to be eunuchs. She dresses "in the garment of a eunuch" and here the Greek clearly means garments of the sort a eunuch wears rather than garments belonging to some specific eunuch, and adorns herself after the manner of a eunuch (this later becomes a convenient explanation for her pierced ears) with earrings. *Vita Sta. Matrona* in *Acta Sanctorum* (Brussels: Socios Bollandianos, 1910), vol. 3, pp. 813–22. Women ascetics often cross-dressed and posed as eunuchs. This is discussed in Sebastian P. Brock and Susan Ashbrook Harvey, *Holy Women of the Syrian Orient* (Berkeley and Los Angeles: University of California Press, 1987), p. 59, and is particularly well handled in J. Anson, "The Female Transvestite in Early Monasticism: The Origin and Development of a Motif," *Viator* 5 (1974).

35. Harriet Whitehead, "Institutionalized Homosexuality in Native North America," in Sherry B. Ortner and Whitehead (eds.), *Sexual Meanings: The Cultural Construction of Gender and Sexuality* (Cambridge: Cambridge University Press, 1981), p. 97, in a discussion of American Indians, makes a statement that could easily apply to the Byzantine context. "For the American Indians occupational pursuits clearly occupy the spotlight, with dress/demeanor coming in a close second. Sexual object choice is part of the gender configuration, but its salience is low; so low that by itself it does not provoke the reclassification of the individual to a special status. In the Western system, the order of salience is virtually the reverse."

36. See Diogenes Laertius, *Vitae Philosophorum*, ed. H.S. Long, *Diogenes Laertii*, bk. 6, sec. 39, l. 4 for an early example, and Skylitzes, *Synopsis historiarum*, p. 131, l. 22 for a later example. When Basil I became emperor the eunuch who understood the treasury accounts had to explain them to him. Through this eunuch Basil learned who had received money unlawfully and forced its restoration. Nikephoros Bryennios, the Younger, *Histoire*, ed. P. Gautier (Brussels, 1975), p. 56, praises the eunuch Nikephoritzes's diligence, intelligence and knowledge of state affairs. A good example of a helpful eunuch involved in a real estate transaction can be found in the *Life of Sta. Euphrosyna the Younger* in *Acta Sanctorum* (Brussels: Socios Bollandianos, 1910), vol. 3, p. 871.

37. See, e.g., Skylitzes, *Synopsis historiarum* p. 179, l. 73; Sokrates, *History of the Church*, p. 690; *Theophanis Continuatus*, p. 406. "Basil the patricius and prefect of the holy bedchamber wrapped the emperor Constantine's body for burial as was customary."

38. See, e.g., Michael the eunuch, who attended Alexius Komnenus at his

death. Anna Komnena, *Alexiade*, ed. B. Leib (with P. Gautier), vol. 3, p. 236, l. 23; and Thomas, a eunuch from Lesbos who came to Constantinople to find work and established himself as a bloodletter at court. John Kinnamos, *Epitome rerum ab Joanne et Alexio Comnenis Gestarum*, ed. Augustus Meineke (Bonn, 1836), p. 296.

39. For example, it is regularly suggested that the emperor Theodosius took Chrysaphius as a lover. See John Malalas, *Chronographia*, ed. L. Dindorf (Bonn, 1831), p. 363. For a later example see Skylitzes's comments about the emperor Romanos. Skylitzes, *Synopsis historiarum*, p. 248, l. 5.

40. Psellus, *Chronographia*, bk. 2, p. 27 and bk. 5, p. 111.

41. *Theophanis Continuatus*, p. 466. The government of the empress Zoe is the best-known example of this phenomenon. John the Orphanotrophos attempted to limit her power by replacing her eunuch staff with his own female relatives. Skylitzes, *Synopsis historiarum*, p. 506.

42. Of course, the most important sacred space, for the emperor, was the palace. This is so obvious that our sources rarely mention it. But Nicetas Choniates also tells us that the eunuchs who guarded the royal forest and hunting preserve, space exclusively used by the emperor, treated it, too, as sacred space and would not let wood be cut there even though it was desperately needed to rebuild the navy. Choniates, *Nicetae Choniatae Historia*, ed. Ioanne Aloysius van Dieten (Berlin, 1975), p. 540, l. 87.

43. Procopius of Caesarea, *Procopii Caesariensis Opera Omnia*, ed. Jacobus Haury (Leipzig: Teubner, 1962), vol. 2, bk. 6, ch. 16.

44. Agathias, *Historiarum Libri Quinque*, ed. Rudolfus Keydell (Berlin: de Gruyter et Socios, 1967), bk. 1, ch. 8.

45. Leo the Deacon, *Historiae libri X*, 107.

46. Nikephoros Bryennios, *Nicephore Bryennios Histoire*, ed. and trans. Paul Gautier (Brussels: Societatem "Byzantion," 1975), bk. 4, ch. 32.

47. The entry of eunuchs into monasteries was often restricted. Along with women and young boys they could not enter the monasteries on Mount Athos, for example. The explanation given for these regulations was that the sight of women, boys or eunuchs offered assistance to the devil in his ongoing temptations of monks. Not all monasteries turned away eunuchs, and there were some houses founded specifically for eunuchs. See P. Placidus de Meester, *De Monachico Statu Iuxta Disciplinam Byzantinam: Statuta Selectis Fontibus et Commentariis Instructa* (Typis Polyglottis Vaticanis, 1942), p. 167, for a summary of legislation on this matter. Theophylaktos, Archbishop of Ohrid, *Discours, Traités,*

Poésies, ed. Gautier (Thessalonike: 1980), p. 328, mentions a number of mon-asteries founded specifically for eunuchs, including one on Mount Athos. In his note to this section of the text Gautier suggests that the founding of special monasteries just for eunuchs was not exceptional. He specifically mentions the monastery founded by the eunuch Eutropius in Palestine near Jericho and the monastery founded in the capital by Michael Attaliates in the eleventh century. In his preface to the above text, Gautier (pp. 115–17) discusses the specific tex-tual problems surrounding the possibility that there was a monastery for eunuchs on Mount Athos.

48. A few famous examples are the Patriarch Ignatius, the son of Michael Rangabe, castrated to eliminate any claims he might have to the throne; the Patriarch Methodius; the Patriarch Polyeuktos in the reign of Constantine Porphyrogenitus, who was raised and educated in Constantinople, castrated by his parents, and became a monk; the Patriarch Germanus, castrated as political punishment; and the Bishop of Nicomedia, a castrated relative of the emperor Michael. See Skylitzes, *Synopsis historiarum*, p. 106, l. 20; p. 87, l. 15; p. 244, l. 89; p. 400, l. 29. But Skylitzes is not totally comfortable with the idea that castrated men might rise to high Church office. He tells us that the Patriarch Methodius became a eunuch with the help of St. Peter, to whom Methodius prayed for release from sexual desires. Skylitzes is very critical when Michael appoints a eunuch as Bishop of Nicomedia. He tells us that John the Orphan-otrophos, a famous eunuch and head of the government under the emperor Michael, hoped to become Patriarch, and takes relish in John's failure. It would be interesting to know how frequently eunuchs crossed over from careers in the Church to careers in court and vice versa. Indications of career crossover are scattered and uncommon. This may reflect the nature of our sources. Chroni-cles say little about the inner workings of the Church hierarchy. While chronicles might identify a churchman as a eunuch, they rarely detail his professional back-ground. Conversely ecclesiastical sources treat court eunuchs in the same way. The obvious crossover involves the common situation in which a powerful court eunuch becomes a monk and lives out the remainder of his life in a monastery. This echoes patterns followed by the upper levels of the aristocracy. It is also important to remember that monasteries were often places of incarceration to which court eunuchs were sent by the emperor. So, entrance into the monastic life has limited value as an indicator that court eunuchs could move into the Church hierarchy. For examples of this phenomenon see Skylitzes, *Synopsis his-toriarum*, p. 190, l. 60 and l. 89; p. 240, l. 68; p. 398, l. 85. This lack of evi-

dence for crossover from the court into the Church offers evidence, admittedly negative, for the argument that court and household eunuchs were acculturated into gender patterns that were not acceptable in the Church. Though not a Patriarch, the great saint and thinker Symeon the New Theologian, may have been a eunuch serving at court under the sponsorship of his uncle, chamberlain to Basil II and Constantine VII. Rosemary Morris makes an excellent argument for this in "The Political Saint of the 11th Century" in Sergie Hackel (ed.), *The Byzantine Saint* (London: St. Vladimirs, 1981). Examples of ecclesiastical eunuchs coming to court are only slightly easier to find. In the reign of Constantine Monomachus (1042-55) the army was put under the control of a eunuch named Nicephorus, a priest who had served Monomachus when he was still a private citizen. "Eager for the splendor and glory of the profane life, Nicephorus left the priesthood." See Skylitzes, *Synopsis historiarum*, p. 464, l. 14. John, Bishop of Sidon, a eunuch, made a similar move into government service. See Attaleiates, *Historia*, eds. W. Brunet de Presle and I. Bekker (Bonn, 1853), p. 180.

49. Eusebios, *Commentarius in Isaiam*, in ed. J. Ziegler, *Eusebius Werke, Band 9: Der Jesajakommentar* [*Die griechischen christlichen schriftsteller* (Berlin: Akademie, 1975)], vol. 1, p. 45, l. 22 and l. 37; and Athanasius, *Orations against the Arians*, in *P.G.*, vol. 26, col. 128, l. 27, recognize this problem, yet offer hope for salvation for eunuchs who lead godly lives.

50. In modern translations the term "eunuchs" is often omitted: εἰσὶν γὰρ εὐνοῦχοι οἵτινες ἐκ κοιλίας μητρὸς ἐγεννήθησαν οὕτως, καὶ εἰσὶν εὐνοῦχοι οἵτινες εὐνουχίσθησαν ὑπὸ τῶν ἀνθρώπων, καὶ εἰσὶν εὐνοῦχοι οἵτινες εὐνούχισαν ἑαυτοὺς διὰ τὴν βασιλείαν τῶν οὐρανῶν.

51. Nazianzos, *Grégoire de Nazianze: Discours 32-37*, ed. Claudio Moreschini (Paris: Cerf, 1985), ch. 16, p. 305, says that some men are born eunuchs, but they should not think too well of themselves because their chastity has not been tested. Beyond this he considers that the passage was intended to apply to all men. Thus those who are "born eunuchs" are those who are born good by nature; those who are "made eunuchs by men" are those who have received the word of God from the Church, which knowledge has removed their passions; and those who are "made eunuchs for the kingdom of heaven" are those who have become holy without the help of earthly teachers.

52. Epiphanius, *Panarion*, ed. Karl Holl, in *Die Grieschen Christlichen Schriftsteller der Ersten Drei Jahrhunderte 2* (Leipzig: Hinrichs, 1915), p. 361.

53. Clement of Alexandria, *Stromata Buch I-VI*, eds. Otto Stählin and Ludwig Früchtel (Berlin: Akademie, 1985), bk. 3, p. 1.

54. Eusebios, *Ecclesiastical History*, vol. 6, p. 29.

55. Athanasius, *Homily on the Song of Songs*, in *P.G.*, vol. 27, col. 1332.

56. John Chrysostom, *Homily XXXV on Chapter XIV of Genesis*, in *P.G.*, vol. 58, col. 599.

57. Canon law is careful to distinguish between the man who castrates himself and the man who is castrated by another against his will or accidentally. Only the latter could become priests. See n.1 above.

58. Theophylaktos, Archbishop of Ohrid, *The Defense of Eunuchs*, in ed. P. Gautier, *Discours, Traités, Poésies* (Thessalonike: 1980), pp. 287–331.

59. Theophylaktos felt a need for a word that would express the collectivity of eunuchs and embrace them in an institutional setting. To do this he used the Greek term εὐνουχισμός, which I have translated as "eunuchism."

60. Theophylaktos, "The Defense of Eunuchs," p. 291. In doing this he is following conventions that are common in agricultural texts of the period, since *testiculated* is a term commonly used of uncastrated farm animals, rams and billy goats.

61. Tribonian was a court official and jurist at the court of Justinian I. He was born some time before 500 C.E. and died about 542. He served as a member of the commission that drafted the *Codex Justinianus*.

62. Theophylaktos, *The Defense of Eunuchs*, p. 199, l. 19.

63. *Ibid.*, p. 317, l. 7.

64. The author obviously does not believe that an intelligent person would suggest that monks, like eunuchs, are ill omened. Yet in saying this he admits that at least some people believe this of eunuchs and suggests that in some way eunuchs and monks are alike and whatever attributes they share create the idea that they are unlucky and perhaps magical. Obviously neither procreates. Both wear distinctive clothing and are acculturated into a specific way of life and demeanor. Both have access to and control over sacred space. There are scattered, veiled references to the special powers of both eunuchs and monks throughout our sources, but they are difficult to analyze and remain, at this point, only a source of speculation.

CHAPTER TWO: LONDON'S SAPPHISTS

1. An earlier version of this essay was printed in Julia Epstein and Kristina Straub (eds.), *Body Guards: The Cultural Politics of Gender Ambiguity* (New York: Routledge, 1991). I am grateful to the publishers and the editors of the volume for their willingness to have the essay reprinted. I began my study of sodomy

with "London's Sodomites: Homosexual Behavior and Western Culture in the Eighteenth Century," *Journal of Social History* 11 (1977). I subsequently discussed the new historiography in "Sodomitical Subcultures, Sodomitical Roles, and the Gender Revolution of the Eighteenth Century: The Recent Historiography," *Eighteenth-Century Life* 9 (1985) and in Robert P. Maccubbin (ed.), *'Tis Nature's Fault: Unauthorized Sexuality during the Enlightenment* (New York: Cambridge University Press, 1987) and "Gender and the Homosexual Role in Modern Western Culture: The 18th and 19th Centuries Compared," in Dennis Altman et al., *Homosexuality, Which Homosexuality?* (Amsterdam and London: An Dekker/Schorer, GMP, 1989). As preliminaries to the chapters on sodomy in my forthcoming *The Sexual Life of Eighteenth-Century London*, I have presented new evidence and argument in "The Birth of the Queen: Sodomy and the Emergence of Gender Equality in Modern Culture, 1660–1750," in Martin B. Duberman, Martha Vicinus and George Chauncey, Jr. (eds.), *Hidden from History: Reclaiming the Gay and Lesbian Past* (New York: New American Library, 1989); "Sodomitical Assaults, Gender Role, and Sexual Development in Eighteenth-Century London," *Journal of Homosexuality* 16 (1988), and in *The Pursuit of Sodomy: Male Homosexuality in Renaissance and Enlightenment Europe*, Kent Gerard and Gert Hekma (eds.) (New York: Harrington Park, 1989); "Sodomy Transformed: Aristocratic Libertinage, Public Reputation and the Gender Revolution of the 18th Century," *Journal of Homosexuality* 19 (1990), and in *Love Letters between a Certain Late Nobleman and the Famous Mr. Wilson*, ed. Michael S. Kimmel (New York: Haworth Press, 1990); and "Sex, Gender, and Sexual Identity in Modern Culture: Male Sodomy and Female Prostitution in Enlightenment London," *Journal of the History of Sexuality* 2 (1991). In a short essay I tried to place the eighteenth-century change in long-term cultural history: "England," in Wayne Dynes (ed.), *The Encyclopedia of Homosexuality*, 2 vols. (New York: Garland, 1990), vol. 1, pp. 354–58. I have been greatly helped in conceptualizing the number of bodies and genders that can exist in a society, and how they can be combined, by Gilbert Herdt, "Mistaken Gender," *American Anthropologist* 92 (1990); Walter L. Williams, *The Spirit and the Flesh* (Boston: Beacon, 1986).

2. Earlier studies include Sheridan Baker, "Henry Fielding's *The Female Husband*: Fact and Fiction," *PMLA* 74 (1959); Elizabeth Mavor, *The Ladies of Llangollen* (Harmondsworth, Eng.: Penguin, 1973); Lillian Faderman, *Surpassing the Love of Men* (New York: Morrow, 1981); Terry Castle, "Matters Not Fit to Be Mentioned: Fielding's *The Female Husband*," *ELH* 49 (1982); K.V. Crawford, "The Transvestite Heroine in 17th-Century Popular Literature," Ph.D.

dissertation, Harvard University, 1984; Dianne Dugaw, "Balladry's Female War-
riors: Women, Warfare and Disguise in the 18th Century," *Eighteenth-Century
Life* 9 (1985) and *Warrior Women and Popular Balladry 1650–1850* (New York:
Cambridge University Press, 1989); Lynne Friedl, " 'Passing Women': A Study
of Gender Boundaries in the Eighteenth Century," in G.S. Rousseau and Roy
Porter (eds.), *Sexual Underworlds of the Enlightenment* (Manchester: Manchester
University Press, 1987). There are two general surveys: Vicinus, " 'They Wonder to Which Sex I Belong': The Historical Roots of the Modern Lesbian Identity," in Altman et al., *Homosexuality, Which Homosexuality?*; Rudolph M. Dekker
and Lotte C. van de Pol, *The Tradition of Female Transvestism in Early Modern
Europe* (Basingstoke, UK: Macmillan; New York: St. Martin's, 1989). I have tried
to make some comments in my "London's Sodomites," p. 13, and in *Homosexuality, Which Homosexuality?*, pp. 158–61, but my argument in the last of these is
considerably modified in this essay; I unwisely said what I did before I had
sufficiently considered the material I had gathered. The existing historiography
(on which I relied) was misleading in its emphasis on the late-nineteenth-century
origins of the lesbian role. It is likely that an already-existing role was becoming more important at that point in time. Women in the late nineteenth century must have begun to define themselves more as female as a result of their
relations to other women than they had done previously.

3. *The Wandering Whore*, 6 parts (London, 1660–1663), part 4, p. 5; part 3,
p. 9; reprint, ed. Randolph Trumbach (New York: Garland, 1986); Joseph Addison, *The Drummer* (1716), act iv, scene 1; [Jonathan Wild], *An Answer to a late
insolent libel* (London, 1718), p. 30; Robert Halsband, *Lord Hervey* (Oxford:
Oxford University Press, 1973), pp. 109–11; Alexander Pope, *Poems*, ed. John
Butt (New Haven, CT: Yale University Press, 1963), pp. 607–08; Joseph Spence,
Observations, Anecdotes and Characters of Books and Men, 2 vols., ed. J.M. Osborn
(Oxford: Clarendon, 1966), vol. 1, p. 80, no. 188; *Oxford English Dictionary*,
s.v. molly: cf. Trumbach, "Birth of the Queen," p. 137.

4. *The Guardian*, ed. J.C. Stephens (Lexington, Kentucky: University Press
of Kentucky, 1982), no. 149, p. 488; *The Spectator*, ed. D.F. Bond (Oxford:
Clarendon, 1965), 5 vols., vol. 4, pp. 28–29, no. 435; vol. 2, p. 390, no. 229;
see also Dugaw, *Warrior Women*, pp. 133–34. For the eighteenth-century English
Sappho, see Lawrence Lipking, "Sappho Descending: Eighteenth-Century Styles
in Abandoned Women," *Eighteenth-Century Life* 12 (1988), which does not deal,
however, with Sappho in the more libertine tradition, which makes clear her
taste for girls. Joan DeJean, *Fictions of Sappho, 1546–1937* (Chicago: Univer-

sity of Chicago Press, 1989), finds the eighteenth-century French Sappho to have been entirely domesticated into a tragic heterosexuality. But in the seventeenth and the nineteenth centuries, she was presented, as well, as either lesbian or whore. This fits the pattern of Enlightenment domestication of women's sexuality. However, this domestication was not necessarily oppressive, since it aimed to free women from the stigma of an irrational and irrepressible sexuality. But the emergence of the modern sapphic role at the end of the eighteenth century also meant that the "lesbianism" of the seventeenth and the nineteenth centuries had different meanings when attributed to Sappho: the first was likely to be combined with desire for men, the latter to be exclusively directed toward women. DeJean is aware of the late-eighteenth-century libertine use of Sappho's name to describe the new sapphic role, but she discounts its significance because it was not taken up into the fictionalized lives of Sappho and because she presumes a continuous lesbian identity across time. She does say (p. 120) that, "before the late nineteenth century, the two traditions – fictions of Sappho and fictions of the lesbian – were never to intersect." It was probably a reflection of the varying public respectability of libertine as opposed to domesticated texts. Peter Tomory, "The Fortunes of Sappho: 1770-1850," in Graeme W. Clarke (ed.), *Rediscovering Hellenism* (Cambridge: Cambridge University Press, 1989), is not helpful and conflates two quotations from Addison. The complaints about women's hermaphroditical clothes went back to the early seventeenth century: see Crawford, "Transvestite Heroine," pp. 146-52; and R.V. Lucas, "*Hic Mulier*: The Female Transvestite in Early Modern England," *Renaissance and Reformation* 12 (1988); Susan S. Shapiro, "Amazons, Hermaphrodites and Plain Monsters: The 'Masculine' Woman in English Satire and Social Criticism from 1580-1640," *Atlantis* 13 (1987).

5. *Tractatus de Hermaphroditis: Or a Treatise of Hermaphrodites* (London, 1718), pp. 58, ii–iv, 14–16, 19–49; *The History of the Human Heart* (London, 1749), pp. 20-21.

6. *Onania; or the heinous sin of self-pollution* (London, 1723) and its *Supplement* (n.d.), pp. 151-62; reprint, ed. Trumbach (New York: Garland, 1986).

7. *Ibid.*

8. *Onania, Supplement*, pp. 162–66; James Parsons, *A Mechanical and Critical Inquiry into the Nature of Hermaphrodites* (London, 1741), p. 33.

9. *Gazetteer and New Daily Advertiser*, May 30, 1770, and June 1, 1771.

10. Parsons, *Hermaphrodites*, pp. 2, 3, 9 and xlvii; J.N. Katz, *Gay/Lesbian Almanac* (New York: Harper & Row, 1983), pp. 71-72.

11. Parsons, *Hermaphrodites*, pp. 25, 28, xvii and xlvii; Nicholas Venette, *The Mysteries of Conjugal Love Revealed* (London, 1710). Traditional public attitudes toward hermaphrodites, and the mid-eighteenth-century change in opinion are discussed in: Pierre Darmon, *Trial By Impotence* (London: Chatto & Windus, 1985), pp. 40–51; Epstein, "Either/Or – Neither/Both: Sexual Ambiguity and the Ideology of Gender," *Genders* 7 (1990); Ann Rosalind Jones and Peter Stallybrass, "Fetishizing Gender: Constructing the Hermaphrodite in Renaissance Europe," in Epstein and Strauss, *Body Guards*. Gary Kates, "D'Eon Returns to France: Gender and Power in 1777," in Epstein and Strauss, *Body Guards*, discusses the famous eighteenth-century case of the Chevalier D'Eon, whose name was used by Havelock Ellis to classify what was later termed transsexualism; but Kates is more interested in showing that D'Eon was not a transsexual than in asking how D'Eon may have fitted into the eighteenth-century classifications of hermaphrodite, passing woman and effeminate sodomite. For women's bodies as imperfect versions of men's, see Thomas Laqueur, "Orgasm, Generation and the Politics of Reproductive Biology," in Catherine Gallagher and Laqueur (eds.), *The Making of the Modern Body* (Berkeley and Los Angeles: University of California Press, 1987), and *Making Sex: Body and Gender from the Greeks to Freud* (Cambridge, MA: Harvard University Press, 1990).

12. Giovanni Bianchi, *[An] historical and physical dissertation on…Catherine Vizzani*, trans. with commentary by John Cleland (London, 1751), pp. 65–66. This was identified as Cleland's by Roger Lonsdale, "New Attributions to John Cleland," *Review of English Studies* 30 (1979). Dekker and van de Pol, *Female Transvestism*, pp. 47–72, agree with Cleland. But the English material I present does not, and in any case, Dekker and van de Pol's case is weakened by their failure to look for evidence of sexual relations between women outside of the context of cross-dressing. Such evidence exists for the Netherlands. See Theo van der Meer, *De Wesentlijke Sonde van Sodomie en andere Vuyligheeden* (Amsterdam: Tabula, 1984), and more clearly in his "Tribades Tried: Female Same-Sex Offenders in Late Eighteenth-Century Amsterdam," *Journal of the History of Sexuality* 1 (1991).

13. Greater London Record Office (*hereafter* GLRO): MJ/SR/2344, New Prison list; Friedl, *Sexual Underworlds*, p. 259 n.66; *Annual Register* 16 (1773), p. 111 and 20 (1777), pp. 191–92; *London Chronicle*, March 22–25, April 5–8, 1760.

14. *London Chronicle*, February 16–18, 1764; for East: *Annual Register* 9 (1766), pp. 116 and 144; *London Chronicle*, September 7–9, 1766.

15. GLRO: MJ/SR/2023, Westminster house of correction list; MJ/SR/

3462, R.480; Corp. of London R.O.: Mansion House Justice Room Minute Book, June 30, 1790.

16. John Ashton, *Eighteenth Century Waifs* (London, 1887), pp. 177-202; *The Female Soldier* (London, 1750), pp. 71-73, 103-105, 121-30 (her courting of women) and pp. 141-42; *The British Heroine* (London, 1742), p. v; John Dryden, *Poems 1693-1696*, ed. A.B. Chambers et al. (Berkeley: University of California Press, 1974), Satyr VI, ll.369-70. Since cases of passing women can be hard to find, I list some that are not discussed in my text. They were found mostly in the *London Chronicle* (LC) between 1759 and 1765 but some are from the *Annual Register* (AR). 1) A woman in Edinburgh who served three years as a soldier, married a wife, and was discovered when under a cure in the infirmary (LC, June 7-9, 1759, p. 548). 2) Barbara Hill, who worked as a stonecutter and a farmer's servant and drove a postchaise in London, married a woman and was discovered when she enlisted in the army (LC, January 31-February 2, 1760, p. 117). 3) Betty Blandford enlisted in a regiment of horse soldiers, was discovered, discharged and sent to Bridewell (LC, February 5-7, 1760, p. 134). 4) Hannah Whitney at Plymouth served five years as a marine and discovered her gender to escape prison (AR 4 [October 1761], p. 170). 5) A woman was discovered on a ship at Plymouth; she was going to look for her husband (AR 4 [August 1761], p. 144). 6) Ann Holt enlisted to search for her sweetheart, whom she found and married (LC, July 21-23, 1763, p. 79). 7) A girl in Surrey stole cattle when dressed as a boy; she was mad (LC, October 5-8, 1765, p. 336; October 22-24, 1765, p. 392). 8) A woman enlisted in the East-India Company to go looking for her husband in India (AR 12 [November 1769], p. 148). 9) A woman on a man-of-war at Chatham came to London from Hull looking for her sweetheart (AR 14 [January 1771], p. 71). 10) Mrs. Cole died at Poplar after serving on ships as a sailor; she had become a woman again on inheriting a small fortune (AR 25 [September 1782], p. 221). 11) A woman served for fourteen years in the dockyards at Deptford, but was later married and had children (LC, July 28-31, 1787, p. 199). 12) A man convicted of horse stealing at Stafford was a woman (LC, September 6-8, 1791, p. 238). 13) Jane Cox of Piddle was found drowned; she had been very tall and strong and had served for many years as a sailor and a soldier (LC, January 29-February 1, 1791, p. 110). There are two patterns in this material: women searching for husbands and sweethearts and women looking for adventure or more interesting work. It is apparent that those women who stayed in civilian life were less likely to be found out than those who enlisted in the army or the navy. There is little evidence of attraction to

women as a motive: two of the thirteen married women and one courted a young woman. Four of them were married to men.

17. *The Genuine History of... Sally Salisbury* (London, 1723), p. 33; *London Chronicle*, January 28–31, 1764; *Appleby's Original Weekly Journal*, August 8, 1719; GLRO: DL/C/172, f. 105; Charlotte Charke, *Narrative of the Life* (London, 1755), pp. 88, 90, 139 and 273; reprint, ed. L.R.N. Ashley (Gainesville, FL: Scholars' Facsimiles & Reprints, 1969); Fidelis Morgan, *The Well-Known Trouble-maker: A Life of Charlotte Charke* (London: Faber & Faber, 1988), pp. 129–30 and 206–207.

18. Charke, *Narrative*, pp. 190–91, 198, 206, 214, 224, 226, 245 and 274 (Mr. & Mrs. Brown); 106–13, 162–64 (courting women); 91–92, 94, 144 (a favorite with the whores); 17, 26, 29–33 (her early years); 51–77 (her first marriage); 139, 258 (her family's reaction). Friedl, *Sexual Underworlds*, p. 242, cites her novel *The History of Henry Dumont* (1756), pp. 60, 66–67. See also S.M. Strange, "Charlotte Charke: Transvestite or Conjurer," *Restoration and 18th-Century Theatre Research* 15 (1976), who tries to distance Charke from the transvestite role by stressing that she made her career playing breeches' parts (or male roles) on the stage. But going about constantly in male clothes was quite a different matter, as her family was aware. It was a practice that tied her to the patterns of life of the cross-dressing woman that were separate from those of the theatrical world. Furthermore, by transvestism Strange probably means the modern sapphic role, not the eighteenth-century passing woman. On the breeches' part, see Pat Rogers in P.G. Boucé (ed.), *Sexuality in Eighteenth-Century Britain* (Totowa, NJ: Manchester University Press; Barnes & Noble, 1982); and Kristina Straub, *Sexual Suspects: Eighteenth-Century Players and Sexual Ideology* (Princeton: Princeton University Press, 1991). (I am critical of Straub's formulations. See my review in *Eighteenth-Century Studies* 26 [1992–93].)

19. H. Montgomery Hyde, *The Love That Dared Not Speak Its Name* (Boston: Little, Brown, 1970), pp. 37–40.

20. Mary Delariviere Manley, *Novels*, ed. Patricia Köster (Gainesville: University Presses of Florida, 1971), 2 vols.: I cite the pages of the eighteenth-century edition.

21. Cleland, *Memoirs of a Woman of Pleasure* (1748–49), ed. Peter Sabor (Oxford: Oxford University Press, 1985); for "lying in state," see the expert testimony of that accomplished libertine, Colonel Francis Charteris, *Select Trials at the Sessions House of the Old Bailey*, 4 vols. (London, 1742), vol. 3, pp. 199 and 206; reprint, ed. Randolph Trumbach (New York: Garland, 1985); the num-

bers of men with two women come from my research on London prostitution; H.F.B. Compston, *The Magdalen Hospital* (London: Society for Promoting Christian Knowledge, 1917), p. 62 n.2.

22. *Private Correspondence of Sarah Duchess of Marlborough*, 2 vols. (London, 1832), vol. 1, p. 253; *Horace Walpole's Correspondence*, eds. W.S. Lewis et al., 48 vols. (New Haven, CT: Yale University Press, 1937–83), vol. 20, p. 53; vol. 9, p. 171 and n.8.

23. *Tractatus*, pp. 41–42; Henry Fielding, *The Female Husband* (London, 1746), pp. 21 and 23; Baker, "Fielding's *Female Husband*," pp. 220, 222 and 223. Jill Campbell's account of Fielding's interest in these matters misses two points. She fails to see that Fielding's concern with effeminate fops, beaus and castrati is to be set in the context of the emergence of the role of the effeminate male sodomite and that Fielding is trying to suggest that there is likely to appear a parallel role for women who have relations with other women, dress in men's clothes and use an artificial penis. The "Farinellos, all in wax" (p. 67) may explicitly have been little dolls, but the pause in the dialogue and the husband's hatred that his wife "should be fond of anything but himself" would strongly have suggested to the knowing that they were the same dildos that figure so prominently in Mary Hamilton's story (" 'When Men Turn Women': Gender Reversals in Fielding's Plays," in Felicity Nussbaum and Laura Brown [eds.], *The New Eighteenth Century* [New York: Methuen, 1987]). Castle, " 'Matters Not Fit to Be Mentioned,' " notes Fielding's ambiguous feelings of attraction and disapproval toward the cross-dressing woman who uses a dildo.

24. Bianchi, *Vizzani*, pp. 34–35, 43 and 53–55. Faderman, *Surpassing Love*, saw that it was the usurpation of male prerogatives that was controversial. She was also aware that among libertines sex between women was acceptable when it did not exclude sex with men. But she placed the emergence of the lesbian role at the end of the nineteenth century and did not interpret her eighteenth-century material in the light of sodomite and sapphist roles.

25. *Thraliana; The Diary of Mrs. Hester Lynch Thrale*, 2d ed., 2 vols., ed. K.C. Balderston (Oxford: Clarendon, 1951), pp. 595 n.1, 949 and n.3, 740, 850–51, 868 and n.3 and 922 (for women) and *passim* (for men).

26. *Walpole's Correspondence*, vol. 24, pp. 234–35; *Thraliana*, pp. 1–2, 770 and 949; *The Farington Diary*, 7 vols., ed. James Greig (London: Hutchinson, 1922–26), vol. 1, pp. 233–34; *A Sapphic Epistle from Jack Cavendish to . . . Mrs. D***** (1782), p. 5. There is a biography of Mrs. Damer by Percy Noble, *Ann Seymour Damer: A Woman of Art and Fashion 1748–1828* (London: Paul, Trench,

Trubner, 1908), the tone of which is set on the first page by the statement that she was "irreproachable in moral character." The gossip about her sexual tastes may have begun as early as 1778, when Lady Sarah Lennox wrote that "as for the *abuse* she has met with, I must put such nonsense out of the question, and in everything else her conduct is very proper" (Countess of Ilchester and Lord Stavordale, *The Life and Letters of Lady Sarah Lennox 1745-1826* [London: J. Murray, 1902], p. 286). Mrs. Damer was the half-sister of the wife of Lady Sarah's brother. Lady Sarah seems to have been well informed about the details of the Damers' unhappy marriage and Mrs. Damer's early widowhood (pp. 250-52, 261-62). Horace Walpole, who was Mrs. Damer's godfather, was very circumspect in what he wrote of her. Walpole's biographers suppose that he fell in love with Mary Berry, but it is apparent that the really intense relationship in this circle was between Berry and Mrs. Damer. See R.W. Ketton-Cremer, *Horace Walpole* (Ithaca, NY: Cornell University Press, 1964); Brian Fothergill, *The Strawberry Hill Set: Horace Walpole and His Circle* (Boston: Faber & Faber, 1983).

27. Mavor, *Ladies*, pp. 73-99, 167-68 and 196-99; on female friendship in the earlier period, see Irene Q. Brown, "Domesticity, Feminism, and Friendship: Female Aristocratic Culture and Marriage in England, 1660-1760," *Journal of Family History* 7 (1982); Janet Todd, *Women's Friendship in Literature* (New York: Columbia University Press, 1980). Faderman, in her pioneering *Surpassing Love*, began her discussion of the eighteenth century with a relatively brief treatment of hermaphrodites and passing women but then dealt with most of her material under the rubric of romantic friendship. The sapphist role (and Mrs. Damer) was absent from her text. By contrast I devote the third section of this essay to sexual relations and not to friendship. It is likely that Butler and Ponsonby, who figured so prominently in Faderman's account of friendship, were in fact a sapphist development in the tradition of female friendship. Other female couples in the romantic tradition did not use the hermaphroditic dress that Butler and Ponsonby wore. Two other points in Faderman's discussion are open to question. She says that the libertine position on sex between women was a male one. But it is apparent that Mrs. Manley (who is not discussed by Faderman) was a libertine. Secondly, Faderman claims that romantic friendship was a psychic compensation in a world of loveless, arranged marriages. Brown argues on the contrary that such friendships should be understood in the contexts of domesticity and romantic marriage that Lawrence Stone and I have described. See Lawrence Stone, *The Family, Sex and Marriage in England, 1500-1800* (New York: Harper & Row, 1977), and Trumbach, *The Rise of the Egalitarian Family*

(New York: Academic Press, 1978). Some of the difficulties in interpreting female friendship when the language of male-female erotic love is used by one woman for another are laid out in Harriet Andreadis, "The Sapphic-Platonics of Katherine Philips, 1632–1664," *Signs* 15 (1988). Alan Bray has tried to argue that the customs of male friendship can hardly be distinguished from those of erotic attraction between males: "Homosexuality and the Signs of Male Friendship in Elizabethan England," *History Workshop Journal* 29 (1990). But he fails to distinguish friendship between two adult male equals from the desire of a man for an adolescent boy, which was then the dominant form of sexual relations between males. Montaigne (cited in Faderman, *Surpassing Love*, p. 65) was aware that the inequalities of age in the latter sort of relationship made it more like the love of men for women than the love between male equals: erotic attraction was presumed to flourish only across the divides of patriarchy – the old for the young, the male for the female, the powerful for the weak. It may then be that Katherine Philips's use of the language of male-female love to describe her affection for women is not a sign of erotic attraction at all. Instead, it is an instance of a woman's acceptance of patriarchal subordination. Platonic friendships between women could not be described in the language of the nonerotic friendship between dominant male equals. Philips could use for women's friendship only the love language of subordination, which was usually an erotic language. Twentieth-century readers should always be aware that, before 1700, the structures of patriarchy were in control of expressions both of friendship and of erotic attraction. The distinctions of heterosexuality and homosexuality, although they are so salient for us, did not exist for the seventeenth-century woman or man.

28. Isaac Kramnick, *The Rage of Edmund Burke* (New York: Basic Books, 1977), pp. 83–87; *The Correspondence of Edmund Burke*, 10 vols., ed. T.W. Copeland and J.A. Woods (Chicago: University of Chicago Press, 1958–78), vol. 6, pp. 130–32. Discussions of the sapphic tastes of Marie Antoinette may be found in two recent essays and the further literature they cite: Jeffrey Merrick, "Sexual Politics and Public Order in Late Eighteenth-Century France: The *Memoires secrets* and the *Correspondence secrète*," *Journal of the History of Sexuality* 1 (1990), pp. 68–84; Lynn Hunt, "The Many Bodies of Marie Antoinette: Political Pornography and the Problem of the Feminine in the French Revolution," in Hunt (ed.), *Eroticism and the Body Politic* (Baltimore: John Hopkins University Press, 1991). It is likely that some of this material is evidence for the development in France of a late-eighteenth-century sapphist role. See Marie-Jo Bonnet, *Un choix*

sans équivoque (Paris: Denoel, 1981). For what it is worth, Marie Antoinette approved of Mrs. Damer when she met her: *Walpole's Correspondence*, vol. 6, p. 127.

CHAPTER THREE: SODOMY AND THE PURSUIT OF A
THIRD SEX IN THE EARLY MODERN PERIOD
Abbreviations used in notes are as follows: AHK, Archief Hervormde Kerk (Records Reformed Church); ARA, Algemeen Rijksarchief (National State Archive); DTB, Doop-, Trouw- en Begraafboeken (records of baptism, marriage and burial); GAA, Gemeente Archief Amsterdam (Municipal Archive Amsterdam); GADo, Gemeente Archief Dordrecht (Municipal Archive Dordrecht); GADH, Gemeente Archief Den Haag (Municipal Archive The Hague); GAR, Gemeente Archief Rotterdam (Municipal Archive Rotterdam); GAU, Gemeente Archief Utrecht (Municipal Archive Utrecht); HGH, Hoog Gerechtshof (High Court); HJK, Hoge Justitie Kamer (Court of Groningen); HS, Handschrift (manuscript); HvH, Hof van Holland (Court of Holland); HvU, Hof van Utrecht (Court of Utrecht); NA, Notarieel Archief (notary records); ORA, Oud Rechterlijk Archief (local court records); PGNH, Provinciaal Gerechtshof Noord-Holland (Provincial Court North Holland); RAG, Rijksarchief Groningen (State Archive Groningen); RANH, Rijksarchief Noord-Holland (State Archive North Holland); RAZ, Rijksarchief Zeeland (State Archive Sealand); RAU, Rijksarchief Utrecht (State Archive Utrecht); REA, Rechtbank van Eerste Aanleg (local court records); RvS, Raad van State (State Council); SA, Schepen Archief (local court records); StS, Staatssecretarie (State Secretariat).

1. Hubert Kennedy, *Ulrichs: The Life and Works of Karl Heinrich Ulrichs, Pioneer of the Modern Gay Movement* (Boston: Alyson, 1988).

2. Gert Hekma, *Homoseksualiteit, een Medische Reputatie. De Uitdoktering van de Homoseksueel in Nederland* (Amsterdam: SUA, 1987); Jeffrey Weeks, *Coming Out: Homosexual Politics in Britain from the Nineteenth Century to the Present* (London: Quartet, 1977).

3. Michel Foucault, *History of Sexuality: Vol. 1*, trans. Robert Hurley (New York: Random, 1978).

4. Hekma, "Homosexual Behavior in the Nineteenth-Century Dutch Army," *Journal of the History of Sexuality* 2.2 (1991).

5. Randolph Trumbach, "Gender and the Homosexual Role in Modern Western Culture: The 18th and 19th Centuries Compared," in Dennis Altman et al., *Homosexuality, Which Homosexuality?* (Amsterdam and London: An Dekker/Schorer, GMP, 1989).

6. Theo van der Meer, *Sodoms Zaad in Nederland. Vervolging, Sociale-Organisatie en Percepties van Homoseksueel Gedrag van de Late Middeleeuwen tot en met het Begin van de Moderne Tijd* (Amsterdam, 1994).

7. Peter Burke, *Popular Culture in Early Modern Europe* (New York: New York University Press, 1978).

8. Dirk Arend Berents, "Homoseksualiteit en criminaliteit in de middeleeuwen," *Groniek* 12 (1980).

9. Jan Boomgaard, *Misdaad en Straf in Amsterdam: Onderzock naar de Strafrechtspleging van de Amsterdamse Schepenbank, 1490–1552* (Zwolle: Waanders, 1992); van der Meer, "Zodoms Zaat in de Republick. Stedelijke homoseksuele subculturen in de achttiende eeum," in Hekma and H. Roodenburg (eds.), *Soete, Minne en Helsche Boosheit. Seksuele Voorstellingen in Nederland, 1300–1850* (Nijmegen: SUN, 1988).

10. Dirk Jaap Noordam, "Homosexualiteit en sodomie in Leiden, 1533–1811," *Leids Jaarboekje* 75 (1983); J. van Haastert, "Beschouwingen bij de criminele vonnissen van de schepenbank van de stad Breda uit de jaren 1626 tot 1795," *Jaarboek van de Geschied- en Oudheidkundige Kring van Stad en Land van Breda "De Oranjeboom"* 29 (1976); van der Meer, *Sodoms.*

11. Van der Meer, *Sodoms.*

12. G. Kuijk and R. Valens Nip, "Saeye zonden," *Groniek* 16 (1982); R.I.A. Nip, "Bengaert Say, een 15 de eeuws ambtenaar," *Holland* 15 (1983).

13. ARA HvH 466, fo 49, 98v–99r; HvH 5875; HvH 5851, fo 11v–13v.

14. Litius Wielandt (1654), ARA HvH 5248.2; Sigismundus Pape (1684), HvH 5337.1.

15. GAU RA 2236 (1676), between fo 474–475.

16. GAU 2236 (1713–1727), fo 930–933.

17. GAR SA 141; SA 250, fo 200r–203r; SA 251, fo 15r–16r; SA 299.

18. GAR SA 127v–129v.

19. GAR SA 177, fo 55v–58r; SA 253, fo 186r–194r.

20. The jurist Van Zurck mentioned in *Codex Batavurs* (Delft, 1727) that this penalty was carried out in 1686 in Amsterdam. I have found no court records or verdicts that confirm this. However, in 1730 two men in this city suffered this penalty. It is unlikely that the court did not act on a precedent. For the blackmail cases: (1689) GAA 5061-334, fo 77v–275v; 5061-596; (1715) 5061-372, fo 116r–119v; 5061-608.

21. ARA HvH 5374.18. In these records, there are references to sodomy trials by the local court in The Hague. Obviously, this court destroyed any evi-

dence of sodomy trials before 1730. See van der Meer, *Sodoms.*

22. *Europische Mercurius* (1730), vol. 1, p. 283.

23. *Resolutien Staten van Holland en Westvriesland* (1730), pp. 430–31.

24. Van der Meer, *De Wesentlijke Sonde van Sodomie en Andere Vuyligheeden. Sodomietenvervolgingen in Amsterdam 1730–1811* (Amsterdam: Tabula, 1984).

25. Rudolf Dekker and Lotte van de Pol, *The Tradition of Female Transvestism in Early Modern Europe* (London: Macmillan, 1989); van der Meer, "Tribades on Trial: Female Same-Sex Offenders in Late Eighteenth Century Amsterdam," *Journal of the History of Sexuality* 1.3 (1991).

26. In the case of heterosexual public indecency, a usual minimum penalty of three months' imprisonment and a fine of eight guilders was applied. It is interesting to note that as early as 1826 ten men who had been found guilty of homosexual public indecency in Amsterdam appealed their case, successfully contesting the public nature of their acts. My preliminary research into these cases indicates that they became crucial in the nineteenth-century debate on the legal and political definition of "public" and "private."

27. Van der Meer, *Sodoms.*

28. GAU REA 15b, REA 16.

29. RANH PGNH 114, no. 609.

30. Florike Egmond, "De hoge jurisdicties van het 18e-eeuwse Holland. Een aanzet tot de bepaling van hun aantal, ligging en begrenzing," *Holland* 19 (1987).

31. Arend Huusen, Jr., "De rechtspraak in strafzaken voor het Hof van Holland in het eerste kwart van de achttiende eeuw," *Holland* 8 (1976).

32. Van der Meer, *De Wesentlijke.*

33. G.M. Cohen Tervaert, *Historische-Juridische Beschouwing over een Reeks Crimineele Processen, Gevoerd in 1731 in den Rechtstoel Oosterdeel-Langewold* (The Hague: Mouton, 1921); Boomgaard.

34. Huussen, Jr., "Prosecution of Sodomy in Eighteenth-Century Frisia, Netherlands," in Kent Gerard and Hekma (eds.), *The Pursuit of Sodomy: Male Homosexuality in Renaissance and Enlightenment Europe* (New York and London: Haworth, 1988).

35. Florike Egmond, "Fragmentatie, rechtsverscheidenheid en rechtsongelijkheid in de Noordelijke Nederlanden tijdens de zeventiende en achttiende eeuw," in Sjoerd Faber (ed.), *Nieuw Licht op Oude Justitie. Misdaad en Straf ten Tijde van de Republiek* (Muiderberg: Coutinho, 1989).

36. Van Der Meer, *Sodoms,* and *De Wesentlijke.*

37. W. van Iterson, *Geschiedenis der Confiscatie in Nederland. Een Rechtshis-*

torische Studie aan de Hand van Noord-Nederlandse, een Aantal Zuid-Nederlandse en Andere Bronnen (Utrecht: H. de Vroede, 1957).

38. Jan Wagenaar, *Vaderlandsche Historie, Vervattende de Geschiedenissen der nu Verenigde Nederlanden, Inzonderheid van Holland*, 21 vols. (Amsterdam, 1729–45), vol. 19, p. 41.

39. English newspapers like *The Free Britton* and the *St. James Evening Post*, in particular, spread stories about such unrest. Inquiries made by the ambassador in England found that such stories originated at the London Stock Exchange but were derived from correspondents in Holland; *Resolutien Staaten Generaal* (1730), pp. 422-74.

40. ARA HvH 291.

41. Van der Meer, *Sodoms*, and "De geboorte van een homoseksuele minderheid," in M. Gijswijt-Hofstra, *Eeen Schijn van Verdraagzaamheid. Afwijking en Tolerantie in Nederland van de Zestiende Eeuw tot Heden* (Hilversum: Verloren, 1989).

42. Leo Boon, "Those Damned Sodomites: Public Images of Sodomy in the Eighteenth Century Netherlands," in Gerard and Hekma (eds.), *Pursuit of Sodomy*.

43. Cohen Tervaert, *Historische-Juridische*.

44. Between 1749 and 1752 several arrests on sodomy charges were made in Amsterdam, The Hague and Delft. GAA RA 5061-536, 44r–54v; GADH OA 5719; RA 3; ARA HvH 5458.9; HvH 303; GADe ORA 51, 90r–91r; ORA 84, 45r. None of the men involved was actually convicted because of sodomy. Court records in Delft refer to "numerous" men who had fled The Hague in 1749. In the same year the prosecutor of the Court of Holland was not allowed by the court to provide information about sodomites to the local court in The Hague; ARA HvH 303. Aside from that, in 1749 riots also occurred in The Hague between Jews and members of a diplomatic delegation from Tripoli after a Jewish boy had been raped by a member of this delegation. ARA HvH 415, 215r–234v; HvH 5449.15.

45. Van der Meer, *De Wesentlijke*.

46. Van der Meer, *Sodoms*.

47. ARA HvH 5661, fo 115r–117r. See also Isaac van den Berg, *Nederlands Advys Boek*, 2 vols. (Amsterdam, 1694); and Pieter Loens, *Regtelyke Aanmerkingen omtrent Eenige Poincten Concernerende de Execrabele Sonde tegens de Natuur* (Rotterdam, 1760).

48. Sjoerd Faber, *Strafrechtspleging en Criminaliteit in Amsterdam, 1680-1811* (Arnhem: Gouda Quint, 1983).

49. Van der Meer, *Sodoms.*

50. Garroting meant that the culprit was put at a stake and strangled from behind with a cord. GAA 5029 (1730).

51. Trumbach, "Gender."

52. ARA HvH 5851, fo 11v–13v.

53. Berents, "Homoseksualiteit."

54. *Ibid.*

55. ARA HvH 5673.

56. RAZ HS 867.

57. GADe ORA 48, 13r–v.

58. GAA 5061–534; 5061–580, fo 106v.

59. GADH RA 106, fo 3r–4r.

60. ARA HvH 5248.2.

61. ARA HvH 5337.1.

62. Van den Berg, *Nederlands Advys Boek.*

63. Bruce Rodgers, *The Queens' Vernacular, a Gay Lexicon* (San Francisco: Straight Arrow Books, 1972).

64. GAA 5061–334, fo 94r.

65. ARA HvH 5374.18.

66. GAR SA 121, fo 218.

67. Van der Meer, *Sodoms.*

68. ARA HvH 5661, 103v–105r.

69. ARA HvH 5420.3.

70. Van der Meer, *De Wesentlijke.*

71. Van der Meer, "Zodoms Zaat in de Republiek," and *De Wesentlijke.*

72. Hester Lunsingh Scheurleer, "Diefstal, prostitutie en andere slechtigheden. Vrouwen in Amsterdamse Confessieboeken uit de achttiende eeuw," in *Vijfde Jaarboek Vrouwengeschiedenis* (Nijmegen: SUN, 1984).

73. GAU RA 2244 (1750–I).

74. See n.29.

75. Van der Meer, *Sodoms.*

76. Van der Meer, "Zodoms Zaat."

77. GAR SA 145, fo 214.

78. See list in GAU RA 2227.

79. Van der Meer, "Zodoms Zaat."

80. Van der Meer, *Sodoms,* and *De Wesentlijke.*

81. GADo ORA 312.

82. Philip Christian Molhuysen et al., *Nieuw Nederlandsch Biografisch Woordenboek*, 10 vols. (Leiden: A.W. Sijthoff, 1911–37).

83. In the notarial records of GADH there are numerous references to Husson's financial dealings with others, from the early 1770s on. Most of these others were prosecuted between 1774 and 1779. See van der Meer, *Sodoms*.

84. ARA HvH 5510.6; GAA 5061–538, fo 197–198.

85. ARA HvH 5515.1. These letters were found with others in the luggage of Floris Husson when he was arrested in Amsterdam. They were sent to the local court in The Hague and to the Court of Holland, where they were copied. Only the copies of the letters of van Amerongen and Mulder survived.

86. GAA 5061–536, fo 89r–112r.

87. Pieter Spierenburg, *The Spectacle of Suffering: Executions and the Evolution of Repression: From a Preindustrial Metropolis to the European Experience* (Cambridge: Cambridge University Press, 1984).

88. Van der Meer, *Sodoms*.

89. GAU RA 2244 (1730-I); GAU RA 2236 (1730), fo 434–441.

90. GAU Records Reformed Orphanage 47, fo 271–275; GAA 5061–53, fo 384–449; 5061–538, fo 9–55.

91. ARA HvH 5661, fo 203r–212v.

92. ARA HvH 5420.3.

93. Arie Theodorus Deursen, *Plain Lives in a Golden Age: Popular Culture, Religion and Society in Seventeenth-Century Holland* (Cambridge: Cambridge University Press, 1991).

94. Quoted in P.J. van Dranen and H. Lewandowski, *Beschavings- en Zedengeschiedenis van Nederland* (Amsterdam, 1731), p. 265.

95. GAU RA 2244 (1730-I).

96. GAU RA 2244 (1730-II).

97. Van der Meer, *Sodoms*.

98. ARA HvH 5420.3.

99. Compare ARA HvH 5420.3.

100. GAU RA 2227.

101. Van der Meer, "Gezangen in den Kerker. De Temige gedichten van een sodomiet," *Homologie* 12.1 (1990).

102. GAR ORA 251, fo 15r–16r.

103. Van der Meer, *Sodoms*.

104. RAG HJK 1995.

105. GAU RA 469-13.

106. GAA 5061-538, fo 287.

107. GAA 5061-640M2.

108. Van de Pol, "Seksualiteit tussen middeleeuwen en moderne tijd," in Harry Peeters et al. (eds.), *Vijf Eeuwen Gezinsleven, Liefde, Huwelijk en Opvoeding in Nederland* (Nijmegen: SUN, 1988).

109. ARA HvH 5420.3.

110. GAA Library B 54 HS Diary Jacob Bicker Raije, 295.

111. GAA 5061-537, fo 426.

112. ARA HvH 5420.3

113. GAA 5061-491, fo 48, 64.

114. ARA HvH 5248.2.

115. ARA HvH 5337.1.

116. Alan Bray, "Homosexuality and the Signs of Male Friendship in Elizabethan England," *History Workshop Journal* 29 (1990).

117. RAZ, Records Vrije van Sluis, 1695.

118. ARA HvH 5420.3.

119. The letters were copied to be used by the prosecutor. The originals have been lost. The copies are to be found in GADo ORA 312.

120. ARA HGH 395. The file contains three original love letters from Jan van Zaanen in Leiden to Kees Cornelissen in Amsterdam. The letters had been confiscated after the latter's arrest in that city for public indecency. After his conviction, Cornelissen appealed to the High Court, and the evidence – including the letters – was turned over to that court.

121. Justus van Effen, *De Hollansche Spectator* (Maart: n.p., 1732), p. 71. Leo Boon, "Those Damned Sodomites," wrongly claimed that van Effen referred to sodomites with this expression.

122. GAU RA 2244 (1731-I).

123. GAA 5061-536, fo 35v.

124. ARA HvH 4733.

125. GAU RA 469-27.

126. GAA 5061-540, fo 36.

127. ARA HvH 5374.1.

128. GAU RA 2244 (1730-I).

129. ARA HvH 5030.1.

130. GAR SA 239 A.

131. GAA 5061-536, 46v, 48r-v.

132. GAA 5061-537, fo 343.

133. GAA 5061-539, fo 328-330.

134. GAA 5061-536, fo 47v.

135. Florike Egmond, *Banditisme in de Franse Tijd. Profiel van de Grote Neder-landse Bende 1790-1799* (Soest: de Bataafse Leeuw, 1986).

136. GAA NA 13294, no. 419.

137. Compare Hekma, "Homosexual Behavior," and van der Meer, *Sodoms.*

138. It is rather curious, of course, that historiography would use such a metaphor for an era that was long thought to be a period of political and economic decline as well.

139. GADH RA 111, fo 86v-87v.

140. GAA 5061-537, fo 410.

141. GADH AHK 289. Both their names are listed in 1791.

142. ARA HvH 5420.3

143. GADH RA 43. A description of his appearance is also to be found in the *Rotterdamsche Courant*, August 24, 1797.

144. ARA HvH 5510.6.

145. ARA HvH 4733.

146. ARA HvH 5420.3.

147. GAA 5061-538, 226.

148. GAU RA 2244.

149. Jan Oosterhof, "Sodomy at Sea and at the Cape of Good Hope During the Eighteenth Century," in Gerard and Hekma (eds.), *Pursuit of Sodomy.*

150. Van der Meer, *De Wesentlijke.*

151. RAU HvU 97.1.

152. GAA 5061-536, fo 43Br-43Gv.

153. Teela M. Aerts, "Het verfoeijelijke crimen van sodomie: Sodomie op VOC-Schepen in de 18e eeuw," *Leidschrift* 4 (1988).

154. GAU RA 2227; RA 2236 (1727-1740), fo 994-1001; B.R. Burg, *Sodomy and the Pirate Tradition: English Sea Rovers in the Seventeenth-Century Caribbean* (New York: New York University Press, 1984).

155. GAU RA 2244 (1730-I).

156. ARA HvH 5420.3.

157. So many variables are involved that it makes little sense to quantify this material here.

158. Noordam, "Homosexualiteit."

159. Herman Diederiks, *Een stad in Verval. Amsterdam omstrecks 1800, Demografisch, Economisch, Ruimtelijk* (Amsterdam, 1982).

160. GADH DTB.

161. GAA DTB.

162. GAA 5072-55 HS Weveringh, fo 40.

163. GAA 5061-537, fo 388.

164. ARA HGH 632, no. 392.

165. ARA StS 355, no. 138.

166. ARA StS 6, no. 12.

167. GAU RA 2244 (1730-I).

168. ARA HvH 5515.1.

169. GADH NA 4201, no. 1157.

170. Van der Meer, *Sodoms.*

171. GADH NA 111, fo 280r-281r, fo 282r-283r; NA 113, fo 183r-v.

172. ARA HvH 4582.

173. Van der Meer, *Sodoms.*

174. GAA 5061-538, fo 301.

175. ARA HvH 5472.

176. Trumbach, "Gender."

177. Donald Haks, *Huwelijk en Gezin in Holland in de 17 en 18e Eeuw. Processtukken en Moralisten over Aspecten van het Laat 17e en 18e-eeuwse Gezinsleven* (Assen: Van Gorcum, 1982).

178. Thomas Laqueur, *Making Sex: Body and Gender from the Greeks to Freud* (Cambridge, MA: Harvard University Press, 1990).

179. Marinus Johannes Antonie de Vrijer, "De storm van het crimen nefandum in de jaren 1730-1732," in *Nederlandsch Archief voor Kerkgeschiedenis, XXV/XXVI* (The Hague, 1933).

180. Herman Roodenburg, *Onder Censuur. De Kerkelijke Tucht in de Gereformeerde Gemeente van Amsterdam, 1578-1700* (Hilversum: Verloren, 1990).

181. J. Hondius, *Swart Register van Duysent Sonden* (Amsterdam, 1679).

182. Hendricus Carolus van Byler, *Helsche Boosheit of Grouwelyke Zonde van Sodomie* (Groningen, 1731), p. 78.

183. Van der Meer, *Sodoms.*

184. Jacobus Viverius, *De Winter Avonden of Nederlandsche Vertellingen* (Rotterdam, 1636).

185. Donald Haks, "Libertinisme en Nederlands Verhalend Proza, 1650-1700," in Hekma and Roodenburg (eds.), *Soete Minne en Helsche Boosheit.*

186. Judges would often look for earlier precedents, as can be seen in their notes. Compare van der Meer, "Tribades." In 1798 a judge from Amsterdam, in

a tract on the question of whether the recently proclaimed separation of Church and State meant that the sodomite bill of 1730 was abolished, argued against the abolition, claiming that he had copies of court records of sodomy trials that clearly showed how evil sodomites were; see G.J. Gales, *Rechtsgeleerd Onderzoek* (Amsterdam, 1798). Such copies indeed existed; see van der Meer, *De Wesentlijke.*

187. Van der Meer, *Sodoms.*

188. Van Byler, *Helsche Boosheit.*

189. Lucien von Römer, "Der Uranismus in den Niederlanden bis zum 19.Jahrhundert, mit besonderer Berücksichtigung der grossen Uranierverfolgung im Jahre 1730," *Jahrbuch für Sexuelle Zwischenstufen* 8 (1906); van der Meer, *De Wesentlijke.*

190. Van der Meer, *Sodoms*, and *De Wesentlijke.*

191. Anton Blok, "Theatrische strafvoltrekkingen onder het ancien régime," *Symposion* 1 (1979).

192. Leonardus Beels, *Sodoms Zonde en Straffe of Strengwraakrecht over Vervloekte Boosheit* (Amsterdam, 1730); Coenraat Mel, *Het Gruwlyk Sodom Gestraft* (Amsterdam, 1731); Jean Frédéric Ostervald, *Verhandeling tegen de Onkuischheit* (Amsterdam, 1730); Albertus Royaards, *Nodige en Tydige Waarschouwing aan Sodoms Grouwelyke Zonde en Vreeselyke Straffe* (Nijmegen, 1731); van Byler, *Helsche Boosheit*; Tako Hajo van den Honert, *De Grouwelikheid en Verfoeyelikheid der Hoerery, Wegens de Nu Doorgebrookene Schandelijkheeden ter Waarschouwing Voorgestelt* (Leiden, 1730).

193. David M. Halperin, *One Hundred Years of Homosexuality and Other Essays on Greek Love* (New York: Routledge, Chapman & Hall, 1990).

194. Compare Peter Brown, *The Body and Society: Men, Women and Sexual Renunciation in Early Christianity* (New York: Columbia University Press, 1988).

195. Haks, *Huwelijk en Gezin*; van Byler, *Helsche Boosheit.*

196. *Nadere Bedenkingen over het Straffen van Zekere Schandelyke Misdaad* (Amsterdam, 1777).

197. Van der Meer, *Sodoms.*

198. Van Byler, *Helsche Boosheit*, pp. 121–22.

199. *Ibid.*, p. 130.

200. Laqueur, *Making Sex.*

201. Van Byler, *Helsche Boosheit*, p. 51.

202. I. Leonard Leeb, *The Ideological Origins of the Batavian Revolution: History and Politics in the Dutch Republic, 1747–1800* (The Hague: Nijhoff, 1973).

203. Compare van Byler, *Helsche Boosheit.*

204. Van der Meer, "Jakob Campo Weyerman en de Sodomietenvervolgingen van 1730," *Mededelingen van de Stichting Jakob Campo Weyerman* 16.2 (1993).

205. Pieter Loens, *Regtelyke Aanmerkingen.*

206. Jakob Campo Weyerman, *Godgeleerde Zeedekundige en Historische Bedenkingen over den text des Apostels Pauli aen de Romeynen, Cap. I vers 27* (Amsterdam, 1730), pp. 2–8.

207. Van der Meer, *Sodoms.*

208. GADH RA 31.

209. GAU RA 469-16.

210. Cohen Tervaert, *Historische-Juridische.*

211. Van der Meer, *De Wesentlijke.*

212. GAA 5061-604M-2.

213. Spierenburg, *Spectacle of Suffering.*

214. Van der Meer, *De Wesentlijke.*

215. ARA RvS 796-I.

216. GAR ORA 250, fo 118v–121r.

217. GAA 5061-50.

218. GAU RA 2244 (1751-I). It involves a copy of a record from Delft that was sent by the court to Utrecht.

219. Franciscus Lievens Kersteman, *Hollandsch Rechtsgeleerd Woordenboek* (Amsterdam, 1768), p. 528.

220. *Nadere Bedenkingen*, p. 8.

221. Trumbach, "The Birth of the Queen: Sodomy and the Emergence of Gender Equality in Modern Culture, 1600-1750," in Martin Duberman, Martha Vicinus and George Chauncey (eds.), *Hidden from History: Reclaiming the Gay and Lesbian Past* (New York: New American Library, 1989).

222. Kersteman, *Hollandsch*, p. 528.

223. *Nadere Bedenkingen*, p. 9.

224. Van der Meer, *Sodoms.*

225. ARA HvH 5661, fo 103r–119v.

226. GAA 5072-50 HS Weveringh, fo 32.

227. GAU RA 469-13.

228. GAU RA 2244 (1762-II).

229. ARA HGH 664.

230. ARA HvH 5506.4.

231. GAA 5061-536, fo 43 Ir.

232. Hekma, "Homosexual Behavior."

233. Van der Meer, *De Wesentlijke.*

234. Van der Meer, "Gezangen."

235. Van der Meer, *Sodoms.*

236. GAU RA 2244 (1730-I).

237. GAU RA 2236 (1727-1750), fo 380; RA 2236 (1751-1758), fo 953.

238. GAA 5061-538, fo 22.

239. Weyerman, *Godgeleerde,* pp. 77-78, referred to a Dutch translation of Rochester's seventeenth-century *Sodom or the Quintessence of Debauchery,* which contains one of the most notorious statements about a "rake" keeping his catamite on his one arm and his mistress on the other.

240. GAU RA 2244 (1730-I).

241. Van Deursen, *Plain Lives.*

242. Roodenburg, *Onder Censuur.*

243. Van der Meer, *Sodoms.*

244. GADH NA 4589, no. 80.

245. ARA HvH 5515.1.

246. ARA HvH 5472.

247. Loens, *Regtelyke Aanmerkingen,* p. A-2.

248. ARA HvH 5510.6.

249. GAA 5061-536, fo 181.

250. ARA HGH 395.

251. ARA HVH 5420.3.

252. ARA HvH 5515.1.

253. GADo ORA 312.

254. GAA 5061-539, fo 328-66.

255. ARA HGH 395.

256. GAA 5061-539, fo 82.

257. Hendrik Herderschee was quite an opportunist in these matters. While in prison he started to write poems published – *Gezangen in den Kerker* (Songs in prison) – in 1819 by a benefactor, Willem Goede. Although nowhere in his poems did he refer to the actual reason he was convicted, Herderschee, like the Church ministers in 1730, blamed his craving for luxury and gluttony for his youthful misdemeanors. It won him the support of the poet laureate of his day, Hendrik Tollens, and an early release from prison; van der Meer, "Gezangen."

258. GAA 5061-539, fo 125.

259. ARA HvH 5248.2.

260. ARA HvH 5374.1.

261. ARA HvH 5420.3.

262. ARA HvH 5661, fo 203r–212v.

263. Van der Meer, "Zodoms Zaat."

264. GAA 5061-536, fo 67r.

265. GAA 5061-536, fo 50r.

266. GAA NA 13294, no. 419.

267. Noordam, "Homosexualiteit."

268. Roodenburg, *Onder Censuur.*

269. ARA HvH 5420.3.

270. GAA 5061-537, fo 384–398.

271. ARA HvH 328; GADH OA 774, fo 42r–83v.

272. *Ibid.*

273. GAU RA 2244 (1732).

274. GAA 5061-334, fo 77v–275v.

275. GAA 5061-392, fo 94r; 5061-393, fo 11v–29v.

276. GAA Library B 54 HS Diary Jacob Bicker Raije, fo 38.

277. ARA HvH 5506.4.

278. ARA HGH 395.

279. Herman Franke, *Twee Eeuwen Gevangen. Misdaad en Straf in Nederland* (Utrecht: Het Spectrum, 1990).

280. ARA REA The Hague 15, 31 no. 141.

281. GAA 5061-539, fo 328–374; 5061-540, fo 1–42.

282. ARA HvH 5432.

283. GAA 5061-388, 27v–31r.

284. GAA 5072-55 HS Weveringh, fo 307.

285. *Alle de Copyen van Indagingen als mede alle de Gedichten op de Tegenwoordige Tyd Toepasselyk,* 2 vols. (Amsterdam, 1730); *Schouw-toneel soo der Geëxecuteerden als Ingedaagde over de Verfoeilijcke Misdaad van Sodomie,* 2 vols. (1730).

286. Bray, *Homosexuality in Renaissance England* (London: GMP, 1982); Trumbach, *Sodomy Trials. Seven Documents* (New York and London: Garland, 1986).

287. *Pleidooi of Regtbank tegen alle Debauchante Quaadlevende en Ontaarde mannen, van deze Tegenwoordige Tyd. Door een Voornaam Liefhebber* (Amsterdam, 1730), p. 2.

288. Weyerman, *Godgeleerde Zeedekundige en Historische Bedenkingen over den text der Spreuken Salomons, Kap. 28. Vaers 15, 17* (Amsterdam, 1730), p. 28.

289. Weyerman (1677–1747) was on a constant collision course with the

legal authorities. He ended his life in prison after being sentenced in 1738 for blackmail.

290. Machteld Bouman, "Het verbod op de vrijmetselarij in 1735. Een herziene analyse van de motieven," *Skript* 9 (1988).

291. GAA 5061-537, fo 343.

CHAPTER FOUR: "A FEMALE SOUL IN A MALE BODY"

1. For an overview of this discussion of sexuality, see Annemarie Wettley, *Von der "Psychopathia sexualis" zur Sexualwissenschaft* (Stuttgart: Enke, 1959); Georges Lanteri-Laura, *Lecture des perversions. Histoire de leur appropriation médicale* (Paris: Masson, 1979); Frank Sulloway, *Freud, Biologist of the Mind* (New York: Basic Books, 1979), ch. 8; on homosexuality, see Gert Hekma, *Homoseksualiteit, een medische reputatie. De uitdoktering van de homoseksueel in negentiende-eeuws Nederland* (Amsterdam: SUA, 1987), ch. 2; and for Hirschfeld, see Manfred Herzer, *Magnus Hirschfeld. Leben und Werk eines jüdischen, schwulen und sozialistischen Sexologen* (Frankfurt/New York: Campus, 1992).

2. Magnus Hirschfeld and Max Tilke, *Die Transvestiten: Eine Untersuchung über den erotischen Verkleidungstrieb* (Berlin: Pulvermacher, 1910).

3. In this essay all terms as used by the cited authors will be indicated with quotation marks; "same-sex preference" will be used as the general expression.

4. Pivotal in the debate on the history of homosexuality has been the work of Michel Foucault, especially his *History of Sexuality: Vol. 1* (New York: Random House, 1990), although the theme is discussed only on pp. 42–44; for the discussion on the gender inversion of homosexuals the work of Randolph Trumbach has been important; see his essay in this volume, and "Gender and the Homosexual Role in Modern Western Culture: The 18th and 19th Centuries Compared," in Dennis Altman et al., *Homosexuality, Which Homosexuality?* (Amsterdam and London: An Dekker/Schorer, GMP, 1989).

5. The best studies on Tissot and masturbation are Théodore Tarczylo, *Sexe et liberté au siècle des Lumières* (Paris: Presses de la Renaissance, 1983) and Jean Stengers and Anne Van Neck, *Histoire d'une grande peur: la masturbation* (Brussels: Editions de l'Unversité de Bruxelles, 1984).

6. J.B.F. Descuret, *La Médecine des passions* (Paris: Béchet et Labé, 1841).

7. Heinrich Kaan, *Psychopathia sexualis*, unpublished dissertation, University of Leipzig, 1844.

8. Claude François Michéa, "Des Déviations de l'appétit vénérien," *Union médical*, July 17, 1849, pp. 338–39.

9. Balzac used this term in his *Splendeur et misères des courtisanes* (1834); see Claude Courouve, *Vocabulaire de l'homosexualité* (Paris: Payot, 1985), p. 215.

10. Johann Ludwig Casper, "Über Nothzucht und Päderastie und deren Ermittlung seitens des Gerichtsartztes: Nach eigenen Beobachtungen," *Viertel-jahrsschrift für gerichtliche und öffentliche Medicin* 1 (1852), and *Handbuch der gerichtlichen Medicin*, vol. 2 (Berlin: Hirschwald, 1858).

11. In 1859, the philosopher Arthur Schopenhauer discussed pederasty as a result of senility; see his *Die Welt als Wille und Vorstellung*, 4th ed. (Leipzig: P. Reclam, 1873), pp. 643–51.

12. See Jörg Hütter, *Die gesellschaftliche Kontrolle des homosexuellen Begehrens: Medizinische Definitionen und juristische Sanktionen im 19. Jahrhundert* (Frankfurt: Campus, 1992), pp. 68–71.

13. Ambroise Tardieu, *Etude médico-légale sur les attentats aux moeurs* (Paris, 1857; 5th ed., Paris: Baillière, 1867), pp. 197–210.

14. Richard von Krafft-Ebing, *Psychopathia sexualis mit besonderer Berück-sichtigung der conträren Sexualempfindung: Eine klinisch-forensische Studie* (Stuttgart: Enke, 1886).

15. See Hütter, *Kontrolle*, p. 108, with a tabulation of the results of the changes in medical and legal circles.

16. Hieronymus Fränkel, "Homo mollis," *Medizinische Zeitung* 22 (1853).

17. F. Dohrn, "Zur Lehre von der Päderastie," *Vierteljahrsschrift für gericht-liche und öffentliche Medicin* 8 (1855).

18. Karl Heinrich Ulrichs, "Vier Briefe," *Jahrbuch für sexuelle Zwischenstufen* (Leipzig, 1899), vol. 1, pp. 35–70; reprinted in *Documents of the Homosexual Rights Movement in Germany, 1836–1927*, ed. Jonathan Katz (New York: Arno, 1975). Pages cited below refer to this last facsimile edition.

19. *Ibid.*, p. 59. *Geschlechtlich* has the same ambivalence as "sexual" has in English, referring to both gender and sexuality.

20. *Ibid.*, pp. 44 and 50.

21. *Ibid.*, p. 55.

22. *Ibid.*, p. 54.

23. On Ulrichs, see Hubert Kennedy, *Ulrichs: The Life and Works of Karl Heinrich Ulrichs, Pioneer of the Modern Gay Movement* (Boston: Alyson, 1988); Ulrichs's twelve books and pamphlets on Uranian love (eleven between 1864 and 1870 and a kind of afterword in 1879) were reprinted by Magnus Hirschfeld (in a slightly changed form) as *Forschungen über das Rätsel der mannmännlichen Liebe* (Leipzig: M. Spohr, 1898; reprint, New York: Arno, 1975). References will

be to the 1975 reprint. Only in his main book, *Memnon* (1868), in *Forschungen*, was the phrase "*anima muliebris in corpore virili inclusa*" used, for the first time to my knowledge (p. 195).

24. For the German laws on homosexuality, see Hütter, *Kontrolle*, and Fritz Eduard Rosenberger, *Das Sexualstrafrecht in Bayern von 1813–1870* (Marburg, 1973).

25. [Alois Geigel], *Das Paradoxon der Venus Urania* (Würzburg, 1869), p. 14; reprinted in Joachim S. Hohmann (ed.), *Der Unterdrückte Sexus: Historische Texte und Kommentare zur Homosexualität* (Lollar: Achenbach, 1977).

26. See Ulrichs, *Inclusa* (1864), in *Forschungen*, pp. 16–25, and *Memnon* (1868), in *Forschungen*, pp. 26–33; in *Memnon*, he states that the body of the Uranian is not fully masculine and the soul not completely feminine (p. 195).

27. On Carl Ernst Wilhelm von Zastrow, see *Capri: Zeitschrift für schwule Geschichte* 2.2 (Sept. 1988), pp. 3–14, with some documents and an introduction by Manfred Herzer.

28. See his *Vindicta* (1865), in *Forschungen*, pp. 38–41, and most clearly and fully in *Ara spei* (1865), in *Forschungen*, pp. 61–98, esp. p. 84.

29. See esp. Ulrichs, *Inclusa* (1864), in *Forschungen*, p. 46.

30. For Virchow, see his letter to Ulrichs, cited in *Ara spei* (1865), in *Forschungen*, p. 72; Geigel, *Paradoxon*, p. 34. Otto Weininger developed a comparable theory. He believed that men and women were never entirely masculine or feminine but that in coupling, they realize complete masculinity and femininity with the lacking masculinity of the man being compensated for by that of the woman. The theory could also be applied to same-sex couples and thus corroborates Ulrichs's view; see Weininger, *Geschlecht und Charakter: Eine prinzipielle Untersuchung* (Vienna/Leipzig: Braumuller, 1903).

31. See esp. Ulrichs, *Memnon* (1868), in *Forschungen*, pp. 51–57, after which he continues with the possibility of *Virilisierung* (masculinization) of Uranians because they wish to be men or to conform to social, masculine norms, with the parallel possibility of Uranization of Dionian men.

32. Later, Karl Günter Heimsoth developed a special theory of *Homophilie*, or sexual attraction between similar poles (virile man with virile man or woman), contra the idea of sexual attraction between opposites, which he named "*Heterophilie*"; see his dissertation, *Hetero- und Homophilie...* (Rostock, 1925).

33. [Karl Maria Kertbeny], *Paragraph 143 des preussischen Strafgesetzbuches...* (Leipzig: Serbe, 1869); reprinted in *Jahrbuch für sexuelle Zwischenstufen* 7 (1905);

and *Das Gemeinschädliche des par. 143 des preussischen Strafgesetzbuches...* (Leipzig: Serbe, 1870).

34. Virchow was one of the experts who signed the "Gutachten der Königlichen wissenschaftlichen Deputation für das Medizinalwesen" (1869), reprinted in *Jahrbuch für sexuelle Zwischenstufen* 7 (1905).

35. Alexander Lacassagne, "Péderastie," in *Dictionnaire encyclopédique des sciences médicales* (Paris: Asselin, 1886), vol. 74, pp. 239–59; Julien Chevalier, *De l'Inversion de l'instinct sexuel au point de vue médico-légale* (Lyon, 1885); Alfred Binet, *Le Fétichisme dans l'amour* (Paris, 1888); Jean-Martin Charcot and Valentin Magnan, "Inversion du sens génital," *Archives de neurologie* 3–4 (1882); Magnan, "Des Anomalies, des aberrations et des perversions sexuelles," *Annales médico-psychologiques* 43 (1885); Benjamin Ball, *La folie érotique* (Paris: Baillière, 1888); and Paul Moreau, *Des Aberrations du sens génésique* (Paris: Asselin, 1880).

36. Cesare Lombroso, "Amore nei pazzi," *Archivio di psichiatria, anthropologia criminale e scienze penale* 2 (1881); Arrigo Tamassia, "Sull'inversione dell'istinto sessuale," *Rivista sperimentale di freniatria e medicina legale* 4 (1878); Paolo Mantegazza, *Gli amori degli uomini* (Milan, 1886); Benjamin M. Tarnowsky, *Die krankhaften Erscheinungen des Geschlechtssinnes* (Berlin, 1886), which appeared a year earlier in Russia; Havelock Ellis and John Addington Symonds, *Sexual Inversion* (London: Wilson and MacMillan, 1897); Nicolaas Bernard Donkersloot, "Klinisch-forensische betekenis der perverse geslachtsdrift," *Geneeskundige Courant* 37.8–14 (1883); Arnold Aletrino, "La Situation sociale de l'uraniste," *Congrès international de l'anthropologie criminelle: Compte rendu des travaux de la cinquième session* (Amsterdam, 1901).

37. The term was introduced with the establishment of the *Zeitschrift für Sexualwissenschaft*, edited by Magnus Hirschfeld. The journal existed for only one year. The main books of the new sexology were Albert Moll, *Untersuchungen über die Libido sexualis* (Berlin: Fischer, 1897); Sigmund Freud, *Drei Abhandlungen zur Sexualtheorie* (Vienna/Leipzig: Deuticke, 1905); and Iwan Bloch, *Das Sexualleben unserer Zeit in seinen Beziehungen zur modernen Kultur* (Berlin: L. Marcus, 1906).

38. Karl Frierich Otto Westphal, "Die conträre Sexualempfindung," *Archiv für Psychiatrie und Nervenkrankheiten* 2 (1869), p. 107.

39. He thus confused theories on innate vs. learned sexual inversion, since an apparantly innate characteristic, the neuropathic condition, was caused by social circumstances, that is, by insufficient nutrition. This mixing of biological and social (and also geographical) causes was typical of all theories of degen-

eration since Bénédict August Morel's seminal *Traité des dégénérescences physiques, intellectuelles et morales de l'espèce humaine* (Paris: Baillière, 1857).

40. See, for example, H. Gock, "Beitrag zur Kenntniss der conträren Sexualempfindung," *Archiv für Psychiatrie und Nervenkrankheiten* 5 (1875); in two cases of a male and female, both Jewish, on p. 574, the author states that Jews have a strong sexual drive; F. Servaes, "Zur Kenntniss von der conträren Sexualempfindung," *Archiv für Psychiatrie und Nervenkrankheiten* 6 (1876); Stark (no first name given), "Über conträre Sexualempfindung," *Allgemeine Zeitschrift für Psychiatrie und psychisch-gerichtliche Medicin* 33 (1877).

41. Von Krafft-Ebing, "Über gewisse Anomalien des Geschlechtstriebes…," *Archiv für Psychiatrie und Nervenkrankheiten* 7 (1877), pp. 307–08.

42. Von Krafft-Ebing, *Psychopathia sexualis*, 5th enlarged ed. (Stuttgart: Enke, 1890), pp. 121–23.

43. Th. Ramien [= Hirschfeld], *Sappho und Sokrates oder wie erklärt man die Liebe der Männer und Frauen zu Personen des eigenen Geschlechts?* (Leipzig, 1896).

44. "Petition an die gesetzgebenden Körperschaften des deutschen Reiches behufs Abänderung des par. 175…," *Jahrbuch für sexuelle Zwischenstufen* 1 (1899).

45. Von Krafft-Ebing, "Neue Studien auf dem Gebiete der Homosexualität," *Jahrbuch für sexuelle Zwischenstufen* 3 (1901).

46. Elisar von Kupffer, "The Ethical-Political Significance of Lieblingminne," in Harry Oosterhuis and Hubert Kennedy (eds.), *Homosexuality and Male Bonding in Pre-Nazi Germany: The Youth Movement, the Gay Movement, and Male Bonding before Hitler's Rise. Original Transcripts from Der Eigene, the First Gay Journal in the World* (New York: Haworth, 1991). This collection gives an excellent overview of this movement, its theories and its political standpoints (which covered the full political spectrum from Nazi right to anarchist left).

47. Von Kupffer, *Lieblingsminne und Freundesliebe in der Weltliteratur: Eine Sammlung mit einer ethisch-politischen Einleitung* (Berlin, 1900).

48. Subtitled *Die physiologische Freundschaft, ein normaler Grundtrieb des Menschen und eine Frage der männlichen Gesellungsfreiheit* (Berlin: Verlag Renaissance, 1904).

49. Benedict Friedländer, "Schadet die soziale Freigabe des homosexuellen Verkehrs der kriegerischen Tüchtigkeit der Rasse? Ein vorläufiger Hinweis," *Jahrbuch für sexuelle Zwischenstufen* 7 (1905); reprinted in his posthumous collection of essays *Die Liebe Platons im Lichte der modernen Biologie* (Berlin: Zack, 1909).

50. Friedländer, *Renaissance des Eros Uranios* (1904; New York: Arno, 1975), esp. p. 222.

51. See Friedländer, "Sieben Thesen," written some days before his suicide in 1908, in *Die Liebe Platons*, pp. 277–78; trans. as "Seven Propositions," in Oosterhuis and Kennedy (eds.), *Homosexuality and Male Bonding*. For a balanced evaluation of the political philosophies of Die Gemeinschaft, see Oosterhuis, "Male Bonding and Homosexuality in German Nationalism," in Oosterhuis and Kennedy (eds.), *Homosexuality and Male Bonding*. Other theorists who came up with comparable combinations of male bonding and homoeroticism were Hans Blüher, *Die deutsche Wandervogelbewegung als erotisches Phänomen* (Berlin: Weise, 1912); and Gustav A. Wyneken, *Eros* (Lauenburg: Saal, 1921).

52. Edwin Bab, "The Women's Movement and Male Culture" (1903), in Oosterhuis and Kennedy (eds.), *Homosexuality and Male Bonding*.

53. Both Jacob Anton Schorer, the leader of the Dutch chapter, and Luciën S.A.M. von Römer had been in Berlin for sometime, were *Obmanner* of the WHK, contributed to the *Jahrbuch* and supported Hirschfeld's theory in their publications.

54. For the Uranian poets, including Symonds and Raffalovich, see Timothy d'Arch Smith, *Love in Earnest: Some Notes on the Lives and Writings of English "Uranian" Poets from 1889 to 1930* (London: Routledge and Kegan Paul, 1970).

55. The literature from and about Symonds and Carpenter is abundant. Carpenter's main texts are *Homogenic Love and Its Place in a Free Society* (Manchester, 1894) and *The Intermediate Sex* (London: Swan Sonnenschein, 1908). He also edited an anthology of homoerotic poetry, *Ioläus: An Anthology of Friendship* (London, 1902), as did von Kupffer. Symonds's contributions are *A Problem in Greek Ethics* and *A Problem in Modern Ethics*, both published privately, and *A Problem in Greek Ethics* was incorporated in his joint enterprise with Ellis, *Sexual Inversion*, which appeared after his death in 1893. See also his *Memoirs*, ed. Phyllis Grosskurth (New York, 1985).

56. Marc André Raffalovich, *Uranisme et unisexualité: Etude sur différentes manifestations de l'instinct sexuel* (Paris/Lyon: Storck, 1895). This book was an apology for male love, in which he also criticized Oscar Wilde, whose legal prosecution took place the same year in England.

57. André Gide, *Corydon* (Paris: Editions de la nouvelle revue française, 1924). For the background on Gide's theories of homosexuality, see Patrick Pollard, *André Gide: Homosexual Moralist* (New Haven, CT: Yale University Press,

1991), e.g., pp. 26-27, where inverts, sodomites and pederasts are discussed. Marcel Proust held more strictly to Hirschfeld's theory. For Proust's theory of homosexuality, see J.E. Rivers, *Proust and the Art of Love: The Aesthetics of Sexuality in the Life, Times and Art of Marcel Proust* (New York: Columbia University Press, 1980).

58. L. Canler, *Mémoires de Canler, ancien chef de la police de Sureté* (Paris, 1862; 3rd ed., 1882), vol. 2, pp. 118-23. Information on French gay terminology can be found in Claude Courouve, *Vocabulaire de l'homosexualité masculine* (Paris: Payot, 1985), but neither here nor elsewhere could I find information on "*persilleuse*."

59. Jeffrey Weeks, "Inverts, Perverts, and Mary-Annes: Male Prostitution and the Regulation of Homosexuality in England in the Nineteenth and Early Twentieth Century," *Journal of Homosexuality* 6.1-2 (Fall/Winter 1980-81), pp. 113-34.

60. Reprinted in *Documents of the Homosexual Rights Movement in Germany, 1836-1927* (New York: Arno, 1975).

61. *Documents*, p. 64ff.: "*normalgeschlechtlich*" is comparable to "trade" in the American gay slang of the 1950s.

62. Research for the period 1830-1909 for Amsterdam Court, 1870-1909 for The Hague and 1830-99 for Haarlem.

63. See Gert Hekma, "Homosexual Behaviour in the Nineteenth-Century Dutch Army," *Journal of the History of Sexuality* 2.2 (October 1991), and "Wrong Lovers in the Nineteenth-Century Netherlands," *Journal of Homosexuality* 13.2-3 (1986-87).

64. See Hekma, *Homoseksualiteit*, pp. 250-58, where the cases are summarized.

65. See Richard Ellman, *Oscar Wilde* (London: Hamilton, 1987); Henri Peyre, *Rimbaud vu par Verlaine* (Paris: Nizet, 1975); and Frédéric Bastet, *Louis Couperus: Een biografie* (Amsterdam: Querido, 1987).

66. On the new models of masculinity, see George L. Mosse, *Nationalism and Sexuality: Respectability and Abnormal Sexuality in Modern Europe* (New York: Fertig, 1985); J.A. Magnan and James Walvin (eds.), *Manliness and Morality: Middle-Class Masculinity in Britain and America, 1800-1940* (New York: St. Martin's Press, 1987).

67. See Walter L. Williams, *The Spirit and the Flesh: Sexual Diversity in American Indian Culture* (Boston: Beacon, 1986), pp. 192-96 ("Survival of Berdache Shamanism").

68. In this respect, I doubt Marjorie Garber's claim (in *Vested Interests: Cross-dressing and Cultural Anxiety* [New York: Routledge, 1992]) that transvestism as an expression of a crisis in categories subverts the binary gender system. The gender-crossing of homosexuals can also function as a *confirmation* of the binary system and as an effective way to prevent other homosexuals from coming out. It can work both ways, depending on the social situation.

69. See, for example, the essay by Trumbach in this volume along with his many other articles on the subject; Theo van der Meer, *De Wesentlijke Sonde van Sodomie en Andere Vuyligheeden. Sodomietenvervolgingen in Amsterdam 1730-1811* (Amsterdam: Tabula, 1984); Rictor Norton, *Mother Clap's Molly House: The Gay Subculture in England 1700-1830* (London: GMP, 1992).

70. Hekma et al., *De roze rand van donker Amsterdam: De opkomst van een homoseksuele kroegcultuur 1930-1970* (Amsterdam: Van Gennep, 1992).

71. Similar arguments are brought forward by John Marshall, "Pansies, Perverts and Macho Men: Changing Conceptions of Male Homosexuality," in Kenneth Plummer (ed.), *The Making of the Modern Homosexual* (London: Hutchinson, 1981); and Jamie Gough, "Theories of Sexual Identity and the Masculinization of the Gay Man," in Simon Sheperd and Mick Wallis (eds.), *Coming On Strong: Gay Politics and Culture* (London: Unwin Hyman, 1989).

72. Gilbert Herdt suggests that the different styles of coming out by successive cohorts of homosexual men follow each other and occur within quite definite periods; see his " 'Coming Out' as a Rite of Passage: A Chicago Study," in Herdt, *Gay Culture in America: Essays from the Field* (Boston: Beacon, 1992), esp. pp. 33-34. My suggestion is that different styles can coexist for longer periods. It is not a question of following each other but of one style adding to another.

73. See Mark Booth, *Camp* (London: Quartet, 1983); see also Esther Newton, *Mother Camp: Female Impersonators in America*, 2nd ed. (Chicago: University of Chicago Press, 1979).

CHAPTER FIVE: WOMAN BECOMES MAN IN THE BALKANS
Parts of this chapter are reprinted by permission and with minor alterations from my "Mannish Women of the Balkan Mountains" in *From Sappho to de Sade: Moments in the History of Sexuality*, edited by Jan Bremmer (New York and London: Routledge, 1989, 1991). The research on which this essay is based has partly been made possible by grant no. 500-276-302 of the Netherlands Organization of Scientific Research (NWO/SSCW). I owe much gratitude to Gilbert

Herdt for his encouragement and useful hints. Without his support and enthusiasm, I probably would have continued my too often idle reverie on the unfolding Yugoslavian tragedy.

In this essay I have omitted the diacritical signs on Serbo-Croatian consonants. Albanian nouns are given as often as possible in their indefinite form. For geographical terms the Serbo-Croatian spellings are used for (formerly) Yugoslavian locales (with the exception of "Belgrade" instead of "Beograd"), and Albanian spelling for the sites in the Albanian state. Personal names are spelled according to the language actually spoken by the people concerned.

1. Rudolf Dekker and Lotte van de Pol, *The Tradition of Female Transvestism in Early Modern Europe* (London: Macmillan, 1989).

2. Julie Wheelwright, *Amazons and Military Maids: Women Who Dressed as Men in Pursuit of Life, Liberty and Happiness* (London: Pandora, 1989).

3. See, for example, Christopher Boehm, *Montenegrin Social Organization and Values: Political Ethnography of a Refuge Area Tribal Adaptation* (New York: AMS Press, 1983), and *Blood Revenge: The Enactment and Management of Conflict in Montenegro and Other Tribal Societies* (Philadelphia: University of Pennsylvania Press, 1987).

4. Mary Douglas, *Purity and Danger* (London: Routledge & Kegan Paul, 1966), and *Natural Symbols* (London: Cresset Press, 1970).

5. See, for example, Kirsten Hastrup, "The Semantics of Biology: Virginity," in Shirley Ardener (ed.), *Defining Females: The Nature of Women in Society* (Oxford: Croom Helm, 1978).

6. Some examples are Marina Warner, *Alone of All Her Sex: The Myth and the Cult of the Virgin Mary* (London: Weidenfeld & Nicolson, 1976), and *Joan of Arc: The Image of Female Heroism* (New York: Knopf, 1981); Willy Jansen, *Women Without Men: Gender and Marginality in an Algerian Town* (Leiden: Brill, 1987).

7. Milan Jovanovic-Batut, "Cudna prilika (S moga puta po Crnoj Gori)," *Branik* (Dec. 12–24, 1885). Instead of "Mikas" this source mentions the (more usual) male name "Miras," which must be either a mistake or a printer's error, since Marijana Gusic (see n.9) as well as my informants all agree on the name Mikas.

8. The name Mikas was usually employed in its vocative form "Mikasu"; the same holds true for the nouns used as terms of address.

9. Gusic (-Heneberg), "Etnografski prikaz Pive i Drobnjake," *Narodna starina* 9 (1930), p. 198; "Ostajnica-tombelija-virdzin kao drustvena pojava," in *Treci kongres folklorista Jugoslavije* (Cetinje: Obod, 1958), pp. 57–58, and "Pravni

polozaj ostajnice-virdjinese u stocarskom drustvu regije Dinarida," in Vasa Cubrilović (ed.), *Odredbe pozitivnog zakonodavstva i obicajnog prava o sezonskim kretanjima stocara u jugoistocnoj Evropi kroz vekove* (Belgrade: Srpska akademija, 1976), p. 280.

10. In Serbo-Croatian past participles clearly display gender.

11. Compare Petar Milatovic, "Tobelija: Obicaj koji prkosi prirodi," *Politikin zabavnik* 29 (Nov. 1985), pp. 14–15. I thank Father Gjergj Marstijepaj O.F.M. of Tuzi for providing me with information on Tonë from the death registry.

12. Tonë (definite form Tona) is the female derivation of Ton (definite form Toni).

13. Karl Steinmetz, *Ein Vorstosz in die nordalbanischen Alpen* (Leipzig: Hartleben, 1905), pp. 50–52; Dragoslav Antonijevic, "Die Frau als Träger epischen Tradition bei einigen Balkanvölkern," *Balcanica* 1 (1970), pp. 221 and 225; Tihomir Djordjević, "Zavetovane devojke kod Arbanasa," *Sveslovenski Zbornik* (1930), p. 64.

14. Gusic, "Pravni polozaj," pp. 272–73.

15. On the Catholic connection, see René Grémaux, "Joan of Arc, Albanian Style," *Frontier: Religion East and West* (April–June 1992), pp. 10–11, and "Franciscan Friars and the Sworn Virgins of the North Albanian Tribes," *Religion, State and Society* 20.3-4 (1992). For a comparison see Grémaux, "Between Approval and Disapproval: Religious Authority and the Balkan Social Males (Catholic, Orthodox, Muslim)," paper presented in group C of the SISWO Conference, "Sexual Cultures in Europe," Amsterdam, June 24–26, 1992, pp. 41–50.

16. In 1992, a Montenegrin refugee residing in the Netherlands told me that Stana Cerovic had recently died. As yet I have received no confirmation of this.

17. The son of Borika's married sisters confided to me that the Cerovic family has about twenty female members who have remained single since partners from equal or higher-ranking families were unavailable.

18. Milatovic, "Tobelija," pp. 14–15.

19. Mirko Barjaktarovic, "Problem tobelija (virdzina) na Balkanskom poluostrvu," *Glasnik etnografskog muzeja* 29 (1966), pp. 276–77; Valbona Begolli, *Pozita e gruas në Kosovë me një vështrim të posaçem në të drejtën zakonore* (Pristina: Rilindja, 1984), p. 40.

20. Tatomir Vukanovic, "Virdzine," *Glasnik muzeja Kosova i Metohije* 6 (1961), p. 92; cf. Djordjević, *Nas narodni zivot* (Belgrade: Srpska Knjizevna Zadruga, 1923), p. 62.

21. Vukanovic, "Virdzine," p. 92.

22. Barjaktarovic, "Problem," pp. 276-77.

23. Shtjefën K. Gjeçov, *Kanuni i Lekë Dukagjinit* (Shkodër: Shtypshkroja françeskane, 1933; reprint New York: Gjonlekaj, 1989), 19, art. 29.

24. In Serbian ethnography this issue sparked controversy between Milenko Filipovic and Barjaktarovic, in which the former claimed sexual freedom and the latter sexual continence: Filipovic, "M. Barjaktarovic – Prilog proucavanju tobelija (zavetovanih devojaka)," *Glasnik etnografskog instituta srpske akademije* 1 (1952); Barjaktarovic, "Odgovor D-ru Milenku Filipovicu," *Glasnik etnografskog instituta srpske akademije* 2/3 (1953-54).

25. See, for example, Gordon Rattray Taylor, *Sex in History* (New York: Ballantine, 1954), p. 215.

26. Spiridion Gopcevic, *Oberalbanien und seine Liga: Ethnographisch-politisch-historisch* (Leipzig: Duncker and Humblot, 1881), p. 460, and *Das Fürstentum Albanien* (Berlin: Paetel, 1914), pp. 109-10.

27. Steinmetz, *Ein Vorstosz*, p. 50.

28. During his stay in tribal northern Albania of the late 1920s, Carleton S. Coon met a sworn virgin, dressed in women's clothes, who "spent the night" with one of his horsedrivers. Coon, *The Mountains of Giants: A Racial and Cultural Study of the North Albanian Mountain Ghegs* (Cambridge, MA: Peabody Museum, 1950), p. 25.

29. M. Edith Durham, *High Albania* (London: Arnold, 1909), p. 80; S.S., "Osobita Srbska Devoika," *Srbska novina ili magazin za hudozestuo, knjizestvo i modu* (March 16, 1838); Filipovic, "Has pod Pastrikom," *Djela* 2 (1958), p. 59; Dervis Korkut, "T. Djordjevic, Nas narodni zivot VI, Beograd 1932," *Zapisi* (Sept. 1932), p. 172.

30. Ernesto Cozzi, "La donna albanese con speciale riguardo al diritto consuetudinario delle Montagne di Scutari," *Anthropos* 7 (1912), p. 321.

31. Viktor Dvorsky, *Černohorskoturecká hranice od ústí Bojany k Tařе* (Prague: Rozpravy Česke Akademie, 1909), p. 130.

32. See also Coon, *Mountains*, p. 25.

33. Pelja Osman, "Tombelije," in *Gajret: Kalendar za godinu 1940 1358-1359 po hidzri* (Sarajevo, 1939), p. 167. This slaughter is perhaps the same one mentioned by Milenko Wesnitsch, "Die Blutrache bei den Südslaven," *Zeitschrift für vergeleichende Rechtswissenschaft* 8 (1889), p. 470.

34. V. Milosavleviq, "Virgjineshat (tybelijet) – Fli të votrës familjare," *Rilindja* 10.16 (1958), p. 12; Vukanovic, "Virdzine," p. 92; Barjaktarovic, "Problem," pp. 274-76; R. Reshitaj, "Fshehtësia e gjatë njëzet vjet," *Rilindja* 11.11-

22.11 (Nov. 22, 1978). Rexhai Surroi's novel *Besniku* (1st ed. Pristina: Rilindja, 1959) is based on this case.

35. Durham, *High Albania*, p. 80. Fortunately Durham also had less negative experiences with "Albanian virgins," as she preferred to call them. See, for example, pp. 101–02.

36. Durham, "High Albania and Its Customs in 1908," *Journal of the Royal Anthropological Institute of Great Britain and Ireland* 40 (1910), pp. 460–61.

37. The institution of blood-sisterhood (Serb.: *posestrimstvo*; Alb.: *motërí*) is the counterpart of blood-brotherhood (Serb.: *pobratimstvo*; Alb.: *vëllamí*). For both forms of ritual kinship see, for example, Friedrich S. Krauss, *Sitte und Brauch der Südslaven* (Vienna, 1885), pp. 619–43; S. Ciszewski, *Künstliche Verwandtschaft bei den Südslaven* (Ph.D. dissertation, Leipzig, 1897).

38. Vukanovic, "Virdzine," p. 111. In some parts of Montenegro blood-sisterhood was rare, and the few who concluded this bond made a secret of it "so that they could not be blamed for it": A. Jovicevic ("Svagdasnji obicaji-Rijecka Nahija u Crnoj Gori," *Zbornik za narodni zivot i obicaja Juznih Slovena* 11 [1906], p. 65), to whom we owe this information, explains it by reference to the minor social function and importance of blood-sisterhood as compared to blood-brotherhood. In my opinion, the alleged objectionable sexual practices between blood-sisters need to be included in the explanation. See also E.E. Evans-Pritchard, "Sexual Inversion among the Azande," *American Anthropologist* 72 (1970), p. 1432.

39. Stevan Ducic, *Zivot i obicaji plemena Kuca* (Belgrade: Srpski etnografski zbornik, 1931), pp. 235–36.

40. Barjaktarovic, "Prilog proucavanju tobelija (zavetovanih devojaka)," *Zbornik filozofskog fakulteta* 1 (1948), p. 346.

41. Vukanovic, "Virdzine," pp. 97–98, "Position of Women among Gypsies in the Kosovo-Metohija Region," *Journal of the Gypsy Lore Society* 40.3/4 (1961), p. 92, and *Romi (Cigani) u Jugoslaviji* (Vranje: Nova Jugoslavija, 1983), p. 152. My informants called Shefkije's partner Rukë (Ruka) and not Madzupka, the name mentioned by Vukanovic.

42. Vukanovic, personal communication.

43. Gusic, "Ostajnica," pp. 57 and 64, and "Pravni polozaj," pp. 274–75.

44. Johann (= Ivan) Zovko, "Ursprungsgeschichten und andere Volksmeinungen," *Wissenschaftliche Mittheilungen aus Bosnien und der Hercegovina* 1 (1893), p. 444.

45. Ivan (= Johann) Zovko, "Junakinje," *Glasnik zemaljkog muzeja u Bosni i*

Hercegovini 6 (1892), p. 270.

46. See, for example, Dekker and van de Pol, *Tradition*.

47. Vukanovic, "Virdzine," pp. 81 and 96, and personal communication.

48. See, for example, Elisabeth Tietmeyer, *Frauen heiraten Frauen: Studien zur Gynaegamie in Afrika* (Hohenschäftlarn: Renner, 1985).

49. Compare Ian Whitaker, "'A Sack for Carrying Things': The Traditional Role of Women in Northern Albanian Society," *Anthropological Quarterly* 54 (1981), p. 151. Several classificatory fictions in an African society are dealt with in Friedrich Klausberger, "Die Hochzeit des toten Jünglings: Rechtsfiktionen im Dienst der Fortpflanzung (Boma-Murle)," *Anthropos* 81 (1986).

50. Ljiljana Gavrilovic, "Tobelije: Zavet kao osnov sticanje prava i poslovne sposobnosti," *Glasnik etnografskog muzeja* 47 (1983), pp. 78–79, and personal communication. See also Vukanovic, "Virdzine," p. 92.

51. Korkut, "T. Djordjević," p. 172.

52. Vukanovic, "Virdzine," p. 89. For Albanian widows from Kosovo who adopted male clothing and assumed the position of master of the house, see Svetozar Tomic, "Jedan pogled na pogrebne narodne obicaje," *Brastvo* 30.50 (1939), p. 101.

53. Micun Pavicevic, "Crnogorke u pricama i anegdotama," *Letopis Matice Srpske* 103.325 (1930) (about the Montenegrin Milica Rovacka), p. 49.

54. Milorad Medakovic, *Zivot i obicaji Crnogoraca* (Novi Sad, 1860), p. 23n (the person is the same as referred to in n.53).

55. Vukanovic, "Virdzine," p. 96, refers to a Serbian from the mid-nineteenth century living in Sredacka Zupa in Kosovo-Metohija.

56. Durham, *High Albania*, pp. 460–61. On Durham's ambivalent gender role, cf. Dea Birkett, "Bucks, Brides, and Useless Baggage: Women's Quest for a Role in Their Balkan Travel," in John B. Allcock and Antonia Young (eds.), *Black Lambs and Grey Falcons: Women Travellers in the Balkans* (Bradford: Bradford University Press, 1991), p. 164.

57. Most information on the property rights of (Albanian) sworn virgins according to local custom is to be found in Giuseppe Valentini, "La famiglia nel diritto tradizionale albanese," *Annali lateranensi* 9 (1945), pp. 29–33.

58. In the literature it is often generally claimed that by adopting the masculine status the original female protected status was lost; see, for example, Boehm, *Blood Revenge*, p. 250 n.2. Vukanovic, however, states that traditional standards of feuding prohibited the killing of sworn virgins. They enjoyed tabolike status ("Virdzine," pp. 89 and 109).

59. Margaret Hasluck, in J.H. Hutton (ed.), *The Unwritten Law in Albania* (Cambridge: Cambridge University Press, 1954), pp. 223 and 256.

60. Article 1229-VIII of the northern Albanian codex of customary law states: "Virgins (women who dress like men): are not distinguished from other women, except that they are free to sit among men, but without the right to vote and speak." Gjeçov, *Kanuni*, p. 108.

61. See, for example, Barjaktarovic, "Tombelije," *Zeta: Nedeljni list* 9 (1939), p. 4.

62. On women acting as heads of households, see Petar S. Vlahovic, "Zene u nasem narodnom zivotu – staresine kucnih zadruga," *Borba*, April 19, 1953, p. 10. Filipovic, "Zene kao narodni glavari kod nekih balkanskih naroda," *Godisnjak balkanoloskog instituta* 2 (1961), pp. 139–57, deals with the topic of Christian Balkan women who, because of their immunity, could act as village elders in confrontation with Ottoman overlords, whereas men easily succumbed to the enemy's violence. Neither of the authors mentions cross-dressing as part of this role inversion.

63. Harold Garfinkel, *Studies in Ethnomethodology* (Englewood Cliffs, NJ: Prentice-Hall, 1967).

CHAPTER SIX: POLYNESIAN GENDER LIMINALITY
THROUGH TIME AND SPACE

1. This essay is based on fieldwork which was conducted in Vava'u, Tonga, in 1978–79 and 1981, and on Nukulaelae Atoll, Tuvalu, in 1980–82, 1985, 1990 and 1991. It was funded at various times by the National Science Foundation, the Harry F. Guggenheim Foundation, the Wenner Gren Foundation and the Fondation de la Vocation. A Rockefeller Fellowship at the Center for Pacific Islands Studies at the University of Hawaii in 1991–92 afforded me the time to think about the issues presented here in a stimulating environment, intellectually and otherwise. I thank Ian Condry, Tamar Gordon, Vili Hereniko, Alan Howard and Jeannette Mageo, whom I bullied into providing detailed criticisms on a draft of this essay at very short notice. I am particularly indebted to Hal Scheffler for his close reading of this piece, and for gently coaxing me away from facile conclusions on issues of gender and sex over the years.

Polynesia roughly includes all islands and island groups that fall within a triangle with New Zealand, Hawaii and Easter Island as its apexes. There are also isolated Polynesian communities scattered on the fringe of Melanesia and Micronesia, the so-called Polynesian Outliers, about which nothing will be said

in this essay. While the region displays a certain amount of cultural homogene-
ity, its western boundaries are fuzzy: the islands of Rotuma and Fiji, whose inhabitants do not speak Polynesian languages, resemble Polynesian societies in many
respects. It is customary to divide Polynesia proper into Western Polynesia,
which includes principally Tonga, Samoa and the smaller island groups in their
vicinity, and Eastern Polynesia, made up of Hawaii, New Zealand and all island
groups east of the Cook Islands. This division is based in part on very general
cultural patterns that distinguish the two subregions.

2. See, e.g., Suzanne J. Kessler, "The Medical Construction of Gender: Case
Management of Intersexed Infants," *Signs* 16 (1990); Thomas Laqueur, *Making
Sex: Body and Gender from the Greeks to Freud* (Cambridge, MA: Harvard Univer-
sity Press, 1990); Gayle Rubin, "The Traffic in Women: Notes on the 'Political
Economy' of Sex," in Rayna R. Reiter (ed.), *Toward an Anthropology of Women*
(New York: Monthly Review Press, 1975); Judith Shapiro, "Transsexualism:
Reflections on the Persistence of Gender and the Mutability of Sex," in Julia
Epstein and Kristina Straub (eds.), *Body Guards: The Cultural Politics of Gender
Ambiguity* (New York: Routledge, 1991).

3. Robert J. Morris, "*Aikāne*: Accounts of Hawaiian Same-Sex Relationships
in the Journals of Captain Cook's Third Voyage (1776–80)," *Journal of Homosexuality* 19.4 (1990), proposes that, in Hawaii at the time of contact, a "homosexual" was referred to as *aikāne* (which in contemporary Hawaiian translates
roughly as "friend") and that the word *māhū* was subsequently borrowed from
Tahiti. But the argument rests on a rather uncritical reading of the already equivocal historical records and fails to make problematic the categories to which
these terms refer. Raleigh Watts, "The Polynesian Mahu," in Stephen O. Murray
(ed.), *Oceanic Homosexualities* (New York: Garland, 1992), p. 171, provides "to
spring up, to grow" as a secondary meaning of the word *māhū*; however, this is
the translation of an entirely different word, *mahu*, with no etymological connection to *māhū*.

4. Arnold van Gennep, *The Rights of Passage* (1909), trans. Monika B.
Vizedom and Gabrielle L. Caffee (London: Routledge & Kegan Paul, 1960);
Victor Turner, *The Forest of Symbols: Aspects of Ndembu Ritual* (Ithaca, NY:
Cornell University Press, 1967), and *The Ritual Process: Structure and Anti-
structure* (Chicago: Aldine, 1969).

5. Compare Gilbert Herdt, "Representations of Homosexuality: An Essay
on Cultural Ontology and Historical Comparison," *Journal of the History of
Sexuality* 1 (1991).

6. See Jeannette M. Mageo, "Male Transvestism and Cultural Change in Samoa," *American Ethnologist* 19 (1992); Kris Poasa, "The Samoan Fa'afafine: One Case Study and Discussion of Transsexualism," *Journal of Psychology and Human Sexuality* 5.3 (1992); Bradd Shore, "Sexuality and Gender in Samoa: Conceptions and Missed Conceptions," in Sherry B. Ortner and Harriet Whitehead (eds.), *Sexual Meanings: The Cultural Construction of Gender and Sexuality* (Cambridge: Cambridge University Press, 1981).

7. Shapiro, "Transsexualism," pp. 268–70.

8. Tamar Gordon, personal communication.

9. Evelyn Blackwood, "Breaking the Mirror: The Construction of Lesbianism and the Anthropological Discourse on Homosexuality," *Journal of Homosexuality* 11.3/4 (1986).

10. Louis Antoine de Bougainville, *A Voyage Round the World Performed by Order of His Most Christian Majesty in the Years 1766, 1767, 1768, and 1769*, trans. John R. Foster (London: Nourse & Davies, 1772), pp. 217–19.

11. Marshall Sahlins, *Historical Metaphors and Mythical Realities: Structure in the Early History of the Sandwich Island Kingdom* (Ann Arbor: University of Michigan Press, 1981), and *Islands of History* (Chicago: University of Chicago Press, 1985).

12. Orsmond, Journal, October 24, 1827, London Missionary Society Archives, cited in Douglas Oliver, *Ancient Tahitian Society*, 3 vols. (Honolulu: University of Hawaii Press, 1974).

13. Neil Gunson, *Messengers of Grace: Evangelical Missionaries in the South Seas, 1797–1860* (Melbourne: Oxford University Press, 1978), p. 195.

14. Gavan Daws, *A Dream of Islands: Voyages of Self-Discovery in the South Seas* (Milton, Queensland: Jacaranda, 1980); Greg Dening, *Islands and Beaches: Discourse on a Silent Land, Marquesas 1774–1880* (Honolulu: University Press of Hawaii, 1980); T. Walter Herbert, Jr., *Marquesan Encounters: Melville and the Meaning of Civilization* (Cambridge, MA: Harvard University Press, 1980).

15. Jefferson, Journal, June 8, 1799, London Missionary Society Archives, cited in Oliver, *Ancient Tahitian Society*.

16. Edward Edwards and George Hamilton, *Voyage of H.M.S. Pandora Despached to Arrest the Mutineers of the 'Bounty' in the South Seas, 1790–91*, ed. Basil Thompson (London: Edwards, 1915), p. 113.

17. William Bligh, *The Log of the Bounty*, 2 vols., ed. Owen Rutter (London: Golden Cockerel, 1937), vol. 2, p. 17.

18. George Mortimer, *Observations and Remarks Made During a Voyage to*

the Islands of Teneriffe, Amsterdam, Maria's Islands near Van Diemen's Land; Otaheiti, Sandwich Islands; Owhyhee, the Fox Islands on the North West Coast of America, Tinian, and from Thence to Canton, in the Brig Mercury, Commanded by John Henry Cox, Esq. (London: Printed for the author, 1791), p. 47.

19. Quote in Anne Salmond, Two Worlds: First Meetings Between Maori and Europeans, 1642–1772 (Auckland: Viking, 1991), pp. 251–52.

20. The situation obviously strikes an enduring chord in Western lore: for example, it is the central theme of a short story by contemporary New Zealand writer John Cranna in Visitors (Auckland: Reed, 1989).

21. Michel Foucault, The History of Sexuality: Vol. 1, trans. Robert Hurley (New York: Viking, 1980); Arnold D. Harvey, "Prosecutions for Sodomy in England at the Beginning of the Nineteenth Century," Historical Journal 21 (1978); George Sebastian Rousseau, "The Pursuit of Homosexuality in the Eighteenth Century: 'Utterly Confused Category' and/or Rich Repository," in Robert P. Maccubbin (ed.), 'Tis Nature's Fault: Unauthorized Sexuality During the Enlightenment (Cambridge: Cambridge University Press, 1987); Randolph Trumbach, "Modern Prostitution and Gender in Fanny Hill: Libertine and Domesticated Fantasy," in Rousseau and Roy Porter (eds.), Sexual Underworlds of the Enlightenment (Chapel Hill: University of North Carolina Press, 1988).

22. See essay by Trumbach, this volume. See also Trumbach, "London's Sodomites: Homosexual Behavior and Western Culture in the Eighteenth Century," Journal of Social History 11 (1977), "Gender and the Homosexual Role in Modern Western Culture: The 18th and 19th Centuries Compared," in Dennis Altman et al., Homosexuality, Which Homosexuality? (Amsterdam and London: An Dekker/ Schorer, GMP, 1989), "The Birth of the Queen: Sodomy and the Emergence of Gender Equality in Modern Culture, 1660–1750," in Martin Duberman, Martha Vicinus and George Chauncey, Jr. (eds.), Hidden from History: Reclaiming the Gay and Lesbian Past (New York: Meridian, 1989), and "Sex, Gender, and Sexual Identity in Modern Culture: Male Sodomy and Female Prostitution in Enlightenment London," Journal of the History of Sexuality 2 (1991).

23. Jeffrey Weeks, Sex, Politics and Society: The Regulation of Sexuality Since 1800 (London: Longman, 1981), p. 100.

24. Arthur Gilbert, "Sodomy and the Law in Eighteenth- and Early Nineteenth-Century Britain," Societas 8 (1978).

25. Gilbert, "Sexual Deviance and Disaster During the Napoleonic Wars," Albion 9 (1977).

26. Robert J. Corber, "Representing the 'Unspeakable': William Godwin

and the Politics of Homophobia," *Journal of the History of Sexuality* 1 (1990), pp. 86–97.

27. Gilbert, "The *Africaine* Courts-Martial: A Study of Buggery and the Royal Navy," *Journal of Homosexuality* 1 (1974), and "Buggery and the British Navy, 1700–1861," *Journal of Social History* 10 (1976).

28. Edwin N. Ferdon, *Early Tahiti as the Explorers Saw It, 1767–1797* (Tucson: University of Arizona Press, 1981), proposes that "male homosexuality" in Tahiti was introduced by early European sailors and that "once [it] was accepted as a way of life for some Tahitian men, transvestism followed as a logical sequel" (p. 154). This unlikely scenario is founded on severe conceptual confusions and flawed logic.

29. John Martin, *An Account of the Natives of the Tonga Islands in the South Pacific Ocean with the Original Grammar and Vocabulary of Their Language Compiled and Arranged from Extensive Communications of Mr William Mariner, Several Years Resident in Those Islands*, 2 vols. (London: Murray, 1817).

30. Mageo, "Male Transvestism."

31. Robert Borofsky and Alan Howard, "The Early Contact Period," in Borofsky and Howard (eds.), *Developments in Polynesian Ethnology* (Honolulu: University of Hawaii Press, 1989).

32. It is particularly suggestive that contemporary Samoans are notoriously concerned with presenting an idealized "official" depiction of their culture to outsiders, as we know from the Freeman-Mead noncontroversy of the early 1980s. Significantly, there is little room for *fa'afāfine* in this depiction.

33. More detailed (although frequently confused and uninformative) were semipopular accounts in the "sexual life in the South Seas" genre published at various times in the twentieth century, beginning of course with Margaret Mead's *Coming of Age in Samoa* (New York: Morrow, 1928) and including such works as George Biddle, *Tahitian Journal* (Minneapolis: University of Minnesota Press, 1968), Bengt Danielsson, *Love in the South Seas* (New York: Reynal, 1956), Donald S. Marshall and Robert C. Suggs, *Human Sexual Behavior* (New York: Morrow, 1971), and Suggs, *Marquesan Sexual Behavior* (New York: Harcourt, Brace & World, 1966).

34. Ernest Beaglehole and Pearl Beaglehole, *Pangai: A Village in Tonga* (Wellington: The Polynesian Society, 1941). On Tonga, see also Edward W. Gifford, *Tongan Society* (Honolulu, HI: Bishop Museum, 1929); on the Marquesas, see Edward S.C. Handy, *The Native Culture in the Marquesas* (Honolulu, HI: Bishop Museum, 1923); on Pukapuka, Beaglehole and Beaglehole, *Ethnology*

of Pukapuka (Honolulu, HI: Bishop Museum, 1938); see Howard and Borofsky, "Introduction," in Howard and Borofsky (eds.), *Developments,* for a description of the historical context of these works.

35. Herdt, "Representations," pp. 489 and 607; Jan Van Baal, "The Dialectics of Sex in Marind-anim Culture," in Herdt (ed.), *Ritualized Homosexuality in Melanesia* (Berkeley and Los Angeles: University of California Press, 1984), p. 128. Berdaches are most cogently treated in Charles Callender and Lee M. Kochems, "The North American Berdache," *Current Anthropology* 24 (1983); Robert Fulton and Steven W. Anderson, "The Amerindian 'Man-Woman': Gender, Liminality, and Cultural Continuity," *Current Anthropology* 33 (1992); Will Roscoe, *The Zuni Man-Woman* (Albuquerque: University of New Mexico Press, 1991), and essay in this volume; and Whitehead, "The Bow and the Burden Strap: A New Look at Institutionalized Homosexuality in Native North America," in Ortner and Whitehead (eds.), *Sexual Meanings*; see also Roscoe, "Bibliography of Berdache and Alternative Gender Roles Among North American Indians," *Journal of Homosexuality* 14.3/4 (1987).

36. Several lines of argumentation are suggestive. In contrast with Native North America, Polynesian societies were generally not subjected to systematic annihilating efforts on the part of colonizing populations, with the possible exception of Hawaii and New Zealand. While North American berdache traditions died out with the contexts that supported them, the cultural setting in which Polynesian gender liminality is embedded never disappeared. The contrast with Melanesian "ritualized" homosexuality is more difficult to explain, although the central role that sexuality plays in the definition of the phenomenon and the particular virulence of modern-day missionary intrusion may be implicated in its disappearance.

37. Robert I. Levy, "The Community Function of Tahitian Male Transvestism: A Hypothesis," *Anthropological Quarterly* 44.1 (1971), and *Tahitians: Mind and Experience in the Society Islands* (Chicago: University of Chicago Press, 1973).

38. Mageo, "Male Transvestism"; Shore, "Sexuality and Gender."

39. Levy, "Community Function," p. 14.

40. See Herdt, "Introduction," in this volume.

41. For journalistic accounts, see Walter L. Williams, "Sex and Shamanism: The Making of a Hawaiian Mahu," *The Advocate* 417 (1985); Carol E. Robertson, "Art Essay: The Māhū of Hawai'i," *Feminist Studies* 15 (1989).

42. I use the phrase "homosexual behavior" here to refer to encounters between biologically male entities in which at least one party experiences erotic

arousal of some kind. Even though sexual encounters with gender-liminal individuals bear some similarity to heterosexual encounters, they are decisively not the same. In particular, while liminal individuals acquire some of the sexual attributes of women, they do not *become* women in the eyes of society, nor do they cease to be men. The terms *homosexual* or *homoerotic* are thus relevant here.

43. On Samoa, see Mageo, "Male Transvestism," p. 450; on Tahiti, see Levy, *Tahitians*, p. 139.

44. Callender and Kochems, "Men and Not-Men: Male Gender-mixing Statuses and Homosexuality," *Journal of Homosexuality* 11.3/4 (1985).

45. Foucault, *History of Sexuality: Vol. I*; John D'Emilio and Estelle B. Freedman, *Intimate Matters: A History of Sexuality in America* (New York: Harper & Row, 1988); Weeks, *Sexuality and Its Discontents: Meanings, Myths, and Modern Sexualities* (London: Routledge & Kegan Paul, 1985); on the individualist imperative and capitalism, see, e.g., Richard Sennett, *The Fall of Public Man* (New York: Knopf, 1977).

46. Gender liminality comes in full bloom in such contexts as dances and in urban Polynesia's bars and discotheques. These are precisely the contexts in which heavy drinking takes place among nonliminal men, and the image of the staggering young buck harassing the gender-liminal person is familiar throughout the Polynesian area.

47. Danielsson et al., "Polynesia's Third Sex," *Pacific Islands Monthly* 49.8 (1978). In Western Samoa, tensions between liminal and nonliminal men appear to be increasing as a non-*fa'afafine* homosexual identity emerges, at odds with "traditional" Samoan ways of understanding sexuality and personhood, and as Western-style gay activism trickles back from the Samoan immigrant community in New Zealand (Douglass St. Christian, personal communication). However, explaining violence against liminal individuals as the sole result of emergent modernity in the Pacific Islands presupposes a romanticized view of Polynesia that has no validity outside the Western imagination.

48. Levy, *Tahitians*.

49. Herdt, "Representations," pp. 619–20.

50. Compare Mageo, "Male Transvestism," p. 453.

51. An exception to this pattern is sexual encounters with male Western tourists, which Tongans (and Western Polynesians in general) do not hesitate to engage in. However, I surmise that in such encounters the Westerner is aligned with the *fakaleitī*. The political and economic contexts in which such encounters are embedded, which deserve further scrutiny, increasingly resemble the

heterosexual encounters between tourists and Palestinian men in Jerusalem's Old City described in Glenn Bowman, "Fucking Tourists: Sexual Relations and Tourism in Jerusalem's Old City," *Critique of Anthropology* 9 (1989).

52. Levy, *Tahitians*, p. 138. Gifford, *Tahitian Society*, p. 204, notes that his Tongan informant in the 1920s talked about the gender-liminal person as a hermaphrodite. Early travelers, like Bligh (*Log of the Bounty*, vol. 2, pp. 16–17), also tended to merge the two categories when speaking of the *māhū* in Tahiti, demonstrating that the eighteenth-century English naturalizations of gender resembled those of modern-day Polynesians.

53. Herdt, "Representations," p. 626.

54. Mageo, "Male Transvestism," p. 453.

55. Laurie K. Gluckman, "Lesbianism in the Maori," *Australian and New Zealand Journal of Psychiatry* 1 (1967), and "Transcultural Consideration of Homosexuality with Special Reference to the New Zealand Maori," *Australian and New Zealand Journal of Psychiatry* 8 (1974).

56. Levy, *Tahitians*, p. 140.

57. Mageo and St. Christian, personal communication.

58. Levy, *Tahitians*, pp. 232–39.

59. For a concise discussion of this problem see Sally McConnell-Ginet, "Language and Gender," in Frederick J. Newmeyer (ed.), *Linguistics: The Cambridge Survey* (Cambridge: Cambridge University Press, 1988), vol. 4, pp. 76–77.

60. Elinor Ochs, "The Impact of Stratification and Socialization on Men's and Women's Speech in Western Samoa," in Susan U. Philips, Susan Steele and Christine Tanz (eds.), *Language, Gender, and Sex in Comparative Perspective* (Cambridge: Cambridge University Press, 1987).

61. Levy, *Tahitians*, p. 233.

62. Oliver, *Two Tahitian Villages: A Study in Comparison* (Laie, HI: Institute for Polynesian Studies, Brigham Young University, 1981), pp. 68–86; Biddle, *Tahitian Journal*, p. 63.

63. Oliver, *Two Tahitian Villages*, p. 146.

64. Joel C. Kuipers, "Talking about Troubles: Gender Differences in Weyéwa Ritual Speech Use," in Jane M. Atkinson and Shelly Errington (eds.), *Power and Difference: Gender in Island Southeast Asia* (Stanford, CA: Stanford University Press, 1990).

65. Anna Meigs, "Multiple Gender Ideologies and Statuses," in Peggy R. Sanday and Ruth G. Goodenough (eds.), *Beyond the Second Sex: New Directions in the Anthropology of Gender* (Philadelphia: University of Pennsylvania Press,

1990); Alice Schlegel, "Gender Meanings: General and Specific," in Sanday and Goodenough (eds.), *Beyond the Second Sex.*

66. Micaela di Leonardo, "Introduction: Gender, Culture, and Political Economy: Feminist Anthropology in Historical Perspective," in di Leonardo (ed.), *Gender at the Crossroads of Knowledge: Feminist Anthropology in the Postmodern Era* (Berkeley and Los Angeles: University of California Press, 1991); Sandra Morgen, "Gender and Anthropology," in Morgen (ed.), *Gender and Anthropology: Critical Reviews for Research and Teaching* (Washington, DC: American Anthropological Association, 1989); Rubin, "The Traffic in Women"; on Polynesia, Ortner, "Gender and Sexuality in Hierarchical Societies: The Case of Polynesia and Some Comparative Implications," in Ortner and Whitehead (eds.), *Sexual Meanings.*

67. Biddle, *Tahitian Journal*, p. 64.

68. Mageo, "Male Transvestism." Incidental reports suggest that parody is not an essential feature of *fa'afafine* identity in Samoa and that contemporary Tahitian *māhū* do engage in caricatural portrayals of femininity in some contexts.

69. See, e.g., Barbara A. Babcock-Abrahams, " 'A Tolerated Margin of Mess': The Trickster and His Tales Reconsidered," *Journal of the Folklore Institute* 11 (1974), and "Too Many, Too Few: Ritual Modes of Signification," *Semiotica* 23 (1978); Gregory Bateson, *Steps to an Ecology of Mind* (New York: Ballantine, 1972); Bruce Jackson, "Deviance as Success: The Double Inversion of Stigmatized Roles," in Barbara A. Babcock (ed.), *The Reversible World: Symbolic Inversion in Art and Society* (Ithaca, NY: Cornell University Press, 1978); James Peacock, "Symbolic Reversal and Social History: Transvestites and Clowns of Java," in Babcock (ed.), *Reversible World*; Turner, *Forest of Symbols.*

70. Levy, "Community Function," p. 20.

71. Levy, *Tahitians*, p. 234.

72. F. Allan Hanson and Louise Hanson, *Counterpoint in Maori Culture* (London: Routledge & Kegan Paul, 1983); Ortner, "Gender and Sexuality"; Shore, "Sexuality and Gender"; Valerio Valeri, *Kingship and Sacrifice: Ritual and Society in Ancient Hawaii* (Chicago: University of Chicago Press, 1985); on culinary prohibitions, see Oliver, *Ancient Tahitian Society*, pp. 224–27.

73. Shore, *Sala'ilua: A Samoan Mystery* (New York: Columbia University Press, 1982), and "Sexuality and Gender."

74. See Penelope Schoeffel, "Gender, Status, and Power in Samoa," *Canberra Anthropology* 1 (1978), for a slightly divergent analysis.

75. Mageo, "Male Transvestism."

76. The play between different aspects of womanhood, particularly those that invoke oppositions between virginal and nonvirginal status, or virtue and promiscuity, is not the exclusive monopoly of Samoan gender liminals. It is a common theme in Western drag shows and also surfaces in such contexts as Madonna's music video "Like a Virgin," in which the performer sings the refrain while simulating sexual motions.

77. Warren J. Blumenfeld and Diane Raymond, *Looking at Gay and Lesbian Life* (New York: Philosophical Library, 1988), p. 105.

78. Watts, "The Polynesian Mahu," p. 171; see also Murray, "Austronesian Gender-defined Homosexuality: Introduction," in Murray (ed.), *Oceanic Homosexualities*.

79. Herdt, "Representations."

80. George Devereux, "Institutionalized Homosexuality among the Mohave Indians," *Human Biology* 9 (1937); cf. Herdt, "Representations."

81. Whitehead, "The Bow and Burden Strap."

82. See Serena Nanda, *Neither Man nor Woman: The Hijras of India* (Belmont, CA: Wadsworth, 1990), and also her essay in this volume.

83. Levy, *Tahitians*, p. 133.

84. Nanda, *Neither Man nor Woman.*

85. Unni Wikan, "Man Becomes Woman: Transsexualism in Oman as a Key to Gender Roles," *Man*, n.s., 12 (1977).

86. Mageo, "Male Transvestism."

87. Shore, *Sala'ilua*; Eleanor R. Gerber, "Rage and Obligation: Samoan Emotions in Conflict," in Geoffrey M. White and John Kirkpatrick (eds.), *Person, Self, and Experience: Exploring Pacific Ethnopsychologies* (Berkeley and Los Angeles: University of California Press, 1985); Ochs, "The Impact of Stratification."

88. Niko Besnier, "Literacy and the Notion of the Person on Nukulaelae Atoll," *American Anthropologist* 93 (1991); Howard, "Ethnopsychology and the Prospects for a Cultural Psychology," in White and Kirkpatrick (eds.), *Person, Self, and Experience*; Karen L. Ito, "Affective Bonds: Hawaiian Interrelationships of Self," in White and Kirkpatrick (eds.), *Person, Self, and Experience*; Kirkpatrick, *The Marquesan Notion of the Person* (Ann Arbor: UMI Research Press, 1983).

89. Mageo, "Male Transvestism," p. 452.

90. Compare Peacock, "Symbolic Reversal," on transvestism and clowning in Java.

91. Victor Turner, *Blazing the Trail: Way Marks in the Exploration of Symbols*, ed. Edith Turner (Tucson: University of Arizona Press, 1992).

92. Shore, *Sala'ilua*, pp. 258–59.

93. Dieter Christensen and Gerd Koch, *Die Musik der Ellice-Inseln* (Berlin: Museum für Völkerkunde, 1964); Besnier, "Involvement in Linguistic Practice: An Ethnographic Appraisal," *Journal of Pragmatics* (in press).

94. Shore, "The Absurd Side of Power in Samoa," paper presented at the Conference on Leadership in Oceania: For Raymond Firth on the Occasion of his 90th Birthday, London, 1991.

95. Lila Abu-Lughod, "Writing Against Culture," in Richard G. Fox (ed.), *Recapturing Anthropology: Working in the Present* (Santa Fe, NM: School of American Research Press, 1991); Babcock-Abrahams, " 'A Tolerated Margin,' " and "Too Many, Too Few"; Turner, *Blazing the Trail*.

96. On *rabisman*, see Marie Reay, "The Politics of a Witch-Killing," *Oceania* 47 (1976).

97. Marilyn Strathern, "Self-Interest and the Social Good: Some Implications of Hagen Gender Imagery," in Ortner and Whitehead (eds.), *Sexual Meanings*, and "Domesticity and the Denigration of Women," in Denise O'Brien and Sharon W. Tiffany (eds.), *Rethinking Women's Roles: Perspectives from the Pacific* (Berkeley and Los Angeles: University of California, 1985).

98. David D. Gilmore, *Manhood in the Making: Cultural Concepts of Masculinity* (New Haven, CT: Yale University Press, 1990), p. 207.

99. The blanket characterization of certain "non-Western" societies as "nonhomophobic" common in this literature deflects attention from examining the nature of homophobia in any society. Walter W. Williams, "Benefits for Nonhomophobic Societies: An Anthropological Perspective," in Warren J. Blumenfeld (ed.), *Homophobia: How We All Pay the Price* (Boston: Beacon, 1992), is a good illustration of how problematic such reasoning can be.

100. Herdt, "Representations," p. 489.

101. For a review, see Geoffrey M. White, "Ethnopsychology," in Theodore Schwartz, White and Catherine A. Lutz (eds.), *New Directions in Psychological Anthropology* (Cambridge: Cambridge University Press, 1992).

102. See Richard J. Perry, "Why Do Multiculturalists Ignore Anthropologists?" *Chronicle of Higher Education*, March 4, 1992, p. A–52.

103. Besnier, "The Demise of the Man Who Would Be King: Sorcery and Ambition on Nukulaelae," *Journal of Anthropological Research* (in press).

104. Besnier, "Heteroglossic Discourses on Nukulaelae Spirits," paper presented at the Annual Meeting of the Association for Social Anthropology in Oceania, New Orleans, 1992.

105. Erving Goffman, *Stigma: Notes in the Management of Spoiled Identity* (Englewood Cliffs, NJ: Prentice-Hall, 1964).

106. Shore, "Sexuality and Gender."

107. Howard and Kirkpatrick, "Social Organization," in Howard and Borofsky (eds.), *Developments in Polynesian Ethnology*.

108. Harold W. Scheffler, "Sexism and Naturalism in the Study of Kinship," in di Leonardo (ed.), *Gender at the Crossroads of Knowledge: Feminist Anthropology in the Postmodern Era* (Berkeley and Los Angeles: University of California Press, 1991).

109. George B. Milner, "Problems of the Structure of Concepts in Samoa: An Investigation of Vernacular Statement and Meaning," Ph.D. thesis, University of London, 1968, pp. 185–86.

110. Howard and Kirkpatrick, "Social Organization"; Ortner, "Gender and Sexuality"; Sahlins, *Islands of History*; Shore, "Sexuality and Gender."

111. Pauline Paine, "Introduction: Sex and Gender in Oceania," *Nexus* 2.1 (1981); Robertson, "Art Essay."

112. Besnier, "Heteroglossic Discourses."

113. The literature on Polynesian gender liminality has yet to address the relationship between liminality and church-based morality. Yet Christianity in one form or another is the principal reference point for morality in virtually all contemporary Polynesian societies. Even if Christian discourse is silent on the topic everywhere in the region, this fact alone is interesting, given the contrast with Christianity's strident obsession with sexual and gender diversity in such societies as North America.

114. The logic underlying this account lends contemporary support for one of the explanations that Oliver puts forth for the presence of *māhū* in precontact Tahiti: "males unable or unwilling to play the physically demanding and often hazardous roles expected of Maohi [i.e., traditional Tahitian] men in climbing, canoeing, fighting, and so forth, were permitted and, perhaps, even encouraged or required to play female roles" (Oliver, *Ancient Tahitian Society*, p. 1112). I am much less enthusiastic about Oliver's other conjectures, to the effect that the elaboration of the *māhū* was the result of the numerical preponderance of men and of the sexual freedom that reigned in precontact Tahiti.

115. Whitehead, "The Bow and Burden Strap," p. 107.

116. Louis Joseph Bouge, "Un aspect du rôle rituel du 'Mahu' dans l'ancien Tahiti," *Journal de la Société des Océanistes* 11 (1955).

117. Herdt, *The Sambia: Ritual and Gender in New Guinea* (New York: Holt,

Rinehart & Winston, 1987); Herdt (ed.), *Rituals of Manhood: Male Initiation in New Guinea* (Berkeley and Los Angeles: University of California Press, 1982); and Herdt (ed.), *Ritualized Homosexuality in Melanesia* (Berkeley and Los Angeles: University of California Press, 1984).

118. Besnier, "Authority and Egalitarianism: Discourses of Leadership on Nukulaelae Atoll," paper presented at the Conference on Leadership in Oceania: For Raymond Firth on the Occasion of his 90th Birthday, London, 1991.

119. Wikan, "Man Becomes Woman."

120. In urban centers, there are incidental reports of gender-liminal persons engaging in economically driven prostitution targeting principally Western tourists; see Danielsson et al., "Polynesia's Third Sex"; Deborah F. McFarlane, "Trans-sexual Prostitution in Polynesia," *Pacific Islands Monthly* 55.2 (1983), and "Trans-sexual Prostitution in New Zealand: Predominance of Persons of Maori Extraction," *Archives of Sexual Behavior* 13 (1984). How the emergence of this phenomenon articulates with "traditional" concepts of gender liminality is an important question. But it is clear that the phenomenon is a development on preexisting patterns that involve no such economic dimension.

121. See also Herdt, "Representations," p. 487.

CHAPTER SEVEN: HOW TO BECOME A BERDACHE

I am grateful for the comments and suggestions of David Schneider, Martin Ottenheimer, Stephen Murray, Eric Ramirez, Evelyn Blackwood, Jane Collier, Wesley Thomas and members of the Affiliated Scholar seminar at the Institute for Research on Women and Gender at Stanford. Special thanks are due to Dr. James Brust for permission to use the rare photograph of "Squaw Jim" (see figure 7.2).

1. Rene Goulaine de Laudonniere, in ed. Richard Hakluyt, *The Principal Navigations, Voyages, Traffiques, and Discoveries of the English Nation* (Glasgow: MacLehose & Sons, 1904), vol. 8, pp. 453-54, vol. 9, pp. 16, 56 and 69; Jacques Le Moyne, in Stefan Lorant (ed.), *The New World: The First Pictures of America* (New York: Duell, Sloan & Pearce, 1965), p. 69; Francisco de Pareja, Jerald T. Milanich and William C. Sturtevant (eds.), *Francisco Pareja's 1613* Confessionario: *A Documentary Source for Timucuan Ethnography*, trans. Emilio F. Moran (Tallahassee, FL: Division of Archives, History, and Records Management, Florida Department of State), pp. 39 and 43; Andrés González de Barcia, *Barcia's Chronological History of the Continent of Florida*, trans. Anthony Kerrigan (Gainesville: University of Florida Press, 1951), pp. 117–18, 306.

2. Matilda C. Stevenson, "The Zuñi Indians: Their Mythology, Esoteric Fra-

ternities, and Ceremonies," *Twenty-third Annual Report of the Bureau of American Ethnology, 1901-1902* (Washington, DC: Government Printing Office, 1904), p. 374. For a listing of tribes with berdache roles, see Will Roscoe, "Bibliography of Berdache and Alternative Gender Roles among North American Indians," *Journal of Homosexuality* 14.3-4 (1987). The geographic focus on North America, which this essay inherits, is arbitrary. Roles comparable to berdache status existed and continue to exist among various native people of Central and South America. See, e.g., Stephen O. Murray, *Male Homosexuality in Central and South America, Gai Saber Monograph* 5 (1987); Peter Fry, "Male Homosexuality and Spirit Possession in Brazil," in Evelyn Blackwood (ed.), *The Many Faces of Homosexuality* (New York: Harrington Park, 1986); Walter L. Williams, *The Spirit and the Flesh: Sexual Diversity in American Indian Culture* (Boston: Beacon Press, 1986), ch. 7; Beverly Chiñas, "Isthmus Zapotec 'Berdaches'," *Newsletter of the Anthropological Research Group on Homosexuality* 7 (May 1985); Stephen W. Foster, "A Bibliography of Homosexuality Among Latin-American Indians," *The Cabirion and Gay Books Bulletin* 12 (1985).

3. There are no reliable data at present for estimating the frequency and number of berdaches in traditional times, although careful work in census records and oral histories may make it possible to estimate the numbers of berdaches in some tribes in the late nineteenth century. Accounts suggest that in small tribes there might be only one or two berdaches in a given generation. In larger communities, however, their numbers were sufficient for them to be recognized as a social group.

4. See Roscoe, "Bibliography," p. 155, table 1.

5. See Claude Courouve, "The Word 'Bardache'," *Gay Books Bulletin* 8 (1982). *Berdache* is a serious misnomer, encompassing significant diversity within a term whose historical meaning has little in common with Native American traditions. Nonetheless, this should not be an excuse for discounting the striking consistency in the presence and construction of multiple genders in the New World. To do so would continue the dissimulation that has historically obfuscated the Western view of gender diversity.

6. For a detailed discussion of these points, see Gilbert Herdt, "Representations of Homosexuality: An Essay on Cultural Ontology and Historical Comparison," *Journal of the History of Sexuality* 1.3-4 (1991).

7. See, e.g., Elsie C. Parsons, "The Zuñi Ła'mana," *American Anthropologist* 18.4 (1916); Ruth Benedict, *Patterns of Culture* (Boston: Houghton Mifflin, 1959), pp. 262-65.

8. Relevant works by the authors are all cited in Roscoe, "Bibliography."

9. Jonathan N. Katz, *Gay American History: Lesbians and Gay Men in the U.S.A.* (New York: Crowell, 1976); Harriet Whitehead, "The Bow and the Burden Strap: A New Look at Institutionalized Homosexuality in Native North America," in Sherry B. Ortner and Whitehead (eds.), *Sexual Meanings: The Cultural Construction of Gender and Sexuality* (New York: Cambridge University Press, 1981).

10. Charles Callender and Lee M. Kochems, "The North American Berdache," *Current Anthropology* 24.4 (1983). See also Callender and Kochems, "Men and Not-Men: Male Gender-Mixing Statuses and Homosexuality," in Blackwood (ed.), *The Many Faces of Homosexuality*; Beatrice Medicine, " 'Warrior Women' – Sex Role Alternatives for Plains Indian Women," in Patricia Albers and Medicine (eds.), *The Hidden Half* (Lanham, MD: University Press of America, 1983); Blackwood, "Sexuality and Gender in Certain American Indian Tribes: The Case of Cross-Gender Females," *Signs: The Journal of Women in Culture and Society* 10.1 (1984); Roscoe, "Bibliography," "We'wha and Klah: The American Indian Berdache as Artist and Priest," *American Indian Quarterly* 12.2 (1988), "The Semiotics of Gender on Zuni Kachinas," *The Kiva* 55.1 (1990), "That Is My Road: The Life and Times of a Crow Berdache," *Montana: The Magazine of Western History* 40.1 (Winter 1990) and *The Zuni Man-Woman* (Albuquerque: University of New Mexico Press, 1991); Williams, *Spirit and the Flesh*. Anthropological interest in berdaches has developed in tandem with renewed interest on the part of American Indians. In 1975, the Gay American Indian organization was founded in San Francisco, to be joined in the 1980s by similar groups in cities throughout North America. These organizations foster interest in and a sharing of berdache traditions among individuals of diverse tribal backgrounds. Paula Gunn Allen, Beatrice Medicine, Maurice Kenny, Midnight Sun, Richard La Fortune, Terry Tafoya and M. Owlfeather are among the American Indian writers and scholars who have written on the subject. See, e.g., Roscoe (ed.), *Living the Spirit: A Gay American Indian Anthology* (New York: St. Martin's, 1988).

11. See the examples summarized in Roscoe, "Bibliography," p. 167.

12. See Callender and Kochems, "North American Berdache," p. 499; Williams, *Spirit and the Flesh*, pp. 87–109; Roscoe, "Bibliography," pp. 158–59.

13. See Williams, *Spirit and the Flesh*, pp. 93–95.

14. For We'wha, Klah and Osh-Tisch, see my biographical studies cited in n.10. For Qánqon, see Claude E. Schaeffer, "The Kutenai Female Berdache: Courier, Guide, Prophetess, and Warrior," *Ethnohistory* 12.3 (1965); for Run-

568

ning Eagle, see James W. Schultz, *Running Eagle: The Warrior Girl* (Boston: Houghton Mifflin, 1919); for Woman Chief, see Edwin T. Denig, "Indian Tribes of the Upper Missouri: Report to the Honorable Isaac S. Stevens," in J.N.B. Hewitt (ed.), *Forty-sixth Annual Report of the Bureau of American Ethnology, 1928-1929* (Washington, DC: Government Printing Office, 1930), pp. 433-34.

15. See David F. Greenberg, "Why was the Berdache Ridiculed?" in Blackwood (ed.), *The Many Faces of Homosexuality*, pp. 179-90.

16. See Greenberg, *The Construction of Homosexuality* (Chicago: University of Chicago Press, 1988), pp. 77-88; Williams, *Spirit and the Flesh*, ch. 7 and passim; and the useful discussion of the problems of interpretation in Suzanne J. Kessler and Wendy McKenna, *Gender: An Ethnomethodological Approach* (Chicago: University of Chicago Press, 1985), pp. 29-41.

17. Roscoe, "Bibliography," pp. 154-70.

18. See *ibid.*, pp. 162-63; Callender and Kochems, "North American Berdache," pp. 448-49; Greenberg, *Construction of Homosexuality*, pp. 44-45.

19. See, e.g., works by Blackwood, Medicine, Williams and me cited in n.10 above.

20. For the canonical statement on berdaches as gender-crossers, see Henry Angelino and Charles Shedd, "A Note on Berdache," *American Anthropologist* 57.1 (1955).

21. M. Kay Martin and Barbara Voorhies, *Female of the Species* (New York: Columbia University Press, 1975), p. 86; cf. Kessler and McKenna, *Gender*, p. 29.

22. Sue-Ellen Jacobs, "Comment on 'The North American Berdache,'" *Current Anthropology* 24.4 (1983). See also Jacobs and Jason Cromwell, "Visions and Revisions of Reality: Reflections on Sex, Sexuality, Gender, and Gender Variance," *Journal of Homosexuality* 23.4 (1992).

23. Blackwood, Review of *The Spirit and the Flesh: Sexual Diversity in American Indian Culture*, by Williams, *Journal of Homosexuality* 15.3-4 (1988). For a negative view on multiple genders see Alice Schlegel, "Gender Meanings: General and Specific," in Peggy R. Sanday and Ruth G. Goodenough (eds.), *Beyond the Second Sex: New Directions in the Anthropology of Gender* (Philadelphia: University of Pennsylvania Press, 1990), p. 39.

24. Examples of all these are provided in my studies of Zuni, Navajo and Crow berdaches. See sources cited in n.10 above.

25. For a listing of native language terms by linguistic family, see the Glossary in Roscoe, "Bibliography," pp. 138-53.

26. Of course, many groups have no single term for "man" or "woman" as

classes of persons but a set of terms for males and females at different points in life and in different relations to others. Similarly, the Cheyenne recognized not one but two categories of berdaches. The *heeman* (often written *hemaneh*) was a berdache "having more of the male element," whereas the *hetaneman* had "more of the female element" (Rodolphe C. Petter, *English-Cheyenne Dictionary* [Kettle Falls, WA: n.p., 1915]). I am indebted to Winfield Coleman for this reference.

27. See Roscoe, *Zuni Man-Woman*, ch. 6; Berard Haile, *Women Versus Men: A Conflict of Navajo Emergence* (Lincoln: University of Nebraska Press, 1981), pp. 11, 18–32; Robert H. Lowie, "Myths and Traditions of the Crow Indians," *Anthropological Papers of the American Museum of Natural History* 25.1 (1918).

28. Medicine, "Warrior Women," p. 269.

29. Whitehead, "The Bow and the Burden Strap," pp. 90-93; Williams, *Spirit and the Flesh*, pp. 11, 233-34.

30. Callender and Kochems, "North American Berdache," p. 446. In a bibliography on alternative gender roles in North America, I was able to cite documentation on female berdache roles in sixty-three tribes (see Roscoe, "Bibliography"). In fact, the historical literature and early ethnographies are notoriously deficient on all matters relating to American Indian women, so that definitive statements concerning the distribution of female berdaches seem unwarranted at this point.

31. Whitehead, "The Bow and the Burden Strap," p. 91; Sabine Lang, *Männer als Frauen – Frauen als Männer: Geschlechtsrollen-wechsel bei den Indianer Nordamerikas* (Hamburg: Wayasbah, 1990), (English summary in *Society of Lesbian and Gay Anthropologists Newsletter* 13.2) takes a similar position.

32. Blackwood, "Sexuality and Gender," p. 29.

33. Roscoe, *Zuni Man-Woman*, pp. 27-28, 232.

34. The use of the term *gender* specifically to oppose the social to the natural dimensions of sex roles, and thereby question the relationship between them, is fairly recent. Donna Haraway, *Simians, Cyborgs, and Women: The Reinvention of Nature* (New York: Routledge, 1991), p. 133, traces the current American usage of the term to the "gender identity" research of the psychoanalyst Robert J. Stoller beginning in the late 1950s; cf. Kessler and McKenna, *Gender*, p. 7.

35. See, e.g., n.74 below.

36. See Judith Shapiro, "Transsexualism: Reflections on the Persistence of Gender and the Mutability of Sex," in Julia Epstein and Kristina Straub (eds.),

Body Guards: The Cultural Politics of Gender Ambiguity (New York: Routledge, 1991).

37. Roscoe, *Zuni Man-Woman*, p. 132.

38. Whitehead, "The Bow and the Burden Strap," p. 85; cf. Greenberg, *Social Construction of Homosexuality*, p. 40.

39. Whitehead, "The Bow and the Burden Strap," p. 107.

40. *Ibid.*, pp. 108–09; cf. Lang, *Männer als Frauen*. Subsequent writers have offered only minor modifications to Whitehead's argument. Callender and Kochems emphasize the significance of beliefs concerning the spirituality of berdaches and point out that women's autonomy in North American societies was often based on food production as well as the manufacture of durable goods. Their most significant disagreement with Whitehead concerns her contention that berdaches reinforced masculine supremacy. They cite various examples of women encouraging and supporting males who chose to become berdaches and note that it is unlikely such a role could have flourished without the explicit approval of women ("North American Berdache," p. 456). Blackwood criticizes Whitehead's reliance on anatomical sex. She argues that "native conceptualizations of gender do not contain an invariable opposition of two roles" and points to the "unimportance of biological sex to the gender role" assumed by individuals in many tribes (Blackwood, "Sexuality and Gender," p. 42).

41. Whitehead, "The Bow and the Burden Strap," p. 83.

42. Callender and Kochems, "Men and Not-Men," p. 166. See also Jacobs and Cromwell, "Visions and Revisions of Reality," pp. 45 and 62.

43. See Gayle Rubin, "The Traffic in Women: Notes on the 'Political Economy' of Sex" in Rayna R. Reiter (ed.), *Toward an Anthropology of Women* (New York: Monthly Review, 1975).

44. There is a burgeoning literature on all these subjects. For a cogent theoretical critique of the sex/gender binary, see Judith Butler, *Gender Trouble: Feminism and the Subversion of Identity* (New York: Routledge, 1990). For a survey of shifting definitions of sex in Western history, see Thomas Laqueur, *Making Sex: Body and Gender from the Greeks to Freud* (Cambridge, MA: Harvard University Press, 1990).

45. Whitehead, "The Bow and the Burden Strap," pp. 90–91.

46. Callender and Kochems, "North American Berdache," p. 456, also point out that a prestige-based hypothesis does not sufficiently account for widespread beliefs attributing berdaches with holiness and supernatural power. These beliefs are far more elaborate than necessary to account for a variation in occupational

THIRD SEX, THIRD GENDER

preferences. Even so, Whitehead's model represents an advance over Robert L. Munroe, John H. Whiting and David Hally, "Institutionalized Male Transvestism and Sex Distinctions," *American Anthropologist* 71 (1969), who link the presence of "institutionalized male transvestism" to a relative lack of sex distinctions – defined as the use of sex as a discriminating factor in prescribing behavior and membership. They fail to identify the correlates of these sex distinctions in the division of labor, however, and without this linkage, degree of sexual differentiation remains an inherently subjective and ethnocentric measure. Although certain activities or behaviors may not be coded for gender in some societies, this does not mean that distinctions between gender roles were unclear in the minds of natives or that these differences, wherever they were perceived, were not strongly defended and maintained. In a subsequent article, Robert L. and Ruth H. Munroe ("Male Transvestism and Subsistence Economy," *Journal of Social Psychology* 103 [1977]) report a higher incidence of "male transvestism" in societies where males contribute 50 percent or more of subsistence. Again, this analysis leaves no room for the role of native belief systems. I believe the cultural *value* placed on women's work and women's role in controlling the distribution of their products will prove more reliable correlates of berdache statuses than absolute contribution to subsistence, which has rarely been measured by objective means and is subject to random variation due to environmental and historical causes.

47. It is also helpful to keep in mind that many of the tribes most strongly associated with the Plains warrior stereotype were sedentary, horticultural societies before contact and the acquisition of horses and guns.

48. Le Moyne, *New World.* See sources on Florida berdaches cited in n.1.

49. Alfred Bowers, *Hidatsa Social and Ceremonial Organization*, Bureau of American Ethnology Bulletin no. 194 (Washington, DC: Government Printing Office, 1965), pp. 105, 115, 132, 159, 166–68, 256, 259–60, 267, 315, 325–27, 330, 427, 438; Williams, *Spirit and the Flesh*, p. 81; A.B. Holder, "The Bote: Description of a Peculiar Sexual Perversion Found among North American Indians," *New York Medical Journal* 50.23 (1889), p. 623; cf. Royal B. Hassrick, *The Sioux: Life and Customs of a Warrior Society* (Norman: University of Oklahoma Press, 1964), p. 133.

50. E. Adamson Hoebel, *The Cheyennes: Indians of the Great Plains* (New York: Holt, Rinehart & Winston, 1960), pp. 77–78. Hay, attempting to account for William A. Hammond's otherwise implausible account of how men were recruited into the berdache role at Acoma and Laguna, has pointed out that

Pueblo medicine societies occasionally resorted to a form of involuntary recruitment; see Hammond, *Sexual Impotence in the Male and Female* (Detroit: Davis, 1887), pp. 163-67. Hay speculates that the procedures Hammond describes may reflect (in a distorted fashion) the existence of a berdache religious society (personal communication).

51. Greenberg's citations in support of Iroquois and Coastal Algonquian berdache roles are faulty (*Social Construction of Homosexuality*, pp. 40-41). I find no positive evidence of berdache roles for these groups in either François Xavier de Charlevoix, who describes Illinois berdaches but only vaguely refers to the Iroquois having lost their reputation for "chastity" as a result of their contact with the Illinois ("Les Iroquois en particulier étoient assez chastes, avant qu'ils eussent Commerce avec les Illinois, & d'autres Peuples voisins de la Louysiane"; see Charlevoix, *Journal d'un Voyage fait par Ordre du Roi dans l'Amerique Septentrionale*, vol. 3, *Histoire et Description Generale de la Nouvelle France* [Paris: Nyon Fils, 1744], p. 303); George H. Loskiel, who accuses the Delaware and Iroquois of "unnatural crimes" (Loskiel, *History of the Mission of the United Brethren among the Indians in North America*, trans. Christian I. La Trobe [London: Printed for the Brethren's Society for the Furtherance of the Gospel, 1794], p. 14); or Charbonneau, who makes no reference to the Iroquois at all ("Charbonneau behauptete sogar, dass in dieser Hinsicht die Bardaches den Weibern vorgezogen würden") (quoted in Maximilian Prince of Wied, *Reise in das Innere Nord-America in den Jahren 1832 bis 1834*, vol. 1 [Koblenz: J. Hoelscher, 1839]). Nor do the citations Greenberg refers to in Ferdinand Karsch-Haack, *Das Gleichgeschlechtliche Leben der Naturvölker* (Munich: Ernst Reinhardt, 1911), pp. 328-30, provide the evidence needed to conclude that these groups had berdache roles.

52. Jacques Marquette, "Of the First Voyage Made by Father Marquette," in Reuben G. Thwaites (ed.), *The Jesuit Relations and Allied Documents* (Cleveland: Burrows, 1900), vol. 59, p. 129. See also Raymond E. Hauser, "The *Berdache* and the Illinois Indian Tribe during the Last Half of the Seventeenth Century," *Ethnohistory* 37.1 (1990).

53. For example, Squaw Sachem (Massachusetts), Weetamoo (Pocaset), Awashonks (Sannet) and Magnus (Narragansetts) in Samuel G. Drake, *The Aboriginal Races of North America...* (New York: Alden, 1880), pp. 105, 187-90, 239, 240, 244, 248-57. For women's economic roles, see Howard S. Russell, *Indian New England Before the Mayflower* (Hanover, NH: University Press of New England, 1980).

54. Whitehead, "The Bow and the Burden Strap," p. 111.

55. This count is based on the tribal identifications used in vols. 7 and 8 of the Smithsonian's *Handbook of North American Indians*. Northwest Coast tribes with berdache roles include Eyak, Tlingit, Haida, Haisla, Bella Bella, Bella Coola, Kwakiutl, Nootkans, Quileute, Central Coast Salish (Squamish), Southwestern Coast Salish (Quinault), Southern Coast Salish (Nisqually), Siuslawans, Athapaskans (Tututni), Hupa, Yurok and Tolowa. For sources, see Roscoe, "Bibliography."

56. Franz Boas, *The Mythology of the Bella Coola Indians*, Memoirs of the American Museum of Natural History, no. 2, pt. 2 (New York, 1898), pp. 38–40; T.F. McIlwraith, *The Bella Coola Indians*, 2 vols. (Toronto: University of Toronto Press, 1948), vol. 1, pp. 45–46, 53, 265; vol. 2, pp. 148, 179, 188–94.

57. Some additional evidence of how berdache status was incorporated into social-ranking systems comes from the Tlingit and Northwest California tribes. Frederica De Laguna, "Tlingit Ideas about the Individual," *Southwestern Journal of Anthropology* 10 (1954), pp. 178 and 183, reports the Tlingit belief that the "half-man, half-woman" was a reincarnation of a particular clan's ancestor. Theoretically, only members of this clan became berdaches. De Laguna introduces these comments by stating that the presence of "institutionalized berdaches or transvestites" was denied. However, several historical sources refer to the presence of Tlingit berdaches. See Étienne Marchand, in C.P. Claret Fleurieu (ed.), *A Voyage Round the World Performed during the Years 1790, 1791, and 1792, by Étienne Marchand* (London: Longman, Rees, Cadell, Davies, 1801), vol. 1, p. 370; and H.J. Holmberg, *Ethnographische Skizzen über die Völker des Russischen Amerika* (Helsinfors: Friis, 1855), part 1, pp. 120–21. In a similar vein, Arthur R. Pilling notes that the known berdaches from northwest California tribes all came from fairly small, aristocratic families (Pilling, "Zuni Men-Women and the U.S. Census," unpublished manuscript, 1993). George Devereux, "Institutionalized Homosexuality of the Mohave Indians," *Human Biology* 9 (1937), p. 502, also reports a belief among the Mohave that berdaches tended to come from prominent families. See also Callender and Kochems, "North American Berdache," p. 453. Comparative studies will be especially important in resolving the question of prestige differentiation and the elaboration of gender categories. It would appear that the hijras of India, for example, represent an instance of an alternative gender status within a large-scale, ranked society, but the economic functions of the role are minor in relation to its gendered, sexual and spiritual aspects (see Serena Nanda, this volume). A similar example is provided

by the *galli* priests of Cybele and Attis in the ancient Greco-Roman world.

58. Roscoe, "Making History: The Challenge of Lesbian and Gay Studies," *Journal of Homosexuality* 15.3-4 (1988).

59. I also proposed the concept of "sociosexual specialization" as a culturally neutral term defining a field of study concerned with homosexuality in the broadest sense — i.e., encompassing its associations with gender variation as well as sexuality. This synthetic term helps avoid the pitfalls of deploying such ethnocentric categories as "the sexual" or "the erotic," which may not be universally relevant. Since writing this essay, James Clifford pointed out to me the relevance of Rodney Needham's work on polythetic classification; see Needham, *Against the Tranquility of Axioms* (Berkeley and Los Angeles: University of California Press, 1983).

60. Jane F. Collier and Sylvia J. Yanagisako, "Toward a Unified Analysis of Gender and Kinship," in Collier and Yanagisako (eds.), *Gender and Kinship: Essays Toward a Unified Analysis* (Stanford: Stanford University Press, 1988), p. 44.

61. See, e.g., J. Owen Dorsey, "A Study of Siouan Cults," *Eleventh Annual Report of the Bureau of American Ethnology, 1889-1890* (Washington, DC: Government Printing Office, 1890), p. 379; Alice C. Fletcher and Francis La Flesche, "The Omaha Tribe," *Twenty-seventh Annual Report of the Bureau of American Ethnology, 1905-1906* (Washington, DC: Government Printing Office, 1911), p. 133; John Treat Irving, Jr. and John F. McDermott (eds.), *Indian Sketches Taken During an Expedition to the Pawnee Tribes, 1833* (Norman: University of Oklahoma Press, 1955), pp. 93-95; Victor Tixier and McDermott (eds.), *Tixier's Travels on the Osage Prairies* (Norman: University of Oklahoma Press, 1940), p. 234. Although Callender and Kochems present a table listing tribes in which childhood inclination determined berdache status and those in which visions were considered the precipitating factor, they acknowledge that these modes of entry were not necessarily exclusive. In fact, a close examination of case histories shows that berdache-specific dreams and visions typically served to confirm childhood preferences. Even when dreams were the primary precipitating factor, adoption of berdache occupations typically followed.

62. Benedict, *Patterns of Culture*, p. 87.

63. For sources, see Roscoe, "Bibliography," *Zuni Man-Woman*, p. 5.

64. Pueblo women's role in agricultural production has been overlooked. Women assisted men in many aspects of planting, tending and harvesting corn, frequently accompanying them to the field. Once corn was harvested and stored, they had complete discretion over its distribution. Finally, women at Zuni and

most other Pueblos up to the present maintain highly productive gardens where a variety of vegetables and herbs are grown.

65. See the analysis of this myth and notes on related data from Acoma, Laguna and Hopi in Roscoe, *Zuni Man-Woman*, ch. 6 and pp. 251–52.

66. Jacobs, "Comment," p. 460. See also Jacobs and Cromwell, "Visions and Revisions of Reality," pp. 54–56.

67. For sources on the association of the moon and Plains berdache status, see Callender and Kochems, "North American Berdache," p. 451.

68. Willard W. Hill, "The Status of the Hermaphrodite and Transvestite in Navaho Culture," *American Anthropologist* 37 (1935).

69. Williams, *Spirit and the Flesh*, p. 199.

70. For an example of the latter, see the photograph of a Navajo berdache by A.C. Vroman taken in the 1890s (nos. V713, V714, Vroman Collection, Seaver Center for Western History Research, Natural History Museum of Los Angeles County).

71. Hill, "Status," p. 274.

72. Gary Witherspoon, *Language and Art in the Navajo Universe* (Ann Arbor: University of Michigan Press, 1977), p. 142.

73. I am indebted to Wesley Thomas for his translation of this term. See also Robert W. Young and William Morgan, *The Navajo Language: A Grammar and Colloquial Dictionary* (Albuquerque: University of New Mexico Press, 1980), p. 525.

74. Witherspoon, *Language and Art*, p. 49. This also helps explain confusion over the statements of some informants that "real" Navajo berdaches were hermaphrodites. "Sex" is the outer expression of an inner form, and the inner form is considered to precede the outer. The body of the berdache was therefore assumed to be the reflection of an inner form, which was double-sexed. In other words, physiology was expected to follow psyche.

75. For an overview of Navajo economy and history, see David M. Brugge, "Navajo Prehistory and History to 1850," in Alfonso Ortiz (ed.), *Handbook of the North American Indian* (Washington, DC: Smithsonian Institution Press, 1983), vol. 10.

76. See Roscoe, "We'wha and Klah."

77. Karl W. Luckert, *The Navajo Hunter Tradition* (Tucson: University of Arizona Press, 1975), pp. 174–77. On Begochidiin, see Stanley A. Fishler, *In the Beginning: A Navaho Creation Myth*, University of Utah Anthropological Papers, no. 13 (Salt Lake City: University of Utah Press, 1953), pp. 2, 11, 14–17; Wash-

ington Matthews, *Navaho Myths, Prayers, and Songs*, University of California Publications in American Archaeology and Ethnology, no. 5 (Berkeley: University of California Press, 1907), pp. 58–60; Berard Haile, *Love-Magic and Butterfly People* (Flagstaff: Museum of Northern Arizona Press, 1978), pp. 83–90, 161; Hasteen Klah, *Navajo Creation Myth: The Story of the Emergence*, compiled by Mary C. Wheelwright, Navajo Religion Series, vol. 1 (Santa Fe, NM: Museum of Navajo Ceremonial Art, 1942); Hill, *The Agricultural and Hunting Methods of the Navaho Indians*, Yale University Publications in Anthropology, no. 18 (New Haven, CT: Yale University Press, 1938), pp. 99, 126, *Navaho Humor*, General Series in Anthropology 9 (Menasha, WI: Banta, 1943), p. 8; Gladys A. Reichard, *The Story of the Navajo Hail Chant* (New York: Gladys A. Reichard, 1944), pp. 47–49, *Navaho Religion: A Study of Symbolism* (Tucson: University of Arizona Press, 1983), pp. 59, 77, 184, 386–90; Donald Sandner, *Navaho Symbols of Healing* (New York: Harcourt Brace Jovanovich, 1979), pp. 38, 76, 77; Wheelwright, *Hail Chant and Water Chant*, Navajo Religion Series, no. 2 (Santa Fe, NM: Museum of Navajo Ceremonial Art, 1946), pp. 5–8, 33–40, 120.

78. Yet another mythological berdache appears in the Navajo origin myth and is referred to simply as "Nádleehé." This figure presides over and arbitrates a temporary division between the men and the women. See Haile, *Women Versus Men*, pp. 11, 18–32.

79. The concern with real vs. pretend *nádleehé* (see, e.g., Hill, "Status," p. 273; Haile, *Love-Magic*, p. 161ff.) may reflect a feeling on the part of some nonberdache Navajos that individuals with secular motives were taking advantage of these new opportunities.

80. Devereux, "Institutionalized Homosexuality."

81. "Report of Alarcon's Expedition," in George P. Hammond and Agapito Rey (eds.), *Narratives of the Coronado Expedition 1540–1542* (Albuquerque: University of New Mexico Press, 1940), pp. 130, 148; Pedro Font, *Font's Complete Diary: A Chronicle of the Founding of San Francisco*, trans. Herbert E. Bolton (Berkeley: University of California Press, 1931), p. 105.

82. For example, see Holder, "Bote," p. 624.

83. Devereux, "Institutionalized Homosexuality," p. 522.

84. Victor W. Turner, *The Ritual Process: Structure and Anti-structure* (Chicago: Aldine, 1969). The *alyha·* initiation is related in Alfred L. Kroeber, *More Mohave Myths*, Anthropological Records, no. 27 (Berkeley: University of California Press, 1972), p. 20; and Devereux, "Institutionalized Homosexuality," pp. 506–509.

85. Kroeber, *Handbook of the Indians of California* (New York: Dover, 1976), pp. 748-49, *More Mohave Myths*, pp. 17-20.

86. Kroeber, *More Mohave Myths*, p. 18.

87. Compare the story of Cane, Kroeber, *Seven Mohave Myths*, Anthropological Records, no. 11, pt. 1 (Berkeley: University of California Press, 1948), pp. 8-9.

88. Kroeber, *More Mohave Myths*, p. 20.

89. Kroeber, *Handbook*, p. 730, fig. 60a; Edith S. Taylor and William J. Wallace, "Mohave Tattooing and Face-painting," *The Masterkey* 21.6 (1947), fig. 6a.

90. Devereux, "Institutionalized Homosexuality," p. 510.

91. *Ibid.*, p. 519.

92. Herman Grey, *Tales from the Mohaves* (Norman: University of Oklahoma Press, 1970), p. 10.

93. Devereux, "Institutionalized Homosexuality," p. 503.

94. Kenneth M. Stewart, "Mohave," in Ortiz, *Handbook of North American Indians*, vol. 10, pp. 57-59; Devereux, *Mohave Ethnopsychiatry: The Psychic Disturbances of an Indian Tribe* (Washington, DC: Smithsonian Institution Press, 1969), p. 232.

95. Herdt, "Representations," 494.

96. See, e.g., Anne Bolin, *In Search of Eve: Transsexual Rites of Passage* (South Hadley, MA: Bergin & Garvey, 1988). This appears to be changing, however. Some transsexuals for political and personal reasons are choosing not to assimilate to the "opposite sex," freely acknowledging their previous lives in another gender and rejecting traditional images of femininity. See Sandy Stone, "The *Empire* Strikes Back: A Posttranssexual Manifesto," in *Body Guards*, pp. 280-304.

97. Devereux, "Institutionalized Homosexuality," p. 514.

98. Devereux, "Mohave Indian Autoerotic Behavior," *Psychoanalytic Review* 37.3 (1950), pp. 206-207.

99. See Devereux, "Cultural and Characterological Traits of the Mohave Related to the Anal Stage of Psychosexual Development," *Psychoanalytic Quarterly* 20 (1951).

100. *Ibid.*, p. 403; Kroeber, *More Mohave Myths*, p. 5.

101. Devereux, "Institutionalized Homosexuality," pp. 498-99. Devereux describes the case of a Mohave man who engaged in both active and receptive anal intercourse while in prison but was not considered a berdache. See also the interview with a gay Mohave man, who specialized in crafts and was teased

but accepted by other Mohaves, in Bob Waltrip, "Elmer Gage: American Indian," *ONE Magazine* 13.3 (1965).

102. For recent work on berdache-type roles in other parts of the world, see Callender and Kochems, "Men and Not-Men"; Murray, "Third (and Fourth?) Sex Araucanian Shamans," in *Male Homosexuality in Central and South America*, pp. 159–64; Murray (ed.), *Oceanic Homosexualities* (New York: Garland, 1992); and Carol E. Robertson, "The Māhū of Hawai'i," *Feminist Studies* 15.2 (1989).

CHAPTER EIGHT: HIJRAS

1. I am grateful to the following individuals who gave me helpful comments on parts of this essay: Randolph Trumbach, Charles Brooks, Owen Lynch, Betsy Hegeman and most especially Gilbert Herdt. I would also like to thank the PSC-CUNY Research Foundation for the financial support of the fieldwork on which this article is based.

A role similar to the hijras exists in South India; see Nicholas J. Bradford, "Transgenderism and the Cult of Yellamma: Heat, Sex, and Sickness in South Indian Ritual," *Journal of Anthropological Research* 39.3 (1983). The force of this role, called *jogappa*, comes from its erotic, sacred, female character. In my earlier ethnography on the hijras, *Neither Man nor Woman: The Hijras of India* (Belmont, CA: Wadsworth, 1990), I did not sufficiently emphasize this aspect of the hijra role, a perspective that I try to incorporate in this essay.

2. Wendy Doniger O'Flaherty, *Women, Androgynes, and Other Mythical Beasts* (Chicago: University of Chicago Press, 1980).

3. Alf Hiltelbeitel, "Siva, the Goddess, and the Disguises of the Pandavas and Draupadi," *History of Religions* 20.1–2 (1980).

4. O'Flaherty, *Siva: The Erotic Ascetic* (Chicago: University of Chicago Press, 1973).

5. Frederique Apffel Marglin, "Female Sexuality in the Hindu World," in Clarissa Atkinson, Constance H. Buchanan and Margaret R. Miles (eds.), *The Immaculate and the Powerful* (Boston: Beacon Press, 1985).

6. Sudhir Kakar, *The Inner World: A Psychoanalytic Study of Childhood and Society in India* (Delhi: Oxford University Press, 1981).

7. Vern Bullough, *Sexual Variance in Society and History* (Chicago: University of Chicago Press, 1976).

8. *Ibid.*

9. Kushwant Singh, *Delhi, a Novel* (New Delhi: Penguin, 1991).

10. O'Flaherty, *Women*, p. 299.

11. O'Flaherty, *Siva*, p. 318.

12. Denzil Charles Jelf Ibbetson, Edward MacLagan and Horace Arthur Rose, *A Glossary of the Tribes and Castes of Punjab and the North-west Frontier Province* (Lahore: Civil and Military Gazette Press, 1911), vol. 2, p. 331.

13. O'Flaherty, *Women*.

14. Laurence W. Preston, "A Right to Exist: Eunuchs and the State in Nineteenth Century India," *Modern Asian Studies* 21.2 (1987), p. 373.

15. S.N. Ranade, "A Study of Eunuchs in Delhi," unpublished manuscript, Government of India, Delhi.

16. O'Flaherty, *Siva*.

17. *Ibid.*, p. 131.

18. Hiltelbeitel, "Siva," p. 168.

19. See Pauline Kolenda, "Untouchable Chuhras Through Their Humor: 'Equalizing' Marital Kin Through Teasing, Pretense, and Farce," in Owen M. Lynch (ed.), *The Social Construction of Emotion in India* (Berkeley and Los Angeles: University of California Press, 1990), for an insightful study of the ambivalence surrounding sexuality in North Indian kinship systems as a basis for humor.

20. Victor Turner, *The Ritual Process: Structure and Anti-structure* (Ithaca, NY: Cornell University Press, 1969).

21. Bradford, "Transgenderism."

22. Akos Ostor, Lina Fruzzetti and Steve Barnett (eds.), *Concepts of Person: Kinship, Caste, and Marriage in India* (Cambridge, MA: Harvard University Press, 1982).

23. Richard Lannoy, *The Speaking Tree* (New York: Oxford University Press, 1975); O'Flaherty, *Siva*.

24. Serena Nanda, "Deviant Careers: The Hijras of India," in Morris Freilich, Douglas Raybeck and Joel Shavishinsky (eds.), *Deviance: Anthropological Perspectives* (Westport, CT: Greenwood, 1991).

25. Trikoli Nath Madan, "The Ideology of the Householder among the Kashmiri Pandits," in Ostor et al. (eds.), *Concepts*.

26. There are many fewer female ascetic roles in India than male ascetic roles. For a description of one such role, see Peter Phillimore, "Unmarried Women of the Dhaula Dhar: Celibacy and Social Control in Northwest India," *Journal of Anthropological Research* 47.3 (Fall 1991). The role Phillimore describes as *sadhin*, or female ascetic, contains some of the marks of an alternative gender role but is not comparable to the hijras in its meanings or cultural potency.

27. John Money and Claus Wiedeking, "Gender Identity Role: Normal Differentiation and Its Transpositions," in Benjamon B. Wolman and Money (eds.), *Handbook of Human Sexuality* (Englewood Cliffs, NJ: Prentice-Hall, 1980).

28. Money and Anke A. Ehrhardt, *Man and Woman, Boy and Girl: The Differentiation and Dimorphism of Gender Identity from Conception to Maturity* (Baltimore: Johns Hopkins University Press, 1972).

29. Herdt, "Mistaken Gender: 5-alpha Reductase Hermaphroditism and Biological Reductionism in Sexual Identity Reconsidered," *American Anthropologist* 92 (1990).

30. Kakar, *Inner World*, p. 77. For a critique of Kakar as too Freudian and individualized (rather than "dividualized"), see Stanley Kurtz, *All the Mothers Are One* (New York: Columbia University Press, 1992).

31. Kakar, *Inner World*, p. 158.

32. *Ibid.*, p. 95.

33. O'Flaherty, *Women*, p. 280.

34. Ranade's study (n.15 above), pp. 72–74, carried out under the auspices of the Indian government, of one hundred hijras in Delhi reported that, of the Hindu hijras (33 percent of his sample were Muslims) who gave information, 27 percent were from the higher castes and 23 percent from the scheduled (formerly "untouchable") castes. Well over three quarters of the total sample came from families of very poor landless farm laborers; the remainder came from families of small shopkeepers or low-paid occupations such as peons, drivers or tailors. Most of their families included no literate persons, although 5 percent of the families included one member who had passed high school. The one upper-caste (brahman) man I knew of who was categorized by his relations as "intersexed" never married and was sent to the United States to pursue an academic career.

35. Alan Roland, "Toward a Psychoanalytic Psychology of Hierarchical Relationships in Hindu India," *Ethos* 10.3 (1982).

36. Preston, "Right to Exist," p. 380.

37. *Ibid.*

38. *Ibid.*

39. Ranade, unpublished manuscript.

40. Dilip Bobb and Chhotabhai Jethabhai Patel, "Fear Is the Key," *India Today*, September 15, 1982, pp. 84–85.

41. Ibbettson et al., *Glossary.*

42. Ranade, unpublished manuscript, p. 72.

43. Robert L. Munroe and Ruth H. Munroe, "Male Transvestism and Subsistence Economy," *Journal of Social Psychology* 103 (1977); Munroe, John W.M. Whiting and David J. Hally, "Institutionalized Male Transvestism and Sex Distinction," *American Anthropologist* 71 (1969).

CHAPTER NINE: MISTAKEN SEX

1. This chapter is an enlarged version of an article published in the *American Anthropologist* 92 (1990), pp. 333–46, as "Mistaken Gender: 5-Alpha Reductase Hermaphroditism and Biological Reductionism in Sexual Identity Reconsidered." Permission to reprint the text is gratefully acknowledged to the American Anthropological Association. Material on the ethnographic setting has been reproduced in revised form from Gilbert Herdt and Robert J. Stoller, "Semen Depletion and the Sense of Maleness," *Ethnopsychiatrica* 3 (1980), pp. 79–116. The earlier version from the *American Anthropologist* was commented on by the following colleagues, to whom I am grateful: Andrew Boxer, Norman Bradburn, Joseph Carrier, Julian Davidson, John DeCecco, Daniel Freedman, Paul Friedrich, Martha McClintock, John Money, Steven Murray, Robert LeVine, Bennett Simon, Robert J. Stoller, Richard Shweder and Donald Tuzin.

Julliane Imperato-McGinley et al., "Steroid 5-alpha Reductase Deficiency in Man: An Inherited Form of Male Pseudohermaphroditism," *Science* 186 (1974).

2. Imperato-McGinley et al., "Androgens and the Evolution of Male-Gender Identity among Male Pseudohermaphrodites with 5-alpha Reductase Deficiency," *New England Journal of Medicine* 300 (1979), pp. 1235–36.

3. Herdt and Julian Davidson, "The Sambia 'Turnim-man': Sociocultural and Clinical Aspects of Gender Formation in Male Pseudohermaphrodites with 5-alpha Reductase Deficiency in Papua New Guinea," *Archives of Sexual Behavior* 17 (1988).

4. Herdt, *Guardians of the Flutes* (New York: McGraw-Hill, 1981).

5. Herdt and Stoller, "Sakulambei – A Hermaphrodite's Secret: An Example of Clinical Ethnography," *Psychoanalytic Study of Society* 11 (1985).

6. See Herdt, *Sambia: Ritual and Gender in New Guinea* (New York: Holt, Rinehart & Winston, 1987); Herdt and Davidson, "Sambia 'Turnim-man' "; Herdt and Stoller, *Intimate Communications: Erotics and the Study of Culture* (New York: Columbia University Press, 1990).

7. Michel Foucault, *The History of Sexuality: Vol. 1*, trans. Robert Hurley (New York: Viking, 1980), p. 38.

8. On the metaphor of "construction," see Carole S. Vance, "Anthropol-

ogy Rediscovers Sexuality: A Theoretical Comment," *Social Science and Medicine* 33 (1991); Ruth Benedict, "Continuities and Discontinuities in Cultural Conditioning," *Psychiatry* 1 (1938); Margaret Mead, *Sex and Temperament in Three Primitive Societies* (New York: Morrow, 1935); Bronislaw Malinowski, *Sex and Repression in Savage Society* (Cleveland: Meridian, 1927). A review of these is offered in Herdt and Stoller, *Intimate Communications.*

9. Hans Gsorg Gadamer, *Truth and Method* (New York: Crossroad, 1965).

10. Charles Darwin, *The Descent of Man and Selection in Relation to Sex* (London: J. Murray, 1871); Roberta L. Hall, ed., *Sexual Dimorphism in Homo Sapiens: A Question of Size* (New York: Praeger, 1982).

11. Isaac D. Balbus, *Marxism and Domination* (Princeton, NJ: Princeton University Press, 1982); Nancy Chodorow, *The Reproduction of Mothering* (Berkeley and Los Angeles: University of California Press, 1978); Michelle Z. Rosaldo and Louise Lamphere, "Introduction," in Rosaldo and Lamphere (eds.), *Woman, Culture, and Society* (Stanford, CA: Stanford University Press, 1974); Peggy R. Sanday, *Female Power and Male Dominance* (Cambridge: Cambridge University Press, 1981).

12. Such studies are reviewed in Herdt, *Guardians*; Jeffrey Weeks, *Sexuality and Its Discontents* (London: Routledge & Kegan Paul, 1985), pp. 79–91.

13. Robert B. Edgerton, *Rules, Exceptions, and Social Order* (Berkeley and Los Angeles: University of California Press, 1985), pp. 77–78, and "Pokot Intersexuality: An East African Example of Sexual Incongruity," *American Anthropologist* 66 (1964).

14. See my Introduction, this volume; see also Weeks, *Sexuality*; and Vance, "Anthropology Rediscovers Sexuality."

15. Herdt, "Representations of Homosexuality in Traditional Societies: An Essay on Cultural Ontology and Historical Comparison. Part I," *Journal of the History of Sexuality* 2 (1991).

16. Stoller, *Sex and Gender* (New York: Science House, 1968).

17. See Charles Callender and Lee M. Kochems, "The North American Berdache," *Current Anthropology* 24 (1983); Harriet Whitehead, "The Bow and the Burden Strap: A New Look at Institutionalized Homosexuality in Native North America," in Sherry B. Ortner and Whitehead (eds.), *Sexual Meanings* (Cambridge: Cambridge University Press, 1981); Walter Williams, *The Spirit and the Flesh* (New York: Beacon, 1986).

18. Mead, "Cultural Determinants of Sexual Behavior," in *Sexual and Internal Secretions* (Baltimore: Williams & Wilkins, 1961), p. 1453.

19. On postnatal gender change, see Money and Anke Ehrhardt, *Man and Woman, Boy and Girl* (Baltimore: Johns Hopkins University Press, 1972). For a critique, see Lawrence Kohlberg, David Ricks and John Snarey, "Childhood Development as a Predictor of Adaption in Adulthood," *Genetic Psychology Monographs* 110 (1984).

20. Clifford Geertz, "Common Sense as a Cultural System," in *Local Knowledge* (New York: Basic Books, 1983), pp. 80–84.

21. Willard Williams Hill, "The Status of the Hermaphrodite and Transvestite in Navaho Culture," *American Anthropologist* 37 (1935), p. 274.

22. *Ibid.*, p. 275.

23. Richard Hoffman, "Vices, Gods, and Virtues: Cosmology as a Mediating Factor in Attitudes Toward Male Homosexuality," *Journal of Homosexuality* 9 (1984); Money, "Hermaphroditism," in Albert Ellis and Albert Aberbanel (eds.), *The Encyclopedia of Sexual Behavior* (New York: Hawthorn, 1961).

24. Vern Bullough, *Sexual Variance in Society and History* (Chicago: University of Chicago Press, 1976), p. 113.

25. Susan Gelman, Pamela Collman and Eleanor E. Maccoby, "Inferring Properties from Categories versus Inferring Categories from Properties: The Case of Gender," *Child Development* 57 (1986).

26. Herdt, *Sambia.*

27. Sigmund Freud, *Three Essays on the Theory of Sexuality* (1905), *Standard Edition of the Complete Psychological Works of Sigmund Freud*, vol. 8 (London: Hogarth, 1953).

28. Herdt, "Representations."

29. Herdt, "Developmental Continuity as a Dimension of Sexual Orientation across Cultures," in David McWhirter, June Reinisch and Stephanie A. Sanders (eds.), *Homosexuality and Heterosexuality: The Kinsey Scale and Current Research* (New York: Oxford University Press, 1990).

30. See Money and Ehrhardt, *Man and Woman*, for a primary review of hermaphroditic conditions; for an update, see Imperato-McGinley et al., "The Impact of Androgens on the Evolution of Male Gender Identity," in S. Jerome Kogan and E.S.E. Hafez (eds.), *Pediatric Andrology* (The Hague: Martinus Nijhoff, 1981); Robert T. Rubin, Reinisch and R.F. Haskett, "Postnatal Gonadal Steroid Effects on Human Behavior," *Science* 211 (1981); and Stoller, *Sex and Gender*, Vol. 2: *The Transsexual Experiment* (New York: Aronson, 1975).

31. Imperato-McGinley et al., "Steroid 5-alpha Reductase Deficiency."

32. Imperato-McGinley et al., "Androgens."

33. *Ibid.*, p. 1234.

34. *Ibid.*

35. Money, J.G. Hampson and J.L. Hampson, "An Examination of Some Basic Sexual Concepts: The Evidence of Human Hermaphroditism," *Bulletin of Johns Hopkins Hospital* 97 (1955).

36. Albert Ellis, "The Sexual Psychology of Human Hermaphrodites," *Psychosomatic Medicine* 7 (1945).

37. Money and Ehrhardt, *Man and Woman.*

38. Stoller, *Sex and Gender.*

39. Ehrhardt and Heino Meyer-Bahlburg, "Effects of Prenatal Sex Hormones on Gender-related Behavior," *Science* 211 (1981); Ehrhardt, "The Psychobiology of Gender," in A. Rossi (ed.), *Gender and the Life Course* (New York: Aldine, 1985), p. 84ff.; Melvin M. Grumbach and F.A. Conte, "Disorders of Sexual Differentiation," in Jean D. Wilson and Daniel W. Foster (eds.), *Williams's Textbook of Endocrinology,* 7th ed. (Philadelphia: Saunders, 1985); Arye Lev-Ran, "Gender Role Differentiation in Hermaphrodites," *Archives of Sexual Behavior* 3 (1974).

40. See Money, "Gender Identity and Hermaphroditism: Letter," *Science* 191 (1976); Meyer-Bahlburg, "Hormones and Psychosexual Differentiation: Implications for the Management of Intersexuality, Homosexuality and Transsexuality," *Clinics in Endocrinology and Metabolism* 11 (1982); Ehrhardt, "Psychobiology," p. 87; see also Grumbach and Conte, "Disorders," p. 382ff. It is important to note, however, that some, such as Money and Ehrhardt, who have been most critical of the work, are also strong proponents of the theory it challenges.

41. Money, "Gender Identity"; Edward Sagarin, "Sex Rearing and Sexual Orientation: The Reconciliation of Apparently Contradictory Data," *Journal of Sex Research* 11 (1975).

42. Rubin et al., "Effects," p. 1322.

43. Ehrhardt, "Psychobiology"; Ehrhardt and Meyer-Bahlburg, "Effects"; Rubin et al., "Effects."

44. Imperato-McGinley et al., "Steroid 5-alpha Reductase Deficiency," p. 1215.

45. Imperato-McGinley et al., "Androgens," p. 1234.

46. Sagarin, "Sex Rearing," p. 331.

47. Imperato-McGinley et al., "Androgens," p. 1234.

48. Meyer-Bahlburg, "Hormones," p. 686.

49. Sagarin, "Sex Rearing."

50. Imperato-McGinley et al., "Androgens," p. 1213.

51. *Ibid.*, p. 1235.

52. Theodore Brameld, *The Remaking of a Culture* (New York: Harper, 1959), p. 108; Susan E. Brown, "Love Unites Them and Hunger Divides Them: Poor Women in the Dominican Republic," in Rayna R. Reiter (ed.), *Toward an Anthropology of Women* (New York: Monthly Review Press, 1975), pp. 323-25; James G. Leyburn, *The Haitian People* (New Haven, CT: Yale University Press, 1966), p. 197; Thomas E. Weil et al., *Area Handbook for the Dominican Republic*, 2nd ed. (Washington, DC: Government Printing Office, 1973), pp. 65-76.

53. On Puerto Rico, see Brameld, *Remaking*, p. 108; on Jamaica, see Barry Floyd, *Jamaica: An Island Microcosm* (New York: St. Martin's, 1979), p. 66; on Black Caribs, see Virginia Kerns, *Women and the Ancestors* (Urbana: University of Illinois Press, 1983), pp. 89-103; on Haiti, see Leyburn, *Haitian People*, pp. 196-97ff.

54. Howard J. Wiarda and Michael J. Kryzanek, *The Dominican Republic* (Boulder, CO: Westview, 1982), p. 19.

55. On the Zapotec third sex, cf. Anya P. Royce, "Masculinity and Femininity in Elaborated Movement System," in Reinisch (ed.), *Masculinity and Femininity: Basic Perspectives* (New York: Oxford University Press, 1987), pp. 339-409.

56. Imperato-McGinley et al., "Impact of Androgens," p. 101; see also Richard Green, *The "Sissy Boy Syndrome" and the Development of Homosexuality* (New Haven, CT: Yale University Press, 1987), p. 44.

57. Imperato-McGinley et al., "Impact of Androgens."

58. *Ibid.*, p. 100.

59. Milton Diamond, "Sexual Identity and Sex Roles," in Bullough (ed.), *The Frontiers of Sex Research* (Buffalo, NY: Prometheus, 1979); Kathryn E. Hood, P. Draper, Lisa J. Crockett and Ann Petersen, "The Ontogeny and Phylogeny of Sex: A Biopsychosexual Synthesis," in D. Bruce Carter (ed.), *Current Conceptions of Sex Roles and Sex Typing* (New York: Praeger, 1987), p. 59.

60. Green, *"Sissy Boy Syndrome"*; Money, "Sin, Sickness, or Society?" *American Psychologist* 42 (1987).

61. Imperato-McGinley et al., "Androgens," p. 1234; see also Imperato-McGinley et al., "Impact of Androgens."

62. Marshall H. Klaus and J.H. Kennel, *Maternal-Infant Bonding* (St. Louis: Mosby, 1976); Foucault, *The Birth of the Clinic*, trans. A.M.S. Smith (New York: Pantheon, 1973).

63. John H. Gagnon, "Sex Research and Social Change," *Archives of Sexual Behavior* 4 (1975).

64. Imperato-McGinley et al., "Reply to J. Money's Letter," *Science* 196 (1976), p. 872.

65. Paula Brown, *New Guinea Highland Peoples* (New York: Cambridge University Press, 1978); Herdt, "Introduction," in Herdt (ed.), *Ritualized Homosexuality in Melanesia*, paperback ed. (Berkeley and Los Angeles: University of California Press, 1993); Shirley Lindenbaum, "Variations on a Sociosexual Theme in Melanesia," in Herdt (ed.), *Ritualized Homosexuality in Melanesia* (Berkeley and Los Angeles: University of California Press, 1984).

66. Daniel Carleton Gajdusek, "Urgent Opportunistic Observations: The Study of Changing, Transient and Disappearing Phenomena of Medical Interest in Disrupted Human Communities," in *Health and Disease in Tribal Societies* (Amsterdam: Elsevier/Excerpta Medica, North Holland, 1977).

67. On the Hua, see Anna S. Meigs, *Food, Sex, and Pollution: A New Guinea Religion* (New Brunswick, NJ: Rutgers University Press, 1984), p. 93; on the Bimin-Kuskusmin, see Fitz John P. Poole, "Coming into Social Being: Cultural Images of Infants in Bimin-Kuskusmin Folk Psychology," in Geoff M. White and John Kirkpatrick (eds.), *Person, Self, and Experience* (Berkeley and Los Angeles: University of California Press, 1985), p. 229.

68. Poole, "Transforming 'Natural' Woman: Female Ritual Leaders and Gender Ideology among Bimin-Kuskusmin," in Ortner and Whitehead (eds.), *Sexual Meanings*.

69. Reviewed in Herdt and Davidson, "Sambia 'Turnim-man.'"

70. Herdt, *Sambia*, pp. 63–64; Herdt and Stoller, "Sakulambei."

71. Herdt and Stoller, *Intimate Communications*, ch. 7.

72. Reviewed in Herdt, *Guardians of the Flutes*, and *Sambia*.

73. This conviction is held to be self-evident even though Sambia clearly recognize that other mammals, like opossums and dogs, do possess semen and are "naturally" able to grow, attain biological male maturity and reproduce. Obviously, homosexual fellatio has many aspects among Sambia, including symbolic ones, so this sketch cannot do justice to the fuller manifestations of the cultural system; see Herdt, *Guardians of the Flutes*.

74. On the Keraki, see Francis Edgar Williams, *Papuans of the Trans-Fly* (Oxford, UK: Clarendon Press, 1936); Herdt, "Introduction"; Bruce M. Knauft, *South Coast New Guinea Cultures* (New York: Cambridge University Press, 1993). It should be noted that ritual homosexuality is more frequent than thought in

the Pacific, and somewhere between 10 percent and 20 percent of all traditional societies in Melanesia practice it (see Herdt, "Ritualized Homosexuality in Melanesia: An Introduction," in the 1984 edition of *Ritualized Homosexuality in Melanesia*). Female homosexual ceremony of this type is, however, very rare. Obviously the male hegemony and social controls of the warriorhood are related to this form of institutionalized male bonding. As a generalized social form, the Melanesian practice is age-structured homosexuality, a variant of homoeroticism known from many tribal and archaic societies; David Greenberg, *The History of Homosexuality* (Chicago: University of Chicago Press, 1988).

75. Herdt, *Guardians of the Flutes*.

76. *Ibid.*

77. *Ibid.*

78. See Herdt and Davidson, "Sambia 'Turnim-man,' " for a clinical study.

79. *Ibid.*

80. Herdt and Stoller, "Sakulambei."

81. Herdt, *Guardians of the Flutes*.

82. Herdt and Stoller, "Sakulambei."

83. On this, cf. Herdt, *Guardians of the Flutes*.

84. Herdt and Davidson, "Sambia 'Turnim-man.' "

85. Herdt and Stoller, "Sakulambei."

86. On the proper initiation, see Herdt, *Sambia*. On Saku's ritual development, see Herdt and Stoller, "Sakulambei." On nosebleeds, see Herdt, "Sambia Nosebleeding Rites and Male Proximity to Women," *Ethos* 10 (1982).

87. Herdt and Stoller, *Intimate Communications*.

88. Don S. Gardner, "A Note on the Androgynous Qualities of the Cassowary: Or, Why the Mianmin Say It Is Not a Bird," *Oceania* 55 (1984); Herdt, *Guardians of the Flutes*.

89. John R. Baker, "Notes on New Hebridean Customs, with Special Reference to the Intersex Pig," *Man* 28 (1928).

90. Poole, " 'Natural' Woman," and "Coming."

91. Herdt, *Guardians of the Flutes*, ch. 8.

92. Robert I. Levy, *The Tahitians* (Chicago: University of Chicago Press, 1973).

93. Compare Foucault, *Herculine Barbin*, trans. Robert McDougall (New York: Pantheon, 1980).

94. Compare Imperato-McGinley et al., "Steroid 5-alpha Reductase Deficiency."

95. Stoller, *Sex and Gender*, vol. 2.

96. Mead, "Cultural Determinants," p. 1476.

97. Money and Ehrhardt, *Man and Woman*; Ehrhardt, "Psychobiology"; Maccoby, "Gender Identity and Sex Role Adoption," in H.A. Katchadourian (ed.), *Human Sexuality* (Berkeley and Los Angeles: University of California Press, 1979).

98. Green, *"Sissy Boy Syndrome"*; Stoller, *Sex and Gender*, vol. 5.

99. Imperato-McGinley et al., "Steroid 5-alpha Reductase Deficiency"; Sagarin, *Sex Rearing.*

100. Pat Caplan, "Introduction," in Caplan (ed.), *The Cultural Construction of Sexuality* (London: Tavistock, 1987), p. 21.

101. Weeks, *Sexuality.*

102. Greenberg, *History.*

103. *Ibid.*; Hoffman, "Vices," p. 42.

104. Maccoby, "Gender Identity," p. 195.

CHAPTER TEN: TRANSCENDING AND TRANSGENDERING

1. I want to give special thanks and appreciation to Gilbert Herdt for his invaluable and incisive comments and helpful suggestions for this chapter from its inception and throughout its revision. I am extremely grateful to Vern and Bonnie Bullough for their careful reading, thorough and insightful critique and graciousness in helping me. Unfortunately, their landmark book, *Cross Dressing, Sex and Gender* (Philadelphia: University of Pennsylvania Press, 1993) was not available at the time of this writing. I am indebted to Tom Henricks, who provided me with his expertise on developing my research methodology, as well as intellectual engagement and supportive guidance. Many thanks to Linda Martindale for her excellence in manuscript preparation and her editorial skills.

See Anne Bolin, Review of *Gender Blending: Confronting the Limits of Duality*, *Journal of the History of Sexuality* 2.3 (1992), "Gender Subjectivism in the Construction of Transsexualism," *Chrysalis Quarterly* 1.3 (1992), *In Search of Eve: Transsexual Rites of Passage* (South Hadley, MA: Bergin & Garvey, 1988), "Transsexuals and Caretakers: A Study of Power and Deceit in Intergroup Relations," *City and Society* 1.2 (1987), and "Transsexualism and the Limits of Traditional Analysis," *American Behavioral Scientist* 31.1 (1987).

2. Although I refer to such groups as male-to-female transsexuals, male transvestites and transgenderists, this should not be construed as a statement of representativeness but merely as a literary convenience. My findings were

based on a limited population using a snowball sampling technique. While generalization was sacrificed, I feel I have helped make visible the diversity within the transgendered community by the detail and substance provided by ethnographic and textual materials.

3. A number of member terms are used to generally denote that group of people whose genitals, status, appearance and behaviors are not in congruence with the Western schema that mandates an essential relationship between sex and gender (i.e. genitalia, status, appearance and gender role). Some refer to the "transgendered community" or more cursively "the gender community." Ariadne Kane, Director of the Human Achievement and Outreach Institute, prefers the term "the paraculture" to include alternative life-styles of individuals who cross-dress. While gay cross-dressers or female impersonators are not usually included as transgenderists, this is not invariable. In addition, sexual eroticism varies among those identified as transgenderists.

4. Jason Cromwell continues by stating that female-to-male transsexuals "by not altering their bodies through surgery (or only moderately so)...can be dismissed as 'masculine women' " ("Talking About Without Talking About: The Use of Protective Language Among Tranvestites and Transsexuals," paper presented at the Annual Meeting of the American Anthropological Association, Chicago, November 20–24, 1991, p. 38). See also Cromwell, "Fearful Others: The Construction of Female Gender Variance," unpublished paper, University of Washington, Seattle, n.d.; Holly Devor, *Gender Blending: Confronting the Limits of Duality* (Bloomington: Indiana University Press, 1989). Outside of Cromwell's work, there is a dearth of sociocultural studies on female-to-male transgendered people. Vern Bullough and Bonnie Bullough's (personal communication) broad historical perspective identifies cross-dressing as primarily a phenomenon among women with male cross-dressing as only a very recent phenomenon.

5. Bolin, *In Search of Eve*, pp. 32–39.

6. This approach is in the genre of interpretive anthropology, defined as a covering label for a diverse set of reflections on both the practice of ethnography and the concept of culture. It includes a view of culture as negotiated meanings that can be "read" (or analyzed) as a text by the ethnographer and "read" and "decoded" by the natives. See George E. Marcus and Michael M.J. Fischer, *Anthropology as Cultural Critique: An Experimental Moment in the Human Sciences* (Chicago: University of Chicago Press, 1986), pp. 25 and 30; Clifford Geertz, "Deep Play: Notes on the Balinese Cockfight," in Geertz (ed.), *Myth, Symbol, and Culture* (New York: Norton, 1972), and "Making Experience, Authoring

Selves," in Victor W. Turner and Edward M. Bruner (eds.), *The Anthropology of Experience* (Urbana: University of Illinois Press, 1986); Victor Turner, *Dramas, Fields, and Metaphors: Symbolic Action in Human Society* (Ithaca, NY: Cornell University Press, 1974), and *The Forest of Symbols: Aspects of Ndembu Ritual* (Ithaca, NY: Cornell University Press, 1967).

7. Effecting the construction of the identity was information available in the popular media, newsletters and magazines of various male-to-female transsexual and male transvestite organizations, as well as the professional medical-psychological literature.

8. Esther Newton, *Mother Camp: Female Impersonation in America* (Englewood Cliffs, NJ: Prentice-Hall, 1972), pp. 338–39.

9. Susan Sontag, "Notes on Camp," in *Against Interpretation and Other Essays* (New York: Dell, 1970), pp. 277–78.

10. Michel Foucault, "Technologies of the Self," in Luther B. Martin et al. (eds.), *Technologies of the Self: A Seminar with Michel Foucault* (Amherst: University of Massachusetts Press, 1988); Catherine Gallagher and Thomas Laqueur, *The Making of the Modern Body* (Berkeley and Los Angeles: University of California Press, 1987); Susan R. Bordo, "The Body and the Reproduction of Femininity: A Feminist Appropriation of Foucault," in Alison M. Jaggar and Bordo (eds.), *Gender/Body/Knowledge: Feminist Reconstructions of Being and Knowing* (New Brunswick, NJ: Rutgers University Press, 1989), and "Reading the Slender Body," in *Body/Politics: Women and the Discourses of Science* (New York: Routledge, 1990), pp. 83–112.

11. Dallas Denny, "The Politics of Diagnosis and a Diagnosis of Politics," *Chrysalis Quarterly* 1.3 (1992), pp. 10, 18–19.

12. Suzanne J. Kessler and Wendy McKenna, *Gender: An Ethnomethodological Approach* (New York: Wiley, 1978), p. 153.

13. *Ibid.*, pp. 142–55.

14. See John Money and Anke A. Ehrhardt, *Man and Woman, Boy and Girl* (Baltimore: Johns Hopkins University Press, 1972), pp. 109–10.

15. *Ibid.* See also Michael D. Lemonick, "Genetic Tests under Fire," *Time*, February 24, 1992, p. 65.

16. Bolin, "Transsexualism and the Limits of Traditional Analysis"; Will Roscoe, *The Zuni Man-Woman* (Albuquerque: University of New Mexico Press, 1991); Walter L. Williams, *The Spirit and the Flesh: Sexual Diversity in American Indian Culture* (Boston: Beacon Press, 1986).

17. Kessler and McKenna, *Gender*, p. 4.

18. Kath Weston, *Families We Choose: Lesbians, Gays, Kinship Between Men, Between Women* (New York: Columbia University Press, 1991).

19. Bullough, "Crossdressing: Crossgender, Perceptions, Ideals and Realities," paper presented at the Fantasia Fair Conference, Cape Cod, MA, Oct. 18, 1992.

20. Harry Benjamin subsequently founded the Harry Benjamin International Gender Dysphoria Association, an organization for professionals with gender-dysphoric clients, i.e., people requesting hormonal and surgical reassignment; see Jack C. Berger et al., *Standards of Care: The Hormonal and Surgical Sex Reassignment of Gender Dysphoric Persons* (Galveston, TX: The Harry Benjamin International Gender Dysphoria Association, 1980), p. 3. Benjamin published the first medical article on the subject as well as organized the first symposium at the Association for the Advancement of Psychotherapy in 1953; see Benjamin, "Introduction," *Transsexualism and Sex Reassignment* (Baltimore: Johns Hopkins University Press, 1969), pp. 2–5.

21. Benjamin, *The Transsexual Phenomenon* (New York: Julian, 1966), p. 14, and "Introduction," p. 3.

22. Richard Green and Money, "Preface," in Green and Money (eds.), *Transsexualism and Sex Reassignment Surgery* (Baltimore: Johns Hopkins University Press, 1969).

23. Benjamin, *The Transsexual Phenomenon*, pp. 17–22.

24. Benjamin, "Introduction," p. 22.

25. W.J. Meyer, P.A. Walker and Z.R. Suplee, "Survey of Transsexual Hormonal Treatment in Twenty Gender-Treatment Centers," Janus Information Facility, Department of Pediatrics and Psychiatry and Behavioral Sciences, University of Texas Medical Branch at Galveston, n.d., pp. 3–4.

26. Emily Martin, "The Cultural Construction of Gendered Bodies: Biology and Metaphors of Production and Destruction," *Ethnos* 54.3–4 (1989).

27. Bolin, "A Transsexual Coming of Age: The Cultural Construction of Adolescence," in Tony L. Whitehead and Barbara Reid (eds.), *Gender Constructs and Social Issues* (Urbana: University of Illinois Press, 1992), and *In Search of Eve*.

28. Bolin, *In Search of Eve*, p. 15.

29. Bolin, "A Transsexual Coming of Age."

30. Bolin, *In Search of Eve*, pp. 106–20.

31. This is the description of Sasha, a presurgical male-to-female transsexual, hormonally reassigned as female who was in a sexual relationship with a self-identified lesbian.

32. Although *transgenderist* has a generic quality and may be used to include both biological males and females, my discussion continues to focus on gender variance among physiological males.

33. American Psychiatric Association, *Diagnostic and Statistical Manual of Mental Disorders*, 3rd ed. (Washington, DC: American Psychiatric Association, 1980).

34. Denny, "Politics of Diagnosis."

35. This is not to suggest that these are the only three social influences shaping twentieth-century gender-variant identities. Vern and Bonnie Bullough emphasize the great contribution of Virginia Prince in constructing the current transvestite identity and that as other individuals gain ascendance more options will be made available other than the classic married heterosexual transvestite. In addition, the Bulloughs explore in their recent book *Cross Dressing, Sex and Gender* the importance of homophobia in shaping cross-gendered identities, particularly that occurring from within the gender community (personal communication).

36. Denny, "Politics of Diagnosis."

37. *Ibid.*, p. 13.

38. *Ibid.*, p. 17.

39. *Ibid.*, p. 12.

40. Bolin, *In Search of Eve*, pp. 51–52.

41. Denny, "Politics of Diagnosis," p. 11.

42. *Ibid.*, p. 19.

43. Human Outreach and Achievement Institute, *A Gender Glossary* (South Portland, ME: Human Outreach Institute, n.d.); Merissa Sherrill Lynn, "Definitions of Terms Used in the Transvestite-Transsexual Community," *Tapestry* 51 (1988).

44. Lynn, *Definitions of Terms Commonly Used in the Transvestite/Transsexual Community* (Wayland, MA: IFGE Educational Resources Committee, n.d.), p. 9.

45. Denny, "Dealing with Your Feelings," *AEGIS Transition Series* (Decater, GA: Aegis, 1991), p. 6.

46. Holly Boswell, "The Transgender Alternative," *Chrysalis Quarterly* 1.2 (1991).

47. *Ibid.*, p. 29.

48. *Ibid.*, pp. 30–31.

49. American Psychiatric Association, *Diagnostic and Statistical Manual of*

Mental Disorders, 3rd ed. revised (Washington, DC: American Psychiatric Association, 1987).

50. Boswell, "Getting It Together in the Gender Community," n.d., p. 22.

51. Erving Goffman, *Interaction Ritual* (Garden City, NY: Doubleday, 1967), and *Stigma: Notes on the Management of a Spoiled Identity* (Englewood Cliffs, NJ: Prentice-Hall, 1963).

52. "The Second Annual New Woman's Conference" (Wayland, MA: IFGE, The New Woman Caucus, 1992).

53. Boswell, "Getting It Together."

54. Bolin, "The Splendor of Gender: Socio-Cultural Contributions to Gender Variance," address delivered to the Second Annual Oklahoma Conference of the Society for the Scientific Study of Sex, Edmond, OK, September 30–October 1, 1988.

55. Serena Nanda, "The Hijras of India: Cultural and Individual Dimensions of an Institutionalized Third Gender Role," *Journal of Homosexuality* 11 (1986), and *Neither Man nor Woman: The Hijras of India* (Belmont, CA: Wadsworth, 1990); Roscoe, *Zuni Man-Woman*; Williams, *The Spirit and the Flesh*.

56. Marcus and Fischer, *Anthropology as Cultural Critique*, p. 32.

57. Evidence of this pattern is found in a variety of sources. For example, Wendy Parker makes reference to the 1969 Stonewall resistance by "street queens" among her list of dates in "Historical Facts of Interest to the Gender Community," thereby recognizing a commonality between "street queens" and transgenderists. According to one consultant, efforts at integrating the gay community into transgender community conferences have begun with invitations to various local gay communities in the host city. In fact, the Human Achievement and Outreach Institute incorporated two gay interns working at the 1992 Fantasia Fair. The two interns spoke about an effort by their regional gay community center to be more incorporative and less stigmatizing of the "drag queen" community. They took their role as interns very seriously in terms of wanting to learn more about the diversity of cross-dressing. These two young men regarded themselves as quite different from gay female impersonators whose cross-dressing was performance oriented. They viewed themselves as part of a new younger generation of cross-dressers in the gay community. While gay camp allows for contrasting expressions of gender (see Sontag, "Notes on Camp"), the interns' presentation lacked the contrasts and the hyperglamorous attributes. Like many but certainly not all of the cross-dressers at the Fantasia Fair, the interns dressed so as to pass. This represents a new construction of an identity

within the gay community that blends attributes of heterosexual cross-dressing with gay female impersonation.

58. Midnight Sun, "Sex/Gender Systems in Native North America," in Roscoe (ed.), *Living the Spirit: A Gay American Indian Anthology* (New York: St. Martin's, 1988), p. 33.

59. Roscoe (ed.), *Living the Spirit*, p. 3. For the purposes of this analysis, the issue of whether the berdache can be framed in Western terms, e.g., homosexuality and transsexualism, is not relevant. What is important are the uses made of the berdache by the diverse constituencies in the gender community and the gay and lesbian communities.

60. Roscoe, "Writing Gay and Lesbian Culture(s): An Impossible Possibility," paper presented at the Annual Meeting of the American Anthropological Association, Chicago, November 20-24, 1991, p. 1.

61. Bolin, "Flex Appeal, Food, and Fat: Competitive Body Building, Gender and Diet," *Play and Culture* 5.4 (1992), "Flex Appeal: Women, Body Image and Identity," paper presented at the Annual Meeting of the American Anthropological Association, Chicago, November 20-24, 1991, and "Gender Bending."

62. Bolin, "Flex Appeal, Food, and Fat," p. 87.

63. Robert W. Duff and Lawrence K. Hong, "Self-Images of Women Body-Builders," *Sociology of Sport Journal* 1.4 (1984).

64. Bolin, "Flex Appeal, Food, and Fat," and "Vandalized Vanity: Feminine Physiques Betrayed and Portrayed," in Frances E. Mascia-Lees and Patricia Sharpe (eds.), *Tattoo, Torture, Mutilation, and Adornment: The Denaturalization of the Body in Culture and Text* (Albany: State University of New York Press, 1992).

65. For further discussion, see Bolin, "Flex Appeal: Women, Body Image and Identity," "Flex Appeal, Food and Fat"; Alan Klein, "Body Double: Ethnography Meets Post-Modernism in the Gym," in *Little Big Men: Gender Construction and Bodybuilding Subculture* (Albany: State University of New York Press, in press).

66. Michael Kimmel, "After Fifteen Years: The Impact of the Sociology of Masculinity on the Masculinity of Sociology," in Jeff Hearn and David Morgan (eds.), *Men, Masculinities and Social Theory* (Boston: Unwin Hymin, 1990), p. 99.

67. Janice M. Irvine, *Disorders of Desire: Sex and Gender in Modern American Sexology* (Philadelphia: Temple University Press, 1990), p. 231.

68. Cromwell, "Fearful Others," pp. 16-17.

69. M. Kay Martin and Barbara Voorhies, *Female of the Species* (New York: Columbia University Press, 1975), p. 84.

70. Randolph Trumbach, "London's Sapphists: From Three Sexes to Four Genders in the Making of Modern Culture," in Julia Epstein and Kristina Straub (eds.), *Body Guards* (New York: Routledge, 1991), p. 112, and in this volume.

Contributors

Niko Besnier is associate professor of anthropology at Yale University. He has been conducting field work in Western Polynesia since 1978, principally on Nukulaelae Atoll (Tuvalu).

Anne Bolin is professor of anthropology at Elon College and the author of *In Search of Eve: Transsexual Rites of Passage*.

René Grémaux is fellow of the Foundation for the Social-Cultural Sciences of the Netherlands Organization of Scientific Research.

Gert Hekma is a lecturer in gay studies at the University of Amsterdam. He is the co-editor of *The Pursuit of Sodomy: Male Homosexuality in Renaissance and Enlightenment Europe* and of two forthcoming books, *Sexual Cultures in Europe* and *Male Homosexuality and the Socialist Left*.

Gilbert Herdt is professor of human development at the University of Chicago and director of the Center for Culture and Mental Health. He is the author of numerous books and articles, including *Ritualized Homosexuality in Melanesia, Gay and Lesbian Youth* and *The Time of AIDS: Social Analysis, Theory, and Method*.

Serena Nanda is chair of the department of anthropology at John Jay College of Criminal Justice, City University of New York. She is the author of *Neither Man nor Woman: The Hijras of India* and *Cultural Anthropology*, and co-author of *American Cultural Pluralism and Law*.

597

KATHRYN M. RINGROSE is a lecturer in history at the University of California, San Diego. She is currently completing a study of Byzantine conceptions of gender and sexuality.

WILL ROSCOE is an affiliated scholar at the Institute for Research on Women and Gender at Stanford University and research associate at the Center for Education and Research on Sexuality at San Francisco State University. He is the author of *The Zuni Man-Woman*.

RANDOLPH TRUMBACH is professor of history at Baruch College, City University of New York. He is the author of *The Rise of the Egalitarian Family* and is presently completing a two-volume study of sexual life in eighteenth-century London.

THEO VAN DER MEER, a fellow of the Foundation for Historical Research of the Netherlands Organization of Scientific Research, is the author of *De Wesentlijke Sonde van Sodomie en Andere Vuyligheeden*.

Index

Bougainville, Louis-Antoine de, 289-90.
Bouge, Louis Joseph, 323.
Bowers, Alfred, 347.
Brahma, 385.
Brand, Adolf, 227-28.
Bray, Alan, 163.
Brazil, 56.
Brederode, Gerardus, 166.
Brown, Peter, 509 n.5.
Bullough, Vern, 455.
Burg, Barry Richard, 172.
Burke, Edmund, 134.
Burma, 54.
Butler, Eleanor, 133-34.
Butler, Judith, 45.
Byzantine society, 38; aristocratic male ideal, 107; church in, 99-102, 108; ecclesiastical male ideal, 107-108; emperor's court in, 96-97, 508-509 nn.1, 2; gender and social roles in, 94-97; ladder metaphor of gender, 105, 107-108; sexuality in, 108.

CADOGAN, WILLIAM, 119.
Callender, Charles, 300, 332, 338, 344-45, 571.
Camp, 49, 239, 451, 594 n.57.
Campbell, Jill, 525.
Canler, L., 230-31.
Cape of Good Hope, 171.
Cappadocia, 510 n.9.
Carlier, François, 230-31.
Carpenter, Edward, 47, 75-76, 235.
Casper, Johann Ludwig, 137, 216-18.
Caste, 394; and hijras, 409.
Castrati, 48, 98, 498 n.128.
Castration, 71, 86, 88, 90-94, 98-99, 104-106, 507-508 n.1, 510 n.9, 511 nn.16, 17, 518 n.57; and Byzantine Church, 100-101; and child's character, 102, 105; in Hindu sects, 376-77.
Catamites, 331.
Catholicism, 183.

Catullus, 228.
Cebuan society, 69.
Celibacy, 99, 104-108, 278; and Byzantine church, 100-101; and Calvinism, 183; in Kangra, 70; oaths of, 268-69.
Cengic, Smailaga, 257.
Charcot, Jean-Martin, 223.
Charke, Charlotte, 124-25, 524.
Chevalier, Julien, 223.
Children: in antiquity, 90; and berdaches, 355; in Greek ladder metaphor, 87; and sexual development, 112.
China, 48.
Chivy, John, 122.
Christianity, 85, 104, 108; and liminality, 565 n.113; priests, 86; early, 504 n.210. See also Byzantine society, Dutch Reformed Church.
Chromosomal sex, 30.
Claes, Coman, 149.
Class. See Social class.
Classificatory schemes, 15, 17, 34, 53, 423-24, 443-44, 499 n.142; among Sambia, 68; in Balkans, 277, 281; in Byzantine sources, 87-90; hijra, 70-71; in Hinduism, 375; in medical sexology, 30-31; in urban Brazil, 56.
Cleland, John, 121, 125-27, 129-30.
Clement of Alexandria, 89, 100.
Clothing: of berdaches, 339, 359-60; and female androgynes, 116; in sodomitical network, 167-68. See also Cross-dressing.
Coke, Edward, 119, 126.
Collier, Jane, 349-50, 353.
Colonialism, 63-64.
Coming out, 236, 548 n.72.
Constantine VII, 96.
Constitio Criminalis Carolina, 144.
Cook, James, 292.
Coreal, Francisco, 329-31, 336, 339, 347.
Council of Nicaea, 508 n.1.

mon, 119, 126; Justinian Code, 104; Mosaic, 102, 104, 162; Roman, 85, 102, 104.
Leach, Edmund, 54.
Leo the Deacon, 98, 510 n.7.
Leo the Wise, 508, n.1.
Lesbianism, 288, 448; Westfall on, 224. See also Sapphists.
Lestevenon, Willem Anne, 155.
LeVay, Simon, 16, 47, 498 n.124.
Lévi-Strauss, Claude, 17, 20, 33, 35; theory of kinship, 52.
Levy, Robert, 69, 296, 301, 304, 309, 440; critique of, 305–308.
Lewis, Ann, 123.
Libertinism, 124–25, 148–49, 525 n.24; sexual practices in, 161.
Lieblingsminne, 228.
Liminality, 287, 560 nn.42, 46; and berdaches, 362; and hijras, 387.
Lineage: in Balkans, 243; and marriage between women, 274; and third gender, 278.
Literary criticism, 332.
Liutprand of Cremona, 512 n.21.
Living the Spirit: A Gay American Indian Anthology, 477.
Ljubisa, Visarion, 248.
Loens, Pieter, 201.
Lombroso, Cesare, 217, 223.
London Missionary Society, 290.
Love, 162–66, 228; in emergent modernism, 177; romantic, 36.
Lucian, 510 n.7.
Luckert, Karl, 358.
Lurie, Nancy, 332.
Lynn, Merissa Sherrill, 466.

MACCOBY, ELEANOR E., 445.
Magdalen Hospital, 127.
Mageo, Jeannette, 294, 303, 308, 313.
Magnan, Valentin, 223.
Mahabharata, 375.
Māhū, 440, 443; appearances of, 307; in chiefly circles, 298; cultural functions of, 306–307; early

descriptions of, 291–92; as fuzzy category, 309–10; and hula performance, 299; in hula ritual, 312; as negative image of gender identity, 304–305; semen ingestion by, 323; sexual practices of, 301; and shamanism, 328.
Malinowski, Bronislaw, 34, 36–37, 421, 490 n.25; Sex and Repression in Savage Society, 42; The Sexual Life of Savages, 42–43.
Man and Woman, Boy and Girl, 32.
Manley, Delariviere, 126–28.
Mantegazza, Paolo, 223.
Maori, 292.
Marginalism, 55, 57–58, 245; and berdaches, 362; and eunuch social roles, 97; and hijras, 387; and passing, 79.
Mariner, Will, 294.
Marquesas, 294.
Marquette, 347.
Marriage, 26, 274; avoidance of, 268–69; in Calvinism, 184; egalitarian, 176–77, 211; and gender-liminal Polynesians, 311; ghost, 274; in Hinduism, 394; and homosexuality, 238; of muskobaracas, 274; and sex-reassignment surgery, 454; and sodomites, 173–77.
Martin, M. Kay, 308.
Masculinity: in Balkan culture, 268; Byzantine standards of, 99, 105–106; in eighteenth-century Holland, 170–71, 202–203; and gay style, 238; German ideals of, 228; models of, 234–35; Sambian rituals of, 433–34; and self-control, 185; of sworn virgins, 275–76.
Mastamho, 362, 364.
Masturbation, 117–18, 159–60, 187, 214–17, 299; decriminalization of, 222.
Matavilye, 368.
Mauss, Marcel, 33, 41, 79, 342.
Mavor, Elizabeth, 133.

Ponsonby, Sarah, 133–34.
Poole, Fitz, 431.
Pope, Alexander, 115–16.
Popovic, Djurdja, 271–72.
Portmore, Catherine, 126.
Power, 54–57, 350, 353; and passing, 57–60, 69.
Pregnancy, 201; in Balkans, 269; of berdaches, 361, 367–68.
Prestige systems, 317–18, 348; berdaches in, 346, 574; Mohave, 366; Navajo, 355; Pueblo, 355; women in, 347.
Primitivism, 36–38.
Procopius, 97.
Procreation, 90, 99, 104; in Byzantine church culture, 102, 108; and Calvinism, 183–84; and male ideal, 108.
ProgynonRX, 455.
Prosecution, 208; of hijras, 414; in Netherlands, 139–48, 530 n.26, 531 n.44; of sex crimes, 223; and sodomy, 154.
Prostitution: in Amsterdam, 152–53; female, 221; and gay style, 238; and hijras, 373, 393, 415–16; homosexual, 230, 232; in Polynesia, 327, 566 n.120; in seventeenth-century London, 127; and sexology, 223; sexual practices in, 161; and sodomites, 158–59; and sodomy, 193.
Prussia, 219–20.
Psyche, 62.
Psychic hermaphroditism, 75–76, 220, 226, 494.
Psychoanalysis, 39, 42.
Psychology, 331; and sexual psychopathy, 222–24.
Pulteney, William, 115.
Punishment: death penalty, 162, 181, 189–91; mirror penalties, 191; and penal reform, 193–94. See also Executions.

QÁNQON, 335.
Queens, 238–39, 594 n.57.

Rabisman, 316.
Racism, 27.
Radha, 376.
Raffalovich, Marc André, 229.
Raije, Jacob Bicker, 207.
Rakes, 128, 148, 198.
Read, Kenneth, 24.
Reformism, 75–76.
Reichard, Gladys, 332, 358.
Reinisch, J.M., 427.
Renaissance, 26.
Reproduction, 12, 25–26, 43, 422; ideologies of, 54, 74; and pleasure, 45; and sex differences, 56; in social theory, 34.
Rexhinaj, Curë Prenk, 271–72.
Rijnhart, Samuel, 164–65, 169, 189–90, 198, 202.
Robinson, Paul, 75, 491 n.33.
Roheim, Géza, 38.
Romanos, 86, 509 n.3.
Roscoe, Will, 476–77; The Zuni Man-Woman, 339.
Rousseau, Jean-Jacques, 35–36.
Rubin, Gayle, 45, 52–53, 55, 504 n.226.
Rubin, Robert T., 427.
Running Eagle, 335.

SAKULAMBEI, 16, 420, 437–39.
Salisbury, Sally, 124.
Sambia, 57, 396–97, 420, 432–41, 444, 587 n.73; classificatory schemes among, 68; and developmental theory, 49; feminine socialization in, 435; male initiation ritual, 433–34; sex differences in, 55–56.
Samoa, 43, 294, 304, 314–15, 318; dance forms in, 314–15; fale aitu, 311–12; homosexual behavior in, 299; language, 286, 305; and liminality, 560 n.47; personhood in, 312–13; sexual dimorphism in, 307–308.
Sapphists, 112; appearance of, 121–22; and cross-dressing, 121–25; emer-

Zone Books

The Society of the Spectacle
By Guy Debord

A Vital Rationalist
Selected Writings from
Georges Canguilhem
Edited by François Delaporte

The Invention of Pornography
Edited by Lynn Hunt

Etienne-Jules Marey
By François Dagognet

La Jetée
By Chris Marker

The Accursed Share
Volume I
By Georges Bataille

The Accursed Share
Volumes II & III
By Georges Bataille

Perspective as Symbolic Form
By Erwin Panofsky

Fragmentation and Redemption
By Caroline Walker Bynum

Expressionism in Philosophy:
Spinoza
By Gilles Deleuze

The Poetic Structure of the World
Copernicus and Kepler
By Fernand Hallyn

The Life of Forms in Art
By Henri Focillon

The Normal and the Pathological
By Georges Canguilhem

Masochism
Coldness and Cruelty
By Gilles Deleuze
Venus in Furs
By Leopold von Sacher-Masoch

Theory of Religion
By Georges Bataille

Myth and Society in
Ancient Greece
By Jean-Pierre Vernant

Myth and Tragedy in
Ancient Greece
By Jean-Pierre Vernant and
Pierre Vidal-Naquet

Mitra-Varuna
By Georges Dumézil

Bergsonism
By Gilles Deleuze

Matter and Memory
By Henri Bergson

Your Money or Your Life
By Jacques Le Goff

Foucault/Blanchot
Maurice Blanchot: The Thought
from Outside
By Michel Foucault
Michel Foucault as I Imagine Him
By Maurice Blanchot

Society Against the State
By Pierre Clastres

This edition designed by Bruce Mau
  with Greg Van Alstyne
Type composed by Archetype
Printed and bound Smythe-sewn by Maple-Vail
  using Sebago acid-free paper